Combined with the resources you have trusted to provide you with the best business resources available are:

- **In the News** — New current events articles are added throughout the year. Each article is summarized by our teams of expert professors and is fully supported by exercises, activities, and instructor materials.
- **Online Study Guide** — Four quizzes are linked to each text chapter and include "hints" for each question. Quizzes are graded immediately upon submission to provide immediate feedback on each given answer, and enable students to e-mail results to the instructor.
- **Research Area** — Your own personal resource library includes tutorials, descriptive links to virtual libraries, and a wealth of search engines and resources.
- **Internet Resources** — Discipline-specific sites, including preview information that allows instructors to review site information before viewing the site, ensure the best available business resources found by our learning community.

For the professor

- **Teaching Resources** provide material contributed by professors throughout the world—including teaching tips, techniques, academic papers, and sample syllabi—and **Talk to the Team,** a moderated faculty chat room.
- **Online Faculty Support** includes downloadable supplements, additional cases, articles, links, and suggested answers to Current Events Activities.
- **What's New** gives you one-click access to all newly posted PHLIP resources.

For the student

- **Talk to the Tutor** schedules virtual office hours that allow students to post questions from any supported discipline and receive responses from the dedicated PHLIP/CW faculty team.
- **Writing Resource Center** provides an online writing center that supplies links to online directories, thesauruses, writing tutors, style and grammar guides, and additional tools.
- **Career Center** enables students to access career information, view sample resumes, even apply for jobs online.
- **Study Tips** provide an area where students can develop better study skills.

Online Learning Solutions–

Complete course content is pre-loaded!

Prentice Hall provides rich content available in **your choice** of platforms:

WebCT or Blackboard. You may opt to use our content in its entirety or edit the material to suit your course. Features of each platform may vary but most include:

- **Multiple-Section Chat Rooms**
- **Bulletin Board Conferencing**
- **Online Quizzes and Tests**
- **Course Management with Page Tracking**
- **Calendar and Syllabus Capabilities**

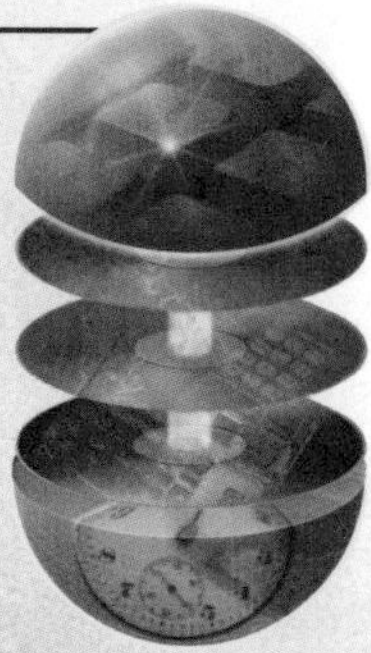

Management Accounting

THE ROBERT S. KAPLAN SERIES IN MANAGEMENT ACCOUNTING

Robert S. Kaplan, Consulting Editor

Management Accounting, 3rd ed.
Atkinson/Banker/Kaplan/Young

The Design of Cost Management Systems, 2nd ed.
Cooper/Kaplan

Modern Management Control Systems
Merchant

Advanced Management Accounting, 3rd ed.
Kaplan/Atkinson

Management Accounting

edition 3

ANTHONY A. ATKINSON
University of Waterloo

RAJIV D. BANKER
University of Texas at Dallas

ROBERT S. KAPLAN
Harvard University

S. MARK YOUNG
University of Southern California

Prentice Hall, Upper Saddle River, New Jersey 07458

Library of Congress Cataloging-in-Publication Data

Management accounting / Anthony A. Atkinson ... [et al.]--3rd ed.
p. cm.
Includes bibliographical references and index.
ISBN 0-13-010195-8
1. Managerial accounting. I. Atkinson, Anthony A.

HF5657.4 .M328 2000
658.15'11--dc21

00-062348

Executive Editor: Debbie Hoffman
Editor-in-Chief: PJ Boardman
Assistant Editor: Kathryn Sheehan
Editorial Assistant: Jane Avery
Director of Development: Steve Deitmer
Developmental Editor: Elissa Adams
Media Project Manager: Nancy Welcher
Marketing Manager: Beth Toland
Marketing Assistant: Jessica Pasquini
Production Editor: Anne Graydon
Managing Editor (Production): Sondra Greenfield
Permissions Coordinator: Suzanne Grappi
Production Manager: Paul Smolenski
Associate Director, Manufacturing: Vincent Scelta
Design Manager: Pat Smythe
Interior Design: Amanda Kavanagh
Cover & Illustration Design: Blair Brown
Manager, Print Production: Christy Mahon
Page Formatter: Ashley Scattergood
Composition: Progressive Information Technology
Full-Service Project Management: Progressive Publishing Alternatives
Printer/Binder: RR Donnelley

Credits and acknowledgments borrowed from other sources and reproduced, with permission, in this textbook appear on appropriate page within text.

10 9 8 7 6 5 4 3 2 1
ISBN 0-13-010195-8

This book *is dedicated to our parents and families*

brief contents

Atkinson
Banker
Kaplan
Young

MANAGEMENT ACCOUNTING

Third Edition

The third edition of Management Accounting has come about after **listening long and hard to the market** and collecting feedback from instructors and students like you.

The result?

A management accounting textbook that offers something the competition can't.

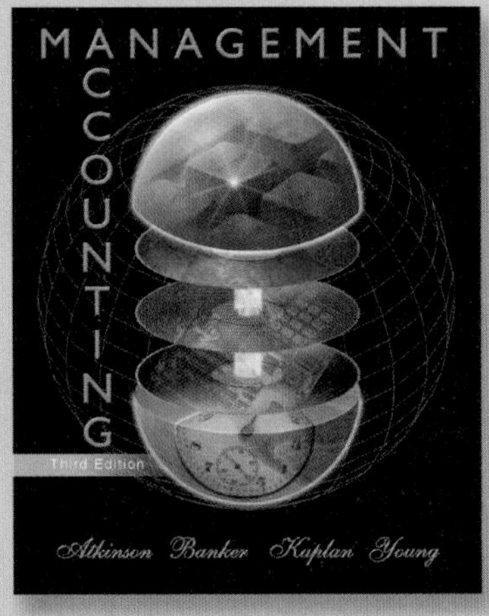

A brand new framework...coverage of ABC and the Balanced Scorecard ***written by Bob Kaplan****...the most compelling real-world examples... testimonials from practitioners on the authoritativeness and practicality of the material...the leading-edge technology...and an unbeatable author team.*

Management Accounting, Third Edition lays out a direct route to Corporate Success!

This book tells it to you straight – what you need to know and why. A revised, trimmed-down framework gives you the benefit of current thinking in management accounting, allowing you to master the concepts and skills critical to your success as a manager.

Let ***Management Accounting, Third Edition*** be your guide for making business decisions in the real business world!

"Management Accounting, Third Edition, is a well received addition to a university curriculum. Companies need financial professionals who know how to communicate not only what a company spent, but also how it consumed that spending and where it provided value and alignment to strategy. The financial skills that are needed are those which allow us to focus on the future as well as the past with a common thread of creating value. This book provides a practical foundation in those skills."

–Ralph W. Canter
Managing Director, KPMG Consulting LLC

"The workplace has changed and so must the workforce. Accountants now must do more than keep the score–they must help make it. The creation and measurement of value is what business is about. The new book provides the reader with the toolset to take on these new challenges. Filled with practical case studies and examples, here's the roadmap to finance's new job requirements."

–Peter A. Zampino,
Director of Research
Consortium for Advanced Manufacturing International

"Management Accounting, Third Edition, is a great synthesis of the latest developments in managerial accounting research and practice. It is a must read for all business students who are seeking the essential skills to become successful managers or entrepreneurs."

–Amanda Woolverton,
MBA student,
University of Southern California

The Unique Kaplan Edge

Why would you want to learn from anyone else?

See the brand new and definitive chapter on Activity-Based Costing, written by Robert Kaplan (Chapter 5), as well as an extensive look at The Balanced Scorecard (Chapter 10).

"This chapter (5) delivers an excellent, simple, well-represented explanation of cost capture systems, suitable for beginners."

–David R. Fordham, James Madison University

"Activity-based costing is a difficult topic for students. The topic was covered quite well (and there were) numerous excellent problems at the end of the chapter."

–Joanne Healy, Kent State University

"We've used ABKY since 1995. The course is case-based and this text complements our strategy of teaching to general managers and integrating management accounting with other core disciplines. From the outset this text has been revolutionary in its focus on creating value through innovative performance measurement and control. This theme resonates with our students who have taken financial accounting, finance, and corporate strategy and understand the importance of securing competitive advantage through distinctive managerial practice."

–Shannon Anderson
Assistant Professor and
Arthur Andersen Faculty Fellow
University of Michigan
Business School

Table of Contents

A New Framework

A New Framework

Atkinson, Banker, Kaplan, and Young offer a new framework designed to address the needs of business managers making decisions. The authors address the following questions:

- What defines the nature, focus, and scope of management accounting? (Chapters 1 and 2)
- What determines the cost of products or customers? How do costs change over the product's life cycle? (Chapter 3)
- What approaches do managers use to compute the costs of their products and services? (Chapters 4 and 5)
- How can we use costs for planning (Chapter 6) and decision-making (Chapters 7 and 8) purposes?
- How can we use revenue and cost information for capacity planning (Chapter 9) and profit planning and evaluation (Chapter 10) purposes?
- How can we manage and control organizational behavior through organization design (Chapter 11) and how does cost information inform the process of control (Chapter 12)?

Focus

Focus

- **Behavioral Issues** (previously Chapter 15) are now incorporated into the text where the material is most relevant.
- **Contemporary Issues** (previously Chapter 13) are now incorporated in the earlier text chapters, offering an up-to-date view of the real world of management accounting.
- **Compensation** (previously Chapter 14) is now incorporated into the new Chapter 10, "Motivating Behavior in Management Accounting and Control Systems."

IN PRACTICE

The Wall Street Journal Workplace-Ethics Quiz

As technology has proliferated in the workplace a number of new ethical questions regarding work behavior have surfaced. See how your responses to these questions in this Wall Street Journal Ethics Quiz compare to national survey data, which appear on the following page.

Office Technology

1. Is it wrong to use company e-mail for personal reasons? ❑ Yes ❑ No
2. Is it wrong to use office equipment to help your children or spouse do schoolwork? ❑ Yes ❑ No
3. Is it wrong to play computer games on office equipment during the workday? ❑ Yes ❑ No
4. Is it wrong to use office equipment to do Internet shopping? ❑ Yes ❑ No
5. Is it unethical to blame an error you made on a technological glitch? ❑ Yes ❑ No
6. Is it unethical to visit pornographic Web sites using office equipment? ❑ Yes ❑ No

Gifts and Entertainment

7. What's the value at which a gift from a supplier or client becomes troubling? ❑ $25 ❑ $50 ❑ $100
8. Is a $50 gift to a boss unacceptable? ❑ Yes ❑ No
9. Is a $50 gift FROM the boss unacceptable? ❑ Yes ❑ No
10. Of gifts and suppliers: Is it OK to take a $200 pair of football tickets? ❑ Yes ❑ No

Source: *The Wall Street Journal*, October 21, 1999, page B1.

*"**In Practice**" boxes provide insights into the challenges today's companies are facing.*

Current Topics

- Activity-Based Costing (Chapter 5)
- Theory of Constraints (Chapter 6)
- Target Costing (Chapter 9)
- Life-Cycle Costing (Chapter 9)
- Kaizen Costing (Chapter 9)
- Benchmarking (Chapter 9)
- Balanced Scorecard (Chapter 10)

"The chapter (9) is easy to read and presents information in a logical, well thought out manner. The discussion of incorporating the entire value chain and total life-cycle costing is strong. The concerns about target costing and kaizen costing are also very helpful in understanding the 'real life' effects of the methods."

–Ann Selk, University of Wisconsin-Green Bay

"I like the inclusion of contemporary topics (for example, target costing, benchmarking, kaizen costing, EVA, balanced scorecard) throughout the book rather than mostly in one chapter."

–Ella Mae Matsumura, University of Wisconsin-Madison

"The principles contained in this book are relevant to us on a daily basis as we make decisions that impact the sales and profits of the Butterfinger candy bar franchise. We use the tools to evaluate media spending, to determine the extent to which we customize product offerings for retailers, to determine when to increase/decrease the number of SKUs in the franchise, to identify significant consumer complaints with the product so as to determine corrective action, etc. This is a must read for anyone interested in growing a business."

–Anne Loveland
Associate Marketing Manager
Nestlé

"ABKY [Atkinson, Banker, Kaplan, Young] have done it again in Management Accounting, 3rd ed.–the authors provide a comprehensive description of the latest and most effective tools in management accounting. The material covered in this book, augmented by numerous examples, provides financial professionals with the skills necessary to move their organizations forward by improving financial and operational performance–enhancing the enterprise's fundamental value. I highly recommend this book and it should be on the bookshelves of every financial professional."

–Brian K. Higgins,
Burke Inc.
National Practice Leader,
Value-Based Management
Burke Strategic Consulting Group

Cutting Edge Technology
completes the package

THE TECHNOLOGICAL EDGE

Manufacturers Build on ERP to Gain an E-Business Edge

As stated in this chapter, organizations can be characterized as a series of activities. The way organizations allocate resources to those activities will depend on the strategies they employ.

A recent study of the 100 Top Innovators in Manufacturing revealed that in 1999, investment in enterprise resource planning (ERP) systems has significantly dominated all other categories in the spending of application dollars (see Exhibit 2-2). The strategy of innovative firms is to invest heavily in ERP and ERP-related applications as springboards to e-business. Rod Johnson, an analyst at AMR Research Inc. in Boston, states, "We're seeing a very dramatic shift among more innovative manufacturing companies. The era from 1993 to the present was all about deploying ERP and improving operational efficiency. The focus now is on systems that can grow revenue and earnings by allowing for a tighter focus on the customer. ERP was the precursor. Now the challenge is to build on that."

New! **"The Technological Edge"** boxes appear in each chapter. They highlight the many ways in which technology is changing the overall business environment.

Examples include:

- Relationship of management accounting to SAP *(Chapter 4)*
- SAP Implementation in Organizations *(Chapter 6)*
- How companies are using the web to conduct business *(Chapter 10)*

"The technology boxes are useful. There is always a need to demonstrate the relevance of the concepts in the context of today's business environment. They also serve to demonstrate how the changes in the environment create the need for new types of management information."

–Mike Evanchik,
University of Maryland,
University College

www.prenhall.com/atkinson

FREE Text-Specific Web Resources

Prentice Hall offers the marketplace's most robust set of free resources, continually updated and checked:

- **In the News**–Keep your class up to date! New Current Events articles are added throughout the year. Each article is summarized by our teams of expert professors and fully supported by exercises, activities, and instructor materials.
- **Free Online Study Guide**–4 Quizzes per chapter! Results from the automatically graded questions for every chapter provide immediate feedback for students and can be e-mailed to the instructor.
- **Internet Resources**–We provide management accounting-specific sites that you can preview. You'll visit the best business resources available.

For the Professor

- **Teaching Resources**, contributed by professors throughout the world, include teaching tips and techniques, academic papers, sample syllabi, and Talk to the Team, a moderated faculty chat room.
- **Online faculty support** includes downloadable supplements, additional cases, articles, links, and suggested answers to Current Events Activities and Internet Exercises.
- **What's New** gives you one-click access to all newly posted PHLIP resources.

For the Student

- **Talk to the Tutor** offers virtual office hours. Students post questions and receive responses within 48 hours from the dedicated PHLIP/CW faculty team.
- **Writing Resource Center** is an online writing center that provides links to online directories, thesauruses, writing tutors, style and grammar guides, and additional tools.

New! MyPHLIP Resources Accompany Text Website

Welcome to MyPHLIP–your personal guide to the free online resources for your book!

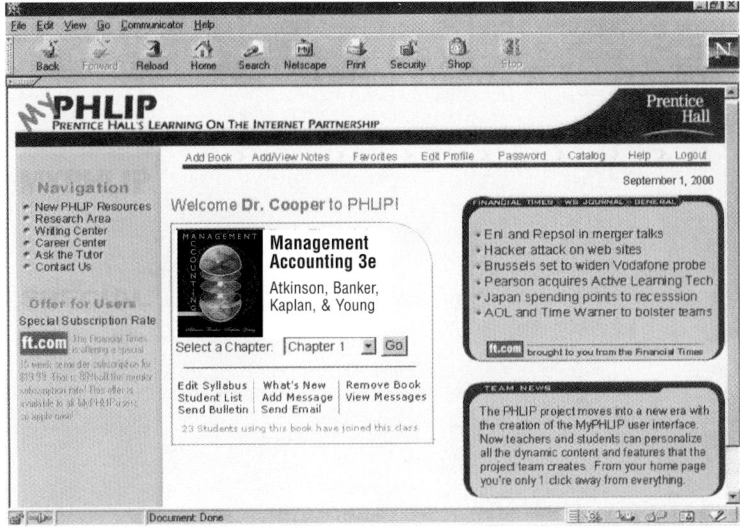

New! Custom-designed distance-learning courses available in WebCT and Blackboard formats:

Now you have the freedom to personalize your own online course materials! Prentice Hall Business Publishing provides the content and support you need to create and manage your own online course materials in WebCT and Blackboard. With quality materials and the best support packages available, we make it easy for you to use these powerful course management tools.

Our Prentice Hall Accounting online courses provide:

- Multiple-Section Chat Rooms
- Bulletin Board Conferencing
- Course Management with Page Tracking
- Calendar and Syllabus Capabilities
- Online Quizzes and Tests
- Gradebook
- "Point and Click" Systems for Course Customization

New MyPHLIP Features:

MyPHLIP pages–your personal access page unites all of your MyPHLIP Prentice Hall texts—only one web site address to remember!

Notes–you can add reminders and references where and when you'd like.

Messages–you can send messages to individual students or to all students linked to your course.

Business Headlines–this feature links you to articles in today's business news!

Instructor Manual–the MyPHLIP Instructor Manual provides tips and suggestions from our PHLIP faculty for integrating PHLIP resources into your course.

Atkinson
Banker
Kaplan
Young

MANAGEMENT ACCOUNTING

Third Edition

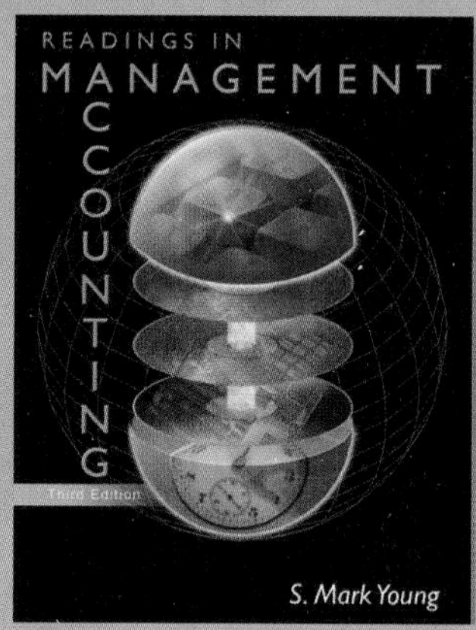

Readings in Management Accounting, Third Edition
By S. Mark Young, University of Southern California

Readings in Management Accounting, Third Edition, contains thirty-nine articles representing state-of-the-art thinking and examples on a wide variety of management accounting topics in many types of service and manufacturing contexts. The readings come from many sources, including *The Wall Street Journal, Management Accounting, Journal of Cost Management, Harvard Business Review,* and others. They present the current thinking on each of the topics covered in the text.

Study Guide by Ella Mae Matsumura and S. Mark Young

To help students prepare for examinations, each chapter in the Study Guide provides:

Learning Objectives – for each chapter
A ***Review of Key Concepts*** section – a summary of key terms and ideas
Check-marked boxes – to focus attention on particular exhibits in the text or key points
Practice Test Questions – including multiple choice and completion questions
Problems – which test knowledge and ability to master the material, are included within the practice tests

EasyABC Quick CD-ROM
Get a jump start on learning and experimenting with activity-based costing! EasyABC Quick helps you create a model of a business and identify and analyze the real costs associated with activities, processes, and products. EasyABC Quick includes extensive online help and is an important tool to help accelerate learning and understanding of activity-based costing.

Also Available:

- Instructor's Resource Manual
- Solutions Manual and Solutions Transparencies
- Test Item File
- PH Custom Test
- Solutions to Spreadsheet Templates
- On Location! Videos
- MyPHLIP/CW Web Site
- WebCT and Blackboard Standard Online Courses
- PowerPoint Presentation
- Study Guide
- EasyABC Quick software
- Spreadsheet Templates

contents

acknowledgments

We would like to take this opportunity to thank the many professors who reviewed this textbook at various stages of its development:

Thomas M. Carment, Northeastern State University
Catherine A. Craycraft, University of New Hampshire
W. Michael Donovan, Southern Maine Technical College
Michael Evanchik, University of Maryland University College
Jane B. Finley, Belmont University
David R. Fordham, James Madison University
Dale R. Geiger, California State University–San Marcos
Donald W. Gribbin, Southern Illinois University–Carbondale
James Haischer, Polk Community College
Joanne P. Healy, Kent State University
Celina L. Jozsi, University of South Florida
Paul E. Juras, Wake Forest University
John Logsdon, Webber College
Suzanne Lowensohn, Barry University
Ella Mae Matsumura, University of Wisconsin–Madison
Ann E. Selk, University of Wisconsin–Green Bay
Gary P. Spraakman, York University
Lourdes F. White, University of Baltimore
Patrick Wilkie, George Mason University

The following people attended the management accounting focus group:

Phillip A. Blanchard, University of Arizona
Robert K. Edney, Rider University
Florence McGovern, Bergen Community College
Rita Kingery, University of Delaware
Kathryn Lancaster, California Polytechnic State University–San Luis Obispo
Harry A. Newman, Fordham University
Kenneth P. Sinclair, Lehigh University
Jeanne H. Yamamura, University of Nevada–Reno

We would also like to thank the people on the Prentice Hall team who contributed to this project: Debbie Hoffman, Kathryn Sheehan, Jane Avery, Beth Toland, Anne Graydon, Diane deCastro, Paul Smolenski, Pat Smythe, and Christy Mahon. In addition, we would like to thank Donna King of Progressive.

The authors and publisher would also like to thank Ella Mae Matsumura for her valuable contributions to completing the ms.

A.A.A.
R.D.B.
R.S.K.
S.M.Y.

Anthony A. Atkinson
is currently the Society of Management Accountants of Ontario Professor in the School of Accountancy at the University of Waterloo. Atkinson received a Bachelor of Commerce and M.B.A. degrees from Queen's University in Kingston, Ontario, M.S. and Ph.D. in Industrial Administration degrees from Carnegie-Mellon University in Pittsburgh, and is a fellow of the Society of Management Accountants of Canada. He has written or co-authored two texts, monographs, and over 35 articles on performance measurement and costing. In 1989, the Canadian Academic Accounting Association awarded Atkinson the Haim Falk Prize for Distinguished Contribution to Accounting Thought for his monograph that studied transfer pricing practice in six Canadian companies. He has served on the editorial boards of two professional and five academic journals and is the Editor of the Journal of Management Accounting Research. Atkinson also served as a member of the Canadian government's Cost Standards Advisory Committee, for which he developed the costing principles it now requires of government contractors.

Rajiv D. Banker
has taught at Carnegie-Mellon University, University of Minnesota, and Dartmouth College. Banker graduated from the University of Bombay at the top of his class and received a doctorate in business administration from Harvard University. He received two awards for teaching excellence at Carnegie-Mellon University and the Outstanding Teacher Award at the University of Minnesota.

Banker has published more than 90 articles in leading research journals in accounting, information systems, computer science, operations management, management science, and economics, including articles in the *Accounting Review, Journal of Accounting and Economics,* and the *Journal of Accounting Research.* He has received five awards for his research articles. Banker's current research in management accounting includes issues pertaining to strategic cost management, activity-based costing, costs of quality, and value of performance-based incentive plans, among other issues. His research has been supported by the National Science Foundation, the Institute of Management Accountants, and several leading corporations.

Robert S. Kaplan

Marvin Bower Professor of Leadership Development, has been at the Harvard Business School since 1984. Previously, he was on the faculty of the Graduate School of Industrial Administration at Carnegie-Mellon University and served as Dean of that school from 1977 to 1983. He received a B.S. and M.S. in Electrical Engineering from M.I.T. and a Ph.D. in Operations Research from Cornell University. In 1994, he was awarded an honorary doctorate from the University of Stuttgart.

Kaplan, a co-developer of both activity-based costing and the Balanced Scorecard, has authored or co-authored ten books and more than 125 papers, which have won numerous awards. Kaplan received the Outstanding Accounting Educator Award in 1988 from the American Accounting Association (AAA) and the 1994 CIMA Award from the Chartered Institute of Management Accountants (U.K.) for "Outstanding Contributions to the Accountancy Profession".

His newest book, co-authored with David Norton, is *The Strategy-Focused Organization: How Balanced Scorecard Companies Thrive in the New Business Environment.* Other books include *Cost and Effect: Using Integrated Cost Systems to Drive Profitability and Performance,* with Robin Cooper, and *The Balanced Scorecard: Translating Strategy into Action* with David Norton, which has been translated into 19 languages.

Kaplan consults on the design of performance and cost management systems with many leading organizations, and regularly offers seminars to executives in North and South America, Europe, Middle East, South Africa, Asia, and Australia/New Zealand.

S. Mark Young

Professor of Accounting at the Leventhal School of Accounting at the University of Southern California, is Associate Editor of the *Journal of Management Accounting Research* and past Associate Editor of *The Accounting Review.* He also serves on several other major editorial boards including *Accounting, Organizations and Society.* Young received an A.B. from Oberlin College, an M.Acc. from The Ohio State University, and a Ph.D. from the University of Pittsburgh. He is the recipient of four outstanding teaching awards at the undergraduate and graduate levels, including the Golden Apple Teaching Award from the MBA Program at USC. He has published over 40 papers and made over 100 presentations of his research in Europe, Asia, Australia, and the United States. Young has been a KPMG Peat Marwick Faculty Fellow and has received research grants from the National Science Foundation, the Institute of Management Accountants, the Consortium for Advanced Manufacturing International, the Institute of Internal Auditors, and the Center for Innovation Management Studies. In 1994, together with coauthor Frank Selto, Young won the Management Accounting Section's (AAA) Notable Contribution to the Management Accounting Literature Award. Most recently, Dr. Young has conducted research or consulted with Nevada Power Company, Texas Instruments, the Economic Analysis Corporation, First Data Corporation, Chrysler, and General Motors.

Management Accounting

chapter 1

Management Accounting: Information that Creates Value

AFTER READING THIS CHAPTER, YOU WILL BE ABLE TO

1. appreciate the important role that management accounting information plays in manufacturing, service, nonprofit, and governmental organizations
2. discuss the significant differences between management accounting and financial accounting
3. understand how different people in the organization have different demands for management accounting information
4. appreciate how management accounting creates value for organizations and how it relates to operations, marketing, and strategy
5. explain why management accounting information must include both financial and nonfinancial information
6. understand why activities should be the primary focus for measuring and managing performance in organizations
7. appreciate the behavioral and ethical issues faced by management accountants

Jerry Marshall

IKON PRINTING

Vincent Daniels, manager of the new retail outlet of Ikon Printing, is pondering the management challenges in his new position. Ikon Printing is a long-established printing company in a major metropolitan area. The new Ikon outlet, located at the edge of the parking lot for Eastern Business School, represents Ikon's attempt to break into the rapidly growing business for retail digital imaging.

The Ikon retail store provides a range of copying and digital imaging services for the business school's students, faculty, and administrators, plus other retail customers. Ikon's primary products are black-and-white copies of documents. Variation exists even in this basic product, however, as consumers can choose from a variety of paper colors, sizes, and quality. Ikon recently purchased a machine that prints color copies from digital input. Color copies also can be produced in a variety of sizes, paper quality, and paper types including transparencies for overhead projection and photographic-quality reproductions. Other printing products include business cards, laminated luggage tags, and name badges for conferences, executive programs, and students.

In addition to physical printing, the Ikon center provides fax services by which individuals can both receive and transmit documents. When incoming faxes are received, a store employee calls the recipient, who stops at the outlet to receive the document. The center also has several personal computers, both Windows-based and Macintosh, which students rent by the hour for basic computer processing, Internet access, e-mail, and prepraring presentations and resumes. Each computer is connected to Ikon's black-and-white and color printers, enabling students to produce paper copies of their presentations and resumes.

Ikon has other machines that assemble printed pages into bound documents. Two different binding types are available. The store also sells a limited selection of office supplies including paper, envelopes, paper clips, glue, binders, tabs, pens, pencils, and marking pens.

Currently, about five employees (including Vincent) work at the retail outlet during prime hours (8 A.M. to 5 P.M.) with two to four people working the evening shift (6 P.M. to midnight) when walk-in business is much slower. The number of people working during the evening hours is determined by the anticipated backlog of reproduction work that will be performed during these hours.

Vincent wonders what financial and operating information he needs to manage the store. Prices for the various products and services have been set based on competitors, such as Kinko's Copying Centers and Staples. Vincent receives a daily report on total sales, broken down by cash sales, credit card sales, and credit sales to various programs at the business school; but he currently does not have a report on expenses such as labor, materials, and equipment for each line of business (black-and-white and color printing, computing, document preparation, fax services, and sales of office supplies). Thus, Vincent is unsure whether each line of business is profitable.

Further, the different business lines require different quantities and types of capital: equipment such as copying and printing machines, computers, and facsimile machines; physical capital such as office space; plus the different inventories of paper types, colors, grades and sizes, and office supplies. Are the profits in each line of business high enough to justify the capital supplied?

Vincent also would like to operate the business more efficiently. What information does he need to improve processes so that he can produce more revenues with the same resources? Is information about production volume, such as number of copies per hour from each machine, sufficient, or should he also be receiving information about the quality and defects associated with each line of business? What about speed of response when customers ask for a rush job? Is he meeting their expectations?

This information seems especially important for the pilot store that Vincent is operating. If the pilot is successful, then the parent company will likely try to open many similar outlets near schools and universities throughout the metropolitan area. For this purpose, the parent company wants to know which business lines are the most profitable, including the cost of capital and space required, so that these lines can be featured at each retail outlet. If some business lines are not profitable, then Ikon probably will not offer those services at newly opened stores unless they are necessary to build retail traffic.

With dozens of stores opening in the next few years, headquarter managers also will need operating information to monitor the performance of each store. This information will help them to take corrective action when a store's performance is not up to standard, and to identify those managers and stores whose performance's are exemplary so that their practices can be shared and transferred to the other stores.

Vincent wonders how he will develop and report the information that he and his managers at corporate headquarters will find useful as they attempt to grow the business and increase profits.

Management Accounting Information

WHAT IS MANAGEMENT ACCOUNTING INFORMATION?

 **Management accounting** has been defined by the professional society, Institute of Management Accountants, as:

> a value adding continuous improvement process of planning, designing, measuring and operating nonfinancial and financial information systems that guides management action, motivates behavior, and supports and creates the cultural values necessary to achieve an organization's strategic, tactical and operating objectives.

Management accounting
A value adding improvement process of planning, designing, measuring, and operating nonfinancial and financial information systems that guides management action, motivates behavior, and supports and creates the cultural values necessary to achieve an organization's strategic, tactical, and operating objectives.

The reported expense of an operating department, such as the assembly department of an automobile plant or an electronics company, is one example of **management accounting information.** Other examples are the calculated costs of producing a product, delivering a service, performing an activity or business process, and serving a customer. In addition, management accounting produces measures of the economic performance of decentralized operating units, such as business units, divisions, and departments. These measures help senior managers assess the performance of the company's many decentralized units. Management accounting information is a primary informational source for decision making, improvement, and control in organizations. Effective management accounting systems can create considerable value to today's organizations by providing timely and accurate information about the activities required for their success.

Management accounting information
Financial and operating data about an organization's activities, processes, operating units, products, services, and customers; e.g., the calculated cost of a product, an activity, or a department in a recent time period.

Traditionally, management accounting information has been financial; that is, it has been denominated in a currency such as \$ (dollars), £ (pound sterling), or ¥ (yen). Recently, however, management accounting information has expanded to encompass operational or physical (nonfinancial) information, such as quality and process times, as well as more subjective measurements, such as customer satisfaction, employee capabilities, and new product performance.

Differences Between Management Accounting and Financial Accounting

Management accounting systems provide information to managers and employees within the organization. **Financial accounting** reports, in contrast, communicate economic information to individuals and organizations that are external to the company. These external constituencies include shareholders, creditors (bankers, bondholders, and suppliers), regulators, and governmental tax authorities.

Financial accounting
The process of producing financial statements for external constituencies—people outside the organization, such as shareholders, creditors, and governmental authorities. This process is heavily constrained by standard-setting, regulatory, and tax authorities and the auditing requirements of independent accountants (contrast with management accounting).

The financial accounting process is constrained by mandated reporting requirements of external regulatory authorities such as the Financial Accounting Standards Board (FASB) and the Securities and Exchange Commission (SEC) in the United States, and the International Accounting Standards Committee for global reporting. In many countries, financial reporting is also influenced by governmental tax agencies. As a consequence, financial accounting tends to be rules driven, and students of financial accounting study the journal entries, procedures, standards, and regulations for producing the mandated financial statements.

For their management accounting systems, however, companies have great discretion to design systems that provide information for helping employees and managers make good decisions about their organization's financial, physical, and human resources. These decisions should lead to lower cost supplier relationships, more profitable products and customers, and more efficient and responsive processes.

To understand how management accounting information helps increase profits, reduce costs, and improve processes, we must focus on the decisions and informational needs of employees and managers, not external constituencies. Exhibit 1-1 provides an overview of the basic features of financial and management accounting and illustrates the contrast between them. In this book, we will focus on how companies' management accounting practices can be derived from the information and decision needs of its managers and employees, not from requirements to prepare statements for external constituencies.

Diversity of Management Accounting Information

We can illustrate the diverse uses for management accounting information with a relatively simple example. Consider the operation of Beck Motors, an automobile dealership. What are the varied uses for operational and financial information in this dealership? How does the demand for managerial accounting information vary among employees at different levels of the dealership?

REPAIR MECHANIC

Dennis Mitchell is an automobile mechanic who repairs and maintains cars. Dennis performs many standard activities for which much prior knowledge already exists. For example, he replaces brakes, installs a new muffler or exhaust system, lubricates the car, changes the oil and oil filter, or performs a tune-up. These tasks have been done millions of times before by mechanics at this dealership and at auto-repair facilities all over the world. Thus, standards have been established for the quantity of time and materials Dennis should take to perform each of these routine maintenance and repair procedures.

Since Dennis may wish to assess his efficiency in performing maintenance and repairs, the management accounting system should provide him with the information about the actual time required and the actual parts and materials used for each job. Dennis can use this information to determine whether he is performing at the normal efficiency assumed in establishing the labor time and materials quantity standards for this activity. In

EXHIBIT 1-1

Financial and Management Accounting Basic Features

	FINANCIAL ACCOUNTING	MANAGERIAL ACCOUNTING
Audience	*External:* Stockholders, creditors, tax authorities	*Internal:* Workers, managers, executives
Purpose	Report on past performance to external parties; contracts with owners and lenders	Inform internal decisions made by employees and managers; feedback and control on operating performance
Timeliness	Delayed; historical	Current, future oriented
Restrictions	Regulated; rules driven by generally accepted accounting principles and government authorities	No regulations; systems and information determined by management to meet strategic and operational needs
Type of Information	Financial measurements only	Financial plus operational and physical measurements on processes, technologies, suppliers, customers, and competitors
Nature of Information	Objective, auditable, reliable, consistent, precise	More subjective and judgmental; valid, relevant, accurate
Scope	Highly aggregate; report on entire organization	Disaggregate; inform local decisions and actions

THE TECHNOLOGICAL EDGE

Enterprise Resource Planning (ERP) Software Automates Companies' Transactions Systems

The world's two largest software companies, IBM and Microsoft, run big parts of their business on software that neither one of them makes. Companies such as SAP, the market leader based in Germany, competes with such companies as PeopleSoft, Oracle, Baan (Netherlands), and J.D. Edwards. In 1997, these companies had $10 billion in revenues, up 40% from 1996.

Enterprise resource planning (ERP) software enables global companies to have completely integrated information systems. A salesman in East Asia enters an order at a local terminal. The transaction is processed by the system and triggers a shipment from Singapore, the closest distribution center to the customer. Inventory lists and parts supplies are updated automatically, and worldwide production schedules and balance sheets immediately reflect the changes. With this capability, salespersons can promise firm delivery dates with more confidence, and managers can assess the impact of decisions about credit terms, inventory, production schedules, and supply-chain management.

Such installations can be extremely expensive, however, thus requiring not only considerable spending on hardware and software, but also on external consultants with the experience to customize the ERP software to individual company needs. The systems also require that companies formalize decision rules and business processses that previously were done casually and informally. The VP for research strategy at AMR (the parent company for American Airlines) commented, "About 80% of the benefits come from what you change in your business. The software is just an enabler. It's like mapping out the entire genetic structure of a human being." Companies must dissect every link in their operational decision-making chains and then reconstruct them to take advantage of the new systems. Excellent project management skills are essential.

Source: Michael H. Martin, "Smart Managing," *Fortune*, February 2, 1998, pp. 149–151.

addition to the quantity of materials and labor time used, some repair jobs may require testing the automobile on specialized equipment or using the special equipment as part of the repair process itself. Dennis will find it helpful to know how much time each job required on specialized equipment. In general, management accountants develop information about the standards for labor time, machine time, and materials usage for repetitive tasks. Employees use these standards to monitor, control, and improve the efficiency with which they use labor, materials, and equipment resources for repetitive tasks.

After Dennis finishes a maintenance or repair procedure, he performs a quality check by starting the car and testing whether it runs properly. If he finds a problem, such as a defective part or a badly installed part, then he replaces or reinstalls the faulty part and continues to work on the car until it works properly. Information about the quality of the work performed, such as number of repair jobs done correctly the first time, will be valuable in assessing how well Dennis is performing his job.

In addition to routine, standard tasks, Dennis occasionally does some nonstandard work. For example, he may repair an engine that is not working properly when neither he nor the car owner initially knows the cause for the malfunction; or, Dennis may repair a car that has suffered considerable damage in an accident. In both cases, the full extent of the required repairs is not known until Dennis starts working on the car. Dennis records the actual time spent on the job, which equipment was used, and for how long the equipment was used as well as the quantity and identity of parts and materials used to bring the car back into working condition. Then the manager of the repair shop will use this information to determine the price charged to the customer for nonstandard repairs.

Informational Summary. The information used by Dennis, a front-line employee, includes data on the quantity of materials, supplies, labor, and machine time used to produce a service. The information also includes data on the quantity of outputs Dennis produced: the number and type of repair jobs completed. Finally, it includes quality information, such as the proportion of repairs successfully completed without additional rework and the number of defects detected while producing the service, plus cycle time information—how long Dennis spent on the job from the time he started work until time of completion.

At this simple level, we can see a role for a wide variety of quantitative information for employees such as Dennis, but so far not much of a role for financial information. This situation is typical of traditional organizations, in which employees and operators are directed to perform prescribed tasks. In such situations, they receive quantitative summaries of their performance but are told little about the economic or financial consequences of the work they perform. We will return to this issue later as we discuss how front-line employees can do their jobs even better if they receive financial information related to their work. For now, assume that production and service workers primarily use quantitative operational data, rather than financial information, for their day-to-day tasks.

In addition to the amount and type of information provided to Dennis, we also should understand with what frequency it should be provided. Dennis produces outputs, such as repaired cars, continually throughout the day. Therefore, he needs daily or even individual job summaries if he is to learn how well he has performed and where opportunities for improvement may exist. Imagine that he received only a monthly report that contained just highly aggregated information:

1. total parts and materials used in car parts
2. total time used during the month to repair cars compared with the total standard time allowed for the repairs
3. total time spent reworking defects during the month

Dennis would not be able to relate such a highly aggregated and delayed report to any of the repair jobs he performed during the month. So this report would not be useful for controlling and improving his job performance. As one financial manager noted,

> To understand the problem of delayed and aggregate . . . information, you could think of the department manager as a bowler, throwing a ball at pins every minute. But we don't let the bowler see how many pins he has knocked down with each throw. At the end of the month we close the books, calculate the total number of pins knocked down during the month, compared this total with the standard, and report this information back to the bowler. If the total number is below standard, we ask the bowler for an explanation and encourage him to do better next period. We're beginning to understand that we won't turn out many world-class bowlers with this type of reporting system.[1]

To summarize, operational-level information should be timely, which means daily or after each job, so that the operator is aware at the time of any discrepancies between actual and standard or historical performance.

MANAGER OF THE SERVICE DEPARTMENT

What are the informational needs of Jennifer Pratt, service department manager of Beck Motors? Jennifer supervises the two dozen mechanics who work in the department, and

[1] R.S. Kaplan, "Texas Eastman Company," Harvard Business School Case #9-130-039, pp. 6–7.

the service representatives who discuss proposed maintenance and repairs with customers and return repaired cars to them.

Jennifer wants information about the use of the service department's resources. Since mechanics are paid for an eight-hour shift regardless if they are working on jobs, she will want a report that compares the number of hours actually spent repairing and maintaining cars with the number of hours for which mechanics are paid. This data will help her determine whether the department currently has unused capacity or whether it is operating at full capacity. If productive work is consistently below capacity (so that mechanics are often not working on jobs), then Jennifer can consider reducing the size of the service department; if the department is consistently working at capacity, then she can contemplate adding additional resources such as extra mechanics and another service bay to handle the greater demand.

To assess the efficiency of the mechanics as measured by the quantity of resources used for maintenance and repairs, Jennifer may want to compare the actual labor times, machine times, and quantity of materials and supplies used on individual jobs to the standards established for those jobs. Jennifer will want to determine which mechanics are working more efficiently than others and which are using more resources than expected. She also will monitor the quality of the work performed—which jobs or mechanics are generating defects, rework, and customer complaints. The information about the efficiency and quality of work performed will direct her attention to mechanics who may need additional education and training so that they can accomplish their jobs more efficiently and with fewer defects. Also, by identifying the highest quality and most productive mechanics, she can encourage them to share their knowledge and techniques with the less productive, more defect-prone mechanics.

In addition to monitoring capacity use, efficiency, and quality of work performed, Jennifer may need information about profitability of the service operation. She will receive a weekly or monthly report on the profit or loss generated by the service department. In addition to this aggregate report, she may want a more detailed report on profitability according to the type of service performed, such as muffler repairs, tune-ups, oil changes, and brake replacements. To prepare this report, management accountants must be able to assign the total service department's expenses to the costs of performing each type of service. Jennifer can then calculate the profitability of each type of service by linking its costs with the revenue generated by the service job. She can use the profitability information on this report to modify prices and to chose an appropriate product mix. For example, she may learn that certain jobs can be performed more efficiently by outsourcing: subcontracting the jobs to local mechanics in the area rather than handling them internally. She also can establish marketing and promotion policies to attract the most profitable maintenance and repair business to the service department. If certain types of jobs appear to be losing money, she can work with the mechanics to see how to perform these jobs at lower cost.

Jennifer also uses the cost estimates for each type of service when she estimates repair costs for used cars acquired as trade-ins when customers purchase new cars. Cost information also helps her make decisions about whether to acquire additional equipment to allow mechanics to perform certain jobs that are not currently possible with existing equipment. In summary, Jennifer will use information about the cost of individual types of maintenance and repair jobs to inform her decisions on the following:

- pricing
- product mix—which repair jobs are more profitable to promote
- capacity expansion—adding service bays, mechanics, or new equipment
- capacity contraction—reducing the number of mechanics
- outsourcing—contracting with local repair shops for certain types of service work
- process improvement—learning how to perform service jobs faster, with fewer defects, and using fewer supplies and materials

- monitoring performance—evaluating the performance of individual mechanics
- bidding for new business

These important decisions—made by middle- and upper-level managers in almost all organizations—require accurate management accounting information about current and future operations.

MANAGER OF THE DEALERSHIP

Barry Beck, president of Beck Motors, is obviously concerned with the overall profitability of the dealership but has less need than Dennis or Jennifer for information to monitor hourly and daily operations, or the profit and loss on individual jobs and car sales. Barry receives a monthly, perhaps weekly, financial report on the dealership's profitability broken down by its major operating departments: new car sales, used car sales, car repairs and service, and parts sales. This report requires a reasonable assignment of dealer expenses to the individual operating departments, which in turn means deciding how much of the dealership's people, building, and equipment resources are devoted to the various lines of business (new car sales, fleet sales, used car sales, repairs and service, and sales of parts).

The information enables Barry to monitor whether any operating department is falling short of its profit plan. It highlights the likely causes of unexpected shifts in profitability, such as variations in volume, mix, quality, and pricing. Barry also will want to compare the performance of his dealership with that of similar dealerships in terms of volume, efficiency, and profitability. This creates a demand for external data about the best practices of competitors or other comparable organizations, a practice called **benchmarking.**

Benchmarking
The process of studying and adapting the best practices of other organizations to improve the firm's own performance and establish a point of reference by which other internal performance can be measured.

Barry will want to see financial and operating statistics on factors that indicate whether the organization is creating long-term value and probability. Examples of such factors include the number of cars sold, the margins on car sales by type of vehicle, revenue per employee in the service department, customer satisfaction indexes, and number of customer complaints.

Many automobile companies now send questionnaires to recent car buyers to assess the quality of the buying experience up through the delivery of the car to the customer. Barry will want to monitor his dealership's scores on this survey over time to ensure that the trend is positive. In addition, he will compare his score with that of other dealers to determine how well his operations are performing relative to competition. As another measure of how well his dealership is doing against competitors, he will measure market share—the percent of total automobile sales and service in his local area that his dealership captures. If customer satisfaction and market share are declining or are below levels of targeted competitors, Barry may need to consider improvements in advertising, sales-force training, pricing, and customer service to regain and enhance his market position. Customer retention—the percent of customers who return to the dealership for their next car purchase—also will be a critical long-term success factor for his company.

The data used by a senior executive such as Barry Beck—the profitability of products, services, and customers; market opportunities and competitive threats; market share, customer loyalty and satisfaction; and technological innovations—are examples of **strategic information** that is critical for informing and guiding the decisions of a company's senior executives.

Strategic information
Information that guides the long-term decision making of the organization. Strategic information can include the profitability of products, services, and customers; competitor behavior and performance; customer preferences and trends; market opportunities and threats; and technological innovations.

Functions of Management Accounting

The example of Beck Motors shows how management accounting information assists several different organizational functions—operational control, product and customer costing, management control, and strategic control—as shown in Exhibit 1-2.

The demand for management accounting information differs at each level of the organization. At the operator (front-line) level where raw materials or purchased parts are converted into finished products and where services are performed for customers

EXHIBIT 1-2

Functions of Management Accounting Information

Operational control	Provide feedback information about the efficiency and quality of tasks performed
Product and customer costing	Measure the costs of resources used to produce a product or service and market and deliver the product or service to customers
Management control	Provide information about the performance of managers and operating units
Strategic control	Provide information about the enterprise's financial and long-run competitive performance, market conditions, customer preferences, and technological innovations

(such as Dennis Mitchell's repair workstation), information is needed primarily to control and improve operations. The information is disaggregate and frequent; it is more physical and operational than financial and economic. As we move higher in the organization, middle managers such as Jennifer Pratt supervise work and make decisions about financial and physical resources, products, services, and customers. These managers may receive management accounting information less frequently, and the information is more aggregate and financial based. Managers use this management accounting information diagnostically; it can alert them to aspects of operations that are different from expectations. Middle managers also use management accounting information to help them make better plans and decisions.

Executives who are at the highest organizational levels, such as Barry Beck, receive management accounting information that summarizes transactions and events occurring at the individual operator, customer, and department levels. They use this information to support decisions that have long-term consequences for the organization. Executives typically receive management accounting information less frequently, as it is used for strategic rather than operational decisions.

Historically, senior-level executives have seen only aggregate financial information to assess the performance of their organizations. Recently, however, senior executives such as Barry Beck have begun to monitor a more balanced set of performance indicators that includes much more nonfinancial information, particularly information about these factors:

1. customers and markets
2. innovations in products and services
3. overall quality, process time, and cost of critical internal processes
4. capabilities of the organization's employees and systems

This more comprehensive set of business performance indicators enables senior executives not only to monitor past performance, but also to understand the drivers of future performance.

From the automobile dealership example, you can see that management accountants must customize both the content and the frequency of management accounting information to the different tasks performed by employees, managers, and executives at each level of the organization. Management accountants cannot expect a single standard

Operational control
The process of providing feedback to employees and their managers about the efficiency of activities being performed.

Product costing
The process of measuring and assigning to products and services the costs of the activities performed to design and produce them.

Customer costing
The process of assigning marketing, selling, distribution, and administrative costs to individual customers so that the cost of serving each customer can be calculated

Management control
The process of providing information about the performance of managers and operating units.

Strategic control
The process of providing information about the competitive performance of the overall business unit, both financially and in meeting customers' expectations.

Data about the resource use and output of this bucket factory are summarized at different levels of frequency and detail to meet the wide range of information needs of managers at different organizational levels in the firm. (Jeff Greenberg/Photo Researchers, Inc.)

set of reports to serve all employee and managerial needs. This need to customize management accounting information to the particular decision, learning, and control needs of employees and managers is an important theme throughout this book.

Management Control: Origins in Twentieth-Century Enterprises

The operations of an automobile dealership are relatively simple in comparison with those of many organizations. The dealership is an example of a company with a limited product line (new cars, used cars, repair parts, and service), in a single industry (retail car sales and service), and operating at a single location. Today many companies, such as General Electric, Motorola, DaimlerChrysler, and Sony, produce diverse products in several different industries in hundreds of plants worldwide. Managers of such large, diversified, and dispersed companies require management accounting information to help them allocate physical, financial, and human resources among their operating divisions and to monitor and control their diverse operations. The origins of using management accounting information in such complex organizations can be traced to the experiences in the early twentieth century of two companies: DuPont and General Motors.[2] As we contemplate changes in management accounting and control systems at the start of the twenty-first century, it will be useful to understand the origins of some of today's most widely used approaches.

[2] See details on the DuPont and General Motors innovations in Chapter 4 of H. Thomas Johnson and Robert S. Kaplan, *Relevance Lost: The Rise and Fall of Management Accounting* Boston: Harvard Business School Press, 1987.

DUPONT AND GENERAL MOTORS: INNOVATIVE MANAGEMENT ACCOUNTING SYSTEMS AT DIVERSIFIED CORPORATIONS

Many innovations in management accounting systems occurred in the early decades of the twentieth century to support the growth of multiple-division diversified corporations, such as DuPont and General Motors. As the DuPont Company expanded, it had to acquire raw materials from many different suppliers, process these materials through many production stages in several different types of plants, and produce a diversified mix of chemical products that were bought by companies in many different industries. The senior executives of such a diversified company devised advanced techniques to coordinate operating activities in their different divisions. These techniques included an **operating budget**—the document that forecasts revenues and expenses during the next operating period including monthly forecasts of sales, production, and operating expenses—and a **capital budget**—the document that authorizes spending for resources with multiyear useful lives, such as plant and equipment.

Operating budget
The document that forecasts revenues and expenses during the next operating period including monthly forecasts of sales, production, and operating expenses.

Capital budget
The management document that authorizes spending for resources, such as plant and equipment, that will have multiyear useful lifetimes.

Return on investment (ROI)
The ratio of net income to invested capital.

Donaldson Brown, the chief financial officer (CFO) of DuPont, developed the vital **return on investment (ROI)** performance measure. The ROI measure combined a profitability measure with a capital intensity measure to produce a single measure of departmental and divisional performance, its return on investment or ROI:

Profitability Measure

Return on sales = Operating income/Sales

Asset or Capital Utilization Measure

Sales/Investment

The ROI calcuation gave DuPont executives a single number to evaluate the performance of their operating divisions:

$$\text{ROI} = \frac{\text{Operating income}}{\text{Investment}} = \frac{\text{Operating income}}{\text{Sales}} \times \frac{\text{Sales}}{\text{Investment}}$$

The senior managers at DuPont used the ROI measure to help them decide which of their divisions should receive additional capital to expand capacity.

Around 1920, Brown left DuPont to become CFO for General Motors under its new chief executive officer, Alfred Sloan. Under Sloan's and Brown's leadership, General Motors introduced many management accounting initiatives to accomplish the company's guiding operating philosophy of "centralized control with decentralized responsibility." Decentralized responsibility refers to the authority that local-division managers had in order to make their own decisions without having to seek higher approval on pricing, product mix, customer relationships, product design, acquisition of materials, and appropriate operating processes. Decentralization allowed managers to use their superior access to information about local opportunities and operating conditions to make better and more timely decisions. Centralized control of decentralized operations was accomplished by having corporate managers receive periodic financial information about divisional operations and profitability. This summary financial information helped assure the senior managers that their division managers were making decisions and taking actions contributing to overall corporate goals.

The General Motors management accounting system enabled a complex organization to plan, coordinate, control, and evaluate the operations of multiple, somewhat independent operating divisions, such as assembly divisions that produced Chevrolet, Pontiac, and Buick automobiles, and component divisions that produced parts such as radiators, batteries, fuel pumps, engines, and transmissions. It enabled the managers of these divisions to pursue aggressively their individual financial, operating, design, and marketing objectives while contributing in a coherent fashion to the overall wealth of the corporation. Sloan's and Brown's initiatives played a critical role in creating an enormously successful enterprise during the 1920 to 1970 time period.

During the past few decades, however, accounting for external constituencies in such companies as DuPont and General Motors became quite challenging because of the increased regulation and numbers of standards for external reporting (from the FASB and SEC, for example, in the United States). The demands of these external constituents led many organizations to place more emphasis on developing information for external financial reporting than for internal managerial decision making and control. As a result, management accounting systems in most organizations stagnated and proved inadequate for the changing and challenging competitive, technological, and market conditions of the late twentieth century. For example, between 1970 and 1990, General Motors experienced severe competitive challenges from European and Japanese carmakers. GM's financial managers who were focused on external reporting requirements did not adapt the management accounting systems that were designed decades earlier by Brown and Sloan. These systems, now obsolete, failed to signal to marketing managers the high costs associated with product and model proliferation, sent distorted signals to product engineers about the costs of their design decisions, and failed to provide front-line employees with accurate and timely feedback on the quality and cycle times of their manufacturing processes.

Management Accounting and Control in Service Organizations

The major changes in the demand for management accounting information experienced by manufacturing companies in recent years also have occurred in virtually all types of service organizations. Service companies have existed for hundreds of years; their importance in modern economies has increased substantially during the twentieth century. See Exhibit 1-3 for examples of service industries and companies.

SERVICE COMPANIES' DEMAND FOR MANAGEMENT ACCOUNTING INFORMATION

Service companies differ from manufacturing companies in several ways. The most obvious difference is that service companies do not produce a tangible product. Less obviously, many employees in service companies such as Ikon Printing have direct contact with customers. Thus, service companies must be especially sensitive to the timeliness and quality of the service that their employees provide to customers. Customers of service companies immediately notice defects and delays in service delivery. The consequences from such defects can be severe, as dissatisfied customers usually choose alternative suppliers after an unhappy experience.

Managers in service companies, however, have historically used management accounting information far less intensively than managers in manufacturing companies. Such a lack of accurate information about the cost of operations probably occurred because many service organizations operated in benign, noncompetitive markets, either highly regulated or government owned (such as national railroads, airlines, postal services, and telecommunications companies). Others, such as local retailers, were subject only to local, not national or global, competition. In these noncompetitive environments, managers of service companies were not under great pressure to lower costs, improve the quality and efficiency of operations, introduce new products that made profits, or eliminate products and services that were incurring losses. Since managers were not making such decisions, their demand for information to help them make such decisions was virtually nonexistent. Consequently, the management accounting systems in most service organizations were simple. They allowed managers to budget expenses by operating department and to measure and monitor actual spending against these functional departmental budgets.

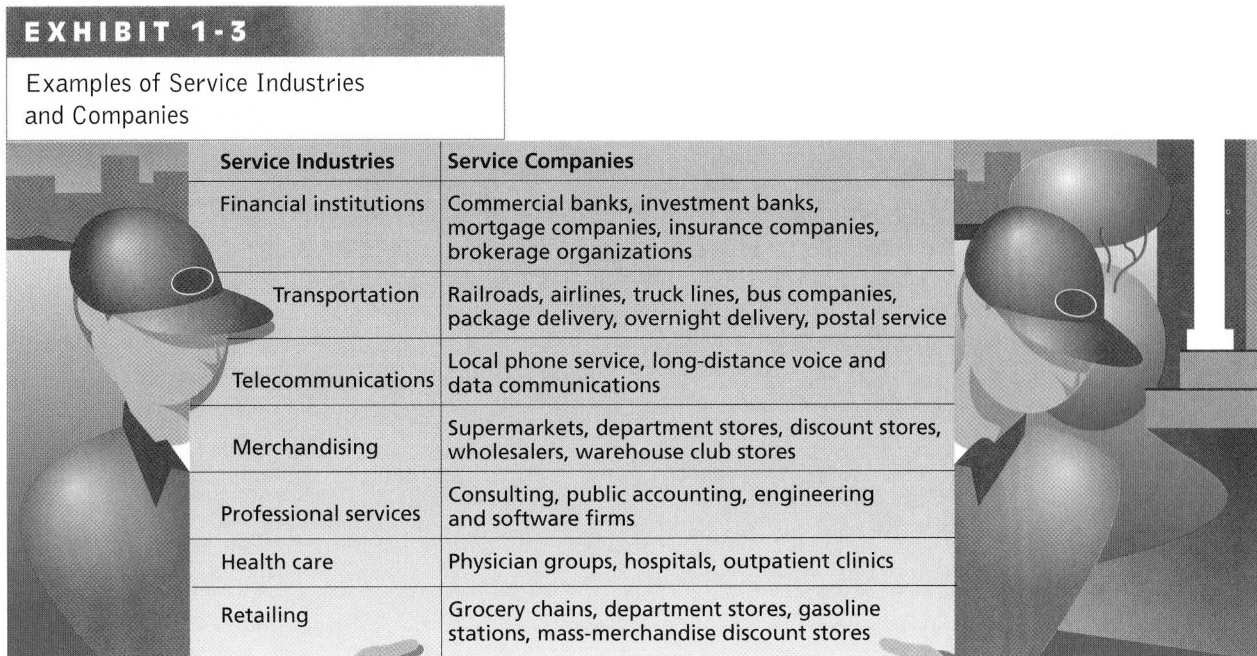

EXHIBIT 1-3

Examples of Service Industries and Companies

Service Industries	Service Companies
Financial institutions	Commercial banks, investment banks, mortgage companies, insurance companies, brokerage organizations
Transportation	Railroads, airlines, truck lines, bus companies, package delivery, overnight delivery, postal service
Telecommunications	Local phone service, long-distance voice and data communications
Merchandising	Supermarkets, department stores, discount stores, wholesalers, warehouse club stores
Professional services	Consulting, public accounting, engineering and software firms
Health care	Physician groups, hospitals, outpatient clinics
Retailing	Grocery chains, department stores, gasoline stations, mass-merchandise discount stores

Changing Competitive Environment

The competitive environment for both manufacturing and service companies has now become far more challenging and demanding. As a consequence, today's companies demand different and better management accounting information.

MANUFACTURING AND SERVICE COMPANIES

Starting in the mid-1970s, manufacturing companies in North America and Europe encountered severe competition from overseas companies that offered higher-quality products at lower prices. Global networks for raising and disbursing capital, for acquiring and transporting raw materials, and for distributing finished goods allowed the best manufacturers in whatever country they were located to access local domestic markets throughout the world. No longer was it sufficient for a company to have cost and quality parity against its domestic competitors. A company could survive and prosper only if its costs, quality, and product capabilities were as good as those of the best companies in the world.

Similarly, the deregulation movement in North America and Europe since the 1970s completely changed the ground rules under which many service companies operated. As in manufacturing companies, managers of service companies now require accurate, timely information to improve the quality, timeliness, and efficiency of the activities they perform, as well as to make decisions about their individual products, services, and customers.

GOVERNMENT AND NONPROFIT ORGANIZATIONS

Government and nonprofit organizations as well as profit-seeking enterprises are feeling the pressures for improved performance. Citizens are demanding more responsive and more efficient performance from their local, regional, and national governments. The U.S. Congress, in 1990, passed the Chief Financial Officers (CFO) Act, which requires each major federal agency to have a chief financial officer who is responsible for "the development and reporting of cost information" and "the systematic measurement of performance." The Government Performance and Results Act (GPRA) of 1993 requires that each U.S. federal agency:

- establish top-level agency goals and objectives, as well as annual program goals;

IN PRACTICE

How EMC Uses Cost Information with Its Suppliers

The EMC Corporation makes data storage systems for large company applications. EMC's business is characterized by rapidly evolving technology, where customers expect both continuous improvement in product capabilities and continuous reductions in price. To support its high-growth strategy, EMC has formed close partnerships with its 25 top-tier suppliers. The company wants more than custom-designed products from its suppliers. It closely watches suppliers' financial statements to ensure that they can keep their costs and prices at very low levels. For some components, such as cabinets, the company monitors the prices and availability of raw materials. In effect, EMC goes directly to its suppliers' suppliers and negotiates prices and volumes with them. For commodity-based parts, such as disk drives, the company monitors industry-wide pricing and availability via market research reports.

EMC also attacks the suppliers' conversion costs (labor and production support expenses). By studying the prices of other subcontractors in the industry and other forms of market research, EMC learns what the production overhead should be for the most efficient producers and what other subcontractors are charging for the same work. This enables EMC to set prices for its suppliers that let them make a profit, but only if they match the cost structure of the most efficient producers in the industry. As one supplier noted, "EMC was trying to make sure they were getting a competitive price. They weren't trying to squeeze us, but it's up to us to run efficiently."

Source: Kris Frieswick, "Up Close and Personal," *CFO Magazine*, April 1998, pp. 87–91.

- define how it intends to achieve those goals; and
- demonstrate how it will measure agency and program performance in achieving those goals.

In signing GPRA, President Clinton announced that the act will:

> chart a course for every endeavor that we take the people's money for, see how well we are progressing, tell the public how we are doing, stop the things that don't work, and never stop improving the things that are worth investing in.

In 1993, Vice President Al Gore, as part of his National Performance Review to "reinvent government," recommended an action to require the Federal Accounting Standards Advisory Board (FASAB) to issue a set of cost accounting standards for all federal activities.

Clearly, to implement these directives, managers of government agencies will need greatly improved management accounting information. In response to the CFO and GPRA acts, FASAB issued a document of "Managerial Cost Accounting and Standards-for the Federal Government."[3] This document stated, "In managing federal government programs, cost information is essential in the following five areas: (1) budgeting and cost control, (2) performance measurement, (3) determining reimbursements and setting fees and prices, (4) program evaluations, and (5) making economic choice decisions." So the demands for cost information in government will be essentially identical to those in for-profit manufacturing and service companies.

Nonprofit organizations also are feeling the pressure for cost and performance measurement. There has been explosive growth in nongovernmental organizations dealing with economic development, the environment, poverty, illiteracy, hunger and malnutrition, and public and private health, plus nonprofit organizations focused on social service and the arts. These organizations are competing for funds from governments, foundations, and private individuals. Increasingly the public and private donors are demanding account-

[3] FASAB Statement of Recommended Accounting Standards, Number 4 (June 1995).

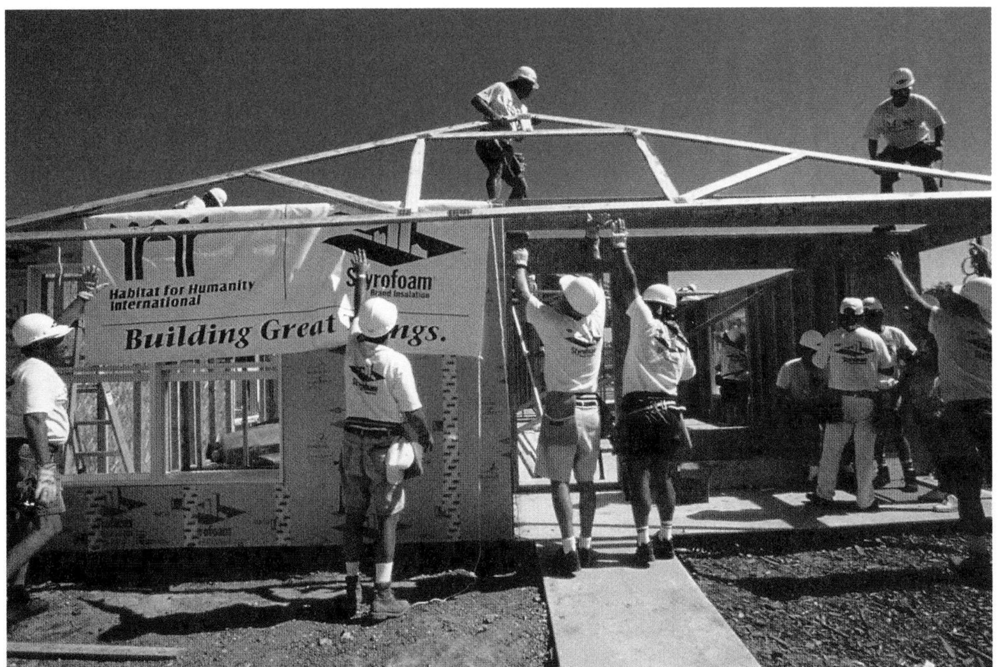

▶ *Government and nonprofit agencies, like Habitat for Humanity, as well as manufacturing and service organizations, are increasingly accountable for the way they use the resources entrusted to them in fulfilling their organizational goals. (Paul S. Howell/Liaison Agency, Inc.)*

ability from the organizations they fund, including measures of effectiveness. That is, are the organizations achieving their intended purpose and measures of efficiency, and are they using their resources productively? Managers of nonprofit organizations, of all types, are looking to adapt management accounting procedures, developed in the private sector, to the demands on them for accountability and cost and performance measurement.

MEASURING AND MANAGING ACTIVITIES AND BUSINESS PROCESSES

The measurement of **activities** will be the key organizing principle for studying management accounting information. Examples of organizational activities are assembling products, processing customer orders, and receiving and storing materials from suppliers. Activities describe how organizational resources and employees accomplish work. Cost systems based on activities, called **activity-based costing,** link organizational spending on resources (people, equipment, materials and supplies, and energy) to the products and services produced and delivered to customers. Activity-based costing will be covered extensively in this book.

We also discuss business **processes,** which represent collections of activities for accomplishing organizational objectives. Procurement, order fulfillment, and customer administration are examples of business processes.

Traditionally, management accounting information has been collected and reported for individual departments. Although cost control at the department level remains important, cost and nonfinancial performance measures, such as process time and quality, also must now be measured for activities and business processes. Such measurements emphasize total cost reduction and process improvement, not just improving efficiencies for individual workers, machines, and departments. The management accounting information will provide managers with better information about current performance so that they can have clearer priorities for where and how to improve activities and processes.

Activities
The work performed within an organization. An activity brings together people, equipment, materials, energy, and other resources to produce a product or service. Activities should be described using verbs: assemble products, set up machines, respond to customer requests, or design a new service.

Activity-based costing (ABC)
System based on activities that links organizational spending on resources to the products and services produced and delivered to customers.

Processes
A series of activities that are linked to perform a specific objective, such as purchasing materials, producing products, maintaining equipment, or servicing customers.

IN PRACTICE

Measuring the Finance Function

Lucent Technologies became a stand-alone company on October 1, 1996, when AT&T separated into three companies. Lucent, supported by Bell Laboratories, designs, develops, manufactures, and markets communications systems and technologies ranging from microchips to corporate, national, and international networks. Lucent's financial executives wanted to produce financial information that would enable them to be a key strategic partner in the formulation and implementation of Lucent strategies. A financial services leadership team was formed to lower the cost of the finance function and improve service to internal customers. Among the team's many initiatives were improvements in measurements and understanding costs.

Measurements. The team created measurements or "vital signs" for key functions. Measurements are either customer focused (measure performance in terms of customer expectations) or efficiency focused (measure internal efficiencies and costs). Examples of customer-focused measurements are response time or ratings from customer satisfaction surveys. Efficiency measurements are used mostly for comparing or benchmarking processes with those of best-in-class firms. Examples are cycle time, rate of defects, and cost per transaction.

Understanding costs. Lucent's financial team knew that tools and techniques for understanding costs and causes of costs, such as activity-based costing (ABC) systems, are common in manufacturing organizations. They recognized that modified versions of ABC also can be used in service organizations for cost reduction programs and for allocating costs equitably among business units. Lucent Financial Systems set up cost pools by financial process. It identified cost drivers such as the number of payroll payments, accounts payable payments, and accounting transactions. It included a process for tracking direct labor by business unit. The ABC approach enabled the financial managers to perform root cause analyses in areas identified as having a high potential for cost savings.

Source: Thomas A. Francesconi, "Transforming Lucent's CFO," *Management Accounting*, July 1998, pp. 22–30.

MANAGEMENT ACCOUNTING AND STRATEGY

A focus on business processes also enables companies to link their management accounting systems to the organization's strategy. Management accounting information can help organizations clarify, communicate, and implement business strategy. For example, such organizations as Dell Computers, CostCo, and McDonald's follow a strategy of operational excellence, in which they emphasize cost leadership and consistent quality. These companies use management accounting information to foster continuous improvement in the cost, quality, and cycle time of their processes. Other companies, such as Intel, Sony, and Merck, follow a strategy of product leadership, in which they develop products that deliver performance superior to that of competitors. These companies need to emphasize activities for innovation and for understanding and anticipating customers' future needs for new products and services. Their management accounting information informs and motivates employees about innovation, product performance and profitability, and new customer opportunities. A third set of companies, such as Home Depot, seek competitive success by offering great customer service, in which they provide customers with a great buying experience. These companies need management accounting information that will provide feedback on ease and speed of purchase, and friendly and helpful employees.

In summary, management accounting systems provide information that helps managers and employees improve their operational performance. The systems also are vital for communicating the strategy of the business and for aligning all organizational activities and processes to help implement the strategy.

Behavioral Implications of Management Accounting Information

We have stressed the role of management accounting information to assist the decisions and problem-solving activities of operators and managers. Information is never neutral, however. Just the act of measuring and informing affects the individuals involved. In physics, the Heisenberg uncertainty principle notes that the act of measuring the position or velocity of a subatomic particle affects the particle's position or velocity. The intrusive effect of measurement is even more pronounced when dealing with humans. As measurements are made on operations and especially on individuals and groups, their behavior changes. People react to measurements. They focus on the variables and behavior being measured and spend less attention on those not measured. Some people have recognized this phenomenon by declaring: "What gets measured gets managed" or "If I can't measure it, I can't manage it."

In addition, as managers attempt to introduce or redesign cost and performance measurement systems, people familiar with the previous systems resist. These people

IN PRACTICE

Airborne Freight: Low Costs to Fly High

"We have a passion about costs," says Airborne Chief Financial Officer Roy Liljebeck. To compete with much larger competitors such as Federal Express and United Parcel Service (UPS), Airborne decided to become the low-cost provider. Average selling, general, and administrative (SG&A) expenses in the industry run about 15.4% of sales; but Airborne maintains its SG&A at around 10%. "What sets us apart is that we have fairly nominal marketing expenses," explains Liljebeck.

Controlling costs in its 260 sales districts is a priority. Part of Airborne's strategy to reduce marketing expenses is to target high-volume customers such as corporations. Airborne doesn't go after the individual consumer. This enables the company to avoid operating expensive retail outlets in high-traffic areas. The corporate headquarters is in a lower-cost part of Seattle's downtown district. Liljebeck reports, "Costs per shipment handled is one of the major concerns for district field managers. It strongly influences their quarterly commission. On the sales side, we're concerned about shipments and revenue." By focusing on marketing cost reduction and cost avoidance, Airborne has kept the size of its sales force stable even as revenues have grown strongly.

To make cost watching part of the corporate culture, the company ties 75% of its employees incentive compensation plan to bottom-line (net profit) performance.

Matthew McVay/Stock, Boston

Source: "Resisting Temptation: The Fourth Annual SG&A Survey," *CFO Magazine,* December 1997, p. 67.

have acquired expertise in the use (and occasional misuse) of the old system and are concerned with whether their experience and expertise will be transferable to the new system. People also may feel committed to the decisions and actions taken based on the information the old system produced. These actions may no longer seem valid based on the information produced by a newly installed management accounting system. Thus, a new management system can lead to embarrassment and threat, a trigger for reactions against change.[4]

Management accountants must understand and anticipate the reactions of individuals to information and measurements. The design and introduction of new measurements and systems must be accompanied by an analysis of the behavioral and organizational reactions to the measurements. Even more importantly, when the measurements are used not only for information, planning, and decision making but also for control, evaluation, and reward, employees and managers place great pressure on the measurements themselves. Managers and employees may take unexpected and undesirable actions to influence their score on the performance measure.

Ethics and the Management Accountant

When management accounting information is used for control, and especially performance evaluation, management accountants may often find themselves in complex situations, fraught with conflict. Pressure may be exerted to influence the numbers to make a favored product, customer, or line of business appear more profitable than it actually is. Department managers may wish to distort information so that the cost of inefficient processes or the existence of substantial amounts of excess capacity is not revealed in a management accounting report. Senior executives whose incentive compensation is based on the reported financial numbers may put pressure on accountants to recognize revenue from a customer early or defer until subsequent periods the recognition of an expense. Or, conversely, executives may wish to recognize certain expenses early or conduct premature asset writedowns so that much higher earnings may be reported in future periods. For example, in the 1980s, executives at Heinz manipulated the reporting of advertising expenses to provide a cushion to manage earnings in future periods. The pressure to manipulate reported results is especially severe when compensation and promotion are strongly linked to the accounting reports, and when executives are highly sensitive to short-term stock price movements.

Ultimately, the way an individual responds to pressure derives from his or her inner values and beliefs; but individuals are also strongly influenced by their perception of organizational standards and norms. If individuals see unethical, even illegal, behavior practiced by coworkers or, worse, superiors and the organization's leaders, they may feel that such behavior is accepted and sanctioned. Unless the individual already has a strong set of personal beliefs and values, he or she may find it difficult to withstand the pressure to "go along with the flow" and participate in this behavior when a difficult, conflicting situation arises. Thus, organizational leadership plays a critical role in fostering a culture of high ethical standards.

Beyond the example set by senior executives, companies can use two types of control systems to foster high ethical standards among their employees: beliefs systems and boundary systems.[5] A **beliefs system** is the explicit set of statements, communicated to employees, of the basic values, purpose, and direction of the organization. Documents such as credos, mission statements, vision statements, and statements of purpose or

Beliefs system
The explicit set of statements, communicated to employees, of the basic values, purpose, and direction for the organization.

[4] C. Argyris and R.S. Kaplan, "Implementing New Knowledge: The Case of Activity-Based Costing," *Accounting Horizons,* September 1994, pp. 83–105.

[5] This treatment is taken from "Beliefs and Boundaries: Framing the Strategic Domain," Chapter 3 in R. Simons, *Levers of Control,* Boston: HBS Press, 1995, pp. 33–58; and R. Simons, "Control in an Age of Empowerment," *Harvard Business Review,* March-April 1995, pp. 80–88.

THE TECHNOLOGICAL EDGE

The Pervasiveness of Management Accounting and Performance Measurement: The Case of the Failed Mars Probes

Since 1992, NASA's management philosophy on space missions is that they have become "faster, better, and cheaper" to develop and execute. This philosophy is consistent with those of many organizations operating in today's global environment; however, it can only succeed if performance is not sacrificed. This does not appear to be the case for NASA, since 7 of the past 16 robotic exploration missions have either failed or developed serious technical difficulties post launch.

Critics have attacked excessive cost cutting as one of the key reasons for failure. The most recent debacle was the disappearance of a $165 million Mars probe as it was approaching the red planet in early December 1999.

Because of the recent failures, NASA is scrutinizing project management by the Jet Propulsion Laboratory (JPL) in Pasadena, which oversees the $356.8 million Mars exploration program. Also under study is Lockheed Martin, principal contractor on the projects.

Lockheed Martin has been forthcoming in its self-assessments, stating that its efforts to meet cost and schedule constraints may have forced the firm not to test the Mars Polar Lander as thoroughly as it should have, and in particular to overlook the retrorockets used for descent to the Martian surface. Further, company officials stated that cost cutting also led them to make choices that perhaps should not have been made, such as foregoing a telemetry transmitter that could have allowed flight operations engineers to keep in contact with the Lander on its descent.

Another concern has been the major cutbacks in Lockheed's engineers, and working conditions that drove assigned personnel too hard. Apparently, it was not uncommon for people to work from 80 to 100 hours a week on the project. Could employee burnout also have played a role?

Apart from the significant scientific loss inherent in the Lander's disappearance, Lockheed will probably forego much of the $12.5 million award fee. NASA is already rethinking features to add back to the next Mars Lander. New communications and hazard avoidance systems (which originally were taken away due to budget constraints) could add as much as $12 million in costs to the new Lander.

The lesson is that while decision makers in all kinds of organizations are now operating in lean environments, critical thinking about what is essential and what is not must occur before final decisions are made. Otherwise, disasters similar to the Mars Lander will continue to occur. If budgets are inadequate to allow the production of a device that will not fail, then it may be time to worry less about severe cost cutting and more about the overall effectiveness and timeliness of the project.

Source: Robert Lee Hotz, "Are Failed Mars Probes the Price of Cost Cutting?" *Los Angeles Times*, December 26, 1999, pp. A1, A45.

values are components in organizations' beliefs systems. For example, Exhibit 1-4 is the Johnson & Johnson credo. J&J senior managers meet regularly with employees throughout the company to review and interpret the credo, being sure every employee understands the company's responsibilities to customers, employees, local communities, and shareholders. The J&J credo played a powerful role when a crisis hit the company several years ago. Newspapers and TV news programs began to report consumers falling

EXHIBIT 1-4

Johnson & Johnson Credo

Our Credo

We believe our first responsibility is to the doctors, nurses and patients,
to mothers and fathers and all others who use our products and services.
In meeting their needs everything we do must be of high quality.
We must constantly strive to reduce our costs
in order to maintain reasonable prices.
Customers' orders must be serviced promptly and accurately.
Our suppliers and distributors must have an opportunity
to make a fair profit.

We are responsible to our employees,
the men and women who work with us throughout the world.
Everyone must be considered as an individual.
We must respect their dignity and recognize their merit.
They must have a sense of security in their jobs.
Compensation must be fair and adequate,
and working conditions clean, orderly and safe.
We must be mindful of ways to help our employees fulfill
their family responsibilities.
Employees must feel free to make suggestions and complaints.
There must be equal opportunity for employment, development
and advancement for those qualified.
We must provide competent management,
and their actions must be just and ethical.

We are responsible to the communities in which we live and work
and to the world community as well.
We must be good citizens — support good works and charities
and bear our fair share of taxes.
We must encourage civic improvements and better health and education.
We must maintain in good order
the property we are privileged to use,
protecting the environment and natural resources.

Our final responsibility is to our stockholders.
Business must make a sound profit.
We must experiment with new ideas.
Research must be carried on, innovative programs developed
and mistakes paid for.
New equipment must be purchased, new facilities provided
and new products launched.
Reserves must be created to provide for adverse times.
When we operate according to these principles,
the stockholders should realize a fair return.

Johnson & Johnson

Courtesy of Johnson & Johnson.

ill and dying after consuming contaminated pills of J&J's best-selling over-the-counter product, Tylenol. Even before much was known about the cause or the pervasiveness of the problem, executives quickly removed the product from every store in the country, a move that restored the company's credibility and enabled a speedy recovery from the unfortunate event. The executives, when later asked to explain the rapidity of their very costly response, unanimously declared that the credo gave them no other choice.

The statements in a beliefs system are intended to inspire and promote commitment to the organization's core values and its purpose for being in business. When conflicting situations arise, however, the lofty rhetoric in the statements will only have true meaning and serve as guides to actions if employees observe senior managers acting according to the statements. In this way, employees learn that the company's stated beliefs represent deeply rooted and actionable values.

Articulate and actionable beliefs systems, however, are not enough. These systems inspire people to higher values and missions but may not contain sufficient clarity to communicate what behavior and actions are unacceptable. So companies also need boundary systems that communicate what actions must never be taken. **Boundary systems** are stated in negative terms, or in minimal standards of behavior. They are intended to constrain the range of acceptable behavior.

Boundary systems Statements that communicate to employees what actions must never be taken; intended to constrain the range of behavior.

People generally want to do the right thing—to act ethically in accordance with the organization's credo, mission, vision, and values statements; but pressures to achieve superior results may lead to situations when individuals are asked to bend the rules. Management accountants, as collectors and reporters of the organization's performance measures, may be more subject to such pressure than many other individuals.

The examples of organizations that do not have clear, enforceable boundary systems often appear on the front pages of newspapers and on television. Violations of ethical norms, society's rules, and the company's own policies may jeopardize an organization's existence (note the severe penalties incurred by institutions such as Kidder Peabody, Baring's Bank, and Sumitomo Metals, when managers or traders took huge, unauthorized risks to generate near-term earnings). Managers in other companies may collude with competitors to set prices or allocate market share, in clear violation of antitrust laws. When discovered, the company, its employees, and its shareholders suffer significant losses.

Codes of conduct should clearly identify forbidden actions, such as bribery, violations of customers' or clients' privacy, and spying on competitors. Boundary systems also include clear communication of the laws under which the company operates. Antitrust laws; zero tolerance for sexual, racial, and gender discrimination and harassment; environmental, health, and safety laws; and foreign corrupt practices regulations are examples of boundary systems that must be understood and adhered to by all employees. Management accountants, like all employees, must be aware of and be deeply committed to act in ways that do not violate their organization's code of conduct and societal laws governing organizational behavior and actions. Management accountants, as designers and custodians of the organization's reporting and control systems, have an additional obligation to ensure that such boundary systems exist in their organization, and that the boundary systems are clearly communicated throughout the organization. They also should monitor that senior executives act quickly and decisively when behavior in violation of these standards is detected. If violations are detected but not acted upon, management accountants can communicate with the audit committee of the board of directors, who are the shareholders and society's representatives in the organization.

Management accountants, as members of a profession, also operate with an additional boundary system, the code of behavior promulgated by their industry and professional association. In the United States, many management accountants belong to the Institute of Management Accountants (IMA). In the United Kingdom and elsewhere in the world, the Chartered Institute of Management Accountants (CIMA) is an important and influential professional association for management accountants. Professional organizations usually establish ethical norms and codes of professional conduct for their members. The professional association can monitor and police its norms and codes through peer reviews. They have procedures for disciplinary action when violations are detected. Exhibit 1-5 contains an extract from the IMA's standard of ethical conduct. Note how many of the guidelines are phrased in terms of what management accountants should *not* do, consistent with how boundary systems operate.

Management accountants, when faced with pressure to manipulate or bias reported numbers, will be guided by their own and the organization's norms and values. The organization's values should be communicated through beliefs systems that inspire individuals about working toward a mission somewhat higher than improving short-term performance. The organization hopes that beliefs systems will support and reinforce the individual's own inner values to act appropriately. But beliefs systems, by themselves, are not sufficient. The management accountant must be aware of the organization's

EXHIBIT 1-5

Extract from "Standards of Ethical Conduct for Management Accountants"

Management accountants have a responsibility to:

- Avoid actual or apparent conflicts of interest and advise all appropriate parties of any potential conflict.
- Refrain from engaging in any activity that would prejudice their ability to carry out their duties ethically.
- Refuse any gift, favor, or hospitality that would influence or would appear to influence their actions.
- Refrain from either actively or passively subverting the attainment of the organization's legitimate and ethical objective.
- Recognize and communicate professional limitations or other constraints that would preclude responsible judgment or successful performance of an activity.
- Communicate unfavorable as well as favorable information and professional judgments or opinions.
- Refrain from engaging in or supporting any activity that would discredit the profession.

Courtesy of the Institute of Management Accountants, Montvale, NJ.

code of conduct, society's laws, and the standards set by his or her professional organization to provide guidance about the behavior and actions that are unacceptable under any circumstances.

Ikon Printing Revisited

Vincent Daniels, the new manager of Ikon Printing's first retail outlet, now understands the considerable opportunities and challenges he faces. He must develop systems that will inform him about the efficiency, cost, and profitability of the various activities performed in his store. Vincent will want a system that provides day-to-day feedback about the efficiency and productivity of the various machines (copies per hour); machine availability and downtime; product defects, rework, customer returns, and defective merchandise; and response times to customer requests. He will want activity-based information about product cost and profitability (black-and-white copying, color copying, facsimile services, document preparation, computer rental, and supplies), and profitability by major customer type (the business school's MBA and executive programs, faculty research, school administration, and other institutional accounts). Such information will help Vincent and Ikon's corporate executives make better pricing decisions for their services and customers, including volume discounts or surcharges for orders with special requirements and services. The information about the most profitable product lines and customer segments will help direct marketing efforts and spending on equipment, space, and inventory to their most profitable uses. Beyond the operational and financial measurements, Vincent may wish to have several nonfinancial measures of the outcomes and the drivers of the outlet's strategy—market share and satisfaction for targeted customers; time, quality, and cost of internal processes; new products and services to offer; employee skills and motivation; and system capabilities. The management accounting information will help Vincent and Ikon Printing operate their business in a way that maximizes long-term performance.

SUMMARY

Management accounting has become an exciting discipline that is undergoing major changes to reflect the challenging new environment that organizations worldwide now face. Accurate, timely, and relevant information about the economics and performance of organizations is crucial to organizational success. This chapter has introduced the different informational needs for operators/employees, middle managers, and senior executives. It described the different tasks that are informed by management accounting information: operational control, product and customer costing, management control, and strategy implementation and control. Individuals will use both financial and nonfinancial information as they perform their tasks. The focus on the costs incurred and the value created by organizational activities and processes will provide a central focus for management accounting information. The design of management accounting systems and the use and interpretation of the management accounting information produced by these systems are now critical to the success of both manufacturing and service organizations in today's globally competitive and technologically challenging environment. This textbook introduces the opportunities for enhancing organizational performance through effective design and use of management accounting systems.

KEY TERMS

activities, 17
activity-based costing, 17
beliefs system, 20
benchmarking, 10
boundary systems, 23
capital budget, 13
customer costing, 11
financial accounting, 5
management accounting, 5
management accounting information, 5
management control, 11
operating budget, 13
operational control, 11
processes, 17
product costing, 11
return on investment (ROI), 13
strategic control, 11
strategic information, 10

ASSIGNMENT MATERIALS

QUESTIONS

1-1 Why do operators/workers, middle managers, and senior executives have different informational needs? (LO 1, 3)

1-2 Why do a company's operators/workers, managers, and executives have different informational needs than shareholders and external suppliers of capital? (LO 2)

1-3 Why may financial information alone be insufficient for the ongoing informational needs of operators/workers, managers, and executives? (LO 3, 4, 5)

1-4 Why might senior executives need measures besides financial ones to assess how well their business performed in the most recent period? (LO 4, 5)

1-5 What forces have caused management accounting systems designed decades ago to become less relevant and less valuable for organizational employees in today's globally competitive environment? (LO 1, 5)

1-6 How does the role for management accounting systems change as the environment becomes more competitive? (LO 4, 5)

1-7 What is the impact of shifting the role of management accounting information from controlling workers and operators to informing the continuous improvement activities of these workers and operators? (LO 6)

1-8 What, if any, are the differences between the management accounting information needed in manufacturing organizations and that needed in service organizations? (LO 1)

1-9 Why is management accounting information important in government and nonprofit organizations? (LO 1)

1-10 What information do employees need about activities performed in the organization? (LO 6)

1-11 How can managers use information on the cost of activities and business processes? (LO 6)

1-12 What information might management accounting systems provide to managers and employees for each of the following strategies: operational excellence, product leadership, and customer service? (LO 4)

1-13 How can management accounting information produce behavioral and organizational reactions? (LO 7)

1-14 How can beliefs systems and boundary systems foster high ethical standards among employees? (LO 7)

EXERCISES

LO 1, 3 **1-15** ***Different information needs*** Consider the operation of a fast-food company with hundreds of retail outlets scattered about the country. Identify the management accounting information needs for the following:

(a) The manager of a local fast-food outlet that prepares food and serves it to customers who walk in or pick it up in a drive-through window

(b) The regional manager who supervises the operations of all the retail outlets in a three-state region

(c) Senior management located at the company's corporate headquarters. Consider specifically the information needs of the president and the vice presidents of operations and marketing.

Be sure to address the content, frequency, and timeliness of information needed by these different managers.

LO 1, 3 **1-16** ***Different information needs*** Consider the operation of a hospital. Identify the management accounting information needs for the following:

(a) The managers of (1) a patient unit, where patients stay while being treated for illness or while recuperating from an operation, and (2) the radiology department, where patients obtain X rays and receive radiological treatment

(b) The manager of the nursing service, who hires and assigns nurses to all patient units and to specialty services such as the operating room, emergency room, recovery room, and radiology room

(c) The chief executive officer of the hospital

Be sure to address the content, frequency, and timeliness of information needed by these different managers.

LO 1, 3 **1-17** ***Different information needs*** Consider the operation of Ikon Printing. Identify the management accounting information needs for the following:

(a) An employee desiring to help serve customers more efficiently and effectively

(b) The manager of a single retail outlet

(c) The president of Ikon Printing

Be sure to address the content, frequency, and timeliness of information needed by these different individuals.

LO 1, 2, 4, 5 **1-18** Consider the descriptions of management accounting provided in Exhibit 1-1 and Exhibit 1-2. Discuss why these responsibilities are viewed as "accounting" and how management accountants interface with other functional areas in fulfilling the stated responsibilities. What skills and knowledge does a management accountant need to fulfill the responsibilities?

PROBLEMS

1-19 ***Differences between financial and managerial accounting*** Many German companies have their management accounting department as part of the manufacturing operations group rather than as part of the corporate finance department. These German companies operate two separate accounting departments. One performs financial accounting functions for shareholders and tax authorities; the other maintains and operates the costing system for manufacturing operations. LO 2

REQUIRED

What are the advantages and disadvantages of having separate departments for financial accounting and management accounting?

1-20 ***Role for nonfinancial information for senior executives*** A recent article on the decline of a U.S. corporation described the information provided and the reward structure of senior managers: "Summarized data on sales and sales growth were displayed on senior executives' instrument panels and the managerial reward system gave generous weight to sales volume. In contrast, the senior executives' dashboard lacked summarized information on field failures, their effect on customer relations, the performance of competing machines, the growing cancer of failure-prone features, and the extent of customer defections."[6] LO 4, 5

REQUIRED

(a) Should senior executives be responsible for delivering excellent financial performance to shareholders, leaving the details of customer relations, engineering design, and manufacturing operations to the vice presidents and managers of these various departments?

(b) Are financial measures alone sufficient to measure the performance of an organization during a period and to use as a basis for compensating the senior executives of an organization? Why or why not?

(c) What problems, if any, arise from monitoring and rewarding senior executives by a combination of financial and nonfinancial measures?

1-21 Sarah Schmit, manager of the Components Division of FX Corporation, is considering a new investment for her division. The division has an investment base of $4,000,000 and an operating income of $600,000. The new investment of $500,000 supports corporate strategy and is expected to increase operating income by $50,000 next year, an acceptable level of return from corporate headquarters' point of view. LO 7

REQUIRED

(a) What is the current return on investment (ROI) for Components Division?

(b) What will the ROI be if Sarah undertakes the new investment?

(c) Suppose Sarah's compensation consists of a salary plus a bonus proportional to her division's ROI. Is Sarah's compensation higher with or without the new investment?

(d) Suggest changes to FX Corporation's management that will better align performance evaluation and compensation with corporate goals.

1-22 ***Differences between financial and managerial accounting*** The controller of a German machine tool company believed that historical cost depreciation was inadequate for assigning the cost of using expensive machinery to individual parts and products. Each year he estimated the replacement cost of each machine and LO 2

[6] J. Juran, "Made in U.S.A.: A Renaissance in Quality," *Harvard Business Review* (July–August 1993).

calculated depreciation, based on the machine's replacement cost, to be included in the machine-hour rate used to assign machine expenses to the parts produced on that machine. Additionally, the controller included an interest charge, based on 50% of the machine's replacement value, into the machine-hour rate. The interest rate was an average of the three- to five-year interest rate on government and high-grade corporate securities.

As a consequence of these two decisions (charging replacement cost rather than historical cost and imputing a capital charge for the use of capital equipment), the product cost figures used internally by company managers were inconsistent with the numbers that were needed for inventory valuation for financial and tax reporting. The accounting staff had to perform a tedious reconciliation process at the end of each year to back out the interest and replacement value costs from the cost of goods sold and inventory values before they could prepare the financial statements.

REQUIRED

(a) Why would the controller introduce additional complications into the company's costing system by assigning replacement value depreciation costs and imputed interest costs to the company's parts and products?

(b) Why should management accountants create extra work for the organization by deliberately adopting policies for internal costing that violate the generally accepted accounting principles that must be used for external reporting?

LO 1, 4, 5 **1-23** ***Role for financial information for continuous improvement*** Consider an organization that has empowered its employees, asking them to improve the quality, productivity, and responsiveness of their processses that involve repetitive work. This work could arise in a manufacturing setting, such as assembling cars or producing chemicals, or in a service setting, such as processing invoices or responding to customer orders and requests. Clearly the workers would benefit from feedback on the quality (defects, yields) and process times of the work they were doing to suggest where they could make improvements. Identify the role, if any, for sharing financial information as well with these employees to help them in their efforts to improve quality, productivity, and process times. Be specific about the types of financial information that would be helpful, and the specific decisions or actions that could be made better by supplementing physical and operational information with financial information.

LO 7 **1-24** ***Ethical issues*** You are employed as a senior manager in an insurance organization. One of your responsibilities is to randomly review claims for reimbursement that have been submitted by people who have traveled on the organization's behalf.

By chance, you have pulled a claim that was submitted by Harold, one of your closest friends. You decide to confront your friend with your findings. Harold, knowing you are a friend, replies: "Sure the claim contains false items. Everybody does it and it is almost expected!"

Stunned by his confession, you tell him that he has to resubmit an accurate reimbursement claim. Harold responds: "Look Mike, I don't feel that I get paid enough in this lousy organization and this is my way of getting a few extra dollars each month. You know how they have been working all of us to death after the layoffs. I'm entitled to this, and I refuse to resubmit the claim."

REQUIRED

(a) What do you think of Harold's argument?

(b) Should you have approached him differently?

(c) What should you do now, and why?

(d) How might the company's control system be designed to foster high ethical standards regarding reimbursement claims and other issues?

CASES

1-25 ***Information for employee empowerment*** A U.S. automobile components plant had recently been reorganized so that quality and employee teamwork were to be the guiding principles for all managers and workers. One production worker described the difference: LO 3

> In the old production environment, we were not paid to think. The foreman told us what to do, and we did it even if we knew he was wrong. Now, the team decides what to do. Our voices are heard. All middle management has been cut out, including foremen and superintendents. Management relies on us, the team members, to make decisions. Salary people help us make these decisions; the production and manufacturing engineers work for us. They are always saying, "We work for you. What do you need?" And they listen to us.

The plant controller commented as follows:

> In traditional factories, the financial system viewed people as variable costs. If you had a production problem, you sent people home to reduce your variable costs. Here, we do not send people home. Our production people are viewed as problem solvers, not as variable costs.

REQUIRED

(a) What information needs did the production workers have in the old environment?

(b) What information do you recommend be supplied to the production workers in the new environment that emphasizes quality, defect reduction, problem solving, and teamwork?

1-26 ***Role for financial information for continuous improvement*** The manager of a large semiconductor production department expressed his disdain for the cost information he was presently given: LO 3, 5

> Cost variances are useless to me.[7] I don't want to ever have to look at a cost variance, monthly or weekly. Daily, I look at sales dollars, bookings, and on-time delivery (OTD)—the percent of orders on time. Weekly, I look at a variety of quality reports including the outgoing quality control report on items passing the final test before shipment to the customer, in-process quality, and yields. Yield is a good surrogate for cost and quality. Monthly, I do look at the financial reports. I look closely at my fixed expenses and compare these to the budgets, especially on discretionary items like travel and maintenance. I also watch headcount.
>
> But the financial systems still don't tell me where I am wasting money. I expect that if I make operating improvements, costs should go down, but I don't worry about the linkage too much. The organizational dynamics make it difficult to link cause and effect precisely.

REQUIRED

Comment on this production manager's assessment of his limited use for financial and cost summaries of performance. For what purposes, if any, are cost and financial information helpful to operating people? How should the management accountant determine the appropriate blend between financial and nonfinancial information for operating people?

[7] We will study cost variances in later chapters. For purposes of working this problem, it is sufficient to recognize that a cost variance represents the difference between the cost actually assigned to a production department and the cost that was expected or budgeted for that department.

LO 1, 4 **1-27** ***Part proliferation: role for activity-based costing*** An article in *The Wall Street Journal* (June 23, 1993) reported on the major changes occurring in General Motors. Its new CEO, John Smith, had been installed after the board of directors requested the resignation of Robert Stempel, the previous CEO.

(John Smith's) North American Strategy Board identified 30 components that could be simplified for 1994 models. GM had 64 different versions of the cruise control/turn signal mechanism. It planned to pare that to 24 versions the next year, and the following year to just 8. The tooling for each one cost GM's A.C. Rochester division about $250,000. Smith said, "We've been talking about too many parts doing the same job for 25 years but we weren't focused on it." [Note that the tooling cost is only one component of the cost of proliferating components. Other costs include the design and engineering costs for each different component, purchasing costs, setup and scheduling costs, plus the stocking and service costs for every individual component in each automobile dealership (including Beck Motors) around the country.]

GM's proliferation of parts was mind-boggling. GM made or bought 139 different hood hinges, compared with 1 for Ford. . . . Saginaw's Plant Six juggled parts for 167 different steering columns—down from 250 the previous year but still far from the goal of fewer than 40 by decade's end.

This approach increased GM's costs exponentially. Not only did the company pay far more engineers than competitors to design steering columns, but it also needed extra tools and extra people to move parts around, and it suffered from quality glitches when workers confused one steering column with another.

REQUIRED

(a) How could an inaccurate and distorted product costing system have contributed to the overproliferation of parts and components at General Motors?

(b) What characteristics should a new cost system have that would enable it to signal accurately to product designers and market researchers about the cost of customization and variety?

LO 4, 6 **1-28** ***Role for activity-based cost systems in implementing strategy*** Consider the case of the Cott Corporation, a Canadian private label producer of high-quality cola beverages. Cott is attempting to get grocery retailers to stock its cola beverages, as a lower price alternative to the international brands. Coca-Cola and Pepsi Cola. The international brands (Coke and Pepsi) deliver directly to the retailer's store and stock their product on the retailer's shelves. Cott, in contrast, delivers to the retailer's warehouse or distribution center, leaving the retailer to move the product to the shelves of its various retail outlets. Cott offers substantially lower prices to the retailers, and, in addition, is willing to work with the grocery retailer to customize the cola beverage to the retailer's specification, develop special packaging for the retailer including labeling the beverage with the retailer's name (a practice known as "retailer branding"; e.g., "Safeway Select Cola"), offer a full variety of carbonated beverages (diet, caffeine free, multiple flavors, multiple sizes, and packaging options), and develop a marketing and merchandising strategy for the retailer for the private-label beverage.

REQUIRED

How can Cott build cost systems to help it implement its strategy successfully? Consider how Cott might measure and manage activities and processes, and relationships with suppliers and customers.

LO 2 **1-29** ***Financial versus management accounting: role for activity-based cost systems in privatization of government services*** The mayor of Gotham City is dissatisfied with rising costs and deteriorating quality of the services provided by the municipal workers, particularly in the transportation department: paving roads, repairing potholes, and cleaning the streets. He is contemplating privatizing these services by outsourcing the business to independent, private contractors. The mayor has demanded that his staff develop an activity-based cost system for municipal services, however, before proceeding with his privatization initiative, declaring, "Introducing competition and privatization to government services requires real cost information. You can't compete out if you are using fake money." Currently, the accounting and financial systems of Gotham City report only how much is being spent in each department, by type of expenditure: payroll, benefits, materials, vehicles, equipment (including computers and telephones) and supplies.

REQUIRED

(a) Before outsourcing to the private sector, why does the mayor want to develop activity-based cost estimates of the current cost of performing these municipal services?

(b) After building activity-based cost models, should this information be shared with the municipal workers? Why or why not? How might the workers use the activity-based cost information?

1-30 ***Comprehensive performance measurement in public and nonprofit organizations*** Organizations in the public and nonprofit sector, such as government agencies and charitable social service entities, have financial systems that budget expenses and monitor and control actual spending. Explain why these organizations should consider developing a comprehensive set of performance measurements (including nonfinancial measures) to monitor and report on their performance. What should be the various perspectives in such a comprehensive set of measurements? LO 1, 5

1-31 ***Ethical issues, revenue recognition*** Read the article, "What's Wevenue?" by Elizabeth MacDonald, in *The Wall Street Journal* (January 6, 2000, p. A1). The article states that managers faced aggressive revenue targets and reports testimony about "a dozen or more accounting tricks that various employees, at various levels of management, had deployed to keep the stock buoyant." LO 7

REQUIRED

(a) What revenue recognition or other accounting-related improprieties does the article report?

(b) How widely known were the improprieties within the company?

(c) Describe the reponsibilities and challenges management accountants and others within the organization face with respect to the accounting issues reported in the article, and explain how organizational leadership or control systems can help foster high ethical standards and help prevent the problems described in the article.

NATURE SCOPE FOCUS

COST BEHAVIOR

COST DECISIONS

PLANNING FOR DECISION-MAKING

PLANNING FOR EVALUATION

ORGANIZATIONAL BEHAVIOR AND DESIGN

chapter 2

The Organization as a System of Activities

AFTER READING THIS CHAPTER, YOU WILL BE ABLE TO

1. understand how organizations define objectives and use these objectives to define operating priorities
2. think of the organization as a sequence of activities in a value chain
3. demonstrate how performance measures help organization members manage the value chain
4. describe the process that organizations can use to reduce costs by focusing on activity performance

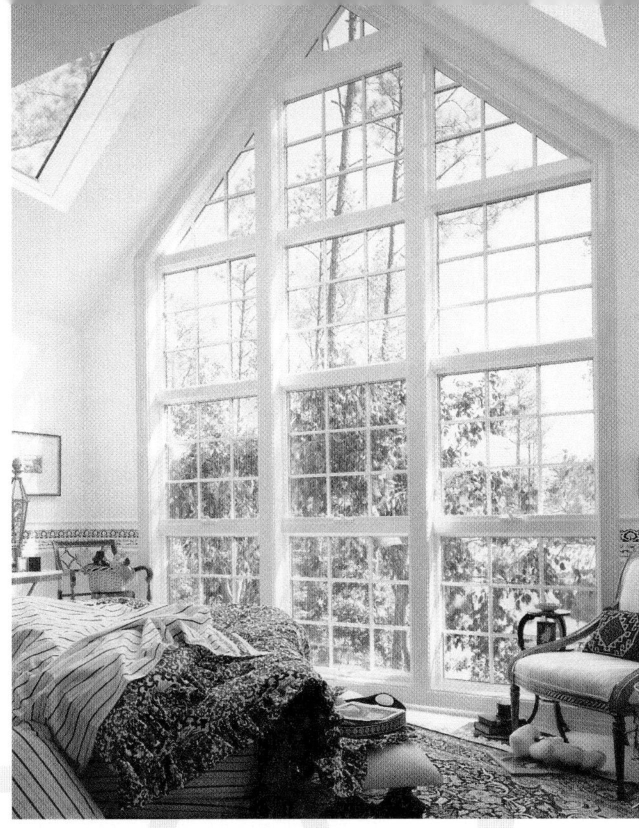

▶ *Windows serve both aesthetic and environmental purposes in residential construction. Customers judge the expected and actual performance of windows by the criteria they deem important. (Anderson Windows, Inc.)*

MIKE'S CUSTOM WINDOWS

Mike's Custom Windows manufactured and supplied windows to the residential construction industry. The residential window industry was characterized by standardization. Window manufacturers supplied a narrow range of standard designs in standard sizes. Large suppliers could supply approximately 20 designs in 10 sizes. The standardization allowed for mass production systems that minimized cost while ensuring a high level of quality.

The market was segregated by two characteristics—the material used in the nonglass parts of the window (which was either wood, vinyl, or metal), and the quality level. Quality levels varied for each material type, but the best windows usually were wood and the lowest quality usually were metal or vinyl.

The existing customization was expensive and required long lead times, since custom windows were made during idle, off-season periods. This meant that builders wanting custom windows needed to order them as far as six months in advance.

Because of the high cost of transportation, the window market was a curious blend of large national manufacturers and local manufacturers. The large manufacturers used their economies of scale, both in manufacturing and logistics, to control the lion's share of the window market and earn the highest margins. Although some local manufacturers developed a high-end product, most usually competed on price at the low-end levels that the larger manufacturers tend to ignore. Almost every manufacturer sold through hardware and building supply stores. Only na-

tional manufacturers had their own showrooms, and these were confined to large urban areas.

Mike's Custom Windows was a small regional supplier that traditionally competed on both quality and price. Its reputation for quality allowed it to gain shelf space with two large building supply chains. Although Mike tried to match the prices of the large suppliers, it was a losing battle. By using highly automated machines, better materials, national distribution deals with a large trucking organization, and a workforce that understood the importance of quality, the large chains were increasing quality and lowering prices. Their strategy was clear—they were reducing the range of products and producing for inventory based on traditional sales patterns.

The result was that the retailers were carrying large inventories with high inventory-related costs, but because the products provided high gross margins (selling price minus acquisition cost), they did not complain. Mike's margins were much smaller and falling as it struggled to meet the larger suppliers' continuous price cuts. Mike's was a family-owned business that had been in operation for more than 30 years, and it had a good image. However, three years of increasing losses convinced the organization that it had two choices—either change the way it did business or get out of the business. The latter was not a choice that the family considered as an alternative.

So Mike's realized that it needed to refocus itself and to develop a competitive advantage that was sustainable. Management realized that the firm had two major strengths, a highly committed workforce and a detailed knowledge of its customers and their requirements in the local building industry. It set out to capitalize on both of them.

The Nature of the Organization's Objectives

Strategy
The process of choosing target customers and deciding how to serve those customers in a unique, sustainable way.

In this section we discuss strategy. **Strategy** is about choosing your target customers and deciding how you are going to serve those customers. Strategic choices are made within the context of the objectives that the organization's principals have set for the organization. For profit-seeking organizations, these objectives are primarily financial such as achieving a target return on investment or earnings per share. Not-for-profit organizations' objectives will usually reflect the beneficiaries that the organizations were created to serve. For this reason, we focus on an organization's customers, as they provide the organization's primary focus.

Once the organization's decision makers decide how the organization will meet its customers' requirements, they design the operating systems or sequence of activities that the organization will use to meet those requirements. This sequence of activities consists of the linked set of activities, both inside and outside the organization, that is used to deliver goods or services to the target customers. To assess the performance of this value chain, organizations develop a system of integrated measures called the performance measurement system. One of these performance measures is costs. With this overview in mind, let us now develop some of the details.

Exhibit 2-1 summarizes the strategic planning perspective. The central element in the exhibit is the target set of customers chosen during the planning process. These

EXHIBIT 2-1

Strategic Planning Elements

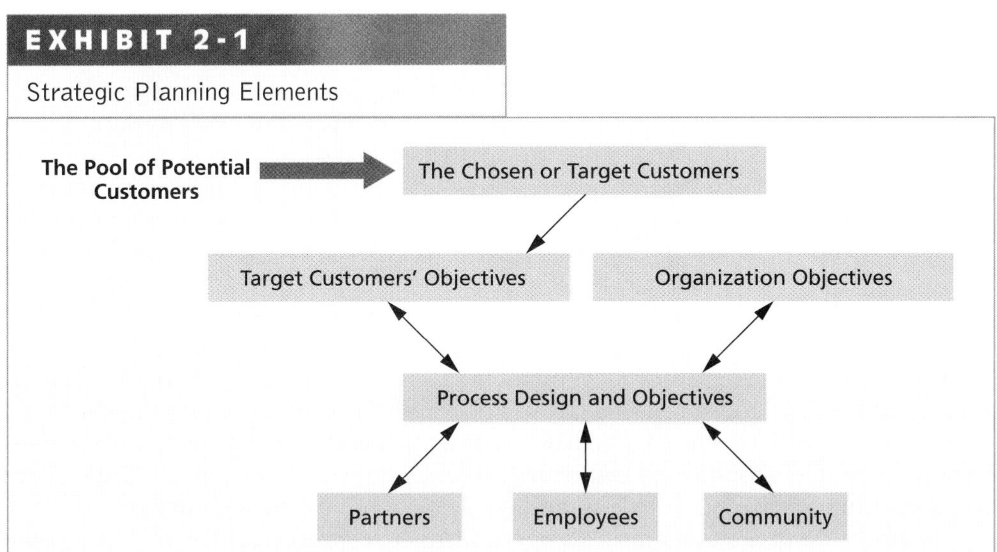

customers have specific requirements that the organization both understands and pursues; thus, the customers' requirements become the organization's requirements. The organization's performance in meeting customers' requirements is monitored and assessed. Measuring performance becomes an element of the organization's management accounting and control system.

What can we say are the objectives of an organization? Quite simply, the organization's objectives are, or at least should be, those of its controlling owners or principals. The primary objective of most profit-seeking organizations, such as DaimlerChrysler, is to provide its shareowners with a return on investment that equals or exceeds that of investments of comparable risk. The primary objective of a not-for-profit organization, such as the Society for the Prevention of Cruelty to Animals, is to provide the greatest level of service to its target community or clients for a given level of cost.

No organization can achieve its primary objective on its own. Profit-seeking organizations need shareowners who provide the primary source of capital. Not-for-profit organizations need principals who reflect the organization's primary reason for exis-

IN PRACTICE

The Nature of Organization Objectives

Peter Drucker describes the importance of having a clear statement of organization objectives as follows: "Because the modern organization is comprised of specialists, each with his or her own narrow area of expertise, its mission must be crystal clear. The organization must be single-minded or its members will become confused. They will follow their own specialty rather than apply it to the common task. They will each define 'results' in terms of their own specialty and impose its values on the organization. Only a focused and common mission will hold the organization together and enable it to produce."

Source: Peter F. Drucker, "The New Society of Organizations," *Harvard Business Review,* Volume 70, Number 5, 1992, pp. 95–104.

tence. Profit-seeking organizations need customers who buy the organization's products (which can be goods or services) and provide these organizations with the funds they need to continue operations. Not-for-profit organizations focus on target communities whose needs they are trying to meet. All organizations need dedicated employees who design and manage the processes that make and deliver their products to their target customers. Many organizations also need the active participation of skilled and committed organization partners, such as suppliers and distributors who provide insights that these organizations need to achieve their objectives. An excellent example of the increasing role of organization partners is the rise of suppliers in the automotive industry. Many suppliers now design and make the products that they supply. Some partners supply capital, raw materials, and components while other partners, such as retailers and transportation specialists, operate between the organization and the final consumer. Organization partners include all outside organizations or individuals with which a particular organization works to achieve its objectives. Examples include suppliers of raw materials, components, and capital and members of the distribution channel between the organization and the final consumer.

Finally, all organizations must design and operate processes that meet the laws and expectations of the broader community. Failure to meet these laws can result in fines, and failure to meet expectations can result in ill will and lost sales. The active consideration of community goodwill is evident in the strong interest in published ratings of organization image. For example, consider the large interest in the annual Fortune list of most admired organizations. Many analysts and organizations believe that high admiration ratings result in higher levels of profit. Other analysts believe that the causal chain goes the other way, that financially successful organizations are highly regarded.

The making of a corporate strategy effectively coordinates the needs of all these groups, called the organization's stakeholders, into a cohesive plan. Stakeholders are the people, groups of people, or institutions that define the organization's success or affect the organization's ability to achieve its objectives. An organization's stakeholders usually include customers, employees, organization partners, owners or principals, and the general community. The contributions and requirements of customers, employees, organization partners, owners or principals, and the broader community serve to define the environment and the general constraints that the organization must recognize in developing and operating its customer-related activities.

Scandinavian Airlines decided that it was in the business of providing services to business travelers and not just providing conventional air carriage services to any traveler. It increased the size of the business class cabin in its aircraft and began operating hotels and other travel amenities that appealed to business travelers. (Scandinavian Airlines System)

Three Levels of Strategy

The three levels of strategy are organizational, business, and operational strategies. **Organizational-level strategy making** is the activity of choosing what business the organization is in. This job is less mundane than you might first imagine. During the 1970s, Coca-Cola was in many different food-related businesses including soft drink beverages, pizza, and wine. Internal analysis suggested that the soft drink business was the most profitable and that the other businesses were inappropriately siphoning organization resources, human and capital, away from the profitable soft drink business since they were not providing or benefiting from organization synergies with the soft drink business. A synergy occurs when a group of activities operating together accomplish more than they can accomplish individually. Consequently, the pizza and wine businesses were sold off and Coke's profits and market valuation soared. Thus, an organization must have focus, so that it can operate effectively and efficiently, and be successful. Think of some successful organizations. Most, like Microsoft and FedEx, have a very narrow product focus. Wal-Mart is a mass merchandiser; everything it does is related to the retail merchandising business. Widely diversified organizations that are successful, such as General Electric, are much less common. They usually consist of highly focused units that operate as separate organizations, each with its own strategy.

Organizational-level strategy making
The process of choosing what business the organization is in.

Choice is the essence of strategy. **Business-level strategy making** means choosing the organization's target customers and the broad approach it will take to meeting their needs. The organization sizes up its strengths and weaknesses and matches them with the opportunities presented by customers and the challenges presented by competitors. The organization must identify the customers whose requirements it is best able to meet. An organization promises its target customers value proposition. **Value proposition** states in a clear and short message the competitive value that the organization will deliver to its target customers—how it will compete for, or satisfy, customers. As an excellent example of a value proposition, the customer service group at the Ford Motor Corporation Customer Service Division developed the following statement:

Business-level strategy making
The process of choosing the organization's target customers and the broad operating decisions necessary to meet its needs.

Value proposition
Clear and short statement of competitive value that the organization will deliver to its target customers—how it will compete for, or satisfy, customers.

Fix it right the first time, on time, at a competitive price in convenient locations.

Ford's value proposition is simple, concise, specific, and direct. It is unequivocal in stating what its customers should expect. It provides a basis for communication between Ford and its customers, and a basis for assessing the performance of internal operations in delivering on this value proposition.

Customers present many different requirements. For example, some gasoline buyers are price sensitive and will buy gasoline wherever the price is lowest, regardless of the location or appearance of the retailer. Moreover, these customers are uninterested in such amenities as full service or a convenience store. Other customers value service and seek amenities such as a convenience store, credit card privileges, location, and appearance.

Note that while customers define their requirements, the organization chooses which customers it intends to pursue. The needs of the organization's target customers therefore reflect a balance between what potential customers want and what the organization believes it can provide. Wal-Mart has chosen to be a mass merchandiser that offers both brand label and private label products to price sensitive customers. The customer niche is very specific. No customer will confuse the selection of clothing products and their prices in a Wal-Mart store with those in a Saks or Neiman-Marcus store. Therefore, Wal-Mart is a mass merchandiser whose strategy is driven by low cost and wide selection. This is Wal-Mart's value proposition.

Southwest Airlines has chosen a niche strategy, by focusing on a narrow range of customers who value low fares and are not particularly concerned about traditional ground or in-flight service amenities. To support this strategy, Southwest Airlines has eliminated the services that its target customers are willing to sacrifice for lower rates and now focuses on developing the highest levels of efficiencies in its operations.

Note also that the organization makes general choices about how it will pursue customers. Some organizations will focus on costs, which is often called a *cost leadership* or operational excellence strategy, and compete by delivering products to its customers at the lowest possible cost. Other organizations such as Southwest Airlines will focus on a niche strategy, often called a customer relationship strategy, and try to meet the unique requirements of a small market segment. Finally, other organizations will compete by continuously bringing new products to the marketplace, sometimes called a product leadership strategy, and abandon older products as they come under intense price competition.

Operational-level (tactical level) strategy
The process of choosing what business the organization is in; reflects the way the organization will pursue its business-level strategy.

The organization's **operational-level (tactical level) strategy** reflects the way the organization pursues its business-level strategy. There are two prominent characteristics of an effective operational-level strategy: It must deliver the organization's value proposition, and it must reflect the organization's strengths. That is, the chosen strategy must reflect what the organization is best at doing and include a better way of creating customer satisfaction than what competitors can accomplish. This better way provides the element of competitive advantage. It should be difficult for competitors to duplicate the processes that the organization has developed to pursue its target customers. This difficulty provides the element of *sustainable* competitive advantage.

Everything that Wal-Mart does at the operational level is designed to meet the strategy of large selection, providing both brand-name and store label products at the lowest possible cost. Wal-Mart's operational activities in this regard include (1) maintaining close relationships with suppliers so that they will provide their products at the lowest possible cost, (2) adopting a highly efficient logistics system, and (3) developing a sophisticated satellite-driven inventory tracking system. When Wal-Mart moves into a new territory, its competitors respond by lowering prices to match those of Wal-Mart; but Wal-Mart's tactical strategies have provided it with a lower cost structure than those of its competitors. The result is that competitors become only marginally profitable, or even unprofitable, when they try to match Wal-Mart's prices. Wal-Mart's low cost and highly integrated value chain have given it a competitive advantage that is sustainable, as competitors cannot emulate or match it. Wal-Mart demonstrates that strategy defines the organization's target customers and market segments, and that the value proposition, in turn, determines the characteristics of the organization's total operational systems. Therefore, strategy provides a focus for activities that the organization must pursue to be successful.

The Nature and Role of Strategy

Customers are the means to the end, the end being achieving the organization's objectives. Therefore, the issue for the firm is not simply to achieve customer satisfaction at any cost. Indeed, high levels of customer satisfaction can be achieved by giving away the organization's goods or services. The issue instead is creating customer satisfaction in a way that allows the organization to achieve its objectives.

STRATEGY AND ITS IMPLICATIONS FOR MANAGEMENT ACCOUNTING AND CONTROL

The strategic planning process matches the objectives of the organization's owners, the requirements of various customers, the skills and capabilities of the organization's

THE TECHNOLOGICAL EDGE

Manufacturers Build on ERP to Gain an E-Business Edge

As stated in this chapter, organizations can be characterized as a series of activities. The way organizations allocate resources to those activities will depend on the strategies they employ.

A recent study of the 100 Top Innovators in Manufacturing revealed that in 1999, investment in enterprise resource planning (ERP) systems has significantly dominated all other categories in the spending of application dollars (see Exhibit 2-2). The strategy of innovative firms is to invest heavily in ERP and ERP-related applications as springboards to e-business. Rod Johnson, an analyst at AMR Research Inc. in Boston, states, "We're seeing a very dramatic shift among more innovative manufacturing companies. The era from 1993 to the present was all about deploying ERP and improving operational efficiency. The focus now is on systems that can grow revenue and earnings by allowing for a tighter focus on the customer. ERP was the precursor. Now the challenge is to build on that."

EXHIBIT 2-2

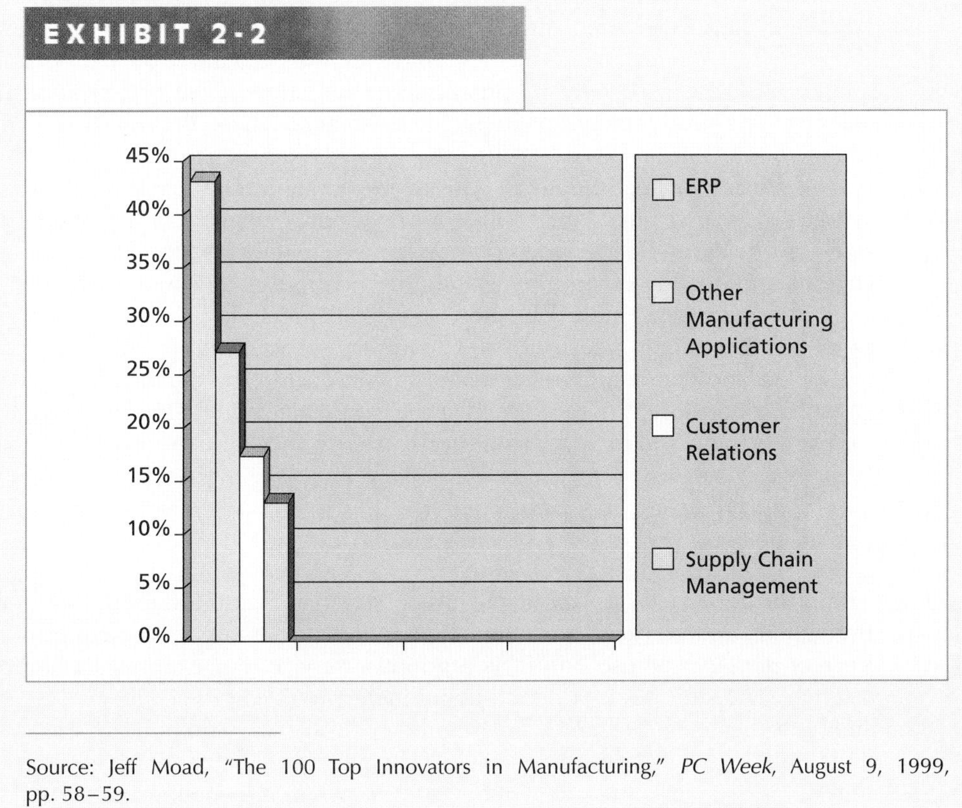

Source: Jeff Moad, "The 100 Top Innovators in Manufacturing," *PC Week*, August 9, 1999, pp. 58–59.

employees, and the potential contributions of business partners. The result is a plan that targets specific customers who have well-defined product requirements or expectations that the firm can satisfy while meeting its objectives. Exhibit 2-1 summarizes this process.

Specifying the organization's target customers and the tactical or operational tools that will be used to pursue them defines what is required of the organization's operating systems. For example, suppose that an organization has committed to a high level of customized service or products. This will require that products be delivered on demand and according to customer specifications. Therefore, relevant measures of organization processes will include response time and ability to meet customer specifications. Note how the process requirements are defined by the target set of customers and by the way the organization decides to pursue them. These process requirements become another element of the organization's management accounting and control system.

Just as the customer requirements define the process requirements, the process requirements define what is required from employees. For example, a highly mechanized and systematized process designed to minimize costs will require very different employee skills than a process designed to be flexible and meet varying customer requirements; hence the difference between a McDonald's and a five-star restaurant. McDonald's is not looking for chefs, but rather for people who can be trained to follow the food-processing rules that are designed to minimize costs and maximize conformance to specification. The five-star restaurant is looking for creativity that culminates in the commercial success of its chefs, and will train and reward them accordingly. The process requirements will thus specify the appropriate performance measures that the organization should use to monitor and manage employee performance.

Other players also can affect the performance of the organization's processes and its ability to meet its target customers' requirements. These members are the organization partners and the general community. We have defined organization partners as organizations or individuals outside the organization that support the organization in its efforts to meet the requirements of its target customers. These organization partners include creditors, suppliers, and groups that provide services in the value chain between the organization and the final consumers. Organization partners provide capital, materials, or services that create value for the final consumers of the organization's services or products. The general community, by creating laws and general social expectations, defines the environment within which the organization's processes must operate. For example, employee safety laws will preclude the use of certain types of processes that might meet customer requirements and be profitable. To the extent that supplier and community relationships are critical to the organization's success, the organization will define performance measures that reflect the expectations of these stakeholders and will monitor its performance on those measures.

The Organization as a Sequence of Activities or a Value Chain

Value chain
The sequence of activities that make or deliver a good or service to customers. Each step in the chain should contribute more to the ultimate value of the product than its cost.

Activity
A unit of work, or task, with a specific goal; a principle that describes and measures how organizational resources and employees accomplish work.

We have talked in general terms about the processes that organizations design and use to deliver goods and services to customers. It is useful to think of an organization as a *sequence of activities* whose output is a good or service. For example, a library lends a customer a needed book; a police department provides protective services to the community; a theater group entertains its audience with a play; and a computer manufacturer builds a laptop computer for a customer. As discussed, an organization's strategy for attracting customers, or its value proposition, is defined by how the organization organizes and manages the sequence of activities that makes and delivers a good or service to its customers. This sequence of activities is also known as a **value chain,** because each step in the chain *should contribute more to the ultimate value of the product than its cost.*

HOW ARE ACTIVITIES DEFINED?

An **activity** is a unit of work, or task, with a specific goal. Activities are important because they create costs. So, as we will see, understanding the nature and reason

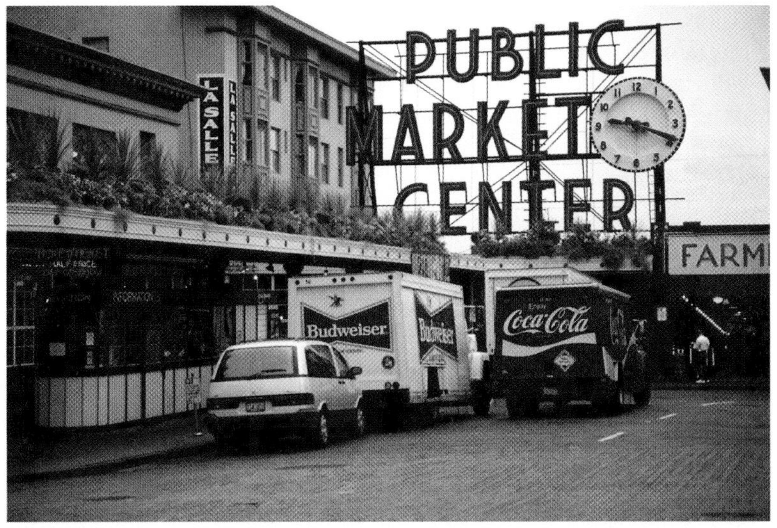
PUBLIC
MARKET
CENTER
FARM
LA SALLE
Budweiser
Coca-Cola

Many order-taking and delivery costs are constant and do not vary with the size of the order. This makes large customers inherently more profitable than small customers. Recently delivery activities have come under intense scrutiny as organizations develop information about which customers are profitable and which are not. (Marjorie Ferrell/ The Image Works)

Customer management activities
A class of activities directed to understanding customer requirements.

Innovation activities
A class of activities that develop new products and services.

Operations activities
A class of activities that include designing systems to handle in-bound logistics; managing suppliers, operations, and manufacturing; and managing the flow of products to customers.

Service activities
A class of activities that provides customers with after-sales service.

Quality
Refers to how well the product's operating characteristics conform to what the organization promises to customers.

Service
The value in use of a good or service.

for an activity is an important step in undertaking cost reductions. Stocking products at Wal-Mart, making a soufflé in a restaurant, interviewing an MBA student for an internship, or setting up a machine in a factory are examples of activities. There are four broad classes of activities in the value chain. Exhibit 2-3 summarizes these activities.

1. **Customer management activities.** These include understanding customer requirements.
2. **Innovation activities.** These include developing products that meet customer requirements.
3. **Operations activities.** These include designing systems to handle inbound logistics; managing suppliers, operations, and manufacturing; and managing the flow of products to customers.
4. **Service activities.** These include providing customers with after-sales service.

Focusing the Value Chain

The firm's target group of customers has specific expectations about the product's price, quality, and service characteristics. **Quality** refers to how well the product's operating characteristics conform to what the organization promises customers. **Service** includes the product's tangible features, such as performance, taste, and functionality, and its intangible features, such as the way customers are treated before, during, and

EXHIBIT 2-3

Key Elements of the Value Chain

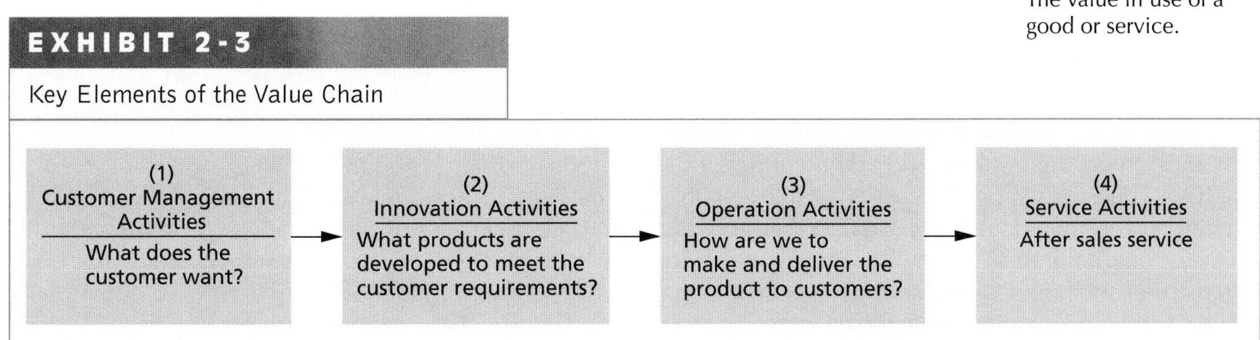
(1)
Customer Management Activities
What does the customer want?
(2)
Innovation Activities
What products are developed to meet the customer requirements?
(3)
Operation Activities
How are we to make and deliver the product to customers?
(4)
Service Activities
After sales service

after the purchase decision. This definition of service is broad and perhaps unfamiliar; however, understanding the breadth of this term is important in what follows. Service is what differentiates products in a world where customers perceive physical goods as commodities. Therefore a meal in a five-star restaurant is a different service than a meal in a fast food restaurant. However if the meal in the fast food restaurant meets its commitments better, it is higher quality. Price refers to the lifetime cost of the product to the customer and includes purchase price, operating costs, maintenance costs, and disposition costs. The organization's target customers define its key success factors, and these, in turn, define what is required from the value chain.

The previous definition of quality is consistent with the standard use of the word in management and production texts. Because this definition differs from its common use in practice, it may be helpful to reiterate that quality refers to conformance to specification and not to product service features. Exhibit 2-4 summarizes the relationship between quality and service.

ORGANIZATION AND PROCESS CONTROL

Organization control
The activity of ensuring that the organization is on track toward achieving its objectives.

Process control
The activity of assessing the ability of each unit in the value chain to meet the requirements of the organization's target customers.

Operations control
The process of providing feedback to employers and their managers about the efficiency of activities being performed.

Organization control is the activity of ensuring that the organization is on track toward achieving its objectives. Organization control includes four components:

1. specifying objectives (plan),
2. communicating objectives to organization members (communicate and implement),
3. monitoring performance relating to objectives (measure), and
4. acting on discrepancies between actual and target performance (revise).

Organization control is a long-run process. Its objectives are achieved by delegating or factoring the responsibility to achieve these objectives to organization processes. In turn, organization processes are controlled using process control.

Process control, or **operations control,** is the activity of assessing the ability of each unit in the value chain to meet the requirements of the organization's target customers. Process control is short-term, sometimes continuous, control, and it measures and compares short-term performance with short-run targets or standards. It focuses on directing, evaluating, and improving the processes that the organization uses to deliver goods and services to its customers. Therefore, what the organization has defined as the quality, service, and cost requirements of its target customers define which performance measures are important in process control.

IN PRACTICE

Cutting Costs and Reducing Service

In their zeal to cut costs, some organizations cut service. Proctor & Gamble and General Foods, large competitors in the coffee market, were slow to react to the customer move to gourmet coffee brands. In fact, a preoccupation with cutting costs led to a decrease in product service as large competitors substituted cheaper robusta beans with higher-quality arabica beans. In another effort to reduce costs, large competitors developed the facilities to process larger batches of coffee, which reduced the processing cost but also reduced the freshness of the resulting product. These manufacturers failed to realize that a significant group of customers were willing to pay more for a better product (that is, higher service) and that their cost-cutting activities were alienating those customers. Cost cutting should focus on eliminating elements of service that customers do not want or unnecessary production steps—not on eliminating services that customers value.

EXHIBIT 2-4

Service and Quality

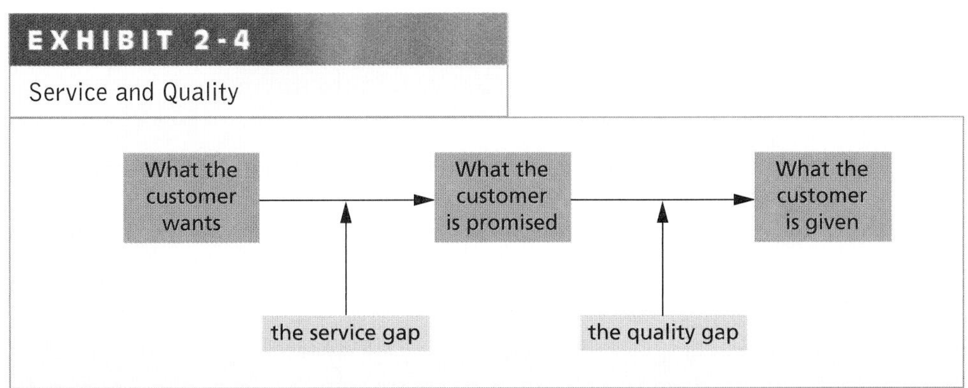

PERFORMANCE MEASUREMENT AND MANAGEMENT ACCOUNTING

Performance measurement, a major management accounting and control activity, evaluates the performance of a single activity and the entire value chain. Performance measurement is perhaps the most important, most misunderstood, and most difficult task in management accounting. An effective system of operations performance measurement includes critical performance indicators or measures that do the following:

Performance measurement
A major management accounting and control process used to evaluate the performance of a manager, activity, or organizational unit.

1. Consider each activity and the organization itself from the *customer's perspective.* That is, what must this activity accomplish so that the organization meets the requirements of its target customers?
2. Evaluate each activity using *customer-validated* measures of performance. That is, do the measures used to evaluate the performance of each activity reflect how the customer perceives or values the activity?
3. Consider all facets of activity performance that affect customers and are therefore *comprehensive.*
4. Provide *feedback* to help organization members identify problems and opportunities for improvement.

Let us consider each criterion in more depth.

Reflecting the Customer Perspective. To support operations control, the firm's performance measures should communicate and summarize the things that are critical to the organization's success in meeting the requirements of its target customers. Although this seems basic, many organizations fail to identify, let alone measure systematically, what their target customers want and value. **Customer-validated performance measures** reflect customer requirements and help employees manage the value chain's processes and activities by concentrating their attention on improving what matters to the customer. For example, if all employees at McDonald's restaurants know that customers require fast service and consistently produced products that are delivered at the lowest possible price and in a clean environment, they can evaluate and manage their activities according to customer requirements even if they do not deal directly with customers. Maintenance personnel can interpret these objectives to mean that equipment should be maintained so that it will not fail and cause service delays, impair quality, or cause excess costs. Housekeeping personnel can ensure cleanliness both inside and outside the restaurant.

Customer-validated performance measures
Tools used to reflect customer requirements and help employees manage the value chain's processes and activities in order to please customers.

Using the Customer's Validation—Outputs and Outcomes. Performance measures should be external, or customer validated, rather than internal to the organization.

IN PRACTICE

The Nature of Effective and Efficient

"Effective" and "efficient" are two terms that management accountants use frequently. Each of these terms has a very special meaning.

Effective is a process characteristic that refers to the ability of a process to achieve its objectives. For example, suppose that a post office is using a mail sorter whose error rate is 3%. The post office buys a new machine with the objective of reducing the error rate. The new machine's error rate is 1.5%. Because the machine has achieved its objective, it is effective.

Efficient is a process characteristic that refers to the ability to use the fewest possible resources to do something. For example, suppose that one steel mill uses 100 tons of raw steel to make 80 tons of finished product and a second steel mill uses 90 tons of raw steel to make 80 tons of the same finished product. The second steel mill is more efficient than the first because it uses less raw steel to produce the same amount of final product.

Effectiveness and efficiency are very different issues that managers attack differently. Effectiveness is determined by the process design, which is evaluated and changed periodically. Efficiency is determined jointly by the process design and how the process operates each day.

Professor Charles T. Horngren, a renowned management accounting educator, made this point when he said "killing a fly with a hammer is effective but it is not efficient."

These customer-validated measures will reflect the requirements of the organization's target customers and are reflected in the organization's value proposition. They should reflect an understanding of the difference between the output and outcome of activities. This requires the ability to define precisely what customers value.

Input
The variables that the organization puts into a process, such as employee time and production costs.

Output
A physical measure of what an activity has produced.

Outcome
The value that a customer places on a product or service.

An **input** is what the organization puts into a process, such as employee time, production cost, or capacity used. An **output** is a physical measure of activity, such as the number of units produced or the amount of time spent being productive. An **outcome** is what the customer values as the result of the activity, such as the number of good units of production or the amount of client satisfaction generated by a service.

Exhibit 2-5 provides some examples of inputs, outputs, and outcomes. Organizations often measure outputs because they are physical and therefore measured easily and objectively. Many organizations assess productivity as the ratio of outputs divided by inputs. For example, fish, meat, and chicken processing plants routinely measure material productivity (or yield) by dividing the weight of salable product produced by the weight of raw material.

Because outcomes are an assessment of customer value, they provide a better measure than inputs or outputs of what the relevant process is contributing to the organization. Outcomes are what the organization specifically is in business to accomplish. Consider how misleading the material productivity measure of output weight divided by input weight might be in a meatpacking plant. The processing operation would get the same performance evaluation from turning into hamburger raw material that might have been processed into filet mignon.

Reflecting Comprehensive Information. An effective program of performance measurement assesses all facets of relevant performance, so that the decision maker is not motivated or influenced to trade off relevant but unmeasured facets of performance for those that are measured. Organizations must avoid falling into the trap

IN PRACTICE

How Continental Airlines Used Performance Measurement for a Corporate Turnaround—Substituting Goals for Rules

Gordon Bethune, Continental's CEO, recalled the situation he inherited. "Continental had become a lousy, unreliable airline. People had stopped using us and for good reason. An airline has no real value unless it's predictable and reliable." But for a decade, Continental's management had been so focused on cutting costs that it provided the worst service in the industry. "We were unpredictable and unreliable, and when you're an airline with that kind of a record, it leaves you with a lot of empty planes."

Bethune learned from the J.D. Power & Associates Airline Customer Satisfaction Study that on-time performance was by far the most important determinant of customer satisfaction; thus, he chose on-time arrivals as the company-wide metric for measuring success. Bethune linked this metric to an incentive plan: Each month that Continental's on-time percentage was in the top five of the U.S. Department of Transportation's rankings, every employee would get $65 extra.

Bethune explained, "How did we get to the $65 figure? We determined what it cost us each month to run flights late—feeding passengers, putting them up overnight, finding them other flights, and finding and delivering baggage that missed connections. We came up with the figure of $5 million per month. Rather than spend this money coping with poor service, we preferred to pay up to half this amount to our employees if they could make our flights run on time. Multiply $65 by 40,000 employees and you get $2.6 million."

In the first month of the program (January 1995), Continental had 71% of its planes land on time, much higher than the 61% achieved a year earlier. Although an improvement, this still left Continental seventh of the top-10 airlines. In February 1995, 80% of Continental's flights landed on time, putting it in fourth place, and for the first time in years, scoring higher than the industry average of 79%. Every employee received a separate check for $65 at the end of the month. In March, Continental finished first in the industry rankings and again in April. After settling a work dispute with its pilots, Continental maintained its record, remaining in the top four for the rest of the year. For 1996, Continental raised the bar, offering a $100 bonus to each employee if the airline could maintain an on-time arrival record of 80% or better. The system continued to evolve to other aspects of customer satisfaction, such as reducing the incidence of lost baggage.

Bethune commented on the impact of setting the right performance measures:

> I can't stress enough that getting people to understand their jobs and how they are measured made their lives easier. This was the complete opposite of how it used to be, with an employee manual that boxed them into ridiculous procedures for every element of their work. Now we give them actual goals instead of rules—and rewards if they make the goals, rather than punishment if they miss them. We have also worked at making the goals really easy to understand: Get the planes to their destinations in a clean, safe, and reliable manner, with their luggage. That's it—that's their job. Now that management is out of their way, the employees do it every day.

Source: "From Worst to First," *Fortune*, May 25, 1998, pp. 185–190.

of thinking, "If we cannot measure what we want, then we will want what we can measure." The difficulty of finding performance measures that are aligned with intended performance, and the problems created when organizations use inappropriate performance measures, is well known in the organization behavior literature. The bottom line is that performance measures will focus behavior on improving those measures and it is foolhardy to assume that unmeasured objectives will be pursued.

EXHIBIT 2-5

Inputs, Outputs, and Outcomes

Organization	Input	Output	Outcome
Goverment Employment Office	Hours of counseling time paid for by the goverment	Number of hours counseled	Number of jobs found that meet clients' legitimate expectations
Police Street Patrols	Cost of patrolling	Hours spent patrolling	Effect of patrolling on crime rate
Research Laboratory	Number of laboratory worker hours paid for	Number of laboratory hours worked	Number of patents produced or the profitability of the products produced
Sawmill	Volume of logs processed	Volume of lumber created	Net realizable value of lumber created

Focusing on a single performance measure when multiple dimensions of performance are required for organization success can have severe consequences, as the following examples show.

- When Domino's Pizza promised its customers it would deliver pizzas to their homes within 30 minutes or provide a $3 refund, it was both defining and guaranteeing its service. What Domino's did not envision or intend was that young, often inexperienced drivers would race through the streets to meet the 30-minute service commitment. Consumers began to complain about the guarantee and told Domino's Pizza franchisees that they would rather wait longer for their pizzas so that these delivery people would drive more slowly and safely. Many Domino's franchisees felt the same way, told their drivers to slow down, and paid the $3 refund routinely and willingly. By focusing only on one facet of performance—speed—Domino's Pizza sent the message to its employees that speed alone, and no other performance facet, such as safety, counted. This matter became a crisis in

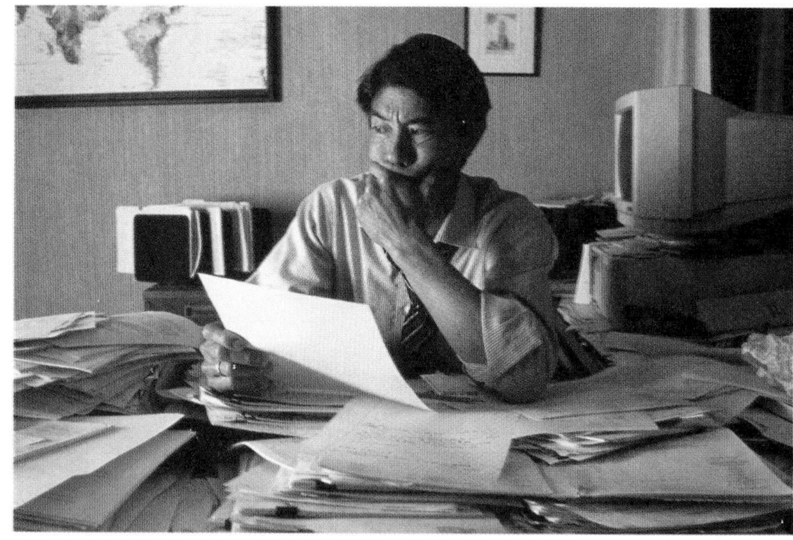

Audit firms invest thousands of hours reviewing audit files and financial statements for accuracy before they are released. The objective is to ensure that the output, for example the financial statement, is the outcome required by the client and regulatory bodies that set accounting standards. (L.D. Gordon/The Image Bank)

IN PRACTICE

Measuring Performance at Federal Express

Federal Express measures 12 attributes of service. It weighs the performance score on each attribute—the higher the customer aggravation caused by the performance failure, the higher the weight assigned to that attribute—to determine an overall service performance score, which it calls the service quality indicator. The score is computed and reported weekly.

Employees use the score to find the root causes of performance failures. For example, if mislabeled packages are causing service failures, procedures are designed to eliminate the causes of packages being mislabeled.

December 1993, when a jury awarded $99 million to a woman who suffered head and spinal injuries after a Domino's Pizza driver ran a red light and broadsided her car. Shortly after this accident, Domino's discontinued its 30-minute delivery guarantee.

- In the late 1970s and early 1980s, the motorcycle manufacturer, Harley Davidson, was struggling. To improve its cash flow, company executives ordered factory personnel to reduce manufacturing and delivery time. The result was that the factory literally followed these instructions and shipped motorcycles they knew were defective, resulting in new motorcycles leaking oil in the dealers' showrooms. When faced with a mounting chorus of complaints from dealers and customers, Harley Davidson realized that the appropriate direction to give to factory personnel was to ship only those motorcycles that were defect-free.

Providing Feedback. Performance measures should be both understandable and tailored to the needs of the people who manage the organization's activities. An effective performance measurement program will help the people who manage the value chain to identify problems and suggest solutions. This attribute reflects the purposeful nature of performance measurement in assessing operations and providing a meaningful guide for improvement. For example, many hotels provide in-room comment cards for their customers to complete. These comments not only provide invaluable insights into quality lapses, instances when the hotel promised but did not deliver, but also serve as a source of suggestions about what new services the hotel should provide.

PERFORMANCE MEASURES AS AIDS IN OPERATIONS CONTROL

Control may be exercised by (1) developing standard procedures that employees are told to follow, or (2) hiring qualified people who understand the organization's objectives, telling them to do whatever they think best to help the organization achieve its objectives, and using the control system to evaluate the resulting performance, thereby assessing how well they have done. For example, to illustrate the first type of control, **task control,** McDonald's restaurants have devised a standard way of cooking a hamburger. As an example of the second type of control, **results control,** a store manager might be told to use her knowledge and skills to design an advertising campaign that will enhance the company's reputation in the local community.

Information is critical to both of these approaches to control. When control is used to *ensure compliance with standard operating procedures*, information is used to motivate people to follow rules and to verify that they follow them. When control

Task control
The process of developing standard procedures that employees are told to follow.

Results control
The process of hiring qualified people who understand the organization's objectives, telling them to do whatever they think best to help the organization achieve its objectives, and using the control system to evaluate the resulting performance, thereby assessing how well they have done.

is used to *motivate people to be creative in meeting customer objectives*, information is used to inform people about the objectives the firm wants to accomplish so that they can be creative and innovative in choosing a course of action that helps the organization achieve its objectives.

Performance Targets

Once the organization has decided what critical performance indicators to measure and has developed a system to capture these measures, it must evaluate performance. Part of the performance evaluation process is to compare realized, or actual, performance with a target performance level. A discrepancy between the actual and planned performance levels (known as a performance variance) signals a potential problem. This, in turn, invokes a problem-solving exercise to determine whether there is a problem and, if so, to solve it.

Organizations develop performance targets in various ways. Many organizations set process performance targets based on *estimated potential.* For example, an engineer might study a bottling machine and conclude, based on its design and operating characteristics, that the machine should be able to fill 2500 bottles per hour.

Other organizations set performance targets based on *improving past performance.* For example, a study of past performance may reveal that workers in a shirt factory complete, on average, 20 shirts per hour. Based on this information, the target for current performance may be to change the way shirts are sewed so that the average performance level becomes 21 shirts per hour. This illustrates the process of **continuous improvement,** which involves continuously making incremental changes to the process to improve process performance. The problem with basing performance standards on either potential or past performance is that these standards provide no sense of urgency. They do not reflect what is going on in the world outside the organization, particularly relative to what competitors are achieving. Internal standards usually are intended to encourage people to work harder or faster rather than smarter. Working smarter requires an emphasis on refining processes and eliminating things that do not improve the product's attributes. Pressures to work harder create organization friction if the people subjected to these standards challenge them either quietly or openly.

Continuous improvement
The act of making incremental changes to the process to improve process performance.

A third approach is to base standards on what the "best in the class" are doing. For example, if the best warehouse operation in the world can find and pick a stockkeeping unit in two minutes, that would be an effective standard to strive to achieve. **Benchmarking** is the process of studying and adapting the best practices of other organizations to improve the firm's own performance. The most effective benchmarking considers practices in *any* industry, not just in the organization's own industry. Moreover, benchmarking is not a prescription for mediocrity—the goal is to lead the industry in terms of efficiency and effectiveness, not simply to conform to the average. Therefore, when your organization is the benchmark, the idea is to continuously improve the benchmark level of performance.

Benchmarking
The process of studying and adapting the best practices of other organizations to improve the firm's own performance and establish a point of reference by which other internal performance can be measured.

A fourth approach is to choose targets that meet or exceed customer expectations: What is required to become the number-one supplier to the organization's target customers?

COST AS A PROCESS PERFORMANCE MEASURE

There are three types of process performance measures: cost, quality, and service which is often equated with time. Historically, management accounting emphasized cost, as information about quality and service could be obtained from direct observation and measurement. Therefore, accountants focused on cost, which management accounting practice uses as a major performance measure. Although cost seems to be a straightforward topic, some cost aspects require careful consideration.

The Role of Costing Information in Managing by the Numbers. In the past, cost information supported a process called **managing by the numbers.** In such an organization, planners first decide the amount of cost reduction required and then reduce each facility's or department's budget by those amounts.

Managing by the numbers
The practice of holding managers responsible for meeting financial targets.

Managing by the numbers has three inherent problems:

1. It is ineffective because it focuses cost-cutting activities on getting employees to work faster, longer, or harder (which will lead to poor quality, poor service, and disgruntled employees) rather than looking for better ways to do the job.
2. It assumes that cost is the only relevant measure of an activity's performance.
3. It does not recognize the reasons for costs in an organization.

In the short-run, a budget cut such as a layoff will cause employees to work harder to do the same jobs in the same way with fewer resources. This regime quickly tires employees. As employees weary of the faster pace, they will slow their work and consequently create managerial pressures to rehire the people who were laid off. Costs will then revert to their previous level. A report by the American Management Association indicates that the slash-and-burn cost cutting of the 1980s actually resulted in organizations as a whole incurring higher costs than those that were cut. This result came about in the form of rising costs of health care due to stress, heart attacks, and strokes for those remaining in organizations.

Organizations that manage by the numbers do not attempt to understand why costs exist in each organization. Rather, they assume that costs are bad and therefore should be eliminated.

A Broader Vision of Costs. Traditionally, organizations used cost information to assess the efficiency of operations and to provide information to evaluate product profitability. In recent years, management accountants have developed a broader vision of how costs can be used and how the type of cost information needed will vary across decision-making contexts.

The notion of life-cycle costing embodies this new perspective on costs. **Life-cycle costing** is a systematic consideration of product costs during the product's lifetime. These include development costs, introduction costs, production costs, distribution costs, after-sales costs, product takeback costs (the cost of recovering post consumer waste), and product abandonment costs. The systematic consideration of these costs during the product development and design stage has important effects on whether to continue with the product and how to price the product. Moreover, classifying product costs provides important insights on how design costs today will affect product costs in the future. In Chapter 9 we return to the insights of life-cycle costing and how it affects design and production decisions.

Life-cycle costing
A systematic consideration of product costs during the product's lifetime.

Understanding the Causes of Costs. Effective cost control requires understanding how the requirements of the organization's target customers create the need for activities and how activities, in turn, create costs. Improving cost performance requires an examination of the need, efficiency, and effectiveness of existing activities and any new activities over the total life cycle of the product or service.

In this approach to cost improvement, a manufacturer, for example, may try to reduce costs by studying its current activities and developing plans to eliminate any whose cost exceeds the value it adds to the product. A study of activities may indicate that 50% of labor costs in the factory relate to handling work in process, which

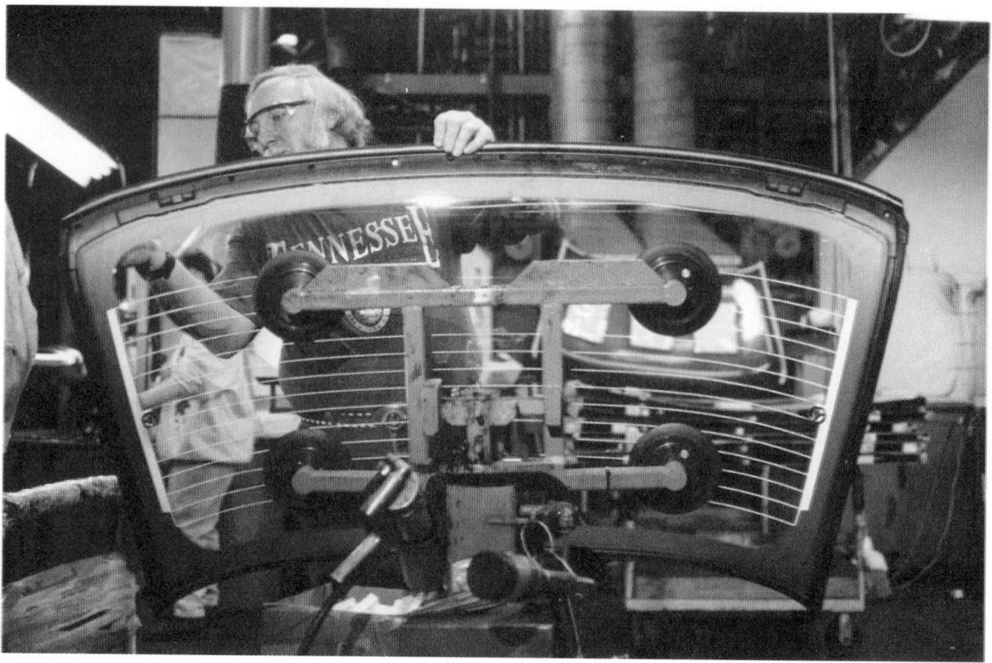

One of the most expensive activities in an organization is the cost of moving work in process around the organization. Many organizations have designed the need to move work in process out of their operations by organizing work into cells, which are self-contained work units that eliminate the need for moving work in process. (F. Hoffmann/The Image Works)

adds nothing to the product attributes that customers value. Instead, handling activities reflects organizational constraints, poor product design, and a poor factory layout. The organization may reduce the need for handling by redesigning the product, simplifying the process used to make it, and rearranging the factory layout to reduce the need for handling. Relative to competitors, who continue to undertake extra handling activities, the organization with improved activity processes would acquire a permanent cost advantage. In the short run, other organizations that had not eliminated handling activities might sprint. However, employees cannot maintain sprints over the long run; they eventually tire of working harder to make up for inefficient product or process designs.

Another important type of cost in many organizations is inspection costs. Inspection activities are required when a process is incapable of defect-free production. To meet the organization's promise of providing a target level of quality to customers when the process is incapable of defect-free production, the organization must identify and eliminate defective production. Customers value quality and not the inspection activity; however, simply eliminating inspections without curing the underlying reasons that cause them would have an adverse effect on the organization. The organization has two choices: eliminate the source of defects in the process, or continue to inspect and try to reduce the cost of inspections.

When possible, the firm should eliminate activities that do not improve the product attributes that customers value, as an effective way to cut costs. Philip Crosby, a quality guru of the 1980s, argued, "Quality is free." Crosby believes that $1 spent in preventing defective production will result in saving at least $1, and usually more, in the costs of detecting and fixing quality problems. Testing this hypothesis is problematic, as the characteristics of each organization and setting will vary. It is likely true that investments in prevention are often, but not always, more than offset by savings in finding and fixing quality problems.

IDENTIFYING AND DEVELOPING USEFUL INFORMATION ABOUT ACTIVITIES

Because of the potential to improve performance that results from improved activity management, many experts argue that organizations should develop activity data. Examples of activity data include the amount of time needed to make and deliver a product or service, the amount of materials handled, the number of moves made, the amount of storage space used on the factory floor, and the level of rework done. The organization manages by using activity data rather than cost data. The activity data not only help identify problems, but in many cases also suggest how to solve them. For example, a manufacturer of computer motherboards maintained a detailed log of all defects found in completed motherboards. This list of defects allowed the organization to identify which step in the process was most problematic and helped to identify defects that were related. Thus, organizations can use activity information as diagnostic information to improve performance.

At the same time, activity costs can help to set priorities for efforts to improve process efficiency or to target certain activities for study and elimination. For example, many managers are stunned when they are confronted with the costs of moving production around a factory floor, which often can exceed 50% of the indirect labor costs in a factory. When confronted with this data, managers might undertake a study to identify ways of organizing production or assembly so that moving work in process around the plant is reduced or even eliminated. One organization used four specialized machines to make different products. Setup costs for the machine were buried in the general plant overhead. When these setup costs were identified, production managers realized that it would be less expensive to dedicate two of the machines to the two products with the highest volume of production, and therefore they eliminated setup costs for those products. For the remaining products, which were produced on nondedicated machines, the organization discovered that the sequence of making products could reduce setup costs. Finally, the organization identified new ways of cleaning, maintaining, and recalibrating machines, which reduced setup costs further.

How Activities Create Costs. The activities required to make and deliver a product to the organization's customers create a demand for resources (materials, labor, and equipment). The acquisition and consumption of these resources create costs, which the accounting system measures. For example, when the organization uses raw materials, costs increase. When the organization acquires capacity, whether human or machine, costs increase. Although important differences exist between different types of costs, as some costs depend on how much you use and other costs depend on how much you acquire regardless if you use the capacity, the idea is that accounting systems track costs created by some underlying activity, whether it is resource use or resource acquisition.

Organizations can reduce costs by eliminating the need for activities, or by improving the performance of existing activities. Before organizations can eliminate activities, such as inspecting or moving work in process, they must eliminate the need that originally caused those activities to be undertaken or they run the risk of impeding the organization's ability to achieve its objectives. This approach is recommended in the emerging literature on environmental cost management, in which many authors are now recommending that organizations take a proactive approach to environmental costs. For example, can the product or process be designed so that it eliminates the need to treat water? This cuts the need for a very costly activity. Some

IN PRACTICE

Nonvalue-Added Activities in Steel Making

A common way of making coil steel is to manufacture the raw steel, cast the raw steel into a large slab, allow the slab to cool, transport the slab to a rolling mill, reheat the slab, and then roll out the slab into the gauge (thickness) required.

Many people recognized that all intermediate steps in this process relating to cooling and reheating the slab were nonvalue-added and created considerable additional costs and time delays. This insight and knowledge drove people in the steel industry to develop a casting machine that could cast thin gauge steel directly from molten steel.

In the last few years this technology has been perfected, and raw steel can be cast into a thickness much closer to the finished gauge. This new technology eliminates all the intermediate steps and therefore the costs associated with making and handling slabs.

organizations are redesigning product packaging so that the need to recover environmentally dangerous post consumer waste is reduced or eliminated. Thus, traditional cost management, which has focused narrowly on the manufacturing or service delivery process, has now given way to a more comprehensive approach. This new approach builds on the idea that modern cost management must include not only post-sale costs such as environmental costs and customer service costs, but also pre-manufacturing costs such as those incurred in the design of a product or service.

The drive to reduce or eliminate activities is important because it allows organizations to permanently reduce the costs of making their goods or services without affecting the value the customer assigns to the product. Process reengineering, or simply **reengineering,** is a popular term that describes this process of finding and eliminating activities.

Reengineering Describes the redesigning or elimination of inefficient processes. Also called process reengineering.

Efficient and Inefficient Activities and Cost Performance. We can classify activities as either efficient or inefficient. An **efficient activity** consumes no excess resources. We can determine whether an activity's performance is efficient by comparing one company's performance with that of competitors, which we defined earlier as benchmarking. For example, General Mills, a maker of breakfast cereals, studied how racecar pit crews organized themselves to accomplish their activities (such as changing tires or adding fuel) in the shortest possible time. General Mills engineers adapted these ideas to develop a system for machinery changeovers in its factories. This system reduced average machine changeover time from 8 hours to *10 minutes*, reduced costs, and increased machine productivity.

Efficient activity An activity that consumes no excess resources.

An **inefficient activity** requires more resources than necessary to produce the desired outcome. Many organizations have adopted the practice of continuously studying existing processes to discover better ways of doing them. Outdated machinery or poor operating procedures may cause activity inefficiencies. The way to improve efficiency may be to provide employees with better work procedures, better designed workstation layouts, and better equipment.

Inefficient activity An activity that requires more resources than necessary to produce the desired outcome.

General Motors set out to improve the assembly process used to make the complicated front seats for its Cadillacs. The assemblers were given worktables on wheels. In addition, the assemblers could adjust the height of the worktables so that they could see their work well and work comfortably. The company also redesigned the process of supplying the parts that went into the seats. The parts were put into bins along a U-shaped path about 10 meters long. The shape and length of the path minimized the distance the assembler had to travel. The bins highlighted inventory levels that, in turn, allowed the reduction of the parts inventory, because everything that was available was displayed and located in one place. At the same time, the bins signaled when to restock parts. The assembler pushed the worktable along the path, taking the needed parts from the bins and assembling them into the seat. These simple changes improved both the efficiency of the assembly process and the quality of the seats.

Making such process improvements requires that we understand how work activities themselves can provide warning signals that something is wrong. **Variances,** which are the differences between planned and actual costs, signal the presence of excessive costs but do not suggest the causes. To improve processes, organizations first must understand how costs behave, to attack their root causes. Cost information also helps organization members identify which activities they should target for cost improvement (in the case of activities that add value from the customers' perspective) or eliminate (in the case of activities that can be eliminated without affecting the organization's strategic potential). Organizations should direct their energies toward those opportunities where the benefits from eliminating or improving activities are the highest.

Variances
The differences between planned and actual costs.

Activity (Value) Analysis. Activity analysis, also known as **value analysis** or **activity-based management,** is an approach to operations control that became popular during the 1980s. An activity is any discrete task that an organization undertakes to make or deliver a product or service. Specifically, activity analysis includes five steps:

Activity analysis
An approach to operations control that involves the five-step process of identifying the process objectives, charting activities, classifying activities, continuously improving processes, and eliminating activities whose costs exceed their value. Also called *value analysis* or *activity-based management.*

1. **Identify the process objectives,** defined by what the organization's target customers want or expect from the process
2. **Chart,** by recording from start to finish, the activities used to complete the product or service.
3. **Classify** activities by comparing their cost with the value they add to the product from the perspective of the customer. Of particular interest are activities (such as moving, storing, or inspecting) that are required because of product or process design inadequacies, but which do not add value from the customer's perspective.
4. **Continuously improve** the efficiency of all activities. Organizations often use benchmarking to support the continuous improvement process. For example, an organization seeking to improve warehouse operations might study them at an

IN PRACTICE

Activity Analysis in a Hospital

A cross-functional team at the Victory Memorial Hospital tackled the problem of customer complaints about excessive waiting times in the emergency room department. The team began by developing a process flow diagram that described every step of a patient's visit to the emergency room department. Then it monitored the waiting times of three types of patients and identified the patient group that experienced the longest delays.

The team then identified the five groups of factors that caused delays: people, machines, materials, methods, and environment. Waiting for test results was a major contributor to waiting time. The team then identified what factors were working against the reduction of waiting time for laboratory results and developed policies and procedures to reduce the delays.

organization such as L.L. Bean, which is renowned for the efficiency and effectiveness of its warehouse operations.

5. **When possible, eliminate activities** whose costs exceed their value by reengineering or redesigning existing processes.

Mike's Custom Windows—Revisited

What have we seen in this chapter that applies to Mike's Custom Windows? First, the organization must focus on its chosen customers and have a specific plan for meeting its customers' requirements in a way that exceeds what its competitors can do. To support this, the organization needs a performance measurement system that monitors how well it is doing in meeting customer requirements and how internal processes, employees, and organization partners are contributing to meeting customer requirements. Let us see how these ideas worked for Mike's.

Market research undertaken for Mike's uncovered four important pieces of strategic knowledge. First, while customers had come to accept the narrow range of styles and sizes, they had no choice because all the manufacturers were moving in this direction—customers still valued the wider range of options. Second, the large chains were only gradually becoming aware of the huge inventory costs that windows created. Third, beyond the opportunity cost of capital tied up in inventory were losses related to both obsolescence and damage while windows were in storage. Lastly, Mike's discovered that the supply cycle was up to 12 weeks for the major suppliers, which meant that stores were often out of popular sizes or styles, and construction projects were delayed. While the big suppliers tried to handle these delays by diverting stock from other areas, their long supply chains simply did not allow prompt responses.

Mike's decided to focus on flexibility and service. Its value proposition became: High quality and high levels of service, measured by shorter lead times, at the lowest possible cost. Flexibility means more styles and sizes, and service means prompt delivery. Planners quickly decided that the only way to meet these dual requirements was to develop (1) production systems that could make customized products quickly and (2) computer-aided design (CAD) systems that could provide manufacturing information directly to computer-controlled production equipment.

This strategy accomplished three objectives. First, it virtually eliminated inventory and most of the costs associated with inventory. This lowered Mike's costs so that even with lower prices Mike's was just as profitable. Second, it met customer requirements for flexibility and service. Third, eliminating inventory while promising prompt delivery made Mike's far more attractive to retailers, who allowed the firm to set up booths in their stores where customers were able to experiment with alternative styles and designs by using simulation software. Moreover, Mike's maintained its own showroom, as well as a web site, so that contractors and customers could deal with Mike's directly if they preferred.

What remained was to develop the systems to deliver this strategy. Benchmarking suggested that the software needed to implement this strategy had been developed in the metal cabinet industry, so CAD modules were developed by making adjustments to existing CAD software. A unique feature was that as the customer experimented with the design, the software provided an estimated cost, guaranteed to be within 10% of the cost of the product. The CAD designs were communicated directly to saw and cutting machines acquired at a relatively low cost. Training was completed in three months.

An unexpected benefit came of this strategic change. As a trial, sales personnel were equipped with laptop computers and were sent out to building sites to demonstrate products to the customers (contractors) and consumers (the homeowners).

Tracking the issuance of building permits identified building sites. By speaking directly with the contractor or the homebuilder on site, the salespeople were able to generate sales directly and confirm delivery dates. This provided longer lead times, which helped production scheduling, because these contacts were usually made about the time that the foundation was poured. Moreover, it allowed the sales personnel to offer additional discounts because of these savings and because the retail store was eliminated. After one year, more than 60% of the business was generated in this way. Mike's considered the new business to be sustainable, as the major competitors were not local and could not easily replicate the local intelligence upon which this strategy was based.

SUMMARY

The organization in its pursuit of objectives or purpose undertakes a sequence of activities designed to deliver a product (a physical good or a service) to its target customers. It is important to evaluate this sequence of activities from the customers' perspectives, as customers ultimately judge the product's acceptability. Service, quality, and cost are universal attributes that customers use to judge products.

Organization members need information about process details, including cost, to manage their sequence of activities by using the fewest possible resources to meet objectives. Helping organization members to develop the systems to capture and interpret this information defines a natural and useful role for management accountants in organizations.

Charting an organization's process activities and identifying those activities whose costs exceed the value they add to the product help organization members continuously strive to improve the value, quality, and cost performance of all activities. In addition, in the longer run it allows organizations to eliminate activities that provide the opportunity for cost reduction without reducing the firm's potential to serve customers.

The activity perspective developed in this chapter provides the foundation for the balance of this book, which explores and develops the ideas and methods that people use to measure, assess, and improve the organization's activities.

SUMMARY EXAMPLE

An article by David Buehlmann and Donald Stover in the November 1993 issue of *Management Accounting* ("How Xerox Solves Quality Problems") describes how Xerox Corporation dealt with a problem that it identified in customer billing. The process began by identifying the billing error rate as 3.54% and estimating the cost of the errors to the organization. The cost of fixing the mistakes and the cost of lost opportunities created by disaffected customers amounted to approximately \$200,000 every six months. The company then formed a cross-functional team to consider the problem. The team first developed a fish bone (Ishikawa) diagram, which resembles the skeleton of a fish. The backbone of the skeleton represents the main problem and the spines represent the identified causes of the main problem. The fishbone diagram had the effect of tying the cross-functional group together into an integrated team who recognized that the problem was multifaceted and multifunctional. The team then followed this process to develop a solution:

1. Identify the problem.
2. Analyze the problem.
3. Generate potential solutions.
4. Select and plan a solution.
5. Implement and evaluate a solution.

The estimated cost of the project was \$7000, and the effect of the solution was to reduce the cost of the billing errors by 54%.

KEY TERMS

Activity, 40
Activity analysis, 53
Activity-based management, 53
Benchmarking, 48
Business-level strategy making, 37
Continuous improvement, 48
Customer management activities, 41
Customer-validated performance measures, 43
Efficient activity, 52
Inefficient activity, 52
Innovation activities, 41
Input, 44
Life-cycle costing, 49
Managing by the numbers, 49
Operational-level (tactical level) strategy, 38
Operations activities, 41
Organization control, 42
Organizational-level strategy making, 37
Outcome, 44
Output, 44
Performance measurement, 43
Process control (operations control), 42
Quality, 41
Reengineering, 52
Results control, 47
Service, 41
Service activities, 41
Strategy, 34
Task control, 47
Value analysis, 53
Value chain, 40
Value proposition, 37
Variances, 53

ASSIGNMENT MATERIALS

QUESTIONS

2-1 Why is the target set of customers the central strategic planning element? (LO 1)

2-2 What are stakeholders? (LO 1)

2-3 Why should stakeholder requirements matter to an organization? (LO 1)

2-4 What are organization objectives? (LO 1)

2-5 What are the distinctions between the three levels of strategy: organizational level, business level, and operational (tactical) level? (LO 1)

2-6 What is a value chain? Provide an example. (LO 2)

2-7 What is an activity? Provide an example. (LO 2)

2-8 How are service and quality defined? Are they related? Explain. (LO 2)

2-9 What elements does price, defined as the lifetime cost of a product to a customer, include? (LO 2)

2-10 What is organization control, and what are its four components? (LO 3)

2-11 What is process, or operations, control? (LO 3)

2-12 What does *effective* mean? (LO 3)

2-13 What does *efficient* mean? (LO 3)

2-14 What are customer-validated performance measures? Provide an example. (LO 3)

2-15 How are outcome and output defined? Are they related? Explain. (LO 3)

2-16 What is task control? Provide an example. (LO 3)

2-17 What is results control? Provide an example. (LO 3)

2-18 What is benchmarking? (LO 3)

2-19 What is managing by the numbers, and what problems are associated with such an approach? (LO 3)

2-20 From the producer's point of view, what costs are included in life-cycle costs? (LO 3)

2-21 How does continuous improvement differ from reengineering? (LO 4)

2-22 How are efficient and inefficient activities defined? (LO 4)

2-23 How can activity, or value, analysis help an organization reduce costs while improving processes? (LO 4)

EXERCISES

2-24 ***Ethics and stakeholders*** Lee and Alex are discussing labeling for product 121, one of their company's products that will be exported overseas to country C. LO 1

Lee: In the US, product 121 must be labeled as possibly hazardous to humans. I think the warning is unnecessary, though, because the amounts shown to present a hazard are much higher than people will encounter with normal use of product 121. Given this evidence, country C's laws do not require us to label the product as possibly hazardous to humans.

Alex: I had a work assignment in country C for two years, and I know that its residents would avoid a product with product 121's US labeling. I think we should leave out the cautionary statement. After all, we'll be in compliance with country C's laws.

REQUIRED

Taking into account the various stakeholders in this situation, discuss reasons for and against putting a cautionary statement on the labels of product 121 that are shipped to country C. What would you recommend?

2-25 ***Defining the organization's environment*** Identify two ways that each of the owner, customer, and community stakeholder groups define the organization's external environment. Why is each group's requirements important to the organization? LO 1

2-26 ***Community satisfaction and owner wealth*** Identify how an organization might learn about how community satisfaction with the organization might translate into increased owner wealth. LO 1

2-27 ***Product service features*** For each of the following products, what are the three most important elements of service: LO 2

(a) television set
(b) university course
(c) meal in an exclusive restaurant
(d) carry-out meal from a restaurant
(e) container of milk
(f) visit to the doctor
(g) trip on an airplane
(h) pair of jeans
(i) novel
(j) university textbook

2-28 ***The elements of quality*** For each of the following products, suggest three measures of quality: LO 2

(a) television set
(b) university course
(c) meal in an exclusive restaurant
(d) carry-out meal from a restaurant
(e) container of milk
(f) visit to the doctor
(g) trip on an airplane
(h) pair of jeans
(i) novel
(j) university textbook

2-29 ***Input, output, and outcome*** Pick any job with which you are familiar. Do not use an example from the text. Give one example each of an input, output, and outcome measure for that job. Do you see any danger in using either input or output measures to assess performance on that job? Why? LO 3

2-30 ***Using results control*** A company that sells life insurance to customers has decided to use results control to control the behavior of its sales staff. What form of results control do you think the company should use in this situation? Why? LO 3

LO 3 **2-31** ***Choosing between task and results control*** Do you think that results control or task control is better suited for controlling the performance of a professional athlete? Why?

LO 3 **2-32** ***Using benchmarking*** Describe how you might use benchmarking to improve your study habits.

LO 3 **2-33** ***Effectiveness and efficiency*** Give an example of an activity that is effective but not efficient. Why do you think that organizations sometimes design processes that accomplish activities effectively but not efficiently?

LO 4 **2-34** ***Process charting*** Briefly chart (that is, specify from start to finish, the activities used to complete the product or service) any process with which you are familiar. Identify two activities in the process that you think are inefficient, and why. You need not make this complicated. Describing something simple, such as borrowing a book from the library, is good enough (but do not use this example).

PROBLEMS

LO 1 **2-35** ***Stakeholders and strategy*** Suppose that you are the owner/manager of a business that provides food catering services.

REQUIRED

(a) Identify your stakeholder groups.

(b) Identify three different approaches that you may use to compete in the food catering market

(c) Identify how you would choose which one of the three competitive approaches identified in (b) you would actually use.

LO 1 **2-36** ***Community expectations*** Use business periodicals and general news sources, such as newspapers and magazines, to identify five examples of community expectations concerning organizations. Each example should clearly identify the community's expectation and should indicate your assessment of the consequences to the organization of not meeting that expectation. *Hint:* Editorial pages often contain commentaries on the social responsibility of business.

LO 2, 3 **2-37** ***Activities and critical performance indicators in a hospital*** What are the key activities in a hospital? What are some critical performance indicators for activities in a hospital?

LO 2, 3 **2-38** ***Activities and critical performance indicators in a convenience store*** Describe the value chain in a neighborhood convenience store. What are some critical performance indicators that might be used to evaluate the key activities?

LO 2, 3 **2-39** ***Critical performance indicators in the personal computer industry*** Identify some critical performance indicators for a manufacturer of personal computers.

LO 2, 3 **2-40** ***Information to evaluate performance*** You have just been made the manager of a group of 45 dry-cleaning outlets that are located in a large metropolitan area. Your company has positioned itself as a niche competitor. You offer personalized customer service and prompt cleaning. As a result, your prices are slightly higher than those of most of your competitors. You have just designed and installed a new system that picks up clothing from each of the outlets, delivers the clothing to the dry-cleaning plant, and returns cleaned clothing to the outlets. How would you evaluate the performance of this process, given the characteristics of your organization?

LO 3 **2-41** ***Choosing information for control*** Suppose that you are the general manager of a large hotel. Identify the daily, weekly, monthly, quarterly, and annual information that you would want to receive to help you manage the hotel. Assume for the sake of discussion that the hotel is divided into five major areas: customer service, housekeeping, restaurant, maintenance, and administration.

2-42 ***Outputs and outcomes*** Choose a familiar activity or process. Define an output and an outcome. (Do not use an example from the text.) Explain how using the outcome measure would be more effective in promoting activity improvement efforts than using the output measure. LO 3

2-43 ***Monitoring materials use*** Organizations in the natural resource sector of the economy, such as pulp and paper, meat packers, and organizations that process ores and metals, have developed and use perhaps the most sophisticated tools for monitoring and managing materials costs. Why do you think this is so? LO 3

2-44 ***Managing by the numbers*** Give an example of managing by the numbers. In view of its limitations, why do you think that managing by the numbers has attracted such a wide following? LO 3

2-45 ***Process charting*** Chart the sequence of activities that occur from the time that you enter a restaurant until the time you leave. Are some of these activities unnecessary, or poorly designed? Does your evaluation of these activities depend on the type of restaurant (i.e., a fast-food restaurant or a formal dining establishment)? LO 2, 4

2-46 ***Identifying stakeholders and strategic performance measures*** Pick any organization that you know or for which you can develop the data that you need to complete this question. (You may find pertinent information in annual reports or company web sites.) Identify the stated stakeholders, the strategy that the organization uses to compete for customers or to meet customers' needs, and performance measures that help the organization track success in meeting its objectives. LO 1, 3

2-47 ***Ethics, social responsibility, and stakeholders*** Some people argue that the only relevant stakeholder to consider in a profit-seeking organization is the owner. These people argue that in competitive markets an organization that pursues social or other goals that increase costs is inappropriately diverting economic resources. They also say that firms pursuing social objectives will be disciplined by the market—that they will suffer losses because their prices can be no higher than the competition while their costs will be higher. Despite this we see many organizations that pursue both social and economic goals. How can such a course of action be rationalized with the economic view, or does this phenomenon call the economic view into question? Explain. LO 1, 3

2-48 ***University mission statement*** A mission statement is an organization's statement of purpose and commitments to each of its major stakeholder groups. Does your university have a mission statement? If so, find and study it. If not, try to compose one so that it addresses the following questions. LO 1, 3

REQUIRED

(a) What stakeholder groups does your university's mission statement specifically identify? Who do you think are the university's stakeholders?

(b) Who is the university's customer? (Be careful, this is a tricky question. Legitimate arguments can be made for each of the following: students, students' parents or sponsors, high school guidance counselors, and prospective employers.)

(c) Some universities identify either alumni or faculty as the university's customer. Explain why you agree or disagree with specifying alumni or faculty as the university's customer.

(d) Has your university developed specific and measurable performance goals relating to each stakeholder group? If so, what do you think of them? If not, what should they be?

LO 1, 3 **2-49** ***Stakeholders, critical performance indicators*** The Liquor Control Board of Ontario (LCBO) is a government agency charged with the acquisition, transportation, storage, and retailing of beverage alcohol in Ontario, Canada's largest province. The following was taken from the LCBO's strategic plan:

Our Commitment

To succeed as a dynamic retailer and progressive organization, the LCBO must continue to foster a climate of trust and co-operation, where corporate values are clearly communicated and responsibilities readily accepted. To our employees, customers, suppliers, government, and communities, we commit the following:

Customers

To exceed our customers' expectations by providing them with service excellence. This will be demonstrated in the selection and quality of our products, the ambiance and convenience of our stores, the professionalism of our employees, and our ongoing commitment to introduce new products and services.

To rigorously test all products sold to our customers to ensure that they exceed established health and quality standards.

To deliver quality customer services throughout our organization by ensuring that every employee's first priority is to serve the customer or to support someone who does.

Employees

To recognize employees' capabilities, empower them to make decisions, impart responsibility for results, and reward their achievements.

To challenge and encourage employees to reach their potential, and coach and support them in their professional development.

To treat employees as individuals, and to value and respect their diversity in experience and perspective.

To create and maintain a workplace environment free from harassment and discrimination.

To respect our employees' right to a healthy and safe working environment, where safe working conditions are promoted and achieved.

To establish a proactive dialogue and positive working relationship with our Union, and to work together with all employees to address the challenges which face the LCBO.

Suppliers

To ensure fairness in our relations with suppliers and trade associations, and to support an equitable system where suppliers can market and sell their products according to customer demand.

Government

To operate our business in a profitable manner on behalf of the people of Ontario, and to support government policies and programs.

Communities

To respond with sensitivity in all our business decisions to the concerns and changing societal values regarding the marketing, distribution, and consumption of beverage alcohol.

> To continually consider and address the environmental implications of our business decisions.
>
> To encourage employees to become involved in their communities by supporting charities and cultural programs, and voluntarily contributing their time and talent to community activities.

As a government agency, the LCBO's sole shareholder is the government. The LCBO is organized into operating groups called divisions. These divisions and their charges are the retail division, operating the LCBO's 815 liquor outlets; merchandising division, acquiring the products that will be stocked in the retail outlets; distribution division, transporting products between suppliers and retail outlets; finance and administrative division, providing financial planning and organization control; human resources division, providing services to employees; information technology division, implementing leading-edge technology; and executive offices, reporting directly to the chief executive officer.

REQUIRED

(a) Name the LCBO's stakeholder groups.

(b) Based on the contents of the commitment statement, identify the LCBO's critical performance indicators for customers, employees, suppliers, and communities.

(c) For each of the organization's operating divisions, except the executive offices division, identify three critical performance indicators.

2-50 ***Performance measurement in the fast-food industry*** Because of the competitiveness of the industry, monitoring performance in a fast-food restaurant is critical for success. LO 2, 3

REQUIRED

(a) On what dimensions does a fast-food restaurant compete?

(b) Identify the major activities in a fast-food restaurant.

(c) Construct a system of critical performance indicators for the major activities you identified.

2-51 ***Performance measurement in the airline industry*** Because of the competitiveness of the industry, monitoring performance in an airline is critical for success. LO 2, 3

REQUIRED

(a) On what dimensions does an airline compete?

(b) Identify the major activities for an airline.

(c) Construct a system of critical performance indicators for the major activities you identified.

CASES

2-52 ***Performance measurement and customer complaints*** While vice chairman of Chrysler Corporation, Bob Eaton made the following observation about Chrysler employees who answered calls from customers with problems or complaints: LO 1, 3

> The people who answer these phones have one of the most important jobs in the company. They are our front lines. They can have a more direct effect on sales than anyone else.

After noting that it can cost as much as five times more to get a new customer than it costs to keep one, and that, on average, a satisfied customer will recount his experience to 5 people and an unsatisfied customer to 35 people, Mr. Eaton went on to say this:

> Even the best salespeople sell only two or three cars a day. Our people on the phones deal with dozens of customers every day. How well they take care of our customers is critical.

REQUIRED

Design a performance measurement system for the Chrysler staff that takes these customer calls.

LO 1, 2, 3, 4 **2-53** ***Vision, strategy, and performance measurement*** Ford Motor Company's 1998 annual report states:

> Ford Motor Company's vision for the future is to deliver superior shareholder returns and to become the world's leading consumer company that provides automotive products and services.

A message from the president and CEO explains:

> What is a consumer company? It's an enterprise that is continuously gathering unfiltered consumer insights worldwide to:

- Connect with current and potential customers and anticipate their present and future needs;
- Translate consumer needs into a competitive advantage, using fast cycle time and generation of breakthrough products and services;
- Focus on building sustained relationships;
- Effectively manage a portfolio of brands; and
- Continuously grow shareholder value

Stating that the consumer focus is the foundation of the company's vision and strategy pyramid, the report continues:

> We are leveraging Ford's five areas of competitive advantage—strong global brands, superior consumer satisfaction and loyalty, best total value to the consumer, nimble organization with leaders at all levels, and corporate citizenship—to drive continuous improvement, and to speed our transformation and growth.

Referring to Ford's four main businesses—Automotive, Ford Credit, Visteon, and Hertz—the president and CEO stated:

> We give each business its own profitability and growth targets. Then, each one breaks down its business into meaningful pieces to grow and improve. We're also pursuing synergies across the four businesses to accelerate growth, sharpen our competitive advantage and improve asset efficiency. We're also maintaining the flexibility to add to, or delete from the portfolio over time, with a focus on superior shareholder value.

Operating priorities and financial milestones are stated for each of the four main businesses. For example, Ford Automotive Operations' stated operating priorities are quality and trust, profitability and business structure, consumer focus and growth, major process improvements, and teamwork and corporate culture. The financial milestones include a return on sales in North America of at least 5%, earnings growth in Europe, improved operating results in South

America, and total costs down $1 billion from 1998, for a constant volume and mix.

REQUIRED

(a) What is the significance of stating the vision as "the world's leading consumer company that provides automotive products and services" rather than "the world's leading automotive company"?

(b) What are some critical performance indicators for Ford in the area of consumer perspectives, and how would you measure the indicators? Consider the broad range of interaction a consumer may have with Ford or its products and services, and also consider environmental issues.

(c) What other critical performance indicators might Ford use, given its stated objectives?

2-54 ***Course registration as a process*** Consider the process of registering for courses at your university or college. LO 2, 3, 4

REQUIRED

(a) Chart the process of registering for courses at your university or college.

(b) As a customer, what criteria do you use to evaluate the registration process?

(c) Label each activity that you have identified in the registration process as efficient or inefficient.

(d) How might the registration process be reorganized to improve or eliminate the inefficient activities, or to improve performance on the evaluative criteria that you think are important?

(e) Which activity would you improve first? Why?

2-55 ***Key objectives and performance measurement*** The fishing products industry has five key objectives: LO 1, 2, 3

1. Keep costs down so that prices can be kept down.
2. Ensure that products meet stated, or expected, quality standards.
3. Ensure that the assigned quota of each species is harvested.
4. Ensure that the fish that are harvested are handled and processed in a way that maximizes their retail value.
5. Support growth by developing new products that are appealing to customers.

There are unique conditions affecting the fishing industry. Harvesting is constrained by two factors. A government regulatory agency sets quotas for each species of fish. The quotas specify the maximum amount of each species of fish that can be caught and the permissible fishing period. Because of equipment failure, weather conditions, and stock depletion, most firms are unable to catch their assigned quota of any given species.

Care has to be taken at each step in the process of harvesting and transporting the fish. During harvesting, too many fish in the nets causes the fish to be crushed and bruised, resulting in a loss of quality. Fish begin to deteriorate the moment they are caught. Therefore, care has to be taken to pack fish in ice in the ship's hold. Similarly, when fish are discharged from the ship's hold into the processing plant, care has to be taken to ensure that they are not damaged or bruised.

Within the processing plant, care has to be taken to ensure that fish are processed rapidly to prevent deterioration, carefully (to ensure that quality standards relating to color, form, and lack of parasites are met), effectively (to ensure that bones, skin, and blood are not left in the fish, and conversely, that excessive amounts of flesh are not removed with the bone), and efficiently (since many of the operations are manual, labor costs are significant).

The Primo Fishing Products Company (PFPC) is organized into three responsibility units: (1) harvesting (the fleet of company-owned ships and their crews used to harvest various species of fish); (2) processing (the processing plants used to process raw fish into the fresh, frozen, and cooked products wanted by the company's customers); and (3) marketing (responsible for creating the demand for the company's products).

Currently, the performance of each of the three responsibility units is evaluated as follows:

UNIT	PERFORMANCE EVALUATION
Harvesting	Tons of fish caught
Processing	Costs relative to standards adjusted for actual volume
Marketing	Sales increases over the previous year

REQUIRED

Assess the current system that is used to evaluate the performance of each responsibility center at PFPC. Make suggestions for any improvements.

LO 1, 2, 3, 4 **2-56** ***Performance measurement and incentive contracting*** Super Copy operates a chain of copy centers located throughout North America. Usually located close to college and university campuses, Super Copy provides a variety of services that are organized into six business areas: (1) normal copying, (2) color copying, (3) binding, (4) graphics services (such as posters and business cards), (5) preparing readings packages for university courses (including obtaining copyright permissions), and (6) basic word-processing services.

Super Copy's approach to business is captured in its motto: *Provide value to the customer while doing it right and fast.* The company's operations manual explains that market intelligence suggests that success in the copy business depends on (1) providing services that customers value: (2) providing a fast response to a customer request; (3) providing clear copies; (4) providing accurate duplication services (for example, ensure that a readings package is not missing any pages and that its pages are properly aligned); and (5) doing all of the above at a competitive cost.

You have recently been appointed the manager of a Super Copy center located near the campus of a small university (about 1800 students) located in a small town (population about 6000) in a predominantly rural area. You and 27 other center managers report to a regional manager. You are paid a salary and a bonus that depends on the measured performance of the center that you manage.

Each quarter, every center manager negotiates performance targets that reflect local conditions and opportunities with the center manager's regional manager in each of the following areas:

1. Sales for each of the six business areas mentioned above
2. Costs as a percentage of sales in each of the six business areas
3. Product quality as determined by a random audit of output conducted during a surprise visit by a team from the regional office
4. Service as determined by the time required to complete a sample of jobs

chosen by the audit teams (all jobs are logged in and logged out on the computer terminal at the customer service counter)

5. Customer satisfaction as determined by a quarterly survey of faculty and students at the nearby university (approved jointly by the center manager and the center manager's regional manager and is conducted by the regional manager's staff)

A performance score is computed as follows:

1. A score is determined for each of the five items of performance.
2. The scores on these five items are added to compute a total score.

The center manager's bonus is the percentage of the center manager's salary represented by the total score. The performance score on each of the five items of performance is determined as follows:

1. three points for meeting target, plus or minus 3%
2. two points for missing target by between 3% and 5%
3. one point for missing target by between 5% and 8%
4. four points for exceeding target by between 3% and 5%
5. five points for exceeding target by between 5% and 8%

Performance that varies by more than 8% of target is excluded from the evaluation and is subjected to an immediate investigation by a committee comprised of (1) the center manager, (2) the regional manager, and (3) the regional controller.

REQUIRED

(a) Evaluate this performance measurement system by indicating why you like, or dislike, each of its relevant features.

(b) As part of your efforts to improve the quality of your products and the services provided to your customers, you have decided to develop a product and service quality monitoring system for your copy center. Suggest what type of system might be useful and why.

2-57 ***Identifying activities that add value from the customer's perspective*** Woodpoint Furniture Manufacturing manufactures various lines of pine furniture. The plant is organized so that all similar functions are performed in one area, as shown in Exhibit 2-6. Most pieces of furniture are made in batches of 10 units. LO 2, 3, 4

Raw materials are ordered and stored in the raw materials storage area. When an order is issued for a batch of production, the wood needed to complete that batch is withdrawn from the raw materials area and taken to the saw area. There the wood is sawed into the pieces that are required for the production lot.

The pieces are then transferred to the sanding and planning area where they are stored awaiting processing in that area. When the machines are free, any sanding or planning is done on all the pieces in the batch. Any pieces that are damaged by the planning or sanding are reordered from the saw area. The other pieces in the lot are set aside in a storage area when pieces have to be reordered from the saw area.

When all the pieces have been sanded or planed, the pieces are then transferred to the assembly area where they are placed in a large bin to await assembly. Pieces are withdrawn from the bin as assembly proceeds. Defective or missing pieces are returned to the saw or sand and plane area where they are remanufactured.

EXHIBIT 2-6

Woodpoint Furniture Manufacturing

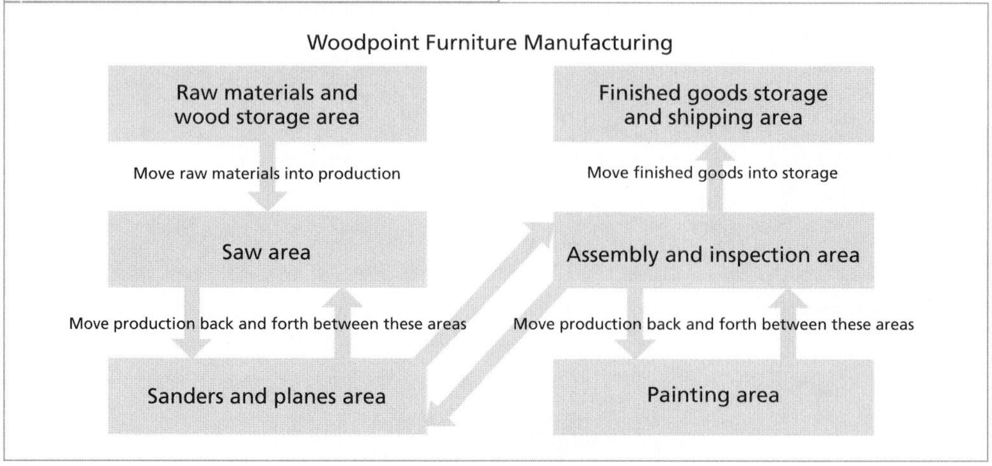

As assembly proceeds or when assembly is completed, depending on the product, any required painting or staining is done in the painting area. Pieces to be stained or painted are transferred back and forth between the assembly and paint area on a trolley. There is a storage area in the paint department for pieces awaiting painting. Whenever assembly is halted to await pieces that have been sent for painting and staining, the rest of the pieces in that batch are put into the storage bin to await the return of the stained or painted pieces.

When assembly is completed, the product is checked by the quality inspector. Any defective products are returned to the appropriate department for rework. When the product is approved, it is packaged and put into final storage to await an order by the customer.

REQUIRED

(a) Chart the process (i.e., specify from start to finish, the activities used) to make furniture in Woodpoint Furniture Manufacturing. Which activities do you think add value from the customer's perspective?

(b) What critical performance indicators would you use to evaluate the performance of this manufacturing operation?

LO 2, 3, 4 **2-58** ***Identifying activities that add value from the customers' perspective*** Consider Exhibit 2-7, which summarizes the activities at Bethlehem Steel Corporation's Sparrows Point plant. The blast furnaces make the iron that is refined into steel. The basic oxygen furnaces and open-hearth furnaces refine the iron into steel. The mix of iron, scrap, and alloys used to make the steel and the characteristics of the furnace determine the steel's properties, which include formability, strength, toughness, hardenability, and corrosion resistance. The continuous slab caster uses the steel from the basic oxygen furnace to make slabs of steel. The steel from the open-hearth furnace is poured into ingot molds for cooling.

When it has cooled and hardened, the steel ingot, weighing between 11,000 and 80,000 pounds, is removed from the mold and stored. When required, the ingots are reheated and moved to the blooming or slabbing mills, which transform the ingots into blooms (square or rectangular shape) or slabs (wide and flat shape), depending on the final product that the ingot will be used to make. This operation also improves the properties of the steel. The

EXHIBIT 2-7

From Modest Beginnings to Quality Steel Products

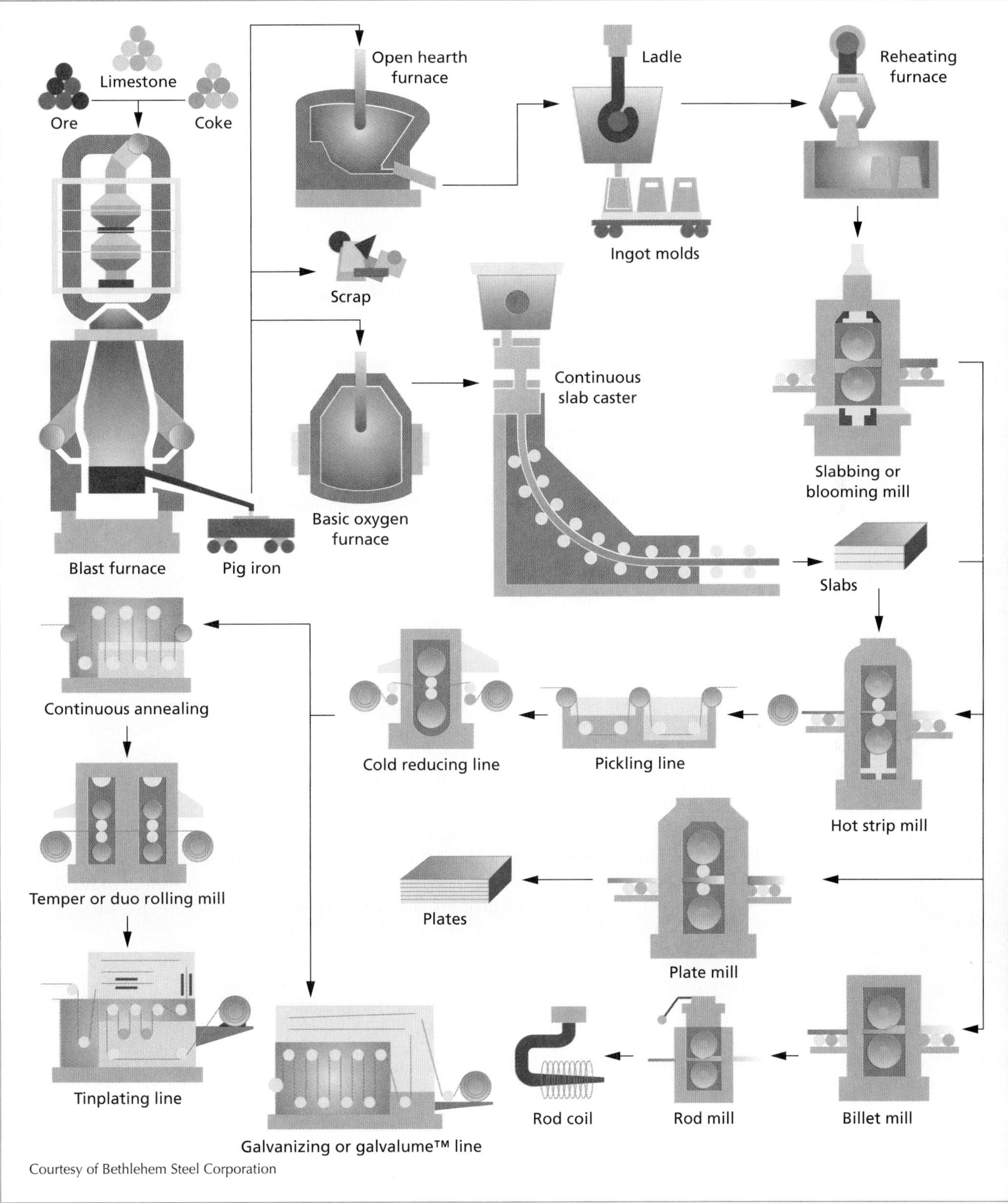

Courtesy of Bethlehem Steel Corporation

billet mill reduces blooms into 4-inch square billets that are shipped to the rod mill, which produces coils of rod that are then transformed into finished items such as wire. Plates are rolled from reheated slabs in the plate mill. The plates must be cut on all sides to the desired dimensions after rolling. Slabs are also used to make strip steel, which is either made into some final products directly or is subjected to finishing operations to make steel sheet or tin-plate.

REQUIRED

(a) What do you think is critical to the customer in making a steel purchasing decision?

(b) Do you see any activities in this process that do not add value from the customer's perspective?

(c) What might be the critical performance indicators in this process?

LO 1, 3, 4 **2-59** ***The clash between reducing costs to improve investor return and providing a work environment that employees expect*** Read the article by Robert Frank in *The Wall Street Journal.*[1] This article describes the clash between an organization that has developed standard operating rules to promote efficiency and quality and the workers who have to follow the rules.

> With a battalion of more than 3,000 industrial engineers, the company dictates every task for the employees. Drivers must step from their trucks with their right foot, fold their money face up, and carry packages under their left arm . . . It tells drivers how fast to walk (three feet per second), how many packages to pick up and deliver a day (400, on average), even how to hold their keys (teeth up, third finger) . . . Those (drivers) considered slow are accompanied by supervisors, who cajole and prod them with stopwatches and clipboards.

The article goes on to identify the pressures put on employees by way of demands for increased productivity and the ability to handle a widening product line. The article mentions that the Teamsters Union, which represents the drivers at UPS, commissioned a study that claimed that the drivers at UPS scored in the 91st percentile of U.S. workers for job stress. One employee observed, "But you just wonder how much more they can squeeze out of us before something breaks." What do you think of this? How can an organization decide when it has gone too far in its cost-cutting efforts?

LO 3, 4 **2-60** ***Developing process performance measures*** Exhibit 2-8 shows the canning cycle for the Coca-Cola bottling operation. Study this diagram, and then identify the production performance measures that you think would be useful to evaluate this process and explain why you would use these performance measures.

[1] Robert Frank, "Driving Harder: As UPS Tries to Deliver More to Its Customers, Labor Problems Grow," *Wall Street Journal,* May 23, 1994, p. A1.

EXHIBIT 2-8

Canning Cycle at Coca-Cola Bottling Operation

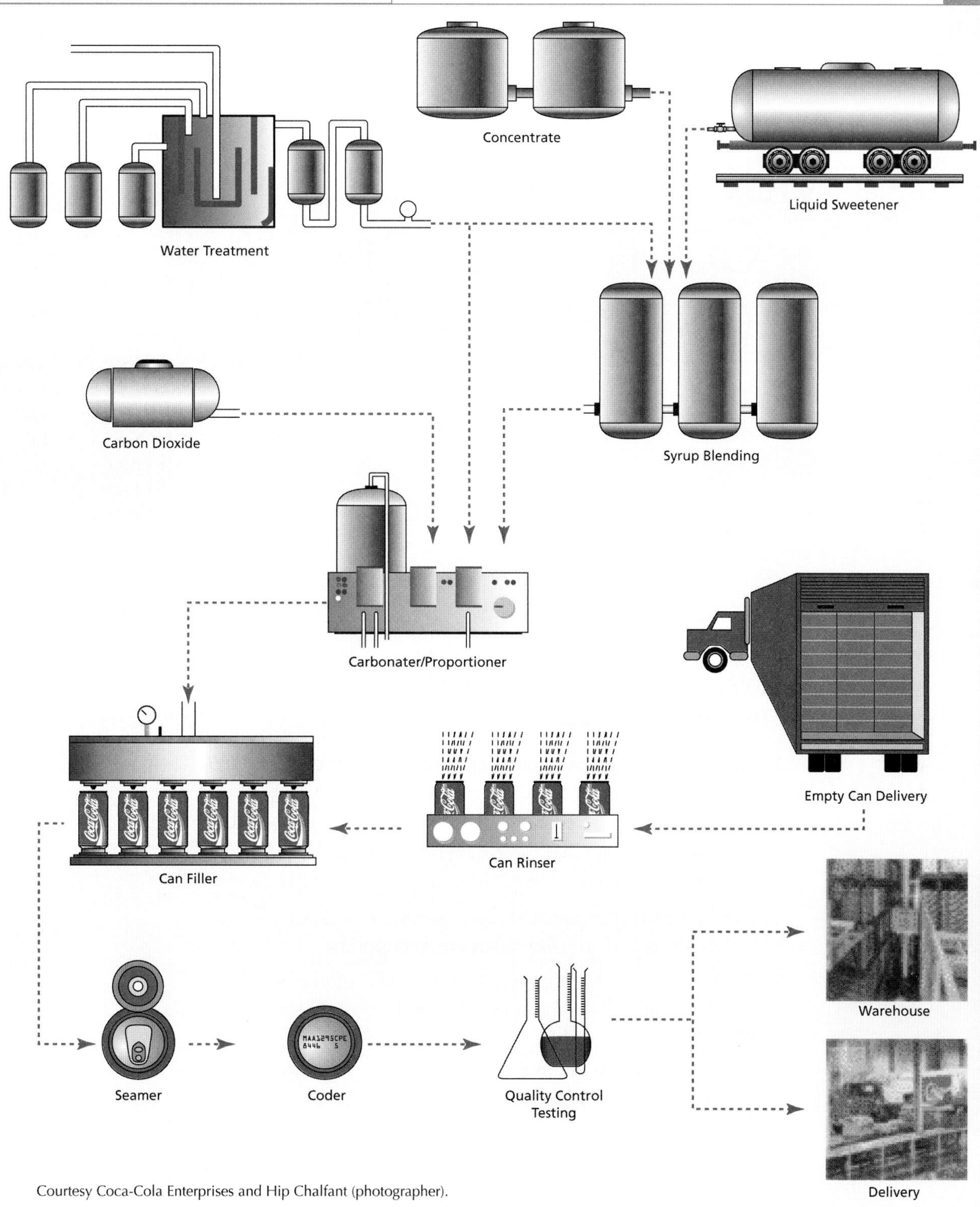

Courtesy Coca-Cola Enterprises and Hip Chalfant (photographer).

chapter 3

Cost Management Concepts and Cost Behavior

AFTER READING THIS CHAPTER, YOU WILL BE ABLE TO

1. explain why the appropriate derivation of a cost depends on how the cost will be used
2. explain why management accountants have developed the notions of long-run and short-run costs and how these different costs are used in decision making
3. state the difference between flexible costs and capacity-related costs and why the difference is important
4. show why the concept of opportunity cost is used in short-run decision making and how opportunity cost relates to conventional accounting costs
5. explain the notion of life-cycle cost and how that idea is used in new product and product purchasing decisions

Bob Daemmrich/Stock, Boston

JOAN'S LANDSCAPING SERVICES

Joan knew that her landscaping business was in trouble. While sales continued to grow, profits had been in a freefall for three years and the situation seemed to be getting worse for Joan's Landscaping Services.

Joan was perplexed about the decline in profits because she believed that her organization was doing everything right. She was hiring well-trained people and ensuring that their training continued after they joined the firm. For conventional landscaping services, Joan met the market price. For specialized services, she had the market virtually to herself and seemed to have all the business she could handle at the prices she charged.

Most landscaping services were relatively competitive because of the low entry costs. Although many organizations did not last long, Joan's was one of the dozen or so in the community that was more than five years old.

Joan was a trained horticulturist, and it showed in her work. While other organizations focused on routine landscaping services including lawn mowing, tree pruning, and other basic maintenance services such as applying lawn chemicals, a major portion of Joan's business came from landscape design and planting. Joan's services were so unique and so well priced that sales were limited only by capacity. In fact, Joan had been expanding her business, since demand seemed insatiable.

As part of her studies in college, Joan took several management courses including two on accounting. She believed she could identify opportunities to improve profit by developing a product line income statement. The results appear in Exhibit 3-1.

The lawn mowing business was mostly under contract. Customers would sign up for the season and pay a quoted rate per cut. The work was straightforward. The lawn was mowed and the edges were trimmed. The layout design business consisted of designing a garden and lawn layout for the customer and then installing

EXHIBIT 3-1

Joan's Landscaping Services

PRODUCT LINE INCOME STATEMENTS			
	LAWN MOWING	LAYOUT DESIGN	OTHER MAINTENANCE
Revenues	$230,000	$175,000	$250,000
Direct Costs	125,000	56,000	145,000
Allocated Costs	105,343	80,153	114,504
Profit	$ –343	$ 38,847	$ –9,504

the approved design. Other maintenance included tree pruning and the application of weed control chemicals.

The direct costs associated with each line of business are the costs of the materials and wages of the people who work in that area. The allocated costs, which total $300,000 in this organization, relate to the office costs and the equipment costs. Since equipment deteriorates with use, Joan figures that equipment costs should be allocated in proportion to revenue since that is a measure of use.

Exhibit 3-1 is a cause of both frustration and concern for Joan. Based on an initial calculation similar to this one, Joan had decided to focus on the layout design business, because it appeared to be the most lucrative and also was subject to the least competition. However, as efforts and sales in the layout design business continued to increase, profits continued to erode at a greater rate. Joan wondered why this was happening.

What Does Cost Mean?

An old adage in management accounting recommends, "different costs for different purposes." This implies, correctly, that there is no single definition of cost. There are two reasons: First, costs are developed and used for some specific purpose, and second, the way the cost is to be used will define the way it should be computed. Remember this adage as you study this chapter.

Management accountants have used different systems, or classifications, to develop cost information. These systems reflect the purposes to which the cost is to be put. These uses include determining whether a new product should be introduced given its prospective price and cost structure, determining whether an existing product should be discontinued, or assessing the efficiency of a particular operation. Let us look at some different systems for organizing costs for different purposes.

WHEN THE PURPOSE IS TO COMPUTE THE COST OF SOMETHING

Cost object
Something for which a cost must be computed.

We begin by describing cost terms that are important when the purpose of costing is to compute the cost of something. A **cost object** is something for which we want to

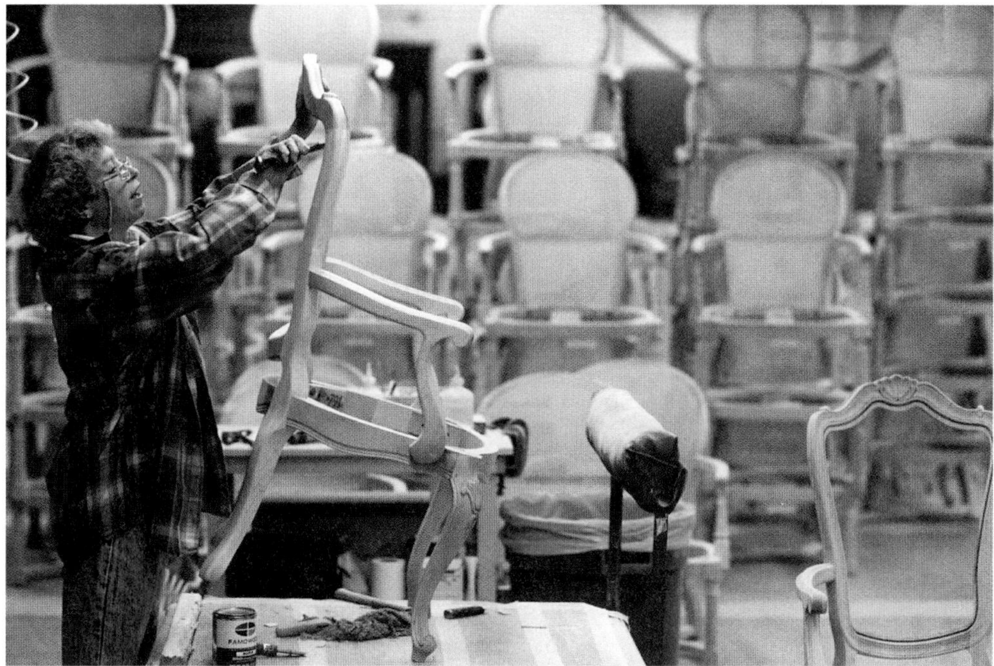

The wood used to make this furniture is a direct cost. The amount of wood used is directly proportional to the units of furniture made. (Liaison Agency, Inc.)

compute a cost. Examples of cost objects include a product, a product line, or an organizational unit such as the shipping department of an on-line retailer. A **direct cost** is a cost of a resource or activity that is acquired for or used by a single cost object. For example, if the cost object were a dining room table, one of the direct costs, called a direct material cost, would be the cost of the wood that went into the dining room table. Similarly, if a manager were hired solely to supervise the production of dining room tables and only dining room tables, that manager's salary would be a direct cost if the cost object were dining room tables. An **indirect cost** is the cost of a resource that was acquired to be used by more than one cost object. For example, the cost of a saw used in a furniture factory to make different products is an indirect cost because it is used to make different products such as dining room tables, china cabinets, and dining room chairs.

Direct cost
A cost of a resource or activity that is acquired for or used by a single cost object.

Indirect cost
A cost of a resource that was acquired to be used by more than one cost object.

Is the salary paid to your accounting instructor a direct or indirect cost? It could be either. If your instructor was hired on a contract to teach only the course you are taking, then his or her salary is a direct cost. If your instructor is paid a salary, which in turn creates the capacity to teach several different courses, his or her salary is an indirect cost.

ORGANIZING COSTS BASED ON THE WAY THEY ARE CREATED

As we will see in this chapter and later in the book, it is sometimes useful to describe costs in terms of how they arise. This perspective on cost definition relies on the notion of flexible and capacity-related resources.

Flexible resources are resources whose costs are proportional to the amount of the resource used. Examples of flexible resources are wood used to make furniture in a factory, electrical power to operate machinery, and fuel used to deliver the furniture to customers. The costs of flexible resources are called **flexible costs.** Flexible costs are always direct costs, but sometimes when it is inconvenient to account for them as

Flexible resources
Those resources whose supply can be adjusted, in the short run, to actual demands (contrast with *committed costs*).

Flexible costs
Those costs that vary with production or sales volumes.

The cost of this production machinery is a capacity-related cost, because the machine cost depends on the amount of capacity acquired and not on how much the machine is used. (Kevin Horan/Stock, Boston.)

direct costs and when the cost is only a small part of total costs, flexible costs are treated as indirect costs. For example, it would be prohibitively costly to measure the amount and therefore the cost of glue used to make a dining room table; therefore, the glue, which is actually a flexible cost, is treated as an indirect cost.

Capacity-related resources
Those resources acquired and paid for in advance of when the work is completed and whose costs depend upon the amounts required rather than the amount used.

Capacity-related costs
The costs associated with capacity-related resources.

Capacity-related resources are acquired and paid for in advance of when the work is done. The costs associated with capacity-related resources are called **capacity-related costs.** Most personnel costs and depreciation on machinery and buildings are examples of capacity-related costs. Note that capacity-related costs depend upon how much of the resource, or capacity, is acquired, rather than on how much is used. Therefore, the amount of capacity-related costs is related to the planned rather than the actual level of activities. Note how this differs from flexible costs, which are directly proportional to the actual level of activity. Capacity-related costs can be direct or indirect. For example, in the case of a multiproduct firm that acquires a climate-control warehouse for the exclusive use of one product, that warehouse cost would be capacity related and direct to the product that uses it. On the other hand, when the capacity of the resource is multipurpose and designed to provide services to many different products, its cost is indirect.

Labor costs have caused both confusion and controversy in costing circles. Labor costs were originally flexible costs, because workers were paid in proportion to the hours that they worked. In fact, some workers are still paid based on the number of hours they work or the amount of work they do (which is called a piece rate system). Despite this, scheduling and union considerations have changed most labor costs into capacity-related costs, because even though many workers are paid on an hourly basis, their wages are guaranteed to be paid, at least in the short run, regardless if work is available. For this reason, most organizations now treat labor costs as capacity related rather than flexible.

How the Use of Cost Information Defines Its Focus and Form

The idea that the use to which a cost is put defines its relevance and appropriate form means that calculating a cost is not an end in itself. A cost number is only valuable if it serves some purpose. There are many purposes for cost information, and it is useful to divide those purposes into external and internal purposes. To see why, let us consider some uses of cost information inside and outside the organization, and then look at some other aspects of cost determination.

USING COST INFORMATION OUTSIDE THE ORGANIZATION

You may be familiar, from a financial accounting course, with the purposes of external reporting of financial measures of performance. The key issues for external users of accounting information are consistency and a reasonably accurate allocation of costs between the income statement (cost of goods sold) and the balance sheet (ending inventory). Since no one is exactly sure how the investors, creditors, and other organization stakeholders use these cost numbers, **generally accepted accounting principles (GAAP),** which prescribe how costs are to be determined for external reporting, focus on process rather than the decision relevance of the resulting cost allocations. The intended result is costs that are computed consistently through time and across different organizations rather than costs that are necessarily useful for a given decision-making purpose. In general, we can say that costs computed for outside users are historical costs that are computed in a standard way because they follow specific rules.

Generally accepted accounting principles (GAAP) The allowable methods for classifying costs for external reporting.

Traditionally, the basic structure of cost accounting systems has reflected the need to determine product costs for external financial statements. This calculation must satisfy external financial reporting requirements imposed by GAAP and also, where they differ from GAAP, by income tax regulations. These external requirements specify which costs to assign to products and thus will appear either as cost of goods sold or inventory as well as which costs to exclude from product cost calculations. When developing costs for external reporting, accounting systems usually classify costs by type and function. The types of costs are product and period costs, and the two broad functional cost classifications are manufacturing and nonmanufacturing costs.

Cost The monetary value of goods and services expended to obtain current or future benefits.

Classifying Costs by Type. GAAP defines **cost** as the monetary value of goods and services expended to obtain current or future benefits. **Expenses** are the costs of goods or services that have expired; that is, they have been used up in the process of creating goods or services. For example, when a furniture maker buys wood to make furniture, the cost of the wood is an asset and appears as part of the organization's inventory. Eventually, when the product into which the wood has been incorporated is sold, the cost of the wood is removed from the organization's assets and is transferred to the income statement where it becomes an expense.

Expenses The costs of goods or services that have expired, that is, have been used up in the process of creating goods and services.

Product costs are incurred to produce the volume and mix of products made during the period. The portion of product costs assigned to the products actually sold in a period appears as expenses (cost of goods sold) in the income statement; the remaining portion of product costs is assigned to the products in inventory and appears as an asset in the balance sheet. Thus, expenses in a fiscal period may not include all the costs (monetary value of goods and services) expended during the year.

Product costs Those costs incurred to produce the volume and mix of products made during the period.

GAAP refers to nonmanufacturing costs, which include administrative, marketing, research and development, and selling costs, as **period costs,** because GAAP does not consider them to be an element of product costs. The main reason is that in GAAP, inventory valuation (the words *product* or *inventory costing* are not used in GAAP) focuses on determining the total cost of existing inventory and not the cost of

Period costs Those costs related to nonmanufacturing costs, including administrative and marketing costs.

▶ *Accountants classify the cost associated with using this advertising space as a period cost. This reflects the conservative accounting assumption that advertising benefits only current period sales. (Sandra Baker/Liaison Agency, Inc.)*

individual items of inventory. GAAP focuses on valuing ending inventory and then allocates any remaining manufacturing costs to cost of goods sold.

Some nonmanufacturing costs, such as selling, clearly do not apply to inventory items since they relate to products that have been sold. Other nonmanufacturing costs (e.g., administrative, research and development, and advertising costs) have such an ambiguous relationship to inventory that GAAP refuses to include these elements of cost in valuing inventory. The reason is that doing so would involve endless and complex rules for organizations to follow so that comparability across organizations could be achieved.

The notions of product and period costs and manufacturing and nonmanufacturing costs, which are important in GAAP, are not particularly useful notions in management accounting, where the objective is to determine all the components, both manufacturing and nonmanufacturing, of the costs associated with a cost object.

Manufacturing costs Those costs incurred inside the factory associated with transforming raw materials into a finished product.

Classifying Costs by Function. GAAP has chosen to use two broad functional cost classifications, manufacturing costs and nonmanufacturing costs.

Manufacturing Costs

Direct manufacturing costs Costs that can be traced easily to the product manufactured or service rendered.

Indirect manufacturing costs All manufacturing costs other than direct manufacturing costs.

Manufacturing costs are all costs incurred inside the factory associated with transforming raw materials into a finished product. These costs include flexible costs related to material and labor and capacity-related costs relating to resources (e.g., machinery and people used inside the factory, and the factory building itself).

Direct manufacturing costs, such as the cost of material or the cost of labor that is paid based on the amount of work done, are traced or assigned to the products that created those costs.

Indirect manufacturing costs are more difficult to trace to products because these costs have a cause-and-effect relationship with capacity rather than with indi-

IN PRACTICE

What Drives Manufacturing Support Costs

Manufacturing executives indicate that controlling and reducing support costs only ranks behind quality and getting new products out on schedule as their primary concern. Support costs as a percent of value added in manufacturing have been increasing steadily over the past 100 years, while the proportion of direct labor costs has been decreasing. (Value added in manufacturing equals direct labor plus manufacturing support costs.) Production managers have been paying increased attention to support costs in today's environment because they have more leverage on improving productivity through cutting support costs than they do through pruning direct labor.

The critical step for managers in controlling support costs lies in developing a model that identifies the forces driving these costs. In a classic paper Miller and Vollman suggest that support costs in a plant are driven not by production volume but by the following four types of manufacturing transactions:

1. *Logistical transactions,* which involve ordering, executing, and confirming the movement of materials from one location to another. These transactions are processed, transcribed, and analyzed by workers on the shop floor as well as by workers in the receiving, expediting, shipping, data entry, and accounting departments.
2. *Balancing transactions,* which ensure that the supplies of materials, labor, and capacity are equal to the demand for these resources. Workers in purchasing; production and materials planning; production scheduling and control; and labor requirements planning take part in these transactions.
3. *Quality transactions,* which comprise quality control, including inspection and rework; quality improvement, including worker training, engineering, and supplier certification; and field support including warranty repairs.
4. *Change transactions,* which update manufacturing information systems to accommodate changes in engineering designs, schedules, routings, standards, materials specifications, and bills of material.

Source: J. G. Miller and T. E. Vollman, "The Hidden Factory," *Harvard Business Review,* September-October 1985, pp. 142–150.

vidual units of production. Therefore, the process of assigning indirect costs to a product involves allocating what is deemed to be a fair share of the indirect cost to the product. Generally, this allocation is based on the product's use of the various capacity resources. Indirect manufacturing costs include those of equipment and the wages and benefits paid to production supervisors and workers who provide the general capacity to undertake production activities in the factory.

Nonmanufacturing Costs

Nonmanufacturing costs include an organization's other costs, as follows:

1. **Distribution costs** involve delivering finished products to customers.
2. **Selling costs** include sales personnel salaries and commissions and other sales office expenses.
3. **Marketing costs** include advertising and promotion expenses.
4. **After-sales costs** involve dealing with customers after the sale and include warranty repairs and the cost of maintaining help and complaint lines.
5. **Research and development costs** include expenditures for designing and bringing new products to the market.

Nonmanufacturing costs
The costs of an organization other than those incurred to produce a product; includes *distribution costs, selling costs, marketing costs, after-sales costs, research and development costs,* and *general and administrative costs.*

In manufacturing organizations costing has traditionally focused on costs incurred inside the factory. However, attention is increasingly turning to understanding the costs associated with dealing with customers such as distribution costs. (Richard Pasley/Stock, Boston)

6. **General and administrative costs** include expenses, such as the chief executive officer's salary and legal and accounting office costs, that do not fall into any of the above categories.

Exhibit 3-2 summarizes the relationship between product and period costs and manufacturing and nonmanufacturing costs.

Like manufacturing costs, nonmanufacturing costs can be flexible or capacity related and direct or indirect. For example, selling commissions are flexible because they vary with the amount sold. Selling commissions also are direct because they are attributable to the product that was sold to earn the commission. The depreciation cost of a warehouse that is used to store many different products is an indirect cost because it is not exclusive to any one product, and it is a capacity-related cost because the depreciation is based on the size of the warehouse and not on the amount of warehouse space used.

EXHIBIT 3-2

Summary of Cost Classifications

PRODUCT (MANUFACTURING) COSTS	PERIOD (NONMANUFACTURING) COSTS
1. direct manufacturing costs	1. distribution costs
2. indirect manufacturing costs	2. selling costs
	3. marketing costs
	4. after-sales costs
	5. research and development costs
	6. general and administrative costs

No one is really sure why GAAP uses this functional approach; the reason is lost in time, but people have different explanations. Perhaps the reason is rooted in some type of responsibility accounting notion that different people are responsible for different functions so we should organize costs by function. Perhaps the reason is that GAAP considers nonmanufacturing costs to be the costs of activities that only benefit sales of the current period so they should be expensed in this period.

Because GAAP considers all nonmanufacturing costs as period costs used to support the sales of products in the current period only, for external reporting purposes GAAP only includes manufacturing costs in calculating the cost of inventory. Traditional cost accounting systems, therefore, provide for the analysis of these costs in detail so that they can be assigned on some sensible basis to products that created those costs.

In principle, cost accounting systems to support managerial decision making can be designed independently of such external reporting requirements. Costing systems designed in the past, however, conserved on information-processing costs by adopting the structure imposed by external reporting requirements. Therefore, most cost accounting systems we observe in organizations today tend to be driven by the rules that determine product costs for inventory valuation and cost of goods sold.

USING COST INFORMATION INSIDE THE ORGANIZATION

Inside the organization costs serve many different purposes. These purposes can be divided into two broad categories: planning and evaluation. Examples of planning purposes occur when cost serves as a reference point for determining the selling price of a prospective product, or when cost is used in a budgeting model to forecast costs under different levels of production and selling activities. Evaluation purposes occur when deciding whether the market price for an existing product makes the product profitable, or when evaluating whether a process is efficient compared with the costs of similar internal or external processes. Some organizations base performance bonuses on cost information. For example, the Scanlon Plan, which was developed in the 1930s, bases workers' rewards on their ability to reduce labor costs below a labor cost standard established in a baseline period.

In summary, decision makers use costs to make decisions and to control the processes they manage. When the decision is known, the cost calculation can be tailored to the specific decision that is being made. That tailoring is the role of the management accountant and the management accounting system.

COST-BENEFIT CONSIDERATIONS IN DEVELOPING COST INFORMATION

We have seen how costs for external reporting are prescribed, whereas costs for internal decision making are optional since they are computed as required for a particular decision. This means that developing cost information for internal decision making is a matter of choice. Because the organization must pay someone to develop cost information, its expected benefits should exceed its development costs.

You might suspect, and it is generally true, that it is difficult to compute the value of using cost information in a particular decision. Nevertheless, the fundamental principle remains: In the cost-benefit tradeoff of developing cost information, the benefit should outweigh the cost. Consider a simple example. Suppose you are making a product that your current costing system estimates has a cost of $19. The product price is $20 and you sell 150,000 units per year. You know that your cost system is rudimentary and that, given the estimated cost of $19, the actual cost could be $16 or $22 with either possibility equally likely. The cost to refine the costing system is $70,000.

The decision here is whether to continue to make and sell the product for the next two years or to abandon it now. Given prior beliefs, the expected value of producing is \$300,000 [(0.5 × 2 × 150,000) × (20 − 16) + (0.5 × 2 × 150,000) × (20 − 22)] and the expected value of abandoning the product now is \$0. Therefore, based on prior beliefs, the product would be produced. With perfect information you can avoid production when the cost is \$22. Associated with the \$22 cost is a loss of \$600,000 [(150,000 × 2) × (20 − 22)]. Since the prior probability is 50% that the cost will be \$22, we can avoid this \$600,000 loss with probability 50% when we have perfect information about costs. Therefore the expected value of perfect information is \$300,000. Therefore, the cost of \$70,000 to refine the costing system is worthwhile, as it is far less than the \$300,000 expected value of the information.

HOW DECISIONS DEFINE THE NATURE OF THE COST REQUIRED

The "different costs for different purposes" adage implies that because cost information is used to inform or guide some decision, that decision will define the nature of the required cost, the way it should be computed, and the value of any cost number. This means a cost number that is useful for one decision may be useless or perhaps even harmful if it is used for another decision. For example, suppose that you were asked to compute the cost of flying one person from London to Zurich. You might start by estimating the cost of the flight including fuel, depreciation on the aircraft, employee salaries, meals, landing fees, and any other related costs. Next you might consider what other company overhead should be added to the above costs to get the total cost of the flight. Finally, you might divide the total cost of the flight by some number (such as the capacity of the aircraft or the number of people on board a particular flight) to get a cost per person. Now suppose that you were told that the flight is going anyway and you must compute the cost of adding one more person to the flight. Would you use the same cost? Not likely. In this latter case you might include only the incremental cost of items such as fuel and meals that are created by adding one more person to the flight. The appropriate cost to use is defined by the context of the decision. The full cost might be used for planning to determine the average ticket price the airline will have to charge if it puts a scheduled flight into operation. The second cost, which we could call an incremental cost, might be used

Because of the huge passenger volumes it is particularly important for airlines to understand cost behavior. Airline planners must ensure in the long run that ticket prices cover capacity-related costs while, at the same time, that short-term pricing uses available capacity. (Etienne De Malglaive/Liaison Agency, Inc.)

What is the cost of going to a movie? (Michelle Burgess/Stock, Boston)

for pricing standby tickets. Using the second cost to develop a long-term ticket pricing strategy would be a disaster because it would ensure the long-run failure of the airline.

DO DIFFERENT COSTS FOR DIFFERENT PURPOSES CAUSE COSTING CHAOS?

At first you might think it curious or even wrong that cost is not a rigid number calculated according to some formal rules. One challenge of working with costs, however, is that they are used in many different contexts. As an example that illustrates a range of possible cost alternatives, suppose we are asked to compute the cost of going to a movie. That task seems somewhat unambiguous until we start thinking about it. Are we talking about historical cost (the cost last week at this theater) or some cost that might exist in the future? If the cost of the movie varies by date or time, by movie or by theater, are we talking about average cost or the cost of a specific movie at a specific location and at a specific time? If there are discount periods, for example matinees or Tuesday evenings, are we talking about the full rate, the discount rate, or the average of the two? Are there other costs? For example, if we expect that the person will pay to hire a baby sitter, pay to park, and will have a drink and a snack, should those costs be added to the admission cost? They might well be considered elements of the total cost of going to a movie. Finally, are there hidden costs? For example, if Mary goes to the movie she will not be able to study for her exam, dropping her expected grade from A to B. The cost that Mary assigns to this grade reduction is an implicit cost associated with going to the movie that she would add to the explicit costs associated with the movie.

But if the question were rephrased as "I promised to pay John's admission to the movie he attended last Thursday, what was the cost?" all ambiguity is resolved, and a specific and relevant cost can be computed. Note that conventional accounting for external reporting avoids all these issues because it is understood that reported cost will be the historical cost for a particular transaction that has already occurred.

OPPORTUNITY COST

Opportunity costs The sacrifices incurred when using resources for one purpose instead of another.

Management accountants often use the concept of opportunity cost. An **opportunity cost** is the sacrifice you make when you use a resource for one purpose instead of another. In the previous example, the reduction in Mary's grade on the exam was her opportunity cost of using her time to go to the movie instead of studying. The opportunity cost of a resource is zero if there is excess capacity of that resource.

To illustrate, suppose that Mount Pleasant Plastics can use an injection-molding machine to produce one of two products: a plastic crate for milk or a plastic container to carry soda bottles. Demand is such that Mount Pleasant Plastics can sell all it makes of either product. The only constraint limiting production is machine time. What would you choose to do? Intuitively you are likely to say, use the machine to make the product that is more profitable. Suppose the milk crates have a profit of $8 and the soda containers have a profit of $5. Which one would you make? The milk crate looks like a better idea, but suppose you discover that it takes one minute to make a milk crate on the machine but only 30 seconds to make a soda carrier. Therefore, the profit per machine minute is $10 if you make soda carriers and $8 if you make milk crates. The soda carrier is a better product because it maximizes the profit for a given supply of machine time.

Opportunity cost is the value of the factor of production in its next best use. In this case, the opportunity cost of machine time is $10 per minute assuming that production is capacity constrained. You should be able to ponder this and conclude that if production is not capacity constrained (for example, it may be constrained by sales or demand considerations), then the opportunity cost of production capacity is $0. Ultimately you will realize that when an organization uses its available resources to maximize its short-run profits, it will simultaneously minimize its opportunity costs.

As you can see, opportunity costs are implicit costs because they do not appear anywhere in the accounting records. Nevertheless, they are important in management accounting, and we will be using this notion at several different places in this book.

COMPARING COST CLASSIFICATION SYSTEMS

The systems of dividing costs into direct and indirect costs and that of dividing costs into flexible and capacity-related costs are different. Therefore, we must be careful when we mix these terms. Exhibit 3-3 summarizes our discussion so far about these four cost concepts.

Recall that since flexible costs vary directly with use, they can be attributed to the cost object that created the use. Therefore, all flexible costs are direct costs. However,

EXHIBIT 3-3

Summary of Direct, Indirect, Flexible, and Capacity-Related Costs

	FLEXIBLE	CAPACITY RELATED
Direct Cost	The cost of a resource whose consumption and cost varies in proportion to product. Example: the cost of crude oil used in a refinery.	The cost of special-purpose capacity (person or equipment) that was acquired for, and used by, only one cost object. Example: the wage paid to a production supervisor who works on one product exclusively.
Indirect Cost	The cost of a resource that is consumed in proportion to production but which is prohibitively expensive to account for as a direct cost. Example: the cost of the stain applied to a dining room table.	The cost of general-purpose capacity (person or equipment) that is used by a number of cost objects. Example: the cost of a warehouse that is used to store the organization's products.

some direct costs are treated as if they were indirect. An example is the cost of miscellaneous supplies in a factory, such as glue that is used in furniture fabrication, lubricating oil that is used in a machine shop, or electricity that is used to power machines in a factory. These costs are really direct costs in that they can be avoided if the cost object to which they relate is not made. But because it would be so costly to account for these costs as direct (imagine calculating the amount of glue or stain that went into making a dining room table), they are treated as indirect costs instead and are applied to production based on some measure of volume, such as production units or direct labor hours worked.

Capacity-related costs can be direct or indirect. For example, if a special-purpose warehouse is designed for, and used by, only one product, the depreciation on that warehouse, which is a capacity-related cost, is also a direct cost to that product. Remember it is exclusivity that defines whether a cost is direct or indirect.

You might wonder whether there are some indirect costs that are not capacity related, that vary directly with volume such as units made or sold. It turns out that there are indirect costs that are not capacity related. It is often incorrectly asserted that all are indirect. In fact, some of the most egregious costing errors have been committed by treating direct capacity-related costs as if they were indirect. Some flexible costs are treated as indirect because it would be prohibitively expensive to account for them as direct costs. It is true, however, that most capacity-related costs are indirect. Can you think of a capacity-related cost that is direct to the unit in which you are enrolled in your university or college? Brant University has an organization unit called the Business School. The Business School is housed in its own building and all classes are taught in that building. Depreciation on that building is a direct cost if the cost object is the Business School, since the building was designed for, and is used exclusively by, the Business School.

HOW PERSPECTIVE DETERMINES THE COST DEFINITION

Continuing the example of the Business School at Brant University, suppose that the Business School has five departments: accounting, marketing, finance, operations management, and management. Suppose that the cost object in some study is the accounting department. In this case, the depreciation on the Business School would be an indirect cost to the accounting department. Why? Because the accounting department is not the exclusive user of the Business School capacity.

So cost is like a chameleon. Its definition can change as the perspective changes. That is another facet of the adage "different costs for different purposes." We might define a cost one way for one decision and another way for another. If this seems confusing at first, remember you can always sort out the direct and indirect classification by using this rule: Direct means that the resource that created the cost was acquired for, and used by, a single cost object.

LONG-RUN AND SHORT-RUN COSTS

Short run is the period over which a decision maker cannot adjust capacity. The level of capacity-related resources, hence of capacity-related costs, is fixed. Therefore, the only costs that vary in the short run are those that vary in proportion to production. Short-run costs are actually flexible costs. If you think of the example discussed earlier in this chapter about computing the cost of flying someone from London to Zurich, short-run costs are those that change when you add one more person to the flight that was going anyway, such as the incremental fuel costs and the incremental meal costs added by one person.

Long-run costs are the sum of flexible and capacity-related costs associated with a cost object, which is most often a product. They are important for product planning purposes because they are an estimate of the cost of all resources consumed to make the product. The price charged for a product must cover its long-run cost for the organization to replace the capacity used to make the product when the capacity deteriorates.

How Organizations Create Costs—An Example

Let us review the definitions of cost and consider how organizations create costs by considering the activities of Fred's Grocery Services.

STARTING UP

Fred Stanford owns and operates a grocery delivery service for a select group of customers. Fred chose his customers using two criteria: First, he knows that they will pay him for his services. Second, they are in a geographical area that Fred can serve reasonably.

On Monday of each week Fred provides his customers with a list of groceries from which they can order. These groceries reflect discounts or bargains that Fred has managed to find at the local farmers' market and through large wholesalers that have excess supply.

Fred's customers value his services because the quality is always high and the prices are low. Fred's customers call in their orders, which Fred delivers at a prearranged time during the following day. Since the availability of bargains is limited, Fred's products are offered on a first-come, first-served basis. Fred usually acquires his products on Saturday and Sunday, and because he has very limited storage space (in a garage that belongs to his parents) and most of the goods he carries are perishable, Fred's objective is to clear his inventory by Friday evening of each week. Fred's costs include the cost of printing the flyers, the cost of acquiring inventory, the cost of maintaining a telephone line (which includes a call answer service), and the expense Fred incurs delivering groceries, which amount to the cost of gasoline since he drives an old vehicle with negligible value.

What are Fred's costs in a start-up phase? The cost of the flyers is an advertising cost that accountants call a discretionary cost. The cost of the merchandise may sound like a flexible cost, but think about its nature. There is no evidence in the case that excess inventory can be returned to the source. Therefore, the cost of the inventory depends on the amount purchased and not the amount used (which, in this case, means sold)—a hallmark of capacity-related costs. This classification choice is confirmed by the observation that Fred's sales are limited by the amount of inventory he acquires—Fred does run out during the week. Note that this capacity-related cost is a fairly short-run cost, as it is committed once, and only for the week. The following week Fred can choose a different level of inventory capacity to hold. Think of how this situation would change if Fred were obligated to buy the same amount each week. That would represent a much longer commitment. The only other cost that Fred incurs is the cost of gasoline related to deliveries. This appears to be a flexible cost in the sense that it depends on the volume of the delivery activities and is incurred in proportion to the number of deliveries made. There is an opportunity cost buried in here, and that is the salary that Fred could earn working elsewhere.

EARLY GROWTH

Word of Fred's reasonable prices and high-quality groceries has spread. The number of Fred's customers has grown and Fred is facing capacity constraints. He can no longer fit his weekly purchases in the garage and he has been forced to lease a small commercial warehouse. One advantage of the warehouse is its large refrigerated area. Fred leases the warehouse on a monthly basis for $3000 per month, which includes utilities and taxes.

THE TECHNOLOGICAL EDGE

Costing Web Sites

After investigating the cost for a medium to large firm to build its first e-commerce site, Gartner Group has found the expensive answer: $1 million.

Although the majority of the cash goes toward labor costs, the opportunity cost is also substantial: Gartner says the cost of building such sites will increase 24% per year over the next two years (see Exhibit 3-4).

EXHIBIT 3-4A

Joan's Landscaping Services

Cost to Develop an E-Commerce Site from Scratch	
Average	$1 Million
Low End	Less than $350,000
High End	More than $2 Million
Time to Complete	
Average	5 months
High End	1 year
Number of Respondents on Budget	None

EXHIBIT 3-4B

Distribution of Costs to Develop an E-Commerce Site

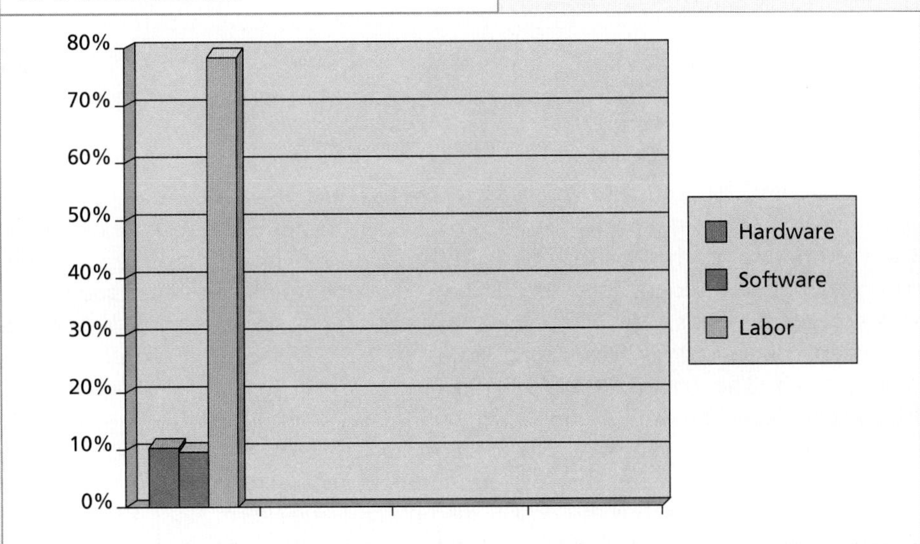

Source: Gartner Group Survey of 20 midsize to large businesses launching a first-phase e-commerce web site. Quoted in *The Industry Standard,* June 14, 1999, p. 102.

Fred has decided that his older car is no longer suitable for grocery deliveries, because it is too small and inconvenient. Fred has purchased a used cube van for $8000. Fred figures that the van will last four years. The insurance on the vehicle will amount to $1500 annually, which Fred pays on a monthly basis. With the addition of the van and the warehouse, Fred's business triples.

Fred's cost structure is now changing. In addition to the costs in the start-up phase, Fred faces new costs: the costs of the warehouse, the van, and the insurance on the van. What type of cost is the warehouse cost? It is a capacity-related cost. Again the cost of the warehouse does not depend upon how much Fred uses it, but on the capacity that Fred acquired. Similarly, the cost of the van, which would be reflected in its depreciation charges, is a capacity-related cost, because the cost of the van does not vary in proportion to any volume measure. However, suppose that Fred believed the van would last for only 100,000 miles and then would have to be scrapped. In that case, the cost might be treated as a flexible cost, because the lifetime of the resource would be based on use rather than time. The vehicle insurance is a capacity-related cost, because it bears no relationship to an underlying volume measure such as number of deliveries, number of customers, or level of sales.

REACHING THE BOUNDARIES OF EXISTING CAPACITY

Fred is having trouble handling order taking because he is spending so much extra time making additional deliveries as his business continues to grow. He hires his sister, Elizabeth, to run the office. Elizabeth's duties are to take telephone orders, schedule deliveries, keep the records for the business, and help in handling the inventory in the warehouse. Fred pays Elizabeth $500 per week.

Fred is under pressure from some customers to accept credit cards. However, for the moment he is resisting and still insists on cash, no personal checks.

Now Fred has added another capacity-related cost since Elizabeth's salary is fixed and does not depend on the underlying volume of activity. Note that it is the increase in sales that has prompted Fred to hire Elizabeth, so you might think that somehow the salary is volume related. But recall the definition of capacity-related cost—it is a cost whose level depends on the amount of resource acquired, not the amount of resource used. Fred is obligated to pay Elizabeth $500 per week whether she is busy or idle.

EXPANDING THE PRODUCT LINE AND ACQUIRING MORE CAPACITY RESOURCES

Faced with demands from many customers, Fred has expanded his product line, which formerly consisted primarily of produce, to include many types of canned goods. Fred purchases the canned goods in truckload lots from a supplier, thereby incurring a moderate discount. Because of the order size required to earn the discount, Fred is no longer clearing his entire inventory each week, and now has a permanent inventory of canned goods. Therefore, Fred has been forced to expand to a larger warehouse unit. The rent is now $5000 per month, but instead of paying monthly and having no lease, Fred must sign a two-year lease.

Again, Fred is on the move, and the cost structure of his business is changing. The larger warehouse means that his commitment to capacity-related costs is now $5000 per month for rent, but the cost is also much longer term since the lease is for two years. This creates more risk for Fred since he is committed to paying that amount even if his business slows. Fred also is now holding inventory, which will create inventory-holding costs such as spoilage and damage and opportunity costs in the form of money that is tied up in inventory and cannot earn a return elsewhere. The cost of the canned goods is a flexible cost, unlike the cost of the produce. Why?

Because the canned goods can be held until they sell, unlike the produce which has to be disposed of if it is not sold.

Perhaps the most interesting development for Fred, from the perspective of a management accountant, however, is the move to multiple product lines. This creates the possibility that Fred might want to compute the profits earned on his two lines of business—produce and canned goods. If he does, the accounting system will create two cost objects, one for the produce and one for the canned goods. When that happens, the costs of the warehouse and the van will be indirect costs and will have to be allocated to each of the product lines using some appropriate basis, so that each product line bears its appropriate share of the cost of the capacity that it uses. However, not all these costs may be indirect. For example, if a portion of the warehouse is refrigerated and only the produce is stored in that area, then all costs relating to refrigeration are related to the produce and all should be assigned to the produce.

REDEFINING THE BUSINESS

Fred is now doing more than $600,000 of business per year. One of Fred's customers remarks, "Hey Fred, you should start your own grocery store." This comment gives Fred cause for thought. Fred never wanted to operate a grocery business. His value proposition was to provide customer service by delivering high-quality merchandise to the customer without requiring the customer to come to a store. Despite his having hired a new employee, Grady, on a part-time basis to help Elizabeth, the order-taking business is again a bottleneck.

Fred starts to think about the internet. He discovers that for $300 per week, a local internet service provider will design and maintain a web site for him. The web site will contain the weekly list of products available, complete with pictures. Fred is intrigued with the idea for two reasons. First, he can provide product availability data so that customers know what products are available and in what quantities, and second, he can change his product list during the week if additional products become available. This deals with two major complaints that customers have: (1) the difficulty of getting through to Elizabeth or Grady on the phone, and (2) when they call, the inconvenience of not knowing product availability.

Fred signs up for the service and tells his customers that prices will be cut 5% for any items ordered via the web site. Within four months, 80% of Fred's business is coming over the web. Fred sells the list of his customers who do not want to move over to the web to his cousin Lemont, who will operate his business in the same way as Fred operated when he was in the start-up phase. With this move, Fred abandons telephone orders and cash and moves exclusively to web-based orders and credit card sales.

What kind of cost is Grady's salary? Since this is a part-time position, Grady's salary is flexible if he is paid only when work is available and only for the work he does. His salary is an incremental cost in the sense that it is created by the expansion and it varies with short-term fluctuations in the underlying volume of activity, which creates a need for his services.

Fred is now committing to a web site that will add more capacity-related costs. Unlike the cost of the truck or the warehouse, which ultimately will have to grow as the business grows, the web site costs will not expand as the business grows. Therefore, this cost might be treated as a business-level or business-sustaining cost that is not allocated to any of the product lines.

CONTINUED GROWTH

Business is booming. Elizabeth has become a full-fledged office manager with a staff of four: an accountant who handles the books and all sales, which are now strictly credit card; a dispatcher who schedules the four drivers needed to handle the volume of deliveries; a purchasing manager who is responsible for finding the best prices for the products stocked; and a warehouse manager. Fred now devotes his time exclusively to making choices about what products to carry. The business is housed in its own building that cost $1 million to purchase. The product line includes produce, packaged meats, many types of household cleaners, and a limited line of dairy items. As always, Fred's value proposition is convenience and costs that are equal to or lower than what is available in the local supermarket.

Note that Fred has now acquired many new capacity-related costs. These costs create business risk, since they are locked in place for an extended period of time. A good example is the cost of the building, which will be reflected in depreciation charges. Fred's story models the general pattern of business growth, in which flexible costs, such as paying people by the hour or renting capacity based on amount used, gradually evolve into committed or capacity-related costs, because the capacity is acquired and paid for irrespective of how much is used.

We will talk more about how cost creation creates a logic for allocating costs to cost objects in Chapter 5.

Cost Structures Today

The composition of manufacturing costs has changed substantially in recent years. In the early 1900s, when many businesses first installed formal cost systems, direct labor represented a large proportion, sometimes 50% or more, of the total manufacturing costs. Direct materials cost was also substantial. As a result, cost accounting systems were designed to focus on measuring and controlling direct labor and materials, and they served this purpose admirably. Capacity-related costs, both direct and indirect, which generally represented a small fraction of total manufacturing costs, were usually accumulated in a single pool and allocated to products in proportion to some volume measure such as the labor or machine hours used by the product.

In today's industrial environment, however, direct labor is only a small portion of manufacturing costs. In the electronics industry, for instance, direct labor costs is often less than 5% of the total manufacturing cost. The cost of direct materials, however, remains important for it represents about 40% to 60% of the costs in many plants.

The big change in cost structure today has been the much higher share of total costs represented by capacity-related costs. This change has occurred because of the shift toward greater automation, which requires more production engineering, scheduling, and machine setup activities; the emphasis on better customer service; and the increase in support activities required by a proliferation of multiple products. In addition to capacity-related manufacturing costs becoming more important, both flexible and capacity-related costs associated with design, product development, distribution, selling, marketing, and administrative activities have increased.

This change in cost structure has caused cost systems that used volume measures to allocate indirect costs to become increasingly inaccurate in computing product costs, because they were designed for manufacturing activities with high direct labor content. Many costs do not vary proportionally with volume. Therefore, an allocation that is volume based has the potential to distort costs. The following example illustrates this idea. Nanticoke Electric has three groups of customers: industrial, commercial, and residential (both single-unit and multiple-unit dwellings). It sells about 1,000,000,000 units of electricity each month to its 455,000 customers. The selling price of the electricity is about $0.50 per unit. A recent costing study has determined that the full manufacturing and distribution cost is about $0.30 per unit. The only other major costs are meter reading costs, which amount to $5 per reading, and billing and processing costs, which amount to $8 per bill. Each customer's meter is

Electric utilities, like many organizations, experience different costs in dealing with different customers. Understanding these differential costs provides important insights in pricing services. (Steve Allen/The Image Bank)

read monthly and bills are prepared monthly. Exhibit 3-5 provides a breakdown of customer types and demand, and the costs of supplying each demand based on the data developed in the special costing study.

The manufacturing and delivery cost for each group is computed by multiplying the total demand for that group by the unit cost of $0.30. The reading and billing cost for each group is computed by multiplying the total reading and billing cost of $13 per customer by the number of customers in that group. The actual cost for each group is the sum of the manufacturing and delivery cost and the reading and billing cost for that group.

Now contrast this information with what is prepared by conventional costing systems. The computed cost for each group is calculated using a simplifying cost allocation approach that is common in traditional costing systems. The total reading and billing costs for all groups are accumulated in a single account. This account totals $5,915,000. This sum is then allocated to the three groups based on demand, which is

EXHIBIT 3-5

Nanticoke Electric Detailed Costing

	INDUSTRIAL	COMMERCIAL	HOME	APARTMENT
Number of Customers	1,000	4,000	150,000	300,000
Total Demand	875,000,000	80,000,000	30,000,000	15,000,000
Mfg and Delivery Cost	262,500,000	24,000,000	9,000,000	4,500,000
Reading and Billing Cost	13,000	52,000	1,950,000	3,900,000
Actual Cost	262,513,000	24,052,000	10,950,000	8,400,000
Actual Average Profit per Customer	$174,987.00	$3,987.00	$27.00	–$3.00

EXHIBIT 3-6

Nanticoke Electric Conventional Costing

	INDUSTRIAL	COMMERCIAL	HOME	APARTMENT
Number of Customers	1,000	4,000	150,000	300,000
Average Demand per Customer	875,000	20,000	200	50
Total demand this Group	875,000,000	80,000,000	30,000,000	15,000,000
Computed Cost this Group	267,675,625	24,473,200	9,177,450	4,588,725
Computed Average Profit per Customer	$169,824.38	$3,881.70	$38.82	$9.70

a volume measure. The total demand by all groups is 1,000,000,000 units. Therefore, the rate per unit of demand for reading and billing costs is $0.005915 ($5,915,000/1,000,000,000). The reading and billing cost allocated to each group is the product of this allocation rate of $0.005915 and its total demand. This allocated cost is then added to the manufacturing and delivery cost for each group to get the computed cost for each group. Exhibit 3-6 summarizes this information. Notice the differences between the actual average profit per customer shown in Exhibit 3-5 and the average profit per customer estimated by the crude costing system shown in Exhibit 3-6.

You might wonder why the costs of reading and billing would be accumulated for all groups and then allocated using a volume measure. Simply, it is an easy and low-cost calculation.

So what is the result? The number shown as the actual average profit per customer is the difference between the total revenue for each customer group and the actual cost divided by the number of customers. The number shown as the computed average profit per customer is the difference between the total revenue for each customer group and the computed cost divided by the number of customers.

You can see the effect of treating the reading and billing costs as if they varied with volume. The computed average cost per customer for the home and apartment customers is overstated. Why? Because a portion of their costs are allocated to the industrial and commercial customers by the inappropriate allocation basis.

The point is that this type of distortion is common in conventional costing systems. Conventional costing takes costs that did not vary proportionally with volume, accumulates them, and then allocates them using a volume measure.

TYPES OF PRODUCTION ACTIVITIES

Traditionally, accountants classified activities into those that varied with volume (leading to what we have called flexible costs), and those that did not (typically leading to supplying capacity and associated committed costs). But this simple dichotomy does not capture the full richness of the types of activities that take place in organizations. The following hierarchy, developed originally for manufacturing operations, gives a broader framework for classifying an activity and its associated costs:

1. unit related
2. batch related
3. product sustaining
4. customer sustaining
5. business sustaining

Unit-Related Activities. Unit-related activities are those whose volume or level is proportional to the number of units produced or to other measures, such as direct labor hours and machine hours that are themselves proportional to the number of units produced. The indirect labor required for quality inspection that checks every item (or 10% or 20% of items) is clearly associated with the number of units produced. Uniform supervision of all activities performed by direct workers requires effort that is associated with the number of direct labor hours. The consumption of lubricating oil for machines and the energy required to operate the machines, as well as the scheduled maintenance of machines after every 20,000 hours or any other specified amount of use, are examples of manufacturing support costs that are proportional to machine hours.

Unit-related activities
Those activities whose volume or level is proportional to the number of units produced or sold.

Since direct labor hours and machine hours themselves increase with the number of units produced, the use of many activities supporting production increases with the level of production. Unit-related activities apply to more than just production activities, however. Loading shipments onto a truck is a unit-related activity, for instance, because it is proportional to the volume of shipments.

Batch-Related Activities. In a production environment, batch-related activities are triggered by the number of batches produced rather than by the number of units manufactured. Machine setups, for instance, are required when beginning the production of a new batch of products. Once the machine has been set up, no additional setup effort is required whether we produce a batch of 100 units or 1000 units of the product. Since the in-process materials for a batch are moved together from one work center to the next, the cost of materials handling also tends to be associated with the number of batches rather than with the number of units in the batches. Similarly, indirect labor for first-item quality inspections (inspections of only the first unit in each batch) involves testing a fixed number of units for each batch produced rather than a percentage of the entire batch. Therefore, the indirect labor required for such inspections also is associated with the number of batches.

Batch-related activities
Those activities triggered by the number of batches produced rather than by the number of units manufactured.

Clerical effort expended to issue purchase orders or to receive materials from suppliers is a support activity associated with the number of purchase orders or with the number of deliveries, rather than with the quantity of materials ordered. However, the support costs of processing the paperwork for purchases depends only on the number of orders rather than the quantity ordered. Production scheduling also is considered a batch-related activity, because it is performed for each production run that needs to be scheduled in a plant, rather than for each unit produced in a production run.

The cost of moving work in process around a factory floor is often proportional to the number of batches since work is often moved in batches. (Shopper/Stock, Boston)

Similarly, many shipping costs may be batch related. For example, if the organization pays the shipper a charge per container or truckload, that unit of shipment is a batch, and the cost of shipping is a batch-related cost, because it depends on the number of batches and not directly on the number or weight of the units shipped.

Product-sustaining activities
Those activities that support the production and sale of individual products but are independent of actual production volumes and batches.

Product-Sustaining Activities. Product-sustaining activities support the production and sale of individual products. The larger the number of products and product lines, the higher the cost of product-sustaining activities. Examples of product-sustaining activities include administrative efforts required to maintain drawings and labor and machine routings for each part; product engineering efforts to maintain coherent specifications such as the bill of materials for individual products and their component parts and their routing through different work centers in the plant; and the process engineering required to implement engineering change orders (ECOs). Engineering efforts to design and test process routines for products and perform product enhancements are other examples of product-sustaining activities. The need to expedite production orders also increases as the number of products and customers serviced by a plant increases. Costs of obtaining patents or regulatory approval, such as Food and Drug Administration approval for new pharmaceutical drugs or food products, increase with the number of products introduced.

Customer-sustaining activities
Those activities that enable the company to sell to an individual customer but are independent of the volume and mix of the products sold and delivered to the customer.

Customer-Sustaining Activities. Shifting from a production to a marketing and sales environment, customer-sustaining activities enable the company to sell to an individual customer but are independent of the volume and mix of the products (and services) sold and delivered to the customer. Examples of customer-sustaining activities include sales calls and technical support provided to individual customers.

Product- and customer-sustaining activities are easily traced to the individual products, services, and customers for whom the activities are performed. But the *quantity* of resources used in these activities are, by definition, independent of the production and sales volumes, and of the quantity of production batches and customer orders. This richer framework enables many more activities to become directly traceable to cost objects, rather than treated as indirect, since they are not proportional to the volumes of production or sales.

Beyond unit, batch, product, and customer-sustaining activities, are other resource supply capabilities that cannot be traced to individual products and customers. These are business-sustaining expenses, such as the cost of a plant manager and administrative staff, and channel-sustaining expenses, such as the cost of trade shows, advertising, and catalogs. The expenses of product-line facility, and channel resources can be assigned directly to the individual product lines, facilities, and channels, but should not be allocated down to individual products, services, or customers.

Business-sustaining activities
Those activities required for the basic functioning of the business, independent of production or sales volumes and mix.

Business-Sustaining Activities. Business-sustaining activities are those required for the basic functioning of the business. These core activities are independent of the size of the organization, or the volume and mix of products and customers. For example, organizations need only one CEO irrespective of their size, and they need to perform certain basic functions, such as registration or reporting, that also are independent of the size of the organization. Similarly, all factories may need one plant manager, one controller or financial manager, one human resource manager, and minimal amounts of activities for housekeeping, maintenance, landscaping, and security. These business-sustaining or facility-sustaining activities are not related to the number of individual products, the number of production runs, or the number of units manufactured and therefore their costs are not allocated to cost objects.

Other Support Activities. There are other support activities that go beyond the basic or core level of business-sustaining activities. The costs of these other sustaining

EXHIBIT 3-7

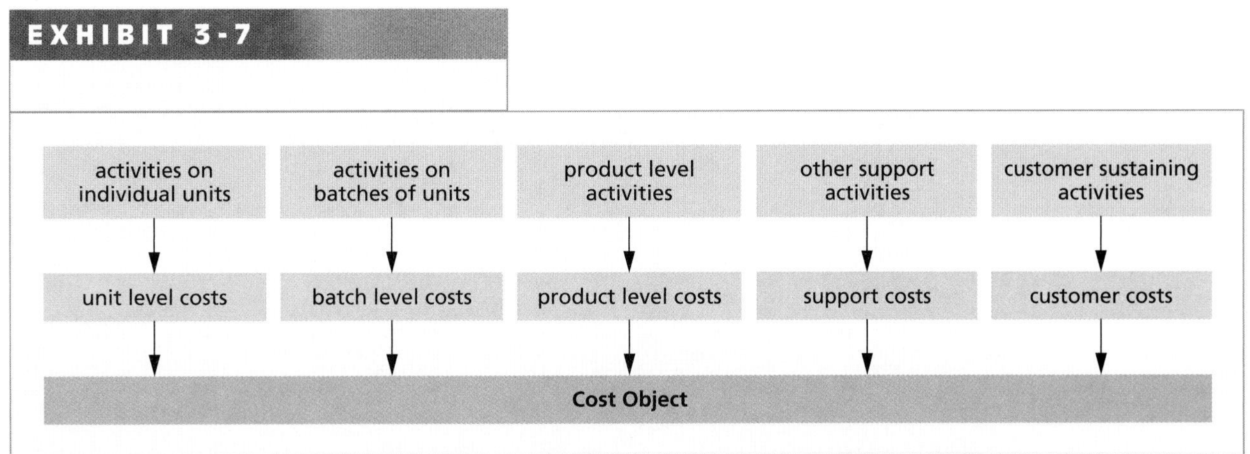

activities vary in proportion to the size or complexity of the organization and are allocated to cost objects in a way that reflects their cause.

Exhibit 3-7 summarizes the five levels of indirect costs that we have just described.

USING THE COST HIERARCHY

The cost hierarchy developed in this section is a model of cost behavior that can be used in two ways: to predict costs and to develop the costs for a cost object such as a product or product line. We will use this hierarchy in Chapter 5 when we discuss activity-based costing systems and in Chapter 11 when we discuss forecasting and budgeting.

UNDERSTANDING THE UNDERLYING BEHAVIOR OF COSTS

If we understand the underlying behavior of costs, we have a basis to predict costs and to understand how costs will behave as volume expands and contracts. Consider the operations of Orillia Novelty Plastics, a small manufacturer of extruded plastics products. Orillia makes three novelty products that customers emboss with their names and use as promotional items. Exhibit 3-8 displays its estimated average monthly production and related demands for raw materials and labor for the next six months. Machine times are not considered because they are budgeted separately. Plastic costs $0.10 per unit and is purchased as needed. All production workers undertake three tasks, setting up the machinery (a batch-related activity), tending the machinery while it is producing (a unit-related activity), and moving work in process around the factory (a batch-related activity). All factory workers are cross-trained so that they can do either run time work or batch work. The total cost of a worker, including wages and fringe benefits, is $25 per hour.

The union contract requires that the number of workers employed can be adjusted only every six months. Therefore, Orillia Plastics must make a six-month commitment to a particular level of worker hours. Based on the projection in Exhibit 3-7, Orillia Plastics has decided to contract for 1500 labor hours per month for the next six months at a total cost of $37,500 (1500 × $25). The difference of $1250 between the contracted ($37,500) cost of labor and the amount estimated, on average, to be needed ($36,250) is a projected excess capacity cost.

Exhibit 3-9 summarizes the production activities for the first month of the six-month contract. Production of item 3 fell, but sales of products 1 and 2 were higher than the average. Study Exhibit 3-9 carefully. Note how the use and cost of plastic follows production up and down. This is the nature of a flexible cost, which depends on the amount used. Note that the cost of labor is stuck at $37,500. Why? Labor is a

EXHIBIT 3-8

Orillia Novelty Plastics
Estimated Monthly Demand

	PRODUCT			
	1	**2**	**3**	**Total**
Units Made	25,000	40,000	10,000	
Plastic per Unit	2	1	3	
Units of Plastic	50,000	40,000	30,000	120,000
Cost of Plastic	$5,000	$4,000	$3,000	$12,000
Run Time Work	0.01	0.005	0.04	
Total Run Time Labor Hours	250	200	400	850
Units per Batch	5,000	4,000	500	
Batches	5	10	20	
Labor Hours per Batch	10	15	20	
Total Batch Labor Hours	50	150	400	600
Total Labor Hours	300	350	800	1,450
Total Labor Cost				$36,250
Total Cost				$48,250

EXHIBIT 3-9

Orillia Novelty Plastics
First Month Production Data

	PRODUCT			
	1	**2**	**3**	**Total**
Units Made	26,000	41,000	8,000	
Plastic per Unit	2	1	3	
Units of Plastic	52,000	41,000	24,000	117,000
Cost of Plastic	$5,200	$4,100	$2,400	$11,700
Run Time Work	0.01	0.005	0.04	
Total Run Time Labor Hours	260	205	320	785
Units per Batch	5,000	4,000	500	
Batches	5	10	16	
Labor Hours per Batch	10	15	20	
Total Batch Labor Hours	52	154	320	526
Total Labor Hours	312	359	640	1,311
Total Labor Cost Used				$32,769
Total Labor Cost Paid				$37,500
Cost Excess Capacity				$ 4,731
Total cost				$49,200

committed or capacity-related cost that has been committed for a six-month period. Like all capacity-related costs, labor cost depends on the capacity acquired and not on the capacity used. Note also that in this case the demand for labor was less than what was available. If the production on products 1 and 2 had shot up even more, the demand for labor may have exceeded the supply and production would have had to be less than the demand.

Suppose after studying Exhibit 3-9, the management at Orillia Plastics undertakes an evaluation of product 3. The cost of the plastic per unit is computed as $0.30 (three units of plastic per unit of product 3 × $0.10 per unit of plastic) and the cost of labor per unit of product 3 as $2 (0.04 run time hours + 20/500 batch time hours × $25 per labor hour) yielding a total cost of materials and labor of $2.30 per unit. Since the selling price of product 3 is only $2.50, and since the $2.30 cost does not include machine-related costs for the production equipment used to make the products or the customer-related costs of shipping and selling, management has decided that the product is a loser and has abandoned it.

Now the question is, what costs will change? Will costs really fall by $18,400 (8000 × $2.30) when product 3 is eliminated? Exhibit 3-10 projects costs with product 3 gone. Note that the total costs are now projected to be $46,800, which is a decline of $2400 (49,200 − $46,800). Why have costs not fallen by the predicted amount of $18,400? Labor costs will remain the same for the life of the six-month contract, regardless if labor is used. After six months (the long run), labor costs will fall by $16,000 (8000 × 2) as a result of this decision, because at that time the labor contract can be renegotiated and labor capacity adjusted downward. In the short run, costs will remain the same. Therefore, in the short run, costs only will decline by the amount of the plastic cost avoided, which is $2400 (8000 × $0.30).

EXHIBIT 3-10

Orillia Novelty Plastics
Drop Product 3

	PRODUCT			
	1	**2**	**3**	**Total**
Units Made	26,000	41,000	0	
Plastic per Unit	2	1	3	
Units of Plastic	52,000	41,000	0	93,000
Cost of Plastic	$5,200	$4,100	$0	$ 9,300
Run Time Work	0.01	0.005	0.04	
Total Run Time Labor Hours	260	205	0	465
Units per Batch	5,000	4,000	500	
Batches	5	10	0	
Labor Hours per Batch	10	15	20	
Total Batch Labor Hours	52	154	0	206
Total Labor Hours	312	359	0	671
Total Labor Cost Used				$16,769
Total Labor Cost Paid				$37,500
Cost Excess Capacity				$20,731
Total Cost				$46,800

In month 3 of the contract, and recognizing that the labor costs are committed, management decides to expand the production of products 1 and 2. From our previous discussion we already know that plastic costs will increase as production of products 1 and 2 increases, but that labor costs will remain fixed at the level of $37,500. The only issue facing management is that the demand for labor of scheduled production cannot exceed the 1500 hours that are available under the contract. Exhibit 3-11 shows that the 1500 labor hours constraint is not exceeded. Recalling our earlier discussion, note that only the cost of plastic has increased to reflect the increased production level. Labor costs have not increased. Why? These are committed costs that will remain unchanged until the end of the six-month period when they will be renegotiated.

Does this mean that for planning purposes organization decision makers should assume labor costs associated with product 1 and product 2 are zero? Of course not! While the incremental costs of increasing the production levels of product 1 and product 2 reflect only the cost of plastic, in the long run when the contract for labor is renegotiated and when organization decision makers are deciding whether to continue making products 1 and 2, the price of these products will have to cover all costs, including the cost of labor. This is the reason why product pricing decisions are based on long-run costs, which include capacity-related costs, and this also is the reason that product costing must reflect the underlying issue of cost behavior. We will take up that issue in Chapter 5.

The important message of this example is that there is a clear difference between the cost of acquiring and the cost of using different resources. For some resources the cost to the organization is proportional to how much is purchased whether or not it is used. For other resources the cost to the organization is proportional to how

EXHIBIT 3-11

Orillia Novelty Plastics
Increased Production of
Products 1 and 2

	PRODUCT			
	1	**2**	**3**	**Total**
Units Made	40,000	70,000	0	
Plastic per Unit	2	1	3	
Units of Plastic	80,000	70,000	0	150,000
Cost of Plastic	$8,000	$7,000	$0	$15,000
Run Time Work	0.01	0.005	0.04	
Total Run Time Labor Hours	400	350	0	750
Units per Batch	5,000	4,000	500	
Batches	8	18	0	
Labor Hours per Batch	10	15	20	
Total Batch Labor Hours	80	263	0	343
Total Labor Hours	480	613	0	1,093
Total Labor Cost Used				$27,313
Total Labor Cost Paid				$37,500
Cost of Excess Capacity				$10,188
Total Cost				$52,500

much is consumed. As we will see in Chapter 5, for purposes of decision making about products, costing systems take a long-run perspective and treat all costs as if they are proportional to the amount that is used. This may serve the needs of some decisions, but treating costs this way can be misleading when the same information is used to develop budgets or to evaluate cost performance. This issue will be taken up in more detail later in this text.

NONMANUFACTURING COSTS AS PRODUCT COSTS

Although we have mentioned nonmanufacturing costs in passing, most of our discussion has focused on manufacturing costs. This is the residual legacy of external reporting, which places most of its attention on isolating and classifying product costs because of their importance in inventory valuation.

For management accountants the issue is quite different. Although manufacturing costs often are the most significant component of total costs, nonmanufacturing costs, such as the costs of research and development, selling, and logistical activities, are large and growing in many organizations. There is an increasing recognition that the management of nonmanufacturing costs is an important contributor to the organization's financial success.

Like manufacturing costs, nonmanufacturing costs include both flexible and capacity-related components. Traditionally management accountants have looked at nonmanufacturing costs as a large pool of costs that should be managed by periodic budget appropriations. For example, expenditures on items such as advertising are determined by what we can afford rather than by the mission we have to accomplish with advertising.

The nonmanufacturing costs that have attracted the most attention are customer-related costs. These include the cost of selling the product to the customer, putting the product in the customer's hands, and providing after-sales support to the customer. These costs can be significant and they can vary widely across different customers.

Many organizations have thus begun to undertake what they call customer accounting, to determine the profitability of dealing with different customers or different types of customers. Customer accounting systems have caused some organizations to abandon certain customers or to provide differential service fees based on the services that customers demand. Because many customer services are proportional to the number of customers rather than the quantity of purchases (recall the billing and meter reading example earlier in this chapter), the effect of replacing traditional costing systems with customer accounting has been to shift costs back from big customers to the smaller customers that create those costs.

Because we need to start somewhere, because manufacturing costs are large, and because we need to avoid overwhelming you with detail, this chapter has focused on manufacturing costs. However, you should remember that nonmanufacturing costs are important and are now attracting considerable attention in many organizations.

LIFE-CYCLE COSTS

We have considered costs used for external reporting and costs used internally to compute the cost of some cost object such as a product or business unit. This discussion has focused on computing the cost of making something and putting it in the customer's hands.

Life-cycle costing is a relatively new perspective that argues that organizations should consider a product's costs over its entire lifetime when deciding whether to introduce a new product. Therefore life-cycle costing is primarily a planning tool, but it has important implications for costing after the product has been introduced.

Life-cycle costing
A systematic consideration of product costs during the product's lifetime.

To understand the notion of life-cycle costing, we need to review briefly the notion of a product life cycle.

There are five distinct stages in a typical product's life cycle. Obviously not all products will follow this pattern. Some products will fail early and have a truncated life cycle.

1. **The product development and planning phase.** In this phase the organization incurs significant research and development costs and product testing costs. Traditional costing often treats these costs as general overhead with two consequences—they are not associated with the product that create the cost, and the total amount of these costs is often either unknown or only vaguely known. Because of the increasing costs of launching products, organizations are devoting more effort to the product development and planning phase, prompting suggestions that the nature and magnitude of these costs should be identified so that when products are initially proposed, planners have some idea of the cost that new product development will inflict on the organization.
2. **Introduction phase.** In this phase the organization incurs significant promotional costs as the new product is introduced to the marketplace. At this stage the product's revenue will often not cover the flexible and capacity-related costs that it has inflicted on the organization.
3. **Growth phase.** During the product growth phase the product's revenues finally begin to cover the flexible and capacity-related costs incurred to produce, market, and distribute the product. There is often little or no price competition. The focus of attention is on developing systems to deliver the product to the customer in the most effective way.
4. **Product maturity phase.** In the product maturity phase price competition becomes intense and product margins (the difference between the product's revenue and flexible costs) begin to decline. While the product is still profitable, profitability is declining relative to the growth phase. During the maturity phase organizations undertake intense efforts to reduce costs to remain competitive and profitable.
5. **Product decline and abandonment phase.** During this phase the product begins to become unprofitable. Competitors begin to drop out—the least efficient first. The remaining competitors find themselves competing for a share of a smaller and declining market. As organizations abandon the product, they incur abandonment costs which can include selling off equipment no longer required or restoring an asset prior to abandoning it (e.g., land reclamation in the case of a mine that has been worked out and is being abandoned.)

From this life cycle, it is apparent that product-related costs occur unevenly over the product's lifetime. This uneven pattern has prompted some people to argue that these costs, particularly costs other than those associated with making the product and delivering it to the customer, should be considered systematically both before and during the product's lifetime.

The motivation for considering costs other than manufacturing and distribution costs before the product is introduced is to ensure that the difference between the product's revenues and its manufacturing and distribution costs cover the other costs associated with developing, supporting, and abandoning the product. The motivation for considering these costs during the product's lifetime is first to identify the magnitude and nature of these costs so that they can be systematically evaluated and managed, and second to develop an understanding of the magnitude of these costs for existing products so that the planners can develop reasonable estimates of the costs that would be associated with new products.

Moreover, some people argue that the product's future costs should be accrued systematically over its lifetime so as to fulfill the principle of matching costs and rev-

Mine operating charters often contain provisions that the mine site must be restored when the mine is abandoned. This abandonment cost is significant and should be considered when the profitability of a proposed new mine is being considered. (Charlie Ott/Photo Researchers, Inc.)

enues. To illustrate, consider the operation of a factory that manufactures transformers. These products use hazardous chemicals and the company knows that when the transformer line is abandoned it will incur significant costs associated with rehabilitating the factory and land where these transformers have been made. Suppose, for the sake of discussion, that this cost amounts to $50 million. If this cost is recognized as a period cost when it is incurred, the implication is that the cost relates to creating revenues in the current period. In fact, that is false. The cost relates to production in the past. It is inappropriate and misleading to match this cost with current revenues, which has led to the proposal that this cost should be recognized during the time the transformers are made. The same argument applies to costs that are unrelated to making or selling the product before and during its lifetime. The argument is that these costs should be capitalized and spread out over the product's lifetime.

Beyond the accounting ends achieved by this uniform recognition of costs that occur discretely over the product's life, some people have suggested that this accrual achieves motivational purposes as well. The argument is that if decision makers are faced with a large cost unrelated to ongoing production in one year, they might want to avoid or at least postpone that cost to a later period in order to smooth income and provide a better level of performance. For example, consider the plight of a mining company that operates coal mines. The company knows that one particular mine has exhausted its economic life and should be closed; however, the company's operating license requires that when the mine is shut, the land be restored to a condition that approximates its original or natural condition. The company knows that this cost will be huge and does not want to burden its current income with that cost, because of the adverse effect that is expected to have on the share price. Rather, the company will wait for a more profitable year to recognize and incur this expense.

Life-cycle costing is a good example of a costing system designed for decision making that has little or no practical relevance in external reporting. Traditionally organizations have resisted developing multiple costing systems, one for internal use and one for external use. However, as the costs of gathering, computing, and handling data have fallen and as the benefits of developing life-cycle costing information have become more apparent, these systems are now being developed in many organizations.

EVALUATING PROFIT PERFORMANCE AT JOAN'S LANDSCAPING

Returning to Joan's Landscaping Services in our chapter-opening vignette, we are now in a position to think about some of the company's problems.

Several hints might suggest the problem. First, Joan has the layout design business to herself and her fees are not a problem for potential customers. This implies that other landscapers believe the layout design business is unprofitable at the prices that Joan is charging. Either Joan is much more efficient than her competitors, or she is seriously underestimating her costs. So the culprit may be the way allocated costs are being handled and a careful study of those costs is needed.

Suppose that an analysis of allocated costs reveals the information shown in Exhibit 3-12. The costs of $300,000 reflect the general business costs (rent on a building where Joan stores her equipment, telephone costs, and billing costs) of about $40,000. The rest of the costs are equipment costs. Moreover, it turns out that none of the equipment, except the trucks, which are shared equally by all businesses, is used in more than one segment of the business.

The allocation rates are computed by dividing the activity cost by the capacity. The allocation amount is computed by multiplying the allocation rate by the capacity used.

The analysis of the equipment used in the business identified that the layout design business used some expensive equipment that tended to reduce labor costs in that division at the expense of higher machine costs. In particular the equipment included a small earthmoving machine and grader, which accounted for the majority of the costs in this division.

With this information, the original profit information can be recast as in Exhibit 3-13.

Note that the unit profit numbers do not include the $40,000 of basic business costs and the $10,000 of unused truck capacity costs because there is no practical way of allocating these costs to any one of the three lines of business. They must be covered by the margins created by each of the three business lines.

Now that capacity-related costs have been properly attributed to each of the three operating businesses, we have a very different picture of this organization. First

EXHIBIT 3-12

Joan's Landscaping

RESOURCE USE INFORMATION

	COST	CAPACITY	RATE	USED	ALLOCATION
Trucks and related costs	$ 40,000	800	$ 50	600	$ 30,000
Lawn mowing equipment	$ 30,000	1,500	$ 20	1200	$ 24,000
Layout design equipment	$120,000	400	$300	400	$120,000
Other maintenance equipment	$ 70,000	700	$100	500	$ 50,000

EXHIBIT 3-13

Joan's Landscaping Services
Product Line Income Statements

	LAWN MOWING	LAYOUT DESIGN	OTHER MAINTENANCE	TOTAL
Revenues	$230,000	$175,000	$250,000	$655,000
Direct Costs	125,000	56,000	145,000	326,00
Margin	$105,000	$119,000	$105,000	$329,000
Cost of Used Capacity				
▪ Own	24,000	120,000	50,000	194,000
▪ Trucks	10,000	10,000	10,000	30,000
Cost of Unused Capacity	6,000	0	20,000	26,000
Unit Profit	$ 65,000	$ –11,000	$ 25,000	$ 79,000
Unused Capacity Cost				10,000
Business-Sustaining Costs				40,000
Organization Profit				$29,000

we see that cutting back on lawn mowing and other maintenance is ill advised. Both units have unused capacity that continue to create the same level of costs as the activity-level contracts. The layout design business is a big loser and the major drain on profits in this business. The costs of the specialized equipment are evidently not being reflected in prices charged for this work. This confirms the original suspicion that Joan's prices are so low that they are encouraging demand and discouraging competition.

Joan needs to raise prices on the layout design business and increase volume in the high margin lawn mowing and other maintenance business to better use available capacity.

SUMMARY

In this chapter we consider various ways that management accountants define costs and study why management accountants compute "different costs for different purposes." We note that costs prepared for the financial statements, which are distributed to people outside the organization and which are used in unspecified ways, focus mainly on the division of costs between manufacturing and nonmanufacturing and between cost of goods sold and ending inventory. The issue in developing costs for external reporting is consistency so that comparison can be made across organizations at a given point in time and trends can be developed for a given organization over time.

When costs are used internally their use is understood so that the cost derivation can be tailored to the decision-making need. We see how different costs might be used to estimate the cost of an airline passenger for long-run and short-run pricing purposes. We consider the notion of opportunity cost and how it provides insights into the short-run allocation of capacity resources.

We explore the nature of short-run and long-run costs and, through an example, illustrate how organizations tend to convert flexible costs into capacity-related costs as they grow and evolve.

We discuss some modern thinking about cost behavior and look at five models of indirect costs (unit related, batch related, product sustaining, customer sustaining, and business sustaining) and how they describe cost behavior in modern organizations. We will exploit these insights in Chapter 5 when we talk about activity-based costing systems.

Finally, we look at the issues in life-cycle costing and how costs tend to be spread unevenly over the product life cycle. Identifying these costs and matching them to the periods to which they provide benefits to the product they sustain provides a number of important insights and behavioral motivations.

KEY TERMS

After-sales costs, 77
Batch-related activities, 91
Business-sustaining activities, 92
Capacity-related costs, 74
Capacity-related resources, 74
Cost, 75
Cost object, 72
Customer-sustaining activities, 92
Direct cost, 73
Direct manufacturing costs, 76
Distribution costs, 77
Expenses, 75
Flexible costs, 73
Flexible resources, 73
General and administrative costs, 78
Generally accepted accounting principles (GAAP), 75
Indirect cost, 73
Indirect manufacturing costs, 76
Life-cycle costing, 97
Manufacturing costs, 76
Marketing costs, 77
Nonmanufacturing costs, 77
Opportunity costs, 81
Period costs, 75
Product costs, 75
Product-sustaining activities, 92
Research and development costs, 77
Selling costs, 77
Unit-related activities, 91

ASSIGNMENT MATERIALS

QUESTIONS

3-1 What are some different uses of cost information? (LO 1)

3-2 Why do different types of cost information need to be reported to support different managerial purposes and decisions? (LO 1)

3-3 What is a cost object? (LO 1)

3-4 How is it possible to distinguish direct costs from indirect costs? (LO 1)

3-5 Explain the difference between flexible costs and capacity-related costs. (LO 3)

3-6 Are flexible costs always direct costs? (LO 1, 3)

3-7 Are capacity-related costs always indirect costs? (LO 1, 3)

3-8 How are costs in a manufacturing firm classified for external reporting? (LO 1, 3)

3-9 Describe the difference between costs and expenses. (LO 1, 3)

3-10 What are the two principal categories into which manufacturing costs are classified? (LO 1, 3)

3-11 What are six categories of costs, classified by function, that are included in nonmanufacturing costs for external reporting? (LO 1, 3)

3-12 Why do traditional cost accounting systems tend to analyze manufacturing costs in greater detail than they do other functional categories of costs? (LO 1, 3)

3-13 What are two broad purposes for which costs are used inside an organization? (LO 1)

3-14 Explain why you agree or disagree with the following statement: "An organization should have the most accurate and complete cost system possible." (LO 1)

3-15 What is an opportunity cost? (LO 1, 4)

3-16 What is the distinction between short run costs and long run costs? (LO 2, 3)

3-17 How has the composition of manufacturing costs changed in recent years? How has this change affected the design of cost accounting systems? (LO 1, 3)

3-18 What are the five categories of production activities? Explain the differences among them. (LO 1, 3)

3-19 Why have customer-related costs attracted increasing attention in recent years? (LO 1, 3)

3-20 What are the five stages in a typical product's life cycle? What is the cost focus in each stage? (LO 5)

EXERCISES

3-21 ***Cost classification by function*** Classify each of the following costs as manufacturing or nonmanufacturing. Further classify nonmanufacturing costs as distribution, selling, marketing, after-sales, research and development, or general and administrative costs. LO 1, 3

(a) Direct labor
(b) Sales commissions
(c) Depreciation on delivery trucks
(d) Salary and bonus for the chief executive officer
(e) Direct materials
(f) Product design staff salaries
(g) Advertising
(h) Property taxes on the corporate headquarters building
(i) Gas and electricity for the factory
(j) Accounting office staff salaries
(k) Operators of product help lines for customers
(l) Customer credit evaluation staff salaries

3-22 ***Components of manufacturing costs*** Classify each of the following manufacturing costs as direct or indirect for products. LO 1, 3

(a) Insurance on manufacturing equipment
(b) Steel plates used in making an automobile body
(c) Wages of assembly workers
(d) Salaries of plant security personnel
(e) Rubber used in making tires
(f) Overtime premiums paid to assembly workers
(g) Depreciation on the factory building
(h) Cost of electric power to operate machines
(i) Production workers' holiday and vacation pay benefits
(j) Wages of materials-handling workers
(k) Grapes used to manufacture wine
(l) Quality inspection costs

3-23 ***Cost classification by activity type*** Classify the following costs as unit-related, batch-related, product-sustaining, or business-sustaining activity costs. LO 1, 3

(a) Direct materials
(b) Setup labor wages
(c) Salaries of plant engineers responsible for executing engineering change orders
(d) Building depreciation
(e) Direct labor wages
(f) Purchase order clerk wages
(g) Product design engineer salaries
(h) Rent for plant building
(i) Quality inspection

(j) Moving materials from one machine to the next
(k) Accounting
(l) Sales support for individual product lines

LO 1, 3 **3-24** ***Cost classification by activity type*** Classify the following costs as unit-related, batch-related, product-sustaining, or business-sustaining activity costs.

(a) Packing labor wages
(b) Materials-handling labor wages
(c) Part administrators' salaries
(d) Plant management salaries
(e) Production scheduling staff salaries
(f) Equipment maintenance
(g) Property taxes
(h) Production expediters' salaries
(i) Insurance for plant facility
(j) Plant security
(k) Workers' training
(l) Electricity usage

LO 3 **3-25** ***Classification of flexible and capacity-related costs*** Classify each of the following as a flexible or capacity-related cost.

(a) Salaries of production supervisors
(b) Steel used in automobile production
(c) Wood used in furniture production
(d) Charges for janitorial services
(e) Commissions paid to sales personnel
(f) Advertising expenses
(g) Salaries of billing clerks
(h) Gasoline used to deliver products
(i) Lubricants for machines
(j) Maintenance for machines

LO 3 **3-26** ***Classification of flexible and capacity-related costs*** Classify each of the following as a flexible or capacity-related cost.

(a) Paper used in newspaper production
(b) Wages of production workers
(c) Salary of the chief executive officer
(d) Glue used in furniture production
(e) Depreciation of factory equipment
(f) Depreciation of shipping truck
(g) Electricity used to operate machines
(h) Boxes used for packing products
(i) Rent for factory building
(j) Factory insurance

LO 1, 3 **3-27** ***Customer-related costs*** Nehls Company is concerned about its growing customer-related expenses. The company currently allocates customer capacity-related support costs on the basis of revenues, at a rate of 30% of sales revenue. After discovering that ordering patterns vary quite dramatically across customers, it proposed a more accurate method that would assign costs of $35 per order. Data on two customers appear below.

	CUSTOMER 1	CUSTOMER 2
Sales	$1200	$1200
Cost of goods sold	750	750
Number of orders per year	2	12

REQUIRED

(a) Compute the customer capacity-related support costs assigned to customers 1 and 2 under the current system.

(b) Compute the customer capacity-related support costs assigned to customers 1 and 2 under the proposed system.

(c) Comment on what the two systems reveal about the profitability of customers 1 and 2.

PROBLEMS

3-28 ***Cost classification*** The L.A. Dress Shop manufactures dresses and decorates them with custom designs for retail sales on the premises. The shop sold 5000 dresses last month. Costs incurred during the last month include the following: LO 1, 3

Cost of fabric used in dresses	$60,000
Wages of dressmakers	5,000
Wages of dress designers	4,000
Wages of sales personnel	1,000
Wages of designers who experiment with new fabrics and dress designs	3,000
Wages of the employee who repairs the shop's pattern and sewing machines	2,000
Salary of the owner's assistant	1,200
Cost of the new sign displayed in front of the retail shop	400
Cost of electricity used in the pattern department	200
Depreciation on pattern machines and sewing machines	10,000
Cost of advertisements in local media	800
Cost of hiring a plane and a pilot to fly along the beach pulling a banner advertising the shop	1,400
Cost of insurance for the production employees	2,000
Rent for the building	6,000

Apportion the rent into different categories based on the following facts. Half of the building's first floor is used for administrative offices. The other half of it is used for a retail sales shop. The second floor is used for making dresses and storing of raw material.

REQUIRED

(a) Classify the above costs into one of the following categories: direct materials costs, direct labor costs, indirect manufacturing (support) costs, distribution costs, selling costs, marketing costs, research and development costs, general and administrative costs. What is the total cost for each category?

(b) Classify the costs as unit-related, batch-related, product-sustaining, or business-sustaining costs. What is the total cost for each category?

LO 1, 3 **3-29 *Cost behavior, cost classifications*** Shannon O'Reilly is trying to decide whether to continue to take public transportation to work or to purchase a car. Before making her decision, she would like to compare the cost of using public transportation and the cost of driving a car.

REQUIRED

(a) What activity measure should Shannon use as she estimates the cost of driving?

(b) What should Shannon view as incremental (flexible or out-of-pocket) costs of driving from home to work?

(c) What are some capacity-related costs of driving a car?

(d) Suppose that if Shannon purchased a car, she would use it to take a two-week scenic vacation by car. What activity measures might Shannon use to estimate her vacation and lodging expenses?

LO 1, 3 **3-30 *Single drivers vs. multiple drivers*** Eagan Electrical Instruments Company estimates manufacturing support as 950% of direct labor costs. Eagan's controller, Jim Becker, is concerned that the actual manufacturing support activity costs have differed substantially from the estimates in recent months. He suspects that the problem is related to the use of only one cost driver. Jim identified the following three additional cost drivers that reflect support activities: number of material moves, number of setups, and number of machine hours. He developed the following rates to estimate manufacturing support activity costs:

MULTIPLE COST DRIVER SYSTEM
$1 per direct labor dollar
$200 per move
$300 per setup
$20 per machine hour

Information for two recent months includes the following:

COST AND QUANTITY	MAY	JUNE
Direct labor cost	$3000	$4200
Number of material moves	50	70
Number of setups	30	40
Number of machine hours	1000	1200

REQUIRED

(a) Estimate manufacturing support costs using the single-driver and multiple-driver systems.

(b) Why do the two sets of estimate differ?

(c) Why will both methods fail to predict accurately the manufacturing support costs? Is one of the two methods likely to be more useful than the other? Explain.

LO 1, 2, 3 **3-31 *Planning activity workloads*** The Abby Corporation, a chain of department stores, estimates the standard workload at its retail outlets in terms of the time required for the activities of (1) hanging new inventory; (2) selling merchandise; (3) handling complaints, inquiries, and returns: (4) taking markdowns; and

(5) counting inventory. The following are the estimated average times for each of these five activities:

ACTIVITY	AVERAGE TIME REQUIRED
Hanging new inventory	1 minute per piece hanged (HANG)
Selling merchandise	10 minutes per customer (CUST)
Handling complaints and returns	15 minutes per complaint (CMPL)
Taking markdowns	2 minutes per piece marked down (MARK)
Counting inventory	0.5 minutes per piece counted (COUN)

The Abby Corporation uses these workload estimates to plan its staffing levels. Past experience indicates that it needs to provide for about 30% more time than the standard workload estimate to ensure that customer service is satisfactory. The Abby Corporation has a policy of hiring only full-time sales consultants working 40 hours a week. The following information pertains to the estimated levels for various activities cost drivers for the four weeks in June:

WEEK	HANG	CUST	CMPL	MARK	COUN
1	5000	4500	500	400	1000
2	6000	5000	400	300	1400
3	5500	4800	600	500	1500
4	6200	5500	550	600	2000

REQUIRED

Determine the number of full-time equivalent sales consultants needed in each of these four weeks.

3-32 ***Cost behavior and decisions*** Second City Airlines operates 35 scheduled round-trip flights between New York and Chicago each week. It charges a fixed one-way fare of $200 per passenger. Second City Airlines can carry 150 passengers per flight. Fuel and other flight-related costs are $5000 per flight. On-flight meal costs are $5 per passenger. Sales commission averaging 5% of sales is paid to travel agents. Flying crew, ground crew, advertising, and other administrative expenditures for the New York-Chicago route amount to $400,000 each week. LO 1, 2, 3, 4

REQUIRED

(a) How many passengers must each of the 70 one-way flights have on average to make a total profit of $700,000 per week?

(b) If the load factor is 60% on all flights (that is, the flights are 60% full), how many flights must Second City Airlines operate on this route to earn a total profit of $500,000 per week?

(c) Are fuel costs flexible or capacity-related?

(d) Second City accepts standby passengers on flights 30 minutes before takeoff if space is available. Assume standby passengers book their tickets through a travel agent, and that the airline pays a flat $6 commission per standby ticket rather than a 5% sales commission. What is the minimum price Second City can charge a standby passenger to cover the incremental costs associated with that passenger?

3-33 ***Cost classification*** Poker's is a small hamburger shop catering mainly to students at a nearby university. It is open for business from 11 A.M. until 11 P.M., Monday through Friday. The owner, Chip Poker, employs two cooks, one server, and a LO 1, 3 part-time janitor. Because there is no space for dining inside the shop, all orders are take-out orders.

Poker's sold 10,000 hamburgers last month. The average hamburger requires 1 hamburger bun, 8 ounces of meat, 4 ounces of cheese, one-eighth a head of lettuce, and $0.07 worth of other ingredients. Costs incurred during the last month include the following:

Meat	$5000
Cheese	1000
Bread	800
Lettuce	600
Other ingredients	700
Cooks' wages	5000
Servers' wages	1500
Janitor's wages	600
Utilities	500
Depreciation on equipment	300
Paper supplies (napkins and bags)	200
Rent	600
Advertisement in local newspaper	300

REQUIRED

(a) Classify these costs into one of the following categories: direct materials, direct labor, indirect manufacturing (support), selling support, and administrative support. What is the total cost for each category?

(b) Classify the costs as unit-related, batch-related, product-sustaining, or business-sustaining costs. What is the total cost for each category?

(c) Suppose that Poker's capacity is 10,000 hamburgers per month with his labor force. If Poker sells only 9000 hamburgers this month, what indirect manufacturing cost per hamburger should Poker assign?

LO 1, 2, 3 **3-34** ***Commitment and consumption of activity resources*** Classic Containers Company specializes in making high-quality customized containers to order. Its agreement with the labor union ensures employment for all its employees and a fixed payroll of $80,000 per month including fringe benefits. This payroll makes available 4000 labor hours each month to work on orders the firm receives. The monthly wages must be paid even if the workers remain idle due to lack of work. If additional labor hours are required to complete jobs, overtime costs $30 per labor hour.

Each job requires four labor hours for machine setup and 0.05 labor hours per container. Flexible costs comprise $1.60 per container for materials and $8.00 per labor hour for manufacturing support expenses. In addition, the firm must pay $20,000 per month for selling, general, and administrative expenses and $36,000 per month lease payments for machinery and physical facilities.

In April 2000, the firm won 90 orders, of which 60 were for 800 containers each and 30 were for 1600 containers each. Determine the total costs for April.

LO 1, 2, 3, 4 **3-35** ***Capacity level, profitability, opportunity cost*** Wedmark Corporation's Cupertino, California, plant manufactures chips used in personal computers. Its practical capacity is 2,000 chips per week. The selling price is $500 per chip. Production this quarter is 1,600 chips per week. Total costs of production this week at 80% of practical capacity level comprise $75,000 of capacity-related costs and $720,000 of flexible costs.

REQUIRED

(a) What will the plant's profit be if it operates at practical capacity?

(b) If the plant's accounting system allocates capacity-related cost using a rate based on its practical capacity level as the base, what is the reported cost per unit?

(c) Suppose that a new customer offers \$480 per chip for an order of 200 chips per week for delivery beginning this quarter. If this order is accepted, production will increase from 1600 chips at present to 1800 chips per week. What is the estimated change in the company's profit if it accepts the order?

(d) Suppose that the new customer in part (c) offered \$480 per chip for an order of 600 chips per week, and Wedmark cannot schedule overtime production. Consequently, it would have to give up some of its current sales to fill the new order for 600 chips per week. What is the estimated change in Wedmark's profit if it accepts this order for 600 chips per week?

3-36 ***Commitment of activity resources*** Crown Cable Company provides cable television service in the Richfield metropolitan area. The company hires only full-time service persons working 40 hours a week at \$18 per hour including fringe benefits. Service persons handle additional service demand by working overtime at the rate of \$24 per hour. The service manager uses standards for estimating the work load and staffing requirements. Each service person can handle an average of six calls in an eight-hour work day. The estimated number of service calls for the first three weeks of October 1999 follow: LO 1, 2, 3

WEEK	SERVICE CALLS
1	1280
2	1340
3	1200

REQUIRED

(a) Determine the number of service persons that will be hired in each of these three weeks to minimize costs.

(b) Estimate the service labor cost for each of the three weeks.

(c) Suppose that the company cannot change the staffing level from week to week. Estimate the service labor costs assuming that the same number (38, 39, 40, 41, 42, 43, 44, or 45) of workers is hired for all three weeks. How much do costs increase under this restriction?

CASES

3-37 ***Flexibility in committing activity resources*** Dr. Barbara Barker is the head of the pathology laboratory at Barrington Medical Center in Mobile, Alabama. Dr. Barker estimates the amount of work for her laboratory staff by classifying the pathology tests into three categories: simple routine, simple nonroutine, and complex. She expects a simple-routine test to require two hours, a simple nonroutine test to require 2.5 hours, and a complex test to require four hours of staff time. She estimates the demand for each of the three types of tests for June through August to be the following: LO 1, 2, 3

MONTH	SIMPLE ROUTINE	SIMPLE NONROUTINE	COMPLEX
June	800	250	450
July	600	200	400
August	750	225	450

Laboratory staff salaries including fringe benefits average $3600 per month. Each worker works 150 hours per month. If the hospital work load exceeds the available staff time, Dr. Barker has the tests performed at a neighboring private pathology laboratory that charges $80 for a simple-routine test, $100 for a simple-nonroutine test, and $160 for a complex test.

Dr. Barker is thinking of employing 20 to 27 workers. Because of the difficulty in hiring reliable workers, Barrington's chief administrator has instructed her to employ laboratory staff for at least one quarter.

REQUIRED

(a) Determine how many workers Dr. Barker should employ to minimize the costs of performing the tests. What is the minimum cost?

(b) Suppose the easy availability of experienced laboratory staff allows Barrington Medical Center to change staffing loads each month. Determine the number of workers Dr. Barker should hire each month in these circumstances. What is the minimum cost?

LO 1, 2, 3 **3-38** ***Commitment and consumption of activity resources*** Steelmax, Inc. sells office furniture in the Chicago metropolitan area. To better serve its business customers, Steelmax recently introduced a new same-day service. Any order placed before 2 P.M. is delivered the same day.

Steelmax hires five workers on an eight-hour daily shift to deliver the office furniture. Each delivery takes 30 minutes on average. If the number of customer orders exceeds the available capacity on some days, workers are asked to work overtime to ensure that all customer orders are delivered the same day. Regular wages are $12 per hour. Overtime wages include a 50% premium in addition to the regular wages.

The Steelmax management has noticed considerable fluctuation in the number of customer orders from day to day over the last three months as shown here:

DAY OF THE WEEK	AVERAGE NUMBER OF ORDERS
Monday	65
Tuesday	70
Wednesday	80
Thursday	85
Friday	95

Steelmax has now decided to pursue a more flexible hiring policy. It will reduce the number of delivery workers to four on Mondays and Tuesdays and increase the number to six on Fridays.

REQUIRED

(a) Determine the total and unit delivery cost when the number of daily customer orders is 70, 80, or 90.

(b) Determine the expected total delivery cost per day and the expected delivery cost per customer order based on both the old and the new hiring policy. What is the expected value per week of the new flexible hiring policy?

3-39 ***Commitment and consumption of activity resources*** Loren's Lawn and Gardening performs various lawn and garden maintenance activities, including lawn mowing, tree and shrub pruning, fertilizing and treating for pests. Unlike other lawn and garden businesses in the city, Loren also specializes in landscape design and planting. Loren is pleased that his design specialty is so much in demand. However, he is concerned because profits have been falling even though sales have been growing over the past few years. In an effort to better understand why profits are falling, Loren prepared the product line income statement below. LO 1, 2, 3

LOREN'S LAWN AND GARDEN
PRODUCT LINE INCOME STATEMENT

	LAWN MOWING	LAYOUT DESIGN	OTHER MAINTENANCE	TOTAL
Revenues	$287,500	$218,750	$312,500	$818,750
Direct Costs	$156,250	$ 70,000	$181,250	$407,500
Allocated Costs	$131,679	$100,191	$143,130	$375,000
Profit	−$ 429	$ 48,559	−$ 11,880	$ 36,250

The lawn mowing business involves mowing lawns and trimming edges for customers who generally sign up for the season and pay a flat fee based on surface area mowed and trimmed. The layout design business involves both designing a garden and lawn layout and installing the design. Other maintenance includes tree and shrub pruning and application of chemicals. The direct costs for each line of business are the costs of the materials and wages of the people who work in that line of business. The remaining costs consist mainly of equipment costs, but also include office costs. After some deliberation, Loren decided to allocate the remaining costs of $375,000 on the basis of revenue, reasoning that revenue is a measure of equipment use.

REQUIRED

(a) Based on the product line income statement above, which business is Loren likely to focus his efforts on? What is the likely result?

A further analysis of the allocated costs produced the information below. General business costs are $50,000, and the remaining $325,000 are equipment costs. The trucks are shared equally by all the segments, but the other equipment is used by only one segment.

LOREN'S LAWN AND GARDEN
RESOURCE USE INFORMATION

	COST	CAPACITY	USED
Trucks & related costs	$ 50,000	800	600
Lawn mowing equipment	$ 37,500	1500	1200
Layout design equipment	$150,000	400	400
Other maintenance equipment	$ 87,500	700	500
	$325,000		

(b) Prepare a new product line income statement similar to Exhibit 3-13.

(c) What advice do you have for Loren?

NATURE SCOPE FOCUS

COST BEHAVIOR

COST DECISIONS

PLANNING FOR DECISION-MAKING

PLANNING FOR EVALUATION

ORGANIZATIONAL BEHAVIOR AND DESIGN

chapter 4

Traditional Cost Management Systems

AFTER READING THIS CHAPTER, YOU WILL BE ABLE TO

1. understand job order costing systems
2. understand how using job bid sheets is effective for estimating product costs in a job order costing system
3. use cost driver rates to apply support activity costs to products
4. discuss why cost systems with multiple cost driver rates give different cost estimates than cost systems with a single rate
5. evaluate a cost system to understand whether it is likely to distort product costs, explain the importance of recording actual costs, and compare them with estimated costs
6. appreciate the importance of conversion costs and the measurement of costs in multistage continuous-processing industries
7. understand the significance of differences between job order costing and multistage-process costing systems
8. understand the two-stage allocation process and service department allocation methods

Bob Daemmrich/The Image Works

MELISSA'S AUTO SERVICE COMPANY

Melissa Wetengel started Melissa's Auto Service Company in 1979. Over a period of two decades, she built it into a business with more than $1 million in billings each year and a strong reputation for high-quality auto repair work. During the last three years, however, Melissa lost a considerable amount of business to quick-service operations such as Burbank Muffler Company for simple jobs including exhaust system replacements. Increased competition from companies such as Burbank cut into her sales volume and profit margins, and her take-home income from the business declined precipitously.

Melissa has expanded her auto shop considerably since its opening. The shop now has five service bays and employs five mechanics, two of whom are highly skilled and trained in doing complex repair jobs. The $60,000 salary and benefits for each expert mechanic exceed the average compensation of the other three mechanics by almost $25,000. The three junior mechanics primarily work on routine repairs such as brake relinings and muffler replacements.

Melissa's accountant, Dee Young, asked Melissa to explain the problem that led to poor financial performance over the last two years: "Melissa, your net income looks terrible. What has happened to your business?"

Melissa responded: "Specialized operators like Burbank Muffler Company have taken away most of my simple repair business with their low prices. How can they price their jobs so low and still make a profit?"

Dee encouraged Melissa with this response: "Let me take a look at your job order costing system. I may be able to find the answer to that question." As the consultation with Dee Young shows, managers today must be able to understand how to calculate the cost of products and services. What costs should be included as part of product costs, and why? How should such costs be calculated, accumulated, and reported to decision makers to help them in their planning and operating decisions?

Cost Management Systems

In this and the following chapter we discuss the topic of cost management systems. Cost management systems have a wide variety of uses, but in these two chapters we focus on their role in measuring the costs of products, services, and customers.[1] Historically, two cost management systems, job order costing and process costing, have been used to cost products and services. Many companies continue to use these two systems. Since the mid-1980s, however, companies have been adopting activity-based costing (ABC) for product and customer costing. In the past, these three systems have been portrayed as distinct; however, all cost systems work in essentially the same way. To start, expense categories are developed and then expenses are mapped to service departments, production centers, or activities. In turn, expenses are then attached to cost objects. The way these links are made and the activities defined is what really differentiates cost management systems. In this chapter we focus on the two traditional methods—job order and process costing systems. Next we discuss activity-based costing systems in Chapter 5.

Job Order And Process Costing Systems

Job order costing system
A process that estimates the costs of manufacturing products for different jobs required for specific customers.

Process costing system
A costing method that computes and allocates an equal amount of cost to each product.

Raw materials inventory
The purchase cost of resources.

A **job order costing system** estimates the costs of manufacturing products for different jobs required for specific customer orders. It is applicable in organizations that treat each individual job as a single unit of output. For instance, a company that makes custom frames to house fine art will use a job order costing system.

A **process costing system**, on the other hand, is applicable when all units produced during a specified time frame are treated as one unit of output. Usually, every unit made during the time period is identical. Fiberglass, for example, is produced in large quantities and then cut into individual units. The total amount of fiberglass made during a specified time is the quantity whose product is to be estimated. Individual products that come from the batch produced in that period are then assigned a unit cost.

Products may differ in their materials content and the hours of labor and machine time required to make them. Products also may differ in the demand they place on support activity resources (a more traditional term is manufacturing overhead), or in response to special customer needs that may lead to customized production, such as when different product characteristics are targeted for different markets. For instance, insulation used in homes in Alaska must, on average, meet more stringent standards than those used in Southern California due to climate differences. With such product and customer variety, managers want to understand the costs of individual products so that they can assess product and customer profitability.

In a traditional job order costing system, detailed records are kept of the flow of costs for each job. The cost flow model essentially uses an inventory concept to track costs, beginning with the **raw materials inventory.** Over a specific time period, the

[1] Other uses for cost management systems are to provide feedback information for operational control and to value inventory for financial statements.

raw materials are transformed by labor and support resources into **work-in-process (WIP) inventory** and then ultimately to **finished goods inventory**. WIP represents the costs of the resources for each job not yet completed. Once the goods have been sold, they are accounted for in the expense category known as cost of goods sold.

Work-in-process (WIP) inventory
The costs of the resources for each job not yet completed.

Many firms are required to bid on jobs before customers decide to place an order with them. To track the flow of costs through a job order costing system, companies use job cost sheets. Costs need to be estimated for each job in order to prepare a bid. Job order costing systems provide the means to estimate these costs.

Finished goods
Inventory that has been completed but not yet sold.

COMPONENTS OF A JOB BID SHEET

Exhibit 4-1 displays a **job bid sheet**, a format for estimating job costs. Famous Flange Company, a manufacturer of a variety of special flanges for several large customers, uses this sheet to bid its jobs. The bid sheet has five distinct panels. Panel 1 identifies the customer, the product, and the quantity of flanges (number of units) required. Panel 2 lists all the materials required to complete the job. For each item of material, the quantity required is estimated based on standard engineering specifications. For instance, each unit of flange L181 requires 2.4 pounds of bar steel stock. Therefore, the order for 1500 units of L181 requires 3600 pounds of bar steel stock. The current price of $11.30 per pound is obtained from records maintained and updated by the purchasing department. With these inputs the cost of bar steel stock required for this job can be calculated as $40,680 ($11.30 price per pound × 3600 pounds).

Job bid sheet
Format for estimating job costs.

EXHIBIT 4-1

Famous Flange Company Job Bid Sheet

	Bid Number: J4369	Date: July 6, 2000		
	Customer: Michigan Motors			
Panel 1	Product: Automobile engine flanges (flange L181)			
	Engineering Design Number JDR-103		Number of Units: 1,500	
	DIRECT MATERIALS	**QUANTITY**	**PRICE**	**AMOUNT**
	Bar steel stock	3600 lb	$11.30	$ 40,680
Panel 2	Subassembly	1500 units	39.00	58,500
	Total direct materials			$ 99,180
	DIRECT LABOR	**HOURS**	**RATE**	**AMOUNT**
	Lathe operators	480	$26.00	$ 12,480
Panel 3	Assembly workers	900	18.00	16,200
	Total direct labor	1380		$ 28,680
	SUPPORT COSTS			**AMOUNT**
	600 machine hours @ $40 support costs			$ 24,000
Panel 4	1380 direct labor hours @ $36.00 per hour			49,680
	Total support costs			$ 73,680
	TOTAL COSTS			**AMOUNT**
	Direct Materials + Direct Labor + Support Costs			$201,540
	Add 25% margin			50,385
Panel 5	Bid price			$251,925
	Unit cost			$ 134.36
	Unit price			$ 167.95

Panel 3 lists the amount of direct labor required for the job.These estimates are obtained from industrial engineering specifications developed on the basis of work and motion studies, or by analogy with comparable standard products. As examples, engineering staff at major steel companies study how workers perform each task necessary to make steel to customer specifications, so that they can estimate how much time each task requires. Similarly, project managers at software development firms compare new project specifications with projects they have managed previously, to estimate the amount of programmer time required to develop new software.

At Famous Flange, industrial engineers have estimated that 0.6 assembly hours are required per flange. Therefore, 900 assembly hours (1500 units × 0.6 hours per unit) are required for 1500 flanges. After estimating the direct labor hours required for a job, Famous Flange must determine a separate wage rate for each grade of labor required for the operations performed to manufacture the flanges. The wage rate for assembly workers is $18 per hour, so the 900 assembly hours are estimated to cost $16,200 (900 hours × $18 wage rate per hour).

Cost driver rate
The amount determined by dividing the activity expense by the total quantity of the activity cost driver.

Job costs
Expenses involved with the direct material, direct labor, and support costs for a job.

Margin
An additional amount added to job costs in order to make a profit.

Bid price
Equals the total job costs plus the margin.

Markup rate
The percent by which job costs are marked up. Also called *markup percentage.*

Rate of return
Ratio of net income to investment.

Full absorption costing
A costing method in which all production costs become product costs.

Variable costing
A costing method in which only flexible costs are included in product costs.

Panel 4 of the bid sheet contains estimates for cost driver (support) costs. Famous assigns support costs to jobs based on the number of machine hours and direct labor hours expected for the job. For this purpose, Famous uses two **cost driver rates**, based on the assumption that all manufacturing support costs are related either to machines or to direct labor.[2] The company classifies manufacturing support costs into two cost pools, based on whether the cost drivers are machine hours or direct labor hours, and computes a separate cost driver rate for each of the two cost pools. (Subsequent sections of this chapter will describe the procedure for calculating cost driver rates in detail.) To obtain the total amount of support costs allocated to the job, an analyst multiplies the number of machine hours (600) and the number of direct labor hours required for the job (1380) by their respective cost driver rates ($40 per machine hour and $36 per direct labor hour). Then the Famous Flange analyst adds the two estimates to obtain a total of $73,680.

600 machine hours	× $40 cost driver rate per machine hour	= $24,000
1380 labor hours	× $36 cost driver rate per labor hour	= $49,680
Total		$73,680

Panel 5 of the job bid sheet shows the total costs estimated for the job, $201,540, obtained by adding the total direct materials, total direct labor, and total support costs ($99,180 + $28,680 + $73,680).

JOB COSTS AND MARKUP

The total direct material, direct labor, and support costs for the job are the **job costs**. Most firms mark up the job costs by adding an additional amount, or **margin**, to make a profit on the job. The total job costs plus the margin equals the **bid price**. At Famous Flange, the **markup rate**, or the percent by which job costs are marked up, is 25%. The markup rate depends on a variety of factors, including the amount of support costs excluded from the cost driver rate (e.g., corporate-level costs), the target **rate of return** (ratio of net income to investment) desired by the corporation, competitive intensity, past bidding strategies adopted by key competitors, demand

[2] There are two traditional forms of product costing known as full absorption and variable costing. Under **full absorption costing,** all production costs, including flexible (or variable) costs and capacity (or fixed) costs, become product costs. Thus, the cost of a unit of product includes direct labor, direct material, and all capacity-related costs. In **variable costing,** only flexible costs are included in product costs. Capacity costs are treated as costs of the period and expensed in the period in which they are incurred. Variable costing is also known as marginal costing or direct costing.

IN PRACTICE

The Cost of Making Bicycles

Henry Horenstein/Stock, Boston

Paramount Cycles, based in Dayton, Ohio, is a manufacturer of high-quality bicycles for children and adults. Their cycles are sold primarily through specialty bicycle shops.

Paramount uses a standard cost accounting system to estimate the cost per bicycle for each model it manufactures. Engineering standards are developed for material quantity and labor hours for each part and for each operation. The industrial engineering department also provides lists for parts and component materials for each bicycle. By multiplying material quantity by estimated cost obtained from the purchasing manager, the finance department is able to calculate direct material cost. Manufacturing records of direct labor hours required for each job are used with labor costs per hour, estimated by the personnel department, to calculate direct labor cost for each bicycle. A cost driver rate is determined by dividing the annual budgeted support cost by the budgeted direct labor dollars to obtain a support cost rate per direct labor dollar. The total of direct material, direct labor, and support costs is used as the cost of a bicycle for both inventory valuation and for product pricing.

conditions, and overall product-market strategies. Pricing is discussed thoroughly in Chapter 7.

The markup rate may differ for different product groups and for different market segments, depending on local conditions. It also may change over time as conditions change. For instance, managers may decide to decrease profit margins when demand is weak and unused production capacity is likely to be available, but may use higher markups to create higher profits when demand is expected to be high and little unused production capacity exists.

DETERMINATION OF COST DRIVER RATES

As discussed, determining realistic cost driver rates has become increasingly important in recent years because support costs now comprise a large portion of the total costs in many industries. Notice that allocated support costs in the Famous Flange example ($73,680) are more than twice the direct labor costs ($28,680) and almost as much as direct materials costs ($99,180). In addition, many firms now recognize that support costs are not related to just one or even two factors, such as direct labor hours or machine hours. Rather, several different factors may be driving costs. Firms are now taking greater care when analyzing support costs by identifying which costs should relate to what cost driver. For instance, costs identified with the activity of setting up machines are related to the cost driver as setup hours. All costs associated with a cost driver, such as setup hours, are accumulated separately. Each subset of total support costs that can be associated with a distinct cost driver is referred to as a **cost pool**.

Cost pool
Each subset of total support costs that can be associated with a distinct cost driver.

Each cost pool has a separate cost driver rate. The cost driver rate is the ratio of the normal cost of a support activity accumulated in the cost pool to the normal level of the cost driver for the activity.

$$\text{Activity cost driver rate} = \frac{\text{Normal cost of support activity}}{\text{Normal level of cost driver}}$$

Recall that the normal cost of the support activity is the cost of the resources committed to the particular activity. The normal level of the activity cost driver is the long-term capacity made available by the amount of resources committed to a support activity. For example, if 10 setup workers are hired at weekly wages including benefits of $810 each, and if each worker has the time to complete 15 setups in a week, then the normal cost for the setup activity is $8100 per week ($810 × 10 workers). This makes available a capacity for performing 150 setups in a week (15 setups × 10 workers). Then the cost driver rate for the setup activity is $54 per setup ($8100 normal cost ÷ 150 setup capacity). The normal cost of a support activity, therefore, excludes fluctuations in costs caused by short-term adjustments such as overtime payments. The normal level of the support activity cost driver also excludes short-term variations in demand as reflected in overtime or idle time. Because the ratio shown in the previous equation is based on normal costs and normal cost driver levels, the rate remains stable over time and does not fluctuate as activity levels change in the short run. As a result, this activity cost driver rate does not change simply because of short-run changes in external factors that do not affect the efficiency or price of the activity resources.

PROBLEMS USING FLUCTUATING COST DRIVER RATES

Consider the support activity cost driver rate based on machine hours at Famous Flange Company. The cost pool includes machine depreciation, maintenance, power, and other machine-related costs. The normal machine-related costs amount to $900,000 per year; the normal capacity made available is 20,000 machine hours per year, or 5000 machine hours (20,000 ÷ 4) per quarter. Therefore, the machine-related cost driver rate is $45 per machine hour ($900,000 ÷ 20,000 hours).

The *actual* machine usage varies each quarter because of fluctuations in demand. Machine hours used are 5400 in the spring quarter, 4500 in the summer, 5000 in the fall, and 3600 in the winter. The normal capacity of 5000 machine hours is exceeded in the spring quarter by operating the machines overtime beyond regular shift hours.

Machine-related costs each quarter are $225,000. If the rate for such costs is based on quarterly cost driver levels instead of the normal levels, then the rate increases as the demand for the machine activity falls, and the rate decreases as the demand increases. For example, as the number of machine hours decreases from 5400 in the spring to 4500 in the summer, the cost driver rate increases from $41.67 per machine hour for spring to $50.00 per machine hour for summer (see Exhibit 4-2). In contrast, the cost driver rate based on normal costs and normal activity levels remains fixed at $45.00 per machine hour ($225,000 ÷ 5000 hours) throughout the year because costs depend on the machine capacity made available and not on the season.

Determination of cost driver rates based on planned or actual short-term usage results in higher rates in periods of lower demand. In such job costing systems, job costs appear to be higher in time periods when demand is lower. If bid prices are based on estimated job costs, then the firm is likely to bid higher prices during periods of low demand when, in fact, it should be thinking about lowering prices to attract

EXHIBIT 4-2

Famous Flange Company Cost Driver Rate and Quarterly Cost Driver Levels

QUARTER	DETAILS*	OVERHEAD RATE PER MACHINE
Spring	$\frac{\$225,000}{5,400}$	$41.67
Summer	$\frac{\$225,000}{4,500}$	50.00
Fall	$\frac{\$225,000}{5,000}$	45.00
Winter	$\frac{\$225,000}{3,600}$	62.50

$$\text{*Cost Driver Rate} = \frac{\text{Quarterly actual costs}}{\text{Quarterly actual machine hours}}$$

business during slow periods. The higher bid price can further decrease demand, which in turn leads to higher cost driver rates and even higher prices. Thus, the firm can enter an unnecessary death spiral as cost driver rates increase, leading to higher bid prices and ultimately even lower demand for its products. Conversely, cost driver rates can appear low in such a cost system when demand is high and capacity is short. This leads the company to attract additional business just when it should be raising prices to ration demand.

Support activity costs are caused by the level of capacity of each activity that is made available rather than by the level of actual usage of these committed resources. Therefore, the activity cost driver rate should be calculated based on the normal cost per unit of the activity level committed. Determining the cost driver rate by dividing the budgeted or actual cost per unit by the budgeted or actual use of that activity will produce misleading product costs.

Melissa's Auto Service Revisited

Let us return to the case of Melissa's Auto Service Company. Dee drew up the following description of the cost accounting system used to prepare bids for Melissa's customers' jobs (see Exhibit 4-3).

SYSTEM DESCRIPTION

A cost estimate is prepared for each customer job, as shown in Exhibit 4-3. After initially checking the customer's car, Melissa prepares a list of replacement parts required (this is her direct materials) required. She consults her authorized dealer price book to obtain list prices for the parts. She also consults her blue book to obtain the number of standard labor hours for the work required to service the car. Then she multiplies standard hours by the combined labor, support activities cost, and markup rate of $61.20 per hour. The combined conversion cost rate includes the following:

mechanic's wages and benefits

shop support activity costs including tools and machine depreciation

markup of 20% to provide a reasonable profit for Melissa

EXHIBIT 4-3

Melissa's Auto Service Cost Estimate for Customer Job

	Estimate Number:	1732		Date: August 9, 2000	
	Customer Name:	Brandon Briggs			
	Address:	43 Bridget Blvd. Bournemouth			
	PARTS				
Direct materials	**Part**	**Quantity**	**List Price**	**Amount**	**Total**
	Muffler	1	$38.00	$38.00	$ 38.00
	Tailpipe	1	15.00	15.00	15.00
	Total parts				$ 53.00
	LABOR				
Direct labor, support costs, and markup	Replacement of exhaust systems 2 hours @ $61.20 per hour				$122.40
	Total labor				$122.40
	Total costs				$175.40
	Prepared by: Melissa Wetengel				

The total cost estimate, or bid price, is the sum of the replacement parts cost and the labor cost charged at the combined labor, support conversion, and markup rate.

Dee investigated further how the combined labor, support activities cost, and markup rate of $61.20 per hour was determined. She examined the accounting and operating records in detail to prepare the following summary of costs budgeted for 2000:

Salaries of two expert mechanics ($60,000 each; total of 3600 billable hours)	$120,000
Salaries of three regular mechanics ($35,000 each; total of 5400 billable hours)	105,000
Fringe benefits	90,000
General and administrative costs	26,000
Depreciation and maintenance on physical facilities, bays, equipment, etc.	64,000
Depreciation and maintenance on special tools and machines (3600 machine hours)	54,000
Total costs	$459,000

The combined processing cost (labor and support activity) driver rate in dollars is determined by dividing the total costs ($459,000) by the total billable hours (3600 + 5400 hours), and then multiplying by 1.20 to represent a markup of 20%.

$$\text{Present cost driver rate} = \frac{\$459{,}000}{3600 + 5400} \times 1.20$$
$$= \$61.20 \text{ per labor hour}$$

Dee determined that Melissa's company had lost considerable business for simple jobs, such as exhaust system replacement and brake relining, that did not require expert mechanics or specialized tools and machines. The present job costing system was deficient in not distinguishing between the expert and regular types of labor and in not recognizing that some of the support activity costs—$54,000 for depreciation and maintenance—resulted from the availability of special tools and machines. Instead the costs of expert and regular labor, special tools, machines were bundled together into a single cost driver rate of $61.20 per labor hour. This type of simple cost system is often referred to as a peanut butter–spreading approach, since the cost of all types of resources—different labor skills, different machine types, and different support resources—are allocated across all jobs regardless if a job uses particular resources.

RECOMMENDED SYSTEM CHANGES

Dee recommended that instead of using a single conversion cost driver rate, Melissa should use the following four different cost driver rates:

1. expert labor wage rate
2. other labor wage rate
3. depreciation and maintenance on physical plant
4. depreciation and maintenance on special tools

The labor and support activity costs should be separated, therefore, into the four cost pools depicted in Exhibit 4-4. To do this, it is necessary first to apportion fringe benefits between the two types of labor costs (expert and regular mechanics) in the ratio of their respective costs. Then the company should determine its labor rates by dividing the total costs for wages and apportioned fringe benefits by the respective billable hours in each labor category and then adding a 20% markup (see Exhibit 4-5). Notice that both support activity costs and markup are included in the labor rate here. In contrast, Famous Flange added markup after determining all product costs—materials, labor, and support activity (see Exhibit 4-1, panel 5). Both methods are common

EXHIBIT 4-4

Melissa's Auto Service
Proposed Cost Pools

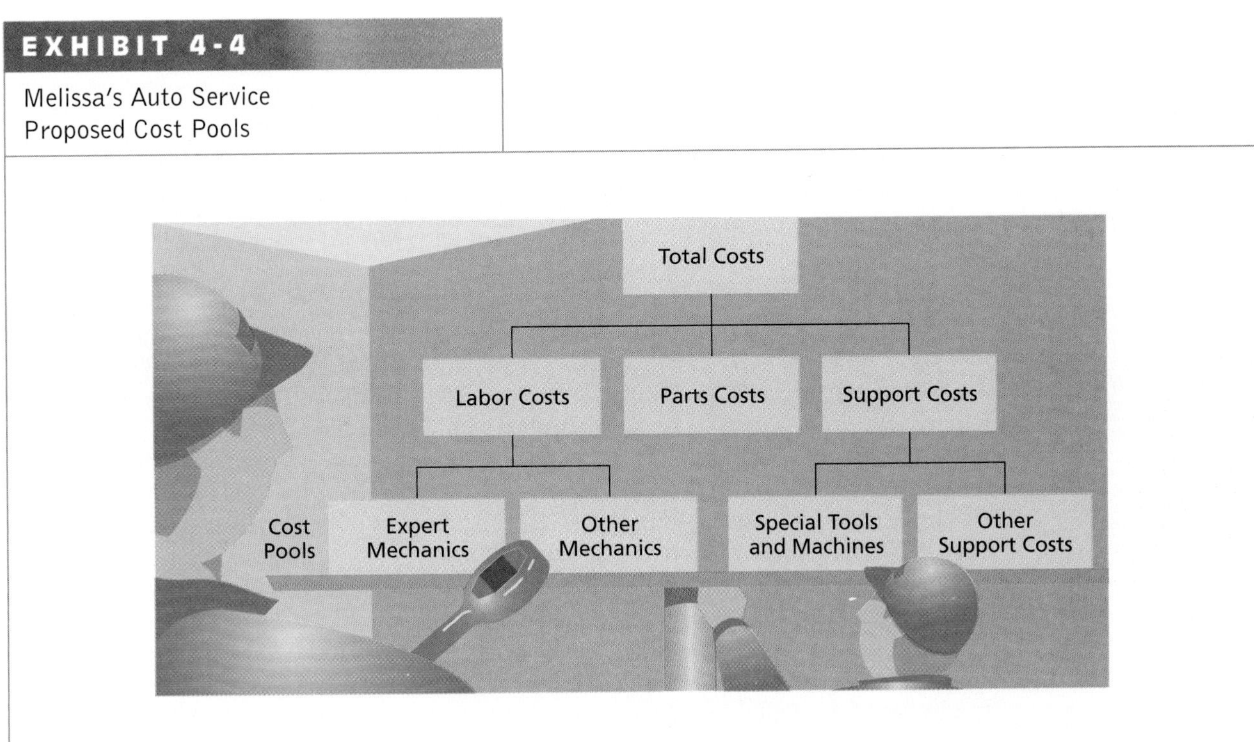

EXHIBIT 4-5

Melissa's Auto Service
Labor Rates

ELEMENTS	EXPERT MECHANICS	OTHER MECHANICS
Wages	$120,000	$105,000
Fringe benefits	48,000	42,000
Total costs	$168,000	$147,000
Markup	20%	20%
Total cost plus markup	$201,600	$176,400
Total billable hours	3,600	5,400
Labor rate per hour	$ 56.00	$ 32.67

$$\frac{\$90{,}000 \text{ benefits} \times \$120{,}000}{\$120{,}000 \text{ salaries of expert mechanics} + \$105{,}000 \text{ salaries of other mechanics}}$$

$$\frac{\$90{,}000 \text{ benefits} \times \$105{,}000}{\$120{,}000 \text{ salaries of expert mechanics} + \$105{,}000 \text{ salaries of other mechanics}}$$

in practice. Melissa's method of calculating a combined conversion cost driver rate is used more in service organizations; Famous's method of separating labor from support costs is common in manufacturing and trading establishments.

The machine-related activity rate for special tools and machines is $18 per machine hour (1.20 markup × $54,000 costs ÷ 3600 hours). The remaining support activity costs comprising general/administrative costs and depreciation/maintenance on physical facilities, bays, and equipment are expected to be related to total labor hours of both types of mechanics. Therefore, the formula to determine the remaining support activity cost driver rate is this:

Support activity cost driver rate

$$= \frac{1.2 \text{ markup} \times (\$26{,}000 \text{ G\&A} + \$64{,}000 \text{ depreciation})}{3600 \text{ expert mechanics' billable hours} + 5400 \text{ other mechanics' billable hours}}$$

$$= \$12 \text{ per labor hour}$$

NEW COST ACCOUNTING SYSTEM ILLUSTRATED

To illustrate how the new cost accounting system provides better information about job costs, Dee picks two representative jobs. Details of the work requirements for these two jobs appear in Exhibit 4-6. The first job involves the replacement of an exhaust system—a simple job that requires neither expert mechanics nor special tools and machines. The second job is relatively complex and involves rebuilding engine flanges.

Under the previous system, job 1732 (replacement of the exhaust system) is costed out at $175.40 [$53.00 parts + (2 hours × $61.20) (old support cost driver rate)], including the 20% markup for profit. Under the new system, the cost of the same job is estimated to be $142.34, including the same 20% markup for profit (see Exhibit 4-7). The new system reveals that job 1732 actually costs less than what appeared to be the case under the previous system. The previous system overcosted the job because the single support activity cost driver rate of $61.20 per labor hour wrongly applied a por-

EXHIBIT 4-6

Melissa's Auto Service Costs under the Old Job Costing System

WORK DESCRIPTION		JOB 1732 REPLACEMENT OF EXHAUST SYSTEM		JOB 2326 REBUILDING ENGINE FLANGES
Parts cost		$53		$412
Labor Hours:				
Expert mechanic hours	0		4	
Other mechanic hours	2		2	
Total labor hours		2		6
Special tools and machine hours		0		4

tion of the expert mechanic wages and special tools and machine costs to the job, although this simple job did not use any of these specialized and expensive resources. Thus, with the new cost system, Melissa's may be able to win back some of its lost business for simple jobs by lowering the price but not the profit margin.

In contrast, the costs of the more complex job 2326 (rebuilding engine flanges) increase from $779.20 [$412 parts + (6 hours × $61.20) (old support activity cost driver rate)] to $845.34 when the new system is used and the higher costs of expert labor and special tools are recognized (see Exhibit 4-7). Thus, the correct assignment of costs reveals that Melissa currently may be underpricing the services of her expert mechanics using special tools. Although this underpricing means that she is getting these more complex jobs, she is making much less profit and perhaps even taking a loss on these jobs than the present costing system leads her to believe. In addition, she is running out of capacity on the relatively more expensive resources for the complex activities by attracting business that does not cover the costs of these resources.

EXHIBIT 4-7

Melissa's Auto Service Costs under the New Job Costing System

	JOB 1732	JOB 2326
Parts cost	$53.00	$412.00
Expert mechanics	0	$224.00 (**4** hours × $56 wage rate)
Other mechanics	$65.34 (2 hours × $32.67 wage rate)	$65.34 (2 hours × $32.67)
Special tools support	0	$72.00 (4 hours × $18 cost driver rate)
Other support	$24.00 (2 hours × $12 overhead rate)	$72.00 (6 hours × $12 cost driven rate)
Total costs	**$142.34**	**$854.34**

IN PRACTICE

Sentry Group—Producing Fireproof Products

Sentry Group, based in Rochester, New York, manufactures fireproof and insulated metal products, including safes, containers, and files for home and office use. Production of steel parts for metal safes starts in the press department where cold-rolled steel is cut to the proper length and width on shear presses. Door jambs and frames are spot-welded to add strength and create a smoother appearance; door hinges are welded to add durability. When all welding is finished, the safe frame and door are filled with vermiculite insulation (a mixture of water, chemicals, and cement) and set aside to cure for 24 hours. When the insulation is dry, safe pieces are cleaned and painted. When the pieces are dry, the safe frame, door, and lock are assembled to form a completed safe, which is then packed for shipment.

Sentry Group uses a standard cost accounting system. Material and labor standards are reviewed annually and updated as necessary. There are six production departments for metal products: press, spot welding, mig welding, insulation, clean and paint, and final assembly. Labor costs for each production department are divided into direct labor and indirect labor (such as materials handling). The direct labor cost of each product is calculated by summing the standard hours per unit for each production department and multiplying the result by the company's average labor rate. Standard materials costs are calculated by the standard price per unit of each item of materials used in its production.

Support costs include five major elements: indirect labor in production departments, other production department costs, general plant costs, shipping and receiving costs, and maintenance costs. The cost driver rate is determined annually by dividing the total support costs of the previous year by the total direct labor costs. The resulting cost driver rate is multiplied by the direct labor content of each product to obtain the support cost per unit of that product. All other manufacturing costs, including engineering, quality control, and materials management—along with selling and general and administrative expenses—are considered period costs and are not included in product costs.

Sentry Group is considering changing to an activity-based costing system to obtain more accurate estimates of its product costs.

Source: "Sentry Group," Harvard Business School, Case 190–124

The difference between the old and the new product costing systems results from the difference in the structure of the cost pools. The new system recognizes two types of labor and support activity costs that include costs of special tools and machines not required for all jobs.

NUMBER OF COST POOLS

You may ask the question: How many cost pools should there be? The number can vary. Cost accounting systems in many German firms use more than 1000 cost pools. The general principle is to use separate cost pools if the cost or productivity of resources is different and if the pattern of demand varies across resources. Exhibit 4-8 displays the trade-offs involved in choosing the level of accuracy of a product costing system. The increase in measurement costs required by a more detailed cost system must be traded off against the benefit of increased accuracy in estimating product costs. If cost and productivity differences between resources are small, having more cost pools will make little difference in the accuracy of product cost estimates. In such a case, the benefits of decreasing errors, such as those that resulted in Melissa's losing simple jobs, will be relatively small and in sufficient to justify the increased cost of more cost pools.

EXHIBIT 4-8

Trade-offs in Choosing the Accuracy of a Costing System

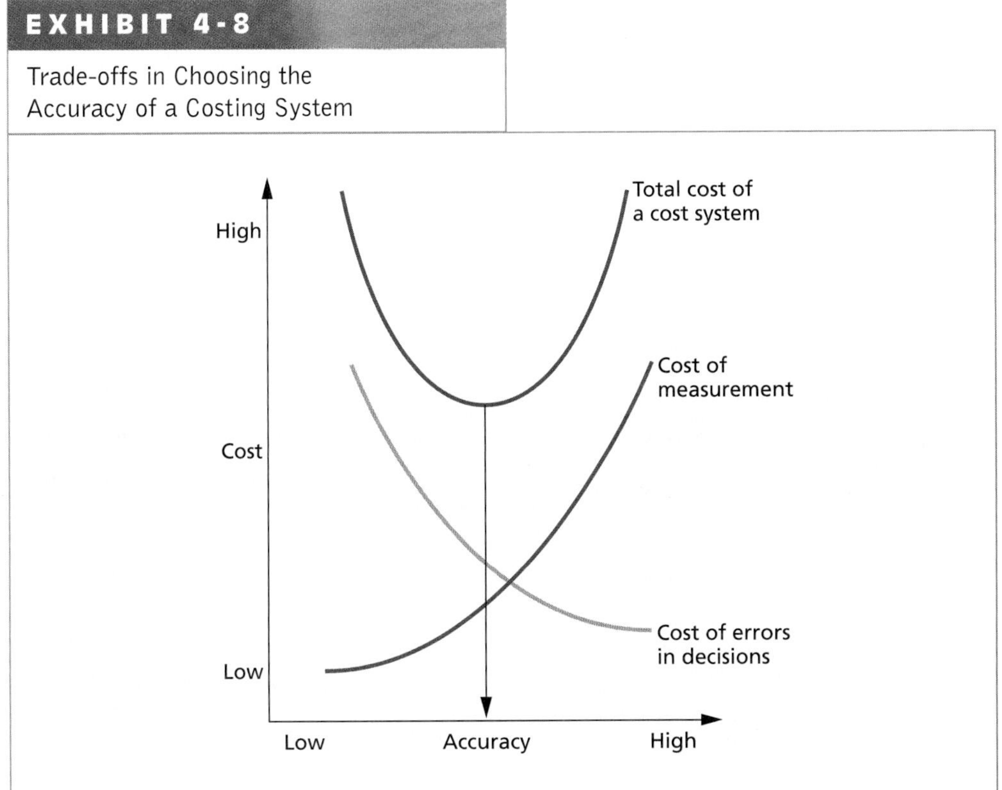

Recording Actual Job Costs

In addition to preparing bids, job order cost accounting systems also record costs actually incurred on individual jobs as they are produced. This process allows comparison of actual costs with the estimated costs to determine whether unexpected variations occurred in the quantity (efficiency) or prices of the various resources used.

Reconsider job J4369 of the Famous Flange Company in Exhibit 4-1. Once Famous has received the customer order and scheduled production, the company prepares a **materials requisition note** listing materials required to begin production. The materials requisition note M47624 lists the bar steel stock required for initial machining work (see Exhibit 4-9). Famous obtains steel requirements from engineering specifications for part design JDR-103 identified in the customer order. On receipt of the materials requisition note, the stores department issues the bar steel stock and moves the materials to the machining department.

Materials requisition note
A list of materials required to begin production.

The 720 pounds of materials issued are for 20% of the total order. The customer requires delivery spread over several months, and Famous Flange schedules production for meeting delivery schedules, a production system called a pull system. This production order is for 300 L181 flanges (20% of the total customer order for 1500 L181 flanges.) (see Exhibit 4-1). Each flange requires 2.4 pounds of materials; therefore, 720 pounds (300 flanges × 2.4 pounds per flange) of bar steel stock has been requisitioned. Since the actual price of bar steel is $11.50 per pound, the actual cost of the requisitioned material is $8280 (720 × $11.50).

Once the machining department receives the materials, the supervisor assigns specific lathe operators to the job. The time the operators spend working on a job is recorded on time cards, as shown in Exhibit 4-10 for machinist William Wiley

EXHIBIT 4-9

Famous Flange Company Materials Requisition Note

Materials Requisition Note Number: M47624 Date: August 2, 2000

From: Machining Department

Approved by: Mike Machina Machining Supervisor

Steve Stuart Stores Supervisor

Job Number: 14369

Engineering Design: JDR-103

Identification Number	Description	Quantity	Rate	Amount
24203	Bar steel stock	720 lb	$11.50	$8280.00

(employee number M16). After the completion of machining work, workers either store the machined bars as work in process or move them to the assembly department if they are scheduled for assembly. The just-in-time pull system that Famous Flange uses moves the materials almost immediately to the next department. The assembly department then prepares an additional materials requisition note to have the stores department issue the appropriate subassemblies. The assembly workers also prepare time cards to record the time they spend on job J4369.

Job cost sheet
Format for recording actual job costs.

Copies of all materials requisition notes and worker time cards are forwarded to the accounting department, which then posts them on a **job cost sheet**, shown in Exhibit 4-11. Even if time cards are recorded in an integrated computerized information system versus a manual accounting system, job cost sheets are prepared using data obtained from actual materials requisition and actual time card records. The time records may be generated by workers entering data into a computer terminal or by passing an electronic wand over a bar code on the job.

Finally, the system calculates total costs for the portion of the job completed. The structure of the job cost sheet is similar to that of the job bid sheet, except that the

EXHIBIT 4-10

Famous Flange Company Worker Time Card

TIME CARD

Employee Number: M16 Name: William Wiley

Date: August 2, 2000 Department: Machining

Checked by: Mike Machina Machining Supervisor

Job Number	Start Time	Stop Time	Total Hours	Wage Rate	Amount
J4369	6:00	10:00	4	$28.00	$112.00
J4362	10:00	1:00	3	28.00	84.00
J4371	2:00	3:00	1	28.00	28.00
Total			8		$224.00

direct materials and direct labor costs on the job cost sheet represent actual costs incurred on the job. Direct materials costs include $11,020 for subassemblies, in addition to $8280 for 720 pounds of bar steel stock recorded in materials requisition note M47624 (see Exhibit 4-9). Referring to Exhibit 4-11, we see that direct labor costs comprise the hours charged by three machinists (M16, M18, M19 lathe operators) and six assembly workers (A25, A26, A27, A32, A34, A35) for this job. (This includes the four hours charged for employee number M16 on August 2 as recorded in the time card in Exhibit 4-10). Support costs are applied to the job based on actual machine hours (117 hours) and direct labor hours (268 hours). The same predetermined support cost driver rates ($40 per machine hour and $36 per direct labor hour) are used as in the job bid sheet because actual total support costs for the plant will not be known until the end of the fiscal period (see Exhibit 4-1, panel 4).

Total costs are determined as before by adding the direct material, direct labor, and support activity costs applied to the job to date. It is now possible to compare these to the costs on the bid sheet. Notice that the actual unit costs of $134.98 ($39,144

EXHIBIT 4-11

Vernon Valve Company Job Cost Sheet

Panel 1

Job number: J4369 — Date: August 12, 2001

Customer: Michigan Motors

Product: Automobile engine valves

Engineering design number: JDR-103

Total number of units ordered: 1500

Panel 2

Materials Requisition Number	Description	Quantity	Price	Amount
M47624	Bar steel stock	720 lb	$11.50	$ 8,280.00
A35161	Subassemblies	290 units	38.00	11,020.00
Total direct materials cost				$19,300.00

Panel 3

Dates	Employee Number	Hours	Rate	Amount
8/2, 8/3, 8/4, 8/5	M16	24	$28.00	$ 672.00
8/2, 8/3, 8/4, 8/5	M18, M19	64	26.00	1,664.00
8/6, 8/7, 8/8, 8/9, 8/10	A25, A26, A27	120	18.00	2,160.00
8/6, 8/7, 8/8, 8/9, 8/10	**A32, A34, A35**	60	17.00	1,020.00
Total direct labor		268		$5,516.00

Panel 4

Support Costs	Amount
117 Machine hours @ $40 per hours	$ 4,680.00
268 Direct labor hours @ $36 per hour	9,648.00
Total support costs	$14,328.00

Panel 5

Total cost	**$39,144.00**
Number of units produced	290
Cost per unit	**$ 134.98**
Projected unit cost	**$ 134.36**

THE TECHNOLOGICAL EDGE

Using the Internet to Reduce Product and Process Costs

Thinking of ways to reduce product and service costs has become a given in today's business environment. Regardless of whether job order and process costing systems are used, engineers and managers are striving to think of ways to streamline operations so that costs can be eliminated. In an age where manufacturing and service have become increasingly more automated, companies are now finding that they can reduce costs significantly by turning to the internet.

Companies are now saving a great deal of money on materials, labor, and support costs using Web-based technology. For example, materials purchasing for many firms is now accomplished on line. The shipping and payment status of these materials can be tracked by both buyers and sellers using the internet. Not only does this practice reduce the cost of the materials, but it also reduces the need for a large procurement department. Employees can also apply for jobs using Web-based application forms, once again reducing the size of the human resources department.

Support costs are also being reduced. Many companies are saving significant money in their technology investments, eliminating the need to purchase and maintain personal computers every couple of years. Instead, companies are buying $500 network computers (that do not use hard drives) that rely on the network for data. With Web technology and browsers, employees can now download the data when needed. Using the Web also reduces computer training costs for employees since mastering a web browser takes very little skill and virtually no education.

Perhaps the most powerful use of internet technology allows employees to integrate and study huge amounts of information that may benefit all parts of their organizations. Web-based systems place data analysis and aggregation into the hands of many, which ultimately can lead to new insights and improvements in the way that products are made and services delivered. These benefits are accomplished in a relatively low-cost way compared with the information environment of the past decade.

Source: R. Lawson, "Achieving 'Net' Results," *Management Accounting*, January 1998, pp. 51–54.

total costs ÷ 290 units produced) for the portion of the job completed through August 12, 2000, are higher than the unit costs of $134.36 ($201,540 total cost ÷ 1500 units) estimated on the job bid sheet (see Exhibits 4-11, panel 5, and 4-1, panel 5).

Multistage Process Costing Systems

For many plants engaged in continuous processing, such as those in the chemicals, basic metals, pharmaceuticals, grain milling and processing, and electric utilities industries, production flows continuously, semicontinuously (that is, continuously but with a few interruptions), or in large batches from one process stage to the next. At each successive process stage, there is further progress toward converting the raw materials into the finished product. In contrast to a job shop manufacturing establishment, in continuous processing it is necessary first to determine costs for each stage of the process and then to assign their costs to individual products.

At this chemical plant, products are manufactured continuously. The process has multiple stages, with different chemical reactions occurring in different cells. (Tom Carroll/Phototake)

The design of product costing systems in such process-oriented plants allows measurement of the costs of converting the raw materials during a time period to be made separately for each process stage. These conversion costs are applied to products as they pass through successive process stages. This system for determining product costs, known as a **multistage process costing system**, is common in process-oriented industries. We also find multistage process costing systems in some discrete-parts manufacturing plants such as those producing automobile components, small appliances, and electronic instruments and computers.

Multistage process costing system
A system for determining job costs in which conversion costs are applied to products as they pass through successive process stages.

The common feature in these settings is that the products manufactured are relatively homogeneous. Few and relatively small differences occur in the production requirements for batches of different products. As a result, it is not necessary to maintain separate cost records for individual jobs. Instead costs are measured only for process stages, and cost variances are determined only at the level of the process stages instead of at the level of individual jobs.

COMPARISON WITH JOB ORDER COSTING

Multistage process costing systems have the same objective as job order costing systems. Both types of systems assign material, labor, and manufacturing support activity costs to products. Some important differences, however, exist between them (see Exhibit 4-12). Note that the factors in column 1 highlight the major points for consideration.

PROCESS COSTING ILLUSTRATED

Consider the product costing system at Calcut Chemical Company's plant that processes organic chemical products through three stages: (1) mixing and blending,

IN PRACTICE

Costing Products at Kenco Engineering

Kenco Engineering, Inc. is a family-owned firm with about $5 million in sales per year. It enjoys a reputation as a producer of high-quality, cutting-edge steel tools impregnated with tungsten. These tools are used in construction, road building, and on mining power equipment. The firm's key proprietary process is merging tungsten carbide chips with a steel plate. When the company's profit margins were good, management felt little need to collect much cost data and control costs. When the company experienced its first losses, however, it was time to implement detailed and accurate cost standards.

The new costing system divides the production process into three stages: tungsten crushing, steel cutting, and conversion processing (merging tungsten and steel). Because crushed tungsten may be purchased on the open market, it is a candidate for outsourcing. Costs assigned to the tungsten-crushing process are based on the long-term costs of operation, which can be avoided if crushed tungsten is purchased from outside. This costing method yields the relevant cost of the process, which management needs in deciding whether to outsource.

In the past, the steel-cutting operation required an overhead crane, a cutting machine, and storage areas because steel was ordered in huge sheets and cut in house. Kenco now has precut steel delivered on a just-in-time basis by a preferred supplier; most internal costs for this operation have been eliminated.

Conversion processing has five distinct steps: bevelling, bolt-hole cutting, tungsten impregnating, straightening, and drilling. The critical, capacity-limiting step is the proprietary tungsten impregnating. Purposely, the other four steps have greater capacity and do not limit this expensive activity. The tungsten process is expected to run 80% of the available time under normal efficient operating circumstances.

There exists only one common cost pool for all five steps of conversion processing. This pool includes costs for all overhead and all labor; they are assigned to the products in the proportion of the time spent on the tungsten-impregnating process based on its normal capacity. Only the time spent on this one step is considered for assigning costs. The other four steps are ignored, because tungsten impregnating is the critical process that cannot be outsourced and therefore limits capacity. For example, reducing setup time in the bevelling step would not reduce production cycle time or generate any cost savings.

The bid sheet at Kenco Engineering breaks the cost of each product into setup, tungsten crushing, steel cutting, conversion processing, and so on. Bid prices also reflect prevailing market forces; therefore, profit margins vary widely from one product to the next. Products with low gross-profit percents receive priority attention from Kenco managers.

Most Kenco products are customized orders, but all products have several attributes in common. Therefore, knowledge from past jobs helps improve efficiency and future bidding. For example, one job required that numerous tungsten strips make several passes through a tungsten-impregnating machine. Analysis of actual job costs revealed a negative gross profit. After engineering consultation, the product was redesigned to use a smaller number of critically placed tungsten strips and the product became profitable.

Source: James T. Mackey and Vernon H. Hughes, "Decision Focused Costing at Kenco," *Management Accounting*, May 1993, pp. 22–26.

(2) reaction chamber, and (3) pulverizing and packing (see Exhibit 4-13). First, Calcut Chemical estimates costs for these three stages, as shown in Exhibit 4-14. These costs include production labor assigned to each stage, support labor performing tasks (such as materials handling and setup), and laboratory testing. We refer to the total cost of all the activities performed at each stage of the process as the conversion costs for that

EXHIBIT 4-12

Differences Between Job Order and Multistage Process Costing Systems

FACTORS	JOB ORDER COSTING SYSTEM	MULTISTAGE PROCESS COSTING SYSTEM
Production	(a) Carried out in many different jobs	(a) Carried out continuously, semi-continuously, or in large batches
Production requirements	(b) Different for different jobs	(b) Homogeneous across products or jobs
Costs	(c) Measured for individual jobs	(c) Measured for individual process stages
Variances	(d) Between actual and estimated direct materials and direct labor costs are determined for individual jobs	(d) Between actual and estimated costs are determined for individual process stages

stage. That is, **conversion costs** are the costs to convert the materials or product at each stage. The total estimated conversion costs for each stage are divided by the corresponding total number of process hours to obtain the estimated conversion cost driver rate per process hour for that stage. Consider two representative products, G307 and G309, manufactured and sold by Calcut Chemical (see Exhibit 4-15). Both products are derivatives of ethyloleate and require the same basic raw materials, which cost $1240 per ton of finished product. The product G309 requires $234 of packing materi-

Conversion costs
Costs of production labor and support activities to convert the materials or product at each process stage.

EXHIBIT 4-13

Calcut Chemical Company Process Flow Diagram

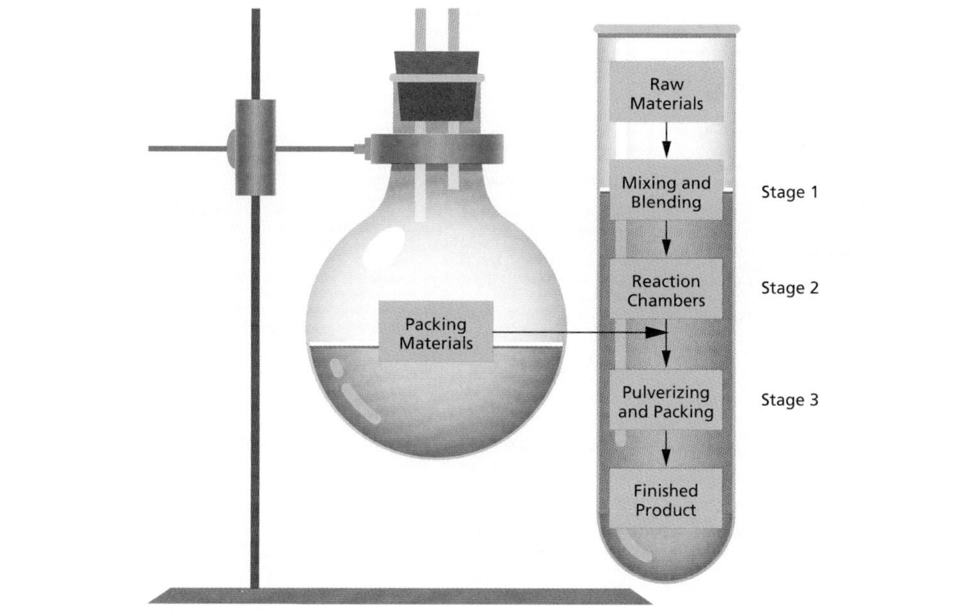

EXHIBIT 4-14

Calcut Chemical Company
Estimated Process Costs for 2000

	MIXING AND BLENDING	REACTION CHAMBERS	PULVERIZING AND PACKING
Production labor	$230,000	$1,040,000	$360,000
Engineering support	20,000	46,000	22,000
Materials handling	18,000	18,000	27,000
Equipment maintenance	10,000	32,000	8,000
Laboratory expenses	20,000	20,000	4,000
Depreciation	40,000	160,000	48,000
Power	32,000	78,000	24,000
General and administrative	16,000	16,000	16,000
Total conversion costs	$386,000	$1,410,000	$509,000
Total number of process hours	8,760	35,040	8,760
Conversion cost per process hour	$44.06	$40.24	$58.11

als per ton, almost 60% more than the $146 of packing materials per ton required for G307. The first product, G307, requires the following:

6 hours per ton for mixing and blending
24 hours of reaction time
4 hours for pulverizing and packing

The second product, G309, requires the same processing time for the mixing and blending and for the reaction chamber stages; But, because of the special requirements of the customers, it needs twice as much processing time for pulverizing and packing (eight versus four hours). Exhibit 4-15 presents the costs per ton of the two products.

EXHIBIT 4-15

Calcut Chemical Company
Product Costs per Ton

COSTS	G307	G309
Materials:		
Raw materials	$1240.00	$1240.00
Packing materials	146.00	234.00
	$1386.00	$1474.00
Conversion costs:		
Mixing and blending	$ 264.36 (6 hr)	$ 264.36 (6 hr)
Reaction chamber	965.76 (24 hr)	965.75 (24 hr)
Pulverizing and packing	232.44 (4 hr)	464.88 (8 hr)
Total conversion costs	$1462.56	$1695.06
Total cost	$2848.56	$3169.00

To determine individual product costs, it is necessary to (1) identify the costs of the material input required at various stages, and (2) add the estimated conversion costs for all the process stages to the material costs. For example, as Exhibit 4-15 shows, material costs per ton of product G307 include $1240 of raw materials required initially for the mixing and blending stage and $146 of packing materials used at the final pulverizing and packing stage.

SUMMARY

This chapter describes two of the most well-known traditional product costing systems—job order and process costing systems. Both costing systems are used to estimate and then measure actual costs of discrete job orders and products produced in continuous process industries. Although they are described here as two different costing systems, many systems observed in practice exhibit elements of both. Both types of cost systems identify materials and labor costs directly with jobs or products. Both systems also assign the remainder of costs to jobs or products on the basis of predetermined cost driver rates.

The support cost driver rate should be determined as the normal cost per unit of capacity of support activity that is made available. If the cost driver rate is based instead on actual or budgeted activity levels that fluctuate over time, then support activity costs will be understated in periods of high demand and overstated in periods of low demand. If product costing systems do not adequately reflect the systematic differences in prices and productivity of materials and labor resources and of factors driving support activity costs, the resultant job or product costs are likely to be distorted. In particular, if there are several grades of labor with widely differing productivity levels and wage rates but only a single common rate is used for all labor, then product costs are likely to be distorted for products that require different grades of labor in different proportions. Similarly, if support costs are caused by multiple cost drivers, but a single cost driver rate is employed to assign all support costs (the peanut butter–spreading approach), then product costs are likely to be distorted for products that require different proportions of the multiple cost drivers.

KEY TERMS

Bid price, 116
Conversion costs, 131
Cost driver rate, 116
Cost pool, 118
Finished goods, 115
Full absorption costing, 116
Job bid sheet, 115
Job cost sheet, 126
Job costs, 116
Job order costing system, 114
Margin, 116
Markup rate, 116
Materials requisition note,125
Multistage process costing system, 129
Process costing system, 114
Rate of return, 116
Raw materials inventory, 114
Variable costing, 116
Work-in-process (WIP) inventory, 115

APPENDIX 4-1

SERVICE DEPARTMENT COST ALLOCATIONS

In this appendix we discuss three ways that companies allocate service department costs to production departments. The three methods are direct allocation, sequential allocation, and reciprocal allocation. The last two are used when service departments consume services provided by other departments. To begin, we discuss the traditional two-stage cost allocation procedure.

Two-Stage Cost Allocations

Traditional cost accounting systems assign operating expenses to products with a two-stage procedure. First, expenses are assigned to production departments and then, in the second stage, production department expenses are assigned to the products. Let us begin by discussing how departmental structure influences the first-stage allocation process and then move to examples of the use of specific allocation methods.

THE EFFECT OF DEPARTMENTAL STRUCTURE ON ALLOCATION

Many plants are organized into departments that are responsible for performing designated activities. Departments that have direct responsibility for converting raw materials into finished products are called production departments. In a manufacturing plant such as PATIENTAID, casting, machining, assembly, and packing are production departments. **Service departments** perform activities that support production, such as machine maintenance, machine setup, production engineering, and production scheduling. All service department costs are indirect support activity costs because they do not arise from direct production activities.

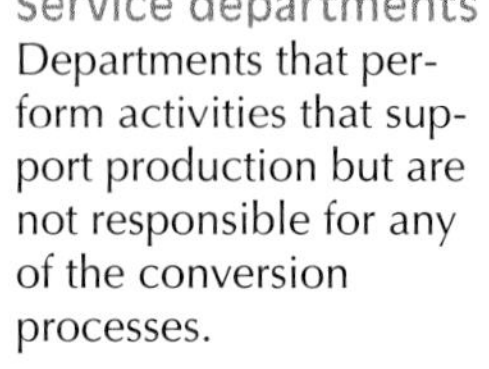
Service departments
Departments that perform activities that support production but are not responsible for any of the conversion processes.

Conventional product costing systems assign indirect costs to jobs or products in two stages. In the first stage, the system identifies indirect costs with various production and service departments, and then all of the service department costs are allocated to production departments. In the second stage, the system assigns the accumulated indirect costs for the production departments to individual jobs or products based on predetermined departmental cost driver rates (see Exhibit 4-16).

The PATIENTAID plant has four production departments: casting, machining, assembly, and packing. In addition, it has five service departments: machine maintenance, machine setup, production scheduling, production engineering, and general and administrative. The cost accounting system accumulates costs separately for each of these nine departments.

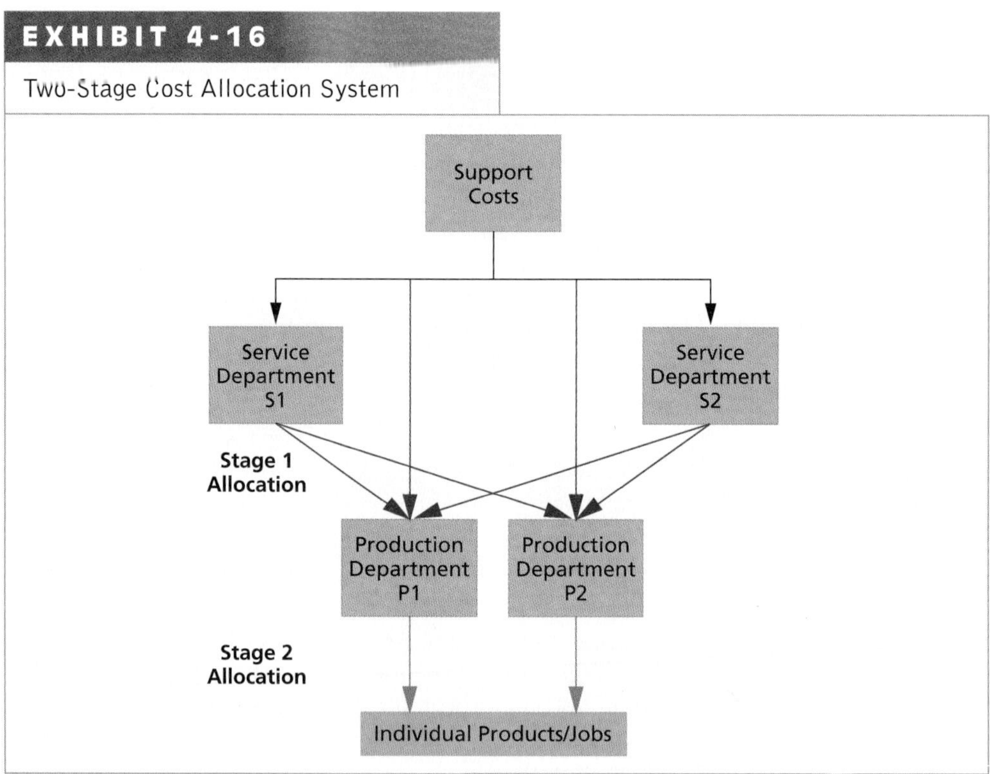

EXHIBIT 4-16
Two-Stage Cost Allocation System

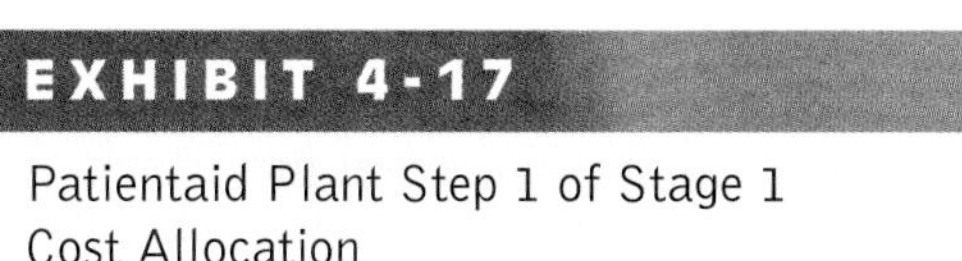
EXHIBIT 4-17

Patientaid Plant Step 1 of Stage 1 Cost Allocation

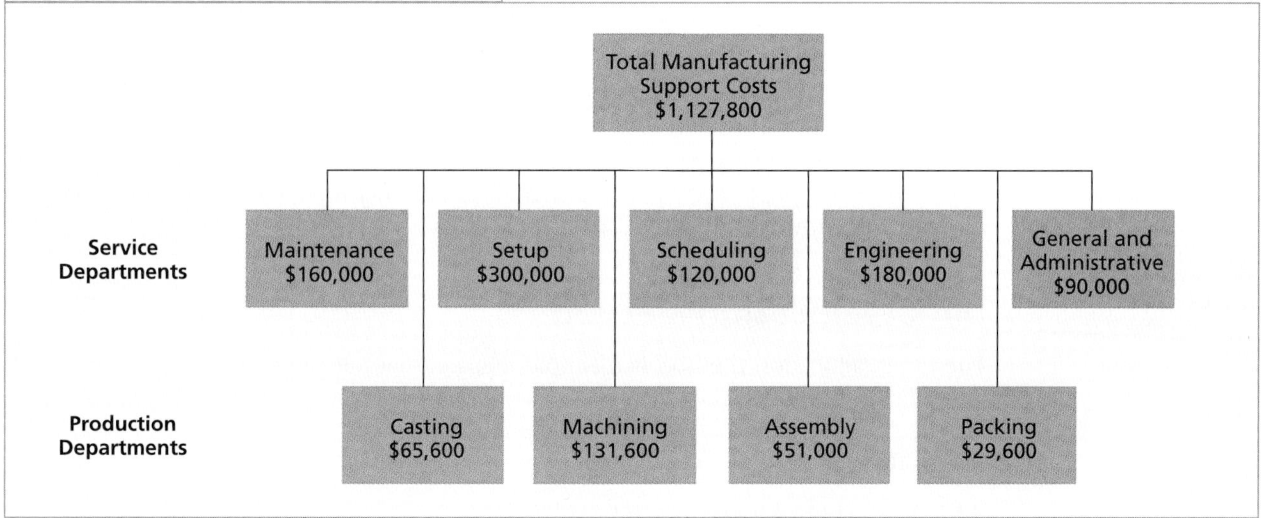

Costs accumulated for the four production departments include supervision, supplies, and machine depreciation costs. Costs for the five service departments include the salaries, wages, and benefits of the engineers and workers who are responsible for these activities as well as the costs of the tools and materials they use. Costs for the general and administrative service department include the salaries and benefits for plant managerial staff, rent, heating and lighting, and janitorial services.

STAGE 1 COST ALLOCATIONS

The first step in Stage 1 of the cost allocation procedure involves estimation of the normal manufacturing support costs incurred in each department. The following summary reflects the total support costs for the nine departments, as depicted in Exhibit 4-17.

PATIENTAID ESTIMATE OF MANUFACTURING SUPPORT COSTS

DEPARTMENTS	SUPPORT COSTS
Production	
Casting	$ 65,600
Machining	131,600
Assembly	51,000
Packing	29,600
Service	
Machine maintenance	160,000
Machine setup	300,000
Production scheduling	120,000
Production engineering	180,000
General and administrative	90,000
Total manufacturing support costs	$1,127,800

Because jobs are worked on in production departments, it is relatively easy to identify the number of direct labor and machine hours for individual jobs in each production department. Conventional costing systems are based on the assumption that we cannot obtain *direct* measures of use of service departments' resources on individual jobs as conveniently as we can of production departments' resources, because jobs are worked on only in production departments. Therefore, conventional costing systems allocate the service department costs first to the production departments before assigning them to individual jobs. This assignment of costs from the service departments to production departments is the second step in Stage 1 of the cost allocation procedure.

As mentioned, there are several different methods of allocating service department costs. These are presented next. We shall describe only the basic principles of **Stage 1 allocations** with reference to a specific method.

Stage 1 allocations Assignment of costs accumulated in the service department directly to the production departments or activities.

Direct Allocation Method

The direct allocation method is a simple method that allocates the service department costs directly to the production departments, ignoring the possibility that some of the activities of a service department may benefit other service departments in addition to the production departments.

ALLOCATION BASES AT PATIENTAID

Allocation of costs requires the identification for each service department of a basis, or cost driver, that best reflects and measures the activity performed by that department. The PATIENTAID plant uses the following bases to allocate service department costs by the direct allocation method.

SERVICE DEPARTMENT	ALLOCATION BASIS
Machine maintenance	Book value of machines in each production department
Machine setup	Number of setups in each production department
Production scheduling	Number of machine hours in each production department
Production engineering	Number of direct labor hours in each production department
General and administrative	Number of square feet occupied by each production department

The allocation bases do not always perfectly reflect the activities that generate service department costs. For example, the number of hours of setup work in each production department is a better basis than the number of setups for allocating setup department costs if the time required per setup differs across production departments. Similarly, expected maintenance hours for each department is a better measure for allocating machine maintenance costs than the book value of machines. However, there must be a trade-off between the additional cost of collecting such information against the potential benefits of the greater accuracy that its use may provide. For instance, PATIENTAID did not believe that the costs of obtaining information about maintenance hours in each department justified the benefit from the greater accuracy it might provide; therefore, the company uses the book value of machines to allocate maintenance costs because this measure is easily available.

It is often difficult to obtain any reasonable measures to allocate the costs of product-sustaining or facility-sustaining activities to production departments. Production scheduling, engineering, and plant administration activities do not benefit specific production departments although their use may differ across different products. PATIENTAID uses machine hours and direct labor hours as the bases to allocate these costs to the production departments. Keep in mind the previous discussion about external financial reporting requirements, such as the valuation of inventory, which have influenced the design of product costing systems in the past. As a result, the

EXHIBIT 4-18

PATIENTAID Allocation Bases Values for Production Departments

Allocation Bases	PRODUCTION DEPARTMENTS				Totals
	Casting	Machining	Assembly	Packing	
Book value of machines	$300,000	$600,000	$180,000	$120,000	$1,200,000
Number of setups	200	400	200	200	1,000
Machine hours	6,000	22,000	9,000	3,000	40,000
Direct labor hours	2,000	11,000	6,000	6,000	25,000
Square feet	6,000	9,000	9,000	6,000	30,000

objective of most conventional product costing systems, such as the one at the PATIENTAID plant, is to assign all manufacturing costs to jobs and products.

Exhibit 4-18 presents the allocation bases and their values for the production departments at PATIENTAID. The allocation of normal costs of the service departments to the production departments is made in proportion to their *respective allocation basis value.*

To complete the allocation procedure for Stage 1, do the following:

1. Obtain the ratio of allocation of machine maintenance service costs to the casting department. To illustrate, consider the ratio 0.250 in the top left corner of Exhibit 4-19. This figure is the ratio of $300,000. (the book value of the machines in the casting department) to $1,200,000 (the total book value of machines in the four production departments).

EXHIBIT 4-19

PATIENTAID Allocation Ratios

Service Department	**Allocation Basis**	**PRODUCTION DEPARTMENTS**				**Totals**
		Casting	**Machining**	**Assembly**	**Packing**	
Machine maintenance	Book value of machines	0.250	0.500	0.150	0.100	1.000
Machine setups	Number of setups	0.200	0.400	0.200	0.200	1.000
Production scheduling	Machine hours	0.150	0.550	0.225	0.075	1.000
Production engineering	Direct labor hours	0.080	0.440	0.240	0.240	1.000
General & administrative	Square feet	0.200	0.300	0.300	0.200	1.000

$$\underbrace{\$300{,}000 \div \$1{,}200{,}000}_{\text{see Exhibit 4-18}} = \underbrace{0.250}_{\text{see Exhibit 4-19}}$$

❷ Determine the amount of service department costs allocated to the production department costs by multiplying the allocation ratio by the corresponding service department costs (see Exhibit 4-20). For example, the casting department receives $40,000 of machine maintenance service department costs.

$$\underbrace{0.250 \times \$160{,}000}_{\text{see Exhibit 4-17}} = \underbrace{\$40{,}000}_{\text{see Exhibit 4-20}}$$

❸ Add the allocated costs from the service departments to the costs originally identified with the production departments.

$$\overbrace{\$65{,}600}^{\text{see Exhibit 4-17}} + \overbrace{\underbrace{\$150{,}400}_{\$40{,}000 + \$60{,}000 + \$18{,}000 + \$14{,}400 + \$18{,}000}}^{\text{see Exhibit 4-17}} = \overbrace{\$216{,}000}^{\text{see Exhibit 4-20}}$$

Stage 1 of the cost allocation procedure is now complete. The $1,127,800 of both service and production departmental costs for the PATIENTAID plant is allocated to the production departments as follows: $216,000 to casting; $503,800 to machining; $232,200 to assembly; and $175,800 to packing (see Exhibit 4-21). During Stage 2 of the allocation procedure, these amounts are used to determine the departmental cost driver rates for assignment of these costs to the jobs worked on in each production department.

Stage 2 allocations Assignment of costs accumulated in production departments and activities to individual products.

STAGE 2 COST ALLOCATIONS

Stage 2 allocations require the identification of appropriate cost drivers for each production department and assign production department costs to jobs and products while they are worked on in the departments. Conventional cost accounting systems

EXHIBIT 4-20

PATIENTAID Allocation of Service Department Costs to Production Departments

	PRODUCTION DEPARTMENTS			
Service Department Costs	**Casting**	**Machining**	**Assembly**	**Packing**
Support costs identified directly in step 1 of stage 1 allocations	$ 65,600	$131,600	$ 51,000	$ 29,600
Allocated from service department in step 2 of stage 1:				
Machine maintenance	40,000	80,000	24,000	16,000
Machine setup	60,000	120,000	60,000	60,000
Production scheduling	18,000	66,000	27,000	9,000
Production engineering	14,400	79,200	43,200	43,200
General and administrative	18,000	27,000	27,000	18,000
Total support costs for the production departments	$216,000	$503,800	$232,200	$175,800

EXHIBIT 4-21

PATIENTAID Plant Step 2 of Stage 1 of the Allocation Procedure

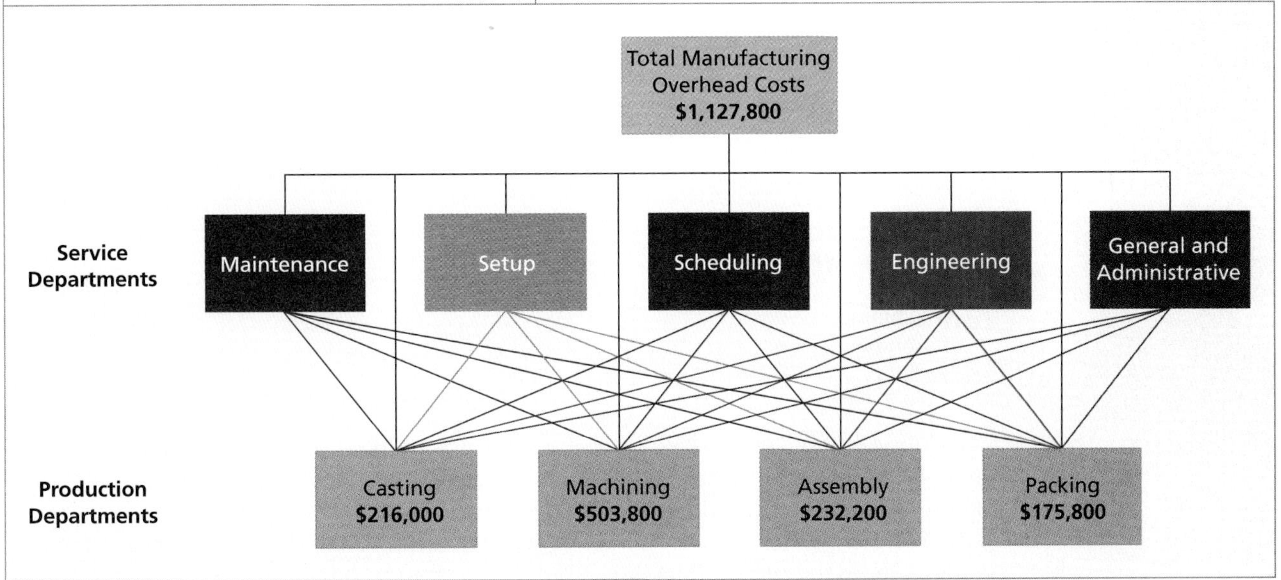

use unit-related cost drivers, such as the number of units made, the number of direct labor hours (or direct labor cost), and the number of machine hours. PATIENTAID uses machine hours as the cost driver for the casting and machining departments because of their high reliance on machines for the operations performed in these departments. The assembly and packing operations are more labor intensive; therefore, PATIENTAID uses direct labor hours as the cost driver in these two departments (see Exhibit 4-22).

Dividing the indirect costs accumulated in each production department by the total number of units of the corresponding cost driver results gives us cost driver rates for each department. To illustrate, the total indirect support costs from Stage 1 are \$216,000 for the casting department, with total machine hours estimated to be 6000. Therefore, the cost driver rate for the casting department is \$36 per machine hour (\$216,000 ÷ 6000).

EXHIBIT 4-22

PATIENTAID Stage 2: Cost Driver Rates for Production Departments

	PRODUCTION DEPARTMENTS			
	Casting	**Machining**	**Assembly**	**Packing**
Total support costs (from step 2 of stage 1)	\$216,000	\$503,800	\$232,200	\$175,800
Allocation basis	Machine hours	Machine hours	Direct labor hours	Direct labor hours
Total machine hours	6,000	22,000	9,000	3,000
Total direct labor hours	2,000	11,000	6,000	6,000
Allocation rate	\$36.00	\$22.90	\$38.70	\$29.30

EXHIBIT 4-23

PATIENTAID Machine and Labor Hours for Two Representative Jobs

	JOB J189-4 (OLD PRODUCT LINE)	JOB J273-2 (NEW PRODUCT LINE)
Machine hours:		
Casting	30	16
Machining	140	56
Assembly	60	24
Packing	20	18
Direct labor hours:		
Casting	18	7
Machining	70	28
Assembly	40	16
Packing	40	16

Support costs are applied to each job as it is worked on in the production departments. Exhibit 4-23 presents data on the number of machine and direct labor hours incurred on two representative jobs, J189-4 and J273-2, in each production department. Job J189-4 involves the production of a batch of 12 units of E189, bacterial analysis equipment in the old product line. Job J273-2 is for the production of a batch of 5 units of E273, one of the new products whose sales have been increasing rapidly.

EXHIBIT 4-24

PATIENTAID Application of Support Costs to Job J189-4

ITEM	COSTS	CALCULATION DETAILS	
Direct materials costs:			
Casting	$ 2,658.40	*given*	
Assembly	1,446.60		
Packing	632.80		
Total materials costs	$ 4,737.80		
Direct labor costs:			
Casting	$ 331.20	18 × $18.40	*given*
Machining	1,666.00	70 × $23.80	
Assembly	632.00	40 × $15.80	
Packing	528.00	40 × $13.20	
Total direct labor costs	$ 3,157.20		
Support costs:			
Casting	$ 1,440.00	40 × $36.00	*see Exhibit 4-22*
Machining	3,206.00	140 × $22.90	
Assembly	1,548.00	40 × $38.70	
Packing	1,172.00	40 × $29.30	
Total support costs	$ 7,366.00		
Total manufacturing costs	$15,261.00		
Number of units	12		
Cost per unit	$ 1,271.75		

Exhibits 4-24 and 4-25 present the costs for direct materials, direct labor, and support costs applied to these two jobs. Recall from Chapter 5 that direct material costs are identified with the jobs based on requisition notes issued for materials required in the casting department, subassemblies required in the assembly department, and packing materials required in the packing department. Direct labor costs are determined by multiplying the number of direct labor hours by the labor wage rate applicable to each department (see Exhibit 4-23). The wage rate is higher in the machining department than in the packing department because more skilled workers are required for machining operations.

To obtain support costs for the jobs J189-4 (Exhibit 4-24) and J273-2 (Exhibit 4-25), multiply the number of machine hours by the departmental cost driver rate for the casting and machining departments, and the number of direct labor hours by the cost driver rate for the assembly and packing departments (see Exhibits 4-22, 4-24, and 4-25). Notice that the number of machine hours and direct labor hours used for these calculations correspond to the amount of time spent on the job in a particular department, rather than on the *totals* for the job in the entire plant. The total manufacturing costs for each job are the sum of the direct material, direct labor, and support costs. To obtain the manufacturing cost per unit, divide total manufacturing costs for the job by the number of units produced in the job.

Distortions Caused by Two-Stage Allocations

Product costing systems installed in many plants employ the two-stage allocation method just described. The structure of these systems, however, can actually distort product costs. Consider the following example.

EXHIBIT 4-25

PATIENTAID Application of Support Costs to Job J273-2

ITEM	COSTS	CALCULATION DETAILS	
Direct materials costs:			
Casting	$1,186.60	*given*	
Assembly	788.80		
Packing	491.40		
Total materials costs	$2,466.80		
Direct labor costs:			
Casting	$ 128.80	7 × $18.40	*given*
Machining	666.40	28 × $23.80	
Assembly	252.80	16 × $15.80	
Packing	211.20	16 × $13.20	
Total direct labor costs	$1,259.20		
Support costs:			
Casting	$ 576.00	16 × $36.00	*see Exhibit 4-22*
Machining	1,282.40	56 × $22.90	
Assembly	619.20	16 × $38.70	
Packing	468.80	16 × $29.30	
Total support costs	$2,946.40		
Total manufacturing costs	$6,672.40		
Number of units	5		
Cost per unit	$1,334.48		

Assume that Minnetka, a company that makes steel valves, has a plant that is organized into three departments: machine setups, which is a service department, and machining and assembly, which are both production departments. Total setup costs of \$200,000 are assigned \$120,000 to the machining and \$80,000 to the assembly departments in proportion to the respective setup hours of 480 and 320 in the two production departments.

The plant manufactures two products, labeled A and B, shown in Exhibit 4-26. From the previous information regarding setup costs, the setup activity costs driver is

$$\$200{,}000 \div (480 + 320 \text{ setup hours}) = \$250 \text{ per hour}$$

Intuitively, it would seem logical to charge products A and B the following for setup costs:

PRODUCT A

$$\$250 \times (5 \text{ setup hours} \div 800 \text{ units}) = \$1.5625$$

PRODUCT B

$$\$250 \times (5 \text{ setup hours} \div 200 \text{ units}) = \$6.2500$$

Let us see now how the two-stage allocation method actually charges setup costs to the products A and B. Stage 2 assigns support costs to products based on machine hours for both production departments at Minnetka. Both products require 0.1 machine hours per unit in each department, machining and assembly. Each department has a total of 8000 machine hours.

$$0.1 \times (64{,}000 + 16{,}000 \text{ units of normal production}) = 8000$$

Therefore, these are the cost driver rates:

MACHINING DEPARTMENT

$$\$15 \text{ per machine hour} = \$120{,}000 \text{ setup costs} \div 8000 \text{ machine hours}$$

ASSEMBLY DEPARTMENT

$$\$10 \text{ per machine hour} = \$80{,}000 \text{ setup costs} \div 8000 \text{ machine hours}$$

Both products A and B are charged \$2.50 per unit for setup costs:

$$\$2.50 = (0.1 \times \$15) + (0.1 \times \$10)$$

Product A is overcosted because it is charged more than its share of setup costs (\$2.50 versus \$1.5625). In contrast, product B is undercosted because it is charged less than the costs of resources actually used for setups of product B (\$2.50 versus \$6.25). Why does the two-stage allocation method distort product costs in this manner?

EXHIBIT 4-26

Minnetka Production Factors Products A and B

Relevant Factors	PRODUCTS A	PRODUCTS B
Batch size in number of units	800	200
Setup hours required:		
Machining	3	3
Assembly	2	2
Normal production in number of units	64,000	16,000
Normal production in number of batches	80	80

Reason for Two-Stage Allocation Distortion

The reason for the distortion is the break in the link between the cause for the support activity costs (setup hours) and the basis for assignment of the costs to the individual products (machine hours). Two related factors contribute to these cost distortions:

1. allocations based on unit-related measures
2. differences in relative consumption ratios

Both products A and B have the same number of machine hours per unit; therefore, both are assigned the same amount of setup costs ($2.50 per unit). In reality, however, the demand for setup activity is less for product A because it is produced in larger batches. It has been charged the same rate as for product B because of the use of machine hours as the cost driver in the second stage of allocations. Conventional two-stage allocation methods use unit-related cost drivers to allocate support activity costs in the second stage, even when the demand for these activities is driven, in fact, by batch-related and product-sustaining cost drivers such as setups and engineering changes.

Cost distortions are greater when the difference between the relative proportion of the cost driver for the activity (setup hours) and the relative proportion of the basis for second-stage assignment of support costs (machine hours) is greater. Product A needs 0.00625 setup hours per unit (5 ÷ 800) on average, but product B needs more—0.02500 setup hours per unit (5 ÷ 200). Both products need the same number of machine hours per unit. The *actual* consumption ratio of product A to product B for setup activity is 1:4 (that is, 0.00625 ÷ 0.02500) based on the ratio of the actual cost driver, setup hours; but the *apparent* consumption ratio used to allocate setup costs is 1:1 based on machine hours (0.1 ÷ 0.1). This difference in the actual cost driver consumption ratio and the unit-level cost drivers used by conventional systems results in overcosting product A and undercosting product B.

Such distortions could be eliminated if we designed a costing system that used the actual cost driver for *each* support activity to assign costs directly to the products. This logic underlies the development of activity-based costing systems discussed in the following chapter.

Two other traditional methods are used to allocate service department costs. These are presented next.

Sequential and Reciprocal Allocation Methods

Sequential and reciprocal allocation methods are used when service departments consume services provided by other service departments. The **sequential allocation method** allocates service department costs to one service department at a time in sequential order. The reciprocal allocation method determines service department cost allocations simultaneously. The specifics of each method are described next.

Sequential allocation method
Allocates service department costs to production departments and other service departments in a sequential order.

SEQUENTIAL ALLOCATION METHOD

Companies use the sequential method under the following condition: There is no pair of service departments in which each department in that pair consumes a significant proportion of the services produced by the other department in that pair. To illustrate this method, consider a plant with two production departments, machining and assembly, and two service departments, power and engineering. Service department costs are allocated on the basis of kilowatt hours and engineering hours, respectively. Exhibit 4-27 displays the directly attributable costs of the four departments and their consumption of the two services.

The sequential allocation method requires that the service departments first be arranged in order so that a service department can receive costs allocated from another service department only *before* its own costs have been allocated to other departments.

EXHIBIT 4-27

Directly Identified Costs and Service Consumption Levels

	SERVICE DEPARTMENTS		PRODUCTION DEPARTMENTS		
Item	**Power**	**Engineering**	**Machining**	**Assembly**	**Totals**
Directly identified costs	$320,000	$180,000	$120,000	$ 80,000	$700,000
Consumption of service:					
Kilowatt hours	0	100,000	480,000	220,000	800,000
Engineering hours	0	0	2,000	2,000	4,000
Allocation ratios:					
Power	0	0.125	0.600	0.275	1.000
Engineering	0	0	0.500	0.500	1.000

Once a service department's costs have been allocated, no costs of other departments can be allocated back to it.

In this example, the power department does not receive engineering services, but the engineering department uses power. Therefore, in the sequential method, the power department costs are allocated first, followed by allocation of the engineering department costs. The total cost of a service department allocated to other departments equals the amount directly identified with the service department *plus* the amount allocated earlier to the service department from other service departments.

$$\textit{Total Costs Allocated} = \textit{Directly Identified Costs} + \textit{Costs Allocated to It}$$

These costs are allocated to the other service and production departments in proportion to their consumption of the service as detailed in Exhibit 4-27. Therefore, for the allocation of the costs of the power department, the allocation ratios in Exhibit 4-27 are based on the consumption of power by the engineering, machining, and assembly departments. The allocation ratios for the engineering service are based on the consumption by the machining and the assembly departments. Exhibit 4-28 shows the resulting allocations.

Power department costs are allocated first because the power department does not consume any other service. Engineering department costs are allocated next. Allocated costs of $220,000 for engineering are the directly identified costs of $180,000 plus the costs allocated to the engineering department from the power department of $40,000. Notice that no costs are allocated back to the power department.

If both service departments in this example consume each other's services, the reciprocal allocation method is appropriate. The sequential method ignores or suppresses such reciprocal relations.

RECIPROCAL ALLOCATION METHOD

The reciprocal allocation method recognizes reciprocal interactions between different service departments. We shall alter the consumption data in Exhibit 4-27 to illustrate this method. Notice that the information in Exhibit 4-29 is the same as that in Exhibit 4-27, except that the power department also consumes 1000 hours of engineering service.

EXHIBIT 4-28

Sequentially Allocated Costs

Item	SERVICE DEPARTMENTS Power	Engineering	PRODUCTION DEPARTMENTS Machining	Assembly
Directly identified costs	$320,000	$180,000	$120,000	$ 80,000
Allocation of power department costs	(320,000)	40,000	192,000	88,000
Allocation of engineering department costs	0	(220,000)	110,000	110,000
Totals	$ 0	$ 0	$422,000	$278,000

The sequential method does not work in this situation because when the engineering department's costs are allocated, 20% must be allocated back to the power department whose costs were already allocated. This would leave unallocated costs in the power department. If we were to allocate this new balance in the power department on the basis of the same allocation ratios as before, we would be left with unallocated costs in the engineering department. In principle, of course, we could repeat these sequential allocations until the unallocated balance of costs became negligible. The same result, however, can be obtained by using the algebraic approach of the reciprocal allocation method.

We shall denote the total costs to be allocated for the power department as P and those for the engineering department as E. Using the equation previously developed, we can find the total costs to be allocated to the power department:

$$\text{Total Costs Allocated} = \text{Directly Identified Costs} + \text{Costs Allocated to It}$$

Because the power department consumes 20% of the engineering services, we have

$$P = \$320{,}000 + 0.2E$$

EXHIBIT 4-29

Directly Identified Costs and Service Consumption Levels

Item	SERVICE DEPARTMENTS Power	Engineering	PRODUCTION DEPARTMENTS Machining	Assembly	Total
Directly identified cost	$320,000	$180,000	$120,000	$ 80,000	$700,000
Consumption of service:					
Kilowatt hours	0	100,000	480,000	220,000	800,000
Engineering hours	1,000	0	2,000	2,000	5,000
Allocation ratios:					
Power	0	0.125	0.600	0.275	1.000
Engineering	0.200	0	0.400	0.400	1.000

Also, because the engineering department uses 12.5% of the power consumed in the plant, we have

$$E = \$180{,}000 + 0.125P$$

Both equations thus recognize that the power department's total costs include a 20% share of the engineering department's total costs, and the engineering department's total costs include a 12.5% share of the power department's costs. We can now solve these two equations simultaneously. For this purpose, we shall substitute the expression for E into the first equation for P.

$$\begin{aligned} P &= \$320{,}000 + 0.20\ (\$180{,}000 + 0.125P) \\ &= \$320{,}000 + \$36{,}000 + 0.025P \\ 0.975P &= \$356{,}000 \\ P &= \$365{,}128 \end{aligned}$$

We also can solve for E by substituting this value of P in the second equation.

$$\begin{aligned} E &= \$180{,}000 + 0.125\ (\$365{,}128) \\ &= \$180{,}000 + \$45{,}641 \\ &= \$225{,}641 \end{aligned}$$

Now that we have determined the total costs for the two service departments, we can calculate the amounts to be allocated to the two production departments using the allocation ratios in Exhibit 4-29. These cost allocations appear in Exhibit 4-30. Notice that the allocations are different from those obtained in the earlier illustration for the sequential method because we began with different data. The power department's total costs were higher because it also consumed some engineering services. Because the machining department consumed a relatively larger amount of power, we find that in this case the costs allocated to it are also higher.

We mentioned that the fundamental assumption of the two-stage allocation method is the absence of a strong direct link between the support activities and the products manufactured. For this reason, service department costs are first allocated to production departments in the conventional two-stage allocation methods, using one of the methods described here. As we will see in the next chapter, activity-based costing rejects this assumption and instead develops the idea of cost drivers that directly link the activities performed to the products manufactured. These cost drivers measure the average demand placed on each activity by the various products. Then activity costs are assigned to products in proportion to the demand that the products place on

EXHIBIT 4-30

Reciprocally Allocated Costs

	SERVICE DEPARTMENTS		PRODUCTION DEPARTMENTS	
Item	**Power**	**Engineering**	**Machining**	**Assembly**
Directly identified costs	$320,000	$180,000	$120,000	$ 80,000
Allocation of power department costs	(365,128)	45,641	219,077	100,418
Allocation of engineering department costs	45,128	(225,641)	90,256	90,256
Totals	$ 0	$ 0	$429,333	$270,666

average on the activities. This usually eliminates the need for the second step in Stage 1 allocations that allocates service department costs to production departments before assigning them to individual jobs and products.

KEY TERMS

Sequential allocation method, 143
Service department, 134
Stage 1 allocations, 136
Stage 2 allocations, 138

ASSIGNMENT MATERIALS

QUESTIONS

4-1 Why are costs estimated for individual jobs? (LO 1, 2)

4-2 What information is presented in a typical job bid sheet? (LO 1, 2)

4-3 What is the source of the information to estimate the cost of materials? (LO 1, 2)

4-4 What is the source of the information to estimate the direct labor cost? (LO 1, 2)

4-5 How are support cost driver rates determined? (LO 1, 2)

4-6 How is support cost estimated for individual jobs? (LO 1, 2)

4-7 What is the markup rate? On what factors does it depend? (LO 1, 2)

4-8 What is a cost pool? Why are multiple cost pools required? (LO 3)

4-9 What problem arises when cost driver rates are based on planned or actual short-term usage instead of normal usage? Why? (LO 3)

4-10 What is the normal cost of a support activity? What is the normal usage level of a cost driver? (LO 3)

4-11 *Use of a peanut butter–spreading approach of a single cost driver rate when there are multiple cost drivers leads to distortions in job costs.* Do you agree with this statement? Explain. (LO 4)

4-12 What are *cost pools?* How is the appropriate number of cost pools selected? (LO 5)

4-13 What is the managerial use of tracking actual costs of individual jobs? (LO 5)

4-14 Why are predetermined cost driver rates used when recording actual job costs? (LO 5)

4-15 What does the term *conversion costs* mean? (LO 6)

4-16 What is the basic procedure for determining product costs in continuous processing plants? (LO 6)

4-17 What are the similarities and differences between job order costing and multistage process costing systems? (LO 7)

4-18 (Appendix) What is the difference between production departments and service departments? (LO 8)

4-19 (Appendix) What are the two stages of cost allocations in conventional product costing systems? (LO 8)

4-20 (Appendix) Why do conventional product costing systems allocate service department costs first to the production departments before assigning them to individual jobs? (LO 8)

4-21 (Appendix) What are the different situations for which direct, sequential, and reciprocal allocation methods are designed? (LO 8)

4-22 (Appendix) Why are conventional two-stage cost allocation systems likely to systematically distort product costs? (LO 8)

4-23 (Appendix) What are two factors that contribute to cost distortions resulting from the use of conventional, two-stage cost allocation systems? (LO 8)

EXERCISES

LO 1, 2, 3 **4-24** ***Job order costing, consulting*** McDonald Consulting computes the cost of each consulting engagement by adding a portion of firm-wide support costs to the labor cost of the consultants on the engagement. The support costs are assigned to each consulting engagement using a cost driver rate based on consultant labor costs. McDonald Consulting's support costs are $5 million per year, and total consultant labor cost is estimated at $2.5 million per year.

(a) What is McDonald Consulting's support cost driver rate?

(b) If the consultant labor cost on an engagement is $20,000, what cost will McDonald Consulting compute as the total cost of the consulting engagement?

LO 3, 4 **4-25** ***Single rate versus departmental rates*** Wright Wood Products has two production departments: cutting and assembly. The company has been using a single predetermined cost driver rate based on plant-wide direct labor hours. That is, the plant-wide cost driver rate is computed by dividing plant-wide support costs by total plant-wide direct labor hours. The estimates for normal costs and normal cost driver levels for 2000 follow:

	CUTTING	ASSEMBLY	TOTAL
Manufacturing support	$25,000	$35,000	$60,000
Direct labor hours	1000	3000	4000
Machine hours	4000	2000	6000

(a) What was the single plant-wide cost driver rate for 2000?

(b) Determine departmental cost driver rates based on direct labor hours for assembly and machine hours for cutting.

(c) Provide reasons why Wright Wood might use the method in (a) or in (b).

LO 4 **4-26** ***Fluctuating cost driver rates, effect on markup pricing*** Toki Company carefully records its costs because it bases prices on the cost of the goods it manufactures. Toki also carefully records its machine usage and other operational information. Manufacturing costs are computed monthly and prices for the next month are determined by adding a 20% markup to each product's manufacturing costs. The support activity cost driver rate is based on machine hours, shown below.

MONTH	ACTUAL MACHINE HOURS
January	1350
February	1400
March	1500
April	1450
May	1450
June	1400
July	1400
August	1400
September	1500
October	1600
November	1600
December	1600

Profits have been acceptable up until the past year, but Toki has recently faced increased competition. The marketing manager reported that Toki's sales force finds the company's pricing puzzling. When demand is high, the company's prices are low, and when demand is low, the company's prices are high. Normal capacity is 1500 machine hours per month. The normal capacity is exceeded in some months by operating the machines overtime beyond regular shift hours. Monthly machine-related costs, all capacity related, are $70,000 per month.

(a) Compute the monthly support cost driver rates that Toki used last year.

(b) Suggest a better approach to developing cost driver rates for Toki, and explain why your method is better.

4-27 ***Process costs*** Health Foods Company produces and sells canned vegetable juice. The ingredients are first combined in the blending department and then packed in gallon cans in the canning department. The following information pertains to the blending department for January 2000. LO 6

ITEM	PRICE PER GAL	GAL
Ingredient A	$0.40	10,000
Ingredient B	0.60	20,000
Vegetable juice		27,000
Materials loss		3,000

Conversion costs for the blending department are $0.55 per gallon for January 2000. Determine the cost per gallon of blended vegetable juice before canning.

4-28 ***Process costs*** Washington Chemical Company manufactures and sells Goody, a product that sells for $10 per pound. The manufacturing process also yields one pound of a waste product called Baddy in the production of every 10 pounds of Goody. Disposal of the waste product costs $1 per pound. During March, the company manufactured 200,000 pounds of Goody. Total manufacturing costs were as follows: LO 6

Direct materials	$232,000
Direct labor	120,000
Manufacturing support costs	60,000
Total costs	$412,000

Determine the cost per pound of Goody.

4-29 ***Service department cost allocation, direct method (Appendix)*** San Miguel Company has two production departments, assembly and finishing, and two service departments, machine setup and inspection. Machine setup costs are allocated on the basis of number of setups while inspection costs are allocated on the basis of number of direct labor hours. Selected information on the four departments follows: LO 8

ITEM	DIRECT COSTS	NUMBER OF SETUPS	DIRECT LABOR HOURS
Machine setup	$40,000	0	0
Inspection	15,000	0	0
Assembly	25,000	300	200
Finishing	20,000	100	500

REQUIRED

(a) Using the direct method, determine the amount of machine setup costs allocated to the two production departments.

(b) Using the direct method, determine the amount of inspection costs allocated to the two production departments.

LO 8 **4-30** ***Sequential allocation (Appendix)*** Cooper Company has two service departments and two production departments. Information on annual manufacturing support costs and cost drivers follows:

	SERVICE DEPARTMENT		PRODUCTION DEPARTMENT	
Item	**S1**	**S2**	**P1**	**P2**
Support costs	$65,000	$55,000	$160,000	$240,000
Direct labor hours	2,000	1,500	2,000	3,000
Number of square feet	800	1,200	2,400	2,600

The company allocates service department costs using the sequential method. First, S1 costs are allocated based on direct labor hours. Next, S2 costs are allocated based on square footage. The square footage for S1 is assumed to be zero for this purpose. Determine the total support costs allocated to each of the two production departments.

PROBLEMS

LO 1, 2, 3 **4-31** ***Job cost sheet*** Portland Electronics, Inc. delivered 1000 custom-designed computer monitors on February 10 to its customer, Video Shack; they had been ordered on January 1. The following cost information was compiled in connection with this order:

Direct materials used:

Part A327: 1 unit costing $60 per monitor
Part B149: 1 unit costing $120 per monitor

Direct labor used:

Assembly: 6 hours per monitor at the rate of $10 per hour
Inspection: 1 hour per monitor at the rate of $12 per hour

In addition, manufacturing support costs are applied to the job at the rate of $5 per direct labor hour. The selling price for each monitor is $350.

(a) Prepare a job cost sheet for this job.

(b) Determine the cost per monitor.

LO 1, 2, 3 **4-32** ***Job cost sheet*** The following costs pertain to job 379 at Baker Auto Shop.

	QUANTITY	PRICE
Direct materials:		
Engine oil	11 ounces	$2 per ounce
Lubricant	2 ounces	3 per ounce
Direct labor	3 hours	15 per hour
Support costs (based on direct labor hours):		10 per hour

Prepare a job cost sheet for Baker Auto Shop.

LO 1, 2, 3, 4, 5 **4-33** ***Job cost sheet, markup, single rate versus departmental rates*** Duluth Metalworks Company has two departments, milling and assembly. The company uses a job costing system that employs a single, plant-wide support cost driver rate to apply support costs to jobs on the basis of direct labor hours. That is, the plant-wide cost driver rate is computed by dividing plant-wide support costs by total plant-wide direct labor hours. The following estimates are for May 2000:

	MILLING	ASSEMBLY
Support costs	$120,000	$160,000
Direct labor hours	8,000	12,000
Machine hours	12,000	6,000

The following information pertains to job 691, which was started and completed during May 2000:

	MILLING	ASSEMBLY
Direct labor hours	10	40
Machine hours	18	8
Direct materials costs	$800	$50
Direct labor costs	$100	$600

(a) Prepare a job cost sheet for job 691.

(b) Assume next that instead of using a single, plant-wide support cost driver rate, the company uses machine hours and direct labor hours as cost drivers for the application of support costs in the milling and assembly departments, respectively. Prepare a job cost sheet for job 691.

(c) Using the costs you computed in parts (a) and (b), determine the bid price that Duluth Metalworks will quote if it uses a 25% markup on total manufacturing cost.

(d) Provide reasons why Duluth Metalworks might prefer the method in (a) or in (b).

4-34 ***Job costing*** The Gonzalez Company uses a job order costing system at its Green Bay, Wisconsin, plant. The plant has a machining department and a finishing department. The company uses two cost driver rates for allocating manufacturing support costs to job orders: one on the basis of machine hours for allocating machining department support costs and the other on the basis of direct labor cost for allocating the finishing department support costs. Estimates for 2000 follow: LO 1, 2, 3, 4, 5

	MACHINING DEPARTMENT	FINISHING DEPARTMENT
Manufacturing support cost	$500,000	$400,000
Machine hours	20,000	2,000
Direct labor hours	5,000	22,000
Direct labor cost	$150,000	$500,000

REQUIRED

(a) Determine the two departmental cost driver rates.

(b) During the month of January 2000, cost records for Job 134 show the following:

	MACHINING DEPARTMENT	FINISHING DEPARTMENT
Direct materials cost	$12,000	$2,000
Direct labor cost	$300	$1,200
Direct labor hours	10	50
Machine hours	80	8

Determine the total costs charged to Job 134 in January 2000.

(c) Explain why Gonzalez Company uses two different cost driver rates in its job costing system.

LO 1, 3 **4-35** ***Job costing*** The Goldstein Company employs a job order cost system to account for its costs. There are three production departments. Separate departmental cost driver rates are employed because the demand for support activities for the three departments is very different. All jobs generally pass through all three production departments. Data regarding the hourly direct labor rates, cost driver rates, and three jobs on which work was done during the month of April 2000 appear below. Jobs 101 and 102 were completed during April, while job 103 was not completed as of April 30, 2000. The costs charged to jobs not completed at the end of a month are shown as work in process at the end of that month and at the beginning of the next month.

PRODUCTION DEPARTMENTS	DIRECT LABOR RATE	COST DRIVER RATES
Department 1	$12	150% of direct material cost
Department 2	18	$8 per machine hour
Department 3	15	200% of direct labor cost

	JOB 101	JOB 102	JOB 103
Beginning work in process	$25,500	$32,400	$ 0
Direct materials:			
Department 1	$40,000	$26,000	$58,000
Department 2	3,000	5,000	14,000
Department 3	0	0	0
Direct labor hours:			
Department 1	500	400	300
Department 2	200	250	350
Department 3	1500	1800	2500
Machine hours:			
Department 1	0	0	0
Department 2	1200	1500	2700
Department 3	150	300	200

REQUIRED

(a) Determine the total cost of completed job 101.

(b) Determine the total cost of completed job 102.

(c) Determine the ending balance of work in process for job 103 as of April 30, 2000.

LO 1, 2, 3, 5 **4-36** ***Job costs and bids; comparing actual and estimated costs*** Brumelle Electronic Company manufactures a variety of electronic components. In April 2000, the company received an invitation from Takayama, Inc. to bid on an order of 1000 units of component ICB371 that must be delivered by August 16, 2000. The following are the standard (estimated) requirements and prices for 1000 units of ICB371:

	QUANTITY	PRICE
Direct material	2000 units	$10 per unit
Direct labor	1000 hours	$10 per hour

The cost of support resources is assigned to jobs based on direct labor hours (a single cost driver rate system). The estimated normal support costs and direct labor hours for 2000 are $300,000 and 50,000 hours, respectively. Brumelle has a policy to add a 20% markup to estimated job costs to arrive at the bid price.

(a) Prepare a job bid sheet to determine the bid price for this job.

Assume next that Takayama, Inc. accepted Brumelle's bid. After producing and delivering the 1000 units of ICB371 to Precision on August 4, Brumelle's management accountants compiled the following information about this job:

	ACTUAL QUANTITY	ACTUAL PRICE
Direct material	2100 units	$9.75 per unit
Direct labor	1000 hours	$11.00 per hour

(b) Prepare a job cost sheet to record the actual costs incurred on this job.

(c) What are some possible explanations for the differences between the actual and the estimated quantities or costs for the job? Are the differences favorable from Brumelle's point of view?

4-37 ***Job bid sheet, direct and sequential allocations (Appendix)*** Sanders Manufacturing Company produces electronic components on a job order basis. Most business is gained through bidding on jobs. Most firms competing with Sanders bid full cost plus a 30% markup. Recently, with the expectation of gaining more sales, Sanders dropped its markup from 40% to 30%. The company operates two service departments and two production departments. Manufacturing support costs and normal activity levels for each department are given below. LO 1, 2, 3, 8

	SERVICE DEPARTMENT		PRODUCTION DEPARTMENT	
Item	**Personnel**	**Maintenance**	**Machining**	**Assembly**
Support costs	$100,000	$200,000	$400,000	$300,000
Number of employees	5	5	5	40
Maintenance hours	1,500	200	7,500	1,000
Machine hours	0	0	10,000	1,000
Direct labor hours	0	0	1,000	10,000

Support costs of the personnel department are allocated on the basis of employees and those of the maintenance department on the basis of maintenance hours. Departmental rates are used to assign costs to products. The machining department uses machine hours, and the assembly department uses direct labor hours for this purpose.

The firm is preparing to bid on a job 781 that requires three machine hours per unit produced in the machining department and five direct labor hours per unit produced in the assembly department. The expected direct materials and direct labor costs per unit are $450.

REQUIRED

(a) Allocate the service department costs to the production departments using the direct method.

(b) Determine the bid price per unit produced for job 781 using the direct method.

(c) Assume that the support costs of the service department incurring the greatest costs are allocated first, and allocate the service department costs to the production departments using the sequential method.

(d) Determine the bid price per unit produced for job 781 using the sequential method in (c).

LO 8 **4-38** ***Direct, sequential, and reciprocal allocation (Appendix)*** Boston Box Company has two service departments, maintenance and grounds, and two production departments, fabricating and assembly. Management has decided to allocate maintenance costs on the basis of machine hours used by the departments and grounds costs on the basis of square feet occupied by the departments. The following data appear in the company's records for 1999:

ITEM	MAINTENANCE	GROUNDS	FABRICATING	ASSEMBLY
Machine hours	0	1,500	12,000	6,000
Square feet	3,000	0	15,000	20,000
Support costs	$18,000	$14,000	$45,000	$25,000

REQUIRED

(a) Allocate service department costs to the production departments using the direct method.

(b) Allocate service department costs to the production departments using the sequential method, assuming that the costs of the service department incurring the greatest cost are allocated first.

(c) Allocate service department costs to the production departments using the reciprocal method.

LO 1, 2, 3, 4, 5 **4-39** ***Single rate versus departmental rates*** Bravo Steel Company supplies structural steel products to the construction industry. Its plant has three production departments: cutting, grinding, and drilling. The estimated support activity cost and direct labor and machine hour levels for each department for June 2000 follow:

	CUTTING	GRINDING	DRILLING
Support activity cost	$42,000	$192,000	$228,000
Direct labor hours	5,000	8,000	12,000
Machine hours	80,000	40,000	30,000

The direct labor and machine hours consumed by job ST101 are as follows:

	CUTTING	GRINDING	DRILLING
Direct labor hours	2,000	2,500	3,000
Machine hours	20,000	3,000	2,000

(a) Assume that a single, plant-wide, predetermined cost driver rate is computed by dividing plant-wide support costs by a basis of plant-wide direct labor hours. Determine the support cost applied to job ST101.

(b) Determine the departmental support cost driver rate and support costs applied to job ST101, assuming that machine hours are used as the cost driver application base in the cutting department and that direct labor hours are used as the cost driver for the grinding and drilling departments.

(c) Explain why Bravo Steel might prefer a plant-wide rate or a departmental support cost driver rate.

LO 1, 3 **4-40** ***Charging for service activity costs*** Airporter Service Company operates scheduled coach service from Boston's Logan Airport to downtown Boston and to Cambridge. A common scheduling service center at the airport is responsible for ticketing and customer service for both routes. The service center is regularly staffed to service traffic of 2400 passengers per week: two-thirds for downtown

Boston passengers and the balance for Cambridge passengers. The cost of this service center is $7200 per week normally, but it is higher during weeks when additional help is required to service higher traffic levels. The service center costs and number of passengers serviced during the five weeks of August follow:

WEEK	COST	BOSTON PASSENGERS	CAMBRIDGE PASSENGERS
1	$7200	1600	800
2	7200	1500	900
3	7600	1650	800
4	7800	1700	850
5	7200	1700	700

How much of the service center costs should be charged to the Boston service, and how much to the Cambridge service?

4-41 ***Job bid price, direct, sequential, and reciprocal allocations (Appendix)*** Sherman Company manufactures and sells small pumps made to customer specifications. It has two service departments and two production departments. Information on March 2000 operations follows: LO 1, 2, 3, 8

	SERVICE DEPARTMENT		PRODUCTION DEPARTMENT	
Item	**Maintenance**	**Power**	**Casting**	**Assembly**
Support costs	$750,000	$450,000	$150,000	$110,000
Machine hours	0	80,000	80,000	40,000
Kilowatt hours	40,000	0	200,000	160,000
Direct labor hours	0	0	100,000	60,000

Separate cost driver rates are determined on the basis of machine hours for the casting department and on the basis of direct labor hours for the assembly department. It takes one machine hour to manufacture a pump in the casting department and 0.5 labor hour to assemble a pump in the assembly department. Direct labor and material costs amount to $32 per pump.

A prospective customer has requested a bid on a two-year contract to purchase 1000 pumps every month. Sherman Company has a policy of adding a 25% markup to the full manufacturing cost to determine the bid.

REQUIRED

(a) What is the bid price when the direct method is used?

(b) What is the bid price when the sequential method that begins by allocating maintenance department costs is used?

(c) What is the bid price when the reciprocal method is used?

CASE

4-42 ***Alternative job costing systems*** Over the past 15 years, Anthony's Autoshop has developed a reputation for reliable repairs and has grown from a one-person operation to a nine-person operation including one manager and eight skilled auto mechanics. In recent years, however, competition from mass merchandisers has eroded business volume and profits, leading the owner, Anthony Axle, to ask his manager to take a closer look at the cost structure of the autoshop. LO 1, 2, 3, 4, 5

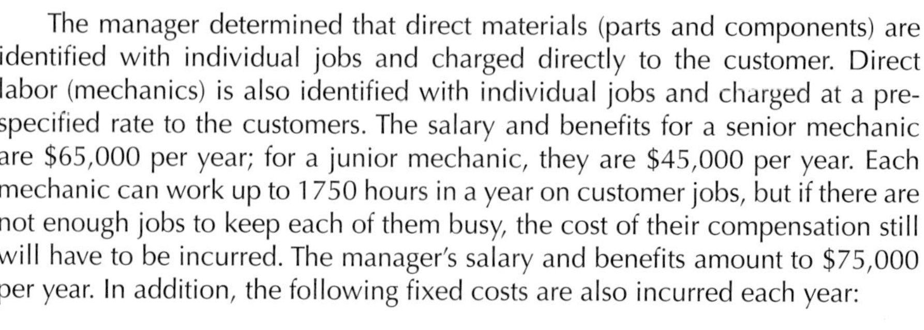

The manager determined that direct materials (parts and components) are identified with individual jobs and charged directly to the customer. Direct labor (mechanics) is also identified with individual jobs and charged at a prespecified rate to the customers. The salary and benefits for a senior mechanic are $65,000 per year; for a junior mechanic, they are $45,000 per year. Each mechanic can work up to 1750 hours in a year on customer jobs, but if there are not enough jobs to keep each of them busy, the cost of their compensation still will have to be incurred. The manager's salary and benefits amount to $75,000 per year. In addition, the following fixed costs are also incurred each year:

Rent	$40,000
Insurance	7,000
Utilities	7,000
Supplies	10,000
Machine maintenance	9,000
Machine depreciation	23,800
Total costs	$96,800

Because material costs are recovered directly from the customers, the profitability of the operation depends on the volume of business and the hourly rate charged for labor. At present, Anthony's Autoshop charges $51.06 per hour for all its jobs. Anthony said he would not consider firing any of the four senior mechanics because he believes it is difficult to get workers with their skills and loyalty to the firm, but he is willing to consider releasing one or two of the junior mechanics.

The present job costing system uses a single conversion rate for all jobs. The cost driver rate is currently determined by dividing estimated total labor and support costs by expected hours charged to customers. The eight mechanics are expected to be busy on customer jobs for 95% of the total available time. The price of $51.06 per hour is determined by adding a markup of x% to the cost driver rate, that is $\$51.06 = [1 + x/100] \times$ cost driver rate. Note that all personnel costs are included in conversion costs at present.

The manager is considering switching to the use of two rates, one for class A repairs and another for class B repairs. Electronic ignition system repairs or internal carburetor repairs are examples of Class A repairs. Class A repairs require careful measurements and adjustments with equipment such as an oscilloscope or infrared gas analyzer. Class B repairs are simple repairs such as shock absorber replacements or exhaust part replacements. Class A repairs can be done only by senior mechanics; class B repairs are done mainly by junior mechanics. Half of the hours charged to customers are expected to be for class A repairs, and the other half are for class B repairs. Because class A repairs are expected to account for all of the senior mechanics' time and most of the machine usage, 60% of the total costs (including personnel costs) are attributable to class A repairs and the remaining 40% to class B repairs.

(a) Determine the markup of x% currently used.

(b) Determine the two new rates, one for class A repairs and another for class B repairs, using the same markup of x% that you determined in (a) above.

(c) The following are expected labor hours anticipated for two customer jobs:

JOB NO.	DESCRIPTION	CLASS A REPAIRS	CLASS B REPAIRS
101	Carburetor repairs	4.5 hr	1.5 hr
102	Exhaust replacement	none	2.0 hr

Determine the price to be charged for each of the two jobs under the present accounting system and under the proposed accounting system.

(d) What change in service mix is likely to result from the proposed price change?

(e) Provide reasons why Anthony might retain the current costing system or change to the proposed costing system.

chapter 5

Activity-Based Cost Management Systems

AFTER READING THIS CHAPTER, YOU WILL BE ABLE TO

1. understand how traditional cost systems, using only unit-level drivers, distort product and customer costs
2. describe why factories producing a more varied and complex mix of products have higher costs than factories producing only a narrow range of products
3. design an activity-based cost system by linking resource costs to the activities performed and then to cost objects, such as products and customers
4. appreciate the role for choosing appropriate activity cost drivers when tracing activity costs to products and customers
5. use the information from a well-designed activity-based cost system to improve operations and make better decisions about products and customers
6. understand the importance of measuring the practical capacity of resources and the cost of unused capacity
7. assign marketing, distribution, and selling expenses to customers
8. analyze customer profitability
9. appreciate the role for activity-based cost systems for service companies
10. discuss the barriers for implementing activity-based cost systems and how these might be overcome

Jay Silverman/The Image Bank

BOOTH MOTORS

Jonathan Kellogg, owner and CEO of Booth Motors, was concerned about the recent declines in profitability of his automobile dealership. Booth was a major midwestern Ford dealer and sales of Ford's popular sports utility vehicles and trucks had been excellent; but many car models that Jonathan had to stock in order to display the full product line stayed on his lot for months. Booth Motors was incurring high expenses to lease land to store these vehicles and high financial charges on the vehicles as well.

Booth Motors had four other related lines of business: used cars, parts, service, and finance and insurance. With $54 million in annual revenues, Kellogg was unsure how profitable each of these lines of business was. Booth spent $48 million purchasing new cars and trucks, used vehicles, and parts. Dealer operating expenses (including employee compensation, insurance, rent, utilities, taxes, advertising, and interest expense) consumed another $5.4 million, leaving Kellogg with a net operating margin of only $600,000. Kellogg felt that as one of the largest auto dealerships in the midwestern United States, Booth should be earning much more than 1% pretax margin on sales. A 1% margin did not adequately compensate him for the capital invested in the dealership, nor did it compensate him for the risks of purchasing and stocking large quantities of vehicles, many of which had to be sold at significant discounts at the end of the model year.

Kellogg understood that there were strong tie-ins across his five lines of business. A new car sale usually involved the purchase of the buyer's existing car, financing and insurance revenues, and future parts and service business. But he still wondered how much each of these business lines was contributing to dealership profitability. If any operated at a loss, he was willing to take actions—such as adjusting prices, modifying product mix, and instituting process improvements—that would enhance dealership profitability. Kellogg was ready to start making tough decisions, both within his dealership and in his negotiations with Ford Motor Company and his financing and insurance supplier. But first he wanted to understand much better the "economic facts" about his dealership. Were all five product lines profitable? Within each product line, especially new vehicle sales, were all products profitable, or were only a few products profitable, with the remainder dragging down profitability?

The existing accounting system at Booth Motors reported the revenues for each of the five product lines and assigned the $48 million in directly attributable costs (i.e., purchased vehicles and parts) to each line. The $5.4 million of operating expense, however, was allocated to each department based on sales. Kellogg believed this allocation did not represent the demands that each product line made on his organizational resources. The system spread all operating expenses uniformly across everything so that it distorted the cost and profitability of individual product lines and products. Kellogg wondered whether advances in cost measurement and management, especially those he had heard were being implemented in the U.S. automobile manufacturing industry, could be applied to his dealership.

Traditional Manufacturing Costing Systems

Manufacturing companies operated for many years with the simple job order and process costing systems described in Chapter 4. These systems assigned direct labor and direct materials costs to products. Indirect costs, such as machine expenses, scheduling, quality control, purchasing, maintenance, supervision, and general factory expenses (for building depreciation, insurance, utilities, and housekeeping) were accumulated as support department expenses. These, in turn, were allocated to production departments in simple proportion to the direct labor hours worked in each department, or sometimes through quite complex schemes.

As an example of the problems of simple cost accounting systems, consider the manufacturing plant of the Cooper Pen Company. Historically, Cooper Pen had been the low-cost producer of traditional BLUE pens and BLACK pens and enjoyed profit margins in excess of 20% of sales. Several years ago, Dennis Selmor, the sales manager, had seen opportunities to expand the business by extending the product line into new products that earned premium selling prices. Five years earlier RED pens were introduced, which required the same basic production technology but could be sold at a 3% premium; last year PURPLE pens were added because of the 10% price premium they could command.

Laura Tunney, the controller of Cooper Pen, had just seen the most recent quarterly financial results of the factory's operations (see Exhibit 5-1) and was keenly disappointed:[1] The new RED and PURPLE pens were more profitable

[1] The results in Exhibit 5-1 only include factory expenses. Excluded are the company's general, selling, and administrative expenses. Were these to be shown, you would see that Cooper was barely breaking even.

EXHIBIT 5-1

Total and Product Profitability, Cooper Pens

	BLUE	BLACK	RED	PURPLE	TOTAL
Production Sales Volume	50,000	40,000	9,000	1,000	100,000
Unit Selling Price	$4.50	$4.50	$4.65	$4.95	
Sales	$225,000	$180,000	$41,850	$4,950	$451,800
Material Costs	75,000	60,000	14,040	1,650	150,690
Direct Labor	30,000	24,000	5,400	600	60,000
Overhead @ 300%	90,000	72,000	16,200	1,800	180,000
Total Operating Income	$ 30,000	$ 24,000	$ 6,210	$ 900	$ 61,110
Return on Sales	13.6%	13.3%	14.8%	18.2%	13.5%

than the high-volume commodity BLUE and BLACK pens, but overall profitability had decreased. Tunney wondered whether the company should continue to deemphasize the commodity products and keep introducing the new specialty colored pens.

Jeffrey Donald, Cooper's manufacturing manager, commented on the changed environment from his perspective:

> Five years ago, life was a lot simpler. We produced just BLUE and BLACK pens in long production runs, and everything ran smoothly, without much intervention. Difficulties started when the RED pens were introduced and we had to make more changeovers. This required us to stop production, empty the vats, clean out all remnants of the previous color, and then start the production of the red ink. Making black ink was simple; we didn't even have to clean out the residual blue ink from the previous run if we just dumped in enough black ink to cover it up. But for the RED pens, even small traces of the blue or black ink created quality problems. And the ink for the new PURPLE pens also has demanding specifications, though not quite as demanding as for RED pens.
>
> We are also spending a lot more time on purchasing and scheduling activities and just keeping track of where we stand on existing, backlogged, and future orders. The new computer system we got last year helped a lot to reduce the confusion. But I am concerned about rumors I keep hearing that even more new colors may be introduced in the near future. I don't think we have any more capability to handle additional confusion and complexity in our operations.

The major task in pen production was preparing and mixing the ink for the different colored pens. The ink was inserted into the pens in a semiautomated process. A final packing and shipping stage was performed manually.

Each product had a bill of materials that identified the quantity and cost of direct materials required for the product. A routing sheet identified the sequence of operations required for each operating step. This information was used to calculate the labor expenses for each of the four products. From this information, it was easy to calculate the direct materials and direct labor costs for each pen. Tunney believed, however, that the assignment of the indirect expenses was probably not accurate. Cooper's indirect expenses (about $180,000 per quarter) were as follows:

Expense Category	Expense
Indirect Labor	$ 60,000
Fringe Benefits	48,000
Computer Systems	30,000
Machinery	24,000
Maintenance	12,000
Energy	6,000
Total	$180,000

Because it was a small company and historically had produced only a narrow range of products (BLUE and BLACK pens), Cooper used a simple costing system. All the plant's indirect expenses ($180,000) were aggregated at the plant level and allocated to products based on their direct labor content. Currently this overhead burden rate was 300% of direct labor cost. Most people in the plant recalled that not too many years ago, before the new specialty products (RED and PURPLE pens) had been introduced, the overhead rate was only 200%.

Limitations of Cooper Pen's Traditional Cost System

Cooper Pen's cost system is adequate for the financial reporting role of inventory valuation. It is simple, easy to use and understand, and applied consistently from year to year. When Cooper's management accountants designed the system years ago, production operations were mostly manual and total indirect costs were less than direct labor costs. Cooper's two products had similar production volumes and batch sizes. Given the high cost of measuring and recording information, the accountants judged correctly that a complex costing system would cost more to operate than the company could recoup in benefits it could provide.

Cooper's environment has now changed. Because of automation, direct labor costs had decreased and indirect expenses had increased. As custom, low-volume products such as red and purple pens were added, Cooper needed more scheduling, setup, and quality control people, plus a computer to track orders and product specifications. The cost system that was adequate when indirect expenses were low and product variety was limited may now be giving distorted signals about the relative profitability of Cooper's different products.

Some improvements to Cooper's cost system might seem obvious. At present, Cooper operates with only a single cost center, the plant. Most companies use many cost centers for cost accumulation. Departments that have direct responsibility for converting raw materials into finished products are called **production departments.** Departments performing activities that support production, such as machine maintenance, machine setup, production engineering, and production scheduling, are **service departments.** Service department costs are typically indirect costs because they cannot be traced directly to products via production activities. If Cooper had multiple production and service cost centers, then it would first allocate service department costs to its production departments and, second, assign the accumulated indirect costs in production departments, going down to individual jobs or products based on predetermined departmental cost driver rates (as discussed in Chapter 4).

Production departments
The departments that have direct responsibility for converting raw materials into finished products.

Service departments
The departments that perform activities that support production but are not responsible for any of the conversion processes.

Even if Cooper Pen used multiple production and service department cost centers, it would still encounter severe distortions in its reported product costs. The distortion arises because of the way production center costs (both the costs incurred within production departments and the costs allocated to them from service departments) are allocated to products. Until quite recently, virtually all manufacturing companies used only unit-level drivers, such as direct labor dollars (the allocation base used by Cooper Pen) for allocating production center expenses to products.

To see why unit-level drivers such as direct labor dollars, direct labor hours, or machine hours lead to product cost distortion in an environment of high product variety, consider the following extreme example of two pen factories:

SIMPLE AND COMPLEX PEN FACTORIES

Simple Factory makes 1 million pens, all the same color: blue. Complex Factory also makes 1 million pens, but of many different colors, sizes, and varieties. In a typical year, Complex Factory produces about 2000 different types of pens ranging from specialty pens with annual production volumes as low as 50 to 100 per year, to higher-volume standard pens (blue and black), whose annual production volumes are each about 100,000 per year.

Even though both factories make the same basic product, Complex Factory requires many more resources to support its highly varied mix. Relative to the blue pen factory, Complex Factory has a much larger production support staff, since it requires more people to schedule machine and production runs, perform setups, inspect items after setup, move materials, ship orders, expedite orders, rework defective items, design new products, improve existing products, negotiate with vendors, schedule materials receipts, order, receive, and inspect incoming materials and parts, and update and maintain the much larger computer-based information system. Complex Factory also operates with considerably higher levels of idle time, setup time, overtime, inventory, rework, and scrap. Since both factories have the same physical output, they both have roughly the same cost of materials (ignoring the slightly higher acquisition costs in Complex Factory for smaller orders of specialty colors and other materials). For actual production, since all pens are about the same complexity, both Simple and Complex Factory would require the same number of direct labor hours and machine hours for actual production (not counting the higher idle time and setup times in Complex Factory). Complex Factory also has about the same property taxes, security costs, and heating bills as Simple Factory; but it has much higher indirect and support costs because of its more varied product mix and complex production task.

Consider now the operation of a traditional cost system, like the one used at Cooper Pens, in the two plants. Simple Factory has little need for a cost system to calculate the cost of a blue pen. The financial manager, in any single period, simply divides total expenses by total production volume to get the cost per blue pen produced. For Complex Factory, the costs of the indirect and support expenses are traced to its various production cost centers, as described in Chapter 4. Once expenses have been accumulated in each production center, they are allocated to products based on the (unit-level) cost driver for that cost center: direct labor, machine hours, units produced, or materials quantity processed. On a per unit basis, high-volume standard blue and black pens require about the same quantity of each of these cost drivers as the very low volume, specialty products. Therefore, Complex Factory's overhead costs would be applied to products proportionally to their production volumes. Blue and black pens, each representing about 10% of the plant's output, would have about 10% of the plants' overhead applied to them. A low volume product, representing only 0.01 of 1% of the plant's output (100 pens per year), would have about 0.01 of 1% of the plant's overhead allocated to it. Therefore, the traditional costing system, even one with multiple production and service cost centers, would report essentially identical product costs for all products, standard and specialty, irrespective of their relative production volumes.

Clearly, however, considerably more of Complex Factory's indirect and support resources are required (on a per-unit basis) for the low-volume, specialty, newly designed products than for the mature, high-volume, standard blue and black pens. Traditional cost systems, even those with hundreds or thousands of production cost centers, will systematically and grossly underestimate the cost of resources required for specialty, low-volume products and will overestimate the resource cost of high volume, standard products. Activity-based cost systems have been developed to eliminate this major source of cost distortion. We will show how they work by returning to the simple situation faced at Cooper Pens.

Activity-Based Cost Management Systems

Activity-based cost (ABC) management system
System based on activities that links organizational spending on resources to the products and services produced and delivered to customers.

Activity-based cost (ABC) management systems trace indirect and support expenses accurately to individual products, services, and customers. ABC systems use a simple two-stage approach that is similar to but more general than the structure of traditional cost systems. Traditional cost systems use actual departments or cost centers for accumulating and redistributing costs. ABC systems, instead of using cost centers for accumulating costs, use activities; that is, rather than asking how to allocate a service department expense to a production department, the ABC system designer asks what activities are being performed by the service department's resources. The resource expenses are assigned to activities based on how much of them are required or used to perform the activities.

TRACING COSTS TO ACTIVITIES

Let us see how this process operated with the Cooper Pen Company. Laura Tunney, controller, started with fringe benefits. She learned that fringe benefits were 40% of labor expenses (both direct and indirect) and could be handled by applying a simple 40% markup to all direct and indirect labor costs.

Tunney then interviewed department heads in charge of indirect labor and found that the people in these departments performed three main activities. About half of indirect labor was involved in scheduling production orders, purchasing, preparing, and releasing materials for the production run, and doing first-item inspection every time the process was changed to a new-colored pen. Tunney aggregated all these tasks into an activity that she called "handle production runs." Another 40% of indirect labor actually performed the physical changeover from one color pen to another, an activity that she labeled "perform setups." While interviewing the supervisors, Tunney learned that the time to change over to BLACK pens was relatively short (about 1 hour), as the previous color did not have to be completely eliminated from the machinery. Other colors required longer changeover times; RED pens required the most extensive changeover to meet the demanding quality specifications for this color. For the remaining 10% of the time, people maintained records on the four products, including making up the bill of materials and routing information, monitoring and maintaining a minimum supply of raw materials and finished goods inventory for each product, improving the production processes, and performing engineering changes for the products. Tunney referred to this activity as "support products."

As she conducted the interviews, Tunney was performing the first two steps for designing an activity-based cost system. She was developing the *activity dictionary,* the list of the major activities performed by the plant's resources (both human resources and, as we will see, its physical resources). She also was obtaining sufficient information to assign resource expenses to each activity in the activity dictionary (50% of indirect labor to "handle production runs," 40% to "perform setups," and 10% to "support products"). Tunney was following a good guideline by using verbs—action words such as *handle, perform,* and *support*—to describe activities. Activities should describe what resources, such as people and equipment are doing.

Tunney next turned her attention to the $30,000 of expenses needed to operate the company's computer system. She interviewed the managers of the data center and the management information system departments and found that most of the computer time and software expenses were used to schedule production runs in the factory and to order and pay for the materials required in each production run. Since

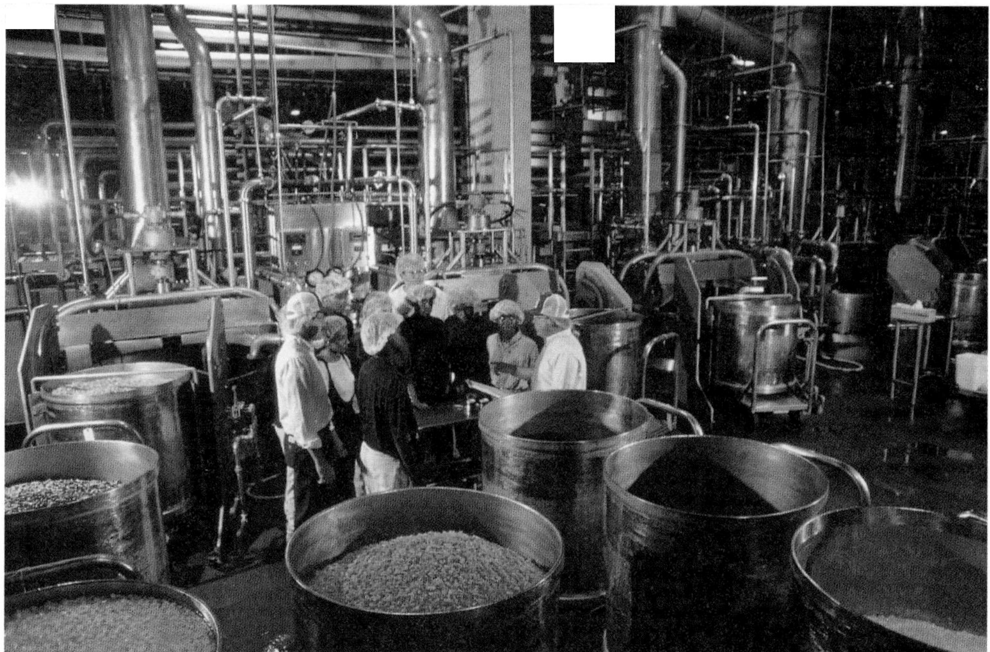

As at Cooper Pens, set-ups such as are done between jobs at the manufacturing company pictured here, are sometimes time consuming and therefore costly. There are many production and operations management techniques for reducing set-up times. Data about the cost of such labor form part of an activity-based costing system. (Will & Deni McIntyre/Photo Researchers, Inc.)

each production run was made for a particular customer, the computer time required to prepare shipping documents and to invoice and collect from a customer also was included in this activity. In total, about 80% of the computer resource was involved in the production run activity. This expense seemed to relate well to the "handle production runs" activity already defined.

Almost all the remaining computer expense (20%) was used to keep records on the four products, including production process and associated engineering change notice information. Tunney believed that this expense should be assigned to "support products," another activity already defined in her activity dictionary.

The remaining three categories of overhead expense (machine depreciation, machine maintenance, and the energy to operate the machines) were incurred to supply machine capacity to produce the pens. The machines had a practical capability of 10,000 hours of productive time that could be supplied to pen production. Tunney added a new activity, "run machines," to represent this production activity.

Tunney noted that even though she had defined only four activities for Cooper's indirect costs, they represented the three different levels of the manufacturing cost hierarchy:

Activity	Cost Hierarchy
Run machines	Unit level
Handle production runs	Batch level
Setup machines	Batch level
Support products	Product sustaining

Finding at least one activity for each hierarchy level gave her confidence that the complexity of the manufacturing process could be captured by the activity-based cost system.

EXHIBIT 5-2

Activities and Activity Expenses

	HANDLE PROD RUNS	SET UP MACHINES	SUPPORT PRODUCTS	RUN MACHINES	TOTAL EXPENSE
Indirect labor and 1/2 fringe	50%	40%	10%		$ 84,000
Computer expense	80%		20%		30,000
Machine depreciation				100%	24,000
Maintenance				100%	12,000
Energy				100%	6,000
Activity Expense	$66,000	$33,600	$14,400	$42,000	$156,000

At this point, Tunney had completed half the design of the new ABC system. She could now relate and assign all indirect and support expenses to production activities. She prepared Exhibit 5-2 to summarize her analysis to date. She also drew a diagram of the process she had followed thus far (see Exhibit 5-3).

The ABC model was only half completed (costs had been accumulated at activities but not yet driven down to products). Yet Tunney already had gotten some important insights from her analysis. Before, she saw only categories of expenses, such as spending on computers, energy, and indirect labor. Now she could see why Cooper Pens was incurring expenditures for these resources. In particular she saw how expensive such activities as handling production runs and setting up machines were. When Cooper produced only BLUE and BLACK pens, there were few production runs and consequently little need to continually set up machines; and since half the setups were to make black ink, the setup activity had been inexpensive. The

EXHIBIT 5-3

ABC — Mapping Resource Expenses to Activities

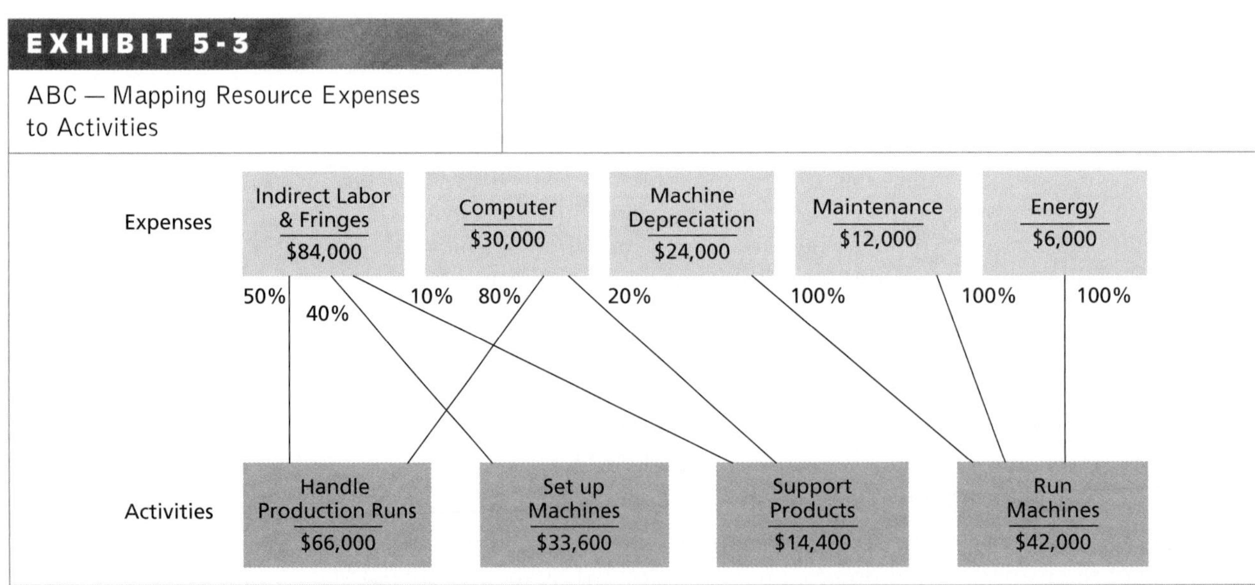

EXHIBIT 5-4

Activity-Based Costing — From Expense Categories to Activities

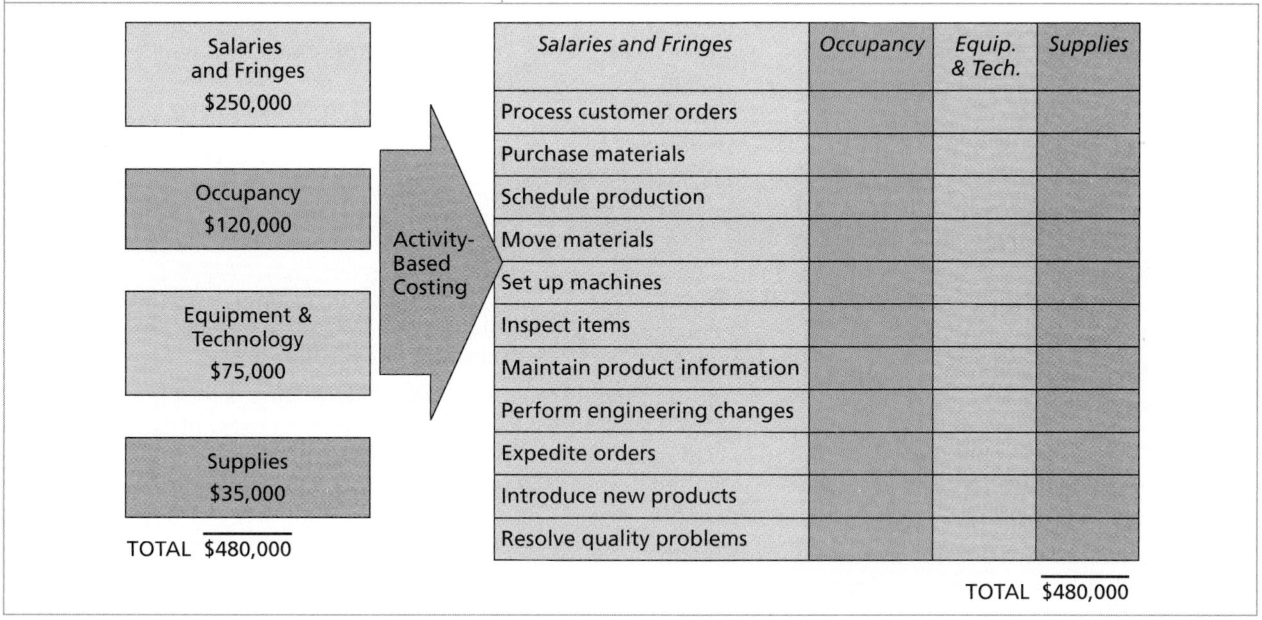

Expense Categories	
Salaries and Fringes	$250,000
Occupancy	$120,000
Equipment & Technology	$75,000
Supplies	$35,000
TOTAL	$480,000

Activity-Based Costing

	Salaries and Fringes	*Occupancy*	*Equip. & Tech.*	*Supplies*
Process customer orders				
Purchase materials				
Schedule production				
Move materials				
Set up machines				
Inspect items				
Maintain product information				
Perform engineering changes				
Expedite orders				
Introduce new products				
Resolve quality problems				
			TOTAL	$480,000

introduction of the new specialty products had led to much higher expenses for the production run and setup activities. The ABC model transformed the focus from what the money was being spent on (labor, equipment, supplies) to what the resources acquired by the spending were actually doing, as we see in Exhibit 5-4.

In the past, industrial engineers at Cooper Pen had studied labor and materials usage closely, because these had been the high cost resources. They were also the primary cost categories featured by Cooper's traditional cost system (which allocated all indirect costs to products using direct labor dollars). The high overhead rate on direct labor seemed to amplify any benefits from direct labor cost savings that the industrial engineers could achieve.

Tunney could now see that it would be worthwhile to have industrial engineers study the way Cooper handled and scheduled production runs and set up machines to uncover new opportunities for cost reduction and process improvement projects. This is an example of **operational activity-based management,** wherein managers use information collected by the ABC system at the activity level to identify promising opportunities for reducing costs in indirect and support activities.

Operational activity-based management
A system that uses information collected by the ABC system at the activity level to identify promising opportunities for reducing costs in indirect and support activities.

TRACING COSTS FROM ACTIVITIES TO PRODUCTS

Tunney now understood how activities, such as scheduling and product support, created a demand for resources. She turned her attention next to understanding why the activities were being performed. She learned, of course, that the activities in the Cooper Pen factory were being performed to support the production of the company's four products. Therefore, the activity expenses should be related in some way to the demands for the activities by the individual products.

Activity cost drivers
Measures that identify the linkage between activities and cost objects; they serve as quantitative measures of the output of activities.

Activity cost drivers identify the linkage between activities and cost objects, such as products, services, and customers. They serve as quantitative measures of the

IN PRACTICE

Using Activity-Based Costing for Operational Improvements

Navistar International Transportation trains project leaders—called Black Belts—in quality management techniques designed to reduce costs through focused projects. The Black Belts use ABC models to identify "low hanging fruit," activities that are easy to eliminate and that do not add value, such as having two people sign off on a $200 invoice. The ABC information helps the Black Belts identify and correct root causes of waste and inefficiencies. The linkage of ABC with the Black Belt program is especially valuable for quantifying the cost savings, using five cost categories:

1. *Cost takeout*—Completely eliminating an activity and the resources formerly used for that activity
2. *Cost avoidance*—Identifying and correcting an error that was not budgeted for correction but would have caused an expense had it not been corrected (e.g., correcting an engineering design flaw before production started)
3. *Reduction of nonvalue-added activities*—Redeploying a resource from a nonvalue-added activity to a value-added activity (e.g., moving a person from the rework area into a production job)
4. *One-time cash flow impact*—Decreasing the demand for cash (such as by reducing the need for equipment or inventory)
5. *Provide growth*—Removing a bottleneck that was causing a capacity constraint (such as by correcting a problem that led to downtime on a critical machine)

Source: M. L. Frigo and H. A. Kos, "Navistar's Dream Team," *Strategic Finance,* August 1999, pp. 38–45.

output of activities. Tunney identified the following activity cost drivers for the activities in her activity dictionary:[2]

Activity	Activity Cost Driver
Handle production runs	Production runs
Set up machines	Setup hours
Support products	Number of products
Run machines	Machine hours
Provide fringe benefits	Direct labor dollars

Activity cost driver rate
The amount determined by dividing the activity expense by the total quantity of the activity cost driver.

Once the activity cost drivers had been determined, Tunney obtained quantitative information on each. She needed to determine the total quantity for each activity cost driver and the quantity of cost driver used by each product.[3] Tunney summarized her findings in Exhibit 5-5.

Tunney now had sufficient information to estimate a complete activity-based cost model for Cooper Pen's factory. She calculated the **activity cost driver rate** by

[2] Examples of other typical activity cost drivers are:

Activity	Activity Cost Driver
Receive materials	Number of material receipts
Introduce new products	Number of new products introduced
Maintain machines	Number of maintenance hours
Modify product characteristics	Number of engineering change notices

[3] Obtaining quantitative information on activity cost driver often requires accessing data from different company information systems, such as the production scheduling system, the engineering system, the sales order system, and the maintenance system. As companies migrate to enterprise resource planning systems, all of these data will reside and be accessible in a data warehouse. The task of building ABC models will become increasingly easier as companies develop more integrated systems.

EXHIBIT 5-5

Activity Cost Drivers

ACTIVITY COST DRIVER	BLUE	BLACK	RED	PURPLE	TOTAL*
Direct labor hr/unit	0.02	0.02	0.02	0.02	2,000
Machine hr/unit	0.1	0.1	0.1	0.1	10,000
Production runs	50	50	38	12	150
Setup time/run	4	1	6	4	
Total setup time (hr)	200	50	228	48	526
Number of products	1	1	1	1	4

*The total labor and machine hours are obtained by multiplying the unit amounts by the quantity of each type of pen sold (from Exhibit 5-1, these quantities are 50,000 BLUE, 40,000 BLACK, 9,000 RED, and 1,000 PURPLE pens).

dividing the activity expense by the total quantity of the activity cost driver, as shown in Exhibit 5-6.

Tunney then multiplied the activity cost driver rate by the quantity of each activity cost driver used by each of the four products, as shown in Exhibit 5-7.

Tunney combined the activity expense analysis for each product with their direct materials and labor costs (from Exhibit 5-1) to obtain a new ABC profitability report (see Exhibit 5-8).

The results were quite different from that based on the traditional cost system (in Exhibit 5-1). Tunney now understood why the profitability of Cooper Pen has deteriorated in recent years. The two specialty products, which the previous cost system had reported as the most profitable, were in fact highly unprofitable. The company had added large quantities of overhead resources—a larger computer system and many more indirect and support employees—to enable these products to be designed and produced. The incremental revenues from sales of the specialty RED and PURPLE pens failed to cover the expenses from the increase in additional support resources required for their production.

The activity-based analysis showed that, contrary to the perspective of the traditional system, the mainstay BLUE and BLACK pens were the only profitable products made by Cooper Pen. These products still had the 20+% profit margins that the company had enjoyed before the new specialty products had been introduced.

EXHIBIT 5-6

Activity Cost Driver Rates

	HANDLE PROD RUNS	SET UP MACHINES	SUPPORT PRODUCTS	RUN MACHINES	TOTAL
Activity Expense	$66,000	$33,600	$14,400	$42,000	$156,000
Activity Cost Driver	Number of runs	Number of setup hours	Number of products	Number of machine hours	
Activity Cost Driver Quantity	150	526	4	10,000	
Activity Cost Driver Rate	$440 per run	$63.88 per hour	$3,600 per product	$4.20 per hour	

EXHIBIT 5-7

Activity Expenses Assigned to Products

	HANDLE PROD RUNS	SET UP MACHINES	SUPPORT PRODUCTS	RUN MACHINES	TOTAL
Activity Cost Driver Rate	$440 per run	$63.88 per hour	$3,600 per product	$4.20 per hour	
Activity Cost Driver Quantity: BLUE	50	200	1	5,000	
Total Activity Expenses: BLUE	$22,000	$12,776	$3,600	$21,000	$59,376
Activity Cost Driver Quantity: BLACK	50	50	1	4,000	
Total Activity Expenses: BLACK	$22,000	$ 3,194	$3,600	$16,800	$45,594
Activity Cost Driver Quantity: RED	38	228	1	900	
Total Activity Expenses: RED	$16,720	$14,565	$3,600	$ 3,780	$38,665
Activity Cost Driver Quantity: PURPLE	12	48	1	100	
Total Activity Expenses: PURPLE	$ 5,280	$ 3,066	$3,600	$ 420	$12,366

EXHIBIT 5-8

Activity-Based Costing Product Profitability Report

	BLUE	BLACK	RED	PURPLE	TOTAL
Sales	$225,000	$180,000	$41,850	$ 4,950	$451,800
Material costs	75,000	60,000	14,040	1,650	150,690
Direct labor	30,000	24,000	5,400	600	60,000
40% fringe on direct labor	12,000	9,600	2,160	240	24,000
Handle production runs	22,000	22,000	16,720	5,280	66,000
Set up machines	12,776	3,194	14,565	3,066	33,600
Support products	3,600	3,600	3,600	3,600	14,400
Run machines	21,000	16,800	3,780	420	42,000
Total expenses	$176,376	$139,194	$60,265	$14,856	$390,690
Operating income	$ 48,624	$ 40,806	($18,414)	($ 9,906)	$ 61,110
Return on sales	21.6%	22.7%	–44.0%	–200.1%	13.5%

Notice that Exhibit 5-8 contained far more information than the highly aggregated report shown in Exhibit 5-1. In that report, a single line item, Overhead, aggregated (inaccurately, as Tunney could now see) the complex set of activities performed by the indirect and support resources for the four products. Now Tunney was able to see a **bill of activities** performed for each product—the set of activities and the costs associated with individual products. She observed that introducing and supporting the two new pen colors (the $3,600 product-sustaining costs) actually exceeded the direct materials and labor costs of the products. Unless the volume of these two specialty products could be increased substantially, they would be unlikely to cover their sustaining expenses.

Bill of activities
The set of activities and costs associated with individual products or customers.

The bill of activities provided numerous insights into ways that managers could transform unprofitable products into profitable ones. For example, Dennis Selmor, in the sales and marketing department, might try to get either higher sales volumes or higher prices to compensate for the large batch and product-sustaining expenses of the specialty pens. In this kind of strategic **activity-based management (ABM),** managers reprice or alter the demand for activities as a way to increase their profitability. Strategic ABM involves decisions on pricing, distribution, product design, and minimum order sizes so that loss products can become profitable.

Activity-based management (ABM)
An approach to operations control that involves the five-step process of identifying the process objectives, charting activities, classifying activities, continuously improving processes, and eliminating activities whose costs exceed their value. Also called *activity analysis* and *value analysis.*

The ABC model also identifies the individual products, services, and customers that are highly profitable (such as Cooper's BLUE and BLACK pens). Marketing and sales managers can use this information to explore whether demand for those highly profitable products, services, and customers can be expanded to generate new revenues that exceed their incremental costs. Thus, with strategic ABM, managers can take actions that shift the activity mix toward more profitable uses.

Jeffrey Donald and other manufacturing people at Cooper Pens can turn their attention from trying to run their production equipment faster (improving the performance of unit-level activities) to learning how to reduce setup times (improving the performance of batch-level activities) so that small batches of the specialty products would be less expensive (require fewer resources) to produce. The high cost of the demanding quality specifications for RED pens, and frequent engineering changes required, can motivate the engineering group to seek ways to design products that would be easier to produce and require fewer modifications once introduced (thereby reducing the resource demands by a product-sustaining activity).

A combination of these action alternatives in pricing, process improvements, and engineering and design improvements would significantly increase Cooper Pen's profitability without compromising its ability to compete in both the high-volume BLUE and BLACK pen markets and the emerging specialty and custom pen segments.

SELECTING ACTIVITY COST DRIVERS

Activity cost drivers are the central innovation of activity-based cost systems as well as the most costly. Therefore, it is worth devoting a little more time to understanding the issues involved in selecting activity cost drivers. The selection of an activity cost driver reflects a subjective trade-off between accuracy and the cost of measurement. An additional consideration is the data requirements from having many activity cost drivers. An ABC system, with 50 activity cost drivers, and 2,000 products would require 100,000 data elements to be estimated (the quantity of each activity cost driver used by each product). Because of the large number of potential activity-to-product linkages, management accountants attempt to economize on the number of different activity cost drivers. For example, activities triggered by the same event—prepare production orders, schedule production runs, perform first part inspections, and move materials—all can use the same activity cost driver: number of production runs or lots produced. ABC system designers can choose from three different types of activity cost drivers: transaction, duration, or intensity (direct charging).

IN PRACTICE

Activity-Based Costing Helps Food Companies Reach Full Potential

Activity-based costing (ABC) has emerged as a key component of the food industry's efficient consumer response (ECR) process. Jack Haedicke, vice president of activity-based management at Kraft Foods, says, "You cannot do ECR unless you understand your internal costs, your costs to serve your customers, and your customers' profitability on your product. If you don't understand ABC, you're not going to be able to partner, to redesign your supply chain, or to understand category profitability when your product gets to the retailer's shelf." A joint industry task force employed ABC techniques to define the specific activities performed by trading partners within each of the several value chains that exist in the grocery industry—self-distributing retailers, wholesaler-supplied systems, and direct store delivery. A study conducted by Ernst & Young in October 1994 found that 41% of food manufacturers were using or piloting an ABC system. The same was true for 26% of distributors, 36% of retailers, and 21% of brokers surveyed. Another 50% of manufacturers said they were planning to pilot an ABC system in the near future, as did 43% of distributors, 29% of retailers, and 48% of brokers.

Activity-based costing also has served as a powerful tool for the management of stock-keeping units (SKUs), that is, the different products carried in inventory. Ralph Drayer, vice president of product supply and customer business development at P&G comments, "When you take an item-by-item elimination approach, you never really achieve the full value of rationalizing your SKU line-up. It's important to really zero-base it, to start from the beginning. We've employed ABC techniques to do that in our ongoing SKU rationalization efforts, enabling us to make effective reductions in our SKUs.

An industry consultant noted that the other major context for applying ABC in grocery companies is to enhance their reengineering efforts. "They are using ABC to ask how big are the activities in each work flow, and how much are they costing. From this data, they can develop a cost baseline for today's process and then show the potential return on investment of the redesigned process, thus adding a dimension of financial support to the business case for process improvement." Drayer of P&G added, "For us, it has certainly heightened the focus on those indirect activities that were not previously analyzed as a contribution to costs of individual items and processes."

At Kraft, ABC is being used to assign corporate costs to a variety of processes and cost objects based on actual resource consumption with the objective of better understanding the company's distribution value chain. These include analyses at the customer and SKU level. Haedicke comments, "We've identified that our cost to serve customers can vary from 1% to 8% of sales through distribution. We consider that a key finding."

Source: *U.S. Distribution Journal,* November 15, 1995, pp. 15–18.

Transaction drivers
Used to count the frequency of an activity, the number of times an activity is performed.

Transaction drivers count how often an activity is performed, for example, the number of setups, number of receipts, and number of products supported. They can be used when all outputs make essentially the same demands on the activity. For example, scheduling a production run, processing a purchase order, or maintaining a unique part number may take the same time and effort independent of which product is being scheduled, which material is being purchased, or which part is being supported in the system.

Transactions drivers are the least expensive type of cost driver but are also the least accurate, because they assume that the same quantity of resources is required every time an activity is performed, as if it were homogeneous across products. For example, use of a transaction driver such as the number of setups assumes that all setups take about the same time to perform. For many activities, the variation in use by individual cost objects is small enough that a transaction driver will be fine for assigning activity expenses to the cost object. If, however, the amount of resources required to perform the activity varies considerably, from product to product, then more accurate and more expensive cost drivers should be used.

Duration drivers represent the amount of time required to perform an activity. Duration drivers should be used when significant variation exists in the amount of activity required for different outputs. For example, simple products may require only 10 to 15 minutes to set up, whereas complex, high-precision products may require 6 hours for setup. Using a transaction driver such as number of setups will overcost the resources required to set up simple products and undercost the resources required for complex products. To avoid this distortion, ABC designers often use a duration driver (such as setup hours) to assign the cost of setups to individual products.

Duration drivers Represent the amount of time required to perform an activity.

Other examples of duration drivers include inspection hours and direct labor hours. In general, duration drivers are more accurate than transactions drivers, but they are much more expensive to implement because the model requires an estimate of the time required each time an activity is performed. With just a transaction driver (such as number of setups), the designer only needs to know how many times a product was setup—information that should be readily available from the production scheduling system. The setup time for each product, however, is an additional and more costly piece of information. The choice between a duration and a transactional driver is, as always, one of economics, balancing the benefits of increased accuracy against the costs of increased measurement.

For some activities, however, even duration drivers may not be accurate enough. **Intensity drivers** directly charge for the resources used each time an activity is performed. Continuing with our setup example, a particularly complex product may require special setup and quality-control people, as well as special gauging and test equipment each time the machine is set up to produce the product. A duration driver, such as setup cost per hour, assumes that all hours are equally costly but does not reflect extra personnel, especially skilled personnel, and expensive equipment that may be required on some setups but not others. In these cases, activity costs may have to be charged directly to the output, based on work orders or other records that accumulate the activity expenses incurred for that output.

Intensity drivers Used to directly charge for the resources used each time an activity is performed.

Intensity drivers are the most accurate activity cost drivers but the most expensive to implement; in effect they require direct charging via a job order costing system to track all the resources used each time an activity is performed. They should be used only when the resources associated with performing an activity are both expensive and variable each time an activity is performed.

The choice of a transaction, duration, or direct charging (intensity) cost driver can occur for almost any activity. For example, for a sales activity such as support existing customers, we could use either a transaction, a duration, or an intensity driver, that is, either

- cost per customer (assumes all customers cost the same);
- cost per customer hour (assume different customers use different amounts of sales resource time, but each hour of support time costs the same); or
- actual cost per customer (actual or estimated time and specific resources, including travel, committed to specific customers).

Often ABC analysts, rather than actually recording the time and resources required for an individual product or customer, may simulate an intensity driver with a weighted index approach. They ask individuals to estimate the relative difficulty of performing the task for one type of product/customer or another. A standard product or customer may get a weight of 1; a medium complexity product/customer can get a weight of 3 to 5, and a particularly complex (demanding) product/customer can get a weight of, say, 10. In this way, the variation in demands for an activity among products and customers can be captured without an overly complex measurement system. Again, the important message is to make an appropriate trade-off between accuracy and the cost of measurement. The goal is to be approximately right; for many purposes, transaction drivers or estimates of relative difficulty may be fine for estimating resource consumption by individual products, services, and customers.

Sometimes project teams get carried away with the potential capabilities of an activity-based cost system to capture accurately the economics of their organization's operations. The teams see diversity and complexity everywhere, and design systems with hundreds or thousands of activities, and specify many duration and intensity activity cost drivers for which data are expensive to collect. For product and customer costing purposes, most companies find that 30 to 50 different activities are sufficient, and choose activity cost drivers that can be obtained rather simply in their organization's existing information system.[4]

The goal of a properly constructed ABC system is to have the best cost system (not the most accurate)—it should balance the cost of errors made from inaccurate estimates with the cost of measurement. Most of the benefits from a more accurate cost system can be obtained with relatively simple ABC systems. Attempting to build an ABC system with 1000 or more activities, and directly charging actual resource costs to each activity performed for each product, service, and customer, leads to an enormously expensive system whose benefits, measured by improvement in decision making, likely exceed the cost of its operations. So cost system designers, like Cooper Pen's Laura Tunney, must make informed judgments about how much complexity is warranted to capture the underlying economics of the organization's operations, without introducing unnecessarily high costs for measurement and data collection.

Measuring the Cost of Resource Capacity

The model estimated by Laura Tunney assigned all resource expenses to activities and then to products. In calculating the activity cost driver rates, Tunney divided the expenses of each activity by the output from that activity (such as number of production runs) to obtain the average cost each time the activity was performed (the "activity cost driver rate"). But suppose more resources have been supplied during a period than were used, for example, the amount of indirect labor supplied could have performed 176 production runs, even though only 150 were scheduled during the quarter. In this case, Tunney would have overestimated the cost of handling each production run. Cooper Pens supplied resources, during the quarter, that cost $66,000. These resources, while used to process only 150 production runs, could actually have handled 176 runs. A better estimate for the cost of resources required to handle each production run is obtained by dividing the activity expense by the **practical capacity** of work it could perform; that is, the activity cost driver rate should be calculated as:

Practical capacity
The amount of work that can be performed by resources supplied for production or service.

$$\text{Cost per production run} = \$66{,}000/176 = \$375 \text{ per run}$$

This amount is considerably below the $440 estimate Tunney calculated based on the actual work performed. The $440 estimate included not only the cost of resources used for the actual production runs handled but also the **cost of unused capacity** for this activity. The cost of unused capacity should not be assigned to products produced or customers served during a period. The activity cost driver rate should reflect the underlying efficiency of the process—the cost of resources to handle each production order—and this efficiency is measured better by using the capacity of the resources supplied as the denominator when calculating activity cost driver rates. The

Cost of unused capacity
An expense determined by the amount of resources unused during production.

[4] One of the main attractions to installation of integrated, enterprise resource planning systems is that many more potential activity cost drivers become automatically available for ABC systems.

numerator in an activity cost driver calculation represents the costs of supplying resource capacity to do work. The denominator should match the numerator by representing the quantity of work the resources can perform.

The cost of unused capacity, however, should not be ignored; it remains someone's or some department's responsibility. Usually you can assign unused capacity after analyzing the decision that led to its creation. For example, if the capacity was acquired to meet anticipated demands from a particular customer or a particular market segment, then the costs of unused capacity due to lower than expected demands can be assigned to the person or organizational unit responsible for that customer or segment. Such an assignment is done on a lump-sum basis; it will be treated as a sustaining, not a unit-level, expense.

If the unused capacity relates to a product line, as when certain production resources are dedicated to individual product lines, then the cost of unused capacity is assigned to the product line where demand failed to materialize. It should not be treated as a general cost, to be shared across all product lines. For example, suppose division management personnel knew in advance that resource supply would exceed resource demand but wanted to retain existing resources for future growth and expansion. Then the unused capacity could be a division-sustaining cost, assigned to the division making the decision to retain unused capacity. In making such assignment of unused capacity costs, we trace the costs at the level in the organization where decisions are made that affect the supply of capacity resources and the demand for those resources. The lump-sum assignment of unused capacity costs provides feedback to managers on their supply and demand decisions.

FIXED AND VARIABLE COSTS IN ACTIVITY-BASED COST SYSTEMS

Even though an ABC system assigns most indirect costs to products, the system does not assume that such costs will vary based on short-term changes in activity volumes. In fact, most indirect expenses assigned by an ABC system are committed costs. The purpose of the ABC assignment is, after all, to help people manage the supply of committed costs since these costs can change based on management's decisions. Committed costs become variable via a two-step procedure. First, demands for resources change because of changes in activity levels. For batch and product-sustaining resources, the activity levels change because of changes in variety and complexity (such as the number of production runs and the number of different products supported). Second, managers make decisions to change the supply of committed resources, either up or down, to meet the new level of demand for the activities performed by these resources.

If activity volumes exceed the capacity of existing resources, the result is bottlenecks, shortages, increased pace of activity, delays, or poor-quality work. Such shortages occur often on machines, but the ABC approach makes clear that shortages can also occur for human resources who perform support activities, such as designing, scheduling, ordering, purchasing, maintaining, and handling products and customers. Facing such shortages, companies typically make committed costs variable: They relieve the bottleneck by spending more to increase the supply of resources to perform work. This is why many indirect costs increase over time.

Demands for indirect and support resources also can decline, either consciously through operational and strategic activity-based management, or inadvertently through competitive or economy-wide forces that lead to declines in sales. Should the demands for batch and product-sustaining resources decrease, few immediate spending reductions will be noticed. Even for many unit-level resources, such as machines and direct labor, reduced demands for work does not immediately lead to spending decreases. People have been hired, space has been rented, computers, telephones, and furniture have been acquired. The expenses for these resources

Unused capacity in some of its low-yielding restaurants led Wendy's management to close 62 locations and sell 200 others to franchisees in 1998. The following year the company also closed all 7 of its unprofitable units in Britain. Some of the resources the company saved showed up in a big boost in Wendy's operating margins and a 20 percent increase in its multimillion dollar ad budget, as the firm refocused its attention on the core U.S. market. (Alan Schein/The Stock Market)

continue even though there is less work for them to perform. The reduced demand for organizational resources does *lower the cost of resources used* (by products, services, and customers), but this decrease is offset by an equivalent *increase in the cost of unused capacity*.

For committed costs to vary downward, after some unused capacity has been created, the organization must actively manage the unused capacity of these resources out of the system. This can be done in either of two ways: Increase the volume of business, or reduce the supply of unused resources. What makes a resource cost "variable" downward is not inherent in the nature of the resource; it is a function of management decisions—first to reduce the demands for the resource, and, second, to lower the spending on it.[5]

Organizations often have unused capacity but do nothing about it. They keep existing resources in place, even though the demands for the activities performed by the resources have diminished substantially. They also fail to find new activities that could be handled by the resources already in place. In this case, the organization receives no benefits from its decisions. The failure to capture benefits from operational or strategic decisions, however, is not due to costs being intrinsically "fixed." Rather, the failure occurs because managers are unwilling or unable to exploit the unused capacity they have created. The costs of these resources is only "fixed" if managers cannot or do not exploit the opportunities from the unused capacity they helped to create.

You can now see that making decisions, such as to reduce product variety, based solely upon resource usage (the ABC system) may be problematic if managers are not able or prepared to reduce spending to align resource supply with the lower levels of demand in the near future. For example, if an action causes the number of production runs to decrease by 10%, no economic benefit will be achieved unless the resources supplied to perform production runs, which are no longer needed, are

[5] Managers do not seem to have any problem recognizing that costs are "variable" in an upward direction. Examination of past history will usually reveal how organizational spending has increased to cope with increased variety and complexity of operations. It's the mechanism for costs to head in the downward direction that has eluded many economists, accountants, and managers.

eliminated or redeployed to higher revenue uses. Consequently, before making decisions based on an ABC model, managers should determine the resource supply implications of their decisions.

Marketing, Selling, and Distribution Expenses: Tracing Costs to Customers

So far in this chapter we have focused only on manufacturing costs and their assignment to products; but companies also incur substantial expenses outside their factories. Especially with the importance of customer satisfaction and market-oriented strategies, the costs of marketing, selling, and distribution expenses have been increasing rapidly in recent years. Many of these expenses do not relate to individual products or product lines, but rather are associated with individual customers, market segments, and distribution channels. For example, in a large mutual fund company, the cost of marketing products, such as 401k retirement programs, directly to companies is very different from that of reaching millions of retail customers. The size and revenue of accounts also differ substantially between corporate and individual retail customers. Companies need to understand the cost of selling to and serving their diverse customer base.

Take the case of two customers, Alpha and Beta, served by the Anders Wire Company. Both customers were approximately the same size, with sales revenue of about $320,000 per year. Anders Wire used a conventional cost accounting system in which marketing, selling, distribution, and administrative expenses were allocated to customers based on sales revenue. These expenses were approximately 35% of total sales. Thus, the income statements for the two customers were virtually identical:

	ALPHA	BETA
Sales	$320,000	$315,000
CGS	154,000	156,000
Gross margin	$166,000	$159,000
MSDA expenses* (@35% of sales)	112,000	110,250
Operating profit	$ 54,000	$ 48,750
Profit percentage	16.9%	15.5%

*MSDA is marketing, selling distribution, and administrative

Both customers were considered highly important and profitable for the company. Sten Drakenburg, the marketing controller for Anders believed, however, that the reported numbers did not represent the reality of the customer relationships. Sten knew that the account manager for Beta spent a huge amount of time on that account. The customer required a great deal of hand-holding and was continually inquiring whether Anders could modify products to meet its specific needs. Many technical resources, in addition to marketing resources, were required to service that account. Beta also tended to place many small orders for special products, required expedited delivery, and tended to pay slowly, which increased the demands on Anders's order processing, invoicing, and accounts receiving process. Alpha, on the other hand, ordered only a few products and in large quantities, placed its orders predictably and with long lead times, and required little sales and technical support. Drakenburg knew that Alpha was a much more profitable customer for Anders than the financial statements were currently reporting.

THE TECHNOLOGICAL EDGE

ERP and Strategic Activity-Based Management

Companies initially deployed enterprise resource planning (ERP) applications to improve their back-office and manufacturing operations. With these installations, they have generated and made available vast amounts of data on employees, customers, finances, products, inventory, and assets. But few companies have tapped into this information for decision makers, who continue to rely on management accountants to make sense of the raw data. That may change soon.

"We're at the point where the real return from ERP systems becomes the ability to translate raw data into useful information," says Jim Shepherd, an analyst with AMR Research. "Now, people believe they ought to be able to use data to actively support decisions, such as 'Do I buy 1,000 of these parts or 10,000? Do I buy from vendor A or from vendor B?' All day long, these decisions have to get made, and there is a strong body of thinking that ERP applications can and will support these fundamental business decisions."

American Century Investments, a mutual fund company, is testing PeopleSoft's business-intelligence application, called Performance Measurement. Bob Jackson, American Century's CFO, cays Performance Measurement can help determine such things as revenue and profitability per customer. "In the existing world, it would take us four to eight weeks to aggregate the right data and massage it through a bunch of spreadsheets," Jackson says. "In the new world, we could get that information automatically and instantaneously . . . within the application." That means American Century would be able to react to changing market conditions more quickly. Adds Jackson, "This is huge in terms of how we price a new piece of business and how effectively we make adjustments."

Source: "New Value in ERP—Companies Are Adding Business-Intelligence Tools to Their Enterprise Resource Planning Systems to Speed Access to Data and Improve Decision Making," *Information Week*, September 18, 1998.

Drakenburg launched an activity-based cost study of the Anders Company marketing, selling, distribution, and administrative costs. He formed a multifunctional project team that included representatives from the marketing, technical, and administrative departments. The team, like Laura Tunney at Cooper Pens, studied the resource spending in the various accounts, identified the activities performed by the resources, and selected activity cost drivers that could link each activity to individual customers (see Exhibit 5-9).

Notice that because he had excellent data available, Drakenburg could use several intensity drivers (actual freight and travel expenses). He also used transactional activity cost drivers (number of orders, number of mailings) and several duration drivers (estimated time and effort). Note, too, that Drakenburg defined a customer cost hierarchy that was similar to the manufacturing cost hierarchy. For example, some of the activities—handle customer orders, ship to customers—were order related, while others were customer sustaining—service customers, travel to customers, provide marketing and technical support.

After the project team members prepared information about the activity expenses and collected data on all the activity cost drivers, they could assign the marketing, selling, distribution, and administrative expenses directly to customers. The picture of relative profitabilities of Alpha and Beta shifted dramatically, as shown here:

ACTIVITY-BASED COSTING CUSTOMER PROFITABILITY ANALYSIS	ALPHA	BETA
Sales	$320,000	$315,000
CGS	154,000	156,000
Gross margin	$166,000	$159,000
Marketing & technical support	7,000	54,000
Travel to customers	1,200	7,200
Distribute sales catalog	100	100
Service customers	4,000	42,000
Handle customer orders	500	18,000
Warehouse inventory	800	8,800
Ship to customers	12,600	42,000
Total activity expenses	16,200	172,100
Operating profit	$149,800	$(13,100)
Profit percentage	46.8%	(4.2%)

EXHIBIT 5-9

Anders Wire Company Activity Dictionary and Activity Cost Drivers

ACTIVITY	ACTIVITY DESCRIPTION	ACTIVITY COST DRIVER
Provide marketing and technical support	Salaries and benefits of marketing managers and technical support personnel, depreciation and maintenance on facilities and equipment used by them, power, telephone charges, and supplies	Estimated proportion of time spent on each customer
Travel to customers	Travel and entertainment expenditures	Actual expenditures
Distribute sales catalog	Costs of developing, printing, and mailing sales catalog to current and potential customers	Number of mailings
Service customers	Salaries and benefits of customer service representatives and costs of equipment and supplies used by them	Estimated proportion of time spent on each customer
Handle customer orders	Salaries and benefits of administrative staff responsible for contacting customers before receiving and after filling orders, coordinating production to schedule deliveries, invoicing, and collection	Number of orders*
Warehouse inventory for customers	Costs of storing finished goods inventory in the warehouse awaiting shipment to customers	Quantity of inventory and space required by customer
Ship to customers	Costs of shipping finished goods to customers. Some customers required immediate, overnight delivery; others could be serviced using low-cost common carriers.	Actual shipping records

*Weighted index used to distinguish between low cost-to-serve customers who had EDI (electronic data interchange) connections to the company versus high cost-to-serve customers who required manual transactions, and had complex delivery and payment terms.

As Drakenburg suspected, Alpha Company was an incredibly profitable customer. Its ordering and support activities placed few demands on the Anders Wire marketing, selling, distribution, and administrative resources, so that almost all its gross margin dropped to the operating margin bottom line. Beta Company, in contrast, was now seen to be the most unprofitable customer that Anders had. While Drakenburg and other managers at Anders knew intuitively that Alpha was a more profitable customer than Beta, none had any idea of the magnitude of the difference. This pattern has occurred in the ABC customer profitability studies of many companies. The largest customers are either the company's most profitable or its most unprofitable. They are rarely in the middle.

Managing Customer Profitability

A customer-based, activity-based profitability analysis, such as that performed at Anders Wire, gives managers the ability to view all its customers through the lens of a 2×2 diagram (see Exhibit 5-10). The vertical axis shows the net margin earned from sales to the customer. The net margin equals net price, after all sales discounts and allowances, less manufacturing cost (as measured by an ABC product costing model, of course). The horizontal axis shows the cost of serving the customer, including order-related costs plus the specific customer-sustaining marketing, technical, selling, and administrative expenses associated with serving each individual customer, as measured by an ABC customer costing model of these expenses.

This diagram shows that companies can enjoy profitable customers in different ways. Some customers may be highly price-sensitive, demanding low prices and heavy discounting, so net margins are low. But these companies work with their suppliers so that the cost of serving them is also low (because they place large orders, for standard products, with predictable delivery schedules, and use EDI technology). Therefore, they can be profitable customers even with heavy discounts. Customers who are high cost-to-serve (because of small orders, heavy technical and sales

EXHIBIT 5-10

Measuring and Managing Customer Profitability

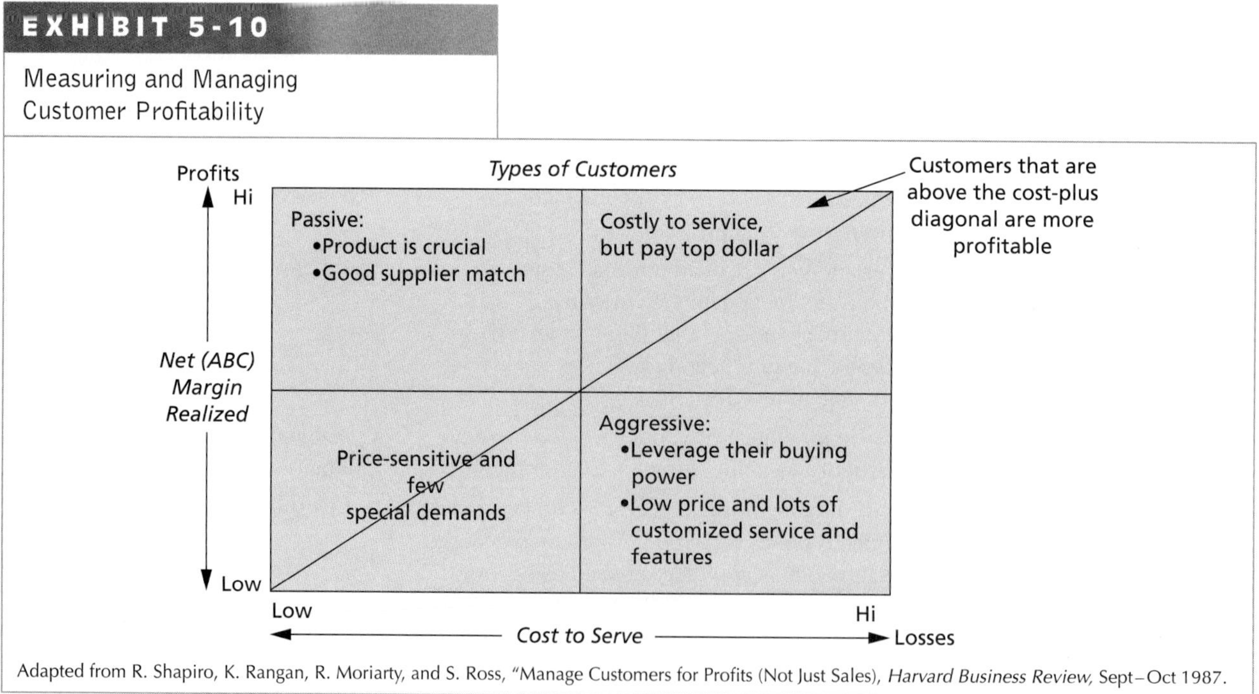

Adapted from R. Shapiro, K. Rangan, R. Moriarty, and S. Ross, "Manage Customers for Profits (Not Just Sales), *Harvard Business Review*, Sept–Oct 1987.

support, expensive delivery requirements, and manual processing of orders) also can be profitable (see the upper right corner of Exhibit 5-10), if the net margins earned on sales to these customers more than compensate for the cost of all the resources deployed for them.

Occasionally, a company may be fortunate to have a customer like Alpha Corporation in the upper-left quadrant of Exhibit 5-10: high margins and low cost-to-serve. These customers should be cherished and protected. Because they could be vulnerable to competitive inroads, managers should be prepared to offer modest discounts, incentives, or special services to retain the loyalty of these "hidden profit" customers if a competitor threatens.

The most challenging customers are found in the lower-right corner: low margins and high cost-to-serve. Such customers are like Beta, the highly unprofitable customer of Anders Wire. Often, the high cost of serving such customers is caused by their unpredictable order pattern, small order quantities for customized products, nonstandard logistics and delivery requirements, and large demands on technical and sales personnel. The company can share this information with the customer, indicate the costs associated with such actions, and encourage the customer to work with the company in a less costly manner. For example, customer costs can be lowered by reducing the number of activities demanded by them and by using technology (EDI) to lower order handling, invoicing, and inventory expenses. The company also can change its pricing practices with such customers. Discounting practices, which formerly were driven by estimated annual volume, could be changed based on individual order size and method of delivery. Price surcharges could be imposed when designing and producing special variants for a customer's particular needs. High shipping costs could be reduced by imposing minimum order sizes or recovered by having the customer pay for freight or special delivery options. All these actions can move the customer in a westerly, more profitable direction on Exhibit 5-10. In all these circumstances, the ABC customer profitability analysis has been used for strategic activity-based management. Managers, with a far more accurate and actionable picture of their customers' profitability, take targeted profit-enhancing actions with individual customers.

Service Companies

We have now articulated the development of activity-based costing and activity-based management in manufacturing settings. Although ABC had its origins in manufacturing companies, many service organizations today are obtaining great benefits from this approach as well. In practice, the actual construction of an ABC model is virtually identical for both types of companies. This should not be surprising, since even in manufacturing companies, the ABC system focuses on the "service" component of companies, not on the direct materials and direct labor costs of manufacturing operations. ABC addresses the support resources that serve the manufacturing process—purchasing, scheduling, inspecting, designing, supporting products and processes, and handling customers and their orders.

Service companies in general are ideal candidates for activity-based costing, even more than manufacturing companies. First, virtually all their costs are indirect and appear to be fixed. Manufacturing companies could at least trace important components of costs, such as direct materials and direct labor, to individual products. Service companies have few or no direct materials and many of their personnel provide indirect, not direct, support to products and customers.[6] Consequently, service companies do not have direct product or customer costs to serve as convenient allocation bases.

[6] Or the direct contact that a service employee has with a customer is so brief that detailed measurement of the time elapsed is not considered to be cost-effective.

IN PRACTICE

ABC and the Post Office

The United States Postal Service (USPS), working with a consulting firm, conducted an activity-based cost study of its key revenue collection processes and market strategy for a national credit card and debit card program. The team identified unit, batch, and product-sustaining activities; resources for each of the activities; and the transaction volumes for each activity. Unit activity was the acceptance and processing of a payment by item. Batch activities involved closeout at the end of the day, consolidation, and supervisory review. Product activities included maintenance charges for bank accounts and deposit reconciliation, and terminal maintenance and training for credit and debit cards.

The analysis led to quantifying the benefits and costs from introducing credit and debit cards, and identified significant opportunities for process improvements. As the report summarized: "Credit and debit card processing costs for retail window transactions become cost effective once total card revenue exceeds 3%–4% of total revenues from retail transactions. As card volume continues to displace cash and check transactions, card costs become even more advantageous." Based on the study and benefits from enhanced customer satisfaction, the USPS Board of Governors approved the rollout of the new payment mechanism.

Source: T. Carter, A. Sedaghat, and R. Williams, "How ABC Changed the Post Office," *Management Accounting,* February 1998, pp. 28–36.

The large component of apparently fixed costs in service organizations arises because, unlike manufacturing companies, they have virtually no material costs—the prime source of short-term variable costs. Service companies must supply virtually all their resources in advance to provide the capacity to perform work for customers during each period. Fluctuations during the period in the demand by individual products and customers for the activities performed by these resources do not influence short-term spending to supply the resources.

Consequently, the variable cost (conventionally defined as the increase in spending resulting from an incremental transaction or customer) for many service industries is essentially zero. For example, a transaction at a bank's automatic teller machine requires an additional consumption of a small piece of paper to print the receipt, but no additional outlay. For a bank to add an additional customer may require a monthly statement to be mailed, involving the cost of the paper, an envelope, and a stamp, but little more. Carrying an extra passenger on an airplane requires an extra can of soda pop, two bags of peanuts (for most coach-class U.S. flights these days), and a minor increase in fuel consumption, but nothing else. For a telecommunications company, handling one more phone call from a customer, or one more data transfer, involves no incremental spending. Therefore, if service companies were to make decisions about products and customers based on short-term variable costs, they would provide a full range of all products and services to all customers at prices that could range down to near zero. But then, of course, the companies would get limited to no recovery of the costs of all the committed resources they supplied that enabled the service to be delivered to the customer.

CUSTOMER COSTS IN SERVICE COMPANIES

Service companies must focus, even more than manufacturing companies, on customer economics. Consider a manufacturing company producing a standard product, or widget. Manufacturers can calculate the cost of producing the widget without regard to how their customers use it; thus the manufacturing costs are "customer independent." Only the costs of marketing, selling, order handling, delivery, and service of the widget might be customer specific. For service companies, in contrast, customer behavior determines the basic operating costs of products.

Consider a standard product such as a checking account. It is relatively straight forward, using ABC methods, to calculate all costs associated with such a checking account. The revenues, including interest earned on monthly balances and fees charged to customers for services, also are easy to attribute to this product. The analysis will reveal whether such a product is, on average, profitable or unprofitable; but such an average look at the product will hide the enormous variation in profitability of this product across customers. One customer may maintain a high cash balance in his checking account and make very few deposits or withdrawals. A second customer may manage her checking account balance very closely, keeping only the minimum amount on hand, and use her account heavily by making many withdrawals and deposits.

As another example, customers of a telecommunications company can order a basic service unit in several different ways—through a phone call, a letter, or a visit to a local retail outlet. The customer may order two phone lines at once or just one; engineers may have to appear to install the new line, or perhaps just make a change in the local switching center. The customer may make only one request or several and can pay either by direct debit, by a mailed check, or in person. The cost of each option is quite different. Therefore, measuring revenues and costs at the customer level provides the company with far more relevant and useful information than at the product level.

In summary, service companies need to identify the differential profitability of individual customers, even those using standard products. The variation in demand for organizational resources is much more customer-driven in service organizations than in manufacturing organizations. A service company can determine and control the efficiency of its internal activities, but customers determine the quantity of demands for these operating activities.

Further, a customer may have more than a single relationship with a service company. In addition to the basic phone line, a telecommunications customer may have a high-speed data line, a long-distance account, a service contract, and equipment rentals. Therefore, before taking drastic action with a customer who has an unprofitable basic phone line, the company's managers should understand all the relationships it has with the customer and act based on total relationship profitability, not just the profitability of a single product.

ABC MODEL FOR A SERVICE COMPANY

The principles for developing an activity-based cost system for a service company are identical to those followed in manufacturing companies. Construct the activity dictionary, assign resource expenses to activities, determine activity cost drivers, calculate activity cost driver rates, and drive activity expenses down to products and customers. Exhibit 5-11 shows a sample of activities and the associated activity cost drivers used in an ABC study of a British retail bank.[7]

Once the ABC model on product and customer profitability has been obtained, service company managers can contemplate the same set of operational and strategic activity-based management actions as their counterparts in manufacturing companies. Companies in financial services (banks, insurance companies, money managers), transportation (airlines, trucking, railroads), telecommunications, wholesale and retail,

[7] S. Datar and R. S. Kaplan, "The Co-operative Bank," HBS Case 9-195-196.

EXHIBIT 5-11

Bank Activities and Activity Cost Drivers

ACTIVITY	ACTIVITY COST DRIVER
Provide ATM service	number of ATM transactions
Clear debit items	number of debits processed
Branch operations for debit items	number of branch counter debits
Issue personal checkbook	number of books issued
Clear credit items	number of credits processed
Lending control and security	number of interventions
Handle customer inquiries	minutes of telephone call time
Marketing and sales activity	number of accounts opened
Computer processing	number of computer transactions
Statements and postage	number of statements issued
Advise on investments and insurance	minutes (hours) of advice provided
Process VISA transactions	number of VISA transactions
Issue VISA statements	number of VISA statements issued
Open/close accounts	number of accounts opened/closed
Administer mortgages	number of mortgages maintained

and health care and even many government agencies are now using activity-based cost analysis to understand and manage the economics of their operations.

Implementation Issues

Although activity-based costing has provided the managers in many companies with valuable information about the cost of their activities, processes, products, services, and customers, not all ABC projects have produced successful outcomes. Companies have experienced difficulties and frustrations in building and using activity-based cost and profitability models. We can identify several of the more common pitfalls that have occurred and ways to avoid them.[8]

1. *Lack of clear business purpose*

   Often, the ABC project is initiated out of the finance or accounting group and is touted as "a more accurate cost system." The project team gets resources for the project, builds an initial ABC model, and then becomes disappointed and disillusioned when no one else looks at or acts upon the new ABC cost and profitability information.

   To avoid this syndrome, all ABC projects should be launched with a specific business purpose in mind. The purpose could be to redesign or improve processes, to influence product design decisions, to rationalize the product mix, or to better manage customer relationships. By defining the business purpose in

[8] The pitfalls described were excerpted from R. Steven Player and David Keys (eds.), *Activity-Based Management: Arthur Andersen's Lessons from the ABM Battlefield* (Wiley Cost Management Series). See also their series of three articles, "Lessons from the ABM Battlefield," *Journal of Cost Management,* Spring 1995, pp. 26–38; Summer 1995, pp. 20–35; and Fall 1995, pp. 31–41.

IN PRACTICE

Barriers to Implementing ABC Systems

Inkslinger, Inc. (a disguised name for a privately held company) contemplated the development of an activity-based costing system to assign indirect labor and overhead costs to the five product line units at its Kentucky plant. The study was triggered by a major capital expansion for a new product line at the plant. The existing cost system used plant-wide overhead rates, so that the cost of the additional equipment and operating expenses raised the costs of the products produced for all five product lines, not just for the unit that installed the new production line. Product managers were beginning to move their production from the Kentucky plant to other facilities, to avoid the higher charges.

Despite the benefits from more accurate cost attribution, Inkslinger decided to delay the development of a more accurate activity-based costing system. The new system was believed to disturb the status quo. It would require organizational members to create an agreed-upon ABC methodology and a standardized activity dictionary across different plants. Also, it would change the measure of product line profitability and affect executives' compensation.

ABC would also affect employee behavior, overthrowing some decision models that had worked for years. Senior managers believed it would be difficult for individuals to cast aside a way of thinking that has kept them employed for many years. They believed it would be even more difficult to accept the new system if individuals were poorly motivated to change because they thought that the cause of the immediate problem—the low sales volume on the new product line—might soon correct itself. Some managers believed that the company might decide to eliminate the new product line because it would be unprofitable, once the cross subsidies created by the existing cost system were eliminated. These managers were concerned that the cost of the remaining products would increase, as the overhead previously allocated to the product line would be applied to the remaining product lines. This, perhaps, could lead to eventual closure of the entire Kentucky plant.

Others were unenthusiastic about ABC because they thought the company needed a simpler cost model, one that was directionally accurate, not perfect, but pointing managers in the right direction for decision making. For these individuals, activity-based costing was perceived as swatting a gnat with a sledgehammer.

Inkslinger decided that implementing ABC was a long-term project. It wanted the new product line to become established before assigning it a full share of activity-based costs. Once the product matures, Inkslinger plans to move in incremental steps toward an ABC system, allowing for a more gradual transition to the new paradigm.

Source: R. J. Palmer and M. Vied, "Could ABC Threaten the Survival of Your Company," *Management Accounting,* November 1998, pp. 33–36.

advance, the team will identify the line manager or department whose behavior and decisions are expected to change as a consequence of the information. The decision maker could be the manufacturing or operations manager (for process improvement), the engineering manager (for product design decisions), the sales organization (for managing customer relationships), or the marketing department (for decisions about pricing and product mix).

It is also important not to oversell what the ABC system is capable of performing. Some project teams, carried away by their enthusiasm, promise that ABC will solve all the company's problems, at least its costing and financial problems. ABC is a strategic costing system; it cannot perform the role of operational control, of providing frequent feedback on process and departmental efficiencies and improvements. Numerous ABC projects were aborted when operating

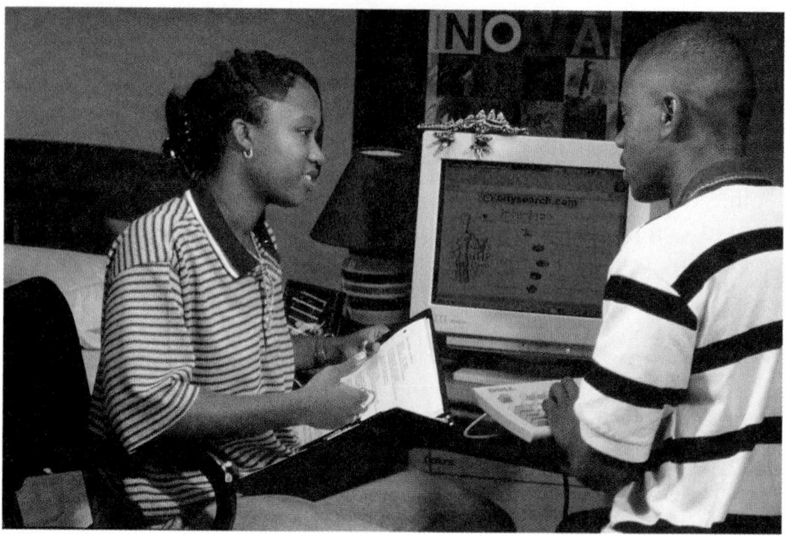

▶ *Several years ago when America Online added one-price Internet access to its payment options, the number of AOL users soared. Even though no two AOL subscribers used the same features of the service or stayed on line for the same length of time, the sheer number of customers, aided by a rapidly rising market for Internet access, allowed the company to make its simple pricing system profitable. (Bob Daemmrich/Stock, Boston)*

managers did not receive frequent feedback on costs and expenses under their responsibility from the new system. For this, companies need a feedback system specifically designed for the purpose.[9] Some projects foundered as the team attempted to have the initial ABC model serve external and regulatory requirements as well. These implementing teams failed to realize that their existing system already worked fine for these purposes and need not be replaced with the ABC system for external audiences.

The primary purpose of the model will also influence the design of the initial model. A model intended primarily for process improvement and process redesign (i.e., operational activity-based management) can have a large number of activities but does not have to be concerned with the availability of information about activity cost drivers. Conversely, for strategic activity-based management (pricing, customer relationships, product mix), the ABC model should be simpler, using fewer than 50 activities, and with data readily available for all the important activity cost drivers. A model intended for product designers and engineers should use activity cost drivers that would be meaningful to this community. Drivers such as number of parts placements, number of unique parts, and number of unique vendors are understandable and actionable to product designers.

2 *Lack of senior management commitment*

A pitfall related to the first problem arises when the finance group undertakes the project without gaining senior management support and buy-in. The rest of the organization then views the project as one done by and for finance people, and, not surprisingly, no one outside the finance organization pays attention to it. As a result, because the finance group is not empowered to make decisions about processes, product designs, product mix, pricing and customer relationship, no actions follow.

The most successful ABC projects occur when a clear business purpose exists for building the ABC model, *and* this purpose is led or at least understood and fully supported by senior line managers in the organization. A steering committee of senior managers from various functional groups and business units can institu-

[9] See R. S. Kaplan, "One Cost System Isn't Enough," *Harvard Business Review,* January–February 1988.

tionalize this support, meeting monthly to review project progress, make suggestions on how to enhance the model, and prepare for the decisions that will be made once the model has been completed.

Even when the ABC project is initiated from the finance group, a multifunctional project team should be formed. The team should include, in addition to a management accountant or other finance group representative, members from operations, marketing/sales, engineering, and systems. In this way, the expertise from diverse groups can be incorporated into the model design and each team member can build support for the project within his or her department and group.

3 *Delegating the project to consultants*
Some projects have failed when they were outsourced to an external consulting company. Consultants may have considerable experience with ABC but limited familiarity with a company's operations and business problems. Nor can they build management consensus and support within the organization to make decisions with the ABC information, or to maintain and update the model after they leave. Even worse, some companies think they can get an ABC system by buying an ABC software package. The software provides a template to enter, process, and report information, but it cannot provide the thinking required to build a cost-effective ABC model.

ABC consultants and ABC software can play a valuable role for many companies, but they are not a substitute for overcoming our first two pitfalls. Successful ABC projects require top management leadership and sponsorship and a dedicated, multifunctional internal project team. These functions cannot be bypassed just because external consultants and prepackaged software have also been purchased.

4 *Poor ABC model design*
Sometimes, even with strong management support and sponsorship, the project team gets lost in the details and develops an ABC model that is both too complicated to build and maintain, and too complex for managers to understand and act upon. Or the model uses arbitrary allocations—frequently percentages, not quantitative activity cost drivers—to map costs from activities to products and customers. The arbitrary allocations create distortions in the model and destroy its credibility among line managers. Often, the final model requires other organizational functions to provide new data and information on a regular basis, that increases their workload, without corresponding benefits to them.[10] Under the burden of poor design, the ABC system soon collapses under its own weight and neglect.

We have stressed in this chapter that ABC model design should be like any design or engineering project, with continual appropriate trade-offs to enable the essential function of the system to be accomplished at minimal additional cost. If the ABC project team keeps end users clearly in mind and gets good advice from its senior management steering committee, it should make good cost-effective design decisions along the way. These decisions can help avoid the problem of having an overcomplex system or misidentified causal relationships between cost objects (products and customers), activities, and resources.

5 *Individual and organizational resistance to change*
Finally, it turns out that not all managers welcome technically superior solutions. Individuals often resist new ideas and change and organizations have great

[10] D. D. Pattison and C. G. Arendt, "Activity-Based Costing: It Doesn't Work All the Time," *Management Accounting,* April 1994, pp. 55–61.

inertia. The resistance to a new ABC model may not be overt. Managers can politely sit through an ABC presentation about product and customer profitability but continue to behave just as they have in the past. Or they will ask the project team to reestimate the model, using a more recent period or at another company site. Sometimes, however, the resistance is more overt. Managers may exclaim the company has been successful in the past with its existing cost system; why does it need a new approach? Or they may accuse the finance people (if it has been a finance-led project; see pitfall 2) of not understanding the complexity of the business or wanting to run the company.

Individual and organizational resistance arises because people feel threatened by the suggestion that their work could be improved.[11] We might not think that a cost model could generate such resistance, but in fact, as we discussed earlier in the chapter, the ABC model could reveal

- unprofitable products,
- unprofitable customers,
- inefficient activities and processes, and
- substantial unused capacity.

Managers responsible for these problems could be embarrassed and threatened by the revelation of apparent bad management "on their watch." Rather than accept the validity of the ABC model and attempt to rectify the problems (which likely occurred because of inadequacies in the previous cost system, not their own negligence or ineptitude), they may deny the validity of the new approach and question the motives of the people attempting to lead the change. Such defensive behavior will inhibit any effective action.

Later in the book we will discuss the behavioral issues that arise when implementing new cost, performance measurement, and management control systems. Resistance is not unique to ABC. It can arise from the introduction of any new measurement or management system, or, indeed, any management change initiative. But as a relatively new costing innovation, activity-based cost systems are prime candidates for triggering individuals' and organizations' negative responses to change initiatives. Dealing with such responses requires skills in recognizing and overcoming defensive behavior, skills that fledgling management accountants may not have been taught in their normal academic studies, nor in their early job assignments.

SUMMARY

In this chapter, we have introduced activity-based cost systems for both manufacturing and service companies. We have shown how ABC systems calculate costs more accurately than traditional cost systems, which rely only on unit-level drivers. ABC systems drive the cost of indirect and support resources—manufacturing resources in factories and marketing, selling, distribution, and administrative resources—to the activities they perform, and then to the cost objects (products, services, and customers) that generate the demand for the activities. In estimating an ABC model, management accountants should estimate activity cost driver rates using the practical capacity of the resources supplied. They should also make appropriate trade-offs in the design of the model, balancing the cost of measurement for more complex models, with the benefits from improved accuracy.

Managers use the information on activity costs to improve organizational profitability. With operational activity-based management, they select high-return

[11] See C. Argyris and R. S. Kaplan, "Implementing New Knowledge: The Case of Activity-Based Costing," *Accounting Horizons,* September 1994, pp. 83–105.

projects for operational improvements. By driving activity costs down to cost objects, managers identify profitable and unprofitable products, services, and customers. They then employ strategic activity-based management, making decisions on pricing, product mix, product design, customer and supplier relationships, and technology that transforms unprofitable products and customers into profitable ones.

Despite the apparent attraction of increased accuracy and managerial relevance from activity-based cost management, individual and organizational resistance can arise to block the effective use of these systems. Management accountants must be sensitive to the conditions that cause such resistance to arise and devise good countermeaures to overcome them.

BOOTH MOTORS: EPILOGUE

Jonathan Kellogg worked with his controller to develop an activity-based cost model of his automobile dealership. Activities for three of the product lines are as follows:

New Vehicle Department	Finance & Insurance (F&I)	Service
Commissions	Commissions	Perform repairs
Interest expense	Sell F&I products	Diagnose problems
Sell new vehicles	Manage lease deals	Generate repair orders
Advertise new vehicles	Manage F&I dept.	Counter, idle time
Store new vehicles	Administer office	Maintain service area
Prepare new vehicles	Prepare documents	Store vehicles
Manage new vehicle deals	Manage cash and finance deals	Process service documents
Perform billing	Process warranty claims	

Activity cost drivers included:

number days on lot	number payables processed
number cash deals	number receipts
number new vehicles sold	number invoices received
number claims processed	weighted CPU time
lot square footage	building square footage
number retail leases	number warranties processed

The product line ABC analysis showed that the Finance & Insurance product line was nearly twice as costly as previously thought and the Service product line was 25% more expensive. Even with the higher expenses attributed to the Finance & Insurance business, however, the ABC analysis showed that the profits from financing and insuring new and used cars accounted for nearly 50% of total dealer profitability. This indicated that the margins from new and used vehicle sales without any financing and insurance tie-ins were only marginally profitable at best.

The most interesting aspect of the analysis occurred when Kellogg extended the ABC analysis down to individual car line vehicles within the new vehicle product line. Only one of the car lines was profitable; for the remaining lines, financing and space costs exceeded the net margin on sales. The profitable car line had the lowest average days on lot. Some of the seemingly most popular car lines, the Taurus and Escort, were the most unprofitable. Apparently, competitive pressure had caused margins on these vehicles to fall below dealer operating expenses for them. While the truck line in aggregate was quite profitable, only two of the eight truck lines (Explorer and Windstar) generated all the profits. In fact the profits from these two lines greatly exceeded the profits from the total truck line, since the other six truck lines lost substantial money.

Kellogg could now see many opportunities for improving his car and truck purchasing and inventory policies. He would have better information when negotiating with customers, including being willing to grant price concessions if customers were financing and insuring their cars through the dealership. He could also assess the lifetime profitability of a customer by linking the margins from new car sales with profits earned from finance and insurance, service work, and parts sales.

KEY TERMS

Activity-based cost (ABC) management systems, 164
Activity-based management (ABM), 171
Activity cost driver rate, 168
Activity cost drivers, 167
Bill of activities, 171
Cost of unused capacity, 174
Duration drivers, 173
Intensity drivers, 173
Operational activity-based management, 167
Practical capacity, 174
Production departments, 162
Service departments, 162
Transaction drivers, 172

SUMMARY PROBLEM

Scott Johnson, controller of Derek Manufacturing, a local machining shop with several numerically controlled machine tools, was contemplating the pricing for a new order that had just arrived. The customer was asking Derek to fabricate 100 units of a complex product that the company had never built before. Derek's engineers would have to spend time developing the process routines to machine the components required for the product. Johnson wondered whether the normal profit percentage of 35% over manufacturing costs would really be adequate for this order.

He knew that materials would cost $12.40 per unit. He estimated that the product would require 0.6 labor hours and 0.8 machine hours per unit once the product had been released into production. The company's direct labor rate was $20 per hour. With Derek's existing, traditional cost system, overhead was applied using both direct labor (at 200% of direct labor dollars) and machine hours (at $70 per hour).

Johnson could easily calculate the estimated cost per unit for the new order:

Materials	$ 12.40
Direct labor: 0.6 × $20	12.00
Direct labor overhead: 200% of $12.00	24.00
Machine hour overhead: 0.8 × $70	56.00
Total costs per unit	$104.40

The total cost for the 100 units would therefore be $10,400 to which Johnson would normally add a 35% markup ($3,640) for a total bid price of $14,094. Johnson was concerned, however, that this bid would not pay for all the engineering time and administrative expenses that would be required for this order.

Fortunately, several months ago, a summer intern from the local college performed a simple activity-based costing study of the company as part of a work-study project. Johnson went into his files, retrieved the study, and saw that the intern had developed the following activity dictionary and estimated activity cost driver rates for each activity.

Activity	Activity Cost Driver Rate
Direct labor processing	$ 50/labor hour
Machine processing	60/machine hour
Purchase and receive components	150/purchase order
Schedule production orders; perform first-item inspection	200/production run
Set up machines	80/setup hour
Process customer orders	100/customer order
Perform engineering design and support	75/engineering hour

Johnson estimated the activity cost driver quantities for some of the activities that the new order would require:

Activity Cost Driver	Quantity (for 100 units)
Number of purchase orders	10
Number of production runs*	6
Average setup time per production run	3 hours
Number of customer orders	1
Engineering design and process time	20 hours

*A separate production run would be required to machine six of the components before assembly into the final product.

REQUIRED

Calculate the activity-based product costs for the new order.

SOLUTION

Materials	$12.40 × 100	$ 1,240
Direct labor	0.6 × 50 × 100	3,000
Machining	0.8 × 60 × 100	4,800
Unit-level expenses		**$ 9,040**
Acquire materials	10 × 150	$ 1,500
Handle production runs	6 × 200	1,200
Set up machines	6 × 3 × 80	1,440
Process customer order	1 × 100	100
Batch-level expenses		**$ 4,240**
Engineering support	20 × 75	$ 1,500
Product-sustaining expenses		**$ 1,500**
Total product expenses		**$14,780**

Johnson could now see that even with a 35% markup, his bid based on conventional costs would not cover the costs of all the resources Derek would be committing to the order. The complex, low-volume product demanded a disproportionate amount of the company's resources to perform batch and product-sustaining activities. For example, this product required six separate production runs to process purchased components. In general, low-volume products, with many specialty components, place high demands on an organization's support resources. The higher prices often charged for such specialized components still may not cover the costs of all the resources used in their design, purchase, fabrication, and delivery.

ASSIGNMENT MATERIALS

QUESTIONS

5-1 What is the difference between *production departments* and *service departments*? (LO 1)

5-2 What are the two stages of cost allocations in conventional product costing systems? (LO 1)

5-3 Why are conventional two-stage cost allocation systems likely to systematically distort product costs? (LO 1, 2)

5-4 What are two factors that contribute to cost distortions resulting from the use of conventional, two-stage cost allocation systems? (LO 1, 2)

5-5 What fundamental assumption implicit in conventional two-stage cost allocation systems is rejected in activity-based costing systems? (LO 1, 2)

5-6 What do the terms *activity cost driver* and *activity cost driver rates* mean? (LO 3)

5-7 What major steps must be performed to determine the activity cost driver rates? (LO 3, 4)

5-8 What are some special considerations in the design of cost accounting systems for service organizations? (LO 9)

5-9 When would you prefer to use the number of setups instead of the number of setup hours as the cost driver measure for the setup activity? (LO 4)

5-10 How do activity-based costing systems avoid distortions in tracing batch-related costs to products? (LO 3, 4)

5-11 Why do conventional product costing systems often exclude selling and distribution costs? (LO 1, 7)

5-12 What recent changes have made it more important to have nonmanufacturing costs assigned to products, product lines, or market segments? (LO 5, 7, 8)

5-13 Why are conventional product costing systems more likely to distort product costs in highly automated plants? How do activity-based costing systems deal with such a situation? (LO 2)

5-14 "Conventional product costing systems are likely to overcost high-volume products." Do you agree with this statement? Explain. (LO 1, 2, 3)

5-15 How are cost drivers selected in activity-based costing systems? (LO 4)

5-16 In activity-based costing, what are the trade-offs made in choosing among transaction, duration, and intensity activity cost drivers? (LO 4)

5-17 Why is practical capacity recommended in calculating activity cost driver rates? (LO 6)

5-18 Why might an organization not experience financial improvement even after using activity-based costing to identify and take action on promising opportunities for process improvements and cost reductions? (LO 6)

5-19 "Activity-based costing systems yield more accurate product costs than conventional systems because they use more cost drivers to assign support costs to products." Do you agree with this statement? Explain. (LO 3, 4)

EXERCISES

LO 4 **5-20** ***Activity cost drivers*** Identify a cost driver for each of the following activities:

(a) Machine maintenance
(b) Machine setup
(c) Utilities
(d) Quality control
(e) Material ordering
(f) Production scheduling
(g) Factory depreciation
(h) Warehouse expense
(i) Production supervision
(j) Payroll accounting
(k) Custodial service
(l) General and administration

LO 1, 2, 5 **5-21** ***Product costing systems and product profitability*** Potter Corporation has gained considerable market share in recent years for its specialty, low-volume, complex line of products, but the gain has been offset by a loss in market share for its high-volume simple line of products. This has resulted in a net decline in its overall profitability. Advise management about specific changes that may be required in its cost accounting system, and explain why the existing system may be inadequate.

LO 3 **5-22** ***Revising an activity-based costing system*** Refer to the Cooper Pen example described in the chapter. Suppose that some unrecorded resource expenses were just discovered at Cooper Pen. Inspection people costing $15,000 per quarter perform quality inspections at the start of each new production run to ensure that the new color being run meets specifications. How should the model be updated to reflect this newly discovered cost?

LO 3, 5, 9 **5-23** ***Activity-based costs*** Friendly Bank is developing an activity-based cost system for its teller department. A task force has identified five different activities: (1) process deposits, (2) process withdrawals, (3) answer customer inquiries, (4) sell negotiable instruments, and (5) balance drawers. By tracing the costs of operating the teller department to these five activities, the task force has compiled the following information regarding support costs and activities for one of its suburban branches.

SUPPORT ACTIVITY	ESTIMATED COST	ACTIVITY COST DRIVER	MONTHLY LEVEL
Process deposits	$29,630	Number of deposits processed	33,250
Process withdrawals	26,080	Number of withdrawals processed	22,750
Answer inquiries	24,860	Number of customer inquiries	45,000
Sell negotiable instruments	4,860	Number of negotiable instruments sold	1,100
Balance drawers	4,290	Number of drawers balanced	1,300
	$89,720		

REQUIRED

(a) Compute the activity cost driver rates for each of the support activities.

(b) The task force has developed the following bill of activities for a typical checking account marketed to retired persons.

SUPPORT ACTIVITY	AVERAGE MONTHLY VOLUME
Process deposits	2.3
Process withdrawals	6.0
Answer customer inquiries	2.1
Sell negotiable instruments	0.5

Estimate the total monthly support costs for this checking account product.

5-24 ***Activity-based costs*** VG Company has identified the following cost pools and cost drivers: LO 3, 5

COST POOLS	ACTIVITY COSTS	COST DRIVERS
Machine setup	$360,000	6,000 setup hours
Materials handling	100,000	50,000 pounds of material
Electric power	40,000	80,000 kilowatt hours

The following information pertains to the production of V203 and G179:

ITEM	V203	G179
Number of units produced	5,000	15,000
Direct materials cost	$25,000	$33,000
Direct labor cost	$14,000	$16,000
Number of setup hours	120	150
Pounds of material used	5,000	10,000
Kilowatt hours	2,000	3,000

Determine the unit cost for each of the two products using activity-based costing.

5-25 ***Activity cost driver rates*** Creathon Company's plant in Columbus, Ohio, manufactures two products: BR12 and BR15. Product BR15 has a more complex design and requires more setup time than BR12. LO 4

Setups for BR12 require two hours on average; setups for BR15 require three hours. Creathon's setup department employs 10 workers whose average wage is $10 per hour; fringe benefits cost 38% of the wages. Other costs for setup activities amount to $25 per setup. Creathon plans to use all 10 workers for 40 hours each for the first three weeks of the winter quarter. The amount of work for these three weeks is as follows:

WEEK	NUMBER OF SETUPS FOR PRODUCT BR12	NUMBER OF SETUPS FOR PRODUCT BR15
1	85	75
2	90	70
3	80	80

REQUIRED

(a) Determine the actual setup activity cost driver rate based on (1) the number of setups and (2) the number of setup hours.

(b) Is either of the two activity cost driver rates or some other rate appropriate in this case? Why?

LO 6 **5-26** Carl's Cornerspot, a popular university eatery in a competitive market, has seating and staff capacity to serve about 600 lunch customers every day. For the past two months, demand has fallen from its previous near-capacity level. Concerned about his declining profit, Carl decided to take a closer look at his costs. He concluded that food was the primary cost that varied with meals served; the remaining costs of $1650 per month were committed in the short run. With demand averaging 550 lunches per day for the past two months, Carl thought it was reasonable to divide the $1650 committed fixed costs by the current average demand of 550 lunches to arrive at an estimate of $3 of support costs per meal served. Noting that his support costs per meal had now increased, he contemplated raising his meal prices slightly. Comment on Carl's choice of activity level for computing costs per meal, and on what will happen if Carl uses his approach if demand decreases further.

LO 8 **5-27** ***Customer profitability*** A credit card company has classified its customers into the following types for customer profitability analysis:

1. Applies for credit card in response to a low introductory interest rate; transfers balance to new account, but when the low introductory rate expires, the customer transfers the balance to an account with a different credit card company that has offered a low introductory rate.
2. Charges a large dollar volume of purchases; pays balance in full on time each month.
3. Carries a high balance; pays only the minimum required payments, but pays regularly with occasional late payments.
4. Carries a high balance; pays at least the minimum payments but does not pay in full, and always pays on time.
5. Carries a low balance; pays at least the minimum payments but does not pay in full, and always pays on time.
6. Does not use the charge account but does not close the account.

Given the following facts, which of the customer types above would you expect to be the most desirable or profitable, the next most profitable, etc., for the credit card company on a long-term basis? Explain your ranking.

- Merchants pay the credit card company a percentage of the dollar sales on each credit card transaction.
- Customers pay no interest on charges for purchases if the balance is paid in full on time each month.
- The credit card company charges a late fee if the customer's payment is late.
- The credit card company incurs costs to send statements to inactive customers.

5-28 Refer to the Inkslinger, Inc. situation described in the "In Practice" box on page 185. What barriers to implementing an activity-based costing system can you identify? How would you respond to the managers' comments? LO 10

PROBLEMS

5-29 ***Comparison of two costing systems*** Normal manufacturing support costs of McInnes Company for September 2000 are as follows: LO 1, 3

COST POOLS	NORMAL COSTS
Power	$ 40,000
Materials handling	90,000
Setups	80,000
Quality inspections	40,000
Total	$250,000

The present cost accounting system allocates support costs to final products based on machine hours. Estimated machine hours for September 2000 are 50,000. After losing several bids recently, Roy McInnes, the president, asked the controller to implement an activity-based costing system, because he was told that activity-based costing provides more accurate product cost estimates. The controller collected the following data:

ACTIVITIES	COST DRIVERS	AVAILABLE CAPACITY	COSTS
Electric power	Kilowatt hours	20,000 kwh	$40,000
Materials handling	Material moves	5,000 moves	90,000
Setup	Machine setups	1,000 setups	80,000
Quality inspection	Number of inspections	2,000 inspections	40,000

The company recently received a request for a bid to supply 1000 units of its product M5. The following estimates were prepared for the production of 1000 units of M5:

ITEM	AMOUNT
Direct material costs	$20,000
Direct labor cost	$18,000
Machine hours	1,800
Direct labor hours	2,000
Kilowatt hours of electricity	2,000
Number of material moves	40
Number of machine setups	5
Number of quality inspections	20

REQUIRED

(a) What is the estimated cost per unit of M5 under the present cost accounting system?

(b) What is the estimated cost per unit of M5 if activity-based costing is used?

LO 1, 3, 4 **5-30** ***Cost distortions*** Ferreira Company has established the following cost pools for 2000:

COST POOLS	COMMITTED COSTS	COST DRIVERS	LEVEL
Maintenance	$ 20,000	Machine hours	10,000
Materials handling	25,000	Number of moves	250
Machine setup	30,000	Setup hours	1,000
Inspection	25,000	Number of inspections	500
Total	$100,000		

The following information pertains to two representative jobs completed during January 2000:

ITEM	J101	J102
Direct materials cost	$10,000	$7,500
Direct labor cost	$ 8,000	$5,500
Number of units	2,000	1,500
Direct labor hours	640	400
Machine hours	700	650
Number of material moves	40	15
Number of setup hours	80	40
Number of inspections	35	15

REQUIRED

(a) Determine the unit cost of each job using machine hours to allocate all support costs.

(b) Determine the unit cost of each job using activity-based costing.

(c) Which of the two methods produces more accurate estimates of job costs? Explain

LO 1, 3 **5-31** ***Cost distortions*** Ehsan Electronics Company manufactures two products, X21 and Y37, at its manufacturing plant in Duluth, Minnesota. For many years the company has used a simple plant-wide manufacturing support cost rate based on direct labor hours. A new plant accountant suggested that the company may be able to assign support costs to products more accurately by using an activity-based costing system that relies on a separate rate for each manufacturing activity that causes support costs.

After studying the plant's manufacturing activities and costs, the plant accountant has collected the following data for 2000:

ITEM	X21	Y37
Units produced and sold	50,000	100,000
Direct labor hours used	100,000	300,000
Direct labor cost	$1,000,000	$4,500,000
Number of times handled	40,000	20,000
Number of parts	12,000	8,000
Number of design changes	2,000	1,000
Number of product setups	8,000	6,000

The accountant has also determined that actual manufacturing support costs incurred during 2000 were as follows:

COST POOL	ACTIVITY COSTS
Handling	$ 3,000,000
Number of parts	2,400,000
Design changes	3,300,000
Setups	2,800,000
Total	$11,500,000

The direct materials cost for product X21 is $120 per unit, while for product Y37 it is $140 per unit.

(a) Determine the unit cost of each product using direct labor hours to allocate all manufacturing support costs.

(b) Determine the unit cost of each product using activity-based costing.

5-32 ***Product profitability analysis*** Kidspack, Inc., has recently expanded its line of backpacks to include high-quality, lightweight hiker backpacks. This new model uses more expensive material and takes longer to produce. While a basic school backpack can be cut and sewn together in 30 minutes, a hiker backpack takes 45 minutes to cut and sew together. The school model is produced in batches of 1000 packs while the hiker model is produced in batches of 100 packs. Each batch requires inspection time of one hour. Using direct labor hours to allocate manufacturing support costs, product profitability is analyzed as follows: LO 1, 3, 4, 5

ITEM	SCHOOL BACKPACKS	HIKER BACKPACKS
Sales	$10.00	$30.00
Less:		
Direct Materials	2.00	10.00
Direct Labor	2.00	3.00
Manufacturing Support	3.00	4.50
Gross Margin	$ 3.00	$12.50
Selling/Administrative	0.50	1.00
Profit	$ 2.50	$11.50
Sales Volume	90,000	6,000

Angel Johnson, the controller at Kidspack, believes that activity-based costing may be a more accurate way of measuring the costs of the two models. He has traced manufacturing support costs to the following activity pools.

		COST DRIVER DEMANDED		
Activity	Activity Costs	Activity Driver	School Model	Hiker Model
Cutting and Sewing	$ 19,800	Direct labor hours	45,000	4,500
Orders	97,500	Number of orders	450	200
Inspections	179,700	Number of inspections	?	?
Total	$297,000			

REQUIRED

(a) The method of assigning costs to individual products does not affect the total manufacturing support costs. Only the amounts assigned to individual products change. Explain why Angel should care about how support costs are assigned to individual products.

(b) Using activity-based costing, calculate the manufacturing support cost per unit for each of the two models.

(c) Analyze product profitability using activity-based costs.

LO 3, 4 **5-33** ***Activity cost drivers*** The Simply French Restaurant has identified the following activities performed by its staff:

Set tables
Seat customers
Take orders
Cook food
Serve orders
Take dessert orders
Serve dessert
Present bills and collect
Clean tables

REQUIRED

(a) For each of the above activities, state whether the number of tables served or the number of customers at the tables is a better cost driver.

(b) What distortions might result in assigning costs if only one of the two drivers in (a) is used?

LO 3, 4, 5, 6 **5-34** ***Cost driver rates with practical capacity*** Kohlman Company manufactures two products: K33 and K77. Estimated unit cost and production data follow:

ITEM	K33	K77
Direct materials cost	$30	$45
Direct labor cost ($12 per hour)	$24	$60
Estimated production in units	400,000	150,000

Manufacturing support costs are estimated to be $6,535,000 for the current year. Activity cost pools and cost drivers are as follows:

Activity	Activity Costs	Cost Driver	Practical Capacity	COST DRIVER UNITS DEMANDED BY K33	COST DRIVER UNITS DEMANDED BY K77
Machine setups	$ 425,000	Setup hours	6,500	2,000	4,200
Purchase ordering	10,000	Number of orders	100	25	50
Machining	6,000,000	Number of machine hours	75,000	40,000	15,000
Inspection	36,000	Number of batches	1,200	400	600
Packing and shipping	64,000	Number of shipments	1,600	80	1,500
Total	$6,535,000				

REQUIRED

(a) Estimate the manufacturing cost per unit of each product if support costs are assigned to products using activity-based cost driver rates based on practical capacity.

(b) Explain why the unit cost for K33 differs from that for K77.

(c) What operational changes might the company take, motivated by analysis of the activity-based cost driver rates?

(d) Compute the variance between the estimated manufacturing support costs and the support costs assigned to the company's products in part (a).

(e) What action steps might the company take based on the variances computed in part (d)?

(f) Should Kohlman base its activity-based cost driver rates on practical capacity or on budgeted usage of the drivers? Explain.

5-35 ***Customer profitability analysis*** Kronecker Company, a growing mail-order clothing and accessory company, is concerned about its growing marketing, distribution, selling, and administration expenses. It therefore examined its customer ordering patterns for the past year and identified four different types of customers, as illustrated below. Kronecker sends catalogs and flyers to all its customers several times a year, and maintains a toll-free number for customers to use when placing orders. Kronecker prides itself on the personal attention it provides shoppers who order on the phone. Orders are taken over the phone or by mail. All purchases are paid for by check or credit card. Kronecker has a very generous return policy if customers are not satisfied with the merchandise received. Customers must pay return shipping charges, but their purchase price is then fully refunded. LO 3, 5, 7, 8, 9

	CUSTOMER 1	CUSTOMER 2	CUSTOMER 3	CUSTOMER 4
Initial sales	$1000	$1000	$2500	$3000
Number of items returned	0	4	2	24
Dollar value of items returned	0	200	500	1500
Number of orders per year	1	6	4	12
Number of phone orders	1	0	0	12
Time spent on phone placing orders	0.25 hours	0	0	1 hour
Number of overnight deliveries	1	0	0	12
Number of regular deliveries	0	6	4	0

Prices are set so that cost of goods sold is about 75% of the sales price on average. Customers pay actual shipping charges, but extra processing is required for overnight deliveries. Kronecker has developed the following activity cost driver rates for its support costs:

ACTIVITY	ACTIVITY COST DRIVER RATE
Process mail orders	$ 5 per order
Process phone orders	$80 per hour
Process returns	$ 5 per item returned
Process overnight delivery requests	$ 4 per request
Maintain customer relations (send catalogs and respond to customer comments or complaints)	$50 per year

REQUIRED

(a) Using activity-based costing, determine the yearly profit associated with each of the four customers described above.

(b) Comment on which customers are most profitable, and why.

(c) What advice do you have for Kronecker regarding managing customer relationships with the different types of customers represented above?

LO 3, 4, 5, 7, 9 **5-36** ***Activity cost driver rates*** The customer billing department at U.S. West Telecommunication, Inc. currently employs 25 billing clerks on annual contract. Each clerk works 160 hours per month. The average monthly wages of billing clerks, including benefits, amount to $2800. Other billing-related costs, including stationery and supplies, are $0.50 per billing.

The two types of customers are residential and business. For residential customers, billing takes on average 10 minutes to prepare; each business customer billing requires 15 minutes.

The following information pertains to the estimated number of customer billings for the months of June and July:

MONTH	BUSINESS CUSTOMERS	RESIDENTIAL CUSTOMERS
June	8,000	12,000
July	6,000	15,000

REQUIRED

(a) If the expected number of billings each month is used to determine a monthly billing activity cost driver rate, what is the activity cost driver rate for each month based on the expected number of billings?

(b) If the expected number of billing labor hours each month is used to determine a monthly billing activity cost driver rate, what is the activity cost driver rate for each month based on the expected number of billing labor hours?

(c) Compare the cost driver rates in (a) and (b) above. Which rate do you recommend? Why?

(d) Can you recommend a better way to estimate the costs of this activity than using either cost driver rate in (a) or (b) above?

LO 3, 4, 5, 8, 9 **5-37** ***Activity-based costing in a health care organization*** In computing the cost of patient stays, Riverside General Hospital assesses physician costs and medication costs directly to each patient. Riverside has examined its support costs for patient stays, resulting in identification of 18 account names, related account expenses, and cost drivers for support costs for the fiscal year 1999:

RIVERSIDE GENERAL HOSPITAL
OPERATING COSTS AND ACTIVITY COST DRIVERS FOR FISCAL YEAR 1999

ACCOUNT NUMBER	ACCOUNT NAME	COST	ACTIVITY COST DRIVER
101	Nursing services	$ 2,973,154	Nursing hours
102	Nursing administration	1,269,762	Nursing hours
103	Pharmacy	496,629	Number of patient days
104	Laboratory	312,347	Number of tests
105	Medical supplies	482,165	Number of patient days
106	Linen and laundry	358,736	Pounds of laundry
107	Dietary	813,148	Number of meals
108	Employee cafeteria	167,239	Number of nurse days
109	Housekeeping	706,308	Square feet of space

110	Medical records and library	250,345	Number of patients
111	Social services	199,026	Number of patients
112	Patient scheduling and administration	60,238	Number of patients
113	Billing and collection	112,280	Number of patients
114	Plant operations	301,238	Square feet of space
115	Plant maintenance	386,622	Square feet of space
116	Medical equipment operations	496,275	Number of procedures
117	Property insurance	38,350	Value of property
118	Depreciation	960,573	Value of property
	Total operating costs	$10,384,435	

REQUIRED

(a) Ana Navarro, Riverside's controller, has suggested using a simpler classification scheme that groups the 18 activities or accounts into unit (patient day)-related, batch (patient)-related, and facility-sustaining activity cost pools. Which of the 18 activities should be included in each of these three cost pools?

(b) Ana believes that 45,606 patient days should be used as the cost driver activity level for the unit-related activity cost pool, and 8,367 patients should be used for the batch-related activity cost pool. Using this cost system, what reimbursement from the insurance company is required to cover at least the unit-related and batch-related costs for a patient who stays in the hospital for 14 days?

(c) What advice would you give Riverside regarding choosing between a cost system with the 18 drivers initially identified and the cost system described in part (b)?

5-38 ***Product cost distortions*** The Manhattan Company manufactures two models of compact disc players: a deluxe model and a regular model. The company has manufactured the regular model for years; the deluxe model was introduced recently to tap a new segment of the market. Since the introduction of the deluxe model, the company's profits have steadily declined and management has become increasingly concerned about the accuracy of its costing system. Sales of the deluxe model have been increasing rapidly. LO 1, 3, 4, 5

The current cost accounting system allocates manufacturing support costs to the two products on the basis of direct labor hours. For 2000, the company has estimated that it will incur $1 million in manufacturing support cost and produce 5,000 units of the deluxe model and 40,000 units of the regular model. The deluxe model requires two hours of direct labor and the regular model requires one hour. Material and labor costs per unit and selling price per unit are as follows:

ITEM	DELUXE	REGULAR
Direct materials cost	$ 45	$30
Direct labor cost	$ 20	$10
Selling price	$140	$80

REQUIRED

(a) Compute the manufacturing support cost driver rate for 2000.

(b) Determine the cost to manufacture one unit of each model.

The company has decided to trace manufacturing support costs to four activities. The amount of manufacturing support cost traceable to the four activities for 2000 are given below:

Activity	Cost Driver	Cost	COST DRIVER DEMANDED Total	Deluxe	Regular
Purchase orders	Number of orders	$ 180,000	600	200	400
Quality control	Number of inspections	250,000	2,000	1,000	1,000
Product setups	Number of setups	220,000	200	100	100
Machine maintenance	Machine hours	350,000	35,000	20,000	15,000
		$1,000,000			

(c) Using the activity-based costing data presented above, compute the total cost to manufacture one unit of each model.

(d) Compare the manufacturing activity resources demanded per unit of the regular model and per unit of the deluxe model. Why did the old costing system undercost the deluxe model?

(e) Is the deluxe model as profitable as the company thinks it is under the old costing system? Explain.

(f) What should Manhattan Company do to improve its profitability?

LO 1, 3, 4, 5 **5-39** ***Activity-based costing*** (Adapted from CMA, June 1992) Alaire Corporation manufactures several different types of printed-circuit boards; however, two of the boards account for the majority of the company's sales. The first of these boards, a TV circuit board, has been a standard in the industry for several years. The market for this type of board is competitive and therefore price sensitive. Alaire plans to sell 65,000 of the TV boards in 2000 at a price of $150 per unit. The second high-volume product, a PC circuit board, is a recent addition to Alaire's product line. Because the PC board incorporates the latest technology, it can be sold at a premium price; the 2000 plans include the sale of 40,000 PC boards at $300 per unit.

Alaire's management group is meeting to discuss strategies for 2000, and the current topic of conversation is how to spend the sales and promotion dollars for next year. The sales manager believes that the market share for the TV board could be expanded by concentrating Alaire's promotional efforts in this area. In response to this suggestion, the production manager said, "Why don't you go after a bigger market for the PC board? The cost sheets that I get show that the contribution from the PC board is more than double the contribution from the TV board. I know we get a premium price for the PC board; selling it should help overall profitability."

Alaire uses a standard cost system, and the following data apply to the TV and PC boards.

ITEM	TV BOARD	PC BOARD
Direct materials	$80	$140
Direct labor	1.5 hours	4 hours
Machine time	0.5 hour	1.5 hours

Variable manufacturing support costs are applied on the basis of direct labor hours. For 2000, variable manufacturing support costs are budgeted at $1,120,000 and direct labor hours are estimated at 280,000. The hourly rates for machine time and direct labor are $10 and $14, respectively. Alaire applies a materials handling charge of 10% of materials cost; this materials handling charge is not included in variable manufacturing support costs. Total 2000 expenditures for material are budgeted at $10,600,000.

Ed Welch, Alaire's controller, believes that before the management group proceeds with the discussion about allocating sales and promotional dollars to individual products, it may be worthwhile to look at these products on the basis of the activities involved in their production. Welch has prepared the following schedule for the management group.

COSTS	BUDGETED COST	COST DRIVER	ANNUAL ACTIVITY FOR COST DRIVER
Material support costs:			
Procurement	$ 400,000	Number of parts	4,000,000
Production scheduling	220,000	Number of boards	110,000
Packaging and shipping	440,000	Number of boards	110,000
Total costs	$1,060,000		
Variable support costs:			
Machine setup	$ 446,000	Number of setups	278,750
Hazardous waste disposal	48,000	Pounds of waste	16,000
Quality control	560,000	Number of inspections	160,000
General supplies	66,000	Number of boards	110,000
Total costs	$1,120,000		
Manufacturing support costs:			
Machine insertion	$1,200,000	Number of parts	3,000,000
Manual insertion	4,000,000	Number of parts	1,000,000
Wave soldering	132,000	Number of boards	110,000
Total costs	$5,332,000		

REQUIRED PER UNIT	TV BOARD	PC BOARD
Parts	25	55
Machine insertions	24	35
Manual insertions	1	20
Machine setups	2	3
Hazardous waste	0.02 lb	0.35 lb
Inspections	1	2

"Using this information," Welch explained, "we can calculate an activity-based cost for each TV board and each PC board and then compare it to the standard cost we have been using. The only cost that remains the same for both cost methods is the cost of direct materials. The cost drivers will replace the direct labor, machine time, and support costs in the standard cost."

REQUIRED

(a) Identify at least four general advantages that are associated with activity-based costing.

(b) On the basis of standard costs, calculate the total contribution expected in 2000 for Alaire Corporation's products: (1) the TV board and (2) the PC board.

(c) On the basis of activity-based costs, calculate the total contribution expected in 2000 for Alaire Corporation's two products.

(d) Explain how the comparison of the results of the two costing methods may impact the decisions made by Alaire Corporation's management group.

LO 1, 3, 4, 5 **5-40** ***Manufacturing support cost driver rates*** (Adapted from CMA, December 1990) Moss Manufacturing has just completed a major change in its quality control (QC) process. Previously, products had been reviewed by QC inspectors at the end of each major process, and the company's 10 QC inspectors were charged as direct labor to the operation or job. In an effort to improve efficiency and quality, a computer video QC system was purchased for $250,000. The system consists of a minicomputer, 15 video cameras, other peripheral hardware, and software.

The new system uses cameras stationed by QC engineers at key points in the production process. Each time an operation changes or there is a new operation, the cameras are moved and a new master picture is loaded into the computer by a QC engineer. The camera takes pictures of the units in process, and the computer compares them to the picture of a good unit. Any differences are sent to a QC engineer who removes the bad units and discusses the flaws with the production supervisors. The new system has replaced the 10 QC inspectors with two QC engineers.

The operating costs of the new QC system, including the salaries of the QC engineers, have been included as manufacturing support in calculating the company's plant-wide manufacturing support cost rate, which is based on direct labor dollars.

Josephine Gugliemo, the company's president, is confused. Her vice president of production hash told her how efficient the new system is, yet there is a large increase in the manufacturing support cost driver rate. The computation of the rate before and after automation is shown below.

ITEM	BEFORE	AFTER
Budgeted support costs	$1,900,000	$2,100,000
Budgeted direct labor costs	1,000,000	700,000
Budgeted cost driver rate	190%	300%

"Three hundred percent," lamented the president. "How can we compete with such a high manufacturing support cost driver rate?"

REQUIRED

(a) Define manufacturing support costs, and cite three examples of typical costs that would be included in this category. Explain why companies develop manufacturing support cost driver rates.

(b) Explain why the increase in the cost driver rate should not have a negative financial impact on Moss Manufacturing.

(c) Explain, in great detail, how Moss Manufacturing could change its accounting system to eliminate confusion over product costs.

(d) Discuss how an activity-based costing system may benefit Moss Manufacturing.

LO 1, 3, 4, 5, 7, 9, 10 **5-41** ***Activity-based costing for services, outsourcing*** Smithers, Inc. manufactures and sells a wide variety of consumer products. The products are viewed as sufficiently profitable, but recently, some product line managers have complained about the charges for the call center that handles phone calls from customers about the products. Product lines are currently charged for call center support costs based on product sales revenues. The manager of product X is particularly upset because he has just obtained a report that includes the following information for last year:

	PRODUCT X	PRODUCT Y
Number of calls for information	2000	4000
Average length of calls for information	3 minutes	5 minutes
Number of calls registering complaints	200	1000
Average length of complaint calls	5 minutes	10 minutes
Sales volume	$400,000	$100,000

Product X is simple to use and consumers have little concern about adverse health effects. Product Y is more complex to use and also has many health hazard warnings on its label. Smithers currently allocates call center support costs using a rate of 5% of net sales dollars. The manager of product X argued that the current system does not trace call center resource usage to specific products. For example, product X bears four times the call center costs that product Y does although there are fewer calls related to product X, and the calls consume far less time.

REQUIRED

(a) What activity cost driver would you recommend to improve on the current system of assigning call center support costs to product lines? Why is your method an improvement?

(b) Suppose Smithers announces that it will now assign call center support costs based on an activity-based cost system that uses minutes of calls as the activity cost driver. Suppose also that the rate is 70 cents per minute. Compare the call center cost assignments to product X and product Y under the previous system and the new activity-based cost system.

(c) What actions can the product managers take to reduce the center costs assigned to their product lines under the previous system and the new system? What other functional areas might help reduce the number of minutes of calls for product Y?

(d) Who might resist implementation of the new activity-based cost system? In your response, discuss possible reactions of the call center staff and other staff who might be affected by efforts to reduce minutes of calls.

(e) From the company's point of view, how might the activity-based costing system help in the assessment of whether to outsource the call center activities?

CASES

5-42 ***Comparison of two costing systems*** The Redwood City plant of Crimson Components Company makes two types of rotators, R361 and R572, for automobile engines. The old cost accounting system at the plant traced support costs to four cost pools: LO 1, 3, 4, 5, 10

COST POOL	SUPPORT COSTS	COST DRIVER
S1	$1,176,000	Direct labor cost
S2	1,120,000	Machine hours
P1	480,000	—
P2	780,000	—
	$3,556,000	

Pool S1 included service activity costs related to setups, production scheduling, plant administration, janitorial services, materials handling, and shipping. Pool S2 included activity costs related to machine maintenance and repair, rent, insurance, power, and utilities. Pools P1 and P2 included supervisors' wages, idle time, and indirect materials for the two production departments, casting and machining, respectively.

The old accounting system allocated support costs in Pools S1 and S2 to the two production departments using *direct labor cost* and *machine hours,* respectively, as the cost drivers. Then the accumulated support costs in pools P1 and P2 were applied to the products on the basis of direct labor hours. A separate rate was determined for each of the two production departments. The direct labor wage rate is $15 per hour in casting and $18 per hour in machining.

	DIRECT LABOR HOURS (DLH)			Direct
Department	**R361**	**R572**	**Total**	**Labor Costs**
Casting (P1)	60,000	20,000	80,000	$1,200,000
Machining (P2)	72,000	48,000	120,000	2,160,000
Totals	132,000	68,000	200,000	$3,360,000

MACHINE HOURS (MH)			
Department	**R361**	**R572**	**Totals**
Casting (P1)	30,000	10,000	40,000
Machining (P2)	72,000	48,000	120,000
Totals	102,000	58,000	160,000

ITEM	R361	R572
Sales price per unit	$19	$20
Sales units	500,000	400,000
Number of orders	1,000	1,000
Number of setups	2,000	4,000
Materials cost per unit	$8	$10

Now the plant has implemented an activity-based costing system. The following table presents the amounts from the old cost pools that are traced to each of the new activity cost pools.

Activity	OLD COST POOLS				
Cost Drivers	**S1**	**S1**	**P1**	**P2**	**Total**
P1-DLH	$ 120,000	0	$120,000	0	$240,000
P2-DLH	240,000	0	0	120,000	360,000
Setup hours	816,000	80,000	240,000	540,000	1,676,000
P1-MH	0	260,000	120,000	0	380,000
P2-MH	0	780,000	0	120,000	900,000
	$1,176,000	$1,120,000	$480,000	$780,000	$3,556,000

Setups for R572 are 50% more complex than those for R361, that is, each R572 setup takes 1.5 times as long as one R361 setup.

REQUIRED

(a) Determine the product costs per unit using the old system. Show all intermediate steps for allocations, including departmental cost driver rates and a breakdown of product costs into each of their components.

(b) Determine the product costs per unit using the new system.

(c) Explain the intuitive reason that the product costs differ under the two accounting systems.

(d) What should Crimson Components do to improve the profitability of its Redwood City plant?

(e) Describe how experienced production and sales managers are likely to react to the new product costs.

5-43 ***Activity-based costing*** The Fishburn plant of Hibeem Electronics Corporation makes two types of wafers, W101 and W202, for electronic instruments. The old cost accounting system at the plant traced support costs to *three cost pools.* LO 1, 3, 4, 5

COST POOLS	SUPPORT COSTS	COST DRIVERS
S	$1,740,000	Machine hours
P1	680,000	—
P2	240,000	—
	$2,660,000	

Pool S included all service activity costs at the plant. Pools P1 and P2 included support costs traced directly to the two production departments, photolithography and assembly, respectively.

The old cost accounting system allocated costs in pool S to the two production departments on the basis of *machine hours.* Then the accumulated costs in P1 and P2 were applied to the products on the basis of direct labor hours. A separate rate was computed for each of the two production departments. The direct labor wage rate is $20 per hour. The following data were compiled from plant records for January:

	DIRECT LABOR HOURS (DLH)		
Department	**W101**	**W202**	**Totals**
Photolithography (P1)	80,000	20,000	100,000
Assembly (P2)	40,000	20,000	60,000
	120,000	40,000	160,000

	MACHINE-HOURS (MH)		
Department	**W101**	**W202**	**Total**
Photolithography (P1)	80,000	30,000	110,000
Assembly (P2)	20,000	15,000	35,000
	100,000	45,000	145,000

ITEM	W101	W202
Sales price per unit	$11.50	$12.25
Sales units	600,000	300,000
Number of orders	1,000	1,000
Number of setups	2,000	4,000
Materials cost per unit	$ 4.00	$ 5.00

Now the plant has implemented an activity-based costing system. The following table presents the amounts from the old cost pools that are traced to each of the new activity cost pools.

Activity Cost Drivers	OLD COST POOLS S	P1	P2	Total
P1-DLH	$ 180,000	$140,000	$ 0	$ 320,000
P2-DLH	120,000	0	60,000	180,000
Setup hours	900,000	390,000	145,000	1,435,000
P1-MH	400,000	150,000	0	550,000
P2-MH	140,000	0	35,000	175,000
	$1,740,000	$680,000	$240,000	$2,660,000

Each W202 setup takes 1.25 times as long as a W101 setup.

REQUIRED

(a) Determine the product costs per unit using the old system. Show all intermediate steps for allocations, including departmental cost driver rates and a breakdown of product costs into each of their components.

(b) Determine the product costs per unit using the new system.

(c) Explain the intuitive reason that the product costs are different under the two accounting systems.

(d) What should Hibeem Electronics Corporation do to improve the profitability of its Fishburn plant?

LO 1, 3, 4 **5-44** ***Activity-based costing*** Sandra Slaughter, senior vice president for sales for Showman Shoes, Inc., noticed that the company had substantially increased its market share for the high-quality boomer boots (BB) and lost market share for the lower-quality lazy loafers (LL). Sandra found that Showman's prices were lower than the competitors' for BB but higher for LL. She did not understand the reasons for these price differences because all companies used the same production technology and were equally efficient.

The manufacturing process is relatively simple. Showman's manufacturing facility has a cutting department and an assembly department. The high-quality BB is produced in small batches (1000 pairs of shoes each) and the lower-quality LL is produced in large batches (3000 pairs each). Sandra has asked you, the company's new controller, to analyze the product costing method to see if the product prices should be changed.

The company currently uses a plant-wide cost driver rate based on direct labor hours. The rate is computed at the beginning of the year using the following budgeted data:

Total manufacturing support costs	$1,200,000
Total direct labor hours	49,000
Total machine hours	49,400
Total setup hours	520

Your assistant has provided you with the following additional information about the production of batches of BB and LL:

Item	EACH BATCH OF (BB): 1000 PAIRS Cutting	Assembly	Totals
Direct labor hours	80	120	200
Machine hours	160	120	280
Setup hours	3	1	4
Direct costs	$7,500	$6,000	$13,500

Item	EACH BATCH OF (LL): 3000 PAIRS Cutting	Assembly	Totals
Direct labor hours	150	180	330
Machine hours	150	120	270
Setup hours	1	1	2
Direct costs	$9,000	$7,200	$16,200

On further inquiry, your assistant has been able to trace the support costs to the two service departments and the two production departments and to identify the following details for potential cost drivers for the service departments.

ITEM	MAINTENANCE	SETUP	CUTTING	ASSEMBLY	TOTALS
Support costs	$160,000	$400,000	$440,000	$200,000	$1,200,000
Direct labor hours	0	0	21,400	27,600	49,000
Machine hours	0	0	27,800	21,600	49,400
Setup hours	0	0	340	180	520

Your assistant has also collected the following information on activities and their cost drivers:

SUPPORT ACTIVITIES	COST	ACTIVITY CATEGORY	COST DRIVER
Maintenance	$160,000	Product sustaining	Machine hours
Setups	400,000	Batch related	Setup hours
Cutting supervision	280,000	Batch related	Setup hours
Cutting depreciation	160,000	Business sustaining	Machine hours
Assembly supervision	160,000	Unit related	Direct labor hours
Assembly depreciation	40,000	Business sustaining	Machine hours

REQUIRED

(a) Using a single, plant-wide cost driver rate based on direct labor hours, determine the costs per pair of BB and LL.

(b) Determine the costs per pair of BB and LL using departmental cost driver rates based on machine hours for the cutting department and direct labor hours for the assembly department. Allocate service department costs using the direct method.

(c) Determine the costs per pair of BB and LL using activity-based costing.

(d) Explain why unit costs for product BB are higher when departmental cost driver rates are used than when a single plant-wide rate is used.

(e) Explain why activity-based costs for product LL are lower than the corresponding costs based on a single plant-wide rate.

5-45 ***Product profitability analysis*** Petersen Pneumatic Company makes three products. Its manufacturing plant in Petersburg has three production departments and three service departments. LO 1, 3, 4, 5, 10

DEPARTMENT	SUPPORT COSTS
Machining (MC)	$ 40,000
Plating (PL)	50,000
Assembly (AS)	15,000
Purchasing and inventory (PI)	50,000
Setup and scheduling (SS)	120,000
Quality control (QC)	70,000

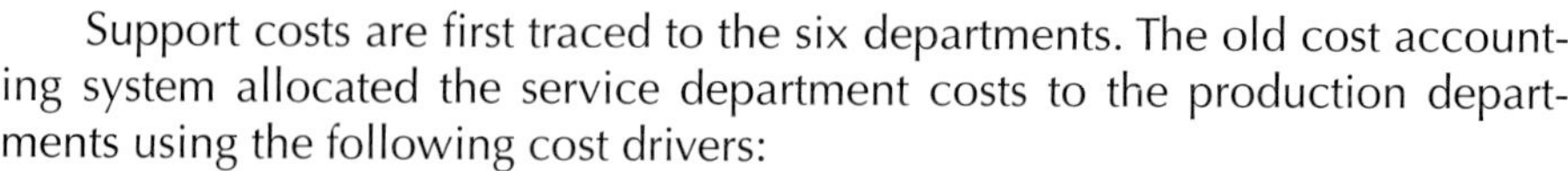

Support costs are first traced to the six departments. The old cost accounting system allocated the service department costs to the production departments using the following cost drivers:

DEPARTMENT	COST DRIVER
PI	Materials cost (MAT)
SS	Direct labor hours (DLH)
QC	Machine hours (MCH)

The old cost accounting system applied support costs to the three products on the basis of direct labor hours. A different cost driver rate was determined for each department. The direct labor wage rate at the plant is $10 per hour.

	DIRECT LABOR HOURS (DLH)			Machine
Department	GT101	GT102	GT103	Hours (MCH)
MC	7,000	2,800	2,200	5,200
PL	3,500	1,700	1,800	1,900
AS	2,500	1,000	1,000	2,900

	PRODUCT SALES		BATCH-RELATED DRIVERS		MATERIALS COST PER UNIT	
Product	Price	Sales Units	Orders	Setups	MC	PL
GT101	$1.25	500,000	25	110	$0.30	$0.10
GT102	1.20	200,000	10	43	0.25	0.10
GT103	1.30	200,000	40	166	0.28	0.10

The profitability of the Petersburg plant has been declining for the past three years despite the successful introduction of the new product, GT103, which has now captured more than a 60% share of its segment of the industry. In an attempt to understand the reasons for its declining profitability, the company has appointed a special task force.

The task force is considering a new cost accounting system based on activity analysis. This system employs five cost drivers: three departmental DLH, setups (SET), and orders (ORD). Each departmental cost pool is divided into homogeneous cost pools identified with a unique driver. The following table presents the percent of the departmental support costs that are put in each of the homogeneous cost pools. The total amounts in the five cost pools are allocated to the three products based on their respective cost drivers.

DEPARTMENT	DLH	SET	ORD
MC	30%	70%	0%
PL	70%	30%	0%
AS	60%	40%	0%
PI	0%	40%	60%
SS	?	?	?
QC	0%	70%	30%

Peter Gamble is the leader of the task force responsible for activity-based cost analysis. He interviewed Nola Morris, who was responsible for the setup and scheduling department, to determine the cost drivers for the departmental support costs.

Gamble: How many people work in the setup and scheduling department?

Morris: I have 12 people who work on setups. Three more are responsible for production scheduling. I spend most of my time supervising them.

Gamble: How do you assign setup workers to production jobs?

Morris: Almost all the time they set up machines in the machining department. The effort depends only on the number of setups.

Gamble: On what does the time spent on scheduling depend?

Morris: It depends on the number of orders.

Gamble: So a large batch or order will require the same amount of setup and scheduling time as a small batch or order.

Morris: Yes, that's right.

REQUIRED

(a) List the reasons that the old cost accounting system at Petersen Pneumatic may be distorting its product costs.

(b) Determine the product cost per unit using both the old and new cost accounting systems. Show all the intermediate steps including the cost driver rates, amounts in the three new cost pools, and a breakdown of product costs into each of their components.

(c) Analyze the profitability of the three products. What insight is provided by the new profitability analysis? What should Petersen Pneumatic do to improve the profitability of its Petersburg plant?

(d) Mike Meservy is a veteran production manager and Shannon Corinth is a marketing manager with considerable experience as a salesperson. Discuss how each of them is likely to react to your analysis and recommendations. Explain how their expected reactions may affect the way you will present your recommendations.

5-46 ***Product profitability analysis*** Pharaoh Phawcetts, Inc. manufactures two models of faucets: a regular and a deluxe model. The deluxe model, introduced just two years ago, has been very successful. It now accounts for more than half of the firm's profits as evidenced by the following income statement for 2000: LO 1, 3, 4, 5, 10

ITEM	TOTAL	REGULAR	DELUXE
Sales	$2,400,000	$1,200,000	$1,200,000
Cost of goods sold	1,540,000	771,000	769,000
Gross margin	$860,000	$429,000	$431,000
Selling/administrative expenses	500,000	250,000	250,000
Net income	$360,000	$179,000	$181,000
Number of units	500,000	300,000	200,000

Its manufacturing plant in Phoenix, Arizona, has two production departments: a machining department and an assembly department. The cost of goods sold included $720,000 in production support costs. The plant accountant traced $192,000 of the production support costs to the machining department and $168,000 to the assembly department. The balance of $360,000 was attributed to the various service departments, and in the existing cost allocation system, the $360,000 was allocated to the machining and the assembly departments in the proportion of their respective machine hours. Next, separate cost drivers were determined for the two production departments based on their respective direct labor hours to assign the support costs to the two products.

Product	TOTAL DIRECT LABOR AND MACHINE HOURS		
	Machining Department	Assembly Department	Totals
Regular	15,000 DLH	3,000 DLH	18,000 DLH
Deluxe	13,000 DLH	5,000 DLH	18,000 DLH
Total DLH	28,000 DLH	8,000 DLH	36,000 DLH
Total machine hours	52,000 MH	8,000 MH	60,000 MH

The direct labor wage rate is $10.00 per hour. Direct materials cost is $0.80 per unit for the regular model and for the deluxe model is $1.10 per unit. An average customer order for the regular model is for 5000 faucets, but for the deluxe model, each order is for 2000 units. The machines required a setup for each order. Three hours are required per machine setup for the regular model; the more complex deluxe model requires five hours per setup.

Pharaoh Phawcett's profitability has been declining for the past two years despite the successful introduction of the deluxe model, which has now captured over a 65% share of its segment of the industry. Market share for the regular model has decreased to 12%. In an attempt to understand the reasons for its declining profitability, the company has appointed a special task force.

The task force is considering a new cost accounting system based on activity analysis. This system employs four cost drivers: two departmental direct labor hours, setup hours, and number of orders. Production support costs are traced to four homogeneous cost pools, each identified with a unique driver as presented in the following table.

Activity Cost Driver	Costs	TRACEABLE NUMBER OF UNITS OF COST DRIVER		
		Total	Regular	Deluxe
Machining DLH	$112,000	?	?	?
Assembly DLH	96,000	?	?	?
Setup hours	272,000	?	?	?
Number of orders	240,000	?	?	?
Total manufacturing support costs	$720,000			

The task force also analyzed selling and administrative expenses. These costs included 5% sales commission on regular models and 10% on deluxe models. Advertising and promotion expenses were $50,000 for the regular model and $90,000 for the deluxe model. The remaining $180,000 of selling and administrative expenses are attributed equally to the two products.

REQUIRED

(a) Determine the product costs per unit using the existing cost accounting system. Show all the intermediate steps including the cost driver rates and a breakdown of product costs into each of their components.

(b) Determine the product costs and profits per unit using the new activity-based costing system. Show all the intermediate steps including the cost driver rates and components of product costs.

(c) Explain the principal reasons that the old cost accounting system at Pharaoh Phawcetts may be distorting its product costs and profitability. Support your answer with numbers when necessary.

(d) Analyze the profitability of the two products. What insight does the new profitability analysis provide? What should Pharaoh Phawcetts do to improve its profitability? What options may be available?

(e) Ryan O'Reilley is a marketing manager with considerable experience as a salesperson. Discuss how he is likely to react to your analysis and recommendations.

5-47 ***Cost distortions*** Sweditrak Corporation manufactures two models of its exercise equipment: regular (REG) and deluxe (DLX). Its plant has two production departments, fabrication (FAB) and assembly (ASM), and two service departments, maintenance (MNT) and quality control (QLC). The parts for each model are manufactured in the fabrication department and put together in the assembly department. The maintenance department supports both production departments, and QLC performs all inspections for both production departments. Each unit of both products needs one inspection in each production department. Each inspection takes 30 and 60 minutes for REG and DLX models, respectively. The two production departments have set the following standards for direct material cost, direct labor cost, and machine hours for each unit of product. LO 1, 3, 4

	FABRICATION		**ASSEMBLY**	
Item	**REG**	**DLX**	**REG**	**DLX**
Direct materials cost	$40.00	$80.00	$10.00	$20.00
Direct labor cost	20.00	40.00	20.00	30.00
Machine hours	2.0	3.0	1.0	2.0

The average wage rate for direct labor is $10 per hour. The following table gives the production volume and support costs for the past two weeks:

	PRODUCTION VOLUME		**SUPPORT COSTS**	
Week	**REG**	**DLX**	**MNT**	**QLC**
45	450	430	$35,000	$6,310
46	450	450	$35,400	$6,350

The present cost accounting system assigns support costs in MNT to the production departments on the basis of machine hours and assigns QLC costs to the two production departments on the basis of the number of inspections. The accumulated costs in FAB and ASM are applied to products based on direct labor hours.

The company is considering implementing an activity-based costing system using machine hours as the cost driver for MNT cost and inspection hours as the cost driver for QLC cost.

REQUIRED

(a) Using the present cost accounting system, determine the product costs per unit for each product for the two weeks.

(b) Using the proposed ABC system, determine the unit product costs for each product for the two weeks.

5-48 ***Identifying activity costs*** Linda Collins is manager in charge of cost analysis and planning at Montex Company. Montex makes steel and brass pumps at its four plants located in Minnesota, Indiana, Illinois, and Michigan. Linda first examined the accounting and payroll records at the Minnesota plant. She organized payroll costs including benefits by department and analyzed expenditure records to identify tools, supplies, and other costs with individual departments. After collecting the departmental cost information, Linda interviewed the departmental managers to identify what activities the personnel in their departments performed. The following table shows the cost associated with two departments, machine setups and quality inspections, and the names of the managers of each department. LO 3, 4, 5

MONTEX COMPANY

Department	Machine Setups	Quality Inspections
Manager	Roger Smith	David Carlson
Wages and benefits	$406,000	$476,000
Tools, supplies, and other costs	110,000	26,000
Initial total costs	$516,000	$502,000
Add: Engineer's wages	0	38,000
Revised total costs	$516,000	$540,000

Edited versions of Linda's interviews with the two managers appear below.

Linda first interviewed Roger Smith, manager of the machine setup department, who has been with Montex Company for 26 years.

Linda Collins: How many people do you have in your department?

Roger Smith: I supervise eight people. We had seven until last June, but because of the high workload we had to add Steve Swanson in the second half of last year. Steve is now a permanent worker in our department.

Linda Collins: What work do they do?

Roger Smith: All my people are responsible for setting up the machines.

Linda Collins: What drives the amount of work that they do?

Roger Smith: Well, setups are required each time they begin a production run. When the machine is available for the production run, our people go and set up the machine and inspect the first item produced to make sure that the machine is set up right.

Linda Collins: So the number of production runs or batches seems to drive your work, not how large a run is?

Roger Smith: Yes, that is really the case. Setting up the machine takes the same time, whether we produce 60 pumps or 5 pumps.

Linda Collins: Do the setups for all batches take about the same amount of time?

Roger Smith: No. There are big differences, depending on the product for which we have to set up the machines. Some products have very complex specifications that require about three hours of setup time. Other products, such as P101, are much simpler, and we can set those up in only one-half hour.

Linda Collins: So the number of setup hours is perhaps the best measure of how much work the setup people perform for the manufacture of a product.

Roger Smith: Yes.

Linda Collins: How many hours of setup work can your crew perform in a year?

Roger Smith: Well, I expect about 1800 hours of productive time per year from each of my people. Last year we had 7.5 workers on average, so there were a total of 13,500 hours available for setup. This year we have 8 workers who will provide a total of 14,400 possible hours for setup.

Linda next interviewed David Carlson, an 18-year veteran at Montex, now in charge of the quality inspection department.

Linda Collins: How many people do you have in the quality inspection department?

David Carlson: I have 12 people in addition to myself. Three of them are responsible for inspecting materials received from our suppliers. The remaining nine are responsible for the final inspection of all our production. I supervise all of their work, so I spend about 25% of my time on receipt inspection and 75% on final inspection.

Linda Collins: Hmm. Let me see. Our payroll records indicate that there are only 11 people reporting to you in your department.

David Carlson: Yes, but Jon Wang from the production engineering department is now permanently assigned to me to help us with our final product inspections.

Linda Collins: (Checking her payroll records) That means I need to add another $38,000 in wages and benefits to your department and subtract it from the production engineering department. Your departmental costs, therefore, are $540,000.

David Carlson: Yes.

Linda Collins: Let me move on. What determines the amount of work for your people who inspect material receipts?

David Carlson: We inspect every lot of materials we receive, so I suppose it is the number of material receipts.

Linda Collins: Does the amount of inspection time depend on the size of the lot?

David Carlson: Not unless it is an exceptionally large lot that we receive only once or twice a year. You see, we randomly inspect a fixed quantity from each batch of incoming materials. It normally takes about one hour to record, inspect, and store each lot we receive.

Linda Collins: How many lots can you receive and inspect in a year with your present staff?

David Carlson: We can do up to 100 per week. Since the plant works 50 weeks in a year, I suppose that means that we can inspect 5000 materials receipts in a year.

Linda Collins: What triggers the work done by your people who are responsible for the final inspection of your production?

David Carlson: Company policy requires us to inspect every unit we produce, so it is the total number of units produced at the plant.

Linda Collins: Do all products require the same number of inspection hours?

David Carlson: Yes. We follow the same procedures for every pump we produce.

Linda Collins: How many pumps can your crew inspect in a year?

David Carlson: We can inspect 5000 pumps in a week, so it means that we can inspect 250,000 pumps in a year. You should realize, of course, that during some weeks when the production level is low in the plant, we do not inspect 5000 pumps and sometimes during peak production periods we work overtime to get the job completed.

REQUIRED

(a) Using the information above, determine cost driver rates for machine setups, inspecting materials from suppliers, and inspecting units produced. Provide justification of your choice of cost drivers, and label your drivers as transaction, duration, or intensity drivers.

(b) Upon viewing the computed cost driver rates, Montex managers suggested exploring reducing inspection of materials purchased from suppliers. What advice would you give management as they pursue this option?

5-49 ***Part proliferation: role for activity-based costing*** Discuss case 1-27. LO 1, 4, 5

5-50 ***Role for activity-based cost systems in implementing strategy*** Discuss case 1-28. LO 3, 4, 5, 7

5-51 ***Financial versus management accounting: role for activity-based cost systems in privatization of government services*** Discuss case 1-29. LO 4, 5, 9, 10

chapter 6

Management Accounting Information for Activity and Process Decisions

AFTER READING THIS CHAPTER, YOU WILL BE ABLE TO

1. explain why sunk costs are not relevant costs
2. analyze make-or-buy decisions
3. demonstrate the influence of qualitative factors in making decisions
4. compare the different types of facilities layouts
5. explain the theory of constraints
6. demonstrate the value of just-in-time manufacturing systems
7. describe the concept of the cost of quality
8. calculate the cost savings resulting from reductions in inventories, reduction in production cycle time, production yield improvements, and reductions in rework and defect rates

S. Mark Young

TOBOR TOY COMPANY

For 45 years, the Tobor Toy Company had been producing high-quality plastic toys for children. The company's best-selling toy was a pricey mechanical toy robot that performed many functions and had several unique features; it commanded a 30% market share. In early 2000, however, Tobor experienced a large drop in sales and market share. After some investigation, this loss was attributed to a significant decrease in the quality of the product and to general delays in getting it to customers. Customers complained that the toy robots failed to perform many of their functions and simply stopped working after several days. The number of returns was astronomical.

Top management decided that the quality of the toy robot needed to be improved dramatically so that the company could regain its reputation and market share. Rumors began to surface that the quality problem was due to deterioration of equipment and an out-of-date production process. Morale among the workers was also poor. Thomas Archer, senior manager of manufacturing, was asked to conduct a thorough investigation and arrive at recommendations for change and improvement.

After several weeks of study, Thomas and a cross-functional team of management personnel documented numerous shop floor problems:

1. *a disorganized, sloppy production system in which piles of both work-in-process and raw materials inventories were scattered over the shop floor.*
2. *a lengthy and complex flow of production*
3. *the use of outdated machinery*

In addition, the quality of the computer chip that allowed the robot to perform its many functions was found to be highly variable, because only some workers focused on their jobs, and thus there were as many defective robots sent back for rework as acceptable ones. Thomas, who had been studying the just-in-time (JIT) manufacturing philosophy, believed that the Tobor Company could benefit greatly from implementing JIT. The just-in-time system seemed to have many advantages, such as streamlining the production process and improving facilities layout, eliminating waste, reducing raw and work-in-process inventories, and generally creating an environment in which producing quality products was rewarded. Further, costs would be easier to control if the company had a well-designed and well-understood production process. Thomas's report to top management raised several questions.

1. *Should many of the existing machines, including the major injection-molding machine, be replaced?*
2. *What should the company do about the local vendor who produced the faulty computer chips?*
3. *Would it make sense to implement an entirely new production process such as JIT?*

After a month of study, top management decided to implement the JIT approach. The cost of implementation and worker training amounted to $300,000. Management personnel wanted to be able to assess the return (benefits) from their investment in JIT. They were adamant that Thomas and his team carefully monitor the quality of products and the changes in the amount of rework. The cost of rework was part of a calculation the company made to determine what it called the cost of quality.

After the first year, Thomas plotted a graph of the rates of major rework, which required scrapping the robot, and minor rework, which included repairs such as realignment of parts and gears, as shown in Exhibit 6-1. Major rework had declined by about 2.5%, whereas the minor rework rate showed a larger decrease of 6.6%.

Thomas believed that improvement in yield rates should improve cycle time, or the time it took to produce the robot from start to finish. On average, he found that cycle time had indeed decreased from 16.4 days to 7.2 days, and that the work-in-process inventory had decreased from $1,774,000 to $818,000, for a savings of $956,000.

Thomas knew that the transition to a full JIT system would take some time, but he also wondered what the bottom-line effect on company profits would be for the year. Would the benefits of less rework, yield increases, and cycle time and inventory reductions be sufficient to offset the $300,000 implementation costs?

In this chapter we will discuss many issues related to how management accounting information is used when making decisions. We discuss what costs are relevant for decisions and provide examples such as how the information can be used in make-or-buy decisions. In addition to understanding what financial information is relevant for decisions, managers in today's business environment also must be well informed about the kinds of activities and processes that generate costs within their facilities. We discuss three types of facility designs, (1) process layouts, (2) product layouts, and

EXHIBIT 6-1

Tobor Toys: Major and Minor Rework Rates

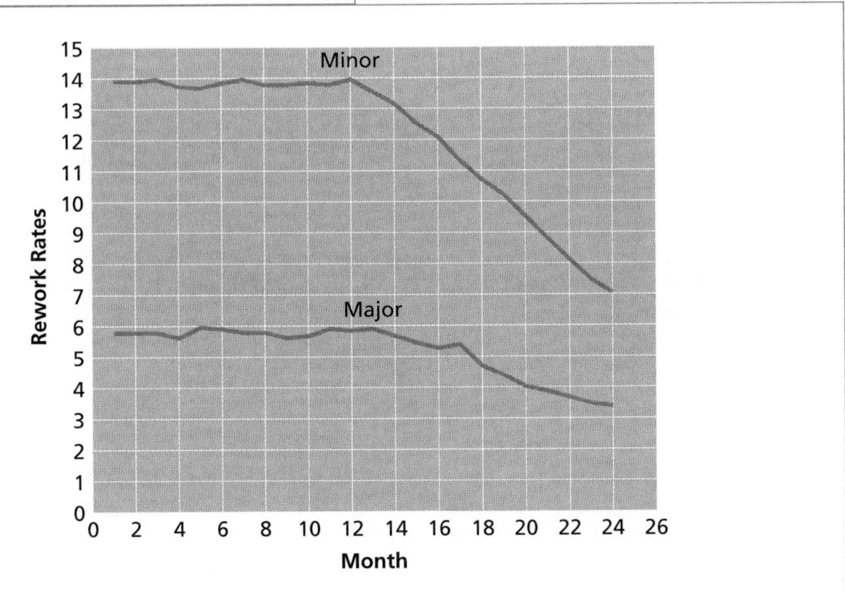

(3) cellular manufacturing, all of which can be used to help organizations reduce costs. We follow this with a discussion of how organizations can reduce costs by ensuring that they focus on improving the quality of their processes. Finally, the just-in-time manufacturing system is presented as a system that integrates many of the ideas we discuss in the chapter.

Evaluation of Financial Implications

Managers must evaluate the financial implications of decisions that require trade-offs between the costs and the benefits of different alternatives. Financial implications are important when considering decisions such as whether to redesign an entire production process or replace existing machines, or whether to buy components from outside subcontractors or make the components in-house (at their own plant). Financial information about the different types of costs form the basis of decisions about the organization's activities and processes, as we saw in the case of the Tobor Toy Company.

Sunk Costs are Not Relevant

Whether particular costs and revenues are relevant for decision making depends on the decision context and the alternatives available. When choosing among different alternatives, managers should concentrate only on the costs and revenues that differ

Relevant costs/revenues Those factors that are affected by a decision.

Sunk costs The costs of resources that already have been committed and cannot be changed by any current action or decision; contrast with *incremental costs.*

across the decision alternatives; these are the **relevant cost/revenues.** The costs that remain the same regardless of the alternative chosen are not considered relevant for the decision.

One category of costs that often causes confusion for decision makers consists of those incurred in the past, or **sunk costs.** These are the costs of resources that already have been committed and cannot be changed by any current action or decision. Because sunk costs cannot be influenced by whatever alternative the manager chooses, they are not relevant to the evaluation of alternatives.

RELEVANT COSTS FOR THE REPLACEMENT OF A MACHINE

Consider the following situation. Bonner Company purchased a new drilling machine for $180,000 from USC Corporation on September 1, 2000, paying $30,000 in cash and financing the remaining $150,000 of the price with a bank loan. The loan requires a monthly payment of $5200 for the next 36 months.

On September 27, 2000, a sales representative of another supplier of drilling machines approached Bonner Company with a newly designed machine that had only recently been introduced to the market. Bertrand Machinery Company, the supplier of the new machine, offered special financing arrangements. It agreed to pay $50,000 for the old USC machine, which would serve as the down payment required for the new Bertrand machine. In addition, Bertrand would require monthly payments of $6000 for the next 35 months.

The new Bertrand design relied on innovative computer chips, which would reduce the labor required to operate the machine. Bonner estimated that direct labor costs would decrease by $4400 per month on the average if it purchased the Bertrand machine. In addition, the new machine would decrease maintenance costs by $800 per month because it had fewer moving parts than Bonner's current machine. The greater reliability of the machine also would allow Bonner to reduce materials scrap cost by $1000 per month. Should Bonner dispose of the USC machine it just purchased on September 1 and buy the new machine from Bertrand Company? What costs are relevant for this decision?

ANALYSIS OF RELEVANT COSTS

If Bonner Company buys the new machine from Bertrand Company, it will still be responsible for the monthly payments of $5200 committed to USC on September 1. Therefore, the $30,000 that Bonner Paid in cash for the USC machine and the $5200 it is committed to pay each month for the next 36 months are sunk costs. Bonner already has committed these resources, and regardless if it decides to buy the new machine from Bertrand, it cannot avoid any of these costs. None of these sunk costs are relevant for the decision.

What costs *are* relevant? The 35 monthly payments of $6000 and the down payment of $50,000 are relevant costs, because they depend on Bonner's decision. In addition, labor, materials, and machine maintenance costs will be affected if Bonner acquires the new Bertrand machine. The expected monthly savings of $4400 in labor costs, $1000 in materials costs, and $800 in machine maintenance costs are relevant. The revenue of $50,000 expected on the trade-in of the old machine is also relevant, because the old machine will be disposed of only if Bonner decides to acquire the Bertrand machine.

Exhibit 6-2 summarizes the relevant costs and revenues of this decision. In a comparison of the cost increases/cash outflows to cost savings/cash inflows, the down payment required for the new Bertrand machine is matched by the expected trade-in value of the USC machine. Furthermore, the expected savings in labor, materials, and machine maintenance costs each month ($6200) are more than the monthly lease payments for the new Bertrand machine ($6000). Thus, it is apparent that

EXHIBIT 6-2

Bonner Company: Relevant Costs and Revenues

COST INCREASES AND CASH OUTFLOWS		COST SAVINGS AND CASH INFLOWS	
1. Down payment on the new Precision machine	$50,000	1. Disposal of the old Newtech machine	$50,000
2. Monthly lease payments on the Precision machine	$ 6,000	2. Monthly cost savings	
		Labor	$ 4,400
		Materials	1,000
		Maintenance	800
			$ 6,200

Source: Jay Heizer and Barry Render, *Production and Operations Management,* 4th ed., 2000. Reprinted by permission of Prentice-Hall, Inc., Upper Saddle River, NJ.

Bonner Company will be better off trading in the USC machine and replacing it with the Bertrand machine.

SUMMARY OF RELEVANT COSTS

Managers must be able to identify the costs and revenues relevant for the evaluation of alternatives. Equally important, they must recognize that some costs and revenues are not relevant in such evaluations. Neither the payments that Bonner has already made on the USC machine nor the remaining monthly payments that it must continue to make are relevant for this evaluation. Both series of payments are sunk costs, because the alternatives available to Bonner do not change the past cash flows or those committed in the future.

ASSUMING RESPONSIBILITY FOR DECISIONS

The correct decision for Bonner Company on a technical level is to dispose of the machine and replace it; however, not all managers would do so, because they are concerned about their reputations within their own organization. Reversing a major decision made only just a month earlier makes the decision look like an error. In many circumstances, by maintaining the original course of action, the manager does not have to reveal that a better decision could have been made.

Three other factors can enter into the decision facing Bonner Company. First, if the manager does not purchase the new machine, then his or her behavior may be viewed as suboptimal in that it ensures lower productivity or performance from the old machine rather than improved performance with the new one. By not making the correct decision now, the manager may incur the effects of a bad decision later.

A second factor to consider is that if the manager admits to making an error when purchasing the old machine, that person might garner more respect from colleagues for accepting the responsibility. Finally, many decision makers have a difficult time distinguishing sunk cost business decisions from sunk cost personal decisions. In contrast to business decisions, the associated costs of previous life decisions can evoke a complex set of personal feelings. As an example, the decision to end a personal friendship or relationship is probably much more complex than the decision to replace a business asset, because the personal decision takes into account one's history with an individual, with all its trials and tribulations. Unlike the case in

IN PRACTICE

Throwing Good Money after Bad

Suppose you are a bank loan officer. A customer with a good credit history comes to you and asks for a $50,000 business startup loan. After careful review of the application, you personally take the initiative to approve the loan. Six months later, the customer shows up in your office and says: "I have some bad news, and I have some good news. The bad news is that the company is having problems. Without additional help we will not survive, in which case you will lose the $50,000. The good news is that I am confident that if you lend us an additional $50,000, we can turn the whole thing around." Do you lend the additional $50,000?

This example, from an article by Professor Dipanker Ghosh, illustrates a current decision that a person faces because of a previous decision. According to the concept of sunk cost, any resources used earlier should not be considered when making future-oriented decisions. Despite this concept, many decision makers continue to pour resources into a highly uncertain project or "throw good money after bad" and escalate their resource commitments.

One of the principal reasons for escalation behavior lies with the characteristics of individual decision makers. For instance, from a psychological standpoint some individuals feel a need to justify a losing project by increasing their commitment in the hope of turning a situation around. These individuals are seeking their own or external justification for their decisions. Other individuals are susceptible to "selective perception" in which they use all available positive information to continue to justify a project but fail to process any negative information that may lead to termination. Still others are affected by whether information is viewed in terms of gains or losses. This concept is known as "framing." When information is framed in terms of gains (for example, the glass is half full), individuals tend to be risk averse; when information is framed in terms of losses (for example, the glass is half empty), individuals tend to be risk seeking. Others engage in "impression management" and resist abandoning a losing project because they believe that giving the project up will diminish their reputation in the eyes of coworkers and superiors.

There are several ways to reduce escalation behavior. First, the performance evaluation system should focus on managers' decision processes rather than decision outcomes. This approach recognizes that a good decision may not lead to a good outcome and can reduce the pressure of justification and decrease the tendency for escalation by allowing managers to terminate a losing project. Both selective perception and framing can be overcome through training in how to evaluate information. Further, the management accountant can play a critical role in helping decision makers by providing information in reports that are clear, precise, timely, and useful. Finally, impression management can be overcome by aligning the outcomes of decisions with the appropriate organizational rewards such as financial compensation, promotions, etc.

Source: Dipanker Ghosh, "Throwing Good Money after Bad," *Management Accounting,* July 1995, pp. 51–54.

the business decision, we do not end a friendship simply because a new friend materializes. Thus, identifying what is relevant and disentangling personal responses when dealing with business decisions are critical tasks for any business decision maker.

Make-or-buy decision A decision in which managers must decide whether their companies should manufacture some parts and components for their products in-house or subcontract with another company to supply these parts and components.

Make-or-Buy Decisions

Management accountants often supply information about relevant costs and revenues to help managers make special one-time decisions. One example is a **make-or-buy decision.** As managers attempt to reduce costs and increase the competitiveness of their products, they face decisions about whether their companies should manufacture some parts and components for their products in-house or subcontract with another company to supply these parts and components. Such make-or-buy decisions illustrate once again how to identify relevant costs and revenues.

Consider the decision faced by Anne Loveland, production manager of Castillo Motors, Inc. The company manufactures about 15% of the lamps required for its automobiles in its own plant near Worthingon, Ohio. Ivonne Castillo, company president, would like to reduce costs. Ivonne has asked Anne to evaluate the possibility of **outsourcing** all the lamps, that is, buying them from an outside supplier instead of manufacturing them in-house. Anne obtains firm quotes from several suppliers for the four types of lamps the company manufactures in-house: standard rear lamps, standard front lamps, multicolored rear lamps, and curved side and rear lamps.

Outsourcing
The process of buying resources from an outside supplier instead of manufacturing them in-house.

Exhibit 6-3 displays details of the two lowest quotes from outside suppliers for a representative lamp in each of the four product lines manufactured in-house. The lowest bid is lower than the total in-house manufacturing cost of each lamp. Should Anne accept the outside bid and terminate the in-house production of these products? What costs must Anne identify and consider when making this decision?

AVOIDABLE COSTS

To answer the previous questions, the decision maker must identify what costs are relevant for the decision. The concept of avoidable costs is useful for Anne to consider. **Avoidable costs** are those eliminated when a part, product, product line, or business segment is discontinued.

Avoidable costs
Those costs eliminated when a part, product, product line, or business segment is discontinued.

If Anne decides to outsource a product, Castillo Motors can avoid certain production costs. If the company purchases the standard rear lamp C-57D directly from the lowest

EXHIBIT 6-3

Castillo Motors, Inc.: Product Costs per Unit and Outside Quotes for Four Representative Products

PRODUCT LINE	STANDARD REAR LAMP	STANDARD FRONT HALOGEN LAMP	MULTICOLORED REAR LAMP	CURVED SIDE AND REAR LAMP
Dimensions	20 cm × 6 cm	14 cm × 4 cm	14 cm × 4 cm	18 cm × 4 cm
Product number	SR214	SF120	MR314	CS418
Product costs per unit:				
Direct materials	$36	$ 49	$ 56	$ 58
Direct labor	22	25	24	28
Unit-related support	14	16	18	20
Batch-related support	10	16	19	22
Product-sustaining overhead	6	12	14	19
Facility-sustaining overhead	8	10	11	14
Total manufacturing costs	**$96**	**$128**	**$142**	**$161**
Bids from outside suppliers:				
Lowest	**$82**	**$109**	**$140**	**$156**
Second lowest	**$88**	**$116**	**$147**	**$164**
Annual production (units)	36,000	48,500	6,800	8,700

bidder, it must pay $2,952,000 ($82 × 36,000) for it. Doing so saves the company $1,296,000 of direct material costs ($36 × 36,000). The firm also could reduce direct labor and supervisory costs and other resources contributing to unit-related support costs. As a result, it can avoid incurring $792,000 of direct labor costs ($22 × 36,000) and $504,000 of unit-related support costs ($14 × 36,000). In addition, with a suitable contraction or redeployment of resources, Castillo Motors can save $360,000 ($10 × 36,000) of batch-related support costs and $216,000 ($6 × 36,000) of product-sustaining support costs.

To decide whether facility-sustaining support costs also are avoidable requires further consideration. Castillo Motors cannot dispose of the part of the plant facility used to support the production of C-57D, because most of the facility-sustaining support costs represent the prorated costs of indivisible common facilities, such as building space and machines, that cannot be eliminated without disposing of the entire machine or building. Nor can these resources be used for other productive purposes or leased to other companies that need space. Therefore, facility-sustaining support costs are unavoidable, or fixed, with respect to a decision to outsource product C-57D.

It is sometimes possible to find an alternative use for the part of the facilities made available by not producing a product. Anne considered the possibility of shifting to the Worthington plant the other production lines manufactured in the same rented facility as the lamps. Castillo Motors could save the facility-sustaining costs for the rental facility by terminating its lease there. Such indirect savings in facility-sustaining costs for the organization are therefore relevant for the decision to outsource product C-57D, because they can arise only if C-57D is outsourced. On further inquiry, however, Anne determined that it would be technically infeasible to transfer the manufacture of the other product lines to the Worthington plant.

To summarize the analysis so far, if product C-57D is outsourced, Castillo Motors can avoid $3,168,000 of manufacturing costs. This is $216,000 more than the total price of $2,952,000 that Castillo Motors has to pay the outside supplier.

Avoidable production costs

Direct material costs	$1,296,000
Direct labor costs	792,000
Unit-related support costs	504,000
Batch-related support costs	360,000
Product-sustaining supports costs	216,000
	$3,168,000
Cost to outside supplier	2,952,000
Increase in profits from outsourcing	$ 216,000

Another way to analyze the decision is to notice that avoidable costs average $88 ($36 + $22 + $14 + $10 + $6) per unit in comparison with the lowest bid of $82 per unit to outsource product C-57D. Therefore, Castillo Motors stands to gain $6 per unit, or $216,000 ($36,000 × $6) overall, and it can apparently lower its costs by buying the parts rather than making them.

QUALITATIVE FACTORS

Are these quantitative estimates of costs and revenues the only relevant considerations for Anne before she decides to outsource C-57D? In fact, for most such decisions several additional factors, which are more qualitative in nature, need to be considered.

A question naturally arises about the permanence of the lower price: Has this supplier chosen to lowball the price to get a foot in the door? If so, after Castillo Motors discontinues the production of C-57D at its Worthington plant and lays off its workers there, will the supplier raise the price for subsequent orders? The reputation of the selected outside supplier is clearly a strong influence on the decision.

Even more important is the reliability of the supplier in meeting the required quality standards and in making deliveries on time. Poor performance on either of these dimensions can result in considerable costs elsewhere for the organization, especially if the outsourced component is critical to the final product. (The same type of qualitative considerations are also important when Tobor Toy Company considers the poor-quality computer chip it has been receiving from its supplier). Lack of availability of the component or a high reject rate can lead to idling of assembly lines and unnecessary delays in meeting customer delivery schedules. Poor quality also creates customer dissatisfaction.

Therefore, many companies have adopted the practice of certifying a small set of suppliers who are dependable and consistent in supplying high-quality items as needed. They provide their **certified suppliers** with incentives, such as quick payments and guaranteed total purchase volumes, so that the suppliers will comply with strict quality and delivery schedules.

Certified suppliers
A set of suppliers who are certified by a company because they are dependable and consistent in supplying high-quality items as needed.

In many industries, technological innovation is an important determinant of competitive advantage. For example, Teijin Electronics Corporation has identified several different technologies that are critical to its business in the next 20 years. It relies on certified suppliers for many of the components of its products, but it has a corporate policy to produce in-house all components that use one of these critical technologies. This policy enables Teijin's research and development staff to experiment, learn, innovate, and implement these critical technologies in-house so that it can retain its leadership and control over innovations in important areas. If it depended on its supplier for innovation, then those benefits also would be available to the supplier's other customers, who could be competitors of Teijin.

Facility Layout Systems

In addition to understanding the relevant costs for many decisions that change the nature of activities and processes, managers must consider the entire operations process within a facility. In this section we discuss the three general types of facility designs: (1) process layouts, (2) product layouts, and (3) cellular manufacturing.

Regardless of the type of facility design, a central goal of the design process is to streamline operations and thus increase the operating income of the system. One method that can guide this process for all three designs is the **theory of constraints (TOC).** This theory maintains that operating income can be increased by carefully managing the bottlenecks in a process. A bottleneck is any condition that impedes or constrains the efficient flow of a process; it can be identified by determining points at which excessive amounts of work-in-process inventories are accumulating. The buildup of inventories also slows the cycle time of production.

Theory of constraints (TOC)
A management approach that maximizes the volume of production through a bottleneck process.

Throughput contribution
The difference between revenues and direct materials for the quantity of product sold.

Investment
The monetary value of the assets that the organization gives up to acquire an asset.

Operating costs
Costs, other than direct materials costs, that are needed to produce a product or service.

The theory of constraints relies on the use of three measures: (1) the throughput contribution; (2) investments, and (3) operating costs. The **throughput contribution** is the difference between revenues and direct materials for the quantity of product sold; **investments** equal the materials costs contained in raw materials, work-in-process, and finished goods inventories; and **operating costs** are all other costs, except for direct materials costs, that are needed to obtain throughput contribution. Examples of operating costs are depreciation, salaries, and utility costs.

The TOC emphasizes the short-run optimization of throughput contribution. Since proponents of the theory view operating costs as difficult to alter in the short run, ABC-type analyses of activities and cost drivers are not conducted. This limits the usefulness of the theory for the longer run. In theory, however, there is no reason why TOC and ABC cannot be used together.

PROCESS LAYOUTS

Process layout
A production design in which all similar equipment or functions are grouped together.

To understand why inventories stockpile in conventional processing systems, and thus increase cycle time, we must understand the conventional way that factory or office facilities are organized. In a **process layout,** all similar equipment or functions are grouped together. Process layouts exist in organizations in which production is done in small batches of unique products. The product follows a serpentine path, usually in batches, through the factories and offices that create it. In addition to these long production paths, process layouts are also characterized by high inventory levels, because it is necessary to store work in process in each area while it awaits the next operation. Often a product can travel for several miles within a factory as it is transformed from raw materials to finished goods.

As an example, the process associated with a loan application at a bank may occur as follows: The customer goes to the bank (a moving activity). The bank takes the loan application from the customer (a processing activity). Loan applications are accumulated (a storage activity), and passed to a loan officer (a moving activity) for approval (both a processing and an inspection activity). Loans that violate standard loan guidelines are accumulated (a storage activity) and then passed (a moving activity) to a regional supervisor for approval (a processing activity). The customer is contacted when a decision has been made (a processing activity), and if the loan is approved, then the loan proceeds are deposited in the customer's account (a processing activity).

In most banks, work in process stockpiles at each of the processing points or stations. Loan applications may be piled on the bank teller's desk, the loan officer's desk, and the regional supervisor's desk. Work-in-process inventory, such as bank loan applications, accumulates at processing stations in a conventional organization for three reasons.

1. Handling work in batches is the most obvious cause of work-in-process inventory in a process layout system. Organizations use batches to reduce setting up, moving, and handling costs; but batch processing increases the inventory levels in the system, because at each processing station all items in the batch must wait while the designated employees process the entire batch before moving all parts in the batch to the next station.

2. If the rate at which each processing area handles work is unbalanced—because one area is slower or has stopped working due to problems with equipment, materials, or people—work piles up at the slowest processing station. Such scheduling delays create another reason why inventory levels increase in a process layout system.

3. Since supervisors evaluate many processing area managers on their ability to meet production quotas, processing station managers try to avoid the risk of having their facility idle. Many managers deliberately maintain large stocks of incoming work in process so that they can continue to work even if the processing area that feeds them is shut down. Similarly, to avoid idling the next processing station and suffering the resulting recriminations, managers may store finished work that they can forward to supply stations further down the line when their stations are shut down because of problems.

Some organizations have developed innovative approaches to eliminating many of the costs relating to moving and storing, which are significant nonvalue-added costs associated with process layout systems. Exhibit 6-4 illustrates the system that Gannett Corporation, the largest U.S. newspaper publisher, has developed. Gannett uses computers and electronic communication in its electronic pagination process to

EXHIBIT 6-4

Using Technology to Reduce Costs in a Process Layout System at Gannett Corp.

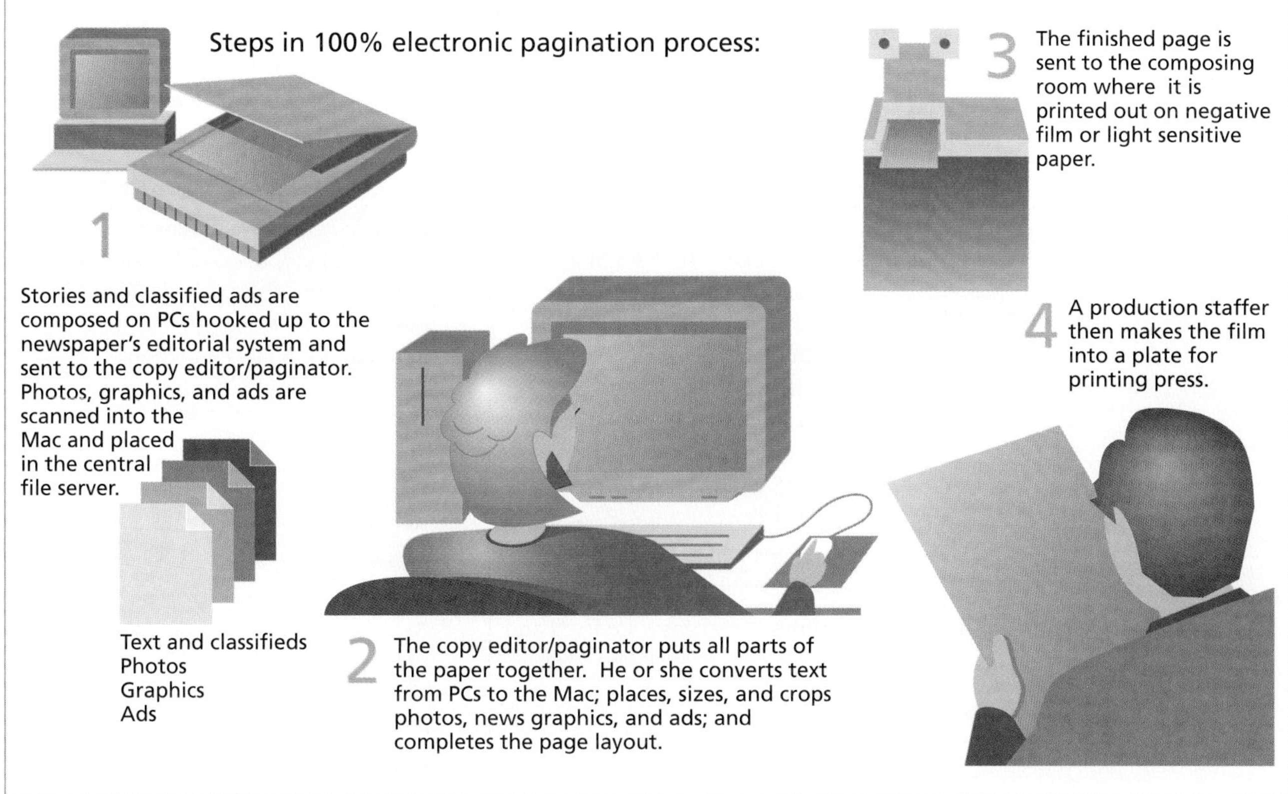

eliminate the physical movement of work in process, thus reducing both cycle time and costs.

Steps in 100% electronic pagination process:
1
Stories and classified ads are composed on PCs hooked up to the newspaper's editorial system and sent to the copy editor/paginator. Photos, graphics, and ads are scanned into the Mac and placed in the central file server.
Text and classifieds
Photos
Graphics
Ads
2
The copy editor/paginator puts all parts of the paper together. He or she converts text from PCs to the Mac; places, sizes, and crops photos, news graphics, and ads; and completes the page layout.
3
The finished page is sent to the composing room where it is printed out on negative film or light sensitive paper.
4
A production staffer then makes the film into a plate for printing press.

PRODUCT LAYOUTS

In a **product layout,** equipment is organized to accommodate the production of a specific product; an automobile assembly line or a packaging line for cereal or milk, for example, is a product layout. Product layouts exist primarily in companies with high-volume production. The product moves along an assembly line beside which the parts to be added to it have been stored. Placement of equipment or processing units is made to reduce the distance that products must travel.

Product layout
A production design in which equipment is organized to accommodate the production of a specific product.

Product layout systems planners often can arrange for raw materials and purchased parts to be delivered directly to the production line where and when they are needed. Suppose that an assembly line is scheduled to handle 600 cars on a given day. The purchasing group knows that these 600 automobiles require 2400 regular tires and 600 spare tires. Under ideal conditions, the purchasing group will arrange delivery of small batches of these tires to the assembly line as frequently as they are needed. However, because each batch of tires from the supplier incurs some batch-related ordering, transportation, and delivery costs, planners may arrange for a few days' worth of tires to be delivered at a time.

Consider the work in process in a cafeteria setting. People pass by containers of food and take what they want. Employees organize the food preparation activities so

IN PRACTICE

ABC versus TOC: Will Ever the Twain Meet?

Proponents of activity based costing (ABC) and the Theory of Constraints (TOC) have been engaging in a somewhat heated debate over the past few years. While proponents on each side are passionate, TOC and ABC have complementary features. What do you think? Below is a side-by-side summary of some of the differences in assumptions between the two approaches:

ASSUMPTIONS	THEORY OF CONSTRAINTS	ACTIVITY BASED COSTING
Objective	Maximize profit via throughput maximization. TOC is not a product costing system. Proponents argue that product costing focuses management's attention locally and does not allow them to understand how the entire throughput process in their organization works.	Produce accurate and relevant information for decision making by tying actual resources consumed to cost objects. Managers need such information to make decisions regarding products, services and customers.
Capacity resources	After capacity has been set, managers will not adjust operating expenses quickly, if at all.	Assumes that managers can alter capacity resources.
Behavior of Labor cost and operating expenses	Assumes these costs are fixed and will not eliminate skilled labor	Assumes that all resources in the short-run are essentially variable and thus able to be reassigned based on activity analysis
Process Improvements	Focus is on increasing throughput by eliminating bottlenecks, and reducing cycle time of products going through the bottleneck.	Determines which activities and processes are adding value and which are not, and which need improvement.
Profit Improvement	Products to manufacture are determined based on their TOC margin and cycle time on the bottleneck.	Product mix and volume decisions are made from a longer-term perspective taking into account the product, channel and customer profitability mix.
Planning Horizon for Product-Mix and Volumes	Short-term oriented and assumes that most costs, except for raw materials, are sunk costs	Long-term oriented and assumes that decisions will be made about less profitable products, channels, and customers.

Source: Gary Cokins, "TOC vs. ABC: Friends or Foes?" ABC Technologies Monograph, 1998. Reprinted by permission of Gary Cokins, garyfarms@aol.com

that the containers are refilled just as they are being emptied—not one unit at a time. For example, the cook does not make and replace one bowl of soup at a time, because the batch-related setup costs of making soup in this fashion will be prohibitively expensive. Reducing setup costs, however, allows for the reduction of batch sizes (the size of the containers) along the line. This reduces the level of inventory in the system and, therefore, costs. It also improves quality while increasing customer satisfaction. The ultimate goal is to reduce setup costs to zero and to reduce

EXHIBIT 6-5

Cellular Manufacturing

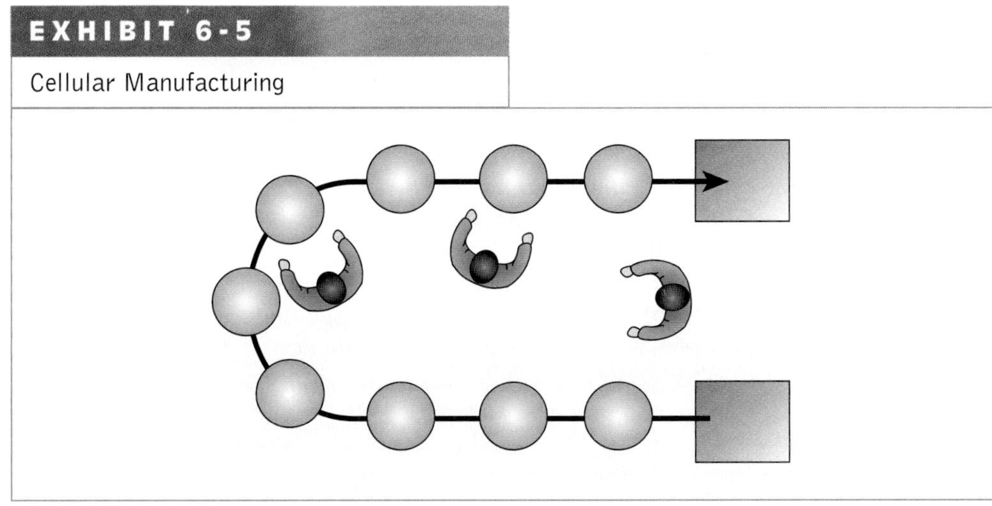

processing time to as close to zero as possible, so that the system can produce and deliver individual products just as they are needed.

CELLULAR MANUFACTURING

The third approach to facilities layout, **cellular manufacturing,** refers to the organization of a plant into a number of cells so that within each cell all machines required to manufacture a group of similar products are arranged in close proximity to each other. As Exhibit 6-5 illustrates, the shape of a cell is often a U shape, which allows workers convenient access to required parts. The machines in a cellular manufacturing layout are usually flexible and can be adjusted easily or even automatically to make different products. Often when cellular manufacturing is introduced, the number of employees needed to produce a product can be reduced due to the new work design. The U shape also provides better visual control of the work flow because employees can observe more directly what their coworkers are doing.

Cellular manufacturing Refers to the organization of a plant into a number of cells so that within each cell all machines required to manufacture a group of similar products are arranged in close proximity to each other.

Inventory Costs and Processing Time

INVENTORY AND PROCESSING TIME

Not only does batch production create inventory costs, but it also creates the delays associated with storing and moving inventory. These delays increase cycle times, thereby reducing service to customers. Delays can happen at any stage of the production cycle, even before manufacturing begins. For example, because of high setup costs, a manufacturer may require that a product be manufactured in some minimum batch size. If a customer order is less than the minimum batch size and if the order cannot be filled from existing finished goods inventory, then the customer must wait until enough orders have accumulated to meet the minimum batch size requirement. It may take a loan officer only five minutes to read and approve a loan application at the bank; however, the application may have to wait for several hours or even days before it reaches the loan officer, because having a clerk run back and forth with each new loan application when it arrives is too expensive.

INVENTORY-RELATED COSTS

Demands for inventory lead to huge costs in organizations, including the cost of moving, handling, and storing the work in process, in addition to costs due to

THE TECHNOLOGICAL EDGE

Cycle Time and Inventory Reduction through SAP

Over the past five years, Colgate-Palmolive, the $9 billion consumer goods company, has been installing SAP AG's complete R/3 suite in all of its global operations. Thus far, the installation is 75% complete. The installation required complete process reengineering of its entire supply chain. In addition, much of the company's technological infrastructure had to be upgraded.

As many companies have discovered, ERP installation is the first step in using the internet to alter company culture and, thus, the way that business is conducted. For example, the company now allows its suppliers direct access to its ERP information through the Web so that *they* can better manage Colgate-Palmolive's inventories—a big step for many companies.

Has the cost been worthwhile? Colgate-Palmolive reports that it has been able to reduce its order-to-shipping cycle time by 50% and drastically reduce the levels of inventories.

Source: Jeff Moad, "PC Week's 1999 Fast-Track Technology Innovators—The 100 Top Innovators in Manufacturing, *PC Week,* August 9, 1999, p. 59.

obsolescence or damage. Many organizations have found that factory layouts and inefficiencies that create the need to hold work-in-process inventory also hide other problems leading to excessive costs of rework.

For example, in batch operations, workers near the end of a process—downstream—often find batch-size problems resulting from the way workers earlier in the process—upstream—have done their jobs. When work is performed continuously on one component at a time, however, workers downstream can identify an upstream problem in that component almost immediately and correct it before it leads to production of more defective components.

COSTS AND BENEFITS OF CHANGING TO A NEW LAYOUT: AN EXAMPLE USING CELLULAR MANUFACTURING

San Rafael Electric Corporation is a leader in the manufacture of small electrical appliances for household and industrial use. It produces a variety of electrical valve controls at its plant in Pasadena, California. Until recently, the plant was organized into five production departments: casting, machining, assembly, inspection, and packing. Now the plant layout has been reorganized to streamline production flows and introduce cellular manufacturing. In the following sections we will take an extended look at both the old and the new, identify the benefits of the new system, and compare the costs and benefits of the two.

The plant manufactures 128 different products that have been grouped into eight product lines for accounting purposes, based on common product features and production processes. Under the old plant layout, the 128 products followed a similar sequence of steps in the manufacturing process (see Exhibit 6-6). Manufacturing of panels for valve controls occurred in large batches in the casting department. Then the manufactured panels were stored in a large work-in-process storage area located near the machining department, where they remained until the lathes and drilling machines were free. After machining, the panels were stored until they were requisitioned for assembly, during which switches and other components received from

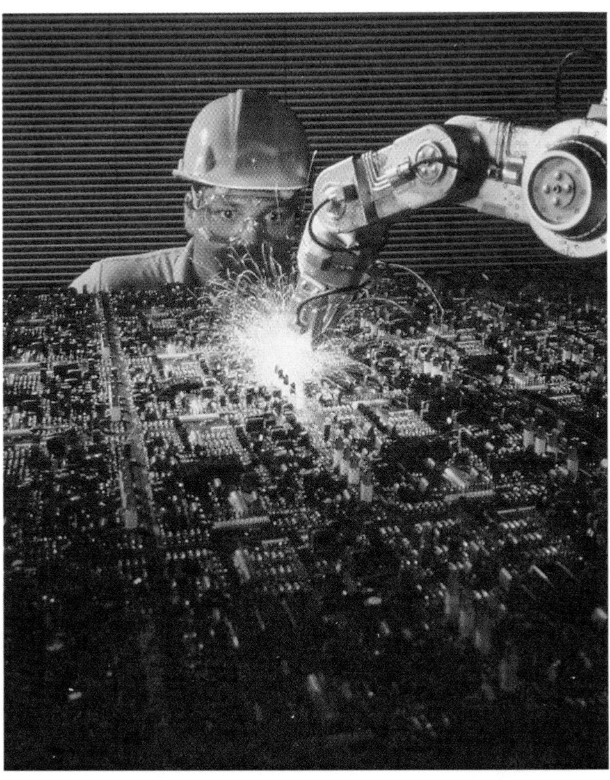

This worker is observing how an industrial robot is performing its tasks. The worker's goal is to find ways to streamline the robot's movement even further to reduce processing time. (M. Tcherevkoff/The Image Bank)

outside suppliers were placed onto each panel. Another storage area located near the assembly department was used for work in process awaiting inspection or packing, which occurred before the panels were packed for shipping. Finally, the packed valve control panels were stored in the finished goods warehouse until they were shipped to distributors and other customers.

This production flow required storage of work-in-process inventory for a long time, and at several times before the beginning of the next production stage. As mentioned, manufacturing **cycle time** is measured as the time from the receipt of the raw materials from the supplier to the delivery of the finished goods to the distributors and customers. At San Rafael, cycle time was 27 days (5 + 1 + 9 + 1 + 1 + 4 + 1/2 + 2 + 1/2 + 3) under the old plant layout. The 4 days during which switches and other components were kept as inventory were not added to the **processing time,** the time expended for the product to be made, because the time spent in inventory represented parallel time with other production activities, such as work-in-process storage and machining. Therefore, the storage requirements for switches and other components did not prolong the time for the total production activity in the plant.

Cycle time
The time required to produce a product from start to finish.

Processing time
Time expended to complete a processing activity.

To evaluate how much of the old cycle time was spent in inventory, we need to know how organizations assess the efficiency of their manufacturing processes. One widely used measure is **manufacturing cycle efficiency (MCE)** and is calculated as follows:

Manufacturing cycle efficiency (MCE)
A measure used to assess the efficiency of a manufacturing process; evaluates how much of the total cycle time was spent in inventory.

$$\text{MCE} = \frac{\text{Processing time}}{\text{Processing time} + \text{Moving time} + \text{Storage time} + \text{Inspection time}}$$

Notice that of the 27 days required for the manufacturing cycle under San Rafael's old system, only 4 days were spent on actual processing [(1 casting) + (1 machining) + (1 assembly) + (1/2 inspection) + (1/2 packing)]. The other 23 days were spent in nonvalue-added activities such as moving, storage, and inspection. The amount of

EXHIBIT 6-6

San Rafael Electric Corporation: Production Flows and Average Time under Old Plant Layout

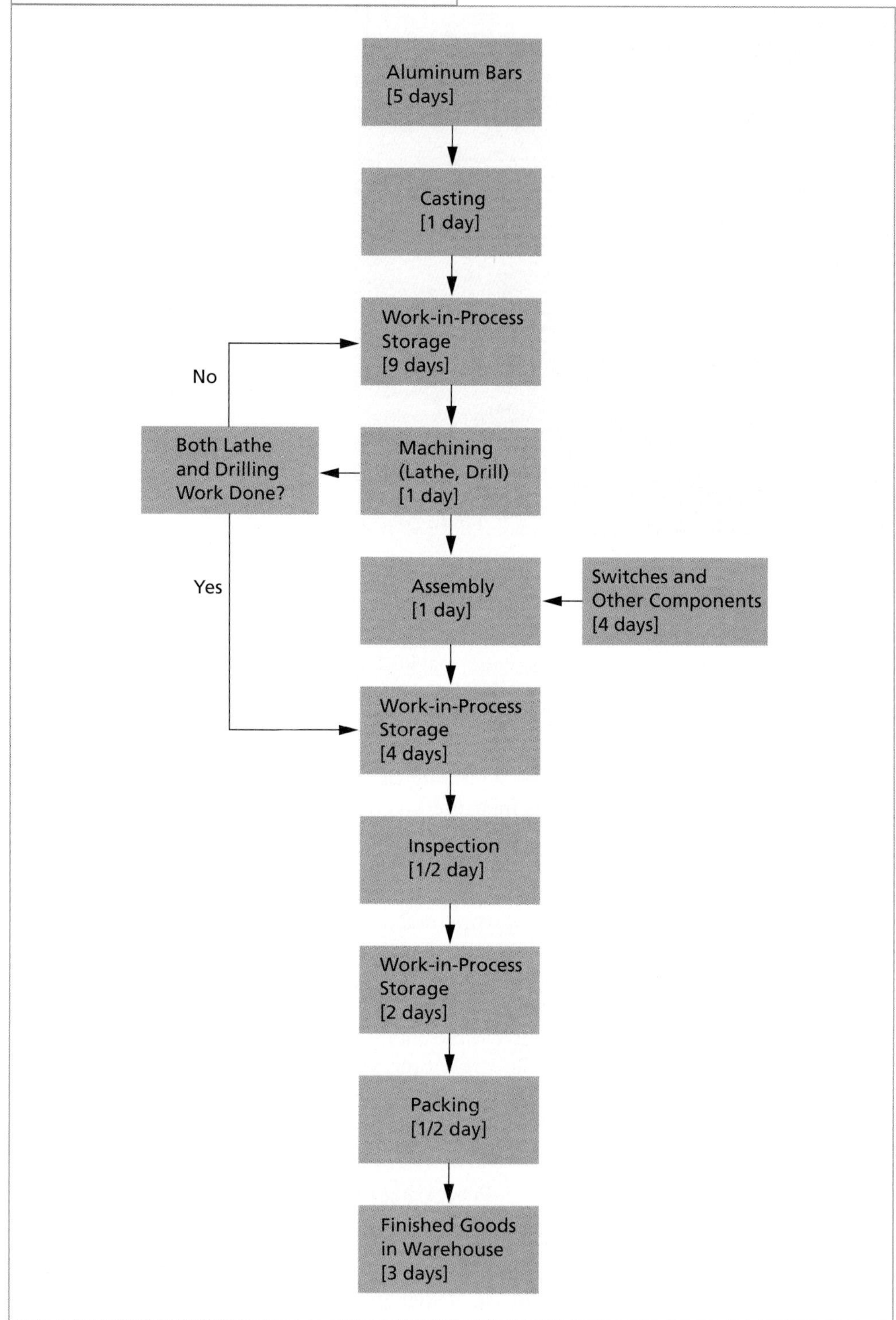

time that materials spent in inventory could be as many as 23 days. The MCE formula reveals that processing time equaled 15% (4 ÷ 27) of total cycle time. These results are representative of many other plants that manufacture products from mechanical or electronic components. We will see shortly how the MCE changes for San Rafael after its reorganization.

Reorganization. A primary objective of the reorganization of the San Rafael plant layout was to reduce the production cycle time. Thus, the plant was reorganized into eight manufacturing cells (corresponding to the eight product lines) in addition to the casting department. Each cell focused on the manufacture of similar products belonging to the same product line.

Exhibit 6-7 depicts the production flows under the new plant layout. While the casting department remains a separate department, the other four operations—machining, assembly, inspection, and packing—are now located in close proximity to each other within each manufacturing cell. Aluminum panels received from the casting department are lathe-machined, drilled, and assembled in the manufacturing cells. Workers in the cells also are responsible for inspection and packing operations. Thus, material handling distances and the time required to move a panel from one process to the next are greatly reduced.

San Rafael Electric also made a transition toward just-in-time production. The change required that there be no work-in-process inventories among the various stages of operations in the manufacturing cells, because panel production flowed immediately from lathe to drilling to assembly to inspection to packing operations. As a result of these steps, the time between operations has been greatly reduced as production is pulled from one stage to the next based on orders for the finished product.

When comparing Exhibits 6-6 and 6-7, notice that San Rafael Electric Corporation did not reduce the amount of time spent on actual manufacturing when it changed the plant layout. The time spent on manufacturing operations after the change (see Exhibit 6-7) is the same as the time spent before the change (see Exhibit 6-6). However, the cycle time is reduced substantially in the new plant layout from 27 to only 12 days. Thus, MCE changes from 15% to 33% (4 ÷ 12). This significant improvement in efficiency over the previous layout comes from eliminating the need for work-in-process inventory between many of the manufacturing operations.

EXHIBIT 6-7

San Rafael Electric Corporation: Production Flows and Average Time under New Plant Layout

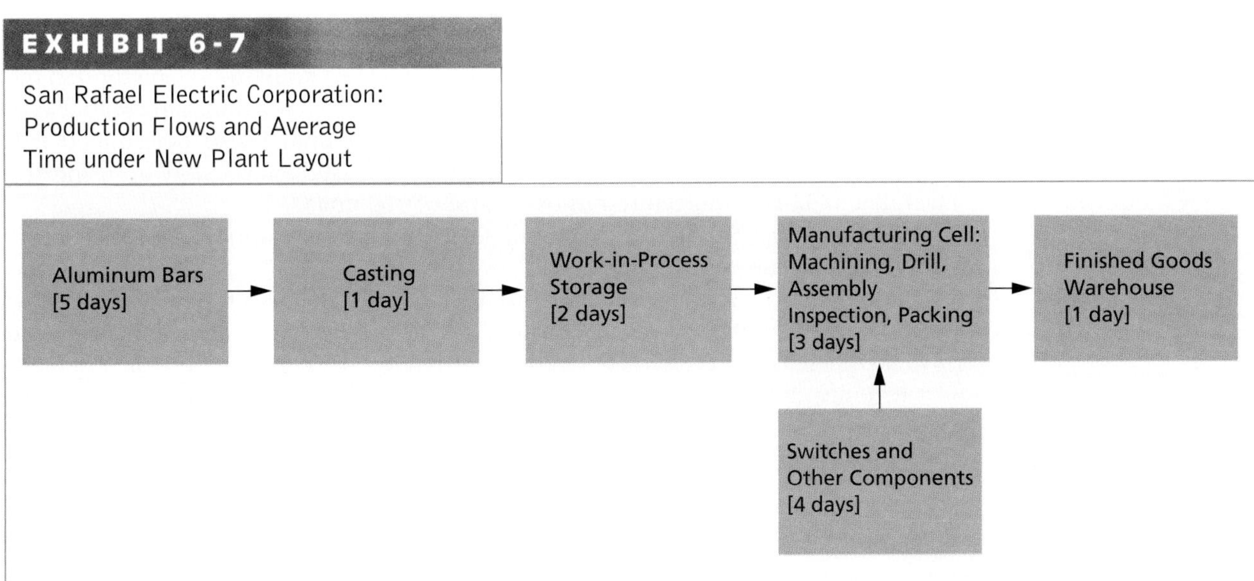

Analysis of Relevant Costs and Benefits. Has this change helped improve the profitability of the Pasadena plant? Mike Richardson, the Pasadena plant controller, identified the following costs associated with the implementation of the changes in the plant layout:

Moving machines and reinstallation	$ 600,000
Training workers for cellular manufacturing	+ $ 400,000
Total costs	$1,000,000

Mike also identified three types of benefits resulting from the plant reorganization: (1) an increase in sales because of the decrease in production cycle time, (2) a reduction in inventory-related costs because of the decrease in the amount and handling of work-in-process inventory, and (3) an improvement in quality since defective processes are detected much faster (at the next processing stage) before many defective items have been produced.

Mike interviewed several production and sales managers to assess the extent of these benefits. He began with Trudie Thomas, a senior sales manager with 17 years of experience at San Rafael.

Mike Richardson: Has the reduction in production cycle time increased sales?

Trudie Thomas: Yes, we have been able to win over many customers from our competitors because we can now quote a much shorter delivery lead time to them. Also, we have been able to retain some of our own customers because we have cut our delivery lead time. We commissioned a market research study to ascertain the impact that reduction in delivery lead time has had on our sales. On the basis of this study, our best estimate is that an increase of $880,000 in sales this year can be attributed to the change in our production cycle time. Details of estimated sales increases for individual products are also provided in this study. I think you'll find it interesting.

Mike next turned to his analyst, Christy Moody, to collect the information necessary to assess the impact of the sales increase on San Rafael profits. Mike asked Christy to determine the contribution margin for the Pasadena plant's products. She returned the next day with several detailed cost accounting reports.

Christy Moody: I've prepared a detailed analysis of the incremental costs for all our products. Here is a summary that gives the totals for all 128 products. (See Exhibit 6-8.) I began with the estimate of the increase in sales for each of the 128 products. Here is an example for product TL32. (See Exhibit 6-9.) I multiplied the 800-unit sales increase by the direct materials cost of $7 per unit, direct labor cost of $4 per unit, and unit-related support of $3 per unit. I also determined that eight additional batches are required for the increased production by using the fact that TL32 is manufactured in batch size of 100 units.

None of the product-sustaining or facility-sustaining support should increase because there are no new products added by increases in size of the plant and no additions to plant machinery. The $10,000 increase in profit is obtained by calculating the difference between the $23,200 increase in sales revenue and the $13,200 increase in costs. The summary in Exhibit 6-8 displays the totals of similar revenue and cost numbers across all of our 128 products.

Mike Richardson: Thanks, Christy, for all your efforts. I see that our best estimate is that the increase in sales resulting from the lower production cycle time has led to an overall increase of $301,000 in profit this year.

Mike next met with Jessica Starr, production and inventory manager at the Pasadena plant, to find out how the reduction in the level of work-in-process inventory affected the consumption of support activity resources.

EXHIBIT 6-8

San Rafael Electric Company Impact of Increase in Sales on Profits

Increase in sales revenue		$880,000
Increase in costs:		
Direct materials	$245,000	
Direct labor	140,000	
Unit-related support	108,000	
Batch-related support	86,000	579,000
Net increase in profit		$301,000

Mike Richardson: Has the change in the plant layout led to changes in the handling and storage of work-in-process inventory?

Jessica Starr: Yes, we have been able to make many changes. We don't need a materials-handling crew to move work-in process inventory from lathes to drilling machines to storage areas on the shop floor. Nor do we need to move and store work-in-process inventory between the assembly, inspection, and packing stages. We did not reduce the number of materials handling workers immediately, but as work patterns stabilized a few weeks after the change in the plant layout, we reduced our materials handling crew from 14 to only 8 workers.

Mike: Were there any other changes in the workload of people performing these support activities?

Jessica: With an almost 70% reduction in work-in-process inventory, down from $2,270,000 to $690,000, we had a corresponding decrease in inventory-related transactions. We did not require as much record keeping for the movement of materials into and out of storage. We expect to be able to reduce our shop-floor-stores staff by 75%, from four workers to only one. So far we have reassigned only one worker, but two more will be reassigned to other production-related tasks next week.

EXHIBIT 6-9

San Rafael Electric Company Profit Impact of Increase in Sales of Product TL32

Increase in sales	(800 units × $29 price per unit)		$23,200
Increase in costs:			
Direct materials	(800 units × $7 cost per unit)	$5,600	
Direct labor	(800 units × $4 cost per unit)	3,200	
Unit-related support	(800 units × $3 overhead per unit)	2,400	
Batch-related support	(800/100 batches × $250 overhead per batch)	2,000	$13,200
Net increase in profit			$10,000

Mike: So far we have talked about personnel. Were any other resources freed up as a result of the reduction in work-in-process inventory?

Jessica: Yes, we need only one-third of the storage space we used earlier for work-in-process inventory. The extra space is idle at present, however, because we haven't yet found an alternative use for it. I don't believe there was any proposal to use that extra space in the three-year facilities plan prepared last month, but eventually as production activity expands we should be able to place new manufacturing cells in the space formerly used to store work-in-process inventory.

Mike: But you don't expect any immediate benefit to arise from the availability of the extra storage space?

Jessica: Yes, that's correct. But there is one more benefit that you shouldn't forget. When some panels are produced in large batches and stored awaiting the next stage of processing, we always find that some of them get damaged in handling, and at times some of them become obsolete because the customer no longer requires them. The change to just-in-time production in the manufacturing cells and the elimination of much of our work-in-process inventory have resulted in a reduction in materials scrap and obsolescence cost from 0.32% of materials cost to only 0.12%.

Mike: Thank you, Jessica. The information you've provided will be very useful in evaluating the impact of the change in the plant layout.

Mike and Christy sat in Mike's office to analyze the information they had collected so far. Facility-sustaining costs pertaining to plant space included building depreciation, insurance, heating, lighting, janitorial services, building upkeep, and maintenance. The support rate for this activity was $108 per square foot. However, Mike and Christy decided that the costs associated with the extra storage space were at present a sunk cost with no cost savings yet realized from freeing up this space.

A check of the materials handling activity costs indicated that the annual wages of workers in this grade averaged $21,000, with 35% more, or $7350 ($21,000 × 0.35) added for fringe benefits. The total materials handling cost savings, therefore, was $170,100 ($28,350 × 6), because the crew size was reduced by six workers.

In a similar fashion, Jessica determined that the annual wages of stores personnel averaged $26,400. With a 35% fringe benefit rate and an expected reduction of three workers, the total annual cost savings was $106,920 ($26,400 × 1.35 × 3).

There can be significant costs involved in financing inventories. Mike estimated the interest rate on bank loans to finance the investment in inventories to be 12% per year. The work-in-process inventory was reduced by $1,580,000 ($2,270,000 − 690,000). This reduced the cost of inventory financing correspondingly by $189,600 ($1,580,000 × 0.12).

Finally, Mike determined that the total annual materials cost was $31,000,000. If the rate of materials, scrap, and obsolescence had remained at the previous 0.32% of materials cost, this loss would have been $99,200 ($31,000,000 × 0.0032). But because of the reduction in the rate to 0.12%, the cost of materials scrap and obsolescence was reduced to only $37,200 ($31,000,000 × 0.0012). This represents a cost savings of $62,000 ($99,200 − $37,200).

Summary of Costs and Benefits. Mike then summarized the information on cost savings resulting from the change in the plant layout (see Exhibit 6-10). He estimated that annual benefits were $829,620. In comparison, the one-time costs of implementing the change were only $1,000,000. If benefits from the changed layout continue

EXHIBIT 6-10

San Rafael Electric Corporation: Annual Benefits Resulting from the Change in Plant Layout

Contribution from increased sales:			
Sales increase	(Exhibit 6–8)	$880,000	
Incremental manufacturing costs	(Exhibit 6–8)	(579,000)	$301,000
Cost savings from work-in-process inventory reduction:			
Cost of financing investment in work-in-process inventory		$189,600	
Cost of materials handling labor		170,100	
Cost of stores labor		106,920	
Cost of materials scrap and obsolescence		62,000	528,620
Total benefits			$829,620

to accrue at the same rate for at least three more months, the total benefits will exceed the amount that San Rafael invested in the project.

$$\$829{,}620 \times 15/12 = \$1{,}037{,}025$$

In other words, the process improvements from the investment would repay the front-end cost in 1.25 years.

The San Rafael case study introduces several important concepts. We have identified several different ways in which new manufacturing practices can improve a plant's profitability. In particular, we have seen that financing is a principal inventory-related cost. It is important to consider this cost, although financing costs are often not emphasized in many traditional cost accounting systems. Streamlining manufacturing processes also reduces the demand placed on many support-activity resources. Activity analysis, therefore, is useful for assessing the potential cost savings that can be realized from more efficient product flows.

Many new manufacturing practices are designed to promote continuous improvement in manufacturing performance by enabling workers to learn and innovate. In this example, changing to a manufacturing cell layout led to improvements in production yield rates and quality, and consequently, improvements in overall plant productivity. In addition, revenues also can increase from shorter lead times to customers.

Cost of Nonconformance and Quality Issues

The previous example shows that cost reduction has become a significant factor in the management of most organizations. Reducing costs, however, involves much more than simply finding ways to cut product design costs, by, for example, using less expensive materials. The premise underlying cost reduction efforts today is to decrease costs while maintaining or improving product quality in order to be competitive. If the quality of products and services does not conform to quality standards, then the organization incurs a cost known as the **cost of nonconformance (CONC) to quality standards.**

Cost of nonconformance (CONC) to quality standards
The cost incurred when the quality of products and services does not conform to quality standards.

Quality may mean different things to different people. It usually can be viewed as hinging on two major factors:

1. satisfying customer expectations regarding the attributes and performance of the product, such as is functionality and features; and
2. ensuring that the technical aspects of the product's design and performance, such as whether it performs to the standard expected, conform to the manufacturer's standards.

QUALITY STANDARDS

Global competition has led to the development of international quality standards. Company certification under these standards indicates to customers that management has committed their company to follow procedures and processes that will ensure the production of the highest-quality goods and services. Exhibit 6-11 presents the ISO9000 Series of Standards developed in Europe and their purposes. The exhibit also provides a sketch of the procedures that organizations need to follow if they

EXHIBIT 6-11

ISO9000 Standards

In Europe in 1987 the International Organization for Standardization (ISO), headquartered in Geneva, Switzerland, developed the ISO9000 Series of Standards. The goal of the 96-member nations is to develop globally recognized quality standards for both products and services. Many types of organizations are interested in becoming IOS9000 registered in order to accomplish the following:

1. Comply with external regulatory agencies,
2. Meet or exceed customer requirements, or
3. Implement a quality improvement program to remain competitive.

ISO guidelines consist of five standards, two of which are general quality management guidelines (ISO9000, ISO9004), and three of which are quality system models (ISO9001, ISO9002, ISO9003). The quality system models are listed below. The first general quality management guideline, ISO9000—*Quality Management and Quality Assurance Standards—Guidelines for Selection and Use,* is used to help a potential registrant decide on which of the three quality system models, ISO9001, ISO9002, or ISO9003, should be selected and followed for a particular application. The second general quality management guideline, IOS9004—*Quality Management and Quality System Elements*—explains how to use each of the three quality system models based on specific elements of the quality management system.

Once an organization has committed to obtaining IOS9000 status it must select a standard from one of the following:

1. ISO9001—*Quality Systems: Model for Quality Assurance in Design and or Development, Production and Installation.* This standard is the most all-encompassing and specifies a supplier's capability to design, supply, and service a product. The standard is designed for the entire life of the product.
2. ISO9002—*Quality Systems: Model for Quality Assurance in Production and Installation:* ISO9002 centers on organizations that produce products, but whose design and servicing are done by others. The requirements are focused at the production and installation stages of the product's life cycle.

3. ISO9003—*Quality Systems: Model for Quality Assurance in Final Inspection and Testing.* This standard applies to contracts between parties in which the supplier has to be able to detect and control any product nonconformance during final inspection and testing. This is the most limited aspect of the ISO standard.

Once an organization has decided on which standard it wishes to follow it can then take the following steps toward ISO9000 registration.

1. *The company must become organized to achieve the standards.* This involves gaining top management support, developing quality policies, and establishing a management review committee and implementation teams.
2. *The current quality management system needs to be evaluated.* In many cases companies determine the current state of their system and identify how big a gap they have to bridge before being able to attain ISO9000 status.
3. *The quality system must be documented.* The gap analysis will guide the level and kind of documentation needed. ISO9000 requires careful documentation objective evidence of performance. Quality manuals, system procedures, work instructions, and quality records need to be developed and/or evaluated.
4. *The quality system must be monitored.* Monitoring involves management reviews of the documented quality system, internal quality audits, and corrective actions.
5. *The organization must be registered to ISO9000.* After the quality system has been functioning for several months, it can choose to undertake an audit to determine if it can achieve ISO9000 registration status. An accredited ISO9000 registrar will undertake a thorough study that will last several days and cost between $5,000 and $20,000 or more depending on the complexity of the organization. A formal audit is conducted and if any nonconformances to the guidelines are found they must be corrected. If the audit team is satisfied with the corrections, the registrar will award certificates of ISO9000 registration.

Source: "Becoming ISO9000 Registered," *Management Accounting, Guideline 25,* 1994, with permission of CMA Canada.

wish to be ISO9000 certified. Exhibit 6-12 details the standards developed in the United States.

COSTS OF QUALITY CONTROL

Our focus in this section on quality is on how to interpret quality costs from a management accounting point of view. Companies have discovered that they can spend as much as 20% to 30% of total manufacturing costs on quality-related processes such as detection and correction of internal and external failure. The best-known framework for understanding **quality costs** classifies them into four categories.

Quality costs
Those costs incurred on quality-related processes; include *prevention, appraisal, internal failure,* and *external failure.*

1. **Prevention costs**
2. **Appraisal costs**
3. **Internal failure costs**
4. **External failure costs**

EXHIBIT 6-12

U.S. Quality Standards

Q series of quality standards The American version of the ISO9000 quality standards.

The American Quality Control Society, in the United States, has developed its own quality standards known as the **Q Series of Quality Standards,** which are similar to those developed in Europe. U.S. organizations wanting to be certified under the Q Series of Quality Standards have to consider and choose one of Q91–Q94. Q90 is the standard that provides an overview of the other standards, the definitions used, and the key concepts related to quality.

1. Q91 is the general standard that is used for design, development, manufacturing, installation, and servicing of products and services.
2. Q92 is meant to provide finer details than Q91 for organizations that engage in manufacturing, installation, and servicing of products or services.
3. Q93 provides finer details than Q91 for organizations that perform inspections and tests and for distributors and value-added contractors.
4. Q94 presents the guidelines for managing and auditing a quality control system.

Source: J. Heizer and B. Render, *Production & Operations Management,* Upper Saddle River, NJ: Prentice-Hall, 1995.

Experience shows that it is much less expensive to prevent defects than to detect and repair them after they have occurred.

Prevention costs Those costs incurred to ensure that companies produce products according to quality standards.

Prevention Costs. Prevention costs are incurred to ensure that companies produce products according to quality standards. Quality engineering, training employees in methods designed to maintain quality, and statistical process control are examples of prevention costs. Prevention costs also include training and certifying suppliers so that they can deliver defect-free parts and materials and better, more robust, product designs.

Appraisal costs Those costs related to inspecting products to ensure that they meet both internal and external customer requirements.

Appraisal Costs. Appraisal costs relate to inspecting products to make sure they meet both internal and external customers' requirements. Inspection costs of purchased parts and materials and costs of quality inspection on an assembly line are considered to be appraisal costs. Examples include inspection of incoming materials, maintenance of test equipment, and process control monitoring.

Internal failure costs The costs incurred when the manufacturing process detects a defective component or product before it is shipped to an external customer.

Internal Failure Costs. An internal failure occurs when the manufacturing process detects a defective component or product before it is shipped to an external customer. Reworking defective components or products is a significant cost of internal failures. The cost of downtime in production is another example of internal failure. Engineers have estimated that the cost of defects rises by an order of magnitude for each stage of the manufacturing process that the defect goes undetected. For example, inserting a defective $1 electronic component into a subassembly leads to $10 of scrap if detected at the first stage, $100 at the next stage, and perhaps $10,000 if not detected for two more stages of assembly.

External failure costs Those costs incurred when customers discover a defect.

External Failure Costs. External failures occur when customers discover a defect. All costs associated with correcting the problem—repair of the product, warranty costs, service calls, and product liability recalls—are examples of external failure costs. For many companies, this is the most critical quality cost to avoid. Not only are costs

EXHIBIT 6-13

Examples of Quality-Related Costs

PREVENTION COSTS	APPRAISAL COSTS
Quality engineering	Inspection/testing of incoming materials
Quality training	Maintenance of test equipment
Statistical process control	Process control monitoring
Supplier certification	Product quality audits
Research of customer needs	

INTERNAL FAILURE COSTS	EXTERNAL FAILURE COSTS
Downtime due to defects	Product liability lawsuits
Waste	Repair costs in the field
Net cost of scrap	Returned products
Rework costs	Product liability recalls
	Service calls
	Warranty claims

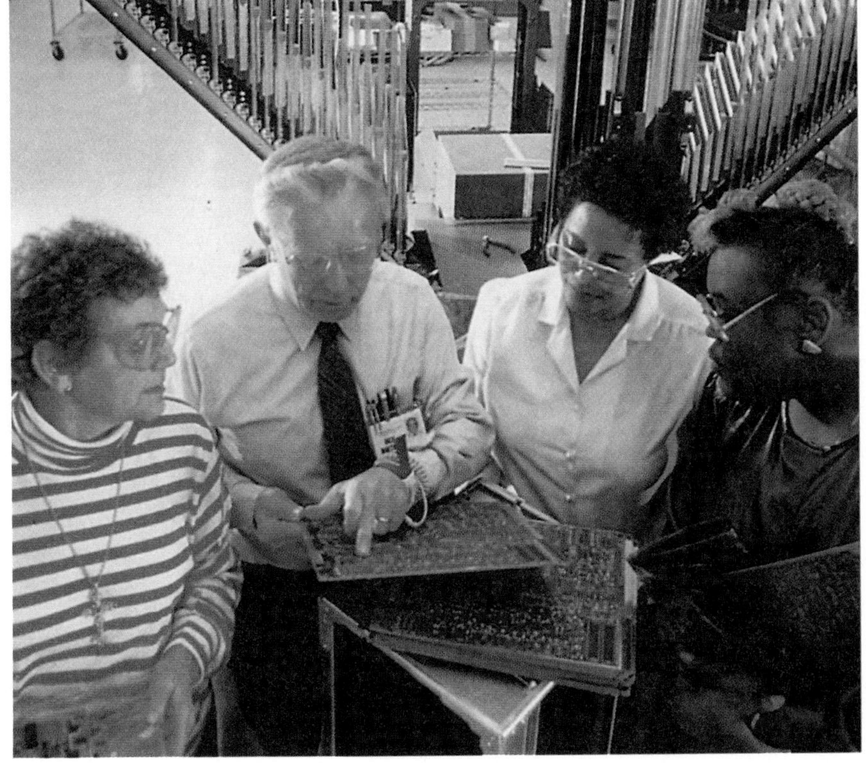

These Motorola employees are discussing ways to prevent defects from occurring on printed circuit boards. Preventing errors at the earliest possible stage will reduce quality costs significantly over the product's life cycle. (Motorola Corporation)

required to fix the problem in the short run, but also customer satisfaction, future sales, and the reputation of the manufacturing organization may be in jeopardy over the long run. Exhibit 6-13 provides examples of the quality costs in each category.

Cost-of-quality (COQ) report
A report that details the cost of maintaining quality production processes and products.

This information is compiled in a **cost-of-quality (COQ) report,** developed for several reasons. First, it illustrates the financial magnitude of quality factors. Often managers are unaware of the enormous impact that rework has on their costs. Second, cost of quality information helps managers set priorities for the quality issues and problems they should address. For example, one trend that managers do not want to see is a very high percentage of quality costs coming from external failure of a product. External quality problems are expensive to fix and can greatly harm the reputation of the product or organization producing the product. Third, the cost of quality report allows managers to see the big picture of quality issues and allows them to try to find the root causes of their quality problems. Fixing the problem at its root will have positive ripple effects throughout the organization, as so many quality issues are interrelated.

Just-in-Time Manufacturing

Just-in-time (JIT) manufacturing
A production process method in which products are manufactured only as needed.

A comprehensive and effective manufacturing system that integrates many of the ideas discussed in this chapter is **just-in-time (JIT) manufacturing.** Recall that the Tobor Toy Company implemented this system in the opening vignette to this chapter.

Just-in-time production requires making a product or service only when the customer, internal or external, requires it. It uses a product layout with a continuous flow—one with no delays once production starts. This means there must be a substantial reduction in setup costs in order to eliminate the need to produce in batches; therefore, processing systems must be reliable.

IMPLICATIONS OF JUST-IN-TIME MANUFACTURING

Just-in-time manufacturing is simple in theory but hard to achieve in practice. Some organizations hesitate to implement JIT, because with no work-in-process inventory a problem anywhere in the system can stop all production. For this reason, organizations that use just-in-time manufacturing must eliminate all sources of failure in the system. The production process must be redesigned so that it is not prohibitively expensive to process one or a small number of items at a time. This usually means reducing the distance over which work in process has to travel and using very adaptable people and equipment that can handle all types of jobs.

At the core of the JIT process is a highly trained workforce whose task is to carry out activities using the highest standards of quality. When an employee discovers a problem with a component he or she has received, it is the responsibility of that employee to call immediate attention to the problem so that it can be corrected. Suppliers must be able to produce and deliver defect-free materials or components just when they are required. In many instances, companies compete with suppliers of the same components to see who can deliver the best quality. At the end of a performance period, the supplier who performs the best will obtain a long-term contract. Preventative maintenance is also employed so that equipment failure is a rare event.

Consider how just-in-time manufacturing can be used at a fast-food restaurant. Some use a just-in-time, continuous-flow product layout, while others use batch production in a process layout. In fact, some fast-food restaurants combine both approaches into hybrid systems that use a batch approach to production and keep inventories at predefined levels. For example, the restaurant may use racks or bins to hold food ready to be sold to the customer and have employees start another batch of production when the existing inventory falls below a line drawn on the bin or rack. At off-peak times, the restaurant may produce to order.

The motivation to use the JIT approach is to improve the quality of the food and to reduce waste by eliminating the need to discard food that has been held in the bin too long. The motivation to use batch production is to sustain a certain level of inventory to reduce the time the customer has to wait for an order. As processing time and setup costs drop, the organization can move closer to just-in-time manufacturing and reduce the waste and quality problems that arise with batch production.

IN PRACTICE

Seeing the Big Picture: Manufacturing, Marketing, and Distribution Activities and the Average Cost of a Compact Disk

While we have focused in this chapter on process and activity decisions related to manufacturing, marketing and distribution activities also need to be scrutinized and improved as their costs are significant in determining product costs. The methods used to reduce cycle time in manufacturing can be applied to both marketing and distribution activities. Further, in the illustration below detailing the breakdown of the average wholesale price of a compact disk (CD), there are a number of other types of costs that need to be managed including record company overhead, recording costs, artist and copyright fees, and so forth. Thus, seeing and managing the "big picture" of the cost of a CD involves an understanding of many organizational functions.

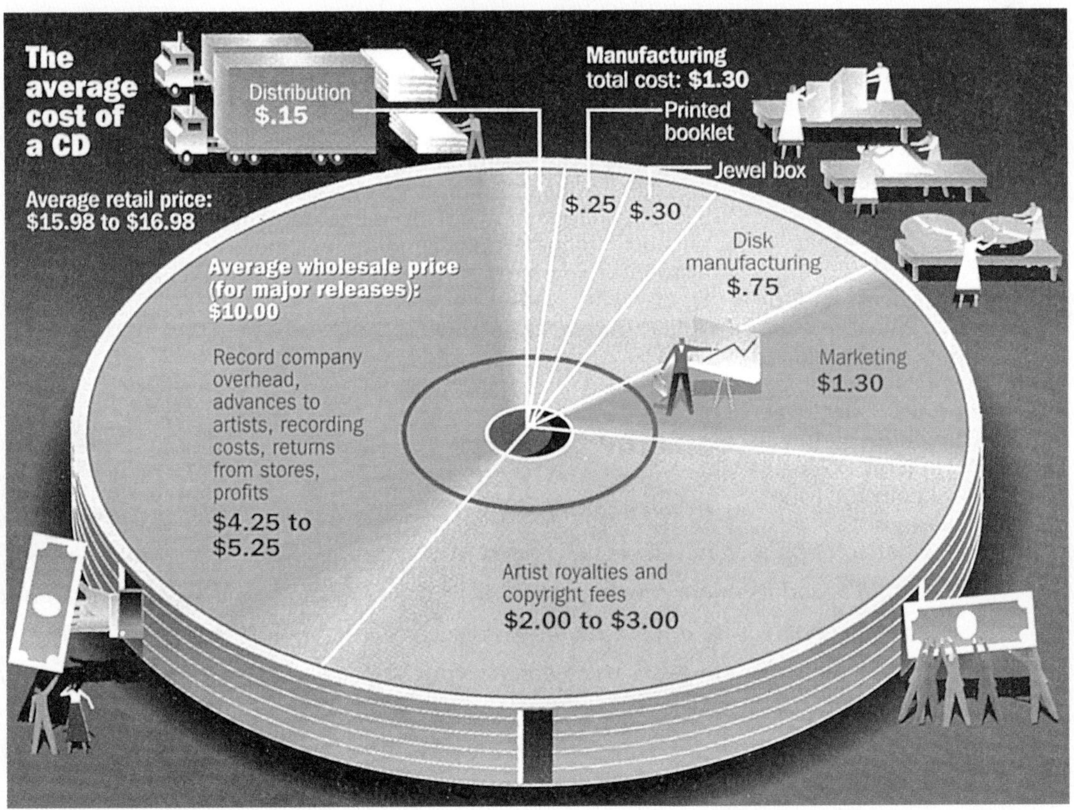

Source: *U.S. News and World Report,* September 25, 1995, p. 68.

JUST-IN-TIME MANUFACTURING AND MANAGEMENT ACCOUNTING

Just-in-time manufacturing has two major implications for management accounting. First, management accounting must support the move to JIT manufacturing by monitoring, identifying, and communicating to decision makers the sources of delay, error, and waste in the system. Important measures of a JIT system's reliability include the following benchmarks of manufacturing cycle effectiveness.

1. Defect rates
2. Cycle times
3. Percent of time that deliveries are on time
4. Order accuracy
5. Actual production as a percent of planned production
6. Actual machine time available compared with planned machine time available

Conventional production systems emphasize labor and machine utilization ratios that encourage large batch sizes and high levels of production. The result is large inventory quantities that lead to long manufacturing cycle times. Therefore, conventional labor and machine productivity ratios are inconsistent with the just-in-time production philosophy, in which operators are expected to produce only what is requested, when it is requested, and on time. The second implication is that the clerical process of management accounting is simplified by JIT manufacturing, because there are fewer inventories to monitor and report.

Just-in-time manufacturing has been a benefit to many organizations. Those interested in implementing this system need to remember several things. First, any significant management innovation, such as ABC or JIT, requires a major cultural change for an organization. Because the central ideas behind JIT are the streamlining of operations and the reduction of waste, many people inside companies are ill-prepared for the change. JIT also can alter the pace of work and the overall work discipline of the organization. It can cause structural changes in such areas as the arrangement of shop floors. Finally, because JIT relies on teamwork, often individuals have to subordinate their own interests to those of the team. Some employees find this difficult, especially if they have come from a work environment where they worked on a single component in relative isolation, or if their personalities are not team oriented.

TOBOR TOY COMPANY REVISITED

We return now to see how Tobor Toy Company fared after its adoption of the JIT manufacturing system. Tobor succeeded in decreasing its major rework rate from 5.8% to 3.3% and its minor rework rate from 13.6% to 7.0%. Major rework required scrapping the robot. Minor rework required correcting the alignment of robot body parts or fixing the ways the gears were functioning, and it had to be done in a specially designated rework area.

As a result of the improvements in rework rates, average production cycle time was reduced by 9.2 days, from 16.4 days to 7.2 days. Average work-in-process inventory was reduced from $1,774,000 to $818,000. Thomas Archer, Tobor Toy's senior manufacturing manager, now had to prepare a report for his chief executive officer detailing how these improvements had affected the company's profits.

PRODUCTION FLOWS

Thomas began by obtaining the new production flowchart shown in Exhibit 6-14. He wanted to assess how the change to the JIT system was progressing. In the first step, the arms and legs of the robot were produced via an injection-molding process in plastic. To accomplish this, metal molds were designed for each component. A measured amount of polypropylene in the form of granules was fed into a horizontal heated cylinder where it was forced into a closed cold mold by a plunger. The liquid plastic entered the mold by means of a channel that led directly into the mold. Runners fed off the channel and moved the liquid plastic to each individual cavity. On cooling, the plastic took the shape of the mold. The process was designed so that each channel produced enough components for 60 robots.

Workers now assembled the various components using the JIT manufacturing system. Other components, such as the computer chip, nylon gears, wheels, and various parts, were added as the production process continued. Although Tobor was striving to eliminate defective robots through the JIT process, achieving this goal was going to take some time. Thus, at the end of the process, any defective robots were rejected and returned for rework or scrapping, depending on the defect. Several finishing

EXHIBIT 6-14

Tobor Toy Company: Production Flowchart

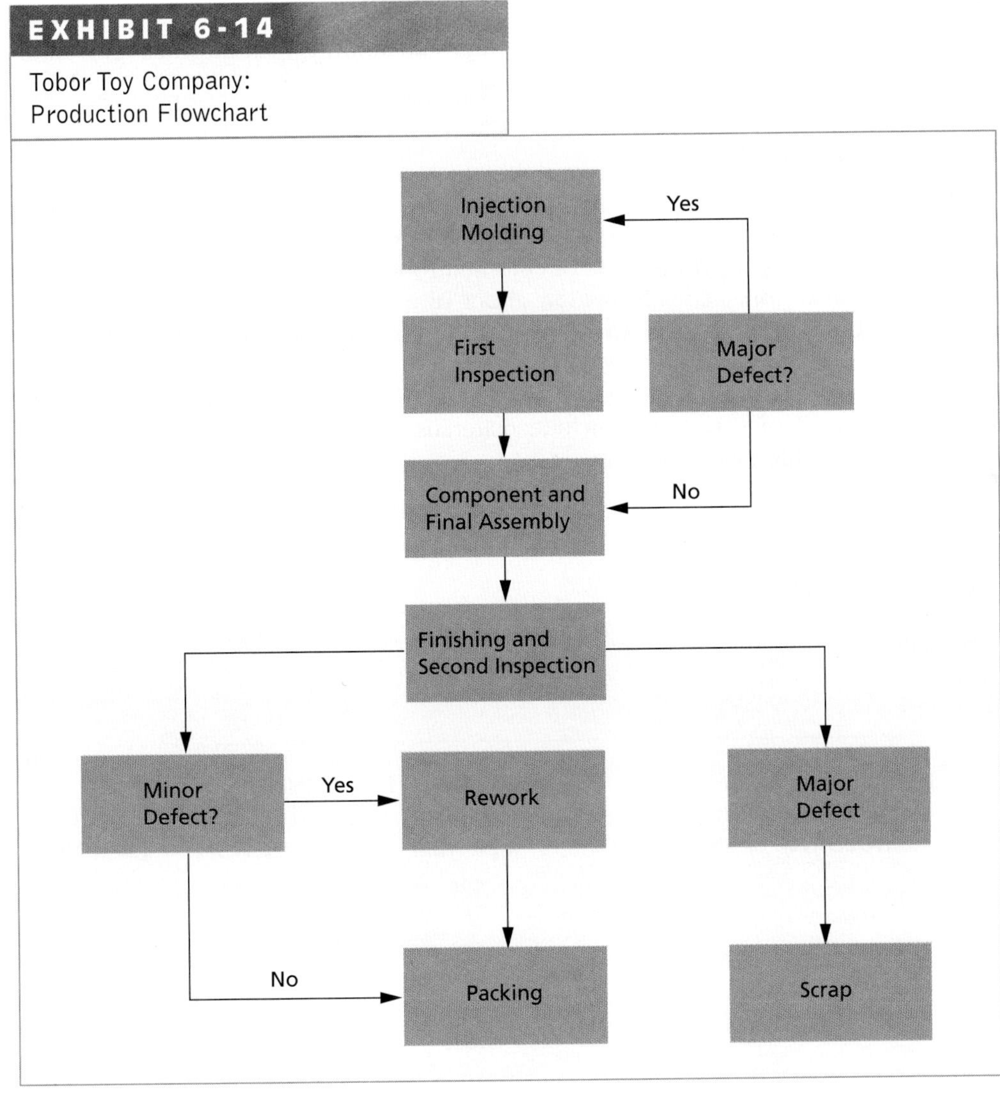

operations and inspections were performed next. Any excess plastic, or flashing, from the molding process was eliminated. The toy robot was then polished to a high gloss. During this process, each robot was inspected. A separate rework area was set aside for correcting the defects and reinserting the robots to ensure that no defects remained. Robots that passed inspection, either before or after rework, were packed and made available for shipment to customers. Thomas concluded that the integration of the JIT system into the overall production flow was relatively successful.

EFFECTS ON WORK-IN-PROCESS INVENTORY

Thomas next turned his attention to records for work-in-process inventory. He had already found that the average WIP inventory decreased by $956,000 after the implementation of the JIT system. He determined from meetings with production personnel that some WIP inventory was still maintained between each pair of successive process stages, because each batch of robots had to await the completion of work on the preceding batch. Thomas could find no detailed records to identify the change in WIP inventory. It was, however, directly influenced by the number of major and minor defects. When defect rates were high, inventory of rejected robots would build up, awaiting rework or scrap. More importantly, production supervisors sought to accumulate a large inventory of work in process in stages occurring after the two inspection points, to enable them to keep busy when many robots were rejected. Therefore, production managers attributed the reduction in work-in-process inventory entirely to reductions in defect rates.

EFFECT ON PRODUCTION COSTS

An important part of Thomas's analysis was an assessment of the impact that the improvement in defect rates had on production costs. Direct materials costs included the cost of the plastic content and the cost of the gears and the computer chip in the robot. The average cost of this type of chip in a robot was $58.

Thomas also collected information about direct labor, unit-related support, and batch-related support costs for each stage of the production process. Exhibit 6-15 includes these costs presented on a unit (robot) basis. Unit-related support costs include labor supervision, plastic, gears, chips, and power costs. Batch-related costs for each batch of 60 robots, which include materials handling and setup of molds, are presented on a unit basis.

EXHIBIT 6-15

Tobor Toy Company: Incremental Conversion Costs per Robot by Production Stages

	INJECTION MOLDING	FIRST INSPECTION	COMPONENT AND FINAL ASSEMBLY	FINISHING AND SECOND INSPECTION	PACKING
Direct Labor (Including Fringe Benefits)	$14	$10	$20	$ 8	$ 6
Unit-Related Support	6	2	12	2	2
Batch-Related Support	8	1	2	1	8
Total Costs	$28	$13	$34	$11	$16

This employee was part of an employee involvement group at a Ford Motor Corporation truck plant that discovered that paint marks and smudges were being caused by paint-booth gloves that were too large and cumbersome. This discovery led to the design and use of the less cumbersome gloves, which reduced the rework cost associated with repainting the damaged parts. (Ford Motor Corporation.)

Thomas excluded product-sustaining and facility-sustaining costs from the analysis. There were no new product introductions or deletions as a consequence of the implementation of the JIT system. The installed plant machine capacity was already greater than its maximum use in recent years, and reductions in defect rates increased the surplus capacity even for the Tobor plant. The company had yet to find new products or new markets that could use this excess capacity; that is, it remained as a sunk cost.

COST OF REWORK

What is the cost of a major defect detected during the first inspection following the injection-molding stage? Because a robot with a major defect cannot be processed further, all incremental conversion costs already incurred on the robot are wasted and all operations must be repeated, incurring the incremental conversion costs again. Recall from our earlier discussion that rework costs are considered internal failure costs. Thomas summarized the costs associated with the correction of a major defect as displayed in Exhibit 6-16 and found that they were $42 per robot.

This estimation includes unit- and batch-related support costs, because more of these costs would be incurred when the entire mold-making, casting, and first-inspection operations were repeated to rectify the major defect. Because there is excess capacity at the plant, product- and facility-sustaining support costs do not increase when repeating production operations are repeated. Therefore, they were not relevant for this analysis. However, if the plant and machine capacity had already been fully utilized and there was no slack to accommodate these repeated operations, the incremental costs of acquiring the additional capacity would be a factor to consider.

Thomas found it somewhat easier to assess the costs of correcting minor defects, which are detected at the second inspection and do not require the rejection of the entire robot. Instead, such minor defects require additional rework operations. Therefore, the incremental costs of correcting minor defects are only the rework costs. Thomas determined that the cost or rework per robot equaled the following:

Direct rework labor	$24
Unit-related support	+ 12
Total cost	$36

EXHIBIT 6-16

Tobor Toy Company: Cost per Unit (Robot) for the Correction of a Major Defect

TYPE OF COST	AMOUNT
Conversion costs for injection molding:	
Direct labor	$14
Unit-related support	9
Batch-related support	5
Costs of first inspection:	
Direct labor	10
Unit-related support	3
Batch-related support	1
Total Costs	$42

Because each robot is reworked independently of the batch in which it was produced, Thomas determined that there were no batch-related support costs. Product- and facility-sustaining support costs also were not relevant because of the excess capacity situation.

Tobor manufactures and sells 180,000 robots each year. Before implementation of the JIT system, on average, 10,440 (180,000 × 0.058) major defects and 24,480 (180,000 × 0.136) minor defects occurred each year. Now, only 5940 (180,000 × 0.033) major defects and 12,600 (180,000 × 0.070) minor defects occur, representing a reduction of 4500 and 11,880 defects, respectively. Therefore, the cost savings of correcting fewer defects because of the JIT system are $189,000 ($42 × 4500) for major rework and $427,680 ($36 × 11,880) for minor rework.

	MAJOR DEFECTS	MINOR DEFECTS
Before JIT	10,440	24,480
After JIT	5,940	12,600
Reduction	4,500	11,880
Cost per correction	× $42	× $36
JIT cost reduction	$189,000	$427,680

COST OF CARRYING WORK-IN-PROCESS INVENTORY

Thomas turned next to the problem of evaluating the cost savings resulting from the reduction in the amount of work-in-process inventory. Interest rates on bank loans to finance the investment in inventories averaged 12.5% per year. With a reduction of $956,000 in WIP inventory ($1,774,000 − $818,000), the cost of financing also decreased by $119,500 ($956,000 × 0.125).

In addition, Thomas estimated that batch-related support costs for various production stages included a total cost of $30 per batch (of 60 robots) that pertained to activities such as work in process, inventory handling, and storage. With the 48.25% reduction in WIP inventory [100 × ($956,000 ÷ $1,774,000)], Thomas expected these related costs also to decrease by about 30%, or equivalently by about $9 per batch ($30 × 0.30). With an annual production of 180,000 robots in 3000 batches (180,000 ÷ 60), Thomas expected a decrease of $27,000 in the costs of work-in-process inventory handling and storage costs ($9 × 3000). As in the case of San Rafael Electric Corporation, however, Thomas's estimate of $27,000 represented the reduction in the demand for these activities because of the reduction in WIP inventory. Over time, these costs should decrease by this amount; but for the reduction to actually occur, the plant management must identify the personnel and other resources committed to this activity and eliminate the resources not required because of the reduction in the demand for them.

BENEFITS FROM INCREASED SALES

Thomas finally decided to evaluate whether the reduction in the production cycle time had resulted in any gains in sales. For this purpose, he met with the marketing manager, Kathie Heine. Kathie pointed out that annual sales had remained stable at around 180,000 robots for the past three years; however, she did believe that the improvement in the production cycle time had an impact on sales. Because of increased competition in the robot market, Kathie had expected to lose sales of about 2000 robots. But the reduction of 6.5 days in the production cycle time had permitted her to respond more aggressively to market demand by offering the robots to customers with a much shorter lead time. Kathie believed that the shorter production cycle time led to maintaining sales of about 2000 robots that otherwise would have been lost. As a result, Tobor had not lost any market share in this market segment.

Thomas determined that the average net selling price (the net of sales commission and shipping costs) for these 2000 robots was $400. Exhibit 6-17 presents his list of the incremental costs for the production of these robots.

EXHIBIT 6-17

Tobor Toy Company: Incremental Costs of Production per Robot

TYPE OF COST	COST PER ROBOT
Direct materials:	
Chip	$ 58.00
All others	32.00
Incremental conversion costs:	
Injection molding	28.00
First inspection	13.00
Component and final assembly	34.00
Second inspection	11.00
Packing	16.00
Prorated rework costs:	
Major defects*	1.40
Minor defects†	2.70
Total incremental costs	$196.10
Average net sales price	$250.00
Contribution margin per robot	$ 53.90

* $\frac{3.3}{100 - 3.3} \times \$42 = \$1.43$

† $\frac{7}{100 - 7} \times \$36 = \$2.71$

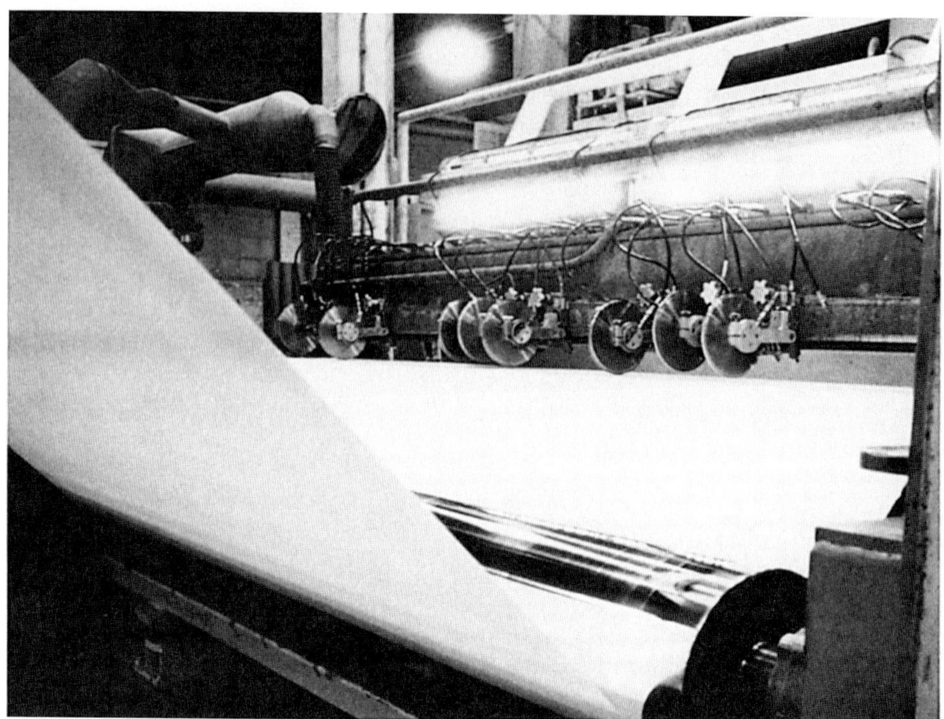

▶ *Customer complaints that paper rolls supplied by Consolidated Papers were breaking in their printing presses led a group of employees at Consolidated Papers to identify the cause. The employees discovered that the breakage occurred because of slight tears at the edges of the paper created when the paper was being trimmed to width during its production. The solution was to design a simple device that held the paper tightly while it was being slit. The cost of this investigation and the device designed to eliminate the problem was justified on the grounds that failing to solve the problem would have cost the company far more in lost sales. (Consolidated Papers, Inc.)*

EXHIBIT 6-18

Tobor Toy Company: Summary of Annual Benefits Resulting from the JIT System

Reduction in rework costs:		
Major rework	$189,000	
Minor rework	427,680	$616,680
Reduction in work-in-process inventory-related costs:		
Financing costs	$107,000	134,000
Inventory handling and storage activity costs	27,000	
Contribution from sales increases resulting from improved production cycle time		108,000
Total Annual Benefits		$858,680

Notice in Exhibit 6-17 that rework costs are prorated over the good units of production. For instance, incremental costs for major rework are $42 for each robot that requires rework. For every 1000 robots produced, an average of 33 robots (1000 × 3.3%) now require major rework. Therefore, the company obtains 967 good robots (1000 − 33). The total incremental major rework cost for 33 robots is $1386 ($42 × 33), which is borne by the 967 good robots at the rate of $1.43 ($1386 ÷ 967) per good robot.

The contribution margin is estimated to be $54 per robot, or $108,000 in total for the 2000 robots ($54 × 2000). Without the JIT system and the consequent reduction in cycle time, this contribution from sales would have been lost.

SUMMARY OF COSTS AND BENEFITS

Exhibit 6-18 displays Thomas's summary of the benefits from the quality improvement program. Total estimated annual benefits of $858,680 are much greater than the one-time costs of $300,000 spent on the JIT system and worker training discussed in the opening vignette to this chapter.

SUMMARY

Managers evaluate the impact of managerial decisions and actions that affect the organization's activities and processes. To support decision making, they must identify the alternatives available and determine how relevant costs and revenues differ for each. As a general rule, sunk costs are not relevant costs.

Managers also must be able to evaluate the financial impact of recent activity and process decisions, such as improved plant layouts that streamline production operations. They need various types of costs and other functional information to assess the impact of decisions affecting an organization's activities and processes. Finally, detailed evaluations of implemented actions may shed light on ways to increase the benefits derived from them.

The JIT manufacturing system has many positive effects on the levels of work-in-process inventory, the cost of support activities of handling and storing work-in-process inventory, and the amounts of major and minor rework. Further, it reduces cycle times so that there are shorter lead times to fulfilling customer orders. All these changes have a very tangible and quantifiable bottom-line effect.

SUMMARY EXAMPLE

VoiceTek Corporation, a major producer of telephone products, is considering the introduction of a videophone targeted to the business market. The proposed price is $1000 per unit. The following cost information is based on the expected annual sales level of 60,000 units for the new product:

$18,000,000	direct material cost
12,000,000	direct labor costs
6,000,000	variable manufacturing support
10,000,000	fixed manufacturing support

The average inventory levels for the videophone are estimated as follows:

Direct material	2 months of production
Work in process (100% complete for materials and 50% for labor and variable manufacturing support)	2 months of production
Finished goods	1 month of production

Annual inventory carrying costs, not included in these variable costs, are estimated to be 10%. In addition, the marketing manager estimates that the total sales revenue of the existing products will be reduced by $12,000,000 once the videophone is on the market. The average contribution margin ratio for the existing products is 30%.

1. Compute the relevant costs (revenues) for the videophone.
2. Should VoiceTek introduce the new product?
3. Determine the breakeven point in units for the videophone.

The following information presents the solution to this problem.

1. Selling price per unit $1000
   Less:
   Variable cost per unit
   Direct materials

   $\$18{,}000{,}000 \div 60{,}000 = \$300$

   Direct labor

   $\$12{,}000{,}000 \div 60{,}000 = \$200$

   Support

   $\$6{,}000{,}000 \div 60{,}000 = \$100$

   Total − 600

   Contribution margin per unit $ 400

   Inventory carrying value
   Direct materials

   $\$300 \times 60{,}000 \text{ units} \times 2/12 = \$3{,}000{,}000$

   Work in process

   $\{\$300 + [(200 + 100) \times 50\%]\} \times 60{,}000 \times 2/12 = \$4{,}500{,}000$

   Finished goods

   $(\$300 + 200 + 100) \times 60{,}000 \times 1/12 = \$3{,}000{,}000$

   Inventory carrying cost

   $(\$3{,}000{,}000 + \$4{,}500{,}000 + \$3{,}000{,}000) \times 10\% = \$1{,}050{,}000$

   Relevant costs
   Increase in contribution margin for sale of videophone

   $\$400 \times 60{,}000 = \$24{,}000{,}000$

   Decrease in contribution margin from cannibalization of existing sales

   $\$12{,}000{,}000 \times 30\% = \$3{,}600{,}000$

   Additional inventory carrying costs

   $1,050,000

   Increase in fixed manufacturing support

   $10,000,000

2. Increase in VoiceTek's operating profit

   $\$24{,}000{,}000 - \$3{,}600{,}000 - \$1{,}050{,}000 - \$10{,}000{,}000 = \$9{,}350{,}000$

   Therefore, VoiceTek should introduce the videophone

3. Let x be the breakeven point in units.

$$\$400 \times x = \$10{,}000{,}000 + \$3{,}600{,}000 + (\$300 \times x \times 2/12 + 450 \times x \times 2/12 + \$600 \times x \times 1/12) \times 0.1$$

$$\$382.5x = \$13{,}000{,}000$$

$$x = 33{,}987 \text{ units}$$

KEY TERMS

Appraisal costs, 240
Avoidable costs, 223
Cellular manufacturing, 229
Certified suppliers, 225
Cost of nonconformance (CONC) to quality standards, 237
Cost-of-quality (COQ) report, 242
Cycle time, 231
External failure costs, 240
Internal failure costs, 240
Investments, 225
Just-in-time (JIT) manufacturing, 242
Make-or-buy decision, 222
Manufacturing cycle efficiency (MCE), 231
Operating costs, 225
Outsourcing, 223
Prevention costs, 240
Processing time, 231
Process layout, 226
Product layout, 227
Q series of quality standards, 240
Quality costs, 239
Relevant costs/revenues, 220
Sunk costs, 220
Theory of constraints (TOC), 225
Throughput contribution, 225

ASSIGNMENT MATERIALS

QUESTIONS

6-1 Why should decision makers focus only on the relevant costs for decision making? (LO 1)

6-2 Are sunk costs relevant? Explain. (LO 1)

6-3 What behavioral factors many influence some managers to consider sunk costs as being relevant in their decisions? (LO 1)

6-4 Are direct materials and direct labor costs always relevant? Explain with examples. (LO 1, 2)

6-5 When are (1) product-sustaining and (2) facility-sustaining (business sustaining) costs relevant? Give examples of each case. (LO 2)

6-6 Why can't we directly compare cash flows at different points in time? (LO 2)

6-7 Are avoidable costs relevant? Explain. (LO 2)

6-8 Give two examples of costs and decision contexts in which the costs are not relevant for a short-term context but are relevant for a long-term context. (LO 2)

6-9 Why are facility-sustaining (business sustaining) support costs often not relevant for make-or-buy decisions? Give an example when facility-sustaining support costs are relevant for a make-or-buy decision. (LO 2)

6-10 What qualitative considerations are relevant in a make-or-buy decision? (LO 2, 3)

6-11 What are the opportunity costs that are relevant in a make-or-buy decision? (LO 2)

6-12 The theory of constraints relies on three measures: *throughput contribution, investments,* and *operating costs.* Define these three measures in the context of the theory of constraints. (LO 4)

6-13 What is the difference between process and product layout systems? (LO 5)

6-14 What is cellular manufacturing? (LO 5)

6-15 How is a just-in-time manufacturing system different from a conventional manufacturing system? (LO 7)

6-16 What creates the need to maintain work-in-process inventory? Why is work-in-process inventory likely to decrease on the implementation of cellular manufacturing, just-in-time production, and quality improvement programs? (LO 5, 7)

6-17 Why are production cycle time and the level of work-in-process inventory positively related? (LO 5, 7)

6-18 List two types of costs incurred when implementing a cellular manufacturing layout. (LO 5)

6-19 What are two types of financial benefits resulting from a shift to cellular manufacturing, just-in-time production, or continuous quality improvements? (LO 5, 7)

6-20 What is meant by the term *cost of nonconformance?* (LO 6)

6-21 Waste, rework, and net cost of scrap are examples of what kinds of quality costs? (LO 6)

6-22 Quality engineering, quality training, statistical process control, and supplier certification are what kinds of quality costs? (LO 6)

6-23 List three examples for each of the following quality costing categories:

(a) prevention costs

(b) appraisal costs

(c) internal failure costs

(d) external failure costs (LO 6)

6-24 What is the additional cost of replacing one unit of a product rejected at inspection and scrapped? (LO 6, 8)

6-25 What is the additional cost if a unit rejected at inspection can be reworked to meet quality standards by performing some additional operations? (LO 6, 8)

6-26 What costs and revenues are relevant in evaluating the profit impact of an increase in sales? (LO 8)

6-27 "Design an accounting system that routinely reports only relevant costs," advised a management consultant. Is this good advice? Explain. (LO 1, 2, 8)

EXERCISES

LO 1, 3 **6-28** ***Relevant costs*** Don Baxter's five-year-old Camaro requires repairs estimated at $5400 to make it roadworthy again. His friend, Mike Blue, suggested that he buy a five-year-old Chevette instead for $5400 cash. Mike estimated the following costs for the two cars:

COSTS	CAMARO	CHEVETTE
Acquisition cost	$24,000	$5,400
Repairs	5,400	0
Annual operating costs:		
Gas, maintenance, insurance	2,900	1,800

REQUIRED

(a) What costs are relevant and what costs are not relevant for this decision? Why?

(b) What should Don do? Explain

(c) What quantitative and qualitative factors are relevant for his decision? Why?

LO 1 **6-29** ***Relevant costs*** Gilmark Company has 10,000 obsolete lamps carried in inventory at a cost of $12 each. They can be sold as they are for $4 each. They can be reworked, however, at a total cost of $55,000 and sold for $10 each. Determine whether it is worthwhile to rework these lamps.

LO 1 **6-30** ***Sunk costs*** Ideal Company's plant manager is considering buying a new grinding machine to replace an old grinding machine or overhauling the old one to ensure compliance with the plant's high-quality standards. The following data are available:

OLD GRINDING MACHINE	
Original cost	$50,000
Accumulated depreciation	40,000
Annual operating costs	18,000
Current salvage value	4,000
Salvage value at the end of 5 years	0

NEW GRINDING MACHINE	
Cost	$70,000
Annual operating costs	13,000
Salvage value at the end of 5 years	0

OVERHAUL OF OLD GRINDING MACHINE	
Cost of overhaul	$25,000
Annual operating costs after overhaul	14,000
Salvage value at the end of 5 years	0

REQUIRED

(a) What costs should the decision maker consider as sunk costs?

(b) List all relevant costs and when they are incurred.

(c) What should the plant manager do? Why?

LO 2 **6-31** ***Make-or-buy, relevant costs*** The assembly division of Cassandra Resolution, Inc. is bidding on an order of 1000 TV sets. The division is anxious to get this order, because it has a substantial amount of unused plant capacity. The variable cost for each TV set is $600 in addition to the cost of the picture tube. The divisional purchasing manager has received two bids for the tube. One is from Cassandra Resolution's picture tube division. This bid is for $55 per picture tube, although its variable cost is only $42 per tube. The other is from an outside vendor for $65 per unit. Cassandra Resolution's picture tube division has sufficient unused capacity for this order.

REQUIRED

(a) Determine the relevant costs for this order for the assembly division under both internal and outsourcing arrangements.

(b) Determine the relevant costs for this order for Cassandra Resolution as a company under each of the sourcing arrangements.

6-32 ***Make-or-buy*** Kane Company is considering outsourcing a key component. A reliable supplier has quoted a price of $64.50 per unit. The following costs of the component when manufactured in-house are expressed on a per-unit basis. LO 2

Direct materials	$23.40
Direct labor	16.10
Unit-related support	14.70
Batch-related support	9.80
Product-sustaining support	22.20
Facility-sustaining support	6.90
Total costs	$93.10

REQUIRED

(a) What assumptions need to be made about the behavior of support costs for Kane?

(b) Should Kane Company outsource the component?

(c) What other factors are relevant for this decision?

6-33 ***Relevant costs in the make-or-buy decision*** Premier Company manufactures gear model G37 used in several of its farm-equipment products. Annual production volume of G37 is 20,000 units. Unit costs for G37 are as follows: LO 2

Direct materials costs	$ 55
Direct labor costs	30
Variable support costs	25
Fixed support costs	15
Total costs	$125

Alternatively, Premier can also purchase gear model G37 from an outside supplier for $120 per unit. If G37 is outsourced, Premier can use the facility where G37 is currently manufactured for production of another gear—model G49. This would save Premier $113,000 in facility rental and other costs presently incurred. Should Premier make or buy G37?

6-34 ***Relevant costs and revenues*** Joyce Printers, Inc. is considering replacing its current printing machines with newer, faster, and more efficient printing technology. The following data have been compiled: LO 1

CATEGORY	EXISTING MACHINES	NEW MACHINES
Original cost	$80,000	$120,000
Annual operating costs	$50,000	$ 30,000
Remaining useful life	5 years	5 years
Salvage value after 5 years	$ 5,000	$ 10,000

The existing machines can be disposed of now for $40,000. Keeping them will cost $20,000 for repair and upgrading. Should Joyce Printers keep the existing printing machines? Explain.

LO 1 **6-35** ***Relevant costs for decision making*** Kentucky Motors has manufactured compressor parts at its plant in Pitcairn, Indiana, for the last 18 years. An outside supplier, Superior Compressor Company, has offered to supply compressor model A238 at a price of $200 per unit. Unit manufacturing costs for A238 are as follows:

Direct materials	$ 80
Direct labor	60
Unit-related support	26
Batch-related support	22
Product-sustaining support	8
Facility-sustaining support	17
Total costs	$213

REQUIRED

(a) Should Superior Compressor's offer be accepted if the plant is presently operating below capacity?

(b) What is the maximum acceptable purchase price if the plant facilities are fully utilized at present and if any additional available capacity can be deployed for the production of other compressors?

LO 6 **6-36** ***Quality cost categories*** Regarding the quality costing categories, how do prevention costs differ from appraisal costs? How do internal failure costs differ from external failure costs?

LO 6 **6-37** ***Quality cost categories*** Of the four quality costing categories, which quality cost is the most damaging to the organization? Explain.

LO 6, 8 **6-38** ***Quality improvement programs and cost savings*** Pyro Valves Company manufactures brass valves meeting precise specification standards. All finished valves are inspected before packing and shipping to customers. Rejected valves are returned to the initial production stage to be melted and recast. As a result of a quality-improvement program, the reject rate has decreased from 6.4% to 5.1%. The following unit cost data are available:

COSTS	CASTING	FINISHING	INSPECTION	PACKING	TOTAL
Direct materials	$225	$ 12	$ 0	$ 8	$ 245
Direct labor	84	121	24	16	245
Variable support	122	164	30	20	336
Fixed support	63	89	16	10	178
	$494	$386	$70	$54	$1,004

Improvements in reject rates have also led to a decrease in work-in-process inventory, from $386,000 to $270,000. Inventory carrying costs are estimated to be 15% per year. Estimate the annual cost savings as a result of the quality improvement, assuming that Pyro sells 10,000 valves each year.

LO 7, 8 **6-39** ***Just-in-time manufacturing and cost savings*** Bogden Company introduced just-in-time manufacturing last year and has prepared the following data to assess the benefits from the change:

CATEGORY	BEFORE THE CHANGE	AFTER THE CHANGE
Production cycle time	68 days	30 days
Work-in-process inventory	$ 160,000	$ 40,000
Total sales	$1,260,000	$1,700,000
Costs as percent of sales:		
Direct materials	30%	25%
Direct labor	22%	15%
Variable support	28%	10%
Fixed support	12%	5%

Inventory financing costs are 15% per year. Estimate the total financial benefits that resulted from the switch to just-in-time manufacturing operations.

6-40 ***Facilities layout*** How would you classify the layout of a large grocery store? Why do you think it is laid out this way? Can you think of any way to improve the layout of a conventional grocery store? Explain your reasoning. (Hint: Think about JIT, cycle time, etc.) LO 5

PROBLEMS

6-41 ***Relevant costs for decision making*** Carmen's Catering provides lunches and dinners for various groups or organizations in the locality. A new customer has approached Carmen's Catering to provide dinner for a special event featuring a well-known speaker, with estimated attendance of 100 people. Carmen suggested two different menus to the customer. The first menu would require materials and direct labor cost of $13 per meal. The second menu would require materials and direct labor cost of $16 per meal. Carmen has developed the following cost analysis for her ongoing operations: LO 1

Event-related support	$ 100
Customer-related support	22
Facility-sustaining support per month	2000

The timing of the new customer's event would present no problems for Carmen's Catering. Carmen would like to know the minimum price she should charge for 100 meals of the first menu, or 100 meals of the second menu.

REQUIRED

(a) In determining the minimum prices, what assumptions need to be made about the behavior of support costs for Carmen's Catering?

(b) What other factors are relevant for this decision?

(c) What prices would you recommend for the first menu or the second menu for the new customer's dinner? Provide reasons for your recommendation.

6-42 ***Relevant cost and revenues: changes in facilities layout*** To facilitate a move toward JIT production, AB Company is considering a change in its plant layout. The plant controller, Anita Bentley, has been asked to evaluate the costs and benefits of the change in plant layout. After meeting with production and marketing LO 1, 5, 8 managers, Anita has compiled the following estimates:

- Machine moving and reinstallation will cost $100,000.
- Total sales will increase by 20% to $1,200,000 because of a decrease in production cycle time required under the new plant layout. Average contribution margin (sales dollars minus variable costs) is 31% of sales.
- Inventory-related costs will decrease by 25% because of an expected decrease in work-in-process inventory. Currently, the annual average carrying value of work-in-process inventory is $200,000. The annual inventory financing cost is 15%.

Should AB implement the proposed change in plant layout? Support your answer.

LO 2 **6-43** ***Relevant costs in the make-or-buy decision*** Tanner Appliance Company manufactures 12,000 units of part M4 annually. The part is used in the production of one of its principal products. The following unit cost information is available on part M4.

Direct materials	$11
Direct labor	9
Unit-related support	4
Batch-related support	5
Product-sustaining support	2
Facility-sustaining support	2
Allocated corporate support	5
Total costs	$38

A potential supplier has offered to manufacture this part for Tanner Appliance for $30 per unit. If Tanner Appliance outsources the production of part M4, 50% of batch-related and 80% of product-sustaining activity resources can be eliminated. Furthermore, the production facility now being used to produce this part can be used for a fast-growing new product line that would otherwise require the use of a neighboring facility at a rental cost of $20,000 per year. Should Tanner Appliance purchase part M4 from the outside supplier? What costs are relevant for this decision? What additional factors should Tanner consider?

LO 1 **6-44** ***Relevant costs: replacement decision*** Anderson Department Stores is considering the replacement of the existing elevator system at its downtown store. A new system has been proposed that runs faster than the existing system, experiences few breakdowns, and as a result promises considerable savings in operating costs. Information on the existing system and the proposed new system follow:

CATEGORY	EXISTING SYSTEM	NEW SYSTEM
Original cost	$300,000	$875,000
Remaining life	6 years	6 years
Annual cash operating costs	$150,000	$ 8,000
Salvage value at present	$100,000	—
Salvage value in 6 years	$ 25,000	$100,000

REQUIRED

(a) What costs are not relevant for this decision?

(b) What are the relevant costs?

LO 1 **6-45** ***Incremental revenues and costs, special order*** Genis Battery Company is considering accepting a special order for 50,000 batteries that it received from a discount retail store. The order specified a price of $4.00 per unit, which reflects a discount of $0.50 per unit relative to the company's regular price of $4.50 per unit. Genis's accounting department has prepared the following analysis to show the cost savings resulting from additional sales:

COSTS	COST PER UNIT WITHOUT THE ADDITIONAL SALES (100,000 UNITS)	COST PER UNIT WITH THE ADDITIONAL SALES (150,000 UNITS)
Variable	$3.30	$3.30
Fixed	$4.20	$3.90

No additional fixed costs will be incurred for this order because the company has surplus capacity. Because the average cost per unit will be reduced from $4.20 to $3.90, Genis's president believes that a reduction in the price to $4.00 is justified for this order.

REQUIRED

(a) Should the order for the 50,000 units at a price of $4 be accepted? What will be the impact on Genis's operating income?

(b) Is the accounting department's analysis the best way to evaluate this decision? If not, what alternative method can you suggest?

(c) What other considerations are important in this case? Why?

6-46 ***Relevant costs: replacement decision*** Syd Young, the production manager at Fuchow Company, purchased a cutting machine for the company last year. Six months after the purchase of the cutting machine, Syd learned about a new cutting machine that is more reliable than the machine that he purchased. The following information is available for the two machines: LO 1

CATEGORY	OLD MACHINE	NEW MACHINE
Acquisition cost	$300,000	$360,000
Remaining life	4 years	4 years
Salvage value now	$100,000	—
Salvage value at the end of 4 years	$ 4,000	$ 6,000

Annual operating costs for the old machine are $140,000. The new machine will decrease annual operating costs by $60,000. These amounts do not include any charges for depreciation. Fuchow Company uses the straight-line depreciation method. These estimates of operating costs exclude rework costs. The new machine will also result in a reduction in the defect rate from the current 5% to 2.5%. All defective units are reworked at a cost of $1 per unit. The company, on average, produces 100,000 units annually.

REQUIRED

(a) Should Syd Young replace the old machine with the new machine? Explain, listing all relevant costs.

(b) What costs should be considered as sunk costs for this decision?

(c) What other factors may affect Young's decision?

6-47 ***ABC and TOC*** Refer to the In Practice entitled "ABC versus TOC: Will Ever the Twain Meet?" on p. 228. Discuss the similarities and differences between activity-based costing and theory of constraints, and situations in which one approach might be preferable to the other. LO 4

LO 5, 7 **6-48** ***Cycle time efficiency and JIT*** Walker Brothers Company is considering installing a JIT manufacturing system in the hope that it will improve their overall manufacturing cycle efficiency. Data from the traditional system and estimates for the JIT system are presented below for their Nosun Product:

TIME CATEGORY	TRADITIONAL SYSTEM	JIT SYSTEM
Storage	4 hours	1 hour
Inspection	40 minutes	5 minutes
Moving	80 minutes	20 minutes
Processing	2 hours	75 minutes

REQUIRED

(a) Calculate manufacturing cycle efficiency under the traditional and JIT systems for the Nosun Product.

(b) Strictly based on your MCE calculations above, should Walker Brothers implement the JIT system? Explain.

LO 5, 7 **6-49** ***JIT and cellular manufacturing*** You are a manufacturing manager faced with the decision to improve manufacturing operations and efficiency. You have been studying both cellular manufacturing and just-in-time manufacturing systems. Your boss expects you to prepare a report covering the costs and benefits of each approach.

REQUIRED

Write a detailed memorandum discussing the costs and benefits of cellular manufacturing versus JIT.

LO 1, 8 **6-50** ***Relevant costs: replacement decision*** Rossman Instruments, Inc. is considering leasing new state-of-the-art machinery at an annual cost of $900,000. The new machinery has a four-year expected life. It will replace existing machinery leased one year earlier at an annual lease cost of $490,000 committed for five years. Early termination of this lease contract will incur a $280,000 penalty. There are no other fixed costs.

The new machinery is expected to decrease variable product costs from $42 to $32 per unit because of improved materials yield, faster machine speed, and lower direct labor, supervision, materials handling, and quality inspection requirements. The sales price will remain at $56. Improvements in quality, production cycle time, and customer responsiveness are expected to increase annual sales from 36,000 units to 48,000 units.

The variable product costs stated earlier exclude the inventory carrying costs. Because the new machinery is expected to affect inventory levels, the following estimates are also provided. The enhanced speed and accuracy of the new machinery are expected to decrease production cycle time by half, and consequently, lead to a decrease in work-in-process inventory level from three months to just one and one-half months of production. Increased flexibility with these new machines is expected to allow a reduction in finished goods inventory from two months of production to just one month. Improved yield rates and greater machine reliability will enable a reduction in raw materials inventory from four months of production to just one and one-half months. Annual inventory carrying cost is 20% of inventory value.

CATEGORY	OLD MACHINE	NEW MACHINE
Average per unit cost of raw materials inventory	$12	$11
Average per unit cost of work-in-process inventory	25	20
Average per unit cost of finished goods inventory	38	28
Selling cost per unit sold	4	4
Variable product cost per unit purchased	42	32

REQUIRED

(a) Determine the total value of annual benefits from the new machinery. Include changes in inventory carrying costs.

(b) Should Rossman replace its existing machinery with the new machinery? Present your reasoning with detailed steps identifying relevant costs and revenues.

(c) Discuss whether a manager evaluated on the basis of Rossman's net income will have the incentive to make the right decision as evaluated in (b) above.

6-51 ***Relevant costs: dropping a product*** Merchant Company manufactures and sells three models of electronic printers. Ken Gail, president of the company, is considering dropping model JT484 from its product line because the company has experienced losses for this product over the last three quarters. The following product-level operating data have been compiled for the most recent quarter. LO 1

CATEGORY	TOTAL	JT284	JT384	JT484
Sales	$1,000,000	$500,000	$200,000	$300,000
Variable costs	600,000	300,000	100,000	200,000
Contribution margin	$ 400,000	$200,000	$100,000	$100,000
Fixed costs:				
Rent	$ 50,000	$ 25,000	$ 10,000	$ 15,000
Depreciation	60,000	30,000	12,000	18,000
Utilities	40,000	20,000	5,000	15,000
Supervision	50,000	15,000	5,000	30,000
Maintenance	30,000	15,000	6,000	9,000
Administrative	100,000	30,000	20,000	50,000
Total fixed costs	$ 330,000	$135,000	$ 58,000	$137,000
Operating income loss	$ 70,000	$ 65,000	$ 42,000	($ 37,000)

In addition, the following information is also available

- Factory rent and depreciation will not be affected by a decision to drop model JT484.
- Quarterly utility bills will be reduced from $40,000 to $31,000 if JT484 is dropped.
- Supervision costs for JT484 can be eliminated if dropped.
- The maintenance department will be able to reduce quarterly costs by $7000 if JT484 is dropped.
- Elimination of JT484 will make it possible to eliminate two administrative staff positions with combined salaries of $30,000 per quarter.

REQUIRED

(a) Should Merchant Company eliminate JT484?

(b) Merchant's sales manager believes that it is important to continue to produce JT484 to maintain a full product line. He expects the elimination of JT484 will reduce sales of the remaining two products by 5% each. Will this information change your answer to (a)? Explain.

LO 1, 8 **6-52** ***Relevant costs: introducing a new product*** Macready Company is considering introducing a new model of personal compact disc players at a price of $105 per unit. Its controller has compiled the following incremental cost information based on an estimate of 120,000 units of sales annually for the new product:

Direct materials cost	$3,600,000
Direct labor cost	$2,400,000
Variable manufacturing support	$1,200,000
Sales commission	10% of sales
Fixed cost	$2,000,000

The average inventory levels for the new product are estimated as follows:

Raw materials	2 months of production
Work in progress (100% complete for materials and 50% complete for labor and variable manufacturing support)	1 month of production
Finished goods	2 months of production

Annual inventory carrying costs not included in the variable manufacturing support listed earlier are estimated to be 12% of inventory value. In addition, the sales manager expects the introduction of the new model to result in a reduction in sales of the existing model from 300,000 to 240,000 units. The contribution margin for the old product is $20 per unit.

REQUIRED

(a) Determine the total impact on Macready's profit from the introduction of the new product.

(b) Should Macready introduce the new product? Explain.

(c) Determine the breakeven point (in units) for the new product. That is, determine the required sales in units for the company to earn zero profit. Assume that sales of the old product decrease by one unit for every two-unit increase in the sales of the new product.

LO 2 **6-53** ***Make-or-buy*** Beau's Bistro has a reputation for providing good value for its menu prices. The desserts, developed by the pastry chef, are one of the distinctive features of the menu. The pastry chef has just given notice that he will relocate to another city in a month, and has volunteered to share some of the dessert recipes with the next pastry chef. Beau has been concerned about the Bistro's declining profits, but is reluctant to raise prices because of the competition he faces. He decided this was an opportune time to consider outsourcing dessert production. Beau solicited bids for dessert production and delivery, and is evaluating two bids, as well as the alternative of hiring a new pastry chef who would make the desserts in-house. The first bid is from a gourmet dessert provider who would fill the Bistro's current dessert demand for $5500 per month, and would periodically introduce new gourmet desserts. The second bid is from a dessert provider who would provide high-quality, traditional desserts to fill Bistro's current demand (in terms of servings) for $5000 per month. Beau has identified the following costs per month if the desserts are made in-house.

Ingredients	$ 500
Pastry chef labor	3500
Assistants' labor	1500
Direct support	200
Total	$5700

REQUIRED

(a) What qualitative factors are relevant for this decision?

(b) Would you advise Beau to outsource dessert production? Provide reasons for your decision.

6-54 ***Outsourcing, ethics*** Hollenberry, Inc. is a successful mail-order catalog business with customers worldwide. The company's headquarters are in a small town some distance from any major metropolitan area. Sales have grown steadily over the years, and the call center facilities are currently inadequate for the sales volume. Management is comparing two alternatives: Expand the call center facilities or outsource the call center operations to a company specializing in such operations. If the call center is outsourced, most of the current employees would lose their jobs because they do not wish to relocate to the new call center location, close to a major metropolitan area. Many of the employees have been with Hollenberry for over 20 years. Regardless of where the call center is located, customers will call a toll-free phone number. If the call center is outsourced, however, more multilingual operators would be available. Hollenberry has identified the following costs: LO 2, 3

Cost of In-House Call Center:

Labor	$650,000
Building rent	60,000
Phone charges	35,000
Other support costs	42,000

If the call center is outsourced, the related office equipment would be sold to the new call center operations for $20,000. The equipment was originally purchased at a cost of $100,000. The building will no longer be rented, and call center employees will have the opportunity to transfer to the outside call center, in which case their salaries will be paid by the outside call center. The other support costs are associated with maintaining the building and office equipment for the current call center.

If Hollenberry outsources the call center and the same number and pattern of calls occurs next year, Hollenberry will pay the new cost center firm $700,000 for the year.

REQUIRED

(a) What costs are relevant for the decision on outsourcing the call center?

(b) What qualitative factors are important in this decision?

(c) What should Hollenberry do? Provide reasons for your recommendation.

6-55 ***Cellular manufacturing and cycle time efficiency*** Ray Brown's company, Whisper Voice Systems, is trying to increase its manufacturing cycle efficiency (MCE). Because Ray has a very limited budget, he has been searching for a way to increase his MCE by using cellular manufacturing. One of Ray's manufacturing LO 5 managers, Maria Lopez, has been studying cellular manufacturing and claims that with minimal cost that includes downtime in the operation she can rearrange existing machinery and workers and improve MCE. Ray is quite skeptical about this and decides to allow Maria to rearrange a small part of his operation. For Ray to be satisfied, he has stated that MCE must increase by 12%. MCE data before and after the rearrangement are as follows:

TIME CATEGORY	BEFORE REARRANGEMENT	AFTER REARRANGEMENT
Inspection	30 minutes	15 minutes
Moving	45 minutes	10 minutes
Processing	70 minutes	30 minutes
Storage	55 minutes	20 minutes

Does the change in MCE meet Ray's requirement? Why or why not?

LO 3, 5 **6-56** ***Facilities layout*** One aspect of facilities layout for McDonald's is that when customers come into the building they can line up in one of several lines and wait to be served. In contrast, at Wendy's, customers are asked to stand in one line that snakes around the front of the counter and wait for a single server.

REQUIRED

(a) What is the rationale for each approach?

(b) Which approach do you favor from (1) a customer's perspective and (2) management's perspective? Explain.

LO 3, 5 **6-57** ***Quality costing: balancing category costs*** Managers concerned with improving quality sometimes have a difficult balancing act given the four types of quality costs that they have to manage. As a new manager, you are trying to figure out a strategy for managing $2 million of quality costs; your total quality costs cannot exceed 4% of sales.

REQUIRED

You need to decide on how much should go into each of the four quality-cost categories. How would you go about allocating these costs? What trade-offs would you have to make as you allocate the costs?

CASES

LO 1, 3 **6-58** ***Relevant costs and revenues; marketing channels*** Diamond Bicycle Company manufactures and sells bicycles nationwide through marketing channels ranging from sporting goods stores to specialty bicycle shops. Diamond's average selling price to its distributors is $185 per bicycle. The bicycles are retailed to customers for $349.

After several years of high sales, Diamond's sales have slumped to 160,000 bicycles per year in the last three years, which is only 70% of its manufacturing capacity. Diamond expects the demand for its products to remain the same in the next few years.

Premier Stores, a nationwide chain of discount retail stores, has recently approached Diamond to manufacture bicycles for Premier to sell. Premier has offered to purchase 40,000 bicycles annually for a three-year period at $125 per bicycle. It is not willing to pay a higher price because it plans to retail the bicycles at only $200. Diamond has not previously sold bicycles through any marketing channel other than specialty stores.

Mike Diamond is the chief executive officer of Diamond Bicycle. Although Premier's offer is well below Diamond's normal price, Mike is interested in the offer because Diamond has considerable surplus capacity. He has been supplied with the following variable product cost information:

Direct material costs	$ 50
Direct labor costs	30
Variable manufacturing support costs	25
Total costs	$105

The direct materials cost includes $2 for embossing Premier's private label on the bicycle.

Fixed support costs total $2,000,000 annually. Diamond also pays its sales staff a 10% commission but will not need to pay any salesperson for the special sale to Premier. Average inventory levels for Premier's offer are estimated to be as follows:

TYPE OF INVENTORY	INVENTORY LEVEL
Raw materials	1 month of production
Work in process	1.5 months of production (100% complete for materials and 50% complete for other variable manufacturing costs)
Finished goods	0.5 month of production

Annual inventory carrying cost is estimated to be 10% of the inventory carrying value. Premier's offer requires Diamond to deliver bicycles to Premier's regional warehouse so that Premier can have ready access to an inventory of bicycles to meet fluctuating market demand. Diamond estimated that about 5% of Diamond's present sales will be lost if Premier's offer is accepted because some customers will comparison shop and find the same quality bicycle available at a lower price in Premier stores.

REQUIRED

(a) Should Mike Diamond accept Premier's offer?

(b) What strategic and other factors should be considered before Mike makes a final decision?

6-59 ***Relevant costs, qualitative factors, costs of quality framework, ethics*** Kwik Clean handles both commercial laundry and individual customer dry cleaning. Kwik Clean's current dry-cleaning process involves emitting a pollutant into the air. In addition, the commercial laundry dry cleaning produces sediments and other elements that must receive special treatment before disposal. Pat Polley, Kwik Clean's owner, is concerned about the cost of dealing with increasingly stringent laws and environmental regulations. Recent legislation requires Kwik Clean to reduce the amount of its air pollution emissions. LO 2, 3, 6

To reduce pollution emissions, Polley is considering the following two options:

Option 1. Invest in equipment that would reduce emissions through filtration. The equipment would involve a large capital expenditure but would bring Kwik Clean into compliance with current regulations for emissions.

Option 2. Invest in a new dry-cleaning process that would eliminate current air pollution emissions, partly through using a different solvent than the one currently used. This option would require an even larger capital expenditure than option 1, but the new equipment would reduce some operating costs. Moreover, Kwik Clean might be able to market its environmentally safer process to increase business.

In evaluating the two options and current operations, Polley has enumerated the following items:

1. The price and quantity of solvent used in current operations (and option 1).
2. The price and quantity of the new solvent that would be used in option 2.
3. The purchase cost of new equipment for option 1 and for option 2.
4. The cost of removing old equipment and installing new equipment under option 2.
5. The purchase price of the filtration equipment in option 1, and useful life of the equipment.
6. The purchase price of the current equipment and remaining useful life.
7. The salvage value of the current equipment, which would be sold under option 2.
8. Polley's salary and fringe benefits.
9. Labor costs for current operations (and option 1) and option 2; labor costs would be lower under option 2 than under option 1.
10. Training costs associated with the new equipment in option 2.
11. Legal fees paid to handle paperwork associated with hazardous waste liabilities connected with the sediments produced when cleaning commercial laundry by the current operations. The same sediments would be produced with the equipment in option 2.
12. Storage and disposal costs associated with the sediments produced when cleaning commercial laundry.
13. Insurance for the equipment and workers. Under option 2, insurance fees would be reduced from the current level.

Polley was concerned about recent events publicized locally. A newspaper article reported that the Occupational Safety and Health Administration (OSHA) fined one of Polley's competitors several thousand dollars for unsafe employee working conditions related to handling solvents. Another business incurred a very expensive cleanup for accidental hazardous waste leakage that contaminated the soil. The leakage received major attention in the local television and radio news broadcasts, and was headlined in the local newspapers.

REQUIRED

(a) Which costs are relevant to Polley's decision between option 1 and option 2?

(b) What qualitative factors is Polley like to consider in making the decision between option 1 and option 2?

(c) Explain how the cost of quality framework of prevention, appraisal, internal failure, and external failure might be applied to operations with environmental pollution, where "failures" are defined as accidental spillage or leakage of hazardous wastes, or illegal levels of pollutants. In which of the four cost of quality categories would you advise Polley to focus her attention?

NATURE SCOPE FOCUS

COST BEHAVIOR

COST DECISIONS

PLANNING FOR DECISION-MAKING

PLANNING FOR EVALUATION

ORGANIZATIONAL BEHAVIOR AND DESIGN

chapter 7

Cost Information for Pricing and Product Planning

AFTER READING THIS CHAPTER, YOU WILL BE ABLE TO

1. show how a firm chooses its product mix in the short term
2. explain how a firm adjusts its prices in the short term depending on whether capacity is limited
3. discuss how a firm determines a long-term benchmark price to guide its pricing strategy
4. evaluate the long-term profitability of products and market segments

Shumsky/The Image Works

HIGH PERFORMANCE SPRINGS

"How can we make a profit if we sell at a price below costs? The cost report I've just received indicates a cost of $2.79 per pound for our 0.50-inch steel springs. If we accept John Lawson's offer to buy 120,000 pounds of 0.50-inch springs at only $2.48 per pound, what benefit do we get? How can we survive in this business if we keep slashing our prices?"

Wendy Stone is the owner of High Performance Springs, a manufacturer of high precision steel springs for industrial customers. She was meeting with Bill Nace, her marketing manager, and Rick Koch, her controller, to evaluate an offer from Lawson Corporation to purchase a large quantity of 0.50-inch springs at sharply reduced prices. Her question followed Rick's comments about the costs and price of this product.

"Our accounting records show that the full cost of the 0.50-inch springs is $2.79 per pound, which breaks down to $1.38 of direct materials, $0.76 of direct labor, and $0.65 of manufacturing support costs. We usually mark up our products 30% over costs, which implies a markup of $0.84 and a price of $3.63 per pound for the 0.50-inch springs. This means that Lawson is demanding a discount of $1.15 per pound, which is almost 32% off our normal price," Rick had observed earlier.

Bill realized that Rick's comments about the product costs and Wendy's reaction to it meant that he could not justify his proposal simply by appealing to the value of developing a reputable firm such as Lawson Corporation as a large customer. He had to make a case for accepting a lower price by comparing the price with the incremental costs (or revenues) of producing the springs. The ***incremental cost per unit*** *of a product is the amount by which the total costs of production and sales increase when one additional unit of that product is produced and sold.*

Incremental cost per unit The amount by which the total costs of production and sales increase when one additional unit of that product is produced and sold.

"It is true that the full cost of the 0.50-inch springs is $2.79, but that includes $0.65 of manufacturing support costs. We know that manufacturing support costs consist of rent, depreciation, insurance, heating and lighting, janitorial services, and so on. These are fixed

costs and will not increase if we accept Lawson's order. So the only costs we need to consider are materials and labor, which add up to only $2.14. Even at a price of $2.48, we can earn a margin of $0.34 per pound," Bill explained.

"Bill is right about rent, depreciation, and insurance being fixed costs," replied Rick. "But such fixed costs are only 60% of our total manufacturing support at present. Support activities also include supervision, setups, and inspection, whose costs will increase if we accept the Lawson order. Variable manufacturing costs for the 0.50-inch springs are $1.38 direct materials, $0.76 direct labor, $0.26 variable support activity costs. This adds up to $2.40 of variable costs, so it seems we would have a contribution margin of $0.08 per pound. But that is before we consider selling and distribution costs, which will, I believe, add another $0.23 to the variable costs of the 0.50-inch springs. I figure the total variable costs to be $2.63 per pound, which is more than the offer of only $2.48 per pound."

Bill asked, "Well, should we counter Lawson's offer by suggesting that we would accept it for a $2.70 price? That would earn us a contribution margin of $0.07 per pound by your calculations."

Before Rick could respond, Wendy interrupted the discussion: "I'm very confused by all this talk about only variable costs. Costs are costs. I pay for rent and insurance just as I pay our workers and our suppliers. If our customers don't pay me a price that covers all our costs—both fixed and variable—I can't possibly make money in this business."

Role of Product Costs In Pricing and Product Mix Decisions

The situation at High Performance Springs exists at most firms whose managers make decisions about establishing or accepting a price for their products. Managers need to determine whether they should offer discounts for large orders or to valued customers. Understanding how to analyze product costs is important for making such pricing decisions. Even when prices are set by overall market supply and demand forces and the firm has little or no influence on product prices, management still has to decide the best mix of products to manufacture and sell. This mix has to take into account the products' market prices, costs, and margins (price less relevant costs), and their use of capacity resources.

Product cost analysis also is significant when a firm is deciding how best to deploy marketing and promotion resources, including how much commission (or how many other incentives) to provide the sales force for different products and how large a discount to offer off list prices. In this chapter we turn to some of the more traditional methods of pricing and consider short- and long-run factors.[1]

[1] In Chapter 9, we discuss target costing and target pricing. These are relatively new methods compared with those discussed in this chapter.

SHORT-TERM AND LONG-TERM PRICING CONSIDERATIONS

Managers must consider both the *short-term* and *long-term* consequences of their decisions. Recall that the costs of many resources committed to activities are likely to be fixed costs in the short term because firms cannot easily alter the capacities made available for many production and support activities. Consequently, for short-term decisions, it is important to pay special attention to whether surplus capacity is available for additional production, or whether shortages of available capacity limit additional production alternatives.

Of special concern when evaluating a particular order is how long a firm must commit its production capacity to fill that order. The length of time is relevant because a long-term capacity commitment to a marginally profitable order may prevent the firm from deploying its capacity for more profitable products or orders, should demand for them arise in the future. Or it could force the firm to add expensive new capacity to handle future sales increases.

If production is constrained by inadequate capacity, managers need to consider whether overtime production or the use of subcontractors can help augment capacity in the short term. In the long term, managers have considerably more flexibility to adjust the capacities of activity resources to match the demand for them in producing various products. Decisions about whether to introduce new products or eliminate existing products have long-term consequences. Therefore, our emphasis is on analyzing how such product decisions will affect the demand placed on the firms capacity resources.

We also classify decisions based on whether the firm can influence the price of its products. If the firm is one of a large number of firms in an industry, and if there is little to distinguish the products of different firms from each other, then economic theory states that prices will be set by the aggregate market forces of supply and demand. Thus, no single firm can influence prices significantly by its own decisions. For instance, in commodity businesses such as grains, meat, and sugar, traders in the commodity markets set prices based on industry supply and demand. Similarly, if prices are set by one or more large firms leading an industry, a small firm on the

EXHIBIT 7-1

Classification of Pricing and Product Mix Decisions

Decision Type	Price-Taker Firm	Price-Setter Firm
Short-term decisions	1	2
Long-term decisions	4	3

Price taker
A firm that accepts the prices set in the marketplace for its products.

Price setter
A firm that can determine the prices its customers will pay for its products.

fringe must match the prices set by the industry leaders. In such a situation, a small firm is a **price taker,** because it chooses its product mix given the prices set in the marketplace for its products.

In contrast, firms in an industry with relatively little competition, who enjoy large market shares and exercise leadership in an industry, must decide what prices to set for their products. Firms in industries in which products are highly customized or otherwise differentiated from each other (because of special features, characteristics, or customer service) also need to set the prices for their differentiated products. Such firms are **price setters.** Once price setters announced their prices, customers place orders and production follows.

We consider four different situations in this chapter, as shown in Exhibit 7-1. We begin the next section by considering the short-term product mix decision of a price taker (quadrant 1 in the exhibit). Then we analyze short-term pricing decisions for a price setter (quadrant 2) and follow with an examination of long-term benchmark prices for a price setter (quadrant 3). Finally, we return to the price-taker firm and consider how it evaluates the long-term profitability of its products and customers (quadrant 4).

Short-Term Product Mix Decisions—Price Takers

Production decisions by a firm with a very small market share in its industry have little impact on the overall industry supply and demand, or on the prices of the firm's products. Such is the case in high-volume manufacturing industries in which the products are standardized and little chance exists to differentiate the products of one firm from those of another (e.g., steel, commodity chemicals, pharmaceuticals, gypsum wall board, and low-end copier machines). The aggregate production decisions of all the firms determine prices in such industries. Or, if there are a few dominating firms, their decisions influence the prices.

A small firm, or a firm with a negligible market share in this industry, behaves as a price taker. It takes the industry prices for its products as given and then decides how many units of each product it should produce and sell. If the small firm demands a higher price for any of its products, it risks losing its customers to other competing firms in the industry, unless it can successfully differentiate its products by offering special features or services. Conversely, if the small firm seeks to increase its market share by asking a price lower than the industry prices, then it risks a retaliatory reduction in prices from its competitors. Lowering the price might result in a price war that would make the firm, and the entire industry, worse off than if the firm had complied with industry prices. This action is particularly painful to smaller firms that have fewer resources to rely on should an unprofitable price war occur.

Giving industry prices, a price taker should produce and sell as much as it can of all products whose costs are less than their prices. Although this may appear to be a simple decision rule, two important considerations complicate matters. First, managers must decide which costs are relevant to the short-term product mix decision. Should all the product costs identified in Chapter 3 be considered, or only those costs that vary in the short term? Second, in the short term, managers may have little flexibility to alter the capacities of some of the firm's resources. For instance, the available equipment capacity may limit the ability of a firm to produce and sell more products whose costs are lower than their prices.

Consider HKTex Company, located in Hong Kong, which sells ready-made garments to discount stores such as Kmart and Wal-Mart. The plant manufactures five types of garments: Exhibit 7-2 presents budgeted production for the third quarter of 2000. The exhibit also displays the minimum sales quantities of each type of garment that must be supplied under long-term contracts with various retail stores. The sales

IN PRACTICE

Newspaper Wars in Britain

Rupert Murdoch controls print and broadcast media around the world: in Australia, Asia, Europe, and North America. His company now owns the *Times,* once the newspaper considered the voice of the British establishment. In 1993, he began a tactical war of price cuts. The *Times* cut its price from the equivalent of about 70 cents to 45 cents. As a result, it gained circulation at the expense of other full-size newspapers, especially the *Daily Telegraph,* the biggest seller, at around one million copies a day.

In June 1994, the *Daily Telegraph* dropped its price to 35 cents. On July 31, 1994, the *Independent* joined the price war, slashing its price to 45 cents from about 75 cents in an attempt to keep pace with its price-cutting rivals. The *Independent's* daily circulation had sunk to 275,000, well below its peak of 400,000, compared with more than 500,000 copies at the *Times* and 400,000 at the *Guardian.* Murdoch promptly cut the *Times* to 35 cents. At these prices, the newspapers began losing millions—one guess is $1.8 million a month for the *Times.* But Murdoch can cover that from his empire's profits until perhaps his rivals collapse. An official board is now looking into charges of predatory pricing, a pricing strategy intended to drive out competitors.

Sources: Anthony Lewis, "Slipping Down the Tabloid Slope," *New York Times,* July 8, 1994; Reuters, "A Price War Grows Hotter," *New York Times,* August 3, 1994.

manager has estimated the maximum sales quantities shown in the last column. His estimates are based on his assessment of the number of orders that can be obtained for delivery in the third quarter of 2000.

Exhibit 7-3 shows unit costs for the five products. Direct material costs are based on estimated materials requirements and their estimated prices. Workers who cut, stitch, and pack are paid on a piece-rate basis. For instance, column 2 (shirts) shows that workers are paid $1.00 for cutting, $0.80 for stitching, and $0.05 for packing one shirt. Inspection labor costs total $7500 per quarter and are assigned to products at the rate of $0.15 per garment. Support activity costs total $10,000 each quarter and are assigned to the 50,000 units budgeted for production at the rate of $0.20 per unit.

Production is limited by the 23,800 machine-hour capacity of the garment manufacturing machines. Exhibit 7-4 displays the number of machine hours required to

EXHIBIT 7-2

HKTex Company
Budgeted Production in Quantities for
2000 (Quarter 3)

GARMENT TYPE	BUDGETED PRODUCTION	MINIMUM SALES	MAXIMUM SALES
Blouses	15,000	5,000	15,000
Trousers	8,000	4,000	9,000
Dresses	5,000	2,000	8,000
Skirts	10,000	6,000	16,000
Shirts	12,000	6,000	14,000
Total units	50,000	23,000	62,000

EXHIBIT 7-3

HKTex Company
Product Costs per Unit

	SHIRTS	DRESSES	SKIRTS	BLOUSES	TROUSERS
Direct materials:					
Textile	$1.80	$6.00	$4.00	$2.00	$4.50
Supplies	0.20	0.90	0.60	0.40	0.60
Total	$2.00	$6.90	$4.60	$2.40	$5.10
Direct Labor:					
Cutting	1.00	1.50	1.00	1.00	1.00
Stitching	0.80	1.80	1.00	0.80	1.00
Inspection	0.15	0.15	0.15	0.15	0.15
Packing	0.05	0.05	0.05	0.05	0.05
Total	$2.00	$3.50	$2.20	$2.00	$2.20
Manufacturing support:					
Utilities	0.03	0.03	0.03	0.03	0.03
Plant administration	0.04	0.04	0.04	0.04	0.04
Machine maintenance	0.02	0.02	0.02	0.02	0.02
Machine depreciation	0.04	0.04	0.04	0.04	0.04
Facility maintenance	0.04	0.04	0.04	0.04	0.04
Facility depreciation	0.03	0.03	0.03	0.03	0.03
Total	$0.20	$0.20	$0.20	$0.20	$0.20
Total product cost per unit	$4.20	$10.60	$7.00	$4.60	$7.50

produce each garment. Note to the considerable differences in the required machine time, ranging from 0.4 hour for one shirt or blouse to 0.8 hour for one dress. The planned production for the third quarter of 2000 is to use all 23,800 machine hours available at present.

With these data, we can evaluate the profitability of the different products and decide the production levels for the five products that will maximize profits for the

EXHIBIT 7-4

HKTex Company
Machine Hour Requirements

GARMENT TYPE	MACHINE HOURS PER UNIT	PRODUCTION IN UNITS	TOTAL MACHINE HOURS REQUIRED
Blouses	0.4	15,000	6,000
Trousers	0.5	8,000	4,000
Dresses	0.8	5,000	4,000
Skirts	0.5	10,000	5,000
Shirts	0.4	12,000	4,800
Totals		50,000	23,800

HKTex Company for the third quarter of 2000. Since HKTex is contemplating short-term adjustments to its product mix, it is necessary to determine what costs will vary with production levels in this period, and then what costs will remain fixed when a change occurs in the production mix.

Clearly, the costs of direct materials and the direct labor that is compensated on a piece-rate basis vary with the quantity of each garment produced. Inspectors are paid a monthly fixed salary, but they are employed as required to support the production of different garments. If production increases, HKTex may have to hire more inspectors. Therefore, inspection labor costs also vary with quantity of production of different garments.

In contrast, the costs of utilities, plant administration, maintenance, and depreciation for the machinery and plant facility will not change with a change in the product mix, because the plant is operating at its full capacity. This analysis assumes these support activity costs are fixed.

The contribution from each of the garments to the firm's profits is determined by subtracting the variable costs from the price of the product. Exhibit 7-5 displays the contribution per unit for the five products, all of which have a positive contribution margin. If its capacity were unlimited, HKTex could produce garments to fill the maximum demand for them. Capacity is constrained, however, and therefore the company must decide how best to deploy this limited resource, as will be discussed.

The total budgeted contribution of $141,600 ($12,000 + $24,000 + $22,000 + $54,000 + $29,600) for the budgeted production is obtained by multiplying the contribution per unit by the budgeted production quantity for each product and then adding them (see Exhibit 7-5). The budgeted profit is $131,600 ($141,600 − $10,000 fixed costs).

This plant works at full capacity to manufacture different apparel in time for the busy sales season. Since the plant capacity cannot be increased readily at short notice, the company evaluates the profitability of different products in the rank order of their contribution per machine hour. (Bill Gallery/Stock, Boston)

EXHIBIT 7-5

HKTex Company
Contribution Margins

GARMENT TYPE	SHIRTS	DRESSES	SKIRTS	BLOUSES	TROUSERS
Price per unit	$5.00	$15.20	$9.00	$8.00	$11.00
Variable costs per unit:					
Textiles	$1.80	$ 6.00	$4.00	$2.00	$4.50
Supplies	0.20	0.90	0.60	0.40	0.60
Cutting labor	1.00	1.50	1.00	1.00	1.00
Stitching labor	0.80	1.80	1.00	0.80	1.00
Inspection labor	0.15	0.15	0.15	0.15	0.15
Packing Labor	0.05	0.05	0.05	0.05	0.05
Total variable costs	$4.00	$10.40	$6.80	$4.40	$7.30
Contribution per unit	$ 1.00	$ 4.80	$ 2.20	$ 3.60	$ 3.70
Machine hours per unit	0.4	0.8	0.5	0.4	0.5
Contribution per machine hour	$ 2.50	$ 6.00	$ 4.40	$ 9.00	$ 7.40
Budgeted production	12,000	5,000	10,000	15,000	8,000
Total budgeted contributions	$12,000	$24,000	$22,000	$54,000	$29,600

Contribution per unit
The price per unit less variable costs per unit.

Notice that the **contribution per unit,** or price per unit less variable costs per unit, is highest for dresses ($4.80). Does that mean that dresses are the most profitable product and that HKTex should produce as many dresses as it can possibly sell? No, because in this case, production is limited by the available machine capacity. The capacity is fixed in the short-term, so HKTex must plan production to maximize the contribution to profit earned for every available machine hour used. Therefore, HKTex should rank-order the products not by their contribution per unit, but by their contribution per machine hour.

Contribution per machine hour
A factor obtained by dividing the contribution per unit by the number of machine hours per unit.

Contribution per machine hour is obtained by dividing the contribution per unit by the number of machine hours per unit. Notice in Exhibit 7-5 that blouses have the highest contribution per machine hour ($9.00); therefore, HKTex should produce a total of 15,000 blouses, the maximum quantity that it can sell in the third quarter of 2000 (see Exhibit 7-2). Trousers have the next highest contribution per machine hour ($7.40), so HKTex should produce a total of 9000 trousers, the maximum it can sell in this quarter. HKTex should continue to decide which products to make by rank-ordering the products by contribution per machine hour. After taking into account existing sales orders, it should make the most profitable products up to the maximum sales potential until it exhausts the entire available machine capacity.

Exhibit 7-6 displays the production quantities that maximize profits in the short term. The minimum production for the five products required under existing sales contracts requires a total of 11,000 machine hours (see column 3). This leaves a balance of 12,800 machine hours of capacity (23,800 − 11,000), which is sufficient to produce the maximum quantities of blouses, trousers, and dresses that HKTex can sell. These three products rank the highest in terms of their contribution per machine hour. The remaining capacity of 1500 machine hours [12,800 − (4,000 + 2,500 + 4,800)] is not adequate to produce the maximum possible quantity of skirts, the next highest ranked product. This remaining capacity is sufficient for the production of only 3000 (1500 ÷ 0.5) additional skirts. No machine capacity remains for the production of any additional shirts, the product with the lowest contribution per machine hour.

EXHIBIT 7-6

HKTex Company
Production Quantities Required to Maximize Profits

GARMENT TYPE	MINIMUM QUANTITY	MACHINE HOURS REQUIRED		ADDITIONAL QUANTITY	MACHINE HOURS REQUIRED
Blouses	5,000	2,000	5,000 × 0.4	10,000	4,000
Trousers	4,000	2,000	4,000 × 0.5	5,000	2,500
Dresses	2,000	1,600	2,000 × 0.8	6,000	4,800
Skirts	6,000	3,000	6,000 × 0.5	3,000	1,500
Shirts	6,000	2,400	6,000 × 0.4	0	0
Totals	23,000	11,000			12,800

To summarize, the available machine capacity should be allocated to the five garments shown in the final production plan in Exhibit 7-7. This production plan yields a profit of $141,500, which is $9900 (about 7.5%) more than the $131,600 profit ($141,600 − $10,000) that HKTex would earn with the original production plan.

This example illustrates the basic principle used to make short-term product mix decisions when prices are unaffected by the quantities sold. With price predetermined, the only short-term decision faced by the manufacturer is how much of each possible product it should produce. The contribution margin *per unit of the constrained resource,* which is machine hours in this example, is the criterion used to decide which products are most profitable to produce and sell at the prevailing prices.

EXHIBIT 7-7

HKTex Company
Final Production Plan

GARMENT TYPE	PRODUCTION QUANTITY EXHIBIT 7-6: MINIMUM/ ADDITIONAL QUANTITIES	TOTAL MACHINE HOURS EXHIBIT 7-4		TOTAL CONTRIBUTION EXHIBIT 7-5 CONTRIBUTION PER UNIT	
Blouses	15,000	6,000	15,000 × 0.4	$ 54,000	15,000 × $3.60
Trousers	9,000	4,500	9,000 × 0.5	33,300	9,000 × $3.70
Dresses	8,000	6,400	8,000 × 0.8	38,400	8,000 × $4.80
Skirts	9,000	4,500	9,000 × 0.5	19,800	9,000 × $2.20
Shirts	6,000	2,400	6,000 × 0.4	6,000	6,000 × $1.00
Totals	47,000	23,800		$151,500	
Less: Fixed Costs				10,000	
Profit				$141,500	

IN PRACTICE

Pricing for No Vacancy

Dismissed by the Walt Disney Company in 1972, Harris Rosen is now one of the most successful independent hotel owners anywhere. A millionaire 100 times over, Harris owns two Quality Inns, a Comfort Inn, the Clarion Plaza, the Omni, and the Rodeway, accounting for 4850 of the Orlando area's 84,400 hotel rooms.

While the average annual occupancy rate in the Orlando area has not exceeded 78.8% in the last decade, Harris's hotels have averaged 96% over that period. The secret behind Harris's ability to fill hotel rooms is fairly simple. Much to his competitor's dismay, he openly cuts prices. When it appears Harris's properties may not fill up, electronic message boards begin flashing $29.95.

He likens this fine-tuning to the airlines' practice of yield management—lowering fares at various times on seats that may otherwise remain unsold. Also used by cruise ships, the technique has not yet caught on in the hotel industry where many operators fret that cutting prices at least openly may tarnish the polished image of their chains. However, if hotel management companies that dominate the industry do not have the foresight to follow his example, Harris maintains that is their problem. "Most of them would rather wind up with empty rooms than drop prices in order to preserve the sanctity of their average daily rates," he scoffs.

Each night at 11 P.M. Harris calls the front desk at each property to see if the hotel is sold out—and if not, why not. In the morning, he is on the phone with the night auditors, recapping the previous day's occupancy rates, average room rates, and food and beverage revenues. Then he discusses the coming day's room rates, that is, the starting rates.

Harris also fills rooms by honoring the rates of the lower-price hotels that send him walk-in customers they cannot accommodate. He also nurtures the group and bus-tour business all year around contrary to the conventional wisdom in the industry, which says to ignore that segment when business is up because it is low profit. Another strategy leading to his success was building the Omni and the Clarion on either side of the Orlando Convention Center, which attracts 2.1 million people a year. Because convention business is usually booked years in advance, the hotel's proximity to the center gives them a buffer against swings in the economic cycle.

Harris says he has so much leeway to move prices because his company's debt is "a minuscule 5% to 10% of the value of its properties, so we don't need to keep rates high to pay off the interest."

Source: Edwin McDowell, "His Goal: No Room at the Inns," *New York Times,* November 23, 1995, pp. C1, C8.

THE IMPACT OF OPPORTUNITY COSTS

Consider next a variation of our analysis so far. Suppose that a new customer that HKTex did not include in its earlier sales forecasts wishes to place an order for 2000 shirts and is willing to pay a price higher than $5 each for this order. How high must the price be to make it profitable for HKTex to accept this special order?

If HKTex produces more shirts, its out-of-pocket costs will increase in the short term by the amount of the variable costs of the 2000 shirts, but a simple comparison of the price with the variable costs shown in Exhibit 7-5 is not adequate for this decision. Because its production capacity is limited, HKTex must cut back the production of some other garment to enable it to produce 2000 additional shirts. Giving up the production of some profitable product results in an opportunity cost, which equals the lost profit on the garments that HKTex can no longer make.

Each shirt requires 0.4 machine hour, so the new order for 2000 shirts requires a total of 800 machine hours (see Exhibit 7-4). To find the capacity of 800 machine hours required to produce the additional shirts, HKTex must forgo a part of the production of some other garment. How should HKTex decide which garment's production to sacrifice? Clearly, it should make the decision that minimizes the opportunity cost. Therefore, HKTex should sacrifice the product currently being produced that has the *lowest* contribution per unit of the constrained resources.

We know from our earlier ranking of the products that of all the products whose production exceeds the minimum required, skirts have the lowest contribution per machine hour (see Exhibit 7-5). To make the special order, HKTex must sacrifice 800 machine hours for the production of skirts. Because each skirt requires 0.5 machine hour, HKTex would be giving up producing 1600 skirts. Each skirt contributes $2.20, so cutting back the production of 1600 skirts causes a sacrifice of $3520 in profits ($2.20 × 1,600).

There is an alternative way to check that the opportunity cost is $3520. The contribution margin per machine hour is $4.40 for skirts, and a cutback of 800 machine hours of production of skirts results in a sacrifice of $3520 of profits ($4.40 × 800).

The cost implication of producing an additional order of 2000 shirts are now clear.

HKTEX COMPANY
COSTS OF PRODUCING 2000 SHIRTS

COST	PER UNIT	TOTAL
Variable cost	$4.00	$ 8,000
Opportunity cost	1.76	3,520
Total	$5.76	$11,520

Incremental costs (or revenues) are defined as the amount by which costs (or revenues) increase if one particular decision is made instead of another. Therefore, if HKTex does not charge a price of at least $5.76 per shirt, the incremental costs, including opportunity costs, will exceed the incremental revenues from this order, and HKTex will be worse off as a result. The lowest price that should be acceptable to HKTex is $11,520 for the order, or $5.76 per shirt.

Also notice that if the price of a shirt is $5.76, the contribution margin per machine hour is $4.40 [($5.76 − $4.00) ÷ 0.4], per the same as that for skirts, whose production is cut back. The basic principle to understand is that HKTex must earn at least as much *contribution margin per machine hour* on the new order as it must sacrifice on the alternative which it must give up.

Short-Term Pricing Decisions—Price Setters

Thus far, we have examined the way managers should adjust their product mix in the short term when the marketplace has determined what prices they can charge for their products. For these types of firms, known as price takers (see quadrant 1 of Exhibit 7-1), the relevant costs for the product mix decision are the short-run variable cost plus any opportunity cost of foregone alternatives.

In many businesses, potential customers request that suppliers bid a price for an order before they decide on the supplier with whom they will place the order. In this section, we examine the relationship between costs and prices bid by a supplier for special orders that do not involve long-term relationships with the customer.

Consider Tudor Rose Tools and Dies Company in Cleveland, Ohio. Tudor Rose manufactures customized steel tools and dies for a wide variety of manufacturing businesses. A new customer, Pyro Industries of Ontario, has asked for a bid on a set of customized tools.

Based on the tool design, production engineers determine the routing through different production departments and estimate the quantity of different materials required for the order and the number of labor hours required in each department. This information is used to prepare a job bid sheet as described in Chapter 3. Then Tudor Rose uses this information, and materials prices and labor wage rates, to estimate the direct materials and direct labor costs displayed in Exhibit 7-8. Support activity costs are assigned to the job based on activity cost drivers and the corresponding activity cost driver rates as described in Chapter 5.

Full costs
Sum of all costs (direct materials, direct labor, and support) assigned to a product.

Cost-plus pricing
A method for setting the price of a product by a markup percentage above cost.

Markup percentage
See *markup rate.*

The **full costs** for the job—that is, the sum of all direct materials, direct labor, and support activity costs—are estimated to be $28,500, consisting of $8400 of direct materials, $9900 of direct labor, and $10,200 of support activity costs. Setting the price of a product also means determining a markup percentage above cost, an approach known as **cost-plus pricing.** The **markup percentage** is determined by a company's desired profit margin and overall rate of return.[2] Tudor Rose has decided that rate is normally to be 40% of full costs.

If Pyro Industries were a regular customer, the bid price would have been $39,900 (1.40 × $28,500). But for this special order from a new customer, what is the minimum acceptable price? It turns out that one of the critical factors to consider is the level of available capacity.

We now consider two distinct cases. We will examine Tudor Rose's pricing decision when there is surplus machine capacity available in the short term to complete the production of the job. Then we will examine the decision when the existing demand for Tudor Rose's services already uses all available capacity and the only way to manufacture the customized tools for Pyro Industries is by working overtime or adding an extra shift.

EXHIBIT 7-8

Tudor Rose Tools and Dies Company
Job Cost Estimate

Direct materials:		
Steel		$ 8,400
Direct labor:		
Lathe	$2,600	
Grinding	3,200	
Machining	4,100	9,900
Manufacturing support:		
Supervision	$3,400	
Batch related	3,700	
Facility sustaining	3,100	10,200
Total costs		$28,500
Markup (40%)		11,400
Bid price		$39,900

[2] There are two traditional methods used to determine the cost base. Companies that use *variable costing* sum all variable costs of manufacturing and base their markup on total variable costs. Those using *full absorption costing* sum all variable and fixed manufacturing costs and base their markup percentage on total manufacturing costs. The markup percentage is often determined using an algorithm based on a rate of return concept.

AVAILABLE SURPLUS CAPACITY

Tudor Rose will incur direct material costs of $8400 to produce customized tools for Pyro Industries. Tudor Rose pays direct production labor on an hourly basis; therefore, these costs will increase by $9900 if the company accepts the Pyro order. In addition, batch-related costs will *increase* by $3700, because a new production batch is needed for the customized tools. The costs supervision and business-sustaining support activities, however, will not increase if additional capacity of these resources is available to meet the production needs of the Pyro Industries order.

Tudor Rose's Incremental Costs

Direct material	$ 8,400
Direct labor	9,900
Batch-related support activities	3,700
Total incremental costs	$22,000

The price that Tudor Rose should charge Pyro Industries must cover these incremental costs for the job to be profitable. In other words, the minimum acceptable price is $22,000 *when surplus production capacity is available.* This is the price at which Tudor Rose will break even on the Pyro Industries order. In practice, Tudor Rose will add a profit margin above incremental costs, and the bid price will be higher than $22,000 depending on competitive and demand conditions. In summary, when excess capacity exists, the *minimum* acceptable price must at least cover the incremental costs that the company will incur to produce and deliver the order.

NO AVAILABLE SURPLUS CAPACITY

If surplus machine capacity is not available, Tudor Rose will have to incur additional costs to acquire the necessary capacity. Tudor Rose often meets such short-term capacity requirements by operating its plant overtime, paying its supervisors overtime wages, and incurring additional expenditures for heating, lighting, cleaning, and

IN PRACTICE

Full Cost-Based Pricing Continues to Be Popular

A 1983 survey of 505 of the largest (Fortune 1000) companies by Govindarajan and Anthony found that over 82% of the companies price their products based on their full costs. Only 17% of the respondents indicated that they rely on variable costs for their product-pricing decisions. This survey also learned that about half of both full cost- and variable cost-based pricing companies relied only on manufacturing costs for their pricing decisions. The other half based their prices on all manufacturing and nonmanufacturing costs.

Eleven years later, Shim and Sudit conducted a similar survey of 141 companies and detected a pattern of reliance on cost data for pricing decisions similar to the earlier survey. The more recent survey included an additional choice for the responding companies, allowing them to indicate that their pricing decisions were based on market forces and not on costs. This survey found that about 70% of the companies used full cost-based pricing, 12% used variable cost-based pricing, and only 18% used market-based pricing. About half of both full cost- and variable cost-based pricing companies continued to rely only on manufacturing costs instead of all costs for their pricing decisions.

Sources: V. Govindarajan and R. N. Anthony, "How Firms Use Cost Data in Pricing Decisions," *Management Accounting,* July 1983, pp. 30–37; E. Shim and E. F. Sudit, "How Manufacturers Price Products," *Management Accounting,* February 1994, pp. 37–39.

Significant overcapacity in the industry caused major price reductions in steel during the 1980s. Intense competition forced mill closings as the industry eliminated underused and inefficient facilities and caused significant upgrading to improve the cost performance of the remaining mills. This steel strip mill at Weirton Steel eliminated several steps in the old process of converting a steel slab into strip steel. The reduction in the industry's excess capacity and improvements in processing have lowered the industry's cost structure and improved its profit performance. (Dean Conger/Corbis)

security. In addition, more machine maintenance and plant engineering activities will be necessary, as past experience has shown that the incidence of machine breakdowns increases during the overtime shift. Under its machinery leasing contract, Tudor Rose also incurs additional rental costs for the extra use of machines when it adds an overtime shift.

Tudor Rose management estimates the amounts of incremental supervision costs (including overtime premium) for the Pyro order at $5100 and the incremental business-sustaining costs at $5400. Thus, the total costs are $10,500 ($5100 + $5400) if overtime is required to manufacture customized tools for Pyro Industries. Therefore, the minimum acceptable price in this case is $32,500 ($22,000 + $10,500). The actual price will depend on the amount of markup over the incremental costs charged by the Tudor Rose Tools and Dies Company.

The principle illustrated here is the same as that described in the previous case. The minimum acceptable price still must cover all incremental costs, but when the firm must acquire additional capacity to satisfy the order, there are more incremental costs involved in the decision to accept or reject the order. In deciding whether to accept the Pyro Industries order and what price to charge for the special order, Tudor Rose must consider the appropriate incremental costs depending on whether surplus production capacity is available. The incremental costs are the relevant costs for such short-run decisions.

Long-Term Pricing Decisions—Price Setters

We now consider price-setter firms that make long-term pricing decisions, as indicated in quadrant 3 of Exhibit 7-1. You may have noticed that the relevant costs for the short-term special order pricing decision differ from the full costs of the job reported in Exhibit 7-8. Full costs include the direct materials, direct labor, and support activity costs assigned based on normal activity cost driver rates. Is there any benefit to reporting this information about full costs to managers who are responsible for the firm's pricing decisions?

In fact, most firms rely on full-cost information reports when setting prices. Typically, the accounting department provides cost reports to the marketing department, which then adds appropriate markups to the costs to determine benchmark or target prices for all products normally sold by the firm.

There is economic justification for using full costs for pricing decisions in three types of circumstances:

1. Many contracts for the development and production of customized products and many contracts with governmental agencies specify that prices should equal full

Most of the cost of providing guest accommodations in a hotel are fixed—a hotel's incremental costs are tied mainly to linen services. Therefore, during off-season in resort areas, hotels often cut their prices significantly to attract customers. Even at these lower prices, a hotel can cover its incremental costs and provide a contribution toward covering fixed costs. Hotels that have peak and off-peak periods plan to recover most of their fixed costs through the prices they charge peak-use customers. (Mandarin Oriental Hotel Group Limited)

THE TECHNOLOGICAL EDGE

When Enterprise System Prices Are Too High, Rent?

Today, the cost of purchasing enterprise financial systems or enterprise resource planning systems can easily run into several million dollars. Savvy executives, for example, Charles Warczak, CIO of Sunburst Hospitality Corporation, are now renting enterprise applications over the Web on a monthly basis. The advantages of renting are many: First, the major barrier to entry, the price of the system, can be reduced significantly by renting. Rental costs tend to be quite modest. Second, many companies do not have the necessary IS personnel to staff the application—and even if they did, the personnel cost can be very high. Third, implementing a system can take up to several years. Application service providers (ASPs), the companies that provide integration services of rented applications, can install a system in 6 to 10 weeks.

Is there a downside? A concern with renting is that once a company allows the ASP to take over and install the system, it may sacrifice the chance to modify the software. In other words, renting may be cheaper, but one may get a system that is not tailored to one's specific needs. Another issue in outsourcing any IT function is to make sure that an appropriate service contract has been agreed upon. Finally, security is a big issue for many companies. Some CIOs do not want to send highly sensitive information over the Web for fear of industrial espionage. Although private leased lines for more secure Web connections are available, they are also 10 times more costly than a regular line. All factors must be weighed before a decision can be made.

Source: Peter Fabris, *CIO Web Business,* May 1, 1999, pp. 44–50.

costs plus a markup. Prices set in regulated industries also are based on full costs.

2. When a firm enters into a long-term contractual relationship with a customer to supply a product, it has great flexibility in adjusting the level of commitment for all resources. Therefore, most activity costs will depend on the production decisions under the long-term contract, and full costs are relevant for the long-term pricing decision.

3. The third situation is representative of many industries. Most firms make short-term adjustments in prices, often by offering discounts from list prices instead of rigidly employing a fixed price based on full costs. When demand for their products is low, the firms recognize the greater likelihood of surplus capacity in the short term. Accordingly, they adjust the prices of their products downward to acquire additional business based on the lower incremental costs they incur when surplus capacity is available. Conversely, when demand for their products is high, they recognize the greater likelihood that the existing capacity of activity resources is inadequate to satisfy all of the demand. Thus, they adjust the prices upward based on the higher incremental costs they incur when capacity is fully utilize. The higher prices serve to ration the available capacity to the highest profit opportunity.

Because demand conditions fluctuate over time, prices also fluctuate with demand conditions over time. For instance, demand in the hotel industry is lower on weekends than on weekdays. Therefore, most hotels offer special weekend rates that are considerably lower than their weekday rates. Many amusement parks offer lower prices on weekdays when demand is expected to be low. Airfares between New York and London are higher in summer, when the demand is higher, than in winter, when the demand is lower. Long-distance telephone rates are lower in the evenings and on the weekends when the demand is lower.

Although fluctuating short-term prices are based on the appropriate incremental costs, over the long term their average tends to equal the price based on the full costs that will be recovered in a long-term contract (see Exhibit 7-9). In other words, the price determined by adding on a markup to the full costs of a product serves as a benchmark or target price from which the firm can adjust prices up or down depending on demand conditions. Most firms use full cost-based prices as target prices, giving sales managers limited authority to modify prices as required by the prevailing competitive conditions.

We have already seen that prices depend on demand conditions. Markups increase with the *strength of demand.* If more customers demand more of a product, then the firm is able to command a higher markup. Markups also depend on the elasticity of demand. Demand is said to be elastic if customers are very sensitive to the price, that is, if a small increase in the price results in a large decrease in the demand. Markups are smaller when demand is more elastic. Markups also fluctuate with the *intensity of competition.* If competition is intense, it is more difficult for a firm to sustain a price much higher than its incremental costs. See Appendix 7-1 for a formal economic analysis of the general pricing decision.

To see how demand elasticity affects the pricing decision, consider the decision by Jim and Barry's Ice Cream Company to increase ice cream prices from $2.40 to $2.50 per gallon. When prices increase, they expect the demand to decline from 80,000 gallons to 75,000 gallons. The incremental cost is $1.60 per gallon of ice cream. How much will the profits increase because of this price increase?

Contribution to profits from each gallon of ice cream increases from $0.80 ($2.40 − $1.60) to $0.90 ($2.50 − $1.60) with the increase in price. The price increase has two effects on profits: (1) It increases the contribution of the units sold (called the "income effect" by economists), but (2) it also decreases the number of units sold and, therefore,

EXHIBIT 7-9

Short-Term Prices Relative to Long-Term Benchmark Price

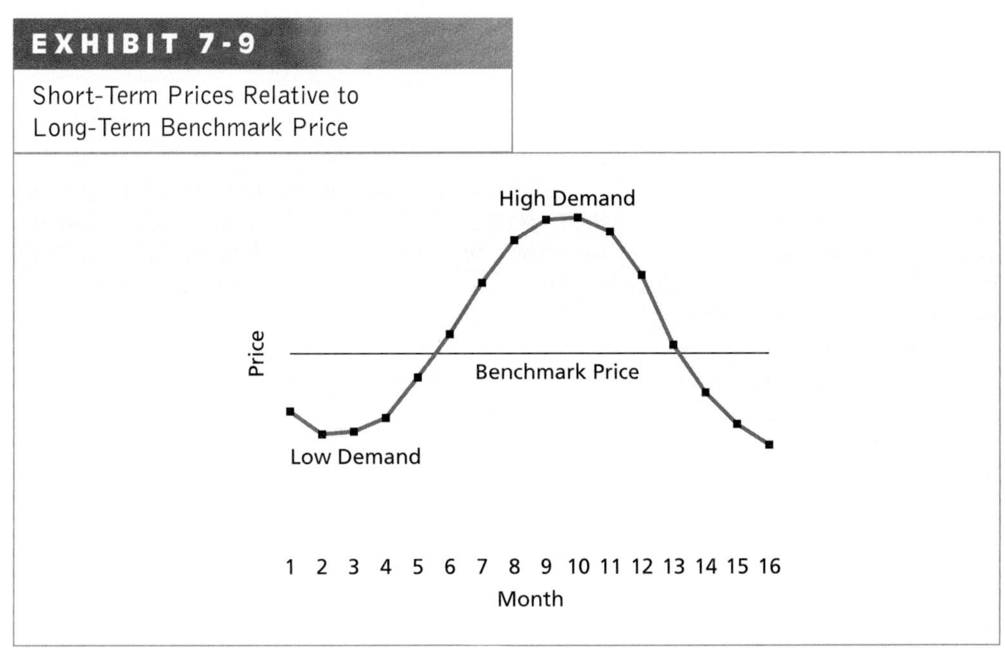

▶ *Companies such as Shell Oil purchase or lease offshore drilling platforms like this one with the belief that the average long-term price of oil products and the cost of alternative sources of crude oil will support its cost recovery. (Shell International)*

the contribution from each unsold unit is lost (called the "substitution effect" by economists). In this case, the increase in contribution is \$0.10 per gallon (\$0.90 − \$0.80), or \$7500 (\$0.10 × 75,000) for the 75,000 gallons of expected sales after the price increase. The decrease in contribution is \$4000 (\$0.80 × 5000) because of the 5000-gallon decline in sales (80,000 − 75,000) of ice cream, which had a contribution margin of \$0.80 per gallon prior to the price increase. Therefore, the net impact of the price increase on profits is an increase of \$3500 (\$7500 − \$4000).

If the demand were more elastic and sales were expected to decline by 10,000 gallons (to 70,000 gallons instead of 75,000 gallons), than the higher price markup would not be advisable. The increase in contribution of \$7000 (\$0.10 × 70,000) then would be more than offset by the decline of \$8000 (\$0.80 × 10,000) due to the sharp decrease in sales. The price increase, therefore, would result in a net decrease of \$1000 (\$7000 − \$8000) in profits.

This example illustrates the important point that when demand is relatively inelastic, profits will usually increase when prices increase. When demand is elastic, however, the quantities sold will decrease sharply when prices increase and profits decrease.

Firms often lower markups for strategic reasons. A firm may choose a low markup for a new product to penetrate the market and win over market share from an established product of a competing firm. Many internet businesses have adopted the strategy of setting low prices to build the business, acquire a brand name, build a loyal customer base, and garner market share. In contrast to this **penetration pricing strategy,** firms sometimes employ a **skimming price strategy,** as in the audio and video equipment industry, where initially a higher price is charged to customers who are willing to pay more for the privilege of possessing the latest technological innovations.

Penetration pricing strategy
The act of choosing a low markup for a new product to penetrate the market and win over market share from an established product of a competing firm.

Skimming price strategy
An act of initially charging customers a higher price, who are willing to pay more for the privilege of possessing a product.

Long-Term Product Mix Decisions—Price Takers

We now turn to quadrant 4 in Exhibit 7-1 which represents a price-taker firm that is making long-term product mix decisions. Decisions to add a new product or to drop an existing product from the portfolio of products usually have significant long-term implications for the cost structure of a firm. Product-sustaining costs—such as product design and engineering, vendor and purchasing costs, part maintenance, and dedicated sales force costs—are relevant costs for such decisions. Batch-related costs—such as setups, materials handling, and first-item inspection (inspection of only the first few items in each batch)—also are likely to change if a change occurs in the product mix in favor of or against products manufactured in large batches.

Bear in mind, however, that managers cannot easily change the amount of resources committed for many product-sustaining and several batch-related activities in the short run. The cost consequences of either introducing a new product or deleting an existing product evolve over time, because both decisions require careful implementation plans stretching over several periods. As a result, managers use the full costs of products, including the cost of using various resources to produce and sustain the product. Recall that such resources include the number of setup staff, the number of product and process engineers, and the number of quality inspectors. Managers use the costs of all resources in their product-related decisions, because in the long term, the firm is able to adjust the capacity of activity resources to match the resource levels demanded by the product quantities and mix.

Comparing product costs with their market prices reveals which products are not profitable in the long term, when firms can adjust activity resource capacities to match production requirements. If some products have full costs that exceed the market price, the firm must consider several options. Although dropping these products appears is to be an obvious option, it may be important to maintain a full product line to make it possible for customers to enjoy one-stop shopping for their orders. But a comparison of the prices with costs still provides a valuable signal to managers because it indicates the *net* cost of the strategy to offer a full product line.

Managers also may consider other options, such as reengineering or redesigning unprofitable products, to eliminate or reduce costly activities and bring their costs in line with market prices. For example, they could improve the production processes to reduce setup times and streamline material and product flows. They also may want to explore market conditions more carefully and differentiate their products further to raise prices and bring them in line with the costs. Firms also can offer customers incentives, such as quantity discounts, to increase order sizes and thereby reduce total batch-related costs. If these steps fail, and if the marketing strategy of offering such a full product line cannot justify the high net cost of such products, then managers must consider a plan to phase out the products from their line. Customers also need to be shifted to substitute products still retained in the company's product line.

A caveat is in order, however. Dropping products will help improve profitability only if the managers (1) eliminate the activity resources no longer required to support the discontinued product, or (2) redeploy the resources from the eliminated

IN PRACTICE

What Can Managers Do to Maintain (or Even Grow) Market Share When Prices Fall Worldwide?

Major structural changes in the way global business has been operating have caused prices to fall. Numerous countries in Asia, Latin America, and Europe have purchased a great deal of manufacturing capacity through debt financing. Using this capacity to produce products has caused competition in export markets to increase and, as a result, export growth for many countries has slowed. Reluctantly, many countries have been forced to devalue their currencies, and thus worldwide prices have fallen.

To maintain market share, companies can either lower their prices or add value to customers in other ways. General Electric has opted for the latter. As an example, Robert Nardelli, president of General Electric's power systems, felt the price pressure especially on new equipment. He instructed his managers to find out how he could provide better service to his top 100 customers. As a result, the company responded with the following: First, it reduced its lead time for replacing old or broken components by 50%. Next, it began to counsel customers on how to better conduct business in Europe and Asia. Third, it began to provide a maintenance staff for equipment upgrades; and finally, it reassigned one-third of its engineers from product development to new service development. Nardelli commented, "If we hadn't reshaped the business, we would still be facing commodity pricing and would have fallen prey to downward spiraling margins . . . but we've actually been able to generate bigger margins."

Source: Ram Charan, "With Capacity Growing, Currencies Tumbling, and Prices Slipping . . . The Rules Have Changed," *Fortune,* March 16, 1998, pp. 159–160.

products to produce more of the profitable products that the firm continues to offer. Costs result from commitments to supply activity resources. Therefore, they do not disappear automatically with the dropping of unprofitable products. Only when companies eliminate or redeploy the resources themselves will actual expenses decrease.

In summary, capacity constraints are likely to be less of a concern for product mix decisions that have long-term effects, because firms can adjust the level of resources committed to most activities in the long run. As a result, a comparison of the price of a product with its activity-based costs provides a valuable evaluation of its long-run profitability.

HIGH PERFORMANCE SPRINGS REVISITED

Should High Performance Springs slash the price of its 0.50-inch springs from $3.63 per pound to $2.48 per pound to obtain business from a reputable customer, the Lawson Corporation? Should it make a counteroffer of $2.70 instead, to cover all its variable manufacturing and selling costs even though full costs amount to $2.79 per pound? How would High Performance cover the related costs if the selling price covers only the variable costs? These were some of the questions raised by Wendy Stone to her controller and marketing manager.

The concepts discussed in this chapter help us to answer these questions. Fixed costs, such as product-sustaining or business-sustaining costs, can be ignored, and variable costs alone are relevant only for analyzing a short-term pricing decision for a period that is too short to adjust the company's resources. For long-term pricing decisions, the costs of many more resources are relevant because firms can adjust the supply of most resources over the long term. If firms set prices to cover only short-term variable costs, they cannot survive in the long term because the existence of costs associated with committed resources will lead to continued losses over the long term.

A case for a lower price for Lawson could be made as a part of a penetration pricing strategy. However, High Performance Springs also must consider the reaction of both its existing customers, who may demand a lower price themselves when they learn that High Performance Springs discounts its regular prices for some customers, and its competitors, who may cut prices to respond to Precision's discounting.

SUMMARY EXAMPLE

We turn now to a numerical example that illustrates some important points discussed in this chapter. Faxtronics, Inc. is a Minnesota-based company that manufactures and sells two models (FM101 and FM102) of high-quality fax modem devices for which the following information is available:

ITEM	COSTS PER UNIT FM101	FM102
Direct materials	$120	$160
Direct labor ($20 per hour)	50	80
Variable support ($5 per machine hour)	20	40
Fixed support	20	20
Total costs per unit	$210	$300
Price per unit	$260	$400

Demand for the two models of fax modem devices has grown rapidly in recent years, and Faxtronics can no longer meet the demand with its current production capacity. At present, the monthly demand is 8000 units for FM101 and 5000 units for FM102. Monthly capacity is limited to 60,000 machine hours.

1. Determine the contribution margin per unit for each of the two products.
2. Determine the product mix that maximizes profits.
3. Suppose Faxtronics has received a special order from a new customer willing to buy 2000 units of FM101 at $300 each. What is the opportunity cost associated with this order?
4. Should Faxtronics accept this order?

The solution to the review problem follows:

1. Contribution margin per unit:

ITEM	FM101	FM102
Selling price per unit	$260	$400
Variable costs per unit		
Direct materials	$120	$160
Direct Labor	50	80
Variable support	20	40
Total variable costs per unit	$190	$280
Contribution margin per unit	$ 70	$120

2. Contribution margin per unit of the scarce resource:

ITEM	FM101	FM102
Contribution margin per unit of product	$70	$120
Number of machine hours per unit	4 (20 ÷ 5)	8 (40 ÷ 5)
Contribution margin per machine hour	$17.50	$ 15.00

With capacity fully utilized, FM101 is a more profitable product because it has a higher contribution margin per unit of the scarce resource (machine hours) than FM102. Therefore, Faxtronic should first satisfy all the demand for FM101 and then use the remaining machine hours of capacity to manufacture FM102. The optimal production plan is as follows:

8000 units of FM101

3500 units of FM102 [60,000 − (8,000 × 4)] ÷ 8

3. Faxtronics has no surplus capacity available for the production of an additional 2000 units of FM101, which requires 8000 (2000 × 4) machine hours. Because FM102 has the lowest contribution margin per machine hour, Faxtronics can make available the capacity (8000 machine hours) necessary for the special order by reducing the production of FM102 by 1000 units (8000 ÷ 8). The contribution margin for these 1000 units of FM102 is $120 per unit. Therefore, the opportunity cost to make 2000 additional units of FM101 is $120 × 1000 = $120,000.

4.

SPECIAL ORDER COSTS	AMOUNT	CALCULATION
Variable cost	$380,000	$190 × 2,000
Opportunity cost	120,000	
Relevant cost	$500,000	
Relevant cost per unit	$ 250	$500,000 ÷ 2,000

Therefore, Faxtronics should accept this order, because the price of $300 is higher than the relevant cost of $250 per unit. Faxtronics will enjoy increased profits by $100,000 [($300 − $250) × 2000] by accepting the special order.

SUMMARY

Managers use cost information to assist them in pricing and in product mix decisions. The manner in which they use cost information in making these decisions depend on whether the firm is a major or minor entity in its industry. If the firm is a major entity, it would be able to influence the setting of prices. If it is a minor entity, the firm would take the industry prices as given and adjust its product mix in response to the prices it could charge. The role of cost information also depends on the time frame involved in the decision. Business-sustaining costs are frequently relevant for long-term decisions, but less often for short-term decisions.

Short-term prices are based on incremental costs that depend on the availability of activity resource capacity. If the capacity is likely to be fully utilized, then the incremental costs of overtime and other means to obtain the additional required capacity are also relevant for the pricing decision. If the firm commits to a price under a long-term contract, the normal costs of all activity resources used in the manufacture and selling of a product are relevant. Interestingly, a long-term price also can serve as a benchmark price around which actual prices may fluctuate when the firm can make short-term price adjustments, depending on the demand conditions prevailing at that point in time.

Short-term product mix decisions also require information on incremental costs that vary in the short term. If the capacity is limited for the short term, managers should use the contribution per unit of the limited capacity as the criterion to rank-order the products in the production plan. For long-term product mix decisions, managers rely on the full costs of products, which reflect the usage of the different activity resources required to design, sustain, produce, and sell the products.

Thus, the nature of the cost information required for pricing and product mix decisions depends on the time frame considered. Regardless of whether the firm is a *price setter* or a *price taker,* full cost information is more useful for long-term decisions. Short-term adjustments require information about costs that vary in the short run.

KEY TERMS

Contribution per machine hour, 276
Contribution per unit, 276
Cost-plus pricing, 280
Full costs, 280
Incremental cost per unit, 269
Marginal cost, 291
Marginal revenue, 291
Markup percentage, 280
Penetration pricing strategy, 287
Price setter, 272
Price taker, 272
Skimming price strategy, 287

APPENDIX 7-1

ECONOMIC ANALYSIS OF THE PRICING DECISION

QUANTITY DECISION

In this chapter, we considered a firm's decision about setting its products' *prices* to maximize its profits or, more broadly, pursuing a strategic goal such as market penetration that would maximize its long-term profits. In contrast, introductory textbooks in economics usually analyze the profit maximization decision by a firm in terms of the choice of a *quantity* to produce. In turn, the quantity choice determines the price of the product in the marketplace.

We first briefly discuss this economic analysis of the quantity choice before examining the pricing decision. We present the quantity choice in terms of equating marginal revenue and marginal cost. **Marginal revenue** is defined as the increase in revenue corresponding to a unit increase in the quantity produced and sold. **Marginal cost** is the increase in cost for a unit increase in the quantity produced and sold. If marginal revenue is greater than marginal cost, then increasing the quantity by one unit will increase profit. If marginal revenue is less than the marginal cost, then it is possible to increase profit by decreasing production. Therefore, management profit is maximized by choosing the production quantity where marginal revenue equals marginal cost.

Marginal revenue
The increase in revenue for a unit increase in the quantity produced and sold.

Marginal cost
The increase in cost for a unit increase in the quantity produced and sold.

Exhibit 7-10 depicts marginal analysis. The marginal revenue curve is decreasing because additional sales quantity is generated only by lowering prices to all buyers. The average revenue curve represents the price itself, because average revenue equals total revenue divided by quantity. To obtain total revenue, it is necessary to

EXHIBIT 7-10

Marginal Analysis of Profit-Maximizing Quantity Choice

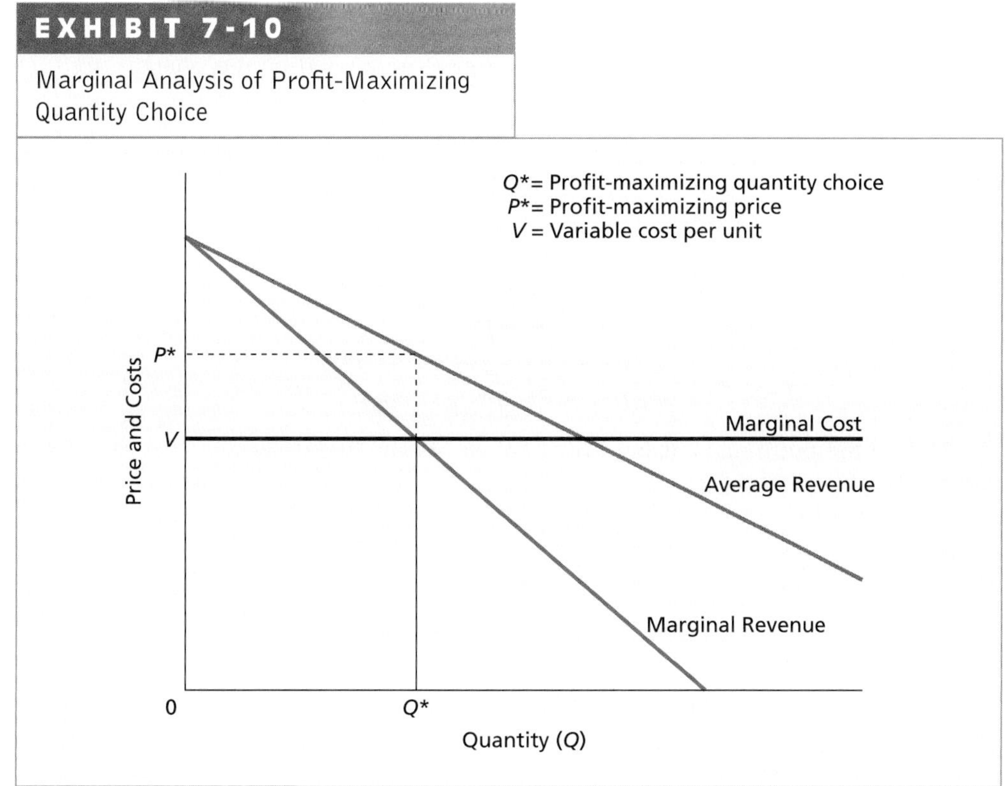

multiply the price by the quantity. Marginal cost is depicted by a horizontal line, because total cost is assumed to increase at a constant rate equal to the variable cost per unit. To determine the profit-maximizing quantity, look for the intersection of the marginal revenue and marginal cost curves, because marginal revenue equals marginal cost at the point of intersection. The profit-maximizing price is the average revenue corresponding to the profit-maximizing quantity.

In this analysis, the firm chooses the quantity level, and the market demand conditions determine the corresponding price. Considered next a firm that must choose a price, not a quantity, to announce to its customers. Customers then react to the price announced and determine the quantity that they demand. In such a case the analysis of the firm's pricing decision cannot be represented graphically as conveniently as in the analysis of the quantity decision previously discussed. Therefore, we shall use instead differential calculus to analyze the firm's pricing decision.

PRICING DECISION

As discussed in Chapter 4, the total costs, C, expressed in terms of its fixed and variable cost components are:

$$C = f + vQ$$

Where f is the fixed cost, v is the variable cost per unit, and Q is the quantity produced in units. Quantity produced is assumed to be the same as quantity demanded. The demand, Q, is represented as a decreasing linear function of the price P:

$$Q = a - bP$$

In general, we may have nonlinear demand functions, but the linear form provides a convenient characterization for our analysis. A higher value of $b \cdot 0$ represents a demand function that is more sensitive (elastic) to price. An increase of a dollar in the price decreases demand by b units. A higher value of $a \cdot 0$ reflects a greater strength of demand for the firm's product. For any given price, P, the demand is greater when the parameter, a, has a higher value.

The total revenue, R, is given by the price, P, multiplied by the quantity sold, Q. Algebraically, we write this:

$$R = PQ = P(a - bP)$$
$$= aP - bP^2$$

The profit, Π, is measured as the difference between the revenue, R, and the cost, C:

$$\Pi = R - C$$
$$= PQ - (f + vQ)$$
$$= P(a - bP) - f - v(a - bP)$$
$$= aP - bP^2 - f - va + vbP$$

To find the profit-maximizing price, P^*, we set the first derivative of profit P with respect to P equal to zero:

$$d^{\Pi}/dP = a - 2bP + vb = 0$$

This equation implies:

$$P^* = (a + vb)/2b = a/2b + v/2$$

LONG-TERM BENCHMARK PRICES

This simple economic analysis suggests that the price depends only on v, the variable cost per unit. Fixed costs are not relevant for the pricing decision. A more complex analysis (not described here) that considers simultaneously the pricing decision and the long-term decisions of the firm to commit resources to facility-sustaining, product-sustaining, and other activity capacities indicates that the costs of these committed resources do play a role in the pricing decision.[3] The costs of these committed activity resources appear to be fixed costs in the short term, but they can be changed in the long term. The prices that a firm sets and adjusts in the short term, based on changing demand conditions, fluctuate around a long-term benchmark price, P^L, that reflects the unit costs of the activity resource capacities:

$$P^L = a/2b + (v + m)/2$$

Here $m = f \div X$ is the cost per unit of normal capacity, X, of facility-sustaining activities. In this case, the degree of price fluctuations around the benchmark price increases with the proportion of fixed costs. As a result, prices appear more volatile in capital-intensive industries, such as airlines, hotels, and petroleum refining, where a large proportion of costs are for facility-sustaining activities.

COMPETITIVE ANALYSIS

How does the pricing decision change when other firms compete in the same industry with products that are similar but not identical to each other? In such a situation, some customers may switch their demand to a competing supplier firm if the competitor reduces its price. Therefore, a firm's pricing decision must consider the prices that may be set by its competitors.

We consider two firms, A and B, and represent the demand, Q_A, for firm A's product as a function of its own price, P_A, and the price, P_B, set by its competitor:

$$Q_A = a - bP_A + eP_B$$

The demand for firm A's product falls by b units for each dollar increase in its own price, but increases by e units for each dollar increase in the competitor's price, because firm A gains some of the market demand that firm B loses.

The profit, P_A, for firm A is represented by the following:

$$\begin{aligned} \Pi_A &= P_A Q_A - (f + vQ_A) \\ &= P_A(a - bP_A + eP_B) - f - v(a - bP_A + eP_B) \end{aligned}$$

Profit maximization requires this:

$$d^{\Pi}_{A} \div dP_A = a - 2bP_A + eP_B + vb = 0$$

Therefore, the profit-maximizing price P^0_A given the other firm's price P_B is:

$$P^0_A = (a + vb + eP_B) \div 2b$$

The pricing decision thus depends on what the competitor's price is expected to be. If the firm expects its competitor to behave as it does and expects it to choose the same price as its own, then we set $P_A = P_B = P^*$ in the equation $a - 2bP_A1 + eP_B + vb = 0$ to obtain:

$$\begin{aligned} a - 2bP^* + eP^* + vb = 0 \\ P^* = a + vb/2b - e \end{aligned}$$

We refer to this price as the equilibrium price, because no firm can increase its profits by choosing a different price provided the other firm maintains the same price P^*. This analysis is based on a concept called Nash equilibrium, for which its discoverer, John Nash, won the 1994 Nobel Prize in Economics.

[3] Rajiv D. Banker and John S. Hughes, "Product Costing and Pricing," The Accounting Review, July 1994, pp. 479–494.

QUESTIONS

7-1 "Prices must cover both variable and fixed costs of production." Do you agree with this statement? Explain. (LO 2, 3)

7-2 Why is the evaluation of *short-term pricing* and product mix decisions different from the evaluation of *long-term pricing* and product mix decisions? (LO 1, 2, 3, 4)

7-3 What distinguishes a *commodity-type business* from other businesses? (LO 1)

7-4 What two considerations complicate short-term product mix decisions? (LO 1, 2)

7-5 What firms are likely to behave as *price-taker* firms? (LO 1, 4)

7-6 What firms are likely to behave as *price-setter* firms? (LO 2, 3)

7-7 "When production capacity is constrained, determine what products to make by ranking them in order of their *contribution per unit*." Do you agree with this statement? Explain. (LO 1)

7-8 "When production capacity is limited and it is possible to obtain additional customer orders, then a firm must consider its *opportunity costs* to evaluate the profitability of these new orders." Do you agree with this statement? What are the opportunity costs in this context? (LO 1, 2)

7-9 What additional costs should a firm consider when making a short-term pricing decision when surplus production capacity is not available and it must employ overtime, extra shifts, subcontracting, or other means to augment the limited capacity? (LO 1, 2)

7-10 Should a firm consider business-sustaining costs in making a short-run pricing decision? Give two examples to illustrate your answer. (LO 1, 2)

7-11 Describe three situations in which there is economic justification for using full costs for pricing decisions. (LO 3)

7-12 How do price markups over costs relate to the strength of demand, the elasticity of demand, and the intensity of competition? (LO 3)

7-13 Why do short-run prices fluctuate over time? (LO 1, 2)

7-14 What strategic reasons may influence the level of markups? (LO 3)

7-15 What options should firms consider when long-run market prices are below full costs? (LO 3, 4)

7-16 Why is full-cost information useful for long-run product mix decisions? (LO 3, 4)

EXERCISES

LO 2 **7-17** ***Special order pricing*** Healthy Hearth specializes in lunches for the health conscious. The company produces a small selection of lunch offerings each day. The menu selections may vary from day to day, but Healthy Hearth charges the same price per menu selection because it adjusts the portion sizes according to the cost of producing the selection. Healthy Hearth currently sells 5000 meals per month, and has sufficient idle capacity to accommodate a recent special order from a government agency to provide 1000 meals next month for senior citizens. Variable costs per meal are $3 per meal, and fixed costs total $5000 per month. Volunteers will deliver the meals to the senior citizens at no charge. The government agency is offering to pay Healthy Hearth $3.50 per meal. What will be the impact on Healthy Hearth's operating income if it accepts this special order?

LO 2 **7-18** ***Special order pricing*** Shorewood Shoes Company makes and sells a variety of leather shoes for children. For its current mix of different models and sizes, the average selling price and costs per pair of shoes are as follows:

ITEM	AMOUNT
Price	$20
Costs:	
Direct materials	$ 6
Direct labor	4
Variable manufacturing support	2
Variable selling support	1
Fixed support	3
Total costs	$16

Shoes are manufactured in batch sizes of 100 pairs. Each batch requires five machine hours to manufacture. The plant has a total capacity of 4000 machine hours per month, but current month production consumes only about 80% of the capacity.

A discount store has approached Shorewood to buy 10,000 pairs of shoes next month. It has requested that the shoes bear its own private label. Embossing the private label will cost Shorewood an additional $0.50 per pair. However, there will be no variable selling support cost for this special order.

Determine the minimum price that Shorewood Shoes should charge for this order. What other considerations are relevant in this decision?

7-19 ***Shelf mix decision*** Superstore is a large discount supermarket. Profits have declined, so the manager has collected data on revenues and costs for different food categories. The data below pertain to some of the frozen foods that Superstore sells. To facilitate comparisons, the manager has listed average price and cost information for each category in equivalent square-foot packages. LO 1

	ICE CREAM	JUICES	FROZEN DINNERS	FROZEN VEGETABLES
Selling price per unit (square-foot package)	$12.00	$13.00	$24.00	$9.00
Variable costs per unit (square-foot package)	$8.00	$10.00	$20.50	$7.00
Minimum square footage required	24	24	24	24
Maximum square footage allowed	100	100	100	100

The manager wants a maximum of 250 square feet devoted to the four categories above.

REQUIRED

(a) Given the manager's constraints, and assuming that the store can sell whatever is displayed on the shelves, what shelf mix (what number of square feet for each category above) will maximize Superstore's contribution margin from these four categories?

(b) What other factors might the manager consider in deciding on the amount of shelf space per category?

7-20 ***Product mix decision*** Boyd Wood Company makes a regular and a deluxe grade of wood floors. Regular grade is sold at $16 per square yard, and the deluxe grade is sold at $25 per square yard. The variable cost of making the regular grade is $10 per square yard. It costs an extra $5 per square yard to make the deluxe grade. It takes 15 labor hours to make 100 square yards of the regular grade and 20 labor hours to make 100 square yards of the deluxe grade. There are 4600 hours of labor time available for production each week. The maximum weekly sales for the regular and the deluxe model are 30,000 and 8,000 square yards, respectively. Fixed production costs total $600,000 per year. All selling costs are fixed. What is the optimal production level in number of square yards for each product? LO 1

LO 1 **7-21** ***Patient mix, ethics*** Willow Way Nursing Home, attempting to improve its profit, adopted a policy of welcoming only residents who are covered by private insurance or by Medicare, or who have sufficient funds of their own to pay the nursing home fees. These groups of residents are clearly the most profitable for Willow Way, but a much larger number of potential residents are covered only by Medicaid, which pays a much lower fee per resident to nursing homes. Other nursing homes welcomed Medicaid patients, reasoning that having such patients covering some of the home's capacity costs was preferable to empty beds. Willow Way, however, turned away potential residents whose only coverage was through Medicaid, and actively encouraged its employees to discharge current residents covered through Medicaid by paying a bonus per Medicaid resident discharged. Employees were also frequently asked to report on their efforts to discharge such residents.

REQUIRED

(a) Evaluate Willow Way's approach to achieving profit for the nursing home, and discuss ethical issues related to their admission and discharge policies.

(b) What options are available to an employee who believes the nursing home's policies are unethical?

LO 2 **7-22** ***Export order*** Berry Company produces and sells 30,000 cases of fruit preserves each year. The following information reflects a breakdown of its costs:

COST ITEM	COSTS PER CASE	TOTAL COSTS
Variable production costs	$16	$480,000
Fixed production costs	8	240,000
Variable selling costs	5	150,000
Fixed selling and administrative costs	3	90,000
Total Costs	$32	$960,000

Berry marks up its prices 40% over full costs. It has surplus capacity to produce 15,000 more cases. A French supermarket company has offered to purchase 10,000 cases of the product at a special price of $40 per case. Berry will incur additional shipping and selling costs of $3 per case to complete this order. What will be the effect on Berry's operating income if it accepts this order?

LO 1, 2 **7-23** ***Extra shift decision*** The manufacturing capacity of Ritter Rotator Company's plant facility is 60,000 rotators per quarter. Operating results for the first quarter of 2000 are as follows:

Sales (36,000 units @ $10)	$360,000
Variable manufacturing and selling costs	198,000
Contribution margin	$162,000
Fixed Costs	99,000
Operating income	$63,000

A foreign distributor has offered to buy 30,000 units at $9 per unit during the second quarter of 2000. Domestic demand is expected to remain the same as in the first quarter.

REQUIRED

(a) Determine the impact on operating income if Ritter accepts this order. What other considerations are relevant in this decision?

(b) Assume that Ritter decides to run an extra shift so that it can accept the foreign order without foregoing sales to its regular domestic customers. The proposed extra shift would increase capacity by 25% and increase fixed costs by $25,000. Determine the impact on operating income if Ritter operates the extra shift and accepts the export order. What other considerations are relevant in this decision?

7-24 ***Export order*** Delta Screens Corporation is currently operating at 60% of capacity in producing 6000 screens annually. Delta recently received an offer from a company in Germany to purchase 2000 screens at $500 per unit. Delta has not previously sold products in Germany. Budgeted production costs for 6000 and 8000 screens follow: LO 2, 3

	NUMBER OF UNITS PRODUCED	
Costs	**6000**	**8000**
Direct materials	$750,000	$1,000,000
Direct labor	750,000	1,000,000
Support	2,100,000	2,400,000
Total costs	$3,600,000	$4,400,000
Full cost per unit	$600	$550

Delta has been selling its product at a markup of 10% above full cost. Delta's marketing manager believes that although the price offered by the German customer is lower than current prices, Delta should accept the order to gain a foothold in the German market. The production manager, however, believes that Delta should reject the order because the unit cost is higher than the price offered.

REQUIRED

(a) Explain what causes the apparent decrease in cost from $600 per unit to $550 per unit when production increases from 6000 to 8000 units.

(b) If the president of Delta Screens Corporation calls on you to resolve the difference in opinions, what will you recommend? Why?

7-25 ***Pricing with elastic demand*** Sunny Valley Orchards is reevaluating the pricing of its fresh-squeezed orange juice in half-gallon containers. Variable costs per half-gallon container of fresh-squeezed orange juice are $1.50. Based on Sunny Valley's market study, the management has determined that the price per half gallon should be between $2.50 and $3.00. Management knows from past experience that demand is affected by price, and estimates the demands shown below for prices between $2.50 and $3.00. Considering only prices in increments of five cents, which price should Sunny Valley choose to maximize its contribution margin from sales of half-gallon fresh-squeezed orange juice? LO 3

PRICE PER HALF GALLON	ESTIMATED DEMAND (HALF-GALLON UNITS) AT GIVEN PRICE
$2.50	75,000
2.55	72,500
2.60	70,000
2.65	67,500
2.70	65,000
2.75	62,500
2.80	60,000
2.85	57,500
2.90	55,000
2.95	52,500
3.00	50,000

LO 3 **7-26** ***Pricing and impact on demand*** Columbia Bicycle Company manufactures and sells 12 different models of bicycles. Columbia is contemplating a 5% price cut across the board for all 12 models. It expects the price cut to result in an 8% increase in the number of units sold of models M124, M126, M128, W124, W126, and W128. Columbia expects the other six models (B112, B116, B120, G112, G116, and G120) to experience a 4% increase in the number of units sold.

The following are the sales prices, variable costs, and sales volume (units) at present. You are required to assess the impact of the price cut on Columbia's profits.

MODEL	SALES PRICE	VARIABLE COSTS	SALES VOLUME
B112	$60	$30	3,000
B116	70	33	4,500
B120	80	36	5,000
G112	60	30	4,000
G116	70	33	4,000
G120	80	36	4,000
M124	100	42	5,000
M126	120	46	5,000
M128	140	50	10,000
W124	100	42	6,000
W126	120	46	7,000
W128	140	40	6,000

LO 3, 4 **7-27** ***Pricing and impact on demand*** Andrea Kimball has recently acquired a franchise of a well-known fast-food and restaurant chain. She is considering a special promotion for a week during which there would be a $0.40 reduction in hamburger prices from the regular price of $1.09 to $0.69. Local advertising expenses for this special promotion will amount to $4500. Andrea expects the promotion to increase sales of hamburgers by 20% and french fries by 12%, but she expects the sales of chicken sandwiches to decline by 8%. Some customers, who may have otherwise ordered a chicken sandwich, now will order a hamburger because of its attractive low price. The following data have been compiled for sales prices, variable costs, and weekly sales volumes:

PRODUCT	SALES PRICE	VARIABLE COSTS	SALES VOLUME
Hamburgers	$1.09	$0.51	20,000
Chicken sandwiches	1.29	0.63	10,000
French fries	0.89	0.37	20,000

Evaluate the expected impact of the special promotion on sales and profits. Should Andrea go ahead with this special promotion? What other considerations are relevant in this decision?

LO 3, 4 **7-28** ***Dropping a product*** Sanders Company recently developed an activity-based costing system, and discovered that one of its products, SM5, does not cover the costs traced to it by the new cost system. Although the current sales price covers the direct material and direct labor costs, it does not cover the manufacturing support costs and customer support costs. The management team initially considered discontinuing production of SM5, but the marketing manager commented that no other local competitors produce SM5. Other than raising the price of SM5, what other actions might Sanders Company explore to increase profitability of SM5?

LO 3 **7-29** ***Pricing using standard hours*** A major automaker collected detailed data on labor hours used by skilled technicians at its auto dealer service departments for different automobile repair jobs. The company then estimated repair times for each type of repair job, and established these estimated times as standards to be used by the dealers in setting prices for the labor portion of the repair jobs. Discuss the advantages and disadvantages of this approach to pricing from the viewpoints of the auto dealer service departments and the customers.

PROBLEMS

7-30 ***Appendix*** Carver Company has a demand function given by this equation: LO 3

$$Q = 400 - (5 \times P)$$

where:
P = price
Q = quantity produced and sold

Carver Company's cost function is given by this equation:

$$C = 2000 + (20 \times Q)$$

Determine the optimal price and the corresponding demand quantity and product unit cost.

7-31 ***Product mix and overtime decisions*** Excel Corporation manufactures three products at its plant. The plant capacity is limited to 120,000 machine hours per year on a single-shift basis. Direct material and direct labor costs are variable. The following data are available for planning purposes: LO 1, 2

PRODUCT	TOTAL UNIT DEMAND FOR NEXT YEAR	SALES PRICE	DIRECT MATERIALS	DIRECT LABOR	VARIABLE SUPPORT	MACHINE HOURS
XL1	200,000	$10.00	$4.00	$2.00	$2.00	0.20
XL2	200,000	14.00	4.50	3.00	3.00	0.35
XL3	200,000	12.00	5.00	2.50	2.50	0.25

REQUIRED

(a) Given the capacity constraint, determine the production levels for the three products that will maximize profits.

(b) If the company authorizes overtime, direct labor cost per unit will be higher by 50% due to the overtime premium. Materials cost and variable support cost per unit will be the same for overtime production as regular production. Is it worthwhile operating overtime?

7-32 ***Capacity and pricing decision*** Hudson Hydronics, Inc. is a corporation based in Troy, New York, that sells high-quality hydronic control devices. It manufactures two products, HCD1 and HCD2, for which the following information is available: LO 1, 2

COSTS PER UNIT	HCD1	HCD2
Direct materials	$ 60	$ 75
Direct labor	80	100
Variable support	100	125
Fixed support	80	100
Total costs per unit	$320	$400
Price	$400	$500
Units sold	2000 units	1200 units

The average wage rate including fringe benefits is $20 per hour. The plant has a capacity of 15,000 direct labor hours, but current production uses only 14,000 direct labor hours of capacity.

REQUIRED

(a) A new customer has offered to buy 200 units of HCD2 if Hudson lowers its price to $400 per unit. How many direct labor *hours* will be required to produce 200 units of HCD2? How much will Hudson Hydronic's profit increase or decrease if it accepts this proposal? (All other prices will remain as before.)

(b) Suppose the customer has offered instead to buy 300 units of HCD2 at $400 per unit. How much will the profits increase or decrease if Hudson accepts this proposal? Assume that the company cannot increase its production capacity to meet the extra demand.

(c) Answer the question in (b) above, assuming instead that the plant can work overtime. Direct labor costs for the *overtime* production increase to only $30 per hour. Variable support costs for overtime production are 50% more than for normal production.

LO 2, 3 **7-33** ***Activity-based costing and markup pricing*** Based on its 1999 activity, the Moose Jaw Manufacturing Company estimates the following manufacturing support costs for 2000 for its plant in Moose Jaw, Saskatchewan.

COST POOL	AMOUNT	ACTIVITY	COST DRIVERS	RATE
Machine operations/ maintenance	$48,000	12,000	Machine hours	$4.00
Supervision	45,000	$225,000	Direct labor dollars	0.20
Materials handling	75,000	100,000	Pounds	0.75
Quality control	66,000	550	Number of inspections	120.00
Machine setups	75,000	250	Production runs	300.00
Total	$309,000			

Moose Jaw's plant manufactures three products: A, B, and C. Data per unit are as follows:

ITEM	PRODUCT A	PRODUCT B	PRODUCT C
Direct materials	$12.00	$15.00	$18.00
Direct labor	$ 9.00	$15.00	$20.00
Machine hours	0.4	0.7	0.9
Pounds	4.0	5.0	7.0
Number of inspections	0.02	0.02	0.05
Number of production runs	0.01	0.01	0.02
1999 Sales price	$40.00	$57.00	$78.00
Maximum demand at 1999 prices	12,000 units	12,000 units	6,000 units
Actual production in 1999	10,000 units	5,000 units	5,000 units

REQUIRED

(a) Determine the product costs using an activity-based costing system.

(b) If Moose Jaw's target prices for each product are 25% above their respective activity-based costs, what are the target prices for products A, B, and C?

(c) At present, production capacity during regular hours is limited to 12,000 machine hours. Capacity can be expanded up to 4000 additional machine hours by using plant overtime. Overtime premium will add 50% to direct labor costs and 30% to each manufacturing support cost pool. If Moose Jaw expands its capacity by using plant overtime to provide an additional 4000 machine hours, what will Moose Jaw's target prices be, using the 25% markup described in part (b)? What issues should the company consider as it decides whether to expand capacity?

7-34 ***Capacity and product mix decision*** Barney Toy Company manufactures large and small stuffed animals. It has a long-term contract with a large chain of discount stores to sell 3000 large and 6000 small stuffed animals each month. The following cost information is available for large and small stuffed animals: LO 1, 2

ITEM	LARGE	SMALL
Price per unit	$32	$21
Variable costs per unit:		
Direct material	$12	$10
Direct labor	6	2
Support	2	1
Fixed costs per unit	3	3
Total unit costs	$23	$16
Estimated demand (inclusive of long-term contract)	15,000	25,000

Production occurs in batches of 100 large or 200 small stuffed animals. Each batch takes a total of 10 machine hours to manufacture. The total machine hour capacity of 3000 machine hours cannot be increased for at least a year.

REQUIRED

(a) Determine the contribution margin per unit for each of the two sizes of stuffed animals.

(b) Determine which size is more profitable to produce. How many units should Barney produce of each size?

(c) Because of an unexpected high demand for stuffed dinosaurs, the discount store chain has requested an additional order of 5,000 large stuffed dinosaurs. It is willing to pay $37 per dinosaur for this special order. Determine the opportunity cost associated with this order.

(d) Should Barney Toy Company accept the order described in (c)? Explain.

(e) Suppose that the company can subcontract the production of up to 10,000 small stuffed animals to an outside supplier at a cost of $22 per animal. How many units of each size (including the special order units) should Barney produce, subcontract, and sell? What other qualitative factors should Barney consider?

7-35 ***Capacity and product mix decision*** Chang Company makes two types of wood doors: standard and deluxe. The doors are manufactured in a plant consisting of three departments: cutting, assembly, and finishing. Both labor and machine time are spent on the two products as they are worked on in each department. LO 1, 2

In planning the production schedule for the next month, management is confronted with the fact that there is a labor shortage, and some machines must be shut down for major maintenance and repair. The following information pertains to the estimated levels of capacity of direct labor hours and machine hours available next month in the three departments:

	DEPARTMENT		
Capacity Available	**Cutting**	**Assembly**	**Finishing**
Machine hours	40,000	40,000	15,000
Labor hours	8,000	17,500	8,000

Direct labor and machine hours required per unit of each product are as follows:

	DEPARTMENTS		
Product Hours	**Cutting**	**Assembly**	**Finishing**
Standard:			
Direct labor hours	0.5	1	0.5
Machine hours	2	2	1
Deluxe:			
Direct labor hours	1	1.5	0.5
Machine hours	3	3	1.5

The estimated demand for the next month is 10,000 units of standard doors and 5000 units of deluxe doors. Unit cost and price information are as follows:

ITEM	STANDARD DOORS	DELUXE DOORS
Unit selling price	$150	$200
Unit costs:		
Direct materials	$60	$80
Direct labor	40	60
Variable support	10	15
Fixed support	10	5

Average wage rate is $20 per hour. Direct labor and machine availability in individual departments cannot be switched from one department to another.

REQUIRED

(a) Determine whether the direct labor hour and machine-hour capacities are adequate to meet the next month's demand.

(b) How many units of each product should the company produce to maximize its profits?

(c) Suggest alternatives the company might consider to satisfy all its customers' demands.

LO 1 7-36 ***Client mix decision*** Loren Lee, a financial planner, contacts and meets with local individuals to assist with financial planning and investments in Loren's employer's investment services company. Loren receives no fee for financial planning advice, but receives a commission on client investments in the investment services company. Commission rates vary across different investment products. Loren's employer pays office and phone costs, and also reimburses Loren for business-related travel. Satisfied clients have recommended Loren to their friends, and Loren now finds himself with more clients than he can handle in the 40 hours per week he would like to work. To analyze where to most profitably spend his time, Loren has classified his current set of customers into the three groups listed below. The hours devoted per customer include direct contact time, travel time, and research and follow-up time for the clients. Loren will introduce clients he is unable to serve to one of his colleagues.

	CUSTOMER GROUP		
	A	B	C
Average investment in company products per month	$900	$600	$200
Hours devoted per customer per month	3	1.5	0.5
Average commission percentage	6%	5%	4%
Current number of customers	20	60	120

Clients in group A are generally interested in hearing about new investment products that Loren's company is offering, and will usually invest sizable amounts in new products after meeting with Loren or conversing with him on the phone. Clients in group B will also invest, but generally in smaller amounts than clients in group A. Clients in group C appreciate meeting with Loren because of the excellent advice he provides in planning for retirement and other future expenses, but have little discretionary income to invest. Group C clients also generally invest in products with a lower commission rate for Loren. However, Loren maintains contact with these clients because he anticipates they will become more profitable as their careers develop.

REQUIRED

(a) Based on the data above, what client mix will maximize Loren's monthly commissions, assuming he works 160 hours per month?

(b) What other factors should Loren consider as he makes his decisions about his client mix?

7-37 ***Short-term pricing*** True Image Printers, Inc. is a corporation based in Oberlin, Ohio, that sells high-quality printers in the Midwest regional market. It manufactures two products, L8011 and L8033, for which the following information is available: LO 2

TRUE IMAGE PRINTERS, INC.
COST INFORMATION ON TWO PRINTERS

	PRODUCT	
Item	**L8011**	**L8033**
Cost per unit:		
Direct materials	$ 300	$ 375
Direct labor	400	500
Variable support	500	625
Fixed support	400	500
Total cost per unit	$1600	$2000
Price	$2000	$2500
Units sold	400 units	200 units

The average wage rate including fringe benefits is $20 per hour. The plant has a capacity of 14,000 direct labor hours, but current production uses only 13,000 direct labor hours of capacity.

REQUIRED

(a) A new customer has offered to buy 40 units of L8033 if its price is lowered to $2000 per unit. How many direct labor hours will be required to produce 40 units of L8033? How much will True Image Printers's profit increase or decrease if it accepts this proposal? All other prices will remain as before.

(b) Suppose the customer has offered, instead, to buy 60 units of L8033 at $2000 per unit. How much will the profits increase or decrease if True Image Printers accepts this proposal? Assume that the company cannot increase its production capacity to meet the extra demand.

(c) Answer the question in (b) above, assuming, instead, that the plant can work overtime. Direct labor costs for the overtime production increase to $30 per hour. Variable support costs for overtime production are 50% more than for normal production.

LO 2 **7-38** ***Bid price*** (Adapted from CMA, June 1991) Marcus Fibers, Inc. specializes in the manufacture of synthetic fibers that the company uses in many products such as blankets, coats, and uniforms for police and firefighters. Marcus has been in business since 1975 and has been profitable each year since 1983. The company uses a standard cost system and applies manufacturing support costs on the basis of direct labor hours.

Marcus has recently received a request to bid on the manufacture of 800,000 blankets scheduled for delivery to several military bases. The bid must be stated at full cost per unit plus a return on full cost of no more than 9% after income taxes. Full cost has been defined as including all variable costs of manufacturing the product, a reasonable amount of fixed support costs, and reasonable incremental administrative costs associated with the manufacture and sale of the product. The contractor has indicated that bids in excess of $25 per blanket are not likely to be considered.

To prepare the bid for the 800,000 blankets, Andrea Lightner, cost accountant, has gathered the following information about the costs associated with the production of the blanket:

COSTS	AMOUNT
Raw materials	$1.50 per pound of fibers
Direct labor	$7.00 per hour
Direct machine costs*	$10.00 per blanket
Variable support	$3.00 per direct labor hour
Fixed support	$8.00 per direct labor hour
Incremental administrative costs	$2500 per 1000 blankets
Special fee**	$0.50 per blanket
Material usage	6 pounds per blanket
Production rate	4 blankets per direct labor hour
Effective tax rate	40%

*Direct machine costs consist of items such as special lubricants, replacement of needles used in stitching, and maintenance costs. These costs are not included in manufacturing support.

**Marcus recently developed a new blanket fiber at a cost of $750,000. In an effort to recover this cost, Marcus has instituted a policy of adding a $0.50 fee to the cost of each blanket using the new fiber. To date the company has recovered $125,000. Andrea knows that this fee does not fit within the definition of full cost as it is not a cost of manufacturing the product.

REQUIRED

(a) Calculate the minimum price per blanket that Marcus Fibers, Inc. could bid without reducing the company's net income.

(b) Using the full cost criterion and the maximum allowable return specified, calculate Marcus Fibers, Inc.'s bid price per blanket.

(c) Without prejudice to your answer to requirement (b) above, assume that the price per blanket that Marcus Fibers, Inc. calculated using the cost-plus criterion specified is greater than the maximum bid of $25 per blanket allowed. Discuss the factors that Marcus Fibers, Inc. should consider before deciding whether to submit a bid at the maximum acceptable price of $25 per blanket.

7-39 ***Product mix and special order decisions*** Holmes Manufacturing Company produces three models of aquastatic controls: A17, B23, and XLT—all of which use the same basic component. The basic components are produced in department A. For model A17, the basic components are finished in department C. For both models B23 and XLT, the basic components undergo further modification in department B before being assembled in department C. Since the modifications for B23 and XLT require similar machines and labor skills, the available capacity of department B can be used for either product. LO 1, 2

COST PER UNIT OF THE BASIC COMPONENT

COST	AMOUNT
Direct materials cost	$ 3.80
Direct labor cost	10.00
Fixed support (allocated based on direct labor hours)	15.00
Total cost per unit	$28.80
Current production volume	4000

PRODUCT COSTS PER UNIT

ITEM	A17	B23	XLT
Selling price per unit	$75.00	$120.00	$160.00
Basic component costs	$28.80	$28.80	$28.80
Direct materials costs	0	$6.00	$4.50
Direct labor costs	$9.00	$20.00	$31.00
Modification hours (department B)	0	0.5 hour	0.75 hour
Finishing hours (department C)	0.3 hour	0.3 hour	0.3 hour
Fixed support (allocated based on direct labor hours)	$9.00	$20.00	$31.00
Total cost per unit	$46.80	$74.80	$95.30
Current production volume	2000	1200	800

REQUIRED

(a) A foreign distributor has asked Holmes to bid on a special order of 1000 units of the basic component. There would be a special shipping charge of

$3200. The Holmes plant has excess capacity to manufacture more than 1000 basic components and this order would not affect sales of the other products. Determine the minimum price that Holmes could offer.

(b) Determine the contribution margin per unit for each of the three products.

(c) Suppose there is excess demand for all three products and the plant is currently operating at capacity. The only change that can be made is shifting workers between department B and department C. Personnel in those two departments are able to work in either area with no loss in efficiency. Determine the optimal monthly production mix of the three products. Check whether your answer changes if the price of model B23 is $140.

LO 2 **7-40** ***Special order decision*** Kirby Company manufactures leather briefcases sold to wholesalers for $37.95. The plant capacity for manufacturing this product is 750,000 units annually, but normal volume is 500,000 units. The unit and total costs at normal volume follow:

TYPE OF COST	UNIT COSTS	TOTAL COSTS
Direct materials	$ 9.80	$ 4,900,000
Direct labor	4.50	2,250,000
Manufacturing support	12.00	6,000,000
Selling and administrative	6.70	3,350,000
Total Costs	$33.00	$16,500,000

Manufacturing support and selling and administrative costs include both variable and fixed costs; fixed manufacturing support costs for the current year are budgeted at $4,500,000; and fixed selling and administrative costs are $2,100,000.

The company has been approached by a prospective customer who has offered to purchase 100,000 briefcases at $25 each. The customer wants the product packaged in large cartons rather than the normal individual containers, and will pick them up in its own trucks. Accordingly, the variable selling and administrative costs will be lower by 60% for this order.

REQUIRED

Determine whether Kirby Company should accept this special order.

LO 1, 2 **7-41** ***Special order pricing, product mix decisions*** (Adapted from CMA, May 1989) Purex Company produces and sells a single product called Kleen. Annual production capacity is 100,000 machine hours. It takes one machine hour to produce a unit of Kleen. Annual demand for Kleen is expected to remain at 80,000 units. The selling price is expected to remain at $10 per unit. Cost data for producing and selling Kleen are as follows:

VARIABLE COSTS PER UNIT:	
Direct materials	$1.50
Direct labor	2.50
Variable manufacturing support	0.80
Variable selling and distribution	2.00

FIXED COSTS PER YEAR:	
Fixed manufacturing support	$100,000.00
Fixed selling and distribution	50,000.00

REQUIRED

(a) Purex Company has an inventory of 2000 units of Kleen that were partially damaged in storage. It can sell these units through regular channels at reduced prices. These 2000 units will be valueless unless sold this way. Sale of these units will not affect regular sales of Kleen. Compute the relevant unit cost for determining the minimum selling price for these units.

(b) Ajax Company has offered to make and ship 25,000 units of Kleen directly to Purex Company's customers. If Purex Company accepts this offer, it will continue to produce and ship the remaining 55,000 units. Purex's fixed manufacturing support costs will decrease to $90,000. Its fixed selling and distribution costs will remain unchanged. Variable selling and distribution costs will decrease to $0.80 per unit for the 25,000 units produced and shipped by Ajax Company. Determine the maximum amount per unit that Purex Company should pay Ajax Company for producing and shipping the 25,000 units.

(c) Purex Company has received a one-time special order for 5000 units of Kleen. Acceptance of this order will not affect the regular sales of 80,000 units. Variable selling costs for each of these 5000 units will be $1.00. Determine the minimum acceptable price for Purex Company for accepting this special order.

(d) Purex Company can use its current facilities to manufacture a product called Shine. Annual production capacity of Shine, which takes 2.5 machine hours per unit to produce, is 50,000 units. The marketing department estimates that 50,000 units of Shine can be sold each year at $16 per unit. Sale of Shine will not affect the demand for Kleen. Cost data for producing and selling Shine are as follows:

VARIABLE COSTS PER UNIT:	
Direct materials	$2.50
Direct labor	4.00
Variable manufacturing support	1.20
Variable selling and distribution	3.30
FIXED COSTS PER YEAR:	
Fixed manufacturing support	$100,000.00
Fixed selling and distribution	50,000.00

Determine the product mix that will maximize Purex Company's profit.

7-42 ***Product mix and overtime decisions*** Refer to the data for Crimson Components Company presented in Problem 5-42. The following additional information is available: LO 1, 2

- The company believes that it cannot change its selling prices.
- All manufacturing support costs described in Problem 5-42 are variable costs.
- All nonmanufacturing costs are fixed.
- The plant has a capacity of 80,000 casting department *machine hours* and 120,000 machining department *machine hours* on a single-shift basis.
- Estimated demand for the next year is 600,000 units of R361 and 800,000 units of R572.

REQUIRED

(a) Determine the total casting department machine hours and machining department machine hours required to produce all of the estimated demand for the next year. In which department is the capacity inadequate to meet estimated demand?

(b) Determine the contribution margins for the two products based on your analysis for requirement (b) in Problem 5-42.

(c) Determine the contribution per machine hour for the department(s) in which capacity is inadequate. Given the capacity constraint(s), determine the production levels for the two products that will maximize profits.

(d) Either or both of the casting and machining departments can be worked overtime. Direct labor cost per unit would be higher by 50% due to the overtime premium. Manufacturing support costs per unit would be the same for overtime production as for normal production. Is it worthwhile operating either department overtime? Explain.

LO 1, 2, 3, 4 **7-43** ***Product mix and special order decisions*** Orion Outdoors Company produces a standard model and a high-quality deluxe model of lightweight tents. Orion's workforce is organized into production teams responsible for cutting, stitching, and inspection activities. Orion has determined that its labor and support costs depend on the number of direct labor hours (cutting, stitching, and inspection), number of batches, and number of shipments. Production information is as follows:

ITEM	STANDARD MODEL	DELUXE MODEL
Direct labor time (cutting and stitching) per tent	10 min.	15 min.
Average batch size	60 tents	30 tents
Direct labor inspection time per batch	2 hrs.	2.5 hrs.
Average size per shipment	60 tents	10 tents
Selling price per tent	$10	$20
Materials costs per tent	$5	$11

Demand for standard and deluxe models is expected to be 6000 and 3000 tents, respectively. Direct labor time available for cutting, stitching, and inspection activities is 2000 hours. The labor cost is $12 per hour, including fringe benefits, and shipping cost is $15 per shipment. Orion produces to demand and maintains no inventory on hand.

REQUIRED

(a) Determine the production quantities for the two models that will maximize profits. Assume in this case that it is not possible to change the number of available labor hours.

Suppose next that labor time available for cutting, stitching, and inspection can be increased as needed. The sales manager has received an offer from Northlands Retail Company for 2000 deluxe model tents at a price of $18.50 each. This order will be produced and shipped in batch sizes of 50 tents. Inspections for this order of deluxe model batches will take 2.5 hours per batch.

(b) Should Orion Outdoors Company accept this order? What other qualitative factors should the company also consider?

7-44 ***Appendix*** Colway Company estimates the relation between the demand for its products and the price it sets, in terms of this equation where: LO 3

Q = the quantity demanded

P = the price of the product

$$Q = a - bP$$

The marketing manager, Trisha Colway, conducted a market research study in fall 1999 that indicated that $b = 500$ and $a = 8400$ on average for the first quarter of 2000.

Capacity costs are m = \$3.00 per unit and variable costs are v = \$8.10 per unit. If committed capacity is exceeded, the variable costs increase to w = \$12.70 per unit.

Trisha determined that the long-term benchmark price is given by this:

$$P^L = \frac{a}{2b} + \frac{v + m}{2}$$

$$= \frac{8400}{2 \times 500} + \frac{\$8.10 + \$3.00}{2}$$

$$= \$13.95$$

Trisha also set the capacity level at $X = 2150$ units.

Colway Company keeps track of demand conditions throughout the quarter. It announces a new price for each week in the Sunday-morning newspaper based on the most current information it has on demand conditions. The following are the estimates of the demand parameter for each of the 13 weeks in the first quarter of 2000.

WEEK t	CURRENT ESTIMATE OF a_t	WEEKLY PRICE P_t
1	8200	\$12.25
2	8350	?
3	8600	?
4	8500	?
5	8400	?
6	8850	?
7	8300	?
8	8050	?
9	8200	?
10	8800	?
11	8350	?
12	7950	?
13	8650	?

The estimate of b remained at $b = 500$ for all 13 weeks. The short-term (weekly) price is set at this if the capacity is *not* exceeded by the realized demand:

$$P_t^* = \frac{a_1}{2b} + \frac{v}{b}$$

It is set at this if the capacity *is* exceeded:

$$P_t^* = \frac{a_t}{2b} + \frac{w}{2}$$

Note that if the price is set at this:

$$P_t^* = \frac{a_t}{2b} + \frac{v}{2}$$

the resultant demand will not exceed the capacity $X = 2150$ only if this occurs:

$$Q = a_t - bP_t = a_t - 500\left(\frac{a_t}{1000} + \frac{8.10}{2}\right) = \frac{a_t}{2} - 2025$$

is less than $X = 2150$, that is, if $a_t < 8350$.

Similarly, if the price is set at this:

$$P_t^* = \frac{a_t}{2b} + \frac{w}{2}$$

the resultant demand will exceed the capacity $X = 2150$ only if $a_t > 10{,}650$.

REQUIRED

(a) Determine the weekly prices, plot them on a graph for each of the 13 weeks, and compare them with the long-term benchmark price. What is the average of the weekly prices?

(b) Determine the total profit over the 13-week period. Repeat the same exercise after setting the capacity (X) at different levels ($X = 1750$, 1950, 2350, 2550). Plot the total profit on a graph against different levels of capacity that you select.

LO 2, 3, 4 **7-45** ***Special order pricing*** (Adapted from CMA, December 1988) The Sommers Company, located in southern Wisconsin, manufactures a variety of industrial valves and pipe fittings that are sold to customers in nearby states. Currently, the company is operating at about 70% capacity and is earning a satisfactory return on investment.

Management has been approached by Glasgow Industries Ltd. of Scotland with an offer to buy 120,000 units of a pressure valve. Glasgow Industries manufactures a valve that is almost identical to Sommers's pressure valve. However, a fire in the Glasgow Industries' valve plant has shut down its manufacturing operations. Glasgow needs the 120,000 valves over the next four months to meet commitments to its regular customers. The company is prepared to pay $19 each for the valves, FOB shipping point, that is, freight and transportation insurance expenses are paid by the buyer, Glasgow Industries Ltd.

Sommers's product cost, based on current attainable standards, for the pressure valve is as follows:

Direct materials	$ 5.00
Direct labor	6.00
Manufacturing support	9.00
Total cost	$20.00

Manufacturing support costs are applied to production at the rate of $18 per standard direct labor hour. This rate is made up of the following components:

Variable manufacturing support	$ 6.00
Fixed manufacturing support	12.00
Cost driver rate	$18.00

Additional costs incurred in connection with sales of the pressure valve include sales commissions of 5% and freight expense of $1 per unit. However, the company does not pay sales commissions on special orders that come directly to management.

In determining selling prices, Sommers adds a 40% markup to product cost. This provides a $28 suggested selling price for the pressure valve. The marketing department, however, has set the current selling price at $27 in order to maintain the company's market share.

Production management believes that it can handle the Glasgow Industries order without disrupting its scheduled production. The order would, however, require additional fixed manufacturing support costs of $12,000 per month in the form of supervision and clerical costs.

If management accepts the order, 30,000 pressure valves will be manufactured and shipped to Glasgow Industries each month for the next four months. Shipments will be made in weekly consignments, FOB shipping point.

REQUIRED

(a) Determine how many additional direct labor hours would be required each month to fill the Glasgow Industries order.

(b) Evaluate the impact of accepting the Glasgow Industries order on Sommers's profit.

(c) Calculate the minimum unit price that Sommers's management could accept for the Glasgow Industries order without reducing its profits.

(d) Identify the factors, other than price, that Sommers Company should consider before accepting the Glasgow Industries order.

7-46 ***Product mix decisions*** (Adapted from CMA, December 1991) Bakker Industries sells three products (products 611, 613, and 615) that it manufactures in a factory consisting of four departments (departments 1 through 4). Both labor and machine time are applied to the products in each of the four departments. The machine processing and labor skills required in each department are such that neither machines nor labor can be switched from one department to another. LO 1, 4

Bakker's management is planning its production schedule for the next several months. There are labor shortages in the community. Some of the machines will be out of service for extensive overhauling. Available machine and labor time by department for each of the next six months is listed below.

	DEPARTMENT			
Monthly Capacity Availability	**1**	**2**	**3**	**4**
Normal machine capacity in machine hours	3500	3500	3000	3500
Capacity of machines being repaired in machine hours	(500)	(400)	(300)	(200)
Available machine capacity in machine hours	3000	3100	2700	3300
Labor capacity in direct labor hours	4000	4500	3500	3000
Available labor in direct labor hours	3700	4500	2750	2600

LABOR AND MACHINE SPECIFICATIONS PER UNIT OF PRODUCT

		DEPARTMENT			
Product	**Labor and Machine Time**	**1**	**2**	**3**	**4**
611	Direct labor hours	2	3	3	1
	Machine hours	2	1	2	2
613	Direct labor hours	1	2	0	2
	Machine hours	1	1	0	2
615	Direct labor hours	2	2	1	1
	Machine hours	2	2	1	1

The sales department's forecast of product demand over the next six months is presented below.

PRODUCT	MONTHLY SALES VOLUME
611	500 units
613	400 units
615	1000 units

Bakker's inventory levels will not be increased or decreased during the next 6 months. The unit price and cost data valid for the next six months are presented below.

	PRODUCT		
Item	611	613	615
Unit costs:			
Direct material	$ 7	$ 13	$ 17
Direct labor			
Department 1	12	6	12
Department 2	21	14	14
Department 3	24	0	8
Department 4	9	18	9
Variable support	27	20	25
Fixed support	15	10	32
Variable selling	3	2	4
Unit selling price	$196	$123	$167

REQUIRED

(a) Determine whether the monthly sales demand for the three products can be met by Bakker Industries's factory. Use the monthly requirement by department for machine hours and direct labor hours for the production of products 611, 613, and 615 in your calculations.

(b) What monthly production schedule should Bakker Industries select to maximize its dollar profits? Support the schedule with appropriate calculations, and present a schedule of the contribution to profit that would be generated by the production schedule selected.

(c) What other alternatives might Bakker Industries consider to be able to supply its customers all the products they demand?

LO 1, 4 7-47 ***Product mix decision*** (Adapted from CMA, June 1990) Sportway, Inc. is a wholesale distributor supplying a wide range of moderately priced sporting equipment to large chain stores. About 60% of Sportway's products are purchased from other companies while the remainder of the products are manufactured by Sportway. The company has a plastics department that is currently manufacturing molded fishing tackle boxes. Sportway is able to manufacture and sell 8,000 tackle boxes annually, making full use of its direct labor capacity at available work stations. The following are the selling price and costs associated with Sportway's tackle boxes.

Selling price per box		$86.00
Costs per box:		
Molded plastic	$ 8.00	
Hinges, latches, handle	9.00	
Direct labor ($15/hour)	18.75	
Manufacturing support	12.50	
Selling and administrative	17.00	65.25
Profit per box		$20.75

Because Sportway believes it could sell 12,000 tackle boxes if it had sufficient manufacturing capacity, the company has looked into the possibility of purchasing the tackle boxes for distribution. Maple Products, a steady supplier of quality products, would be able to provide up to 9000 tackle boxes per year at a price of $68 per box delivered to Sportway's facility.

Bart Johnson, Sportway's product manager, has suggested that the company could make better use of its plastics department by manufacturing skateboards. To support his position, Johnson has a market study that indicates an expanding market for skateboards and a need for additional suppliers. Johnson believes that Sportway could expect to sell 17,500 skateboards annually at a price of $45.00 per skateboard. Johnson's estimate of the costs to manufacture the skateboards is presented below.

Selling price per skateboard		$45.00
Costs per skateboard:		
Molded plastic	$5.50	
Wheels, hardware	7.00	
Direct labor ($15 per hour)	7.50	
Manufacturing support	5.00	
Selling and administrative costs	9.00	34.00
Profit per skateboard		$11.00

In the plastics department, Sportway uses direct labor hours as the cost driver for manufacturing support costs. Included in the manufacturing support for the current year is $50,000 of factory-wide, fixed manufacturing support that has been allocated to the plastics department. For each unit of product that Sportway sells, regardless of whether the product has been purchased or is manufactured by Sportway, there is an allocated $6 fixed support cost per unit for distribution that is included in the selling and administrative cost for all products. Total selling and administrative costs for the purchased tackle boxes would be $10 per unit.

REQUIRED

To maximize the company's profitability, prepare an analysis based on the data presented that will show which product or products Sportway, Inc. should manufacture and/or purchase and will show the associated financial impact. Support your answer with appropriate calculations.

7-48 ***Process or sell decision*** The Troy Company manufactures electronic subcomponents that can be sold at the end of process A or can be processed further in process B and sold as special parts for a variety of electronic appliances. The entire output of process A can be sold at a market price of $2 per unit. The output of process B had been sold at a price of $5.50 for the past three years, but the price has recently fallen to $5.10 on most orders. LO 1

Based on an analysis of the product markets and costs, Toni Tobin, the vice-president of marketing, thinks that process B output should be dropped whenever its price falls below $4.50 per unit. The total available capacity is interchangeable between process A and process B. She recommends that with present prices, all sales should be process B output. Her analysis is summarized below:

OUTPUT OF PROCESS A		
Selling price, after deducting relevant selling costs		$2.00
Costs:		
Direct materials	$1.00	
Direct labor	0.20	
Manufacturing support	0.60	
Cost per unit		1.80
Operating profit		$0.20

OUTPUT OF PROCESS B		
Selling price, after deducting relevant selling costs		$5.10
Transferred-in variable cost from process A	$1.20	
Additional direct materials	1.50	
Direct labor	0.40	
Manufacturing support for additional processing	1.20	
Cost per unit		4.30
Operating profit		$0.80

Direct materials and direct labor costs are variable. All manufacturing support costs are fixed and allocated to units produced based on hours of capacity.

The total hours of capacity available are 600,000. A batch of 60 units requires one hour for process A and two hours of additional processing for process B.

REQUIRED

(a) If the price of process B output for the next year is likely to be $5.10, should all sales be only the output of process B?

(b) What is the lowest acceptable price for process B output to make it as profitable as process A output?

(c) Suppose 50% of the manufacturing support costs are variable. Do your answers to (a) and (b) above change? If so, how?

CASES

LO 1, 3, 4 **7-49** ***Product mix decision*** Aramis Aromatics Company produces and sells its product AA100 to well-known cosmetics companies for $940 per ton. The marketing manager is considering the possibility of refining AA100 further into finer perfumes before selling them to the cosmetics companies. Product AA101 is expected to command a price of $1500 per ton, and AA102 a price of $1700 per ton. The maximum expected demand is 400 tons for AA101 and 100 tons for AA102.

The annual plant capacity of 2400 hours is fully utilized *at present* to manufacture 600 tons of AA100. The marketing manager proposed that Aramis sell 300 tons of AA100, 100 tons of AA101, and 75 tons of AA102 in the next year. It requires four hours of capacity to make one ton of AA100, two hours to refine AA100 further into AA101, and four hours to refine AA100 into AA102 instead. The plant accountant has prepared the following cost sheet for the three products:

Cost Item	AA100	AA101	AA102
		COSTS PER TON	
Direct materials:			
Chemicals and fragrance	$560	$400	$470
AA100	0	800	800
Direct labor	60	30	60
Manufacturing support:			
Variable	60	30	60
Fixed	120	60	120
Total manufacturing costs	$800	$1320	$1510
Selling support:			
Variable	20	30	30
Fixed	10	10	10
	$830	$1360	$1550
Proposed sales level	300 tons	100 tons	75 tons
Maximum demand	600 tons	400 tons	100 tons

REQUIRED

(a) Determine the contribution margin for each product.

(b) Determine the production levels for the three products under the present constraint on plant capacity that will maximize total contribution.

(c) Suppose a customer, Cosmos Cosmetics Company, is very interested in the new product AA101. It has offered to sign a long-term contract for 400 tons of AA101. It is also willing to pay a higher price if the entire plant capacity is dedicated to the production of AA101. What is the minimum price for AA101 at which it becomes worthwhile for Aramis to dedicate its entire capacity to the production of AA101?

(d) Suppose, instead, that the price of AA101 is $1500 per ton and that the capacity can be increased temporarily by 600 hours if the plant is operated overtime. Overtime premium payments to workers and supervisors will increase direct labor and variable manufacturing support costs by 50% for all products. All other costs will remain unchanged. Is it worthwhile operating the plant overtime? If the plant is operated overtime for 600 hours, what are the optimal production levels for the three products?

7-50 ***Pricing decision*** Refer to the data for Sweditrak Corporation presented in Case 5-47. The following additional information is now available. LO 4

The production volume budgeted for each product in weeks 47 to 52 is the same as the volume level in week 46. In early December, the company is considering contracting with a French company to *produce* 400 units of the deluxe model on a four-week trial basis for $200 per unit. Accepting this offer would restrict Sweditrak's own deluxe production to 50 units per week.

REQUIRED

(a) Is it profitable for Sweditrak to accept this offer? What other qualitative factors should Sweditrack also consider in evaluating this offer?

Suppose that Sweditrak is pleased with the quality of the trial shipment and the French company is willing to commit to produce 400 units

of the deluxe model each week for the next three years and charge \$200 per unit. Sweditrak expects the domestic demand for its two models to remain stable at 450 units per week for the next three years. During this three-year period, Sweditrak can adjust the capacity of each department to any desired levels. Capacity changes will result in proportional changes in fixed costs.

(b) What are the relevant costs for this long-term decision?

(c) Will it be profitable for Sweditrak to accept the long-term offer?

LO 3 *7-51* ***Pricing experiment*** This is a pricing experiment in which you will work with a team using cost accounting information in pricing decisions. Each team represents one firm in a market. Each market is completely independent of other markets. Your market has four firms that use similar production technology to produce two types of hiking boots: a lightweight model (*LT*) and a mountaineering model (*MT*). Each firm faces the same demand curves where *P* is your price and *P*1, *P*2, and *P*3 are the other three firms' prices:

$$\text{Demand for } LT = 19{,}919 - 500 \times P + 84 \times (P1 + P2 + P3)$$

$$\text{Demand for } MT = 6{,}632 - 109 \times P + 18 \times (P1 + P2 + P3)$$

Notice that if you increase your price, your demand will fall. If, however, your competitors raise their prices, you will gain some of the market share they lose.

Your instructor will provide you a confidential cost report that you should use in your pricing decisions. No cost data should be shared with other teams.

There will be five periods in this pricing experiment. For each period, your firm must submit the prices at which you are prepared to sell each type of boot. Your firm operates on a just-in-time basis and produces to order. Hence, there are no inventory or production-quantity decisions to be made.

The market share you obtain or the profit you make in any one period will *not* in any form affect your performance in subsequent periods. Your parent company has committed to remain in this market for all five periods. However, your parent company expects you to maximize profits in each period.

You should come to the experiment session with your first set of prices. The prices should be specified in whole dollars only (no cents). Once you have decided on prices, enter the prices on the pricing sheet below and submit it to the instructor. The instructor will determine the quantities sold for each firm and return the pricing sheet to you with a market report (next page) containing the following information: what each firm sold, what prices each

PRICING SHEET

FIRM:__________ MARKET:__________

	Period 1	Period 2	Period 3	Period 4	Period 5
LT—Price					
MT—Price					

MARKET REPORT					
MARKET:________			PRICE:________		

Firm	Lightweight Boots		Mountaineering Boots		Net Income
	Price	Quantity	Price	Quantity	

firm charged, and what the actual net income was for each firm. Then you will need to decide on prices for the next period.

Prior to the experiment session, your team should spend two to three hours understanding the cost and demand structure and thinking about how to set prices. You should also devise a strategy to adjust prices if necessary based on what you observe about your competitors' decisions and about your own and your competitors' performance in each period. Remember the purpose of this experiment is to learn about pricing in a competitive setting.

After participating in the experiment you are required to prepare a report of no more than four typed and double-spaced pages that describe how you determined your costs and pricing rules and how competition affected your pricing. Your report must also include a statement of budget versus actual in the format shown below, together with detailed calculations of the costs of your two products.

STATEMENT OF BUDGET VERSUS ACTUAL

FIRM:____________________ MARKET:____________________

	Period 1	Period 2	Period 3	Period 4	Period 5	Total
Number of LT sold						
Price—LT						
Revenues—LT						
Number of MT sold						
Price—MT						
Revenues—MT						
Total revenues						
Estimated costs—LT						
Estimated costs—MT						
Total costs						
Estimated net income						
Actual net income						
Variance between actual and estimated net income						

chapter 8

Capital Budgeting

AFTER READING THIS CHAPTER, YOU WILL BE ABLE TO

1. recognize the nature and importance of long-term (capital) assets
2. understand why organizations control long-lived assets and short-term assets differently
3. use the basic tools and concepts of financial analysis: investment, return on investment, future value, present value, annuities, and required rate of return
4. use capital budgeting to evaluate investment proposals and recognize how the concepts of payback, accounting rate of return, net present value, internal rate of return, and economic value added relate to capital budgeting
5. evaluate the effect of income taxes on investment decisions and show how to incorporate tax considerations in capital budgeting
6. use what-if and sensitivity analyses in capital budgeting
7. recognize how to include strategic considerations in capital budgeting
8. use post-implementation audits in capital budgeting

The Dow Chemical Company

DOW CHEMICAL PURCHASES UNION CARBIDE

In early August 1999, Dow Chemical Company announced that it was acquiring Union Carbide Corporation for $9.3 billion. This acquisition meant that, in the chemical industry, Dow Chemical became second in size only to DuPont. In response to the announcement, Dow Chemical shares fell approximately 6% and Union Carbide shares jumped approximately 20%.

The acquisition reflected a merger of two organizations with troubled pasts. Dow Chemical was still recovering from the negative image it acquired from producing napalm during the Vietnam War. Union Carbide had never recovered from the effects of a tragic chemical leak at its Bhopal, India, plant, which killed an estimated 10,000 people.

Both Dow Chemical and Union Carbide manufactured primary and intermediate chemicals that were used as inputs to produce final products. This merger reflected a global trend among companies that made primary or intermediate chemical products.

Both Dow and Union Carbide had pursued comparable strategies to preserve sales and market share. They both concentrated on product and process refinements to produce conventional chemicals at the lowest price and actively sought new uses for these primary chemical products. Both organizations had systematically eliminated their investments in consumer products over the previous decade. Industry analysts agreed that Dow Chemical had been more successful in narrowing its focus to concentrate on what appeared to be its core competencies and in reducing its cost structure.

In a news release, Dow Chemical announced that it believed the acquisition would increase its earnings and that rationalization and reengineering would create, within two years, at least $500 million of annual cost savings relative to the *existing cost structures of the two organizations. For example, because the two organizations had complementary products, Dow Chemical could now offer customers a more complete product line to meet their requirements.*

Most analysts accepted these claims and observed that matters could improve even more for the new Dow Chemical, since the prices of primary and intermediate chemicals were expected to rise in the years immediately following the acquisition. However, some analysts questioned the acquisition as a merger of two unattractive and unimaginative organizations.

Long-Term (Capital) Assets

In considering Dow Chemical's acquisition of Union Carbide, reflect back to Chapters 4 and 5, which discussed the cost of capacity resources that organizations purchase in advance and then use for several years to make goods and provide services. These long-term, or capital, assets create the committed costs known as batch-related, product-related, and business-sustaining costs. The significant investment made by Dow Chemical in acquiring Union Carbide illustrates issues addressed in this chapter, including the approach that planners use to evaluate the acquisition of long-term assets that create significant cost commitments.

Cost commitments associated with long-term assets create risk for an organization because they remain even if the asset does not generate the anticipated benefits. In this sense, long-term assets reduce an organization's flexibility. Therefore, organizations approach investments in long-term assets with considerable care.

Organizations have developed specific tools to control the acquisition and use of long-term assets for three reasons:

1. Unlike the case for short-term assets, whose acquisition rate can be modified quickly in response to changes in demand, organizations usually are *committed* to long-term assets for an extended time. This type of commitment creates the potential for either excess or scarce capacity that, in turn, creates excess costs or lost opportunities, respectively.
2. The amount of capital committed to the acquisition of capital assets is usually quite *large;* therefore, acquiring long-term assets creates significant financial risks for organizations.
3. The long-term nature of capital assets creates *technological risk* for organizations.

Capital budgeting is a systematic approach to evaluating an investment in a long-term, or capital, asset. This topic will be discussed later in the chapter.

Investment and Return

By definition, a long-term asset is acquired and paid for before it generates benefits that last two or more years. The fundamental evaluation issue in dealing with a long-term asset is whether its future benefits justify its initial cost.

When most people think of investing in a capacity resource, they think of machinery and equipment. However, many organizations incur significant employee training costs. These expenditures should be evaluated as long-term investments. (Will & Deni McIntyre/Photo Researchers, Inc.)

Investment is the monetary value of the assets that the organization gives up to acquire a long-term asset. **Return** is the increased cash inflows in the future that are attributable to the long-term asset. Investment and return are the foundations of capital budgeting analysis, which focuses on whether the increased cash flows that the organization expects the asset to generate will justify the investment in a long-term asset. The tools and methods used in capital budgeting focus on comparing investment and return or, more generally, the cash outflows and cash inflows associated with a long-term asset.

Investment
The monetary value of the assets that the organization gives up to acquire an asset.

Return
The increased cash inflows in the future attributable to the long-term asset.

Time Value of Money

A central concept in capital budgeting is the **time value of money.** Because money can earn a return, its value depends on when it is received. Like all commodities, money has a cost. The cost of using money is not an out-of-pocket cost, such as the cost of buying raw materials or paying a worker; rather, it is the lost opportunity to invest the money in another investment alternative. For example, if you invest your cash in a stock, you forego the opportunity to deposit it in a savings account and earn interest on it. Therefore, the problem is that investment cash is paid out now and, in return, cash is received in the future. In making investment decisions, then, we must have an equivalent basis to compare the cash flows that occur at different points in time.

Time value of money
The opportunity cost of using money; that is, money like all commodities has a cost and can earn a return, so its value depends on when it is expended or received.

Because money has a time-dated value, the critical idea underlying capital budgeting is that amounts of money received at different periods of time must be converted into their value on a common date to be compared.

SOME STANDARD NOTATION

To simplify our discussion, we use the following notation throughout this chapter.

THE TECHNOLOGICAL EDGE

Can a Return on Human Knowledge be Calculated?

Probably the greatest resource for any organization is its human assets. For over 20 years, companies have been striving to measure the return on investments as they allocate their best minds to new projects. This field is known as knowledge management (KM) and has its roots in the field of quantifying intellectual capital (IC).

For example, can a return be calculated for assigning the best and the brightest employees to a project team to develop a new product? What is the opportunity cost of such a team member? Historically, the focus of capital budgeting has been on calculating returns based purely on cost outlays for buying machinery or equipment. But what about the return for building a team of experts who made the decision to buy the equipment? Was the cost of the team worth the final outcome?

To date, the biggest problem in measuring KM is the difficulty of finding appropriate metrics. In fact, many companies tend to rely on gut feel to evaluate and justify their investments. A recent study showed that only 20% of KM programs used any kind of measures to evaluate how the program affected business performance.

Recently, several approaches have been suggested that tie internal and external organizational goals to specific metrics. These include Robert Kaplan and David Norton's "balanced scorecard approach," as well as the Intellectual Asset Monitor, the Scandia Navigator, and the IC Index. The latter three are similar to the balanced scorecard but emphasize different variables related to people, creativity, and growth.

Although some companies are concerned that focusing on metrics may hinder knowledge work, many are beginning to develop scenarios or business cases that involve justifying their KM investments before they are made. As the demand for new technology and innovation grows, we can expect to see KM investment assessments as a key growth area of management over the coming years.

Source: Dawne Shand, "Return on Knowledge," *Knowledge Management,* April 1999, pp. 32–39.

Number of periods (n) In capital-budgeting analysis, the number of periods, usually measured in months, quarters, or years, whose cash flows a proposed long-term investment will affect.

Future value (FV) The amount that today's investment will be after a stated number of periods at a stated periodic rate of return.

Present value (PV) A future cash flow's value at time zero.

Annuity (a) The equal amount, received or paid at the end of each period for n periods.

Rate of return (r) Ratio of net income to investment.

Abbreviation	Meaning
n	**Number of periods** considered in the investment analysis; common period lengths are a month, a quarter, or a year
FV	**Future value,** or ending value, of the investment n periods from now
PV	**Present value,** or the value at the current moment in time, of an amount to be received n periods from now
a	**Annuity,** or equal amount, received or paid at the end of each period for n periods
r	**Rate of return** required, or expected, from an investment opportunity; the rate of interest earned on an investment

FUTURE VALUE

Because money has time value, it is always better to have money now than in the future. Having \$1.00 today is more valuable than receiving \$1.00 in one year or five years, because the \$1.00 on hand today can be invested to grow to more than \$1.00 in the future.

Consider the difference between having \$1.00 now and \$1.00 a year from now. If you have \$1.00 now, you might invest it in a saving's account to earn 5% interest. After one year, you will have \$1.05. We call this \$1.05 the future value of \$1.00 in one year when the rate of return is 5%. Thus, the future value (*FV*) is the amount that today's investment will be after a stated number of periods at a stated periodic rate of return. The following equation provides the formula for future value:

$$\text{Future value of investment in 1 period} = \text{Investment} \times (1 + \text{Periodic rate of return})$$

$$FV = PV \times (1 + r)$$

Suppose that Bruce Brooks wants to borrow \$10,000 to buy a used car. He plans to repay the loan in full after one year. If the rate of interest is 7% per year, Bruce will have to repay \$10,700 at the end of the year as shown:

$$\begin{aligned} FV &= PV \times (1 + r) \\ &= \$10{,}000 \times (1.07) \\ &= \$10{,}700 \end{aligned}$$

As another example, Frank and Rose Robinson recently inherited \$15,000 from Rose's great aunt. They plan to buy a new home and will use the inheritance as a down payment on the home. However, the home will not be ready for one year. If the money is invested at 9%, how much will Frank and Rose have for their down payment one year from now? The answer is \$16,350 (15,000 × 1.09). In summary, future value is the amount a present sum of money will be worth in the future, given a specified rate of interest and time period.

MULTIPLE PERIODS

Because investment opportunities usually extend over multiple periods, we need to compute future value over several periods. Exhibit 8-1 shows how an initial amount of \$1.00 accumulates to \$1.2763 over five years when the rate of return is 5% per

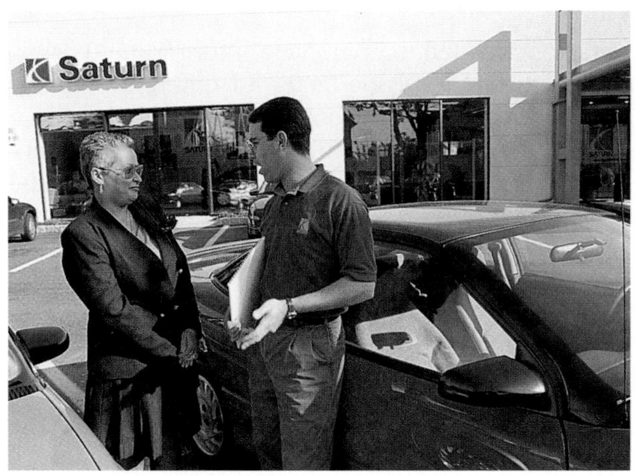

Most people must negotiate a car loan to buy a new car. A financial institution provides a borrower with an amount of cash that the customer uses to acquire the car. In exchange, the borrower sells the financial institution an annuity, which is a promise to pay a stated amount for a stated number of periods. (*Rhoda Sidney/Stock, Boston*)

EXHIBIT 8-1

The Compound Growth of Investment

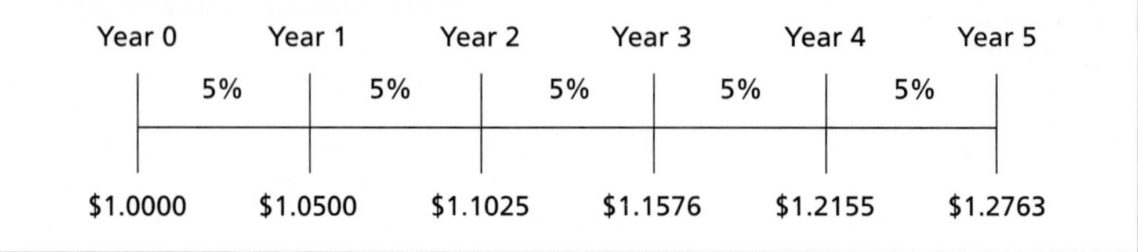

year. The calculations shown assume the following:

1. Any interest earned is not withdrawn until the end of the fifth year; therefore, interest is earned each year on both the initial investment and the interest earned in previous periods, a process that financial analysts call the **compound** effect of interest.
2. The rate of return is constant.

Compound interest When interest earned each year on both an initial investment and the interest earned in previous periods is not withdrawn until the fifth year. Also called the compounding effect of interest.

COMPUTING FUTURE VALUES FOR MULTIPLE PERIODS

It is possible to compute the future value of an investment for multiple periods in a number of ways. These calculations assume that no interest is withdrawn until the end of the investment period.

Calculator Methods. Using a calculator, you can compute future values by either sequential multiplication or exponents.

- Sequential multiplication: Multiply $1.00 by 1.05 five times to compute the future value of $1.00 in five periods when the rate of interest is 5% ($1.2763).
- Exponents: If your calculator can compute exponents directly, you can avoid repeated multiplication by computing $(1.05)^5$ directly.

$$\$1.00 \times 1.05 \times 1.05 \times 1.05 \times 1.05 \times 1.05 = \$1.00 \times 1.05^5$$

These calculations show that the general formula for a future value is

$$FV = PV \times (1 + r)^n$$

This formula is the multiperiod extension of the future value formula presented earlier.

Table Method. Tables provide the factors needed to compute a future value. For example, the table in Exhibit 8-2 provides the future value factor for different numbers of periods and rates of return. If you look down the 5% column and find where that column intersects with the row for five periods, you will find the value 1.2763. Multiply this factor by the amount of the initial investment to find the future value in the required number of periods at the stated rate of return:

$$\begin{aligned} FV_{5\%,\ 5\text{ periods}} &= \$1 \times \textit{future value factor}_{5\%,\ 5\text{ periods}} \\ &= \$1 \times 1.2763 \\ &= \$1.2763 \end{aligned}$$

Suppose a child's parents have just won $100,000 in a lottery. They decide to place $20,000 of this money in a trust fund for their newborn child's education. If the money is invested to earn 7% each year with all interest reinvested, the equation for future value computes the amount to which it will have accumulated after 15 years.

EXHIBIT 8-2

Future Value of $1

PERIOD	2%	5%	7%	10%	12%	15%	17%	20%
1	1.0200	1.0500	1.0700	1.1000	1.1200	1.1500	1.1700	1.2000
2	1.0404	1.1025	1.1449	1.2100	1.2544	1.3225	1.3689	1.4400
3	1.0612	1.1576	1.2250	1.3310	1.4049	1.5209	1.6016	1.7280
4	1.0824	1.2155	1.3108	1.4641	1.5735	1.7490	1.8739	2.0736
5	1.1041	**1.2763**	1.4026	1.6105	1.7623	2.0114	2.1924	2.4883
6	1.1262	1.3401	1.5007	1.7716	1.9738	2.3131	2.5652	2.9860
7	1.1487	1.4071	1.6058	1.9487	2.2107	2.6600	3.0012	3.5832
8	1.1717	1.4775	1.7182	2.1436	2.4760	3.0590	3.5115	4.2998
9	1.1951	1.5513	1.8385	2.3579	2.7731	3.5179	4.1084	5.1598
10	1.2190	1.6289	1.9672	2.5937	3.1058	4.0456	4.8068	6.1917
15	1.3459	2.0789	2.7590	4.1772	5.4736	8.1371	10.5387	15.4070
20	1.4859	2.6533	3.8697	6.7275	9.6463	16.3665	23.1056	38.3376
25	1.6406	3.3864	5.4274	10.8347	17.0001	32.9190	50.6578	95.3962

$$\begin{aligned} FV_{7\%,\ 15\ \text{periods}} &= \$20{,}000 \times \textit{future value factor}_{7\%,\ 15\ \text{periods}} \\ &= \$20{,}000 \times 2.7590 \\ &= \$55{,}180 \end{aligned}$$

From a previous example, suppose that Bruce Brooks believes it will take him three years to accumulate enough money to repay his car loan in one lump sum. If the required interest is 7% per year, the lump-sum loan repayment in three years would be

$$\begin{aligned} FV_{7\%,\ 3\ \text{periods}} &= \$10{,}000 \times \textit{future value factor}_{7\%,\ 3\ \text{periods}} \\ &= \$10{,}000 \times 1.2250 \\ &= \$12{,}250 \end{aligned}$$

Spreadsheet Method. Every computer spreadsheet program can compute future values and all other financial calculations that we describe in this chapter. See the first Excel spreadsheet application (ESS 1) at the top of the next page.

COMPOUND GROWTH OF INTEREST

We have seen that when an amount of money is invested and left to accumulate for multiple periods, the rate of growth is compounded because interest is earned on the interest earned in previous periods. Exhibit 8-3 shows the path of compound growth for various rates of interest. Note that the rate of growth is exponential; that is, growth occurs at an increasing rate.

PRESENT VALUE

An investor may expect a proposed investment to generate benefits in the form of increased cash flow over many periods into the future. The investor must compare these cash flow benefits, or inflows, to the investment's costs, or outflows, to assess the investment. Because money has time value, all cash flows associated with an investment must be converted to their equivalent value at some common date in order for us to make meaningful comparisons between the project's cash inflows and outflows.

ESS 1: COMPUTING FUTURE VALUE

The Excel formula to compute the future value of a single payment is

FV(interest rate, number of periods, payment, present value, type)

where payment is the amount of the payment made each period, and type is 1 if made at the beginning of the period and 0 if made at the end. The default value is zero. The convention in signing payments and interpreting the sign of the amount returned by Excel is that a minus value is an outflow and a positive value is an inflow.

Entering the following in an Excel spreadsheet cell will compute the loan repayment amount for Bruce's loan as −$12,250.43.

= *FV*(0.07,3,,10000,0)

Although any point in time can be chosen as the common date for comparing inflows and outflows, the conventional choice is the point when the investment is undertaken. Analysts call this point *time zero,* or *period zero.* Therefore, conventional capital budgeting analysis converts all future cash flows to their equivalent value at time zero.

Analysts call a future cash flow's value at time zero its present value. The process of computing present value is called **discounting.** Recall the formula for future value:

Discounting
The process of computing present value.

$$FV = PV \times (1 + r)^n$$

EXHIBIT 8-3

Compound Growth for Future Value

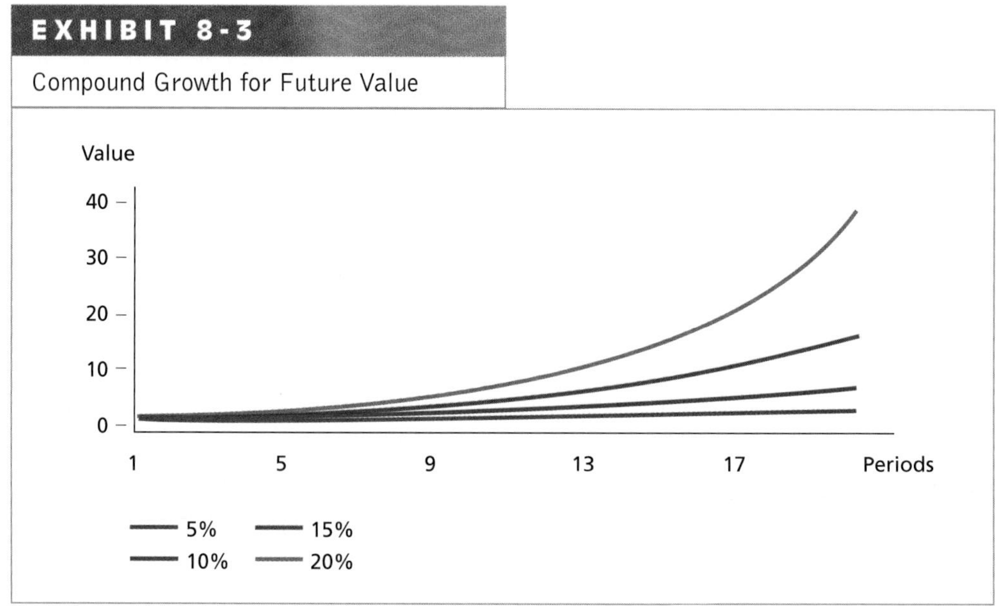

We can rearrange this formula to compute the present value:

$$PV = \frac{FV}{(1 + r)^n}$$

Or,

$$PV = FV \times (1 + r)^{-n}$$

Suppose that the newborn's parents want to accumulate $70,000 over 15 years for their child's education. The parents have idle cash available now to make this investment, which will earn 7% annually. To determine the amount of money they must invest now, we compute the present value of $70,000 with a rate of return of 7%. Use any of the methods described earlier to compute this value.

Calculator Methods. To compute the future value of a present amount of money, use either the sequential division or the exponential method.

- Sequential division: Divide $70,000 by 1.07 15 times.

$$\$70{,}000 \div 1.07 \div 1.07 \div 1.07 \div 1.07 \div 1.07 \div 1.07 \div 1.07 \div 1.07 \div 1.07 \div 1.07 \div 1.07 \div 1.07 \div 1.07 \div 1.07 \div 1.07$$

- Exponents: Evaluate the equation directly:

$$\$70{,}000 \div 1.07^{15}$$

Table Method. Use the appropriate factor shown in Exhibit 8-4.

Spreadsheet Method. See ESS 2 for another Excel spreadsheet application.

ESS 2: COMPUTING PRESENT VALUE

The Excel formula to compute the present value of a single payment is

PV(interest rate, number of periods, payment, future value, type)

where payment is the amount of the payment made each period, and type is 1 if made at the beginning of the period and 0 if made at the end. The default value is zero. The convention in signing payments and interpreting the sign of the amount returned by Excel is that a minus value is an outflow and a positive value is an inflow.

Entering the following in an Excel spreadsheet cell will compute the amount of the initial investment required to accumulate the target amount of $70,000 as −$25,371.22.

= *PV*(0.07,15,,70000,0)

Exhibit 8-4 shows that the factor used to compute present value when there are 15 interest periods and a periodic interest rate of 7% is 0.3624. Therefore, we can

EXHIBIT 8-4

Present Value of $1

PERIOD	2%	5%	7%	10%	12%	15%	17%	20%
1	0.9804	0.9524	0.9346	0.9091	0.8929	0.8696	0.8547	0.8333
2	0.9612	0.9070	0.8734	0.8264	0.7972	0.7561	0.7305	0.6944
3	0.9423	0.8638	0.8163	0.7513	0.7118	0.6575	0.6244	0.5787
4	0.9238	0.8227	0.7629	0.6830	0.6355	0.5718	0.5337	0.4823
5	0.9057	0.7835	0.7130	0.6209	0.5674	0.4972	0.4561	0.4019
6	0.8880	0.7462	0.6663	0.5645	0.5066	0.4323	0.3898	0.3349
7	0.8706	0.7107	0.6227	0.5132	0.4523	0.3759	0.3332	0.2791
8	0.8535	0.6768	0.5820	0.4665	0.4039	0.3269	0.2848	0.2326
9	0.8368	0.6446	0.5439	0.4241	0.3606	0.2843	0.2434	0.1938
10	0.8203	0.6139	0.5083	0.3855	0.3220	0.2472	0.2080	0.1615
15	0.7430	0.4810	**0.3624**	0.2394	0.1827	0.1229	0.0949	0.0649
20	0.6730	0.3769	0.2584	0.1486	0.1037	0.6110	0.0433	0.0261
25	0.6095	0.2953	0.1842	0.0923	0.0588	0.0304	0.0197	0.0105

compute the present value of this investment as follows:

$$\begin{aligned} PV &= \$70{,}000 \times \textit{present value factor}_{7\%,\ 15\ \text{periods}} \\ &= \$70{,}000 \times 0.3624 \\ &= \$25{,}368 \end{aligned}$$

Thus, if the rate of return is 7%, then the parents must invest $25,368 today to accumulate the $70,000 they would like to give their child for the college fund.

DECAY OF A PRESENT VALUE

Invested amounts grow at a compound rate through time, because interest is earned on interest. Similarly, a fixed amount of cash to be received at some future time becomes less valuable as (1) interest rates increase, and (2) the time period before receipt of the cash increases. Exhibit 8-5 shows the nature of the loss of present value with various rates of interest and future cash receipt times. Note that present value decays at a decreasing rate, and that the compounding effect of interest causes the decay to be more rapid as the interest rate increases. This effect causes the decay line to be bowed even more in Exhibit 8-5. The consequence of this decay is that large benefits expected far into the future, when interest rates exceed 10%, will have relatively little current value. This situation mitigates against investment projects that provide benefits well into the future, and so the required rate should be carefully determined. Arbitrarily high interest rates will result in many projects (particularly long-term projects) being inappropriately turned down, because incorrect low values will be assigned to cash flows expected at distant points in the future.

PRESENT VALUE AND FUTURE VALUE OF ANNUITIES

Not all investments have cash outlays at time zero and provide a single benefit at some point in the future. Most investments actually provide a series, or stream, of benefits over a specified period in the future. An investment that promises a constant amount each period over *n* periods is called an n *period annuity*. For example, many lotteries are examples of an *n*-period annuity because they pay prizes in the form of an annuity that lasts, for example, for 20 years.

EXHIBIT 8-5

Present Value Decay

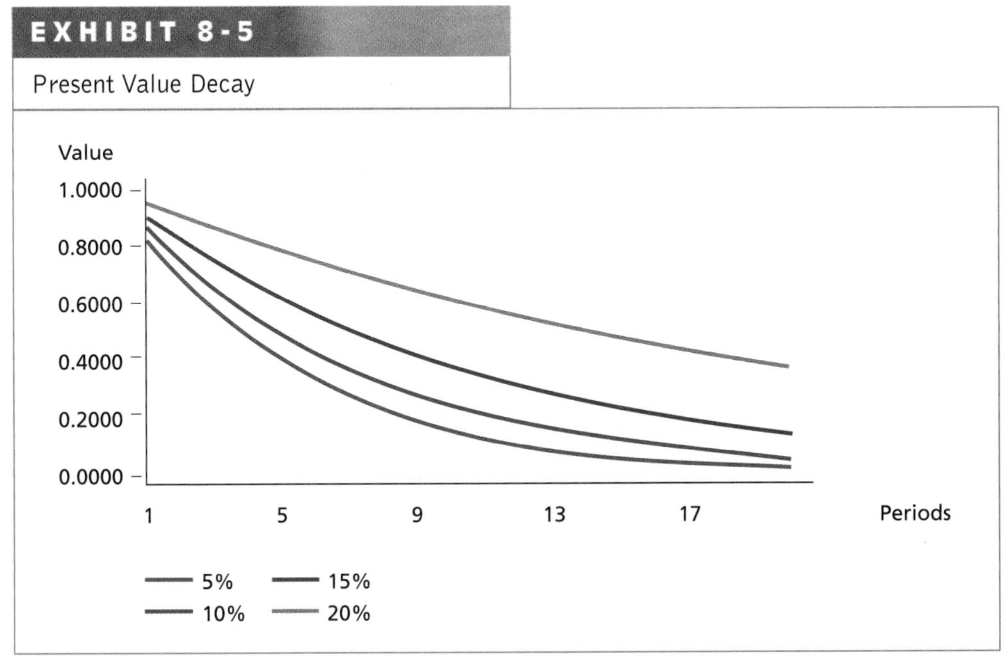

Formulas and financial tables that allow analysts to compute the present value of annuities directly were produced before the widespread availability of calculators and spreadsheets. Today most annuity present value calculations are performed on calculators or computer spreadsheets which can calculate present values directly, so that having knowledge of the formulas and tables themselves is less important. The issue of rounding can be vexing. Because of different ways of rounding, answers found with a regular calculator may vary slightly from those found with a spreadsheet program or financial calculator. Moreover, a column of figures may appear not to sum to the indicated total. This book follows the convention of using the number computed by the specialized calculation or computer. Appendix 8-1 summarizes the formulas for the present and future values of annuities.

To illustrate the idea of an annuity and its present value, suppose that you have won a lottery prize that pays $1 million a year for 20 years. You are interested in

This person has just won the Texas Lottery. The state will pay the winner $50,000 per year for 20 years. Is this lottery prize really worth $1 million ($50,000 × 20)? (Bob Daemmrich/ Stock, Boston)

selling this annuity to raise cash to purchase a business. What is the appropriate value for this annuity today, if the current rate of interest is 7%?

Using a calculator, we can compute the present value of each (20) of the $1 million payments and sum these present values to compute the present value of the annuity. Exhibit 8-6 shows the calculations used to find the present value of the payment in this way. Alternatively, we can use the formula shown in Appendix 8-1 to compute the present value with a single calculation.

Exhibit 8-7 provides the factors used to compute the present value of an annuity for various combinations of periods and interest rates. Using this table we can compute the present value of the lottery annuity as follows:

$$\begin{aligned} PV &= a \times \textit{annuity present value factor}_{7\%,\ 20\ \text{periods}} \\ &= \$1{,}000{,}000 \times 10.594 \\ &= \$10{,}594{,}000 \end{aligned}$$

See ESS 3 for an Excel spreadsheet application.

ESS 3: COMPUTING PRESENT VALUE OF AN ANNUITY

The Excel formula to compute the present value of an annuity payment is

PV(interest rate, number of periods, payment, future value, type)

where payment is the amount of the payment made each period, and type is 1 if made at the beginning of the period and 0 if made at the end. The default value is zero. The convention in signing payments and interpreting the sign of the amount returned by Excel is that a minus value is an outflow and a positive value is an inflow.

Entering the following in an Excell spreadsheet cell will compute the present value of an annuity of $1,000,000 per year for 20 years when the discount rate as 7% is −$10,594,014.25. That is, an outflow of this amount now will produce the 20-year annuity of $1,000,000.

= *PV*(0.07,20,1000000,,0)

Given that zero is the default value, entering the following in the Excel cell will produce the same result:

= *PV*(0.07,20,1000000)

Consider a bond with a face value of $1000 that pays $60 in interest every six months for 10 years, that is, $60 per period for 20 six-month periods and a lump sum of $1000 at the end of the tenth year. If an investor's required return is 5% per six-month period, what would the investor be willing to pay for this bond? Exhibit 8-8 summarizes the cash flows associated with the bond.

There are two components of the cash flow associated with the bond, the periodic interest payments of $60 for 20 periods and the lump-sum payment at the end of the twentieth period. The following formula shows the calculation of the present

EXHIBIT 8-6

Computing the Value of an Annuity

PERIOD	AMOUNT	PV FACTOR	PV
1	$1,000,000	0.9346	$934,579.44
2	1,000,000	0.8734	873,438.73
3	1,000,000	0.8163	816,297.88
4	1,000,000	0.7629	762,895.21
5	1,000,000	0.7130	712,986.18
6	1,000,000	0.6663	666,342.22
7	1,000,000	0.6227	622,749.74
8	1,000,000	0.5820	582,009.10
9	1,000,000	0.5439	543,933.74
10	1,000,000	0.5083	508,349.29
11	1,000,000	0.4751	475,092.80
12	1,000,000	0.4440	444,011.96
13	1,000,000	0.4150	414,964.45
14	1,000,000	0.3878	387,817.24
15	1,000,000	0.3624	362,446.02
16	1,000,000	0.3387	338,734.60
17	1,000,000	0.3166	316,574.39
18	1,000,000	0.2959	295,863.92
19	1,000,000	0.2765	276,508.33
20	1,000,000	0.2584	258, 419.00
Total			$10,594,014.25

EXHIBIT 8-7

Present Value of an Annuity of $1

PERIOD	2%	5%	7%	10%	12%	15%	17%	20%
1	0.9804	0.9524	0.9346	0.9091	0.8929	0.8696	0.8547	0.8333
2	1.9416	1.8594	1.8080	1.7355	1.6901	1.6257	1.5852	1.5278
3	2.8839	2.7232	2.6242	2.4869	2.4018	2.2832	2.2096	2.1065
4	2.8077	3.5460	3.3872	3.1690	3.0373	2.8550	2.7432	2.5887
5	4.7135	4.3295	4.1002	3.7908	3.6048	3.3522	3.1993	2.9906
6	5.6014	5.0757	4.7665	4.3553	4.1114	3.7845	3.5892	3.3255
7	6.4720	5.7864	5.3893	4.8684	4.5638	4.1604	3.9224	3.6046
8	7.3255	6.4632	5.9713	5.3349	4.9676	4.4873	4.2072	3.8372
9	8.1622	7.1078	6.5152	5.7590	5.3282	4.7716	4.4506	4.0310
10	8.9826	7.7217	7.0236	6.1446	5.6502	5.0188	4.6586	4.1925
15	12.8493	10.3797	9.1079	7.6061	6.8109	5.8474	5.3242	4.6755
20	16.3514	12.4622	**10.5940**	8.5136	7.4694	6.2593	5.6278	4.8696
25	19.5235	14.0939	11.6536	9.0770	7.8431	6.4641	5.7662	4.9476

EXHIBIT 8-8

Cash Flows Associated with a 20-Year Bond

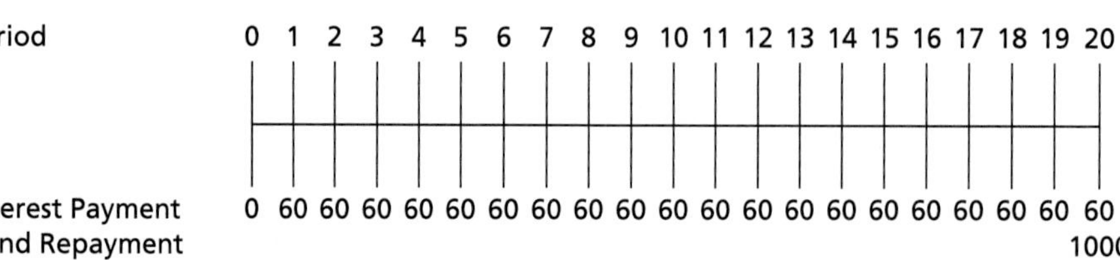

value for the periodic interest payments:

$$\begin{aligned} PV &= a \times \textit{annuity present value factor}_{5\%,\ 20\ \text{periods}} \\ &= \$60 \times 12.4622 \\ &= \$747.73 \end{aligned}$$

The following formula shows the calculation of the present value for the single lump-sum payment of $1000 after 20 periods:

$$\begin{aligned} PV &= FV \times \textit{present value factor}_{5\%,\ 20\ \text{periods}} \\ &= \$1000 \times 0.3769 \\ &= \$376.90 \end{aligned}$$

Therefore, the present value of the bond is $1124.63 ($747.73 + $376.90). The bond sells at a premium—that is, its price is greater than its face value of $1000—because it is paying 6% interest ($60) each period, when the market interest rate is only 5%. A bond that paid only a 4% interest ($40) each period would sell at a discount from its redemption value. You should be able to show that this discount is $124.61.

Computing the Annuity Required to Repay a Loan

We often need to compute the annuity value that a current investment will generate. For example, if you agreed to repay a loan with equal periodic payments, then you are selling the lender an annuity in exchange for the face value of the loan. The factor required to compute the amount of the annuity to repay a present value is simply the inverse of the present value factor for an annuity. Exhibit 8-9 shows these factors for selected periods and rates of return.

In our previous automobile-purchasing example, suppose Bruce discovers that no one will lend him $10,000 to be repaid at the end of three years, because financial institutions reduce risk by requiring periodic loan repayments. Therefore, Bruce must make payments semiannually with a semiannual interest rate of 5%. Bruce's required semiannual payment will be $1970 for three years, as shown in the following calculation:

$$\begin{aligned} a &= PV \times \textit{capital recovery factor}_{5\%,\ 6\ \text{periods}} \\ &= \$10{,}000 \times 0.1970 \\ &= \$1970 \end{aligned}$$

See ESS 4 for an Excel spreadsheet application.

EXHIBIT 8-9

Annuity Required to Repay an Amount of $1

PERIOD	2%	5%	7%	10%	12%	15%	17%	20%
1	1.0200	1.0500	1.0700	1.1000	1.1200	1.1500	1.1700	1.2000
2	0.5150	0.5378	0.5531	0.5762	0.5917	0.6151	0.6308	0.6545
3	0.3468	0.3672	0.3811	0.4021	0.4163	0.4380	0.4526	0.4747
4	0.2626	0.2820	0.2952	0.3155	0.3292	0.3503	0.3645	0.3863
5	0.2122	0.2310	0.2439	0.2638	0.2774	0.2983	0.3126	0.3344
6	0.1785	**0.1970**	0.2098	0.2296	0.2432	0.2642	0.2786	0.3007
7	0.1545	0.1728	0.1856	0.2054	0.2191	0.2404	0.2549	0.2774
8	0.1365	0.1547	0.1675	0.1874	0.2013	0.2229	0.2377	0.2606
9	0.1225	0.1407	0.1535	0.1736	0.1877	0.2096	0.2247	0.2481
10	0.1113	0.1295	0.1424	0.1627	0.1770	0.1993	0.2147	0.2385
15	0.0778	0.0963	0.1098	0.1315	0.1468	0.1710	0.1878	0.2139
20	0.0612	0.0802	0.9440	0.1175	0.1339	0.1598	0.1777	0.2054
25	0.0512	0.0710	0.0858	0.1102	0.1275	0.1547	0.1734	0.2021

ESS 4: COMPUTING THE ANNUITY REQUIRED TO REPAY LOAN

The Excel formula to compute the annuity required to repay a loan is

PMT(interest rate, number of periods, present value, future value, type)

where present value is the amount of the loan or future value is the target amount that is to be accumulated by the annuity payments, and type is 1 if made at the beginning of the period and 0 if made at the end. The default value is zero. The convention in signing payments and interpreting the sign of the amount returned by Excel is that a minus value is an outflow and a positive value is an inflow.

Entering the following in an Excel spreadsheet cell will compute the amount that Bruce has to pay every six months for three years to repay hit $10,000 loan as −$1,970.17.

= *PMT*(0.05,6,10000,,0)

Given that zero is the default value, entering the following in the Excel cell will produce the same result.

= *PMT*(0.05,6,10000)

COST OF CAPITAL

Cost of capital The return that the organization must earn on its investments to meet its investors' return requirements. Also called *risk-adjusted discount rate.*

The **cost of capital,** also known as the risk-adjusted discount rate, is the interest rate organizations use for discounting future cash flows: The cost of capital equals the return the organization must earn on its investment to meet its investors' return requirements. From a financial perspective, when the organization expects to earn less than its cost of capital from a proposed investment, it should return the funds that otherwise would be required for the proposed investment to its providers of capital. If the organization expects to earn more than its cost of capital from a proposed investment, then the investment is desirable, and any surplus that is earned increases the organization's wealth. The cost of capital is the benchmark the organization uses to evaluate investment proposals. The organization's cost of capital reflects (1) the amount and cost of debt and equity in its financial structure, and (2) the financial market's perception of the financial risk of the organization's activities. Finance courses cover in depth the way organizations compute the cost of capital used to evaluate new investments. Although there are several approaches, the most widely used is the weighted average cost of capital method.

Weighted Average Cost of Capital Method. To illustrate, Simple Organization is financed 20% by debt with a pretax cost of 8%, 15% by preferred shares with a pretax cost of 11%, 30% by common equity with a pretax cost of 16%, and 35% by retained earnings with an estimated pretax cost of 14%. Simple's marginal tax rate is 45%. Exhibit 8-10 illustrates calculation of Simple Organization's weighted average cost of capital, which is 12.23%.

EXHIBIT 8-10

Simple Organization Weighted Average Cost of Capital

	PRE TAX COST	AFTER TAX COST	WEIGHT	WEIGHTED AVERAGE
Debt	8%	8%*(1 − .45) = 0.044	20%	0.0088
Preferred Stock	11%	11%	15%	0.0165
Common Stock	16%	16%	30%	0.0480
Retained Earnings	14%	14%	35%	0.0490
Total				0.1223

Capital Budgeting

Capital budgeting A systematic approach to evaluating an investment in a long-term, or capital, asset.

Capital budgeting is the collection of tools that planners use to evaluate the desirability of acquiring long-term assets. Organizations have developed many approaches to capital budgeting. Six approaches are discussed here:

1. Payback
2. Accounting rate of return
3. Net present value
4. Internal rate of return
5. Profitability index

To show how each of these methods works and alternative perspectives, we will apply each to the following investment opportunity.

The investment required to acquire this facility represents a major investment of funds that create significant committed costs. For this reason organizations have developed special tools to evaluate capital investment proposals. (The Coastal Corporation)

SHIRLEY'S DOUGHNUT HOLE

Shirley's Doughnut Hole is considering the purchase of the new automatic doughnut cooker that would cost $70,000 and last five years. It would expand capacity and reduce operating costs, thereby allowing Shirley's to increase profits by $20,000 per year. Shirley's cost of capital is 10%; the new cooker would be sold for $10,000 at the end of five years. Is this investment worthwhile?

PAYBACK CRITERION

The **payback period,** or payback criterion, computes the number of periods needed to recover a project's initial investment. Shirley's initial investment of $70,000 is recovered midway between years 3 and 4, as Exhibit 8-11 shows. Therefore, that payback period for this project is 3.5 years.

Payback period
The number of periods required to recover a project's initial investment.

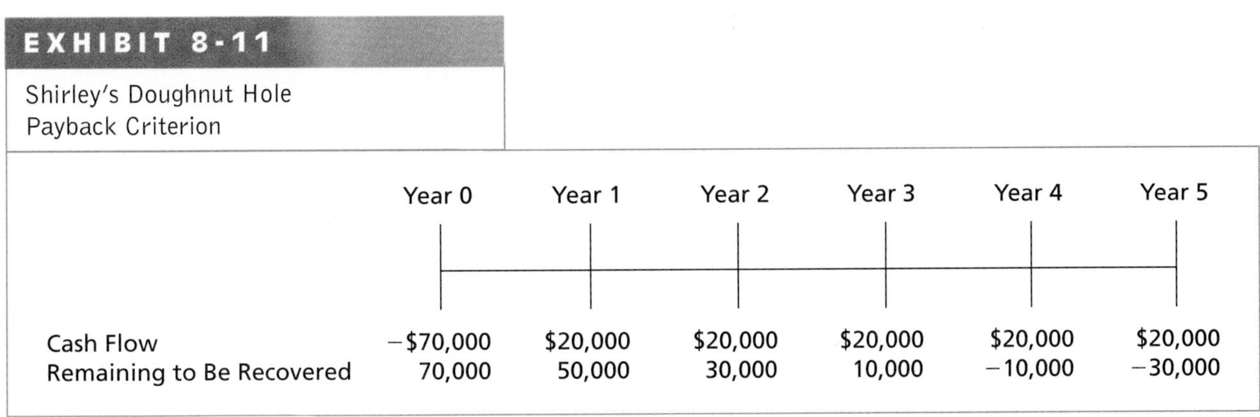

EXHIBIT 8-11

Shirley's Doughnut Hole
Payback Criterion

	Year 0	Year 1	Year 2	Year 3	Year 4	Year 5
Cash Flow	−$70,000	$20,000	$20,000	$20,000	$20,000	$20,000
Remaining to Be Recovered	70,000	50,000	30,000	10,000	−10,000	−30,000

Many people consider the payback period to be a measure of the project's risk. Because the organization has unrecovered investment during the payback period, the longer the payback period, the higher the risk. Organizations compare a project's payback period with a criterion or target, which reflects what the organization thinks is an appropriate level of risk.

The payback criterion has two problems.

1. *It ignores the time value of money.* In the Shirley's example, suppose that the cash flows resulting from the cooker were $60,000 in the first year, $0 in the second year, $0 in the third year, $20,000 in the fourth year, and $20,000 in the fifth year. This set of cash flows has the same payback period, 3.5 years, as the original alternative; however, this alternative would clearly be more desirable because Shirley's recovers $60,000 at the end of year 1. In the first set of cash flows, Shirley's does not recover $60,000 until the end of year 3. With the time value of money, it is always preferable to receive cash earlier. To recognize the time value of money, some organizations use the discounted payback method which computes the payback period but uses discounted cash flows.
2. *It ignores the cash outflows that occur after the initial investment and the cash inflows that occur after the payback period.* Suppose that there are two alternative cooker's that Shirley's is considering: Cooker 1 is as described in the original example; cooker 2 has cash flows that are identical to those of cooker 1 except that its disposal value is $20,000. By any standard, cooker 2 is the better deal; however, the payback method would consider the two alternatives equal because their payback periods are both 3.5 years.

Despite these limitations, repeated surveys of practice have shown that the payback calculation is the most used approach by organizations for capital budgeting. This popularity may reflect other considerations, such as bonuses that reward managers based on current profits, thereby creating a preoccupation with short-run performance.

ACCOUNTING RATE OF RETURN CRITERION

Analysts compute the accounting rate of return by dividing the average accounting income by the average level of investment. Analysts use the accounting rate of return to approximate the return on investment, which is the ratio of the average income from an investment over the average investment level.

To compute the accounting rate of return, the accounting income must be computed first. Suppose that Shirley's decides to depreciate the cooker so that the total amount of depreciation equals the cooker's historical cost less its salvage value. Using the straight-line method, which recognizes an equal depreciation each year, the annual depreciation is $12,000 as shown in the following equation:

$$\begin{aligned}\text{Annual depreciation} &= \frac{\text{Historical cost} - \text{Salvage value}}{\text{Asset life}} \\ &= \frac{\$70{,}000 - \$10{,}000}{5} \\ &= \$12{,}000\end{aligned}$$

Thus, the increased annual income related to the new cooker that Shirley's will report will be $8000 ($20,000 − $12,000). Since all annual incomes are equal in this example, the *average* income will equal the *annual* income.

The average investment for the cooker will be $40,000, as shown in the following equation:

$$\text{Annual investment} = \frac{\text{Historical cost} + \text{Salvage value}}{2}$$

$$= \frac{\$70{,}000 + 10{,}000}{2}$$

$$= \$40{,}000$$

Thus, the accounting rate of return for the cooker investment can be computed as follows:

$$\text{Annual rate of return} = \frac{\text{Average income}}{\text{Average investment}}$$

$$= \frac{8{,}000}{40{,}000}$$

$$= 20\%$$

If the accounting rate of return exceeds the criterion or target rate of return, then the project is acceptable. Like the payback method, however, the accounting rate of return method has a drawback: By averaging, it does not consider the explicit timing of cash flows. However, this method is an improvement over the payback method in that it considers cash flows in all periods.

NET PRESENT VALUE CRITERION

The **net present value (NPV)** is the sum of the present values of all cash inflows and outflows associated with a project. This is the first method we have considered that incorporates the time value of money. Here are the steps used to compute an investment's net present value:

Net present value (NPV)
The sum of the present values of all the cash inflows and cash outflows associated with a project.

Step 1 Choose the appropriate period length to evaluate the investment proposal. The period length depends on the periodicity of the investment's cash flows. The most common period length used in practice is one year, although analysts also use quarterly and semiannual period lengths.

Step 2 Identify the organization's cost of capital, and convert it to an appropriate rate of return for the period length chosen in step 1.

Step 3 Identify the incremental cash flow in each period of the project's life.

Step 4 Compute the present value of each period's cash flow using the organization's cost of capital.

Step 5 Sum the present values of all the periodic cash inflows and outflows to determine the investment project's net present value.

Step 6 If the project's net present value, or residual income, is positive, the project is acceptable from an economic perspective.

In the case of Shirley's, the question is whether the five-year annuity of \$20,000 plus the single salvage payment of \$10,000 after five years justifies the initial \$70,000 investment. Let us follow our six steps to determine the net present value of Shirley's investment.

Step 1 The period length is one year, because all cash flows are stated annually. The convention in capital budgeting is to assume, unless otherwise stated, that the cash flows occur at the end of each period.

Step 2 Shirley's stated cost of capital is 10% per year. Because the period chosen in step 1 is annual, no adjustment is necessary to the rate of return.

EXHIBIT 8-12

A Time Line for Shirley's Doughnut Hole

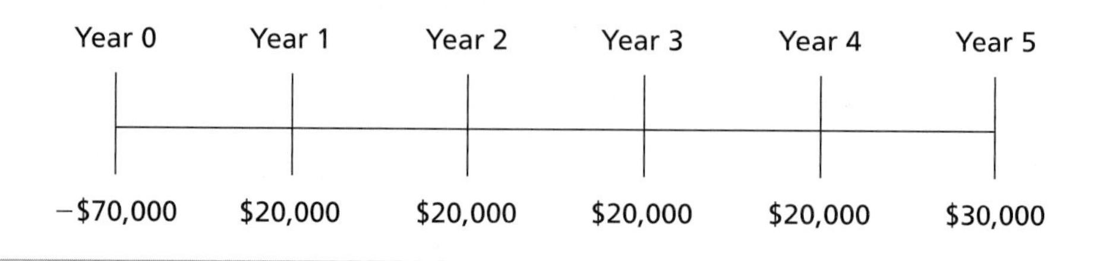

Step 3 The incremental cash flows, as shown in Exhibit 8-12, are a \$70,000 outflow immediately, \$20,000 inflow at the end of each year for five years, and \$10,000 salvage at the end of five years. It is useful to organize the cash flows associated with a project on a time line, as shown, to help identify and consider all the project's cash flows systematically.

Step 4 The present value of a five-year annuity of \$20,000, when the organization's cost of capital is 10%, is \$75,816 as shown in the following equation:

$$\begin{aligned} PV &= a \times \textit{annuity present value factor}_{10\%,\ 5\ \text{years}} \\ &= \$20{,}000 \times 3.7908 \\ &= \$75{,}816 \end{aligned}$$

The present value of the \$10,000 salvage in five years, when Shirley's Doughnut Hole's cost of capital is 10%, equals \$6209:

$$\begin{aligned} PV &= FV \times \textit{present value factor}_{10\%,\ 5\ \text{years}} \\ &= \$10{,}000 \times 0.6209 \\ &= \$6209 \end{aligned}$$

Step 5 The present value of the cash inflows attributable to this investment is \$82,025 (\$75,816 + \$6,209). Because the investment of \$70,000 takes place at time zero, the present value of the total outflows is \$70,000. The net present value, or residual income, of this investment project is \$12,025 (\$82,025 − \$70,000).

EXHIBIT 8-13

Shirley's Doughnut Hole:
Computing Net Present Value

COST OF CAPITAL			10%
Time	**Amount**	**PV Factor**	**PV**
0	(\$70,000.00)	1.0000	(\$70,000.00)
1	20,000.00	0.9091	18,181.82
2	20,000.00	0.8264	16,528.93
3	20,000.00	0.7513	15,026.30
4	20,000.00	0.6830	13,660.27
5	30,000.00	0.6209	18,627.64
Total			\$12,024.95

Step 6 Because the project's net present value is positive, Shirley's should purchase the cooker because it is economically desirable.

Exhibit 8-13 summarizes the individual cash flow calculations for the new doughnut cooker investment. See ESS 5 for an Excel spreadsheet application.

ESS 5: EXCEL SPREADSHEET APPLICATION

COMPUTING AN INVESTMENTS NET PRESENT VALUE Excel has a built-in function to compute a project's net present value.

The function has this form:

NPV(rate, value 1, value 2, . . . , value n)

Suppose that you entered the periodic net cash flows into the following cells in an Excel spreadsheet: −70000 in cell B6, 20000 in cells B7 through B10, and 30000 in cell B11. The net present value function would be this:

= *NPV*(0.1,B7:B11) + B6

This will return the value of $12,024.95. Note that the function assumes that the first cash flow takes place at the end of period 1. Therefore, if there is an initial investment it must be included separately in the expression.

INTERNAL RATE OF RETURN CRITERION

The **internal rate of return (IRR)** is the actual rate of return expected from an investment. The IRR is the discount rate that makes the investment's net present value equal to zero. If an investment's net present value is positive, then it's internal rate of return exceeds its cost of capital; if an investment's net present value is negative, then it's internal rate of return is less than its cost of capital. By trial and error, we can find that the IRR in Shirley's is 16.14% as shown in Exhibit 8-14. Because a 16.14% internal

Internal rate of return (*IRR*) The actual rate of return expected from an investment.

EXHIBIT 8-14

Shirley's Doughnut Hole:
Internal Rate of Return Calculation

INTERNAL RATE OF RETURN		**16.14%**	
Time	**Amount**	**PV Factor**	**PV**
0	($70,000.00)	1.0000	($70,000.00)
1	20,000.00	0.8610	17,220.60
2	20,000.00	0.7414	14,827.45
3	20,000.00	0.6383	12,766.87
4	20,000.00	0.5496	10,992.66
5	30,000.00	0.4733	14,197.51
Total			$ 5.08

rate of return is greater than the 10% cost of capital, the project is desirable. See ESS 6 for an Excel spreadsheet application.

ESS 6: EXCEL SPREADSHEET APPLICATION

COMPUTING AN INVESTMENTS INTERNAL RATE OF RETURN Excel has a built-in function to compute a project's internal rate of return.

The function has this form:

IRR(value 1, value 2, . . . , value n, guess)

Suppose that you entered these periodic net cash flows into the following cells in an Excel spreadsheet: −70000 in cell B6, 20000 in cells B7 through B10, and 30000 in cell B11. The net present value function would be this:

= *IRR*(B6:B11,.10)

The *guess* is your estimate of the project's internal rate of return. You can generally start with a rate like 10% or the organization's cost of capital.

This will return a value of 16.143%. Note that the IRR function assumes that the first cash flow takes place at time zero.

Because a project's net present value summarizes all its financial elements, using the internal rate of return criterion is unnecessary when preparing capital budgets. Moreover, it has some disadvantages.

1. It assumes that an organization can reinvest a project's intermediate cash flows at the project's internal rate of return, which is frequently an invalid assumption.
2. It can create ambiguous results, particularly when we are evaluating competing projects in situations when capital shortages prevent the organization from investing in all projects with a positive net present value and when projects require significant outflows at different times during their lives.

The net present value calculation is a superior alternative to the internal rate of return criterion and requires only one additional piece of information—the organization's cost of capital—for its calculation. However, internal rate of return is pervasive in financial markets and is widely used in capital budgeting (see Exhibit 8-15).

PROFITABILITY INDEX

Profitability index A variation on the net present value method, computed by dividing the present value of the cash inflows by the present value of the cash outflows.

The **profitability index** is a variation on the net present value method. It is used to permit comparisons of mutually exclusive projects with different sizes and is computed by dividing the present value of the cash inflows by the present value of the cash outflows. A profitability index of 1 or greater is required for the project to be acceptable. Consider the two investments with the characteristics described in Exhibit 8-16.

Advocates of the profitability index argue that project A is a better investment because it has a higher profitability index. However, proponents of the net present

EXHIBIT 8-15

Criteria Used for Investment Justification (Percentage of Total Respondents)

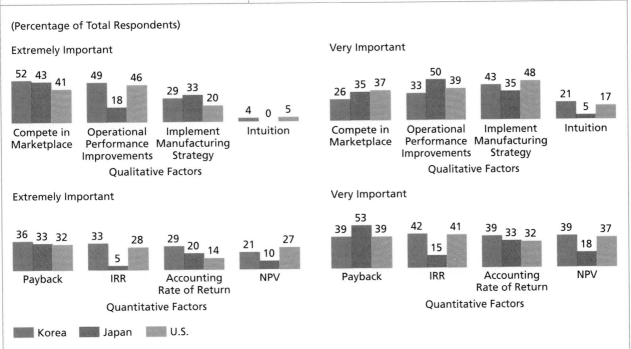

(Percentage of Total Respondents)

Qualitative Factors — Extremely Important

	Korea	Japan	U.S.
Compete in Marketplace	52	43	41
Operational Performance Improvements	49	18	46
Implement Manufacturing Strategy	29	33	20
Intuition	4	0	5

Qualitative Factors — Very Important

	Korea	Japan	U.S.
Compete in Marketplace	26	35	37
Operational Performance Improvements	33	50	39
Implement Manufacturing Strategy	43	35	48
Intuition	21	5	17

Quantitative Factors — Extremely Important

	Korea	Japan	U.S.
Payback	36	33	32
IRR	33	5	28
Accounting Rate of Return	29	20	14
NPV	21	10	27

Quantitative Factors — Very Important

	Korea	Japan	U.S.
Payback	39	53	39
IRR	42	15	41
Accounting Rate of Return	39	33	32
NPV	39	18	37

value method argue that project B is better because it provides a greater wealth increment to the owners than project A.

Returning to Shirley's Doughnut Hole and the net present value criterion section, recall that the present value of the cash inflows was $82,025 and the present value of the cash outflows was $70,000. Therefore, the profitability index for that project was 1.17 (82,025/70,000).

ECONOMIC VALUE ADDED CRITERION

Recently, several analysts and consultants have proposed using the economic value added criterion as a way to evaluate organization performance. Although the criterion is not directly suitable for evaluating new investments, its insights are useful.

Computing economic value added begins by using accounting income calculated according to generally accepted accounting principles (GAAP). Then the analyst

EXHIBIT 8-16

Profitability Indexes Compared

	PV CASH INFLOWS	PV CASH OUTFLOWS	PROFITABILITY INDEX
Project A	$50,000	$40,000	1.25
Project B	$60,000	$50,000	1.20

adjusts accounting income to correct what the proponents of economic value added consider to be its conservative bias.[1] For example, adjustments include capitalizing and amortizing research and development and significant product launch costs, adjusting for the LIFO effect on inventory valuation, and eliminating the effect of deferred income taxes. Next the analyst computes the amount of investment in the organization and derives economic value added as follows:

$$\text{Economic value added} = \text{Adjusted accounting income} - (\text{Cost of capital} \times \text{Investment level})$$

The formula for economic value added is directly related to the net present value criterion. The major difference between the two criteria is that economic value added begins with accounting income, which includes various accruals and allocations rather than net cash flow as does net present value. This is why economic value added is more suited to evaluating and ongoing investment, for example, in a product or a division, than a new investment opportunity.

EFFECT OF TAXES

So far we have ignored the effect of taxes on capital budgeting. In practice, capital budgeting must consider the tax effects of potential investments. The exact effect of taxes on the capital budgeting decision depends on tax legislation, which is specific to a tax jurisdiction. In general, however, the effect of taxes is twofold:

1. Organizations must pay taxes on any net benefits provided by an investment.
2. Organizations can use the depreciation associated with a capital investment to reduce income and offset some of their taxes. The rate of taxation and the way that legislation allows organizations to depreciate the acquisition cost of their long-term assets as a taxable expense varies.

Suppose that Shirley's income is taxed at the rate of 40%. To keep things simple, suppose that the relevant tax legislation requires that Shirley's claim straight-line depreciation of its net investment, which is historical cost less salvage value of long term assets as a tax-deductible expense. If Shirley's after-tax cost of capital is 7%, is the cooker project desirable?

EXHIBIT 8-17

Net Present Value Calculations with Taxes

TIME	CASH FLOW	DEPRECIATION	TAXABLE INCOME	TAX @ 40%	NET CASH FLOW	PV FACTOR	PV
0	($70,000)				($70,000)	1.0000	($70,000)
1	20,000	$12,000	$8,000	$3,200	16,800	0.9346	15,701
2	20,000	12,000	8,000	3,200	16,800	0.8734	14,674
3	20,000	12,000	8,000	3,200	16,800	0.8163	13,714
4	20,000	12,000	8,000	3,200	16,800	0.7629	12,817
5	20,000	12,000	8,000	3,200	16,800	0.7130	11,978
5	10,000	0	0	0	10,000	0.7130	7,130
Total							$ 6,013

[1]For details about these adjustments and about the economic value added method in general, see G. Bennett Stewart, III, *The Quest for Value,* New York: HarperCollins, 1991.

This analysis requires converting all pretax cash flows to after-tax cash flows. In turn, this requires knowing the amount of depreciation that will be claimed each year. Using straight-line depreciation, Shirley's Doughnut Hole will claim $12,000 depreciation each year, as noted earlier.

With this information, we can now compute the after-tax cash flows attributable to this investment. Exhibit 8-17 shows these calculations.

The investment in the cooker provides two after-tax benefits:

1. five-year annuity of $16,800
2. lump-sum payment of $10,000 at the end of five years

Exhibit 8-18 shows a time line of these cash flows.

Because the cooker's book value at the end of five years is $10,000, there is no gain in selling it for $10,000. Rather, its salvage value is treated as a return of capital and is not taxed. When the organization's cost of capital is 7%, the present value of the five-year annuity of $16,800 is $68,883, as shown in the following equation:

$$\begin{aligned} PV &= a \times \textit{annuity present value factor}_{7\%,\ 5\ \text{years}} \\ &= \$16{,}800 \times 4.1002 \\ &= \$68{,}883 \end{aligned}$$

The present value of the lump-sum payment of $10,000 is $7130, as shown in the following equation:

$$\begin{aligned} PV &= a \times \textit{present value factor}_{7\%,\ 5\ \text{years}} \\ &= \$10{,}000 \times 0.7130 \\ &= \$7130 \end{aligned}$$

Therefore, the present value of the incremental inflows attributable to this investment is $76,013 ($68,883 + $7130). Since the $70,000 investment takes place at time zero, the present value of the total outflows is $70,000, and the net present value of this investment project is $6013 ($76,013 − $70,000). Because the project's net present value is positive, it is economically desirable.

Because they operate the equipment and have the most direct knowledge of the conditions under which it will be used, production-level employees are increasingly involved in capital investment decisions. These Mobil Corporation employees are discussing ways to improve the production process that makes wrapping film. (© Cheryl Rossum/Mobil Corp.)

EXHIBIT 8-18

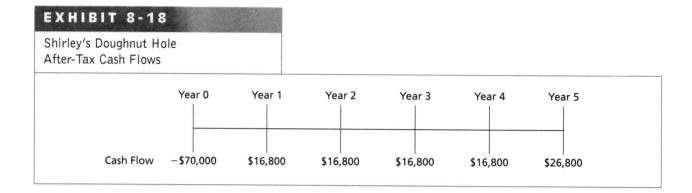

Shirley's Doughnut Hole
After-Tax Cash Flows

	Year 0	Year 1	Year 2	Year 3	Year 4	Year 5
Cash Flow	−$70,000	$16,800	$16,800	$16,800	$16,800	$26,800

Summary Example

Assume that you have the opportunity to invest in a new product that will have a 10-year life. The initial investment is $10 million in machinery and equipment, which will have a salvage value of $200,000 at the end of the tenth year. Your best judgment is that the product will increase profits by $2.5 million in the first year and then incremental profits will decline by 10% per year. Your company faces a marginal tax rate of 40% and its after-tax cost of capital is 7%. Should you invest in this project?

Exhibits 8-19 and 8-20 summarize the details of this problem. We will now consider this investment opportunity from the perspective of the different capital budgeting criteria. In a given capital budgeting situation, an organization may use several of these approaches to evaluate an investment proposal given that the different capital budgeting criteria can rank investment opportunities differently. For example, an organization may turn down a long-lived project with a positive net present value and a long payback period because of risk considerations. Therefore, if an organization is using several capital budgeting criteria, it must develop an individual, and therefore

EXHIBIT 8-19

New Product Evaluation Example

YEAR	CASH FLOW	DEPN.	TAX INC.	TAX @ 40%	ACC. INC.	NCF	PV FACTOR	PV
0	($10,000,000)							($10,000,000)
1	$ 2,500,000	$980,000	$1,520,000	$608,000	$912,000	$1,892,000	0.9346	$ 1,768,224
2	2,250,000	980,000	1,270,000	508,000	762,000	1,742,000	0.8734	1,521,530
3	2,025,000	980,000	1,045,000	418,000	627,000	1,607,000	0.8163	1,311,791
4	1,822,500	980,000	842,500	337,000	505,500	1,485,500	0.7629	1,133,281
5	1,640,250	980,000	660,250	264,100	396,150	1,376,150	0.7130	981,176
6	1,476,225	980,000	496,225	198,490	297,735	1,277,735	0.6663	851,409
7	1,328,603	980,000	348,603	139,441	209,162	1,189,162	0.6227	740,550
8	1,195,742	980,000	215,742	86,297	129,445	1,109,445	0.5820	645,707
9	1,076,168	980,000	96,168	38,467	57,701	1,037,701	0.5439	564,440
10	1,168,551	980,000	(11,449)	(4,580)	193,131	1,173,131	0.5083	596,360
Total								$ 114,469

EXHIBIT 8-20

New Product Evaluation Cash Flow

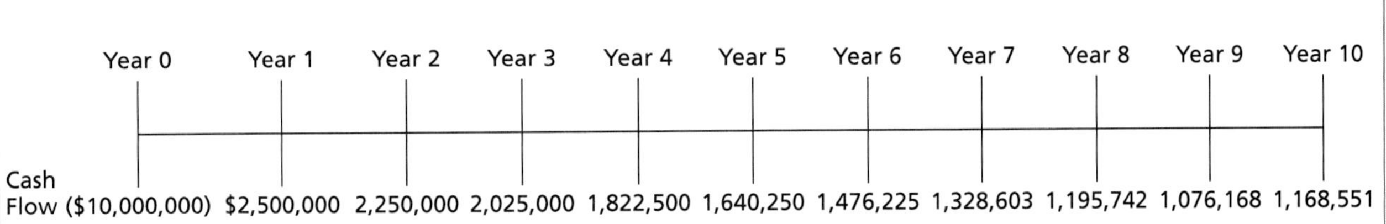

ad hoc, approach to determine how to make choices in situations when different criteria provide different recommendations. Because of its problematic and ad hoc nature, this type of approach is not considered in the following discussion. Instead, we focus on the individual application of each criterion.

PAYBACK CRITERION

Exhibit 8-21 summarizes the information needed to compute the payback period for this project. It shows that the investment is recovered sometime during the seventh year. The payback period value is 6.52, as shown in the following equation:

$$\text{Payback period} = 6 + \frac{\$619{,}615}{\$619{,}615 + \$569{,}547}$$

$$= 6.52 \text{ years}$$

An organization using the payback criterion needs to decide whether it is willing to accept projects with payback periods of this length.

ACCOUNTING RATE OF RETURN CRITERION

From the information given the sixth column of Exhibit 8-19, we can compute the expected average accounting income for this investment, which is $408,982. The

EXHIBIT 8-21

New Product Evaluation Example
Payback Criterion

YEAR	CASH FLOW	DEPN.	TAX INC.	TAX @ 40%	NCF	CUM NCF
0	($10,000,000)				($10,000,000)	($10,000,000)
1	$ 2,500,000	$980,000	$1,520,000	$608,000	$ 1,892,000	(8,108,000)
2	2,250,000	980,000	1,270,000	508,000	1,742,000	(6,366,000)
3	2,025,000	980,000	1,045,000	418,000	1,607,000	(4,759,000)
4	1,822,500	980,000	842,500	337,000	1,485,500	(3,273,500)
5	1,640,250	980,000	660,250	264,100	1,376,150	(1,897,350)
6	1,476,225	980,000	496,225	198,490	1,277,735	(619,615)
7	1,328,603	980,000	348,603	139,441	1,189,162	569,547
8	1,195,742	980,000	215,742	86,297	1,109,445	1,678,992
9	1,076,168	980,000	96,168	38,467	1,037,701	2,716,693
10	1,168,551	980,000	(11,449)	(4,580)	1,173,131	3,889,823

average investment level is \$5,100,000 as shown in the following equation:

$$\text{Average annual investment} = \frac{\text{Initial investment} + \text{Salvage value}}{2}$$
$$= \frac{\$10{,}000{,}000 + \$200{,}000}{2}$$
$$= \$5{,}100{,}000$$

Therefore, the accounting rate of return is 8%, as shown in the following equation:

$$\text{Annual rate of return} = \frac{\text{Average accounting income}}{\text{Average investment}}$$
$$= \frac{\$408{,}982}{\$5{,}100{,}000}$$
$$= 8\%$$

The organization needs to decide whether this accounting rate of return is acceptable.

NET PRESENT VALUE CRITERION

Exhibit 8-19 shows the computation of the net present value of this project, which is \$114,469. Judged by the net present value criterion, this project should be accepted.

INTERNAL RATE OF RETURN CRITERION

The internal rate of return for this project, which can be found by trial and error or by direct calculation using a spreadsheet, is 7.28%. Recall that the internal rate of return is the rate of interest that makes the net present value of this project equal to zero. Because this value exceeds the organization's after-tax cost of capital of 7%, the project would be accepted.

Uncertainty in Cash Flows

Capital budgeting analysis relies on estimates of future cash flows. Because estimates are not always realized, many decision makers like to know how their estimates affect the decision they are making. Estimating future cash flows is an important and difficult task. Cash flow estimation is important because many decisions will be affected by those estimates. It is difficult because these estimates will reflect circumstances that the organization may not have previously experienced.

Most cash flow estimation is incremental, meaning that it is done by projecting previous experience. For example, based on claims from the manufacturer, a new machine might be expected to decrease costs by 10%. Many organizations assume that learning will systematically reduce the costs of a new system or process. Cash flows related to sales of a new product are often estimated based on past experiences with similar products. Whatever the forecast, it usually starts with a previous experience or makes appropriate adjustments.

One approach to estimating cash flows begins by asking the planner to estimate the most likely effect of a decision, such as a cost decrease or a revenue increase, and then to estimate the highest and lowest possible values that could occur. The planner next constructs a normal distribution with a mean equal to the most likely value estimated and a standard deviation equal to the highest estimated value minus the mean, the difference divided by 3.

For example, suppose that Murphy Company is installing a new machine that is expected to improve quality and reduce product cost. The effect will be to increase revenues and decrease manufacturing costs. The planner believes that the most likely net effect will be to increase pretax cash flows by \$100,000 per year; however the

EXHIBIT 8-22

Parkdale Manufacturing
Probability Estimates

USE	PROBABILITY	WEIGHT
50,000 units	0.1	5,000
60,000 units	0.3	18,000
70,000 units	0.3	21,000
80,000 units	0.2	16,000
90,000 units	0.1	9,000
Expected Value		69,000

planner also believes the effect could be as low as $70,000 per year or as high as $130,000. Assuming that the benefits are normally distributed, the standard deviation of the estimated distribution of benefits is $10,000 [($130,000 − $100,000)/3], because only an insignificant probability exists that an observation will be beyond three standard deviations from the mean.

Only the mean or expected value of the estimate is needed for the net present value model, but by developing a distribution of expected outcomes, the planner can develop probabilistic statements about the results. In this example, the planner could say, assuming a normal distribution with a mean of $100,000 and a standard deviation of $10,000, "I believe the probability is about 98% (.9772) that the net cash flow benefit will be at least $80,000."

Another approach for the planner is to identify four or five possible outcomes and to assign a probability of occurring to each one such that the total probabilities assigned equals one. Then the expected value of the estimate is computed by weighting each estimate by its probability. For example, Parkdale Manufacturing is considering adding 100,000 units to existing capacity. Part of the process of evaluating this capacity addition is determining whether it will be used effectively. The planner has developed the estimates shown in Exhibit 8-22.

This calculation suggests that, based on the planner's underlying beliefs, average use will be 69,000 units of new capacity. This estimate would be used in the capital budgeting model to project the revenue and cost effects of the capacity addition.

Project champions sometimes get carried away in estimating the proposed benefits of a new product and can (knowingly or unknowingly) fall into a situation in which they make extravagant claims to get a pet project approved. The bandwagon or groupthink effect often causes a planning group to lose prospective and talk each other into believing something that no member would have accepted individually. Organizations try to mitigate this phenomenon by providing for an evaluation of the results of a capital project after it has been implemented.

What-If and Sensitivity Analysis

Two other approaches to handling uncertainty are what-if and sensitivity analysis. In the Shirley's Doughnut Hole example, Shirley might ask, "What must the cash flows be to make this project unattractive?" Fortunately, we can use computer spreadsheets to answer questions like this.

Most planners today use personal computers and electronic spreadsheets for capital budgeting. The planner can set up a computer spreadsheet to make changes to the estimates of the decision's key parameters. If the analysis explores the effect of a

What-if analysis A type of analysis that explores the effect of a change in a parameter on an outcome.

Sensitivity analysis The analysis of the effect of a change in a parameter on a decision rather than on an outcome.

change in a parameter on an outcome, we call this investigation a **what-if analysis.** For example, the planner may ask, "What will my profits be if sales are only 90% of the plan?" A planner's investigation of the effect of a change in a parameter on a decision, rather than on an outcome, is called a **sensitivity analysis.** For example, the planner may ask, "How low can sales fall before this investment becomes unattractive?"

In a tax situation for Shirley's, suppose the expected incremental cash flows from the operation were only 95% of what was planned, that is, $19,000 instead of $20,000. Is the cooker still an attractive investment? The answer is yes. As shown in Exhibit 8-23, the annual cash benefits need to fall below $17,556 each year before the project becomes economically undesirable. This is a drop of 12% from the estimated amount of $20,000, which is not a big error. Therefore, the decision is sensitive to the estimated benefits.

To illustrate how an organization might deal with uncertainty, consider Southport Consulting. The college and university recruiting season is approaching and Southport Consulting is thinking of hiring new consultants. Each consultant undergoes the training process that costs Southport approximately $30,000. Southport is wondering if this $30,000 cost is justified. The company treats hiring as a capital budgeting exercise. Each entry-level consultant is paid $70,000 per year, including benefits, and generates approximately $80,000 of annual net revenues (revenues less all nonsalary costs related to the revenues). The net contribution of each consultant is thus $10,000 per year.

Southport's consultants are highly prized by client organizations and they are often hired away at higher salaries than Southport can pay and still be profitable. Consultants normally leave at the end of the year, and the probability of keeping a consultant longer than five years is assessed at virtually zero. Exhibit 8-24, which is based on past experience, summarizes the assessed probabilities of keeping the consultant for one through five years, and indicates the present value of the benefits given the organization's cost of capital (12%).

As an exercise, verify the present value of the benefits reported in Exhibit 8-24. For example the value given for year 3 is the present value of a three-year annuity of $10,000 discounted at the rate of 12%. The expected net present value of the net margin contributed by the consultant is $28,367.48, which is less than the $30,000 initial hiring and training costs, suggesting that, given these circumstances, hiring a consultant is not an acceptable investment. (Bonus. Can you show that the minimum

EXHIBIT 8-23

Net Present Value Calculations with Taxes

TIME	AMOUNT	DEPRECIATION	TAX INCOME	TAX @ 40%	NCF	PV FACTOR	PV
0	($70,000)				($70,000)	1.0000	($70,000)
1	17,556	$12,000	$5,556	$2,222	15,334	0.9346	14,330
2	17,556	12,000	5,556	2,222	15,334	0.8734	13,393
3	17,556	12,000	5,556	2,222	15,334	0.8163	12,517
4	17,556	12,000	5,556	2,222	15,334	0.7629	11,698
5	27,556	12,000	5,556	2,222	25,334	0.7130	18,063
Total							$1

EXHIBIT 8-24

Southport Consulting
Present Value of Benefits

YEARS KEPT	PROBABILITY	PRESENT VALUE OF BENEFITS	WEIGHT
1	0.1	$ 8,928.57	$ 892.86
2	0.2	$16,900.51	$ 3,380.10
3	0.3	$24,018.31	$ 7,205.49
4	0.2	$30,373.49	$ 6,074.70
5	0.3	$36,047.76	$10,814.33
Expected Net Present Value			$28,367.48

acceptable annual contribution by a consultant must be approximately $10,576 for the consultant to be attractive under these circumstances?)

Strategic Considerations

So far, we have considered only the profits from incremental revenues or the expected cost savings offered by a long-term asset. The common benefits associated with acquiring long-term assets ignore the assets' strategic benefits, which are of increasing importance. Including strategic benefits in a capital budgeting example is controversial, because they are difficult to estimate and therefore risky to include. However, strategic benefits are, in fact, likely to be no more difficult to estimate than the profits from expected sales or expected cost savings.

Strategic benefits reflect the enhanced revenue and profit potential that derive from some attribute of a long-term asset. Usually long-term assets provide the following strategic benefits:

1. They allow an organization to make goods or deliver a service that competitors cannot, for example, by developing a patented process to make a product that competitors cannot replicate.
2. They support improving product quality by reducing the potential to make mistakes, for example, by improving machining tolerances or reducing reliance on operator settings.
3. They help shorten the cycle time needed to make the product, for example, by implementing one-hour photo developing.

For example, Shirley's may consider investing in a new cooker that can sense when a doughnut is cooked and then eject it automatically. This cooker may offer several benefits.

1. It may allow Shirley to hire less-skilled and lower-paid employees to work in the Doughnut Hole.
2. By compensating for ambient factors such as external temperature and humidity, the cooker may improve the consistency of cooking and, therefore, the quality of the doughnuts. As customers recognize the high quality of the doughnut, they are likely to find Shirley's doughnuts more desirable. In this situation, the benefits from the automatic cooker can include increased sales and lower operating expenses if the competitors do not have this cooker. On the other hand, the automatic cooker can prevent an erosion of sales if Shirley's competitors also purchase it.

Many convenience stores have purchased and installed automatic debit machines. Customers present a bank card and purchases are deducted directly from their bank accounts. Many customers find this service convenient because they can carry less cash. If stores install these machines, the expense involved is a cost of being in business. The failure to provide this service will lead to a loss of sales. The evaluation of the desirability of these machines will include an estimate of the profits lost by not installing them. (Laima Druskis/Photo Researchers, Inc.)

In either situation, acquiring the automatic cooker provides benefits to Shirley's that should be incorporated in the capital budgeting analysis. Moreover, any capital budgeting analysis should reflect the alternatives available to competitors and not simply assume that the status quo will continue indefinitely.

Post-Implementation Audits and Capital Budgeting

Post-implementation audit
The process of revisiting the decision to purchase a long-lived asset.

After-the-fact audits can provide an important discipline to capital budgeting, which is a subjective judgmental process. Revisiting the decision to purchase a long-lived asset is called a **post-implementation audit** of the capital budgeting decision and provides many valuable insights for decision makers.

The decisions that are reached using capital budgeting models rely heavily on estimates, particularly on the project's cash flows and its life. These estimates can come from many sources: past experience, judgment, or the experience of others (e.g., competitors). When estimates are used to support proposals, recognizing the behavioral implications that lie behind them is important. For example, a production supervisor who is anxious to have the latest production equipment may be optimistic to the point of being reckless in forecasting the benefits of acquiring the equipment in terms of cost reduction, quality improvement, and production-time improvements. This behavior is mitigated if people understand that, once equipment is acquired, the company will compare results with the claims made in support of the equipment's acquisition and that higher costs, including depreciation, will be assigned to products or customers produced with or served by this asset.

Many organizations fail to compare the estimates made in the capital budgeting process with the actual results. This is a mistake for three reasons:

1. By comparing estimates with results, the organizations planners can identify where their estimates are wrong and try to avoid making similar mistakes in the future.
2. By assessing the skill of planners, organizations can identify and reward those who are good at making capital budgeting decisions.
3. By auditing the results of acquiring long-term assets, companies create an environment in which planners are less tempted to inflate estimates of the cash benefits associated with their projects in order to get them approved.

Budgeting Other Spending Proposals

Organizations develop spending proposals for discretionary items that are not capital expenditure items, such as research and development, advertising, and training. Such items can provide benefits that will be realized for many periods into the future. However, financial accounting conventions relating to external reporting (GAAP) require that discretionary expenditure items not related to capital be expensed in the periods in which they are made, even if they provide future benefits.

Despite the financial accounting treatment of discretionary expenditures, their magnitude suggests that they should be evaluated like capital spending projects when possible. The approach to analyzing a discretionary expenditure is identical to that used to decide whether to make a capital investment. Planners should estimate the discounted cash inflows (benefits) and discounted cash outflows (costs) associated with any discretionary spending project and accept the project if the net present value of the discounted cash flows is positive.

DOW CHEMICAL'S ACQUISITION REVISITED

This chapter on capital budgeting has provided us with some tools to evaluate the decision by Dow Chemical to pay $9.3 billion to acquire Union Carbide. Obviously we do not have all the facts that senior executives used at Dow Chemical to justify their offer, but we can certainly evaluate the broad parameters of this acquisition using published financial information.

The net income reported by Union Carbide was $403 million and 1998. According to Union Carbide's 10-K filings with the Securities and Exchange Commission, the average annual net income reported by Union Carbide for the last five fiscal years preceding the acquisition was about $586 million.

Assume that Dow Chemical has a cost of capital of 12%. The present value of a perpetual annuity of $403 million is $3.4 billion:

$$\begin{aligned}\textit{Present value of perpetual annuity} &= \textit{Annuity value/Cost of capital}\\ &= 403/.12 = \$3.4 \textit{ billion}\end{aligned}$$

Using the more optimistic estimate for the annual annuity provided by the average income level over the last five years, we compute a present value of $4.9 billion ($586/.12). For the sake of convenience, and to reflect the increased potential for sales from the broader product line and perhaps the more effective management of Union Carbide's former assets by the management team of Dow Chemical, let us use the more optimistic $4.9 billion in our valuation.

In addition, Dow Chemical expects that costs of the merged entity will fall by $500 million per year due to cost rationalization. If we assume that Dow Chemical has a marginal tax rate of 40%, the after-tax amount of the savings is $300 million [$500 million × (1 − tax rate)]. Assuming that this annuity is perpetual, the present value of these cost savings is $2.5 billion ($300/.12). Therefore, we can account for a value of $7.3 billion ($4.9 + $2.5) from this acquisition, and we are left to explain $2 billion ($9.3 − $7.3) or about 23% of the acquisition price.

This seems like a large residual value to explain, but can you think of other sources from which value might accrue in this purchase? In the discussion at the beginning of this chapter, analysts expected the income of primary chemicals to rise in the future, which would increase the value of the income stream that Dow Chemical purchased. But would costs increase as well?

One possibility to explain this gap is Dow Chemical's cost of capital is less than 12%. Suppose Dow Chemical uses an after-tax cost of capital of 10% to evaluate its investments. In this case, the value of the income stream purchased is $5.9 billion ($586/.1) and the value of the cost savings is $3.0 billion ($300/.1), yielding a total of $8.9 billion which is within $500 million of the purchase price.

SUMMARY

This chapter introduces basic capital budgeting concepts. Capital budgeting compares the costs and benefits of a long-term, or capital, asset. The acquisition of long-term assets requires that organizations plan carefully, because these assets involve long-term commitments of huge amounts of money.

Because the cash flows associated with a long-term asset invariably occur at different points in time, and because money has a time value, we use the concept of present value to convert all cash outflows and inflows to a common point in time so that they are comparable.

Taxes affect cash flows in two ways.

1. Taxing authorities defined both the income subject to taxes and the depreciation schedule, which includes the pattern of depreciation and the period over which the depreciation can be recognized in computing taxable income.
2. Taxing authorities set the tax rate that organizations apply to taxable income in determining taxes payable.

Capital budgeting involves uncertainties relating to estimating future cash flows. This includes estimating cost savings resulting from the acquisition of an asset and the amount of increased profits resulting from the increased revenues associated with acquisition of an asset. Planners can use what-if analysis and sensitivity analysis to investigate the effects of forecasting uncertainties on the capital budgeting model.

Because capital budgeting compares the incremental cash inflows and outflows attributable to the acquisition of a long-term asset, it is critical that the baseline, or status quo, position be carefully chosen. For example, if competitors are acquiring equipment to improve quality and retain customers, then the capital budgeting analysis associated with acquiring that equipment must reflect the value and profit losses if the existing equipment is kept while competitors upgrade their equipment.

KEY TERMS

annuity (*a*), 322
capital budgeting, 334
compound interest, 324
cost of capital, 334
discounting, 326
future value (*FV*), 322
internal rate of return (*IRR*), 339
investment, 321
net present value (NPV), 337
number of periods (*n*), 322
payback period, 335
post-implementation audit, 350
present value (*PV*), 322
profitability index, 340
rate of return (*r*), 322
return, 321
sensitivity analysis, 348
time value of money, 321
what-if analysis, 348

APPENDIX 8-1

ANNUITY FORMULAS

To compute the present value of an annuity, use this formula:

$$PV = a \times \left[\frac{(1 + r)^n - 1}{r \times (1 + r)^n}\right]$$

To compute the amount of an annuity that will repay a present value (loan), use this formula:

$$a = PV \times \left[\frac{r \times (1 + r)^n}{(1 + r)^n - 1}\right]$$

APPENDIX 8-2

EFFECTIVE AND NOMINAL RATES OF INTEREST

To this point, we have assumed that the analyst, who makes investment decisions about long-term assets, has been provided with the appropriate periodic rate of return. However, investment situations often specify a rate of return for a period that differs from the period used in the investment analysis. Therefore, you must have a way of converting one periodic rate to another. To do this, we use the notion of nominal and effective rates of interest.

Financial institutions usually express the rate of interest they pay in annual terms. This means that if a financial institution promises a rate of return of 6% on investments, the 6% is the nominal, or stated, annual rate of interest. For example, the bank will say that it will pay "an annual rate of 6% computed and paid quarterly." If a financial institution pays interest quarterly when the nominal rate of interest is 6% per year, interest is paid at the rate of 1.5% (6% ÷ 4) per quarter. Therefore, the effective quarterly rate of interest is 1.5%.

Exhibit 8-25 shows that, under these conditions, $1.00 invested at the beginning of the year accumulates to $1.0614 at the end of the year (4 periods later).

Thus, the effective annual rate of interest is 6.14% rather than the nominal rate of interest of 6%. Why? Periodic compounding has allowed the saver to earn interest on interest earned during the year, which yields a higher return than the nominal rate of return. This is known as the effective rate of interest.

We compute the effective annual rate of interest, r_e, where r_n is the stated, or nominal, annual rate of interest and n is the number of compounding periods per

EXHIBIT 8-25

Compound Growth @ 1.5% Interest

PERIOD	START	INTEREST	END
1	$1.0000	$0.0150	$1.0150
2	1.0150	0.0152	1.0302
3	1.0302	0.0155	1.0457
4	1.0457	0.0157	1.0614

year as follows:

$$r_e = \left(1 + \frac{r_n}{n}\right)^n - 1$$

Consider the interest that a credit card company charges on outstanding monthly balances. The nominal rate of interest is 15%. What is the effective annual rate of interest? Because interest is computed and charged monthly, the effective annual rate of interest is 16.08% as shown in the following equation:

$$\begin{aligned} r_e &= \left(1 + \frac{r_n}{n}\right)^n - 1 \\ &= \left(1 + \frac{0.15}{12}\right)^{12} - 1 \\ &= (1.0125)^{12} - 1 \\ &= 0.1608 \end{aligned}$$

You should consider this fact when you accumulate unpaid charges on your credit card! For example, suppose that a student uses a credit card in January to buy a $500 portable stereo system. The student plans to repay the amount on June 1 upon receipt of a first paycheck from a summer job. The credit card bill arrives on February 1, but the student makes no payment until June 1. Therefore, the bill will accumulate interest for four months. If the stated interest rate on unpaid balances is 15% per year, or 1.25% per month, the amount that the $500 purchase will have accumulated to by June 1 is as follows:

$$\begin{aligned} FV &= P \times \textit{future value factor}_{1.5\%,\ 4\ \text{periods}} \\ &= \$500 \times (1.0125)^4 \\ &= \$500 \times 1.0509 \\ &= \$525.47 \end{aligned}$$

This is a significant amount to consider.

ASSIGNMENT MATERIALS

QUESTIONS

8-1 What is the defining feature of a long-term, or capital, asset? (LO 1)

8-2 What is capital budgeting? (LO 2)

8-3 What are the attributes of long-term assets? Why do organizations use capital budgeting to evaluate the acquisition of long-term assets? (LO 1)

8-4 What are the major objectives in capital budgeting? (LO 1, 2)

8-5 What is an investment? (LO 3)

8-6 What does *return* mean? (LO 3)

8-7 What does *time value of money* mean? (LO 3)

8-8 Is it always true that money now is worth more than the same amount of money received a year from now? (LO 3)

8-9 What is future value? (LO 3)

8-10 What is the role of future value in capital budgeting? (LO 3)

8-11 What does the compounding effect mean? (LO 3)

8-12 What is present value? (LO 3)

8-13 What is the significance and role of time zero in capital budgeting? (LO 3)

8-14 What is discounting? (LO 3)

8-15 Give an example of an annuity. (LO 3)

8-16 What is the cost of capital? (LO 3)

8-17 What is the most widely used approach to computing the cost of capital for evaluating new investments? (LO 3)

8-18 What is the discount rate? (LO 3)

8-19 What does *payback period* mean? (LO 4)

8-20 How is accounting rate of return defined? (LO 4)

8-21 What are inflows and outflows in capital budgeting? (LO 4)

8-22 Why are incremental cash flows important in capital budgeting? (LO 4)

8-23 Why do planners compute the present value of a sum that will be received in the future? (LO 4)

8-24 What is net present value? (LO 4)

8-25 How is the idea of net present value used in capital budgeting? (LO 4)

8-26 What is internal rate of return? (LO 4)

8-27 How would you explain the idea of internal rate of return using nonfinancial terms? (LO 4)

8-28 How is profitability index defined? (LO 4)

8-29 How is economic value added computed? (LO 4)

8-30 Why are post-implementation audits useful? (LO 8)

8-31 *Appendix* What is the difference between the nominal and effective rate of interest? (LO 4)

EXERCISES

8-32 ***Explaining capital budgeting*** How would you describe capital budgeting to someone who is intelligent but knows nothing about the time value of money or the concept of a required return on an investment? LO 1, 2

8-33 ***Quantifying intangible benefits in capital budgeting*** Suppose that you work for a bank and are proposing a system that customers can access from their home computers to do their banking. Only about one-half of the estimated cost of this system can be recovered by decreased clerical time required in the banks. However, you believe that the balance of the cost will be more than made up by improved customer service that will attract more customers. How would you handle this situation in a capital budgeting exercise? LO 1, 2

8-34 ***Evaluating payment alternatives*** Which is a better deal: $1000 at the end of one year or $500 at the end of six months and another $500 at the end of 12 months? Why? LO 3

8-35 ***Explain compounding*** Explain the notion of compounding interest using an example. LO 3

8-36 ***Effect of compounding*** Quintin is now 22 years old and has just started a new job. He is trying to decide whether to start investing for retirement now or to wait several years. Verify that investing a 10% return per year yields approximately the same total accumulation at age 52 for Quintin under the following alternatives: LO 3

(a) Invest $3 per year for 30 years, beginning now.

(b) Invest $5 per year for 25 years, beginning at age 27.

(c) Invest $80 per year for 5 years, beginning at age 47.

8-37 ***The rule of 72*** The "rule of 72" is that the number of periods n that it will take to double an investment whose rate of return is r percent is approximately $72/r$. That is, nr is approximately equal to 72. Verify this approximation for $r = 4, 6, 8$, and 10. LO 3

8-38 ***Valuing an annuity*** You have won a lottery with an advertised prize of $1,000,000. The prize is to be paid in installments of $100,000 per year for the next 10 years. Is this prize really worth $1,000,000? Explain. LO 3

8-39 ***Choosing an annuity*** You have been offered the following two annuities for the same price. Annuity 1 pays $50,000 per year for 10 years. Annuity 2 pays $40,000 per year for 20 years. If your cost of capital is 10%, which of these two annuities is a better deal? Why? LO 3

8-40 ***Cost of capital determinants*** Would you expect the cost of capital to be higher for an electric utility or a genetics laboratory? Explain. LO 3

8-41 ***Weighted average cost of capital*** McDonough Corporation is financed 25% by debt with a pretax cost of 8%, 20% by preferred shares with a pretax cost of 12%, LO 3

35% by common equity with a pretax cost of 16%, and 20% by retained earnings with an estimated pretax cost of 14%. McDonough Corporation's marginal tax rate is 40%. Calculate McDonough's weighted average cost of capital.

LO 4 **8-42** ***Net present value and profitability index*** Lebar Company is considering two mutually exclusive investment alternatives. Lebar has a 10% cost of capital. Cash flow information for the two alternatives appears below.

Initial investment in equipment	$170,000	$100,000
Increase in annual cash flows	$ 50,000	$ 30,000
Life of equipment	5 years	5 years
Salvage value of equipment	0	0

(a) Compute the net present value for each alternative and determine which alternative is more desirable using the net present value criterion.

(b) Compute the profitability index for each alternative and determine which alternative is more desirable using the profitability index criterion.

(c) Why do the rankings differ under the two alternatives? Which alternative would you recommend?

LO 5 **8-43** ***Taxes and capital budgeting*** Describe the effect of taxes in capital budgeting.

LO 5 **8-44** Branson Manufacturing is considering purchasing a piece of equipment costing $45,000. The new equipment would create a new cash inflow of $20,000 for five years. At the end of the five years, the equipment would have no salvage value. The company's cost of capital is 10% and the tax rate is 34%. Assuming the company uses straight-line depreciation for tax purposes, what is the net present value of purchasing the new equipment, taking income taxes into account?

LO 5 **8-45** Simpson Corporation has taxable income of $300,000 and an income tax rate of 34%. Simpson is considering selling an asset whose original cost is $20,000, with $12,000 of it depreciated. How much total after-tax cash will be generated from the sale of the asset for $18,000?

LO 6 **8-46** ***Sensitivity analysis and capital budgeting*** Suppose that you are advising someone who is using capital budgeting to evaluate the purchase of a clothing store. What role might sensitivity analysis play in this evaluation?

LO 6 **8-47** ***Capital budgeting and risk*** Suppose that you are using capital budgeting to evaluate two alternative business opportunities. Both require comparable investments and have comparable average cash flows. However, the cash flows of one business appear to be more volatile than those of the other; that is, the cash flows of this opportunity vary more about its average. Is this an important consideration in capital budgeting?

PROBLEMS

LO 2, 3, 4 **8-48** Discuss the advantages and disadvantages of each of the following as approaches to capital budgeting:

(a) Payback

(b) Accounting rate of return

(c) Net present value

(d) Internal rate of return

(e) Profitability index

(f) Economic value added

8-49 ***Valuing a bond*** A company issues a bond with the following characteristics: LO 3

(a) Semiannual interest payments of $45 for 10 years

(b) A lump-sum repayment of the $1000 face value of the bond after 10 years

If the bond market requires 10% interest compounded semiannually for the debt issued by this company, what is the market price (present value) of this bond?

8-50 ***Valuing zero coupon bonds*** A government issues a savings bond that will pay the holder $1000 in 10 years. (This is called a zero coupon bond.) If the bond market is now requiring 5% annual interest on government debt, what will be the issue price (present value) of this bond? LO 3

8-51 ***Revaluing a bond*** Review the data in question 8-50. Suppose that you purchase that bond. It is now one year later and the bond market now requires 7% interest on government debt. What will you receive for this bond if you sell it today? LO 3

8-52 ***Capital budgeting and sensitivity analysis*** Ritchie's Trucking hauls logs from wood lots to pulp mills and saw mills. Ritchie now operates a single truck and is considering buying a second truck. The total required investment in the truck and trailer would be $130,000. The equipment would have a five-year life and a salvage value of $20,000. Ritchie's cost of capital is 12% and Ritchie faces a marginal tax rate of 35%. You can assume that for tax purposes Ritchie will depreciate the net cost (that is, purchase price less salvage value) of the new equipment on a straight-line basis. LO 4, 6, 7

Adding a second truck would provide two major advantages for Ritchie. First, the new equipment would allow Ritchie to accept business that he now turns down because of a lack of capacity. Ritchie expects that the net cash flow associated with this additional business is about $25,000 per year. Second, the new equipment would allow Ritchie to reduce the cost of current operations primarily by discontinuing the practice of having to pay drivers overtime. This savings would amount to approximately $10,000.

REQUIRED

(a) Using the net present value criterion, is the investment in the new equipment justified?

(b) What is the minimum amount of annual benefit from the investment in the new equipment that will make the project acceptable?

8-53 ***Capital budgeting with taxes and strategic consideration*** Ronnie's Welding uses welding equipment mounted in the bed of a pickup truck to provide on-site welding services. The expected life of his existing equipment is five more years, after which the equipment will be worthless and scrapped for zero salvage. LO 4, 5, 7

Ronnie is considering replacing his existing welding equipment. The new equipment will allow him to do jobs that he must now decline and also reduce the costs of his current jobs. The new equipment should last five years, reduce the operating costs associated with existing jobs by $9000 per year, and attract new jobs that will provide incremental profits of $5000 per year. The purchase price of the new equipment is $50,000, net of what Ronnie could get from selling his old equipment. The salvage value of the new equipment would be $2000 in five years. Assume that Ronnie can borrow money at 12% and that he faces a 40% marginal tax rate. Assume that for tax purposes Ronnie will depreciate the net investment (that is, purchase price less salvage value) on a straight-line basis.

(a) Using the net present value criterion, is this investment desirable?

(b) Suppose that while he is considering this project, Ronnie discovers that the quality of the welds produced by the new machine exceeds the quality of the welds made by the old machine. Because weld quality is related to safety, Ronnie knows that this will be attractive to many of his customers. Suppose that Ronnie believes that if he buys the machine and his competitors do not, the increased profits associated with the new machine will be $8000 instead of the original estimate of $5000. Is this investment desirable?

(c) Ronnie knows that his competitors have access to the same trade information that he does and that he cannot restrict their access to the equipment that he is considering. What do you think would happen if all these competitors purchased the equipment? What do you think would happen if only one competitor purchased the equipment?

LO 3, 4 **8-54** ***Net present value, payback, internal rate of return, and accounting rate of return*** Consider the following two mutually exclusive projects, each of which requires an initial investment of $100,000 and has no salvage value. This organization, which has a cost of capital of 15%, must choose one or the other.

CASH FLOWS OF PROJECTS A AND B		
YEAR	PROJECT A	PROJECT B
1	30,000	$ 0
2	30,000	20,000
3	30,000	20,000
4	30,000	50,000
5	30,000	90,000

(a) Compute the payback period of these projects. Using the payback criterion, which project is more desirable?

(b) Compute the net present value of these two projects. Using the net present value criterion, which project is more desirable?

(c) What do you think about the idea of using the payback period to adjust for risk?

(d) How do you think conventional capital budgeting adjusts for a project's risk?

(e) Compute the internal rate of return for each project.

(f) Assuming that straight-line depreciation is used to compute income, compute the accounting rate of return for these two projects.

(g) What do you think of the accounting rate of return criterion?

LO 4, 6, 7 **8-55** ***Capital budgeting and sensitivity analysis*** Magic Mountain Enterprises runs a ski center. Its 14 downhill runs vary in difficulty from beginner to expert. To attract more customers, Maria Jasper, the owner/manager, is considering developing cross-country ski trails. The cross-country ski trails would take two years to build and would cost $1,000,000 per year to build. The trails would open for business in year 3 and would generate $500,000 per year in net cash flows. Maria has a required return of 12% on all investments.

The land on which the trails would be built is leased. The lease costs are included in the $500,000 annual net cash flow calculation. The lease will expire nine years from now, that is, after the trails have been operated for seven years. There will be no opportunity to renew the lease, and Maria will not be compensated for any of the work done building the ski trails.

(a) Compute the net present value of the decision to enter the cross-country ski business. Should the investment be made? (Ignore taxes in your analysis.)

(b) What is the minimum annual net cash flow from the cross-country ski business during the seven years of operations that would make this investment desirable?

(c) What other factors would you consider in making the decision?

8-56 ***Allocating capital funds and post-implementation audit*** You are the general manager of a consumer products company. One of your major tasks is to approve new product proposals brought to you by the product managers who report to you. The product managers are primarily an aggressive lot who are eager to expand the product lines they supervise. These product managers are paid a wage, which is based in part on the number of products that they supervise. In addition, they receive a bonus that is based on product sales. Each year you receive between 20 and 25 new product proposals. LO 8

Each year the Appropriations Committee gives you a fund that you use to fund new product introductions. This fund is usually in the range of $60 million. On average each new product introduction costs about $10 million. Therefore, you can fund between five and six new product introductions each year.

REQUIRED

(a) What effect do you think post-implementation audits, which compare managerial claims made during new product proposals with actual results, would have on new product proposals?

(b) Do you think that managers would have to be penalized for variances between planned and actual results for the post-implementation audit to have any behavioral effect? If so, how should the company structure the penalty? If not, why would penalties not be necessary?

(c) Do you think that the way managers are paid is appropriate? If so, why? If not, what changes would you suggest?

8-57 ***Effective rate of interest*** Compute the effective annual rate of interest in each of the following cases: LO 3

(a) A bank promises 8% interest compounded annually.

(b) A bank promises 8% interest compounded semiannually.

(c) A bank promises 8% interest compounded quarterly.

(d) A bank promises 8% interest compounded monthly.

(e) A bank promises 8% interest compounded daily.

8-58 ***Finding the interest rate*** You want to borrow $10,000 and repay the loan with equal monthly payments for five years. The bank has advised you that the required monthly payment will be $222.45. What is the monthly rate of interest and the effective annual rate of interest that the bank is proposing to charge you for this loan? LO 3

8-59 ***Accumulating a target level of wealth*** Carolyn Martin, who is now 30, wants to retire at age 60 with $2.5 million in an investment account. If funds can be invested to earn 12% per year compounded annually, what equal annual amount must she invest? What will the required amount be if the funds are invested to earn 12% per year compounded semiannually? LO 3

8-60 ***Accumulating a retirement fund*** Review the data in question 8-59. Suppose that Carolyn decides that it is unrealistic to invest an equal annual amount in her retirement fund. Instead she decides to invest increasing amounts each year. If the amount that she invests each year is 5% more than the amount she invested in the previous year, what amount must she invest in the first year? LO 3

8-61 ***Value in the face of risk*** Return to the data in question 8-39. Suppose that you LO 3 are 65 years old and are deciding which of these two annuities to buy. The proposal is that the annuity will cease upon your death; that is, in the event of your death, the balance of the annuity that you buy will not be paid to your heirs. Choose one of the two annuities showing the basis for your choice.

LO 4, 6 **8-62** ***Capital budgeting and sensitivity analysis*** You work for an automobile company that is considering developing a new car. The product development costs for this new car will be $500 million per year for three years. During the third year of product development, the company will incur $1 billion for manufacturing setup costs. Three years after the start of product development, the company will begin making and selling cars. Production and sales will last seven years, and each car sold will generate an incremental profit of $2500. After seven years, the salvage value associated with the manufacturing facilities will be $200 million. The company's cost of capital is 12%.

REQUIRED

(a) What is the minimum number of cars the company must sell during each of the seven years of the product's life to make this investment desirable under the net present value criterion?

(b) What will the minimum number of vehicles be if the company's cost of capital is 15%? (Ignore taxes when answering this question.)

LO 4, 6 **8-63** ***Capital budgeting and uncertainty*** Jane Eby, the chief financial officer of Baden Discount Enterprises, is faced with choosing between two machines. A new machine is needed to replace an existing machine that makes plastic mop handles for one of the company's most popular products. Jane is not sure about the demand for these mops, but estimates that it would not be less than 20,000 units per year or more than 30,000 units per year for the next five years.

The two machines are the semiautomatic and the automatic, respectively. Relative to the semiautomatic machine, the automatic machine makes the handles more quickly and makes fewer mistakes that require rework. Thus, the total cost per unit for materials and labor for mop handles made by the automatic and semiautomatic machines is not the same. The total unit cost of material and labor for mop handles is $6 on the automatic machine and $8 on the semiautomatic machine.

The automatic and semiautomatic machines cost $500,000 and $300,000, respectively, and both would last five years. After five years of use, either machine could be scrapped for a zero salvage value. This organization has a cost of capital of 12%. (Ignore the effect of taxes when answering this question.)

How should Jane choose between the two machines in this situation? Be specific. You do not have to make a specific decision about one machine or the other, but your recommendation should tell her exactly how she should make the decision.

LO 4, 6 **8-64** ***Capital budgeting and inflation*** Inflation is a general increase in the price level. For example, if the annual cash flows and salvage value in Exhibit 8-17 were subject to inflation at the annual rate of 4%, the cash flows would be those shown in Exhibit 8-26. (Note that, under these conditions, the annual depreciation is now $11,566 [($70,000 − $12,167) ÷ 5].)

However, with inflation, the required rate of return must be increased so that it will provide for both the time value of money and the purchasing power loss due to inflation. In general, the required rate of return is this:

$$(1 + \text{Required rate of return}) = (1 + \text{Real rate of interest}) \times (1 + \text{Inflation rate})$$

$$\text{Required rate of return} = (1 + \text{Real rate of interest}) \times (1 + \text{Inflation rate}) - 1$$

EXHIBIT 8-26

Shirley's Doughnut Hole
Inflation Effects

TIME	AMOUNT	DEPRECIATION	TAX INCOME	TAX @ 40%	NCF
0	($70,000.00)				($70,000.00)
1	20,800,00	11,566.69	9,233.31	$3,693.32	17,106.68
2	21,632.00	11,566.69	10,065.31	4,026.12	17,605.88
3	22,497.28	11,566.69	10,930.59	4,372.23	18,125.05
4	23,397.17	11,566.69	11,830.48	4,732.19	18,664.98
5	36,499.59	11,566.69	12,766.36	5,106.55	31,393.04

$$\text{Required rate of return} = \text{Real rate of interest} + \text{Inflation rate} \\ + \text{Real rate of interest} \times \text{Inflation rate}$$

where the real rate of interest is the return required in the absence of inflation.

(a) Using the appropriate required return, compute the project's net present value.

(b) Why is the net present value of the project lower under conditions of inflation than it was without inflation?

8-65 ***Changing the payment frequency*** Suppose that you are buying a house and require a $200,000 mortgage. You have told the bank that you want to repay your mortgage over 30 years. The bank has indicated that, whatever payment option you consider, you will be charged an effective annual interest rate of 7% on your mortgage. LO 3

REQUIRED

What will be your mortgage payment if you are required to make:

(a) Mortgage payments once a year.

(b) Mortgage payments semiannually.

(c) Mortgage payments quarterly.

(d) Mortgage payments monthly.

(e) Mortgage payments weekly.

(f) Explain any relationship that you see in your responses to parts (a) through (e).

CASES

8-66 ***Sensitivity and what-if analysis*** Your instructor has an Excel spreadsheet for the Shirley's Doughnut Hole example used in the chapter. You will need it to answer this question. The file shows how easily capital budgeting calculations can be done on a computer. (Knowledge and judgment are required to perform capital budgeting analysis; however, the computer makes the necessary calculations easy.) This exercise shows you how quickly you can answer what-if or sensitivity analysis questions after you have set up the spreadsheet. Do not be misled by the simple nature of the problem. The procedure is the same for more complex problems. LO 4, 6

After you retrieve this file, look at the layout of the spreadsheet. The key problem parameters are the initial investment amount in cell D4, the annual

benefits in cell D5, the salvage value in cell D6, the cost of capital in cell D3, and the tax rate in cell D9. The project's net present value is shown in cell D10.

(a) Move to cell D5 and adjust the annual benefits up or down until the amount in cell D10 is zero. (This will be about $17,556.) This is the annual benefit that just makes the project desirable. Note that $17,556 is about 88% of $20,000, the estimated value of the benefit. Therefore, the decision of whether to invest in this project is quite sensitive to our estimate of the cost savings. This causes us to focus our attention on the estimate of cost savings.

(b) Put the value of $20,000 in cell D5. The net present value shown in cell D10 should be $6,013. Now move to cell D3 and experiment with the cost of capital until the net present value in cell D10 is zero. (This will be about 9.94%.) This is 42% more than the estimated required return of 7%, so we would consider the decision to invest in the cooker relatively insensitive to the estimate of the required return.

(c) Put the value of 7% (0.07) in cell D3. Again the net present value shown in cell D10 should be $6,013. Now look at the project life estimate. This simple spreadsheet is not set up in a way that allows us to vary the project life easily, although if you want to, it can be done fairly easily with spreadsheet macros.

(d) Suppose that you want to know if the doughnut cooker investment would be justified if the cooker lasted only four years. Delete row 28. Move to the new cell A28 and enter 4. This terminates the project after four years. However, we must adjust the depreciation so that it is taken over four years instead of five. Move to cell D8 and enter 4. This will adjust the depreciation amount. You can see that the project now has a present value of $1401, which means that the project is undesirable. The decision to buy the cooker is very sensitive to the estimate of the cooker's life.

This simple example gives you the idea of how to use sensitivity analysis to identify what estimates are critical to the project's acceptance or rejection and where to spend more time or money improving the accuracy of estimates used in the analysis.

Suppose that the required return is 9%. If everything else in the problem remains the same, what is the minimum amount of the annual benefits that would make the project desirable?

LO 3, 4, 5, 6, 7

8-67 ***Evaluating an investment proposal under uncertainty*** Serge Martin, general manager of the hapless Hogtown Flyers, is considering the acquisition of Mario Flanagan to bolster his team's sagging fortunes. Mario has played the last two seasons in Europe, so there would be no compensation paid to another team if he is hired. Mario, a prolific scorer, is holding out for a 10-year contract with contract demands of (1) an immediate and one-time payment of $200,000 as a signing bonus and (2) $1,000,000 in salary in the first year. Mario is demanding that his salary increase at the rate of 10% each year.

Serge figures that hiring Mario will increase ticket sales by 35,000 per year. Tickets sell for $20 per game, and total variable costs associated with each customer per game are about $5. In addition, Serge is certain that with Mario, the Flyers will get into the playoffs each year. Getting into the playoffs means sales of at least 50,000 playoff tickets, which sell for $30 each. The variable (unit driven) cost associated with each playoff ticket is about $5. Because the Flyers have the highest ticket prices in the league and would operate at capacity if Mario were signed, Serge does not expect these numbers to change over the life of Mario's contract.

Serge's only concern is that Mario is demanding a guaranteed contract; that is, he will be paid whether he plays or not. Serge is virtually certain that Mario will play for seven years. However, after that, he is uncertain of the possibilities, but certain that whenever Mario stops playing, ticket sales will revert to their current levels.

(a) Prepare a 10-year statement of cash flows associated with this opportunity.

(b) Assume that the Flyer's after-tax cost of capital is 6%. Compute the net present value of this deal if Mario plays for 7 years, 8 years, 9 years, and 10 years. Assume that the Hogtown Flyers face a marginal tax rate of 40% and that any losses on the sports operations can be used to reduce the taxes on other operations.

(c) What would you advise Serge to do?

8-68 ***Evaluating a new technology*** National Courier Company picks up and delivers packages across the country and, through its relationships with couriers in other countries, provides international package delivery services. Each afternoon couriers pick up packages. In late afternoon, the packages are returned to the courier's terminal, where they are placed in bins and shipped by air to National Courier Company's hub. In the hub, these bins are emptied. The packages are sorted and put into different bins according to their destination terminal. Early the next morning, the bins arrive at the various destination terminals, where they are sorted by route, put onto trucks, and delivered. LO 3, 4, 5, 6, 7

An operations study determined that about $2 million of employee time could be saved each year by using a scanning system. Each package's bill of lading would have a bar code that the courier would scan with a handheld scanner when the package is picked up. The shipment would be scanned again as it reaches the terminal, when it leaves the terminal, when it reaches the hub, when it is placed into a bin at the hub, when it arrives at the destination terminal, when it is sorted onto a courier's truck for delivery, and when it is delivered to the customer. Each scanning would eliminate the manual and less accurate completion of a form, thereby providing courier time savings.

The total cost of the scanning system is estimated to be $10 million. It is thought to have a life of six years, after which the equipment will be replaced with new technology. The salvage value of the equipment in six years is estimated to be $500,000.

At the end of each shift, the information from all the scanners will be loaded into National Courier Company's main computer, providing the exact location of each shipment. This tracking information provides for increased security, a lower mis-sort rate, and improved service in tracing shipments that have been mis-sorted. The reduced time spent tracing missing shipments accounts for the balance of the estimated employee time savings. The marketing manager believes that the increased security and service will result in an increased contribution margin of about $1 million per year if competitors do not adopt this technology and National Courier Company does. If competitors buy this technology and National Courier Company does not, it will lose $1 million in contribution margin. If everyone buys this technology each competitor will maintain its current sales level.

If National Courier Company's marginal tax rate is 35% and it has an after-tax cost of capital of 6%, should it make this investment? Assume that National Courier Company will use straight-line depreciation to compute depreciation for tax purposes.

chapter 9

Management Accounting and Control Systems for Strategic Purposes: Assessing Performance over the Entire Value Chain

AFTER READING THIS CHAPTER, YOU WILL BE ABLE TO

1. apply the concept of control
2. identify the characteristics of well-designed management accounting and control systems (MACS)
3. describe the total-life-cycle costing approach to managing product costs over the value chain
4. explain target costing
5. explain Kaizen costing
6. identify environmental costing issues
7. apply the process of benchmarking the best practices of other organizations

Martin Bond/Science Photo Library/Photo Researchers, Inc.

CHEMCO INTERNATIONAL

Nathaniel Young has just been appointed controller of a large chemical company. He is on the fast track, having graduated with a dual concentration in strategy and management accounting from a large Southern California business school only five years earlier. Before going back to school, Nathaniel worked as a management consultant. His most recent job as senior manager of the manufacturing division has been challenging; however, he has performed relatively well despite the poor quality of the data coming out of the company's antiquated management accounting and control system.

Numerous problems seem to plague this system. First, managers find that cost management reports both within and across divisions are often not comparable, given the variety of ways that product costs are generated. Second, information generated by the system is focused solely on the actual manufacturing process itself and does not provide any insight into pre- and postmanufacturing costs such as the cost of developing products or disposing of toxic waste. Since competition in the chemicals industry has increased dramatically, Nathaniel wants to understand all costs related to the life cycle of his products.

Based on his experience as a consultant, Nathaniel has decided to design a management accounting and control system that will generate relevant information. Other managers in his company are not sure whether the change is really necessary. Nevertheless, Nathaniel would like to find out everything he can about how companies in his and other industries have designed their systems. He is also intrigued by how costs can be managed over their total life cycle and, in particular, wants to study how target costing and Kaizen costing can be applied in his company.

Since his company produces chemicals he also is concerned about how to dispose of his products and what their environmental impact may be. The first step is to determine what design principles to follow. Nathaniel decides to study the benchmarking process. He also has heard that another local company just completed the design of a new system, and he decides to call his counterpart at that company to see whether he can gather some benchmarking information.

What are Management Accounting and Control Systems?

Management accounting and control system (MACS)
The larger entity of central performance measurement systems.

In previous chapters we studied different types of cost management systems and the way the information they generated is used in a variety of decision contexts. A cost management system is one of the central performance measurement systems at the core of a larger entity known as a **management accounting and control system (MACS)**. In this and the following chapters we discuss the role that MACS play in helping decision makers determine whether organization level, business level, and operational level strategies (discussed in Chapter 2) and objectives are being met. We begin by presenting the concept of control and then delineate the technical and behavioral characteristics of a well-designed MACS. Because the design of MACS is a large topic, we have divided the discussion into two parts. This chapter will cover the technical aspects of MACS design as well as the ways managers can use benchmarking to gather information about the best practices of others who have implemented new systems. Chapter 10 will focus on the behavioral characteristics of MACS design and cover issues related to human motivation.

The technical characteristics of a well-designed MACS include the scope of the system and the relevance of the information generated. Regarding scope, many MACS measure and assess performance in only one part of the value chain—the actual production process. A major shortcoming is that pre- or postproduction costs associated with products or services are ignored. Since such costs are significant in today's business environment, not having this information puts organizations at a distinct disadvantage when trying to understand the total-life-cycle costs of a product or service, and ways to reduce those costs.

We illustrate the advantages of considering the entire value chain by discussing three contemporary methods: target costing, Kaizen costing, and environmental costing. If well implemented, these methods can help organizations control and reduce costs effectively.

Control
Refers to the set of procedures, tools, performance measures, and systems that organizations use to guide and motivate all employees to achieve organizational objectives.

THE MEANING OF "CONTROL" IN MANAGEMENT ACCOUNTING AND CONTROL SYSTEMS

Broadly speaking, a management accounting and control system generates and uses information to help decision makers assess whether an organization is achieving its objectives. The term **control** in management accounting and control refers to the set of procedures, tools, performance measures, and systems that organizations use to guide and motivate all employees to achieve organizational objectives. A system is **in control** if it is on the path to achieving its strategic objectives and deemed **out of control** otherwise.

In control
Refers to a system that is on the path to achieving its strategic objectives.

Out of control
A state when a system is not on a path to achieving organizational objectives.

For the process of control to have meaning and credibility, the organization must have the knowledge and ability to correct situations that it identifies as out of control; otherwise control serves no purpose. The process of keeping an organization in control consists of five stages as shown in Exhibit 9-1:

1. *Planning* consists of developing an organization's objectives, choosing activities to accomplish the objectives, and selecting measures to determine how well the objectives were met.
2. *Execution* is implementing the plan.
3. *Monitoring* is the process of measuring the system's current level of performance.
4. *Evaluation* occurs when feedback about the system's current level of performance is compared to the planned level so that any discrepancies can be identified and corrective action prescribed.
5. *Correcting* consists of taking the appropriate actions to return the system to an in control state.

Regardless of whether an organization makes cookies, finds job-seekers work, or flies people around the world, the same basic control process applies. One key difference in the control process lies in determining the most appropriate types of performance measures used by an organization. In the following section, we discuss the characteristics that designers consider when developing a management accounting and control system.

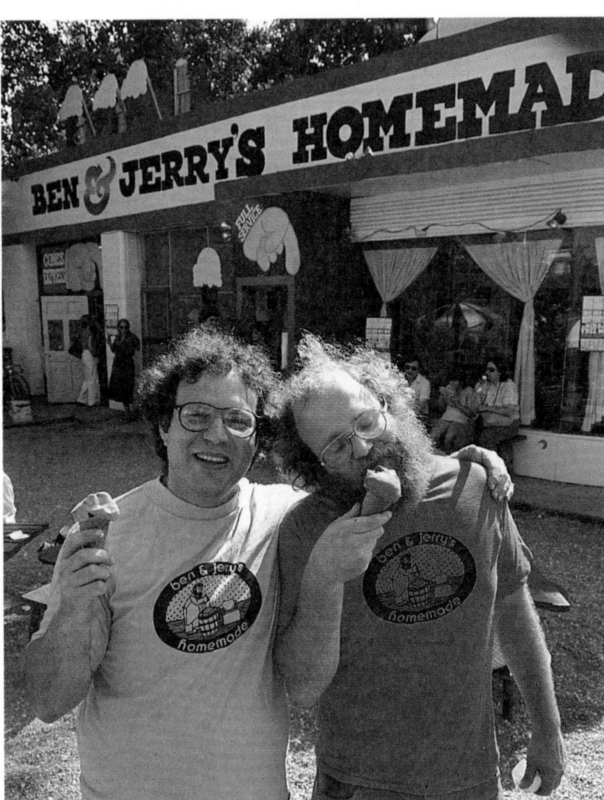

Organizations such as Ben and Jerry's Homemade and the Body Shop are renowned for having both financial and social objectives such as supporting the local community or achieving environmental goals. (Steve Hanson/ Stock, Boston)

EXHIBIT 9-1

The Cycle of Control

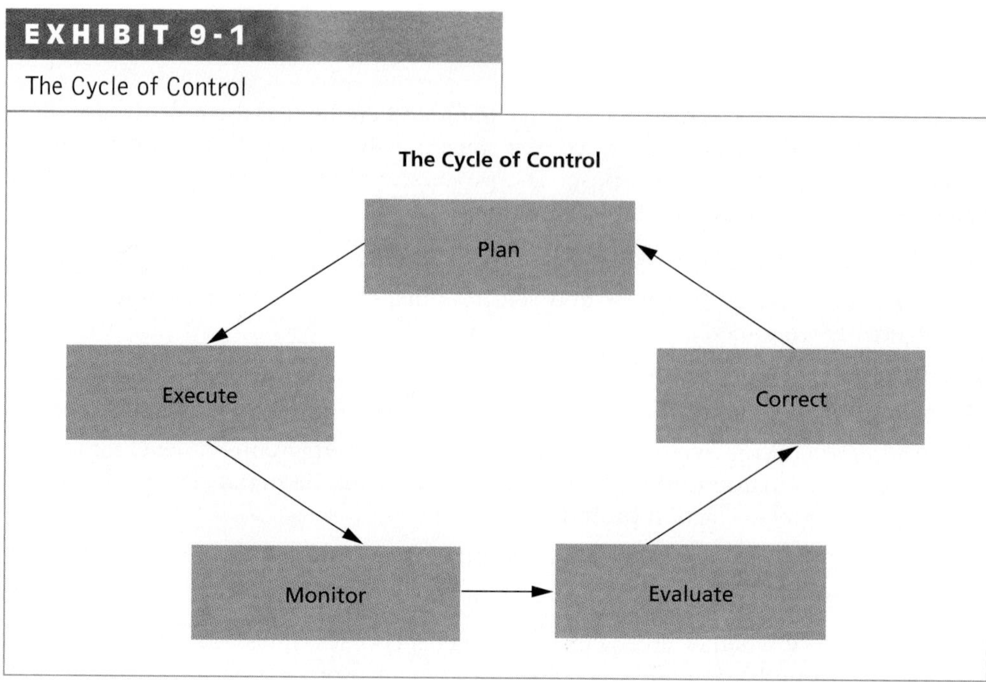

Characteristics of Well-Designed Management Accounting and Control Systems

Designers of management accounting and control systems have both behavioral and technical considerations to meet. Behavioral considerations include the following:

1. embedding the organization's ethical code of conduct into MACS design,
2. using a mix of short- and long-term qualitative and quantitative performance measures (or the balanced scorecard approach),
3. empowering employees to be involved in decision making and MACS design, and
4. developing an appropriate incentive system to reward performance.

In Chapter 10, we discuss these behavioral considerations. For now let us turn to the technical side.

TECHNICAL CONSIDERATIONS

The technical considerations fall into two categories: (1) the **relevance** of the information generated, and (2) the **scope** of the system.

Relevance of information
Refers to how useful information is for organization's decision and control processes.

Scope of a MACS
Includes the entire value chain of the organization.

Relevance of Information. The relevance of the information is measured by four characteristics. The information must be:

1. **Accurate.** As discussed throughout this text, inaccurate information is not relevant or useful for decision making because it is misleading. Designers have to develop a system that leads to the most accurate information possible. For instance, more accurate product costs can be obtained by using systems that trace costs more directly from support activities to products.
2. **Timely.** Accurate information that is late is also of little use for decision making. The MACS must be designed so that the results of performance measurement are

fed back to the appropriate units in the most expedient way possible. The proliferation of high-speed computers, local area networks, and many other forms of technology make the process of providing feedback a real-time possibility in many, if not all, systems.

3. **Consistent.** Designers must structure the MACS to provide a consistent framework that can be applied globally across the units or divisions of an entity. Consistency means that the language used and the technical methods of producing management accounting information do not conflict within various parts of an organization. For example, if two divisions use different costing systems, it is more difficult to understand and compare results across divisions. If one division of an organization uses activity-based costing principles and another division, especially one that is very similar in goals and function to the first, uses volume-based overhead allocation methods, then the information system does not meet the consistency criterion. Or consider the difficulties that would arise if divisions classified the same expense differently, that is, if fringe benefits of workers were classified as direct labor expenses in one division but as indirect labor expenses in another.

4. **Flexible.** MACS designers must allow employees to use the system's available information in a flexible manner so they can customize its application for local decisions. If flexibility is not possible, an employee's motivation to make the best decision may be lessened for the decision at hand, especially if different units engage in different types of activities. For instance, if one division of a company located in Pasadena undertakes new product development and another division in Monterey performs final assembly, each division probably will have different data needs and may use different cost drivers in making its decisions. The performance measures for managing new product development in Pasadena will be quite different from the factors that the Monterey assembly division must use to manage effectively. A well-designed MACS should be able to accommodate the local needs of each division. If not, inaccurate ad hoc local systems may develop, which can lead to poor decisions and confusion between the company's division and upper management.

Scope of the System. The scope of the MACS system must be comprehensive and include all activities across the entire value chain of the organization. For instance, historically, many MACS measure and assess performance in only one part of the value chain—the actual production or throughput process. In this case, the performance of suppliers, the design activities, and the postproduction activities associated with products and services are ignored. Without a comprehensive set of information, managers can only make limited decisions.

THE VALUE CHAIN

In Chapter 2 we defined the value chain as a sequence of activities that should contribute more to the ultimate value of the product than to its cost. Products produced by an organization rely on different activities of the organization and use different resources along the value chain depending on their specifications. Essentially all products flow through the value chain, which begins with research, development, and engineering, moves through manufacturing, and continues on to customers. Depending on the product, customers may require service and will either consume the product (a chocolate bar) or dispose of it after it has served its intended purpose (chemical solvents).

TOTAL-LIFE-CYCLE COSTING

Total-life-cycle costing (TLCC) Describes the process of managing all costs during a product's lifetime.

As products move along the value chain they accumulate costs. **Total-life-cycle costing (TLCC)**[1] is the name we give to the process of managing all costs along the value chain. A TLCC system provides information for managers to understand and manage costs through a product's design, development, manufacturing, marketing, distribution, maintenance, service, and disposal stages.[2] It is also known as managing costs "from the cradle to the grave."

Deciding how to allocate resources over the life cycle usually is an iterative process. Initially a company may decide to spend more on design to reduce the costs of all other subsequent product-related (upstream) costs, such as manufacturing, and service-related costs. At a later time, the company may determine how to reduce those initial design costs as well. Opportunity costs play a heightened role in a total-life-cycle cost perspective, because it is possible to develop only a limited number of products over a particular time period.

Consider the following situation: Managers of the Glendale Company have been developing a new concept for a product they believe will revolutionize their business. Their initial research suggests to them that they can manufacture the product at a reasonably low cost, especially given the new technology that they have just acquired. They begin to consider how they can reorganize their operation to accommodate the production of the new product. Because they have only some preliminary ideas about the feasibility of product design, they approach their research

THE TECHNOLOGICAL EDGE

Aligning IT with the Value Chain in Financial Services

Information technology (IT) has become of central importance to the value chain for financial services. Companies have begun to align IT with their business goals. Some companies create alignment by splitting off a separate electronic commerce group while others form teams of IT people and personnel from other functional areas.

Vincent Philips, vice president of Web systems at Charles Schwab in San Francisco, states, "Marketing people and IT are in the same building and sometimes [on] the same floor. It's a very collaborative effort, where marketing folks talk about different ideas and IT people are there to say, 'We can do it this fast, or we might want to do it this way.'" Schwab also includes IT people in product development meetings to discuss the types of future service issues for customers who are purchasing the products.

Bill Burnham, an e-commerce analyst at Credit Suisse First Boston, in New York says, "We have seen a big explosion in product development as companies move from competing on price to (competing in) product and services offerings. And it will continue as competition intensifies and companies pick their spots. Technology is the bedrock foundation of these businesses. If the technology doesn't work, the business doesn't work."

Source: Martin LaMonica, "Bullish on the Net," *Infoworld,* April 26, 1999.

[1] Another term used for total-life-cycle costs is *whole-life* product costing.

[2] While TLCC has its roots in early-life-cycle costing concepts developed by the U.S. Department of Defense in the 1960s, it has been adopted by commercial organizations only recently.

development and engineering (RD&E) division for further investigation. The report from the RD&E group tells them that the product can be produced, but the cost of developing prototypes is 20 times more than the average prototype cost. RD&E confirms, however, that the actual cost to manufacture the product after the first year will be reasonably low as Glendale gains experience with the new technology.

Thus, the initial life-cycle cost of the product may be quite high, but the manufacturing cost will be relatively low. With this new information, managers of the division now have to determine whether they should forge ahead with new product development from an overall company perspective and given their analysis of opportunity costs.

Numerous life-cycle concepts, such as research development and engineering, and post-sale service and disposal, have emerged in various functional areas of business. Although each concept is useful within its respective area, a TLCC perspective integrates the concepts so that they can be understood in their entirety. From the manufacturer's perspective, total-life-cycle product costing integrates these functional life-cycle concepts: research development and engineering, manufacturing, and post-sale service and disposal. Let us look at each.

Research Development and Engineering Cycle. The **research development and engineering (RD&E) cycle** has three stages:

1. *market research*, where emerging customer needs are assessed and ideas are generated for new products,
2. *product design*, in which scientists and engineers develop the technical aspects of products, and
3. *product development*, in which the company creates features critical to customer satisfaction and designs prototypes, production processes, and any special tooling required.

Research development and engineering (RD&E) cycle
A life-cycle concept that involves market research, product design, and product development.

By some estimates, 80% to 85% of a product's total life costs are committed by decisions made in the RD&E cycle of the product's life.[3] **Committed costs** are those that a company knows it will have to incur at a future date. Decisions made in this cycle are critical, because an additional dollar spent on activities that occur during this cycle can save at least $8 to $10 on manufacturing and postmanufacturing activities, such as design changes or service costs.[4]

Committed costs
Those costs that a company incurs before knowing actual production or sales volumes.

Manufacturing Cycle. After the RD&E cycle, the company begins the **manufacturing cycle** in which costs are incurred in the production of the product. Usually at this stage there is not as much room for engineering flexibility to influence product costs and product design because they have been set in the previous cycle. In Exhibit 9-2 the lower curve illustrates how costs are incurred over both the RD&E and the manufacturing cycle. Note the much higher level of costs incurred during the manufacturing cycle relative to the RD&E cycle. Traditionally, this is where product costing plays its biggest role. Operations management methods, such as facilities layout and just-in-time manufacturing (discussed in Chapter 6), help to reduce manufacturing life-cycle product costs. Over the past decade, in an effort to reduce costs, companies have used management accounting methods such as activity-based cost management to identify and reduce nonvalue-added activities.

Manufacturing cycle
Those costs incurred inside the factory associated with transforming raw materials into a finished product.

Post-Sale Service and Disposal Cycle. The third cycle is the **post-sale service and disposal cycle.** Although the costs for service and disposal are committed in the

Post-sale service and disposal cycle
The portion of the life cycle that begins once the first unit of a product is in the hands of the customer.

[3] This section is based in part on a paper by M. Shields and S. M. Young, "Managing Product Life Cycle Costs: An Organizational Model," *Journal of Cost Management,* Fall 1991, pp. 39–52.

[4] M. D. Shields and S. M. Young, *op cit.,* 1991.

EXHIBIT 9-2

Total-Life-Cycle Costing:
Relationship between Committed Costs and Incurred Costs

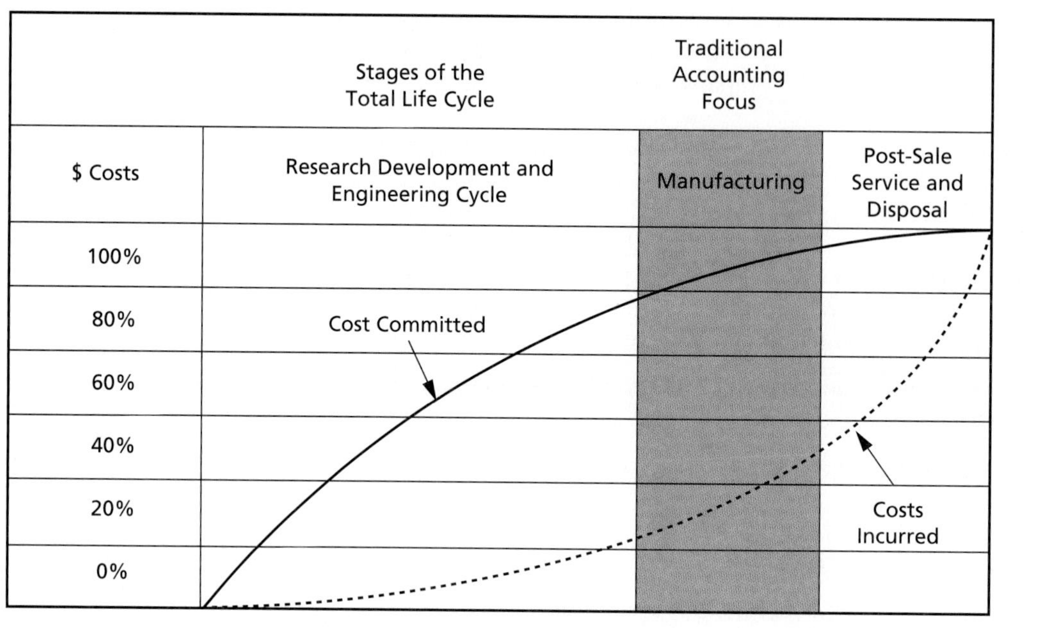

RD&E stage, the actual service cycle begins once the first unit of a product is in the hands of the customer. Thus, this cycle overlaps the manufacturing cycle. The service cycle typically consists of three stages:

1. rapid growth from the first time the product is shipped through the growth stage of its sales,
2. transition from the peak of sales to the peak in the service cycle, and
3. maturity from the peak in the service cycle to the time of the last shipment made to a customer. Disposal occurs at the end of a product's life and lasts until the customer retires the final unit of a product.[5]

Disposal costs often include those associated with eliminating any harmful effects associated with the end of a product's useful life. Products whose disposal could involve harmful effects to the environment, such as nuclear waste or other toxic chemicals, can incur very high costs.

A breakdown of costs for each of the functional life cycles will differ based on the industry and specific product produced. Exhibit 9-3 illustrates four types of products and how the organizations that produce them incur costs over the respective total life cycle of each product.[6]

Exhibit 9-3 shows the variation of costs within the cycles. For instance, the manufacturing cost of the commercial aircraft company is approximately 40% of total

[5] The discussion of the service cycle expands on G. W. Potts, "Exploit Your Product's Service Life Cycle," *Harvard Business Review*, September-October, 1988, pp. 32–36.

[6] The information in this table comes from interviews conducted by Shields and Young, *op. cit.*, 1991. Specific names of companies and products have to remain anonymous due to confidentiality agreements.

EXHIBIT 9-3

Percent of Life-Cycle Costs Incurred across Four Types of Products

STAGE OF LIFE CYCLE	TYPE OF PRODUCT			
Cycle	Combat Jets	Commercial Aircraft	Nuclear Missiles	Computer Software
RD&E	21%	20%	20%	75%*
Manufacturing	45%	40%	60%	*
Service and Disposal	34%	40%	20%	25%
Average Length of Life Cycle	30 years	25 years	2 to 25 years	5 years

*For computer software, both RD&E and manufacturing are often tied directly together.

incurred costs. RD&E and post-sale service and disposal incur 20% and 40%, respectively. An understanding of total-life-cycle costs can lead to cost-effective product designs that are easier to service, and easier and less costly to dispose of at the end of a product's life. Computer software development requires much time in the RD&E stage in order to create and debug the software. It often costs 100 times more to correct a defect in the operating phase for software than in the design phase.[7]

In the following section we discuss the target costing method of management accounting and control that has its focus in the design stage of a product's life cycle, but that also considers all aspects of the value chain and explicitly recognizes total-life-cycle costs.

Target Costing

Target costing is a method of profit planning and cost management that focuses on products with discrete manufacturing processes. The goal of target costing is to design costs out of products in the RD&E stage of a product's total life cycle, rather than trying to reduce costs during the manufacturing stage. Target costing is a relevant example of how a well-designed MACS can be used for strategic purposes, and how critical it is for organizations to have a system in place that considers performance measurement across the entire value chain.

Target costing
A method of cost planning used during the planning cycle to reduce manufacturing costs to targeted levels.

Comparing Traditional Cost Reduction to Target Costing

TRADITIONAL COSTING

Traditional cost reduction in the United States is significantly different from target costing. As shown in Exhibit 9-4, column 1, the traditional costing method begins with market research into customer requirements followed by product specification. Thus, companies engage in product design and engineering and obtain prices from suppliers. At this stage, product cost is not a significant factor in product design. After the engineers and designers have determined product design, they estimate product cost (C_t), where the t subscript indicates numbers derived under traditional thinking. If the estimated cost is considered to be too high, then it may be necessary to modify

[7] See M. A. Cusumano, *Japan's Software Factories,* New York: Oxford University Press, 1991.

EXHIBIT 9-4

A Comparison of the Process of Traditional U.S. and Japanese Cost-Reduction Methods

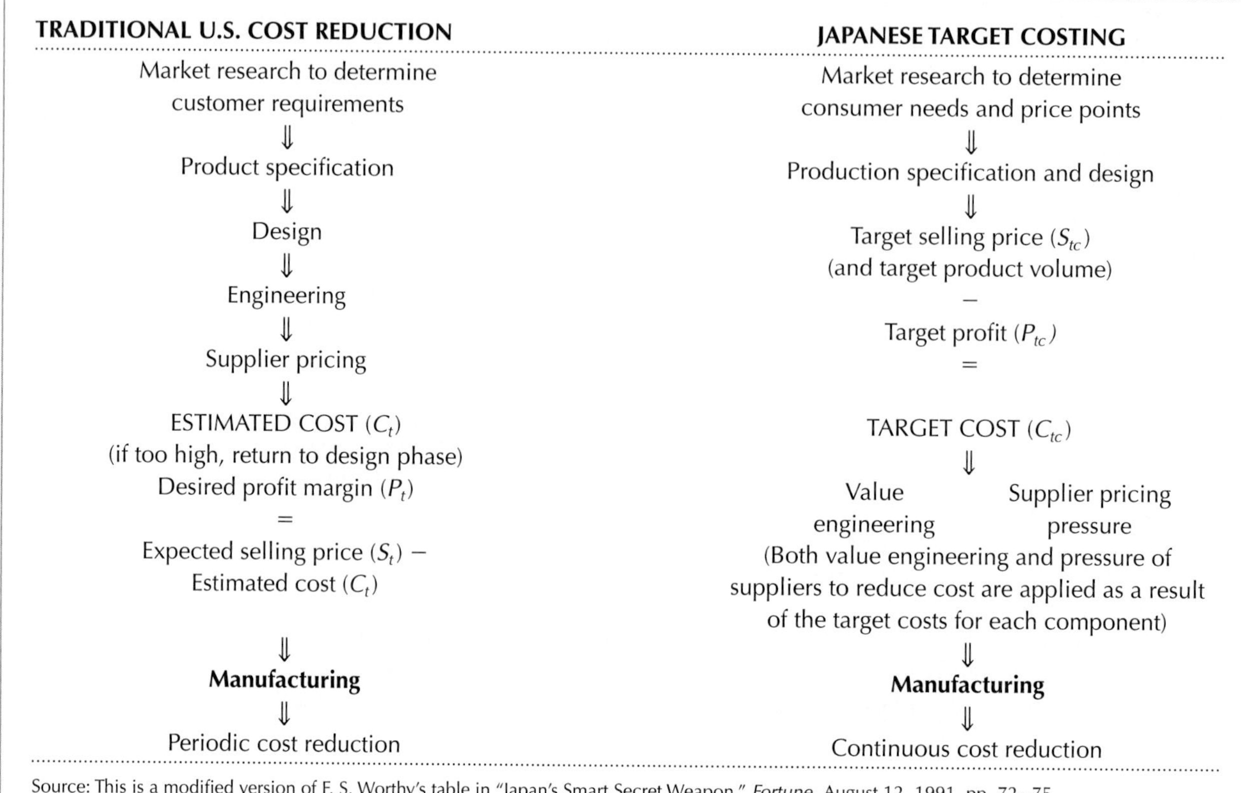

TRADITIONAL U.S. COST REDUCTION	JAPANESE TARGET COSTING
Market research to determine customer requirements	Market research to determine consumer needs and price points
⇓	⇓
Product specification	Production specification and design
⇓	⇓
Design	Target selling price (S_{tc}) (and target product volume)
⇓	−
Engineering	Target profit (P_{tc})
⇓	=
Supplier pricing	TARGET COST (C_{tc})
⇓	⇓
ESTIMATED COST (C_t) (if too high, return to design phase)	Value engineering — Supplier pricing pressure
Desired profit margin (P_t) = Expected selling price (S_t) − Estimated cost (C_t)	(Both value engineering and pressure of suppliers to reduce cost are applied as a result of the target costs for each component)
⇓	⇓
Manufacturing	**Manufacturing**
⇓	⇓
Periodic cost reduction	Continuous cost reduction

Source: This is a modified version of F. S. Worthy's table in "Japan's Smart Secret Weapon," *Fortune,* August 12, 1991, pp. 72–75.

the product design. To find the desired profit margin (P_t), it is necessary to subtract the estimated cost from the expected selling price (S_t). The profit margin is the result of the difference between the expected selling price and the estimated production cost.[8] This relationship is expressed in the following equation:

$$P_t = S_t - C_t$$

In another widely used traditional approach, the cost-plus method, an expected profit margin (P_{cp}) is added to the expected product cost (C_{cp}), where the subscript *cp* indicates numbers derived from the cost-plus method. Selling price (S_{cp}) becomes simply the sum of these two variables. In equation form this relationship is expressed as:

$$S_{cp} = C_{cp} + P_{cp}$$

In both traditional methods, product designers do not attempt to achieve a particular cost target.

In target costing, both the sequence of steps and the way of thinking about determining product costs differ significantly from traditional costing (see Exhibit 9-4, column 2). Although the initial steps, market research to determine customer

[8] Robin Cooper developed the structure for comparing costs in this manner in *Nissan Motor Company, Ltd.: Target Costing System,* Harvard Business School Case #9-194-040.

requirements and product specification, appear similar to traditional costing, there are some notable differences. First, marketing research under target costing is not a single event as it often is under the traditional approach. Rather, while customer input is obtained early in the marketing research process, it is also collected continually throughout the target costing process. Second, much more time is spent at the product specification and design stage in order to minimize design changes during the manufacturing process when they are far more expensive to implement. Third, target costing uses the total-life-cycle concept by making it a key goal to minimize the cost of ownership of a product over its useful life. Thus, not only are costs such as the initial purchase price considered, but also the costs of operating, maintaining, and disposing of the product.[9]

After these initial steps, the target costing process becomes even more distinctive. The next step, determining a target selling price (S_{tc}) and target product volume, depends on the company's perceived value of the product to the customer. The target profit margin (P_{tc}) results from a long-run profit analysis often based on return on sales (net income ÷ sales). Return on sales is the most widely used measure because it can be linked most closely to profitability for each product. The **target cost** (C_{tc}) is the difference between the target selling price and the target profit margin. (Note that the *tc* subscript indicates numbers derived under the target costing approach.) This relationship for the target costing approach is shown in the following equation:

Target cost (C_{tc})
The difference between the target selling price and the target profit margin.

$$C_{tc} = S_{tc} - P_{tc}$$

Once the target cost has been set, the company must determine target costs for each component. The **value engineering** process includes examination of each component of a product to determine whether it is possible to reduce costs while maintaining functionality and performance. In some cases, product design may change, materials used in production may need replacing, or manufacturing processes may require redesign. For example, a product design change may mean using fewer parts or reducing specialty parts if more common components can be used. Several iterations of value engineering usually are needed before it is possible to determine the final target cost. Exhibit 9-5 illustrates a simple example of how to calculate a target cost.

Value engineering
The process of examining each component of a product to determine whether its cost can be reduced while maintaining functionality and performance.

EXHIBIT 9-5

A Target Costing Example

After conducting a marketing research study, Illumina Company decides to produce a new light fixture to complement its outdoor lighting line. According to estimates, the new fixture can be sold at a target price of $20, and the estimated annual target sales volume is 100,000 light fixtures. Illumina has a 20% expected return on sales target. The target cost is computed as follows:

Target sales (100,000 fixtures × $20)	$2,000,000
Less: Target profit (20% × $20/unit × 100,000 units)	400,000
Target cost for 100,000 fixtures	$1,600,000
Unit target cost per fixture ($1,600,000 ÷ 100,000 fixtures)	$16.00

[9] This information comes from S. L. Ansari, J. E. Bell, and the CAM-I Target Cost Core Group, *Target Costing—The Next Frontier in Strategic Cost Management,* New York: McGraw-Hill, 1997.

Two other differences characterize the target costing process. First, throughout the entire process, cross-functional teams made up of individuals representing the entire value chain—both inside and outside the organization—guide the process. For example, it is not uncommon for a team to consist of people from inside the organization (such as design engineering, manufacturing operations, management accounting, and marketing) and representatives from outside the organization (including suppliers, customers, distributors, and waste disposers).

A second difference is that suppliers play a critical role in making target costing work. If there is a need to reduce the cost of specific components, firms will ask their suppliers to find ways to reduce costs. Companies may offer incentive plans to suppliers who come up with the largest cost reduction ideas.[10] Others, however, have begun to use an approach known as supply chain management. **Supply chain management** develops cooperative, mutually beneficial, long-term relationships between buyers and suppliers. The benefits are many. For example, as trust develops between buyer and supplier, decisions about how to resolve cost reduction problems can be made with shared information about various aspects of each other's operations. In some organizations, the buyer may even expend resources to train the supplier's employees in some aspect of the business, or a supplier may assign one of its employees to work with the buyer to understand a new product. Such interactions are quite different from the short-term, antagonistic relationships that are characteristic of a traditional buyer-seller relationship.

Supply chain management
A management system that develops cooperative, mutually beneficial, long-term relationships between buyers and sellers.

CONCERNS ABOUT TARGET COSTING

Although target costing has some obvious advantages, some studies of target costing in Japan indicate that there are potential problems in implementing the system, especially if focusing on meeting the target cost diverts attention away from the other elements of overall company goals.[11] These are some examples:

1. Conflicts can arise between various parties involved in the target costing process. Often companies put excessive pressure on subcontractors and suppliers to conform to schedule and reduce costs. This can lead to alienation and/or failure of the subcontractor. Sometimes design engineers become upset when other parts of the organization are not cost conscious; they argue that they exert much effort to squeeze pennies out of the cost of a product, while other parts of the organization (administration, marketing, distribution) are wasting dollars.
2. Employees in many Japanese companies working under target costing goals experience burnout due to the pressure to meet the target cost. Burnout is particularly evident for design engineers.
3. Although the target cost might be met, development time may increase because of repeated value engineering cycles to reduce costs, which ultimately can lead to the product coming late to market. For some types of products, being six months late may be far more costly than having small cost overruns.

Companies may find it possible to manage many of these factors, but organizations interested in using the target costing process should be aware of them before immediately attempting to adopt this cost reduction method. The behavioral components of MACS design, and in particular the need to motivate but not burn out employees, have to be considered carefully. (We will discuss these issues more fully in

[10] See R. Cooper, *Nissan Motor Company, Ltd.: Target Costing System,* Harvard Business School Case #9-194-040.

[11] See M. Sakurai, "Past and Future of Japanese Management Accounting," *Journal of Cost Management,* Fall 1995; and Y. Kato, G. Boer and C. W. Chow, "Target Costing: An Integrated Management Process," *Journal of Cost Management,* Spring 1995, pp. 39–51.

IN PRACTICE

Cost Savings on Boeing Aircraft Using Target Costing and Value Engineering

Boeing has had considerable success in implementing target costing. Below is a list of Boeing projects and the results obtained using target costing and value engineering.

PROJECT	RESULTS
737 Flight Deck Valve	90% recurring cost reduction 79% part count reduction
737/757 Sidewall Panel Assembly	$14,700 savings per airplane 45% part count reduction
737 #1 Window Replacement	Time reduced from 12 hours to 3 hours
737 Entry Door Operating Force	Improved door forces
737-X Storage Bin Support	50% cost reduction 12 lb per ship set savings

Source: S. Ansari, J. E. Bell, and the CAM-I Target Cost Core Group, *Target Costing—The Next Frontier in Strategic Cost Management,* Irwin Professional Publishing, 1997, pp. 3–4.

Chapter 10.) Despite these criticisms, target costing can provide engineers and managers the greatest leverage to reduce product costs in a critical part of the product life cycle.

Target costing has been in use in Japanese firms for many years. A survey conducted by Kobe University in Japan showed that of those responding, 100% of transportation equipment manufacturers, 75% of precision equipment manufacturers, 88%

Target costs have already been determined for these vehicles before they reach this stage of the manufacturing process. (FUJI Photos/The Image Works)

of electrical manufacturers, and 83% of machinery manufacturers stated that they used target costing.[12] The impetus for such widespread use was diminishing efficiency gains realized in production from using the just-in-time manufacturing system. The Japanese believed that further gains in both manufacturing and service costs could be made if they shifted the focus on cost reduction to the RD&E cycle.[13]

In the United States, target costing has gained momentum as a management method; however, it is not only a method of cost control, but also a comprehensive approach to profit planning and cost management. Companies such as Boeing, Eastman Kodak, and DaimlerChrysler have adopted target costing in parts of their businesses, and in particular, target costing has been applied successfully at Texas Instruments.[14]

Kaizen Costing

Kaizen costing
A costing system that focuses on reducing costs during the manufacturing stage of the total life cycle of a product.

Kaizen costing is similar to target costing in its cost-reduction mission, except that it focuses on reducing costs during the manufacturing stage of the total life cycle of a product. *Kaizen* is the Japanese term for making improvements to a process through small, incremental amounts rather than through large innovations. Kaizen's goals are reasonable, because when the product is already in the manufacturing process it is difficult and costly to make large changes to reduce costs. Kaizen costing contrasts with target costing, which allows many more opportunities to effect change because it occurs much earlier in the product's life cycle.

Kaizen costing is tied into the profit-planning system.[15] In the Japanese automobile industry, for example, an annual budgeted profit target is allocated to each plant. Each automobile has a predetermined cost base, which is equal to the actual cost of that automobile in the previous year. All cost reductions use this cost base as their starting point.

The target reduction rate is the ratio of the target reduction amount to the cost base. This rate is applied over time to all variable costs and results in specific target reduction amounts for materials, parts, direct and indirect labor, and other variable costs. Then management makes comparisons of actual reduction amounts across all variable costs to the preestablished targeted reduction amounts. If differences exist, variances for the plant are determined. Kaizen costing's goal is to ensure that actual production costs are less than the cost base. However, if the cost of disruptions to production are greater than the savings due to Kaizen costing, then it will not be applied.[16] Exhibit 9-6 illustrates one example of determining the total amount of Kaizen costs across multiple plants in a Japanese automobile plant.

COMPARING TRADITIONAL COST REDUCTION TO KAIZEN COSTING

The Kaizen costing system is quite distinct from a traditional standard costing system in which the typical goal is to meet the cost standard while avoiding unfavorable variances. Under Kaizen costing, the goal is to achieve cost reduction targets that are continually adjusted downward. Variance analysis under a standard cost system usually compares actual to standard costs. Under the Kaizen costing system, variance analysis compares the target costs with actual cost-reduction amounts. Kaizen costing

[12] This study is cited in Y. Kato, G. Boer, and C. W. Chow, "Target Costing: An Integrated Management Process," *Journal of Cost Management,* Spring 1995, pp. 39–51.

[13] See R. Cooper and R. Salgmulder, *Target Costing and Value Engineering,* Portland, OR: Productivity Press, 1997; and Yutaka Kato, *Target Costing: Strategic Cost Management,* Nihon Keizai Shinbunsha, 1993.

[14] See J. J. Dutton and M. Ferguson, "Target Costing at Texas Instruments," *Journal of Cost Management,* Fall 1996, pp. 33–38.

[15] This discussion is based on research by Y. Monden and J. Lee, "How a Japanese Auto Maker Reduces Costs," *Management Accounting,* August 1993, pp. 22–26.

[16] See R. Cooper, *When Lean Enterprises Collide,* Boston, Mass.: Harvard Business School Press, 1995.

EXHIBIT 9-6

Computing Kaizen Costs for Plants

Cost savings in Japanese automobile plants involve reducing both committed (fixed) and flexible (variable) costs. Since fixed costs are believed necessary for growth, the main emphasis is on reducing variable costs.

In this example, the total amount of Kaizen costs in all plants determined in a Kaizen planning meeting is designated as *C* in the formulae that follow:

Amount of Actual Cost per Car in the Last Period (*A*)	=	Amount of Actual Cost in the Last Period	÷	Actual Production in the Last Period
Estimated Amount of Actual Cost for All Plants in This Period (*B*)	=	Amount of Actual Cost per Car in the Last Period (*A*)	×	Estimated Production in This Period
Kaizen Cost Target in This Period for All Plants (*C*)	=	Estimated Amount of Actual Cost for All Plants in This Period (*B*)	×	Target Ratio of Cost Decrease to the Estimated Cost

The target ratio of cost decrease to the estimated cost is based on attaining the target profit for the year.

The Kaizen cost target for each plant is determined in the following manner:

Assignment Ratio (*D*)	=	Costs Controlled Directly by Each Plant	÷	Total Amount of Costs Controlled Directly by Plants
Total Kaizen Cost for Each Plant	=	Kaizen Cost Target in This Period for All Plants (*C*)	×	Assignment Ratio (*D*)

The amount of Kaizen cost for each plant is subdivided to each division and subdivisions as costs-reduction goals.

Source: Y. Monden and K. Hamada, "Target Costing and Kaizen Costing in Japanese Automobile Companies," *Journal of Management Accounting Research,* 1991, pp. 16–34. Reprinted by permission of the American Accounting Association.

operates outside the standard costing system, in part because standard costing systems in Japan are oriented toward complying with financial accounting standards.

Another key difference between standard and Kaizen costing has to do with the assumptions about who has the best knowledge to improve processes and reduce costs. Traditional standard costing assumes that *engineers and managers* know best, because they have the technical expertise and can determine procedures that workers are required to perform according to preset standards and procedures. Under Kaizen costing, *workers* are assumed to have superior knowledge about how to improve processes, because they actually work with manufacturing processes to produce products. To facilitate the process, information on actual costs must be shared with front-line employees, which is a significant change for many companies. Thus, another central goal of Kaizen costing is to give workers the responsibility and control to improve processes and reduce costs. Exhibit 9-7 summarizes the differences in philosophy between standard costing and Kaizen costing methods.

CONCERNS ABOUT KAIZEN COSTING

Kaizen costing also has been criticized for the same reasons as target costing has been criticized: The system places enormous pressure on employees to reduce every conceivable cost. To address the problem, some Japanese automobile companies use a grace period in manufacturing just before a new model is introduced. This period,

EXHIBIT 9-7

A Comparison of Standard Costing and Kaizen Costing

STANDARD COSTING CONCEPTS	KAIZEN COSTING CONCEPTS
Cost-control system concept	Cost-reduction system concept
Assumes stability in current manufacturing processes	Assumes continuous improvement in manufacturing
Goal is to meet cost performance standards	Goal is to achieve cost-reduction standards
STANDARD COSTING TECHNIQUES	**KAIZEN COSTING TECHNIQUES**
Standards are set annually or semiannually	Cost-reduction targets are set and applied monthly and continuous improvement (Kaizen) methods are applied all year long to meet targets.
Cost-variance analysis involves comparing actual to standard costs	Cost-variance analysis involves target Kaizen costs versus actual cost reduction amounts
Cost-variance investigation occurs when standards are not met	Investigation occurs when target cost-reduction (Kaizen) amounts are not attained
WHO HAS THE BEST KNOWLEDGE TO REDUCE COSTS?	**WHO HAS THE BEST KNOWLEDGE TO REDUCE COSTS?**
Managers and engineers develop standards as they have the technical expertise	Workers are closest to the process and thus know best

Source: Adapted from Y. Monden and J. Lee, "How a Japanese Auto Maker Reduces Costs," *Management Accounting*, August, 1993, pp. 22–26.

called a *cost-sustainment period*, provides employees with the opportunity to learn any new procedures before the company imposes Kaizen and target costs on them.

Another concern has been that Kaizen costing leads to incremental rather than radical process improvements. This can cause myopia as management tends to focus on the details rather than the overall system.

Environmental Costing

Environmental costing A costing system that computes the cost of the effects an organization has on the environment.

In today's business environment, environmental remediation, compliance, and management have become critical aspects of enlightened business practice. The impact on MACS design and practice of this change is that all parts of the value chain, and thus many kinds of costs, are affected by environmental issues. **Environmental costing** involves selecting suppliers whose philosophy and practice in dealing with the environment matches the buyer's, disposing of waste products during the production process, and addressing post-sale service and disposal issues are being incorporated into cost management systems and overall MACS design.

CONTROLLING ENVIRONMENTAL COSTS

Perhaps the best way to control and reduce environmental costs is to use the activity-based costing method developed in Chapter 5. First, the activities that cause environmental costs have to be identified. Second, the costs associated with the activities have to be determined. Third, these costs must be assigned to the most appropriate products, distribution channels, and customers. As in all types of MACS, it is only when managers and employees become aware of how the activities in which they engage generate environmental costs that they can control and reduce them.

Environmental costs fall into two categories, explicit and implicit. Explicit costs

EXHIBIT 9-8

Bristol-Myers Squibb (Environment 2000 — Product Life Cycle)

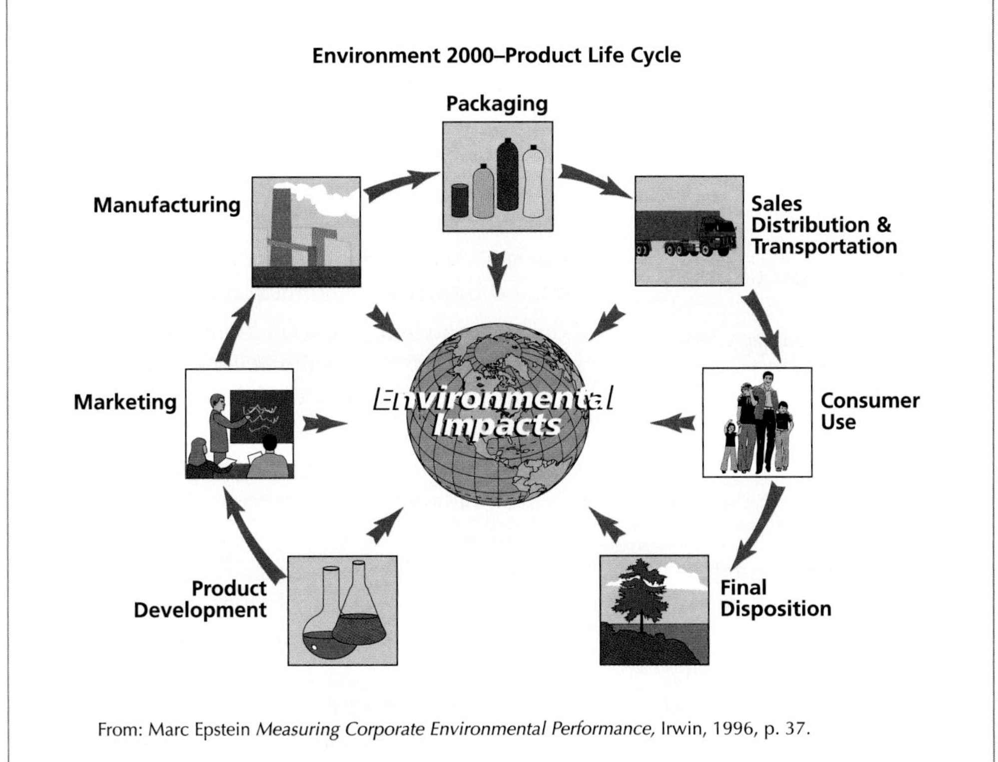

From: Marc Epstein *Measuring Corporate Environmental Performance,* Irwin, 1996, p. 37.

include the direct costs of modifying technology and processes, costs of cleanup and disposal, costs of permits to operate a facility, fines levied by government agencies, and litigation fees. Implicit costs are often more closely tied to the infrastructure required to monitor environmental issues. These costs are usually administration and legal counsel, employee education and awareness, and the loss of goodwill if environmental disasters occur.

Bristol-Myers Squibb has been a leader in environmental, health, and safety (EHS) issues; it launched a firm-wide pollution prevention program in 1992.[17] The program included Product Life Cycle Review teams who identified and reduced any negative environmental health and safety problems in all phases of their products' life cycles (from RD&E through final disposal) (see Exhibit 9-8). In 1997 after five intensive years of study, the teams reached their company goal. The teams also were able to identify potential savings of over $6.5 million in product and process improvements.[18]

Benchmarking[19]

In the opening vignette, Nathaniel Young wanted to change his antiquated MACS to one that would generate relevant information over the entire value chain of his organization. He investigated what other organizations had done to change their MACS.

[17] For more discussion of the issues, see Marc J. Epstein, *Measuring Corporate Environmental Performance,* Chicago: Irwin Professional Publishing, 1996

[18] This information was obtained from the Bristol-Myers Squibb website (www.bristol-meyers.com).

[19] This section is based on research by D. Elnathan, T. Lin, and S. M. Young, "Benchmarking and Management Accounting: A Framework for Research," *Journal of Management Accounting Research,* 1996.

IN PRACTICE

Union Carbide Corporation's Responsible Care Policy

Union Carbide's commitment to health, safety and environmental (HSE) excellence is found in our Responsible Care policy, which has been integrated into our business strategy and HSE management systems:

Union Carbide will conduct its business responsibly and in a manner designed to protect the health and safety of its employees, its customers and the public, and to protect the environment. The company will continue to be a leader within the chemical industry in operational safety performance and in avoidance of injuries, illnesses, accidental releases and incidents.

Programs will be implemented and maintained that provide reasonable assurance that the corporation:

- Complies with all applicable governmental and internal health, safety and environmental requirements.
- Operates plants and facilities in a manner that protects the environment and the health and safety of its employees and the public.
- Develops and produces products that can be manufactured, transported, used and disposed of safely.
- Recognizes and responds to community concerns about chemicals and our operations.
- Makes health, safety and environmental considerations a priority in planning for all existing and new products and processes.
- Reports promptly to officials, employees, customers, and the public information on health or environmental hazards, and recommends protective measures.
- Counsels customers on the safe use, transportation and disposal of chemical products.
- Extends knowledge by conducting or supporting research on the health, safety and environmental effects of products, processes and waste materials.
- Works with others to resolve problems created by past handling and disposal of hazardous substances.
- Participates with government and others to create responsible laws, regulations and standards to safeguard the community, workplace and environment.
- Promotes the principles and practices of Responsible Care by sharing experiences and offering assistance to others who produce, handle, use, transport or dispose of chemicals.

Source: Reprinted by permission of Union Carbide from *1999 Responsible Care Progress Report* found at www.unioncarbide.com.

His research and discussion with another local firm provided him with much information, as discussed next.

Organizations interested in a new management accounting method usually choose one of three ways to learn about and adopt a method.

1. The first is to bring in outside consultants to implement a particular method. Outside consultants can be effective, but costly.
2. A second approach is for organizational members to develop their own systems internally with little or no assistance from outside consultants. Although this approach can be satisfying, it can be highly costly and time consuming, especially if the organization fails in its first few attempts at change.
3. The third approach, known as benchmarking, which we discussed briefly in Chapter 2, requires that organizational members first understand their current operations and approaches to conducting business and then look to the best practices of other organizations for guidance on improving.

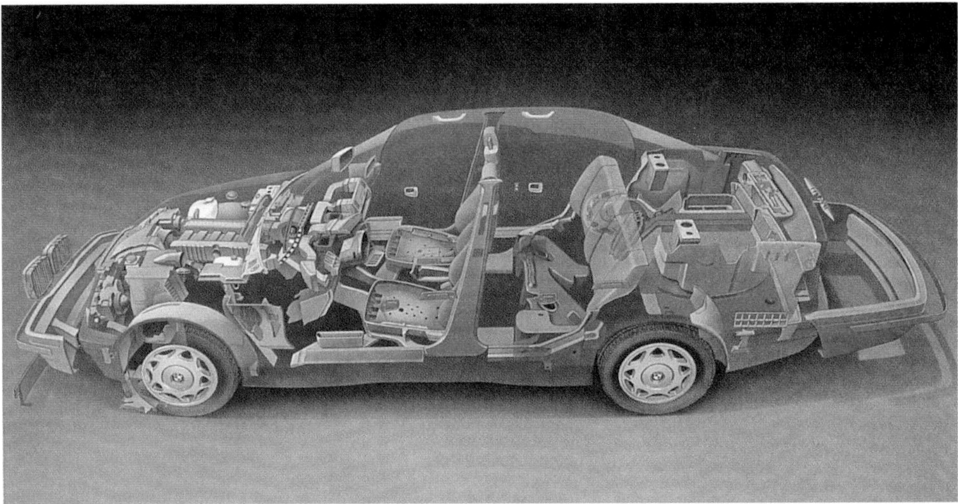

▶ BMW uses parts made of recycled plastics (blue) and those parts that can be recycled (green). So-called green manufacturing and potential legislation for companies to take back used components illustrates decision making based on the total-life-cycle costing concept. Companies can reuse, refurbish, or dispose of a product's components safely and reduce total-life-cycle product costs. (BMW Corporation)

Benchmarking is a way for organizations to gather information regarding the *best practices* of others. It is often highly cost effective, as organizations can save time and money by avoiding the mistakes that other companies have made or by not reinventing a process or method that other companies have already developed and tested. Thus, selecting appropriate benchmarking partners (discussed below) is a critical aspect of the process. The benchmarking process typically consists of five stages that include several organizational/diagnostic, operational, and informational factors. We present each stage below by listing its key factors. Exhibit 9-9 depicts the benchmarking process.

Benchmarking
The process of studying and adapting the best practices of other organizations to improve the firm's own performance and establish a point of reference by which other internal performance can be measured.

STAGE 1: INTERNAL STUDY AND PRELIMINARY COMPETITIVE ANALYSES

In this stage, the organization decides which key areas to benchmark for study, for example, the company's activities, products, or management accounting methods. Then the company determines how it currently performs on these dimensions by initiating both preliminary internal competitive analysis using internal company data and preliminary external competitive analyses using, for example, industry comparisons of quality from publications such as *Consumer Reports* or *J. D. Powers and Associates Reports*. Both types of analyses will determine the scope and significance of the study for each area. Another key factor to remember is that these analyses are not limited only to companies in a single industry. So for example, although Nathaniel Young works in the chemical industry, he could do competitive analyses in any type of organization.

STAGE 2: DEVELOPING LONG-TERM COMMITMENT TO THE BENCHMARKING PROJECT AND COALESCING THE BENCHMARKING TEAM

In this stage, the organization must develop its commitment to the benchmarking project and coalesce a benchmarking team. Because significant organizational change, such as adopting a total-life-cycle costing approach, can take several years,

EXHIBIT 9-9

Stages of the Benchmarking Process

STAGES OF THE BENCHMARKING PROCESS	FACTORS TO CONSIDER
Stage 1: Internal Study and Preliminary Competitive Analyses	Preliminary internal and external competitive analyses Determine key areas for study Determine scope and significance of the study
Stage 2: Developing Long-Term Commitment to the Benchmarking Project and Coalescing the Benchmarking Team	*Developing Long-Term Commitment to the Benchmarking Project:* Gain senior management support Develop a clear set of objectives Empower employees to make change *Coalescing the Benchmarking Team:* Use an experienced coordinator Train employees
Stage 3: Identifying Benchmarking Partners	Size of partners Number of partners Relative position within and across industries Degree of trust among partners
Stage 4: Information Gathering and Sharing Methods	*Type of Benchmarking Information:* Product Functional (process) Strategic (includes management accounting methods) *Method of Information Collection:* Unilateral Cooperative: Database Indirect/third party Group Determine performance measures Determine the benchmarking performance gap in relation to performance measures
Stage 5: Taking Action to Meet or Exceed the Benchmark	Comparisons of performance measures are made

the level of commitment to benchmarking has to be long term rather than short term. Long-term commitment requires (1) obtaining the support of senior management to give the benchmarking team the authority to spearhead the changes, (2) developing a clear set of objectives to guide the benchmarking effort, and (3) empowering employees to make change.

The benchmarking team should include individuals from all functional areas in the organization. Developing a target costing system, for example, would benefit from a total-life-cycle costing perspective, which requires employees from many functional areas. An experienced coordinator is usually necessary to organize the members' team and develop training in benchmarking methods. Lack of training often will lead to the failure of the implementation.

STAGE 3: IDENTIFYING BENCHMARKING PARTNERS

The third stage of benchmarking includes identification of partners—willing participants who know the process. Some critical factors are as follows:

1. size of the partners
2. number of partners
3. relative position of the partners within and across industries
4. degree of trust among partners

Size. The size of the benchmarking partner will depend on the specific activity or method being benchmarked. For example, if an organization wants to understand how a huge organization with several divisions coordinates its suppliers, then the organization would probably seek another organization of similar size for benchmarking. However, size is not always an important factor. For instance, DaimlerChrysler Corporation, a huge corporation, studied L.L. Bean's warehousing method of flowcharting

IN PRACTICE

Benchmarking Speed to Market of Automobile Manufacturers

Benchmarking can take many forms. As the data below illustrate, there is wide variation in the time it takes Japanese and U.S. automobile manufacturers to move from concept approval to the manufacturing of a vehicle. Decreasing the time for development is a critical goal for automobile manufacturers worldwide, since faster development times reduce costs and help manufacturers respond to customer preferences quickly. The data below can be used as a first step to begin the benchmarking process. For example, armed with this information, a competitor may approach Chrysler Corporation to find out how it is able to bring automobiles from concept approval to production in 29 months. The specific approach used to gather the information varies with the kind of relationship that one firm has developed with another.

Source: V. Reitman and R. L. Simison, "Japanese Car Makers Speed Up Car Making," *Wall Street Journal,* December 29, 1995, pp. B1, B5.

QUICKER CARS

Time it takes to develop new vehicle from concept approval to production

AUTO MAKER	CURRENT AVERAGE (MONTHS)	GOAL (MONTHS)	RECORD TIME (MODEL)
Mazda	21	15–18	17 months (Capella)
Toyota	27*	18*	15 months (Ipsum, Starlet)
Mitsubishi	24	18	19 months (FTO)
Nissan	30	20	Not available
Honda	36*	24*	24 months* (CR-V)
Chrysler Corp.	29	24	24 months (Sebring)
Ford	37	24	18 months (European Escort restyling)
GM	46	38	26 months (Yukon, Tahoe)

Source: Auto makers

*Includes design time before concept approval

wasted motion. As a result, Chrysler implemented a method that led to significant changes in the ways that its workers were involved in organizational problem solving.

Number. Initially, it is useful for an organization to consider a wide array of benchmarking partners. However, organizations must be aware that as the number of partners increases, so do issues of coordination, timeliness, and concern over proprietary information disclosure. Researchers argue that today's changing business environment is likely to encourage firms to have a larger number of participants, because increased competition and technological progress in information processing increases benchmarking benefits relative to costs.

Relative Position within and across Industries. Another factor is the relative position of the organization within an industry. In many cases, industry newcomers and those whose performance on leading indicators has declined are more likely to seek a wider variety of benchmarking partners than those who are established industry leaders. Those who are industry leaders may benchmark because of their commitment to continuous improvement.

Degree of Trust. From the benchmarking organization's point of view, developing trust among partners is critical to obtaining truthful and timely information. Most organizations, including industry leaders, operate on a quid pro quo basis, with the understanding that both organizations will obtain information they can use.

STAGE 4: INFORMATION GATHERING AND SHARING METHODS

Two dimensions relating to information gathering and sharing emerge from the literature:

1. type of information that benchmarking organizations collect
2. methods of information collection

Type of Information. There are three broad classes of information on which firms interested in benchmarking can focus. *Product benchmarking* is the long-standing practice of carefully examining other organizations' products. *Functional (process) benchmarking* is the study of other organizations' practices and costs with respect to functions or processes, such as assembly or distribution. *Strategic benchmarking* is the study of other organizations' strategies and strategic decisions, such as why organizations choose one particular strategy over another. Since management accounting methods have become an integral part of many organizations' strategies, benchmarking of these methods would occur as part of the management accounting function.

Unilateral (covert) benchmarking
A process in which companies independently gather information about one or several other companies that excel in the area of interest.

Cooperative benchmarking
The voluntary sharing of information through mutual agreements.

Database benchmarking
A policy in which companies usually pay a fee and in return gain access to information from a database operator.

Methods of Gathering Information. Management accountants play a key role in gathering and summarizing information used for benchmarking. There are two major methods of information collection for benchmarking. The most common can be described as **unilateral (covert) benchmarking,** in which companies independently gather information about one or several other companies that excel in the area of interest. Unilateral benchmarking relies on data that companies can obtain from industry trade associations or clearinghouses of information. A second method is **cooperative benchmarking,** which is the voluntary sharing of information through mutual agreements. The major advantage of cooperative benchmarking is that information sharing occurs both within and across industries. Cooperative benchmarking has three subcategories: database, indirect/third party, and group.

Companies that use **database benchmarking** typically pay a fee and in return gain access to information from a database operator. The database operator collects and edits the information prior to making it available to users. In most cases, there is no direct contact with other firms, and the identity of the source of the data often is not revealed. The database method has the advantage of including a large amount of information in one place; however, insights regarding what the data mean for the firm and how to use the information often are not available.

Indirect/third-party benchmarking uses an outside consultant to act as a liaison among firms engaged in benchmarking. The consultant supplies information from one party to the others and handles all communications. Often the consultant participates in the selection of partners. Since the members may be competitors, they pass information through a consultant so that members remain anonymous. This approach requires that the sources of the information remain confidential.

Indirect/third-party benchmarking
A technique that uses an outside consultant to act as a liaison among firms engaged in benchmarking.

Participants using **group benchmarking** meet openly to discuss their methods. They coordinate their efforts, define common terminology, visit each other's sites, and generally have a long-run association. Typically, firms that engage in cooperative benchmarking abide by a code of conduct that they agree upon prior to the study. As in most interactions, direct contact offers the opportunity for better understanding of the other parties involved and usually is the most effective benchmarking method. This method also is the most costly to implement; therefore, firms must evaluate the cost-benefit tradeoffs.

Group benchmarking
A business alternative in which participants meet openly to discuss their methods.

After the information-gathering process is complete, the participants conducting the benchmarking study determine a **benchmarking (performance) gap** by comparing their organization's own performance with the best performance that emerges from the data. The performance gap is defined by specific performance measures on which the firm would like to improve. Performance measures may include reduced defectives, faster on-time delivery, increased functionality, or reduced life-cycle product costs. Other, more qualitative, measures may include better employee decisions concerning ways to work or solve problems, increased motivation and satisfaction, and improved cooperation and coordination among workgroups and employees.

Benchmarking (performance) gap
The specific performance measure on which a firm would like to improve.

Financial gains such as reduced product costs usually occur as a result of addressing the relevant nonfinancial measures involved. Since most financial gains may take a significant amount of time to be felt, organizations should monitor the nonfinancial variables in the short term. Simply judging the effects of a benchmarking effort in the short term based on financial indicators may lead to premature abandonment of what has been learned during the benchmarking project.

STAGE 5: TAKING ACTION TO MEET OR EXCEED THE BENCHMARK

In the final stage, the organization takes action and begins to change as a result of the benchmarking initiative. After implementing the change, the organization makes comparisons to the specific performance measures selected. In many cases, the decision may be to perform better than the benchmark to be more competitive. The implementation stage, in particular the change process, is perhaps the most difficult stage of the benchmarking process, as the buy-in of organizational members is critical for success. We discuss this issue more fully in chapter 10.

SUMMARY

This chapter is the first of two on management accounting and control system design for strategic purposes. Management accounting and control systems encompass many of the performance measure systems in an organization including its cost management system. The concept of control refers to the set of procedures, tools, performance measures, and systems that organizations use to guide and motivate all employees to achieve organizational objectives. We also identify the technical characteristics of well-designed management accounting and control systems, which include two categories—the relevance of the information and the scope of the system. Four characteristics, accuracy, timeliness, consistency, and flexibility, measure the relevance of the information over the organization's entire value chain.

We also present the total-life-cycle costing concept as a method that accumulates product costs over the entire value chain. In today's business environment, managing cost and other performance variables over the entire value chain has become of paramount importance to competing. Three methods relating to total-life-cycle costing include target costing, Kaizen costing, and environmental costing. Target costing and environmental costing begin in the RD&E stage of the value chain. Using these methods provides organizations with the ability to control and reduce costs at all other stages of the value chain. Kaizen costing is an approach that can be used during the manufacturing process. It enables organizations to make small improvements in products during the production stage. The chapter concludes with a discussion of how managers can use benchmarking to aid them in understanding the best practices of others, and ultimately how to apply what they learn to their own organizations.

KEY TERMS

Benchmarking, 383
Benchmarking (performance) gap, 387
Committed costs, 371
Control, 366
Cooperative benchmarking, 386
Database benchmarking, 386
Environmental costing, 380
Group benchmarking, 387
In control, 367
Indirect/third-party benchmarking, 387
Kaizen costing, 378
Management accounting and control system (MACS), 366
Manufacturing cycle, 371
Out of control, 367
Post-sale service and disposal cycle, 371
Relevance of information, 368
Research development and engineering (RD&E) cycle, 371
Scope of a MACS, 368
Supply chain management, 376
Target cost (C_{tc}), 375
Target costing, 373
Total-life-cycle costing (TLCC), 370
Unilateral (covert) benchmarking, 386
Value engineering, 375

ASSIGNMENT MATERIALS

QUESTIONS

9-1 What does "control" refer to in the context of a management accounting and control system? (LO 1)

9-2 What are the five steps involved in keeping an organization in control? (LO 1)

9-3 What two broad technical considerations must designers of management and control systems address? (LO 2)

9-4 What four components should management accounting and control systems designers consider when addressing the relevancy of the system's information? (LO 2)

9-5 What is the total-life-cycle costing approach? Why is it important? (LO 3)

9-6 What are the three major cycles of the total-life-cycle costing approach in a manufacturing situation? (LO 3)

9-7 What is the difference between committed costs and incurred costs? (LO 3)

9-8 What are the three stages of the research development and engineering cycle? (LO 3)

9-9 What is the post-sale service and disposal cycle? (LO 3)

9-10 What is target costing? (LO 4)

9-11 What are the two essential elements needed to arrive at a target cost? (LO 4)

9-12 What is value engineering? (LO 4)

9-13 In which stage of the total life cycle of a product is target costing most applicable? (LO 4)

9-14 What roles do cross-functional teams and supply chain management play in target costing? (LO 4)

9-15 What is Kaizen costing? (LO 5)

9-16 When is a cost-variance investigation undertaken under Kaizen costing? (LO 5)

9-17 Why is it said that a Kaizen costing system operates "outside of the standard costing system"? (LO 5)

9-18 What are some examples of explicit and implicit environmental costs? (LO 6)

9-19 What is benchmarking and why is it used? (LO 7)

9-20 What are the five stages of the benchmarking process? (LO 7)

9-21 What are the three broad classes of information on which firms interested in benchmarking can focus? Describe each. (LO 7)

9-22 What stage of the benchmarking process is the most important for benchmarking management accounting methods? Why? (LO 7)

9-23 What are the two general methods of information gathering and sharing when undertaking a benchmarking exercise? (LO 7)

9-24 What are the three types of sharing and gathering information under the cooperative form of benchmarking? (LO 7)

9-25 What is a benchmarking (performance) gap? (LO 7)

EXERCISES

9-26 ***Achieving objectives*** Eni Corporation's mission statement includes the following: "Our mission is to continuously improve the company's value to shareholders, customers, employees, and society." Interpret how each of Eni Corporation's stakeholder groups may interpret "the company's value" in the mission statement and, given each group's interpretation, how it may be measured for each group. LO 1

9-27 ***Achieving relevancy in MACS design*** Identify the four components that MACS designers should consider when addressing the relevancy of the system's information, and explain why each component is important. LO 2

9-28 ***Total life cycle in service firm*** Refer to the In Practice entitled "Aligning IT with the Value Chain in Financial Services" on p. 370. Explain how information technology personnel can play an important role in the total life cycle of products or services that financial services firms offer. LO 3

9-29 ***Total-life-cycle costing*** Explain how the total-life-cycle costing approach differs from traditional product costing. LO 3

9-30 ***Benefits of total-life-cycle costing*** Explain the benefits of using a total-life-cycle costing approach to product costing. LO 3

9-31 ***Problems with traditional accounting focus*** What is the traditional accounting focus in managing costs over the total life cycle of a product? What is the problem with this focus? LO 3

9-32 ***Costs committed versus costs incurred*** Review Exhibit 9-2 showing the relationship between committed costs and incurred costs over the total life cycle of a product. Explain what the diagram means and what the implications are for managing costs. LO 3

9-33 ***Post-sale and disposal cycle*** When does the disposal phase of the post-sale and disposal cycle of a product begin and end? LO 3

9-34 ***Target costing*** Explain how target costing differs from traditional cost-reduction methods. LO 4

9-35 ***Target costing equation*** Express the target costing relationship in equation form. How does this equation differ from the other two types of traditional equations relating to cost reduction? Why is this significant? LO 4

LO 4 **9-36** ***Value engineering*** What is the relationship between value engineering and target costing?

LO 4 **9-37** ***Target costing profitability measure*** What is the most widely used profitability measure to develop the target profit margin under target costing?

LO 4 **9-38** ***Implementing target costing*** What are potential problems in implementing a target costing system from a behavioral point of view?

LO 5 **9-39** ***Kaizen versus standard costing*** What factors differentiate Kaizen costing from standard costing?

LO 5 **9-40** ***Target costing versus Kaizen costing*** What is the major difference between target costing and Kaizen costing?

LO 5 **9-41** ***Kaizen costing: knowledge*** According to the Kaizen costing approach, who has the best knowledge to reduce costs? Why is this so?

LO 5 **9-42** ***Kaizen meaning*** What do the terms "Kaizen" and "Kaizen costing" mean? In which stage of the total life cycle of a product is Kaizen costing most applicable? Why?

LO 5 **9-43** ***Kaizen costing*** Under what condition will the cost savings due to Kaizen costing not be applied to production?

LO 6 **9-44** ***Activity-based costing for environmental costs*** How can a firm use activity-based costing to help control and reduce environmental costs?

LO 7 **9-45** ***Benchmarking partners*** What are the key factors in identifying benchmarking partners? Explain why these factors are important.

LO 7 **9-46** ***Benchmarking a target costing system*** As a manager asked to benchmark another organization's target costing system, on what factors would you gather information? Why?

PROBLEMS

LO 3 **9-47** ***Total-life-cycle costing*** Consider the following situation: Your manager comes to you and says, "I don't understand why everyone is talking about the total-life-cycle costing approach to product costing. As far as I am concerned this new approach is a waste of time and energy. I think we should just stick to what we know and that is the traditional approach to product costing."

REQUIRED

Write a memorandum critiquing your manager's view. In the memo, discuss the benefits of adopting the total-life-cycle costing approach.

LO 3 **9-48** ***Total-life-cycle costing versus traditional methods*** Deron Grimes is a traditional manufacturing manager who is only concerned with managing costs over the manufacturing cycle of the product. Arguing that since traditional accounting methods are focused on this cycle, he should not bother with the RD&E cycle because it is separate from his area of manufacturing.

REQUIRED

Write an essay discussing Deron's views. What types of structural and functional changes in organizations may be necessary to help Deron overcome his traditional view?

LO 4 **9-49** ***Target costing: unit cost*** Calcutron Company is contemplating introducing a new type of calculator to complement its existing line of scientific calculators. The target price of the calculator is $75; annual sales volume of the new calculator is expected to be 500,000 units. Calcutron has a 15% return-on-sales target.

REQUIRED

Compute the unit target cost per calculator.

9-50 ***Target costing: return on sales*** Stacy Yoo, president of Caremore, Inc., an appliance manufacturer in Seattle, Washington, has been trying to decide whether one of her product line managers, Bill Mann, has been achieving the company-wide return-on-sales target of 45%. Stacy has just received data from the new target costing system regarding Bill's operation. Bill's sales volume was 300,000 appliances with an average selling price of $500 and expenses totaling $90 million. LO 4

REQUIRED

Determine whether Bill's return-on-sales ratio has met the company-wide target. Has Bill done a good or a poor job? Explain.

9-51 ***Target costing: implementation issues*** Pierre LeBlanc, manager of Centaur Corporation, is thinking about implementing a target costing system in his organization. Several managers have taken him aside and have expressed concerns about implementing target costing in their organization. LO 4

REQUIRED

As an expert in target costing, you have been called in to discuss these concerns and offer advice on overcoming them. Write a memorandum discussing common concerns that managers have about target costing. In the memo, state how you would remedy these concerns.

9-52 ***Traditional cost reduction versus target costing*** Traditional cost reduction in the United States differs significantly from the Japanese method of target costing. LO 4

REQUIRED

Discuss the similarities and differences in the process by which cost reduction under both systems occurs. Be specific in your answer.

9-53 ***Kaizen costing: behavior issues*** Kaizen costing is a method that many Japanese companies have found effective in reducing costs. LO 5

REQUIRED

From a behavioral point of view, answer these questions:

(a) What are the biggest problems in using Kaizen costing?

(b) How can managers overcome these problems?

9-54 ***Benchmarking*** As a manager interested in learning more about target costing, you are contemplating three approaches to obtaining the best information possible. The first is to bring in an outside consultant; the second is to develop your own system inside your organization with little to no outside assistance; and the third is to engage in a benchmarking project with several other firms. LO 4, 7

REQUIRED

Critique each of these approaches, discussing their pros and cons. On what basis will you select your approach to learning about target costing? Explain.

9-55 ***Target costing versus transitional cost-reduction methods*** According to the chapter, the target costing and traditional cost-reduction methods approach the relationships among cost, selling price, and profit margin quite differently. LO 4

REQUIRED

Write an essay that illustrates how the target costing and traditional cost-reduction methods differ, using the appropriate symbols and equations. In addition to the equations, describe how the processes differ in deriving costs.

LO 4 **9-56** ***Target costing and service organization*** Imagine that you are the manager of a large bank. Having heard about a management accounting method called target costing, you are wondering whether it can be applied to the banking industry. In particular, you are trying to determine how to benchmark other organizations to gain more information.

REQUIRED

(a) Can target costing be applied to the banking industry? To what products or services can target costing be applied?

(b) Devise a benchmarking plan for the bank. Your plan should include which banks to benchmark with and the kinds of information sought.

LO 5 **9-57** ***Standard costing versus Kaizen costing*** Many companies are interested in adopting a Kaizen costing approach to reducing costs. However, they are not sure how their current standard costing system will fit with the Kaizen costing approach.

REQUIRED

How do the standard costing system and the Kaizen costing system differ? Can the two systems coexist? Explain.

LO 5 **9-58** ***Kaizen costing versus standard costing*** Your organization, located in Worthington, Ohio, is contemplating introducing Kaizen costing to help with cost reduction. As someone who has an understanding of management accounting, you have been asked for your opinion. Specifically, some of your colleagues are wondering about the differences between standard costing and Kaizen costing.

REQUIRED

Write a report discussing the following:

(a) the similarities and differences between standard costing and Kaizen costing

(b) under what conditions Kaizen costing can be adapted to U.S. organizations

LO 7 **9-59** ***Benchmarking: field exercise with other students*** Assume that you are an average student who has a desire to be one of the best students in class. Your professor suggests that you benchmark the working habits of the best student in the class. You are somewhat skeptical but decide to take on the challenge.

REQUIRED

How would you go about this benchmarking exercise? In answering this question, describe the process that you would undertake in benchmarking the best student, the factors that you would be trying to study, and how you would implement changes to your working habits.

LO 7 **9-60** ***Benchmarking: field exercise in a company*** Benchmarking a product, process, or management accounting method takes a great deal of time and effort. Companies have many choices when it comes to conducting a benchmarking study. For example, in following the five stages of the benchmarking process, companies have to decide on how to proceed, who to select as benchmarking partners, and what information they are willing to share and to gather.

REQUIRED

Locate a company in your local community that has engaged in a benchmarking study. Try to arrange a visit to the company (perhaps through your professor, relative, or friend) in order to talk to employees who have been involved in the benchmarking effort. Using the five-stage process, critique the approach that this company followed. What are the similarities and differences between what this company did and the process described in this chapter? Be specific about the procedures that were used and the variables that were assessed. Finally, what were the results of the benchmarking exercise at this company? Was it a success or a failure? Why?

CASES

9-61 ***Environmental costs, activity-based costing, Kaizen costing*** Evans Co. makes two products, product X and product Y. Evans has produced product X for many years without generating any hazardous wastes. Recently, Evans developed product Y, which is superior to product X in many respects. However, production of product Y generates a hazardous waste. Because of the hazardous wastes, Evans now must deal with hazardous waste disposal, governmental environmental reports and inspections, and safe handling procedures. LO 5, 6

Evans Co. uses a plant-wide rate based on machine hours to assign manufacturing support costs to its two products. Because of concerns about the accuracy of the product costing system, Kim Briggs, the controller, undertook an activity-based costing analysis of the manufacturing support costs. The resulting cost information is summarized in the following table.

	PRODUCT X	PRODUCT Y
Direct costs (material plus labor)	$ 9,000,000	$ 4,000,000
Unit-level support	$ 2,000,000	$ 1,000,000
Batch-level support	$15,000,000	$20,000,000
Product-level support	$ 5,000,000	$20,000,000
Business-sustaining costs	$ 1,000,000	$ 2,000,000
Total machine hours	10,000,000	6,000,000
Number of units	100,000,000	40,000,000

REQUIRED

(a) Compute product costs for products X and Y using a plant-wide rate based on machine hours for manufacturing support costs.

(b) Compute product costs for products X and Y using the activity-based costing figures provided in the table.

(c) Explain the reasons for the differences in cost for each product using the two cost systems. (You may wish to compute unit-level support, batch-level support, product-level support, and business-sustaining costs per unit.)

(d) Evans has been selling products X and Y at a price equal to 1.5 times the product cost computed using the plant-wide rate for manufacturing support costs. Compute these prices and provide recommendations to Evans management concerning profit improvement through pricing changes and cost reduction through manufacturing improvements.

9-62 ***Explicit and implicit environmental costs*** Refer to Case 6-59, which describes Kwik Clean's environmental costs. LO 6

REQUIRED

(a) Identify explicit and implicit environmental costs that Pat Polley has listed.

(b) Are there other environmental costs that Polley should identify?

(c) Prepare a memo to Polly explaining how an activity-based costing approach can help her to control and reduce Kwik Clean's environmental costs.

chapter 10

Motivating Behavior in Management Accounting and Control Systems

AFTER READING THIS CHAPTER, YOU WILL BE ABLE TO

1. discuss the four key behavioral considerations in MACS design
2. explain the human resources model of management
3. discuss task and results control systems
4. apply the ethical control framework to decisions
5. understand the balanced scorecard and its applications
6. discuss the links between different incentive systems and performance

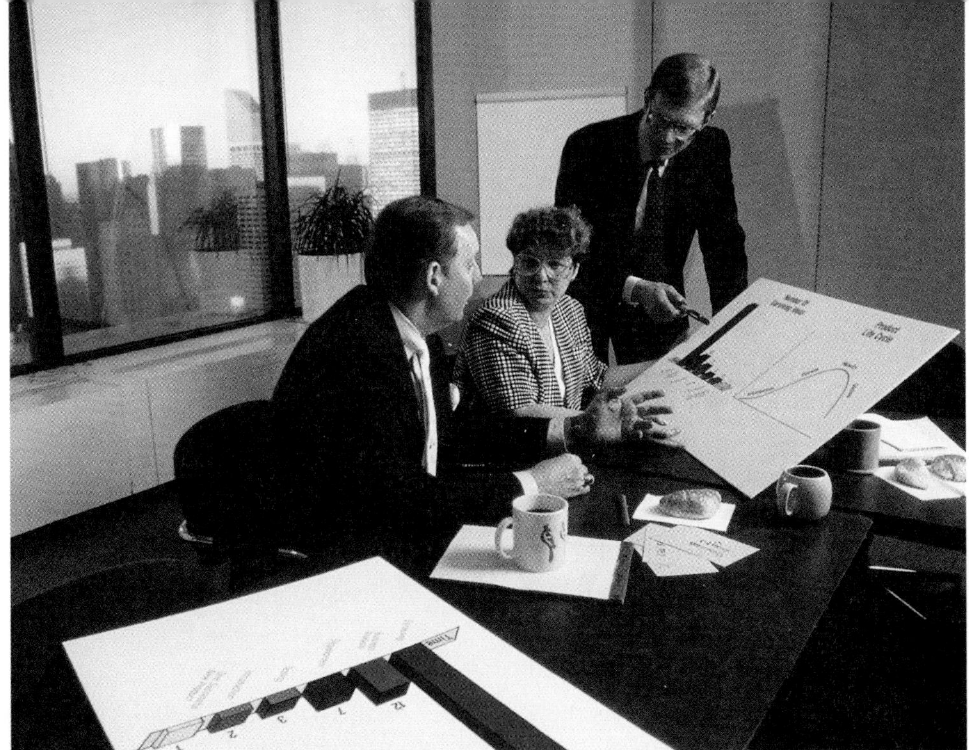

These employees are discussing various aspects of their organization's performance in comparison to their initial plans. (Richard Pasley/Stock, Boston)

CHEMCO INTERNATIONAL—BEHAVIORAL CONSIDERATIONS

As we saw in Chapter 9, Nathaniel Young has been developing the technical side of the new management accounting and control system (MACS) that he plans to implement. At a management briefing, a senior vice president mentioned to him that several managers and their employees were expressing concerns about the proposed changes to the MACS. They wanted to know how the system was designed, whether their performance would be assessed differently, and whether their compensation plans would be altered. They also were uncertain about how the new MACS would alter the organizational work culture.

As he was listening to the discussion, Nathaniel realized that he had committed a major error in his approach—he had not involved enough key people in system design. There were several goals he wanted to achieve with the new MACS. First, he wanted to design a system whose operation on a day-to-day basis was consistent with the company's ethical and cultural norms of behavior. Second, because the previous system had relied myopically on narrow, short-term financial goals, he wanted to encourage broader thinking for all employees through the use of multiple performance measures. In particular, he wanted to encourage a work environment that fostered creativity. Third, and this is where he had really faltered, he wanted to make sure that people were motivated to work at the company. To this end, he had thought about various types of compensation systems to reward superior performance, but he had not considered asking more employees to participate in overall system design. Was it too late to involve them and get their valuable input?

Management Accounting and Control Systems

In Chapter 9 we discussed the technical characteristics of a well-designed management accounting and control system (MACS) and illustrated how these characteristics increase the organization's ability to adapt its measurement systems to changing information needs. However, because human interests and **motivation** can vary significantly, a major role for control systems is to motivate behavior congruent with the desires of the organization.

Motivation
An individual's interest or drive to act in a certain manner.

In this chapter, we turn to the second set of characteristics related to MACS design. Recall that in Chapter 9 we enumerated four major behavioral considerations. These were:

1. embedding the organization's ethical code of conduct into MACS design,
2. using a mix of short- and long-term qualitative and quantitative performance measures (or the balanced scorecard approach),
3. empowering employees to be involved in decision making and MACS design, and
4. developing an appropriate incentive system to reward performance.

Nathaniel Young's dilemma at the beginning of this chapter highlights a key issue that plagues major companies. Although many managers want to do what is best for their companies, they often try to implement new systems without considering the behavioral implications and consequences of a MACS. Unless they pay careful attention to these factors, goal congruence may not occur, motivation could be low, and worst of all, employees may be encouraged to engage in dysfunctional behavior.

Note, however, that these four characteristics do not simply arise by accident in all MACS. Rather, companies whose MACS display these characteristics often subscribe to a particular world view of the role of management that we label the human resource management model of motivation. The development of this view is discussed next, followed by a detailed discussion of the four characteristics.

Scientific management school
A management movement with the underlying philosophy that most people find work objectionable, that people care little for making decisions or showing creativity on the job, and that money is the driving force behind performance.

THE HUMAN RESOURCE MANAGEMENT MODEL OF MOTIVATION

One of the earliest attempts at understanding the role of management, developed at the turn of the century, was the **scientific management school.** The underlying philosophy was that most people found work objectionable, that individuals cared little for making decisions or exercising creativity on the job, and that money was the driving force behind performance. Management believed that employees should follow highly detailed, prescribed procedures and that behavior should be monitored and controlled very carefully through time and motion studies.

Human relations movement
A managerial movement that recognizes that people have needs well beyond performing a simple repetitive task at work and that financial compensation is only one aspect of what workers desire.

The **human relations movement** was the next significant step in the development of managerial views on motivation. This movement recognized that people had needs that went well beyond performing a simple repetitive task at work and that financial compensation was only one aspect of what workers desired. Employees wanted respect, discretion over their jobs, and a feeling that they contributed something valuable to their organization. The human relations movement was the impetus for developing ways to improve morale and job satisfaction and the overall quality of working life.

Human resources model of motivation (HRMM)
A more contemporary managerial view that introduces a high level of employee responsibility for and participation in decisions in the work environment.

Perhaps the most contemporary management view of motivation is the **human resources model of motivation (HRMM).** Based on initiatives to improve the quality of working life, and the strong influence of Japanese management practices, the HRMM introduces a high level of employee responsibility for and participation in decisions in the work environment. The central assumptions of the HRMM are that people find work enjoyable and that they desire to participate in developing objectives, making decisions, and attaining goals in their work environment. Individuals are motivated both by financial and nonfinancial means of compensation. This model also assumes that employees have a great deal of knowledge and information about their jobs, the application of which will improve the way they perform tasks and benefit the organization as a whole. Individuals are thought to be highly creative, ethical, and responsible, and they desire opportunities to effect change in their organizations.

We use the human resource model as the basis for our presentation of the four behavioral considerations in MACS design. Next we discuss the organization's ethical code of conduct.

The Organization's Ethical Code of Conduct and MACS Design

A well-designed MACS should incorporate the principles of an organization's code of ethical conduct to guide and influence behavior and decision making. Ethics is a discipline that focuses on the investigation of standards of conduct and moral judgment. A MACS design that incorporates ethical principles can provide decision makers with guidance as they face ethical dilemmas.

Management accountants often play a significant role in MACS design. Their behavior and decision making are guided by the organization's code of ethical conduct and the ethical standards of their professional association, the Institute of Management Accountants (IMA). For instance, holders of the title, Certified Management Accountant (the certification granted by the IMA), are required to be competent and to always maintain confidentiality, integrity, and objectivity.

The ethical framework embedded in system design is extremely important, because it will influence the behavior of all users. The key user group—managers—interacts a great deal with the MACS. Often managers are subject to intense pressures from their job circumstances and from other influential organizational members to suspend their ethical judgment in certain situations. These pressures include the following:

1. requests to tailor information to favor particular individuals or groups
2. pleas to falsify reports or test results
3. solicitations for confidential information
4. pressures to ignore a questionable or unethical practice

To incorporate ethical principles into the design of a MACS and help managers deal effectively with the previous situations, system designers might attempt to ensure the following:

1. That the organization has formulated, implemented, and communicated to all employees a comprehensive code of ethics. This is often accomplished through the organization's beliefs system as discussed in Chapter 1.
2. That all employees understand the organization's code of ethics and the boundary systems that constrain behavior. Recall from Chapter 1 that boundary systems are designed to specify what actions are appropriate and those that must never be taken.
3. That a system, in which employees have confidence, exists to detect and report violations of the organization's code of ethics.

AVOIDING ETHICAL DILEMMAS

Most organizations attempt to address ethical considerations and avoid ethical dilemmas by developing a code of ethics. Although there is no universal hierarchy of ethical principles, these five categories capture the broad array of ethical considerations: legal rules, societal norms, professional memberships (Certified Management Accountants, etc.), organizational or group norms, and personal norms.

This hierarchy is listed in descending order of authority. For example, an action that is prohibited by law should be unacceptable by society, by one's profession, by the organization, and then by each individual. An action that is legally and socially acceptable, such as strategically underestimating product costs, may, however, be professionally unacceptable and, in turn, unacceptable to the organization and its employees. Unfortunately, any hierarchy of this sort has a number of gray areas, but nevertheless, it provides general guidelines for understanding and dealing with ethical problems that arise.

This ethical hierarchy provides a set of constraints on a decision. In this scheme, ethical conflicts occur when one system of values diverges from a more fundamental system. For example, suppose that the organization's code of ethics commits it to meeting only the letter of the law regarding disclosure of a product defect in one of its manufactured goods that could prove to be hazardous to consumers. However, a broader societal expectation is that organizations should be aggressive in identifying and disclosing potential product defects. An individual decision maker dealing with this situation may face an ethical conflict when the organizational code of ethics implies doing nothing about the defect, since there is no definitive evidence of a product problem. In such cases, broader societal expectations would imply that disclosure is necessary because there is persistent evidence of a problem.

DEALING WITH ETHICAL CONFLICTS

Organizations that formulate and support specific and unambiguous ethical codes can create an environment that will reduce ethical conflicts. One step in avoiding ambiguity or misunderstanding is to maintain a hierarchical ordering of authority, which means that the organization's stated code of ethics should not allow any behavior that is either legally or socially unacceptable. Because most professional codes of ethics reflect broad moral imperatives such as loyalty, discretion, and competence, an organization would create public relations problems for itself if its stated code of ethics conflicted with a professional code of ethics.

Another critical variable that can reduce ethical conflicts is the way that the chief executive and other senior managers behave and conduct business. If these individuals demonstrate exemplary behavior, other organizational members will have role models to emulate. Organizations whose leaders evince unethical behavior cannot expect their employees to behave according to high ethical standards.

In some cases, when organizations develop a formal code of ethics, they can create the potential for explicit ethical conflicts to arise with the code itself. The conflicts that appear most in practice are those between the law and the organization's code of ethics, between the organization's practiced code of ethics and common societal expectations, and between the individual's set of personal and professional ethics and the organization's practiced code of ethics. Any conflicts that remain relate primarily to personal values and norms of behavior that were acceptable prior to the adoption of the organization's new code of ethics but that are now in question.

CONFLICTS BETWEEN INDIVIDUAL AND ORGANIZATIONAL VALUES

People bring personal codes of ethics with them into an organization. If the organization's code of ethics is more stringent than an individual's code, conflicts may arise. But, if adherence to the organization's ethical code is required and enforced, it is possible to diminish ethical conflicts if, as part of the employment contract, the individual is asked and expected to pursue a more stringent code of ethics. Another

IN PRACTICE

Cheats on the Links Are Cheats at the Job

A survey by Hyatt Hotels and Resorts, Golf and the Business Executive, found that almost half of the 401 executives surveyed agreed that the way a person plays golf is very similar to how he or she conducts business affairs. The statistics were very telling: 55% of the surveyed executives admitted cheating at golf at least once, including moving the ball to get a better lie (41%), not counting a missed tap-in (19%), intentionally miscounting strokes (8%), and secretly pocketing a fresh ball while pretending to look for a lost ball in the woods (6%). One-third of the executives who admitted cheating also admitted to pulling fast ones on the job.

Source: M. Quinn, "It's All in the Lie," *Time,* July 26, 1993, p. 54.

possible, and probably more desirable, outcome is that individuals may raise their own ethical standards without conflict.

Difficult issues may arise when the individual's personal code of ethics prohibits certain types of behavior that are legal, socially acceptable, professionally acceptable, and acceptable to the organization. Potential for conflicts in such situations will arise when the action that is unacceptable to the individual is desirable to the organization. As an example, an employee may have deep religious objections to conducting business in any form on a holy day. Working for an organization may require that the person, under these circumstances, do things that he or she finds unacceptable. In this case, the individual is confronted with a personal choice. Unfortunately, the employee may have little institutional support in this situation, but can lobby within or outside the organization to prohibit working on a holy day. This tactic may be effective, or the affected employee may choose not to work for that organization depending on what he or she values most.

CONFLICTS BETWEEN THE ORGANIZATION'S STATED AND PRACTICED VALUES

In some cases, employees will observe management or even senior management engaged in unethical behavior such as management fraud. This type of conflict is the most difficult because the organization is misrepresenting its ethical system, which forces the employee to make a choice between going public with the information or keeping it quiet. In this setting, the employee is in a position of drawing attention to the problem by being a whistle-blower, which many have found to be a lonely and unenviable position. In many instances, though, whistle-blowers have chosen personal integrity over their loyalty to the organization.

Experts who have studied this problem advise that the individual should first ensure that the facts are correct and that a conflict does exist between the organization's stated ethical policy and the actions of its employees in practice. Second, by speaking with superiors, the individual should determine whether this conflict is institutional or whether it reflects the decisions and actions of only a small minority of employees. Faced with a true conflict, the individual has several choices, including:

1. Point out the discrepancy to a superior and refuse to act unethically. This may lead to dismissal, the need to resign from the organization, or the experience of suffering hidden organization sanctions.

2. Point out the discrepancy to a superior and act unethically. The rationale for this choice, which is incorrect, is that the employee believes this affords protection from legal sanctions.
3. Take the discrepancy to a mediator in the organization, if one exists.
4. Work with respected leaders in the organization to change the discrepancy between practiced and stated ethics.
5. Go outside the organization to publicly resolve the issue.
6. Go outside the organization anonymously to resolve the issue.
7. Resign and go public to resolve the issue.
8. Resign and remain silent.
9. Do nothing, and hope that the problem will dissolve.

Although most experts recommend following alternative 4 on this list, it is beyond the scope of this chapter to discuss the efficacy of any of these alternatives other than to mention that there are circumstances that can make any of them appropriate. If the organization is serious about its stated code of ethics, it should have an effective ethics control system to ensure and provide evidence that the organization's stated and practiced ethics are the same. Part of this control system should include a means for employees to point out inconsistencies between stated practices and ethics without fear of retribution. For example, some organizations rely on an ombudsman, and others rely on the internal audit function or an external auditor. Any organization that does not provide a system to protect employees in these situations either is not taking its code of ethics seriously or has an inadequate ethics control system.

THE ELEMENTS OF AN EFFECTIVE ETHICAL CONTROL SYSTEM

Ethical control system
A management control system based on ethics used to promote ethical decision making.

To promote ethical decision making, management should implement an **ethical control system.** The elements of this ethical control system should include the following:

1. A statement of the organization's values and code of ethics written in practical terms, along with examples so that the organization's employees can relate the statement to their individual jobs.
2. A clear statement of the employee's ethical responsibilities for every job description and a specific review of the employee's ethical performance as part of every performance review.
3. Adequate training to help employees identify ethical dilemmas in practice and learn how to deal with those they can reasonably expect to face.
4. Evidence that senior management expects organization members to adhere to its code of ethics. This means that management must:
   - Provide a statement of the consequences of violating the organization's code of ethics.
   - Establish a means of dealing with violations of the organization's code of ethics promptly, ruthlessly, and consistently with the statement of consequences.
   - Provide visible support of ethical decision making at every opportunity.
   - Provide a private line of communication (without retribution) from employees directly to the chief executive officer, chief operating officer, head of human resource management, or someone else on the board of directors.
5. Evidence that employees can make ethical decisions or report violations of the organizations stated ethics (be the whistle-blower) without fear of reprisals from superiors, subordinates, or peers in the organization. This proof usually takes the

IN PRACTICE

The Wall Street Journal Workplace-Ethics Quiz

As technology has proliferated in the workplace a number of new ethical questions regarding work behavior have surfaced. See how your responses to these questions in this Wall Street Journal Ethics Quiz compare to national survey data, which appear on the following page.

Office Technology

1. Is it wrong to use company e-mail for personal reasons? ☐ Yes ☐ No
2. Is it wrong to use office equipment to help your children or spouse do schoolwork? ☐ Yes ☐ No
3. Is it wrong to play computer games on office equipment during the workday? ☐ Yes ☐ No
4. Is it wrong to use office equipment to do internet shopping? ☐ Yes ☐ No
5. Is it unethical to blame an error you made on a technological glitch? ☐ Yes ☐ No
6. Is it unethical to visit pornographic Web sites using office equipment? ☐ Yes ☐ No

Gifts and Entertainment

7. What's the value at which a gift from a supplier or client becomes troubling? ☐ $25 ☐ $50 ☐ $100
8. Is a $50 gift to a boss unacceptable? ☐ Yes ☐ No
9. Is a $50 gift FROM the boss unacceptable? ☐ Yes ☐ No
10. Of gifts from suppliers: Is it OK to take a $200 pair of football tickets? ☐ Yes ☐ No
11. Is it OK to take a $120 pair of theater tickets? ☐ Yes ☐ No
12. Is it OK to take a $100 holiday food basket? ☐ Yes ☐ No
13. Is it OK to take a $25 gift certificate? ☐ Yes ☐ No
14. Can you accept a $75 prize won at a raffle at a supplier's conference? ☐ Yes ☐ No

Truth and Lies

15. Due to on-the-job pressure, have you ever abused or lied about sick days? ☐ Yes ☐ No
16. Due to on-the-job pressure, have you ever taken credit for someone else's work or idea? ☐ Yes ☐ No

Source: *The Wall Street Journal,* October 21, 1999, page B1.

form of an organization mediator who has the authority to investigate complaints, wherever they lead, and to preserve the confidentiality of people who report violations.

6. An ongoing internal audit of the efficacy of the organization's ethical control system.

STEPS IN MAKING AN ETHICAL DECISION

Formal training is part of the process of promoting ethical decision making. After gathering the facts relating to a particular decision and evaluating the alternative courses of action, the decision maker can eliminate possible courses of action that

IN PRACTICE

Answers to Ethics Quiz

Here are the responses based on national cross-sectional survey data of employees at large companies gathered by the Ethics Officer Association, Belmont, Massachusetts, and the Ethical Leadership Group, Wilmette, Illinois.

How do your answers compare? Are you surprised?

1. 34% said personal e-mail on company computers is wrong
2. 37% said using office equipment for schoolwork is wrong
3. 49% said playing computer games at work is wrong
4. 54% said Internet shopping at work is wrong
5. 61% said it's unethical to blame your error on technology
6. 87% said it's unethical to visit pornographic sites at work
7. 33% said $25 is the amount at which a gift from a supplier or client becomes troubling, while 33% said $50, and 33% said $100
8. 35% said a $50 gift to the boss is unacceptable
9. 12% said a $50 gift from the boss is unacceptable
10. 70% said it's unacceptable to take the $200 football tickets
11. 70% said it's unacceptable to take the $120 theater tickets
12. 35% said it's unacceptable to take the $100 food basket
13. 45% said it's unacceptable to take the $25 gift certificate
14. 40% said it's unacceptable to take the $75 raffle prize
15. 11% reported they lie about sick days
16. 4% reported they take credit for the work or ideas of others

Source: *The Wall Street Journal,* October 21, 1999, page B4.

are ethically unacceptable. The decision model in Exhibit 10-1 is one approach to eliminating unacceptable alternatives.

In summary, the organization's code of ethics is integral to MACS design. Both designers and users of the system should remember this fact and rectify any deviations from the code of ethics that the system explicitly or implicitly promotes.

MOTIVATION AND GOAL CONGRUENCE

In addition to fostering ethical behavior and decision making, a central issue in MACS design is how to motivate appropriate behavior at work. When designing jobs and specific tasks, system designers should consider the following three dimensions of motivation:

1. *Direction,* or the tasks on which an employee focuses attention
2. *Intensity,* or the level of effort the employee expends
3. *Persistence,* or the duration of time that an employee will stay with a task or job

Consistent with theories of individual motivation,[1] careful attention to motivation is a key step for the organization and its employees to align their respective goals; this

[1]See Two-Factor Theory by F. Herzberg, "One More Time: How Do You Motivate Employees?," *Harvard Business Review,* January–February 1968, pp. 53–62; Expectancy Theory by V. Vroom, *Work and Motivation,* New York: Wiley, 1964; and Goal-Setting Theory by E. Locke and G. Latham, *A Theory of Goal Setting and Task Performance,* Englewood Cliffs, NJ: Prentice Hall, 1990.

EXHIBIT 10-1

Decision Model for Resolving Ethical Issues

1. **Determine the Facts—What, Who, Where, When, How.**
   What do we know or need to know, if possible, that will help us define the problem?
2. **Define the Ethical Issue.**
   - List the significant stakeholders
   - Define the ethical issues

   Make sure precisely what the ethical issue is, for example, conflict involving rights, questions over limits of disclosure obligation, and so on.
3. **Identify Major Principles, Rules, Values.**
   Determine key principles such as integrity, quality, respect for persons, societal benefits, and costs.
4. **Specify the Alternatives.**
   List the major alternative courses of action, including those that represent some form of compromise or point between simply doing or not doing something.
5. **Compare Values and Alternatives.**
   Determine if there is one principle or value, or a combination, which is so compelling that the proper alternative is clear, for example, correcting a defect that is almost certain to cause loss of life.
6. **Assess the Consequences.**
   Identify short- and long-term positive and negative consequences for the major alternatives. The common short-run focus on gains or losses needs to be measured against long-run considerations.
7. **Make Your Decision.**
   Balance the consequences against your primary principles or values and select the alternative that best fits.

Source: William W. May (Ed.), *Ethics in the Accounting Curriculum; Cases and Readings,* American Accounting Association, Sarasota, Florida, 1990, p. 1.

alignment is known as achieving **goal congruence.** The alignment of goals occurs as employees perform their jobs well and are helping to achieve organizational objectives; they are also attaining their own individual goals such as obtaining promotions, earning financial bonuses, or advancing their careers in other ways.

Goal congruence
The outcome when managers' and employees' goals are aligned with organizational goals.

MACS system designers have to be concerned about how the organization communicates its goals to employees. One method by which organizations motivate other forms of work behavior is through the performance measures it employs, the ways that it provides a voice to employees through participation in decision making, and the rewards that it offers to employees. In addition to incorporating ethical principles, these are the three other behavioral goals discussed at the beginning of the chapter.

In a perfect world, as employers and employees align their goals, employers could simply rely on the concept of **employee self-control,** in which employees monitor and regulate their own behavior and perform to their highest levels. Even if goals are aligned, however, different types of work tasks require different levels of skill, precision, and responsibility. To deal with the variety of tasks that employees face, management often relies on different forms of behavior control at work. The two most common types of control are task control and results control.

Employee self-control
A managerial method in which employees monitor and regulate their own behavior and perform to their highest levels.

Task control
The process of developing standard procedures that employees are told to follow.

Task Control. **Task control** is the process of finding ways to control human behavior so that a job is completed in a prespecified manner. Task control can be broken down into two categories—preventive control and monitoring. In **preventive control,** much if not all of the discretion is taken out of performing a task due to the

Preventive control
An approach to control that focuses on preventing an undesired event.

precision required or the nature of the materials involved. For instance, tasks that require very careful handling such as making silicon wafers or those that use precious metals such as gold often are controlled carefully or are performed by machines or computers. This is not to say that machines are infallible, but rather that the degree of error is probably less than that experienced with humans. Naturally, as the accomplishment of a task requires increasingly greater judgment, the building of preventive control systems becomes more difficult.

Monitoring
Inspecting the work or behavior of employees while they are performing a task.

Monitoring means inspecting the work or behavior of employees while they are performing a task. Monitoring can be accomplished using listening devices or through surveillance. For example, all of us have experienced the situation in which a (sometimes annoying) phone message tells us that the conversation we are about to have with a company representative may be "monitored to ensure quality control." Since monitoring, or listening in to a conversation in this case, is often done randomly, the employee does not know when it will occur and thus will be disciplined to act in a consistent, professional manner at all times. Monitoring also can be accomplished using surveillance. For instance, cameras or "eyes in the sky" are used to observe the actions and behaviors of croupiers at gambling casinos.

Monitoring, however, can have its negative consequences. Some employees feel that being monitored causes them unnecessary stress. These same employees believe that monitoring also undermines the level of trust between employers and employees.

Task control is most appropriate in the following situations:

1. When there are legal requirements to follow specific rules or procedures to protect public safety, for example in the manufacture of prescription drugs, and critical aircraft components, and in the operation of nuclear power generation facilities.

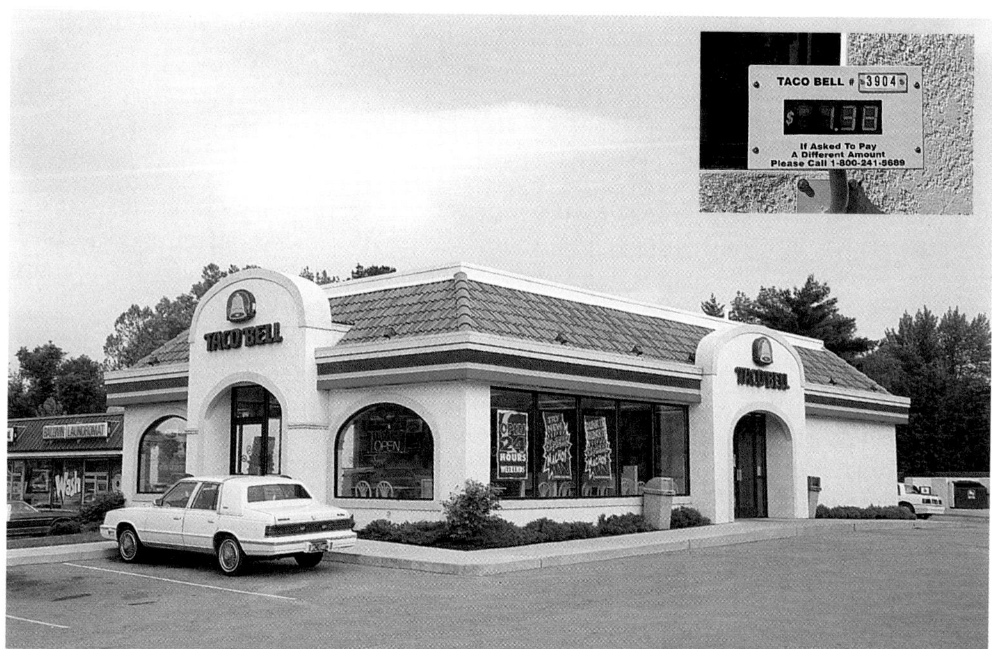

Most organizations require that employees who handle cash provide a cash register receipt to the customer—and some back this up by promising the customer a free meal or a discount if a receipt is not provided. Requiring that the customer receive a cash receipt requires that the sale is entered into the cash register's memory which, in turn, ensures that all incoming cash receipts are recorded—a form of task control that relies on prevention. (David Ulmer/Stock, Boston. Inset: Taco Bell)

THE TECHNOLOGICAL EDGE

Big Brother at Work?

A recent survey conducted by the American Management Association shows that monitoring of company employees is on the rise. Two years ago, the survey reports that 35% of U.S. companies studied employee e-mail. In 1999, the percentage rose to 45%. Companies also are using video surveillance, listening in on phone calls, and installing other types of electronic monitoring. Combining these data, 67% of all companies are monitoring employee behavior in one way or another.

Source: American Management Association Survey, January–March 1999.

EXHIBIT 10-2

Companies Engaged in Electronic Monitoring

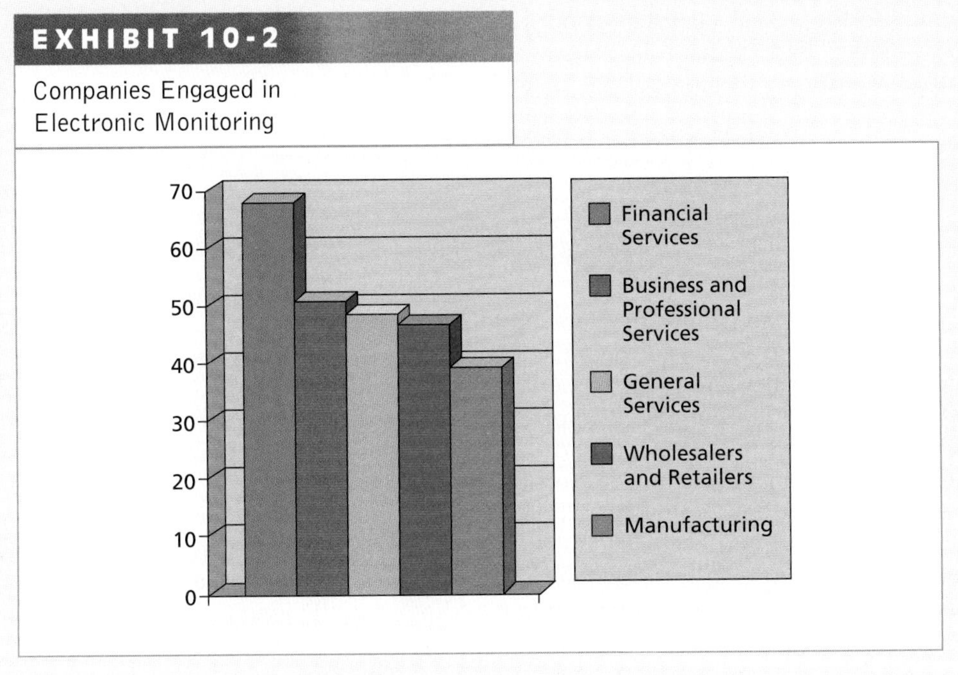

2. When employees handle liquid or other precious assets, to reduce the opportunity for temptation and fraud.
3. When the organization can control its environment and eliminate uncertainty and the need for judgment. In these instances, the organization can develop specific rules and procedures that employees must follow.

Results control The process of hiring qualified people who understand the organization's objectives, telling them to do whatever they think best to help the organization achieve its objectives, and using the control system to evaluate the resulting performance, thereby assessing how well they have done.

Results Control. Rather than directly monitoring and directly controlling tasks, **results control** methods focus on measuring employee performance against stated objectives. For results control to be effective, the organization must have clearly defined its objectives, communicated them to appropriate organization members, and designed performance measures consistent with the objectives. For example, sales people are often evaluated based on the volume of sales they made during a specific time interval. The organization sets standards of performance against which the actual results of an employee's performance are compared. Or, consider a business unit head who must improve her organization's financial performance relative to a prespecified target.

In some instances, task and results controls are used in tandem. As mentioned, phone calls by company salespeople often are monitored to control behavior; however, in addition, these same salespeople often have a weekly sales quota to reach. This is particularly true of salespeople from major long-distance carriers.

Results control is most effective when:

1. Organization members understand the organization's objectives and their contribution to those objectives.
2. Organization members have the knowledge and skill to respond to changing situations by taking corrective actions and making sound decisions.
3. The performance measurement system is designed to assess individual contributions so that an individual can be motivated to take action and make decisions that reflect their own and the organization's best interests.

Central to the design of results control systems is the development of a performance measurement system that fully reflects the multiple objectives and goals of an organization. We discuss this issue in the next section.

Using a Mix of Performance Measures—The Balanced Scorecard Approach

THE NEED FOR MULTIPLE MEASURES OF PERFORMANCE

The old saying, "what gets measured gets done," indicates that the ways in which organizations and individuals measure performance send signals to all employees and stakeholders about what the organization considers as its priorities. If organizations choose performance measures without careful consideration, then noncongruent behavior can occur. For instance, suppose a firm sets up a performance evaluation system that rewards a vendor based *only* on on-time delivery of product. In all likelihood, on-time delivery will be the variable on which the vendor's employees will focus. Since this evaluation would not consider the quality of the goods sent, vendors who supply the merchandise may sacrifice quality for the sake of meeting promised delivery dates. Or they may quote excessively long lead times to ensure that deliveries are not late. Either action could work to the long-term detriment of the organization and the vendor.

Department store managers have discovered that when salespeople are compensated using sales quotas, their attention will be focused on selling as much expensive merchandise as possible. Employees faced with such a situation initially may find that their sales volume is increasing; but, as the competition for customers develops, the work environment may become hostile as salespeople dispute over customers or sales. Another consequence of relying solely on commissions as a motivating tool is that other aspects of the sales function, such as straightening merchandise or restocking shelves, may become lower priorities. Also, customers may return merchandise that has been oversold to them.

Occasionally employees are so motivated to achieve a single goal that they engage in dysfunctional behavior. For instance, consider a company whose single performance measure is whether employees attain their sales quotas. If an employee is worried about being fired, and if there are no other ways to demonstrate good performance, the employee might engage in some undesirable behavior or in what is known as **gaming the performance indicator.** As an example, a salesperson might ask his coworker to give him credit for the colleague's sales bookings. Or, the salesperson may have his friends come into the store, buy merchandise, and then return it

Gaming the performance indicator
An activity in which an employee may engage in dysfunctional behavior to achieve a single goal.

60 days later. In the worst case, the salesperson might engage in **data falsification** by knowingly altering sales booking records in his favor.

Data falsification
The process of knowingly altering company data in one's favor.

In addition to setting up boundary systems so that employees have a clear understanding of what is considered appropriate and inappropriate behavior, organizations also can design performance measurement systems that encourage the desired behavior. One possibility is to use multiple performance measures that reflect the complexities of the work environment and the variety of contributions that employees make. In many of today's manufacturing and service environments, employees, or associates, are being cross-trained to perform a variety of tasks. For instance, at the General Motors Saturn plant, employees are organized into self-managed work teams that follow a product's manufacture from beginning to end. Thus, organizations have an opportunity to design multiple measures to assess the work that is actually being done. Using multiple performance measures also will cause employees to recognize the various dimensions of their work and to be less intent on trying to maximize their performance on a single target at the expense of other aspects of their jobs.

USING A MIX OF QUANTITATIVE PERFORMANCE MEASURES

In addition to using multiple performance measures, MACS designers have to expand their views of the kinds of performance measures to use. For instance, only within the past few years have managers become aware of the need for measures of quality, speed to market, cycle time, flexibility, complexity, innovation, and productivity. Historically, some of these measures, such as quality, were in the hands of industrial engineers, while others, such as speed to market or flexibility, were not measured at all.

There are other new organizational realities that managers should keep in mind. Faced with increasing competitive pressures, many organizations have begun to move away from traditional hierarchical organizations with many layers of management, referred to as tall organizations, to those with fewer and fewer layers, or flat organizations. General Electric, for example, has reduced its hierarchical structure significantly. As the barriers between functional areas such as engineering design, manufacturing, accounting, finance and marketing are being eliminated, employees are working increasingly in cross-functional teams.

Another significant corresponding change is the use of business process reengineering, in which designers begin with a vision of what organizational participants would like their process or product to look like or how they would like it to function and then radically redesign it. Such an approach is significantly different from starting with an existing product or process and then making slight incremental changes. Further, reengineering design changes have led to the need for new informational requirements and measures related to the costs and benefits of innovation. Thus, new measures of performance must take into account group-level performance measures and cross-functional business process measures, not just departmental efficiency and spending measures.

The traditional focus of performance measures in management accounting has been on quantitative financial measures such as cost and profit, rather than quantitative nonfinancial and qualitative measures. Examples of quantitative, nonfinancial measures include yield, cycle time, schedule adherence, number of defectives, market share, and customer retention. Variables such as the image of a product or service, the level of caring of the staff in a hospital, or the reputation of a company are examples of qualitative variables. While they may be more subjective than quantitative variables, many qualitative, variables can now be assessed using psychometric methods developed in the behavioral sciences. Customer satisfaction, for instance, is a qualitative measure, which can now be quantified by using psychological scales. Clearly, measures such as customer satisfaction and employee morale are crucial for both the short- and long-term success of any organization.

THE BALANCED SCORECARD

Balanced scorecard A systematic performance measurement system that translates an organization's strategy into clear objectives, measures, targets, and initiatives organized by four perspectives.

Using the appropriate mix of short- and long-term financial and nonfinancial performance measures, with need for organizations to mobilize and exploit their intangible or intellectual assets as well as their physical, tangible assets, has given rise to a systematic approach to performance measurement known as the **balanced scorecard.** The balanced scorecard is the first systematic attempt to design a performance measurement system that translates an organization's strategy into clear objectives, measures, targets, and initiatives. While organizations have been measuring their own performance in numerous ways, the balanced scorecard integrates the measures used across organizations and, in particular, helps organizations grapple with their intangible or intellectual assets. The focus on intangible assets is a significant advance even for companies known for having sound performance measurement systems.

As mentioned in Chapter 1, a company's intangible assets enable it to do the following:

1. Develop customer relationships that retain the loyalty of existing customers and enable the organization to reach new customer segments.
2. Introduce innovative products and services desired by targeted customer segments.
3. Produce high-quality, customized products and services at low cost and with short lead times.
4. Mobilize employee skills and motivation for continuous improvements in process capabilities, quality, and response times.
5. Deploy information technology, databases, and systems.

The measures derived under the scorecard represent a balance between four measurement perspectives: (1) external financial measures for stakeholders and customers such as return on capital employed, (2) customer measures such as retention and satisfaction, (3) internal business process perspective measures such as cycle time, and (4) measures for learning and growth such as the number of new patents and the development of employee skills. Exhibit 10-3 illustrates the relationships among the four perspectives.

External Financial Perspective. While considered traditional, financial performance measures are still used to determine whether an organization's strategy and objectives are affecting bottom-line financial performance. This perspective continues to be critical for both internal and external stakeholders. Examples of financial measures include operating income, return-on-capital employed, and economic value added.

Customer Perspective. The customer perspective measures the business unit's performance in targeted customer and market segments. The customer perspective typically uses customer outcome measures such as customer profitability, customer retention, customer satisfaction, and market share.

Internal Business Process Perspective. The internal business process perspective focuses on those processes that will increase value to customers and lower costs for improved financial performance. Using analyses that cut across the entire value chain, the internal business process perspective plays two roles. First, measures are developed to assess and improve existing processes. Second, the approach is used to develop new processes and new measures that will affect customer satisfaction and financial performance.

Learning and Growth Perspective. The focus on the learning and growth perspective is to address the three sources of organizational learning and growth: people,

EXHIBIT 10-3

The Balanced Scorecard Provides a Framework to Translate a Strategy into Operational Terms

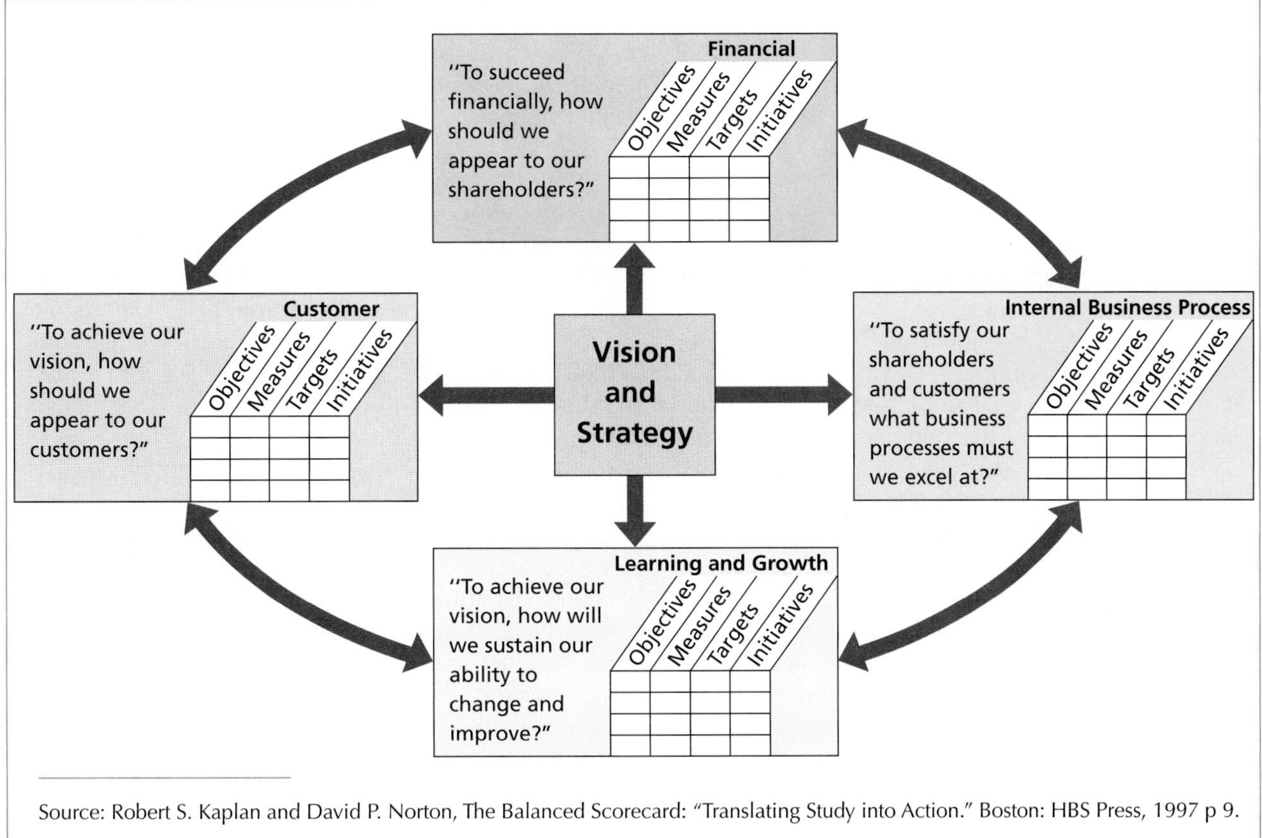

Source: Robert S. Kaplan and David P. Norton, The Balanced Scorecard: "Translating Study into Action." Boston: HBS Press, 1997 p 9.

systems, and organizational procedures. Measures for people include employee satisfaction and retention, training, and skill development. Systems metrics determine whether information systems are producing accurate, reliable, and consistent information that informs managers about their customers and business processes. Organizational procedures can be evaluated by determining whether the organization has specific organizational metrics of success with appropriate reward systems.

Empowering Employees to Be Involved in MACS Design

Empowering employees in MACS design requires two essential elements—allowing employees to participate in decision making and ensuring that employees understand the information they are using and generating.

PARTICIPATION IN DECISION MAKING

Organizations often do not realize that their greatest asset is the people they employ. Encouraging participation has a two-fold benefit for organizations. First, research has suggested that employees who participate in decision making evince greater feelings of morale and job satisfaction. In many instances, these heightened feelings translate into increased productivity as employees begin to feel that they have some ownership and control over what they do at work.

IN PRACTICE

Does the Balanced Scorecard Work?

As a result of massive environmental turbulence such as floods in the southern United States, hurricanes Hugo and Andrew, the LA riots, and other environmental cleanup, Cigna Property and Casualty (P&C) in the early 1990s was operating in the red. In the past, Cigna had used a strategy that led them to chase premium revenue in very difficult markets. Further, they relied solely on financial measures of performance as this is what their underwriters understood.

Gerald Isom, president of Cigna P&C stated, "In the past, the entire focus was on the financial numbers. There was just not nearly enough attention on what causes the numbers to be what they are. The balanced set of measures changed that. It creates a precise vehicle for getting the critical success factors on the table."

As shown in Exhibit 10-4, Cigna has fully utilized all categories of the balanced scorecard. Senior managers believe the scorecard has helped to align individual goals with that of the organizational vision and has provided a new way of organizing work and thinking.

Cigna uses the balanced scorecard in four ways. First, to specify strategy; next, to communicate the strategy downward through three major operating divisions and 20 business units. Third, the scorecard is used for detailed business planning; and fourth, it provides continuous feedback for organizational learning. Approximately 24 scorecards across these business units were developed.

In addition, Cigna developed an interesting compensation plan. At the beginning of every year, all employees receive a fixed number of "position shares." The number of shares received depends on job position. Throughout the year, supervisors award shares to employees based on their performance. Each share starts out with a par value of $10; however, at the time of payout, Cigna determines the value of each share based on balanced scorecard progress. Employees are compensated based on the most relevant scorecard which can be at the corporate, division, or business unit level. Thus, a clerk working in the claims department of the corporate office would earn shares based on the scorecard, but this would be weighted based on the business unit in which they worked, such as workers' compensation.

Does the scorecard work? In the first six months of 1996, Cigna reported a net operating income of $32 million contrasted with a $16 million loss in the first half of 1995. You be the judge!

EXHIBIT 10-4

A Sample Cigna Scorecard

Financial
- Shareholder Expectations
- Operating Performance
- Growth
- Shareholder Risk

External
- Producer Relations
- Policyholder Relations
- Regulatory

Internal Business Process
- Business Growth
- Underwriting Profitability
- Claims Management
- Operating Productivity

Learning and Growth
- Upgrading Competencies
- Information Technology Support
- Support Organization Alignment

Source: Bill Birchard, "Closing the Strategy Gap," *CFO Magazine,* October 1996, pp. 27–36.

Southern Gardens, a Florida based citrus processor and subsidiary of US Sugar, with 190 employees is a company that has enjoyed success with the BSC. It could provide a good picture, and illustrate that a small, agricultural company benefited from the BSC. (Marc Vaughn/ Wragg & Casas Public Relations, Inc.)

Second, except in highly automated industries, people (not machines) still perform the major portion of work and have superior information and an understanding in regard to how work is best accomplished, and consequently, how to improve products and processes. For example, employees in the Sydney branch of ANZAC Company will know more about the way their branch functions than will central headquarters located in Melbourne. Therefore, MACS designers should strongly consider enlisting the participation of the Sydney employees. The same concept applies within a division. Assembly line operators usually know more about the process on which they work than their managers do. Research has shown that participation and communication between local and central offices and between superiors and subordinates result in the transmission of critical information to which central management would otherwise not have access.

EDUCATION TO UNDERSTAND INFORMATION

The second critical element of empowering employees is to ensure that they understand the information they use and on which they are evaluated. Many executives believe that only managers need to understand the information generated by the MACS. Recently, it has become evident to many managers that employees at all levels must understand the organization's performance measures and the way they are computed in order to be able to take actions that lead to superior performance. For example, if employees do not understand how their actions affect a variable such as cycle time (the time it takes for a product or service to be produced or performed from start to finish), then they will not know how to alter their actions to improve cycle time performance. If employees in a manufacturing plant are performing unnecessary actions on an assembly line or are idle, for example, the cycle time performance of their group will be affected. Similarly, at the point of service, or the point where organizational employees interact with customers, delays in the processing of claims will increase cycle time as well.

Consider an airline whose intent is to improve its public image. From time to time, some airlines ask customers to fill out a customer satisfaction survey. If flight attendants have not been educated regarding how each of their actions (such as being rude or slow to produce service) directly affects customer satisfaction, then the airline has failed to do its part to ensure satisfactory performance of one of its key indicators for flight attendants. This is also true in many other types of service organizations. In restaurants or department stores, customers often become frustrated with the level of service. For example, assigning waiters and waitresses in a restaurant to too many tables can cause them to forget customer requests, or if they have annoying personal habits or are extremely clumsy, customers remember the negative experience and may not return. Consider a department store in which sales personnel may be too pushy, too difficult to find for service, or arrogant. A customer may become irritated with such an experience and vow never to shop at that store again.

Unless restaurant owners and department store managers educate their employees about how their actions affect customer perceptions of service quality and repeat business, the energy devoted to improving customer satisfaction is wasted. Studies have shown that, on average, five times as many customers who are dissatisfied with a product or service tell other people about their experience than customers who are satisfied with a product or service. Thus, the reputation of organizations that offer a poorly produced product or a poorly delivered service can be ruined rather quickly. In general, poor or nonresponsive service by employees who have direct contact with customers is usually evidence of poor management, poor training, and poor education rather than an indicator that the employee is not a good worker.

For MACS to function well, employees have to be constantly re-educated as the system and its performance measures change. Without continuous updating of everyone's education, companies cannot be leaders or even players in international markets. In the United States, lack of training is a severe problem. Some studies have shown that U.S. employees receive only one-tenth the training of Japanese employees, for example. Thus, U.S. management cannot expect its employees to be globally competitive if management does not supply them with the necessary training. Ultimately, the concept of continuous education should become so ingrained in employees that continually mastering new skills becomes a job requirement. Organizations that foster such an environment have been labeled learning organizations.

Developing Appropriate Incentive Systems to Reward Performance

The final behavioral consideration in MACS design is to consider the most appropriate reward systems to further motivate employees. We begin by discussing both intrinsic and extrinsic rewards and then focus on the many types of financial reward systems that organizations use.

INTRINSIC REWARDS

Intrinsic rewards Those rewards that come from within an individual and reflect satisfaction from doing the job and the opportunities for growth that the job provides.

Organizations use both intrinsic and extrinsic rewards to motive employees. **Intrinsic rewards** are those that come from within an individual and reflect satisfaction from doing the job and the opportunities for growth that the job provides. In some cases intrinsic rewards reflect the nature of the organization and type of work one is performing. For example, volunteering at a day care center offers no financial compensation but instead provides the volunteer with the feeling or reward that he or she is helping children learn. Even in jobs where people are financially compensated, one of management's most challenging tasks is to design jobs and develop an organizational environment and culture that lead employees to derive intrinsic rewards just by working. Organizations also hope that through the hiring process that they can find a good match between a specific type of job and a specific individual. Because of how intrinsic rewards are derived, manufacturing accounting information has no effect on them.

EXTRINSIC REWARDS

Based on assessed performance, an **extrinsic reward** is any reward that one person provides to another to recognize a job well done. Examples of commonly used extrinsic rewards are meals, tips, cash bonuses, stock bonuses, and recognition in newsletters and on plaques. Extrinsic rewards reinforce the notion that employees have distinguished themselves from the organization. Many people believe that extrinsic rewards also reinforce the common perception that the wage compensates the employee for a minimally acceptable effort and that the organization must use additional rewards or compensation to motivate the employee to provide additional effort.

Extrinsic reward Motivating desired behavior by providing an explicit, usually financial, reward.

CHOOSING BETWEEN INTRINSIC AND EXTRINSIC REWARDS

Many compensation experts believe that organizations have not made enough use of intrinsic rewards. They claim that, given proper management leadership, intrinsic rewards may have motivational effects as strong as or even stronger than extrinsic rewards. The issue of the effectiveness of intrinsic and extrinsic rewards is a topic of heated debate in the management literature. Some argue that people who expect to receive a reward for completing a task or for doing that task successfully do not perform as well as those who expect no reward at all. Others argue that, although this result holds true over a wide range of tasks, people, and rewards, the result is strongest when the job requires creative skills. For some, pay may not be a motivator.[2] This argument is built around the idea that the preoccupation with extrinsic rewards undermines the effectiveness of reward systems and that the design of organizations and jobs should allow employees to experience intrinsic rewards.

The issue remains unresolved; however, one thing is clear: Most organizations have ignored and continue to ignore the role of intrinsic rewards in motivation and blindly accept the view that only financial extrinsic rewards motivate employees. Many people believe that financial extrinsic rewards are both necessary and sufficient to motivate superior performance. Both systematic and anecdotal evidence suggest, however, that financial extrinsic rewards are not necessary to create effective organizations and that performance rewards do not necessarily create them. Whether nonfinancial extrinsic and intrinsic rewards are more or less effective than financial extrinsic rewards in motivating behavior is unresolved. However, both nonfinancial extrinsic and intrinsic rewards have a role to play in most organizations.

Beyond the debate about the relative effectiveness of intrinsic and extrinsic rewards, some people argue that incentive compensation programs in any form are unacceptable. They suggest that organizations must strive to be excellent to survive in a complex and competitive world. Thus, superior and committed performance is necessary for all employees in organizations and is part of the contract of employment, not something that merits additional pay.

Conversely, a large number of organizations rely on extrinsic monetary rewards to motivate performance. Since employees often engage in social comparisons of how they are performing at work, extrinsic monetary rewards are a tangible indicator of how well one is doing relative to others. These organizations base their reward systems to a large extent on information and measures provided by management accounting systems. In the remainder of this section, we focus on the kinds of extrinsic rewards that are most commonly used in organizations.

EXTRINSIC REWARDS BASED ON PERFORMANCE

Incentive compensation, or pay-for-performance systems, are reward systems that provide monetary (extrinsic) rewards based on measured results. Pay-for-performance systems base rewards on achieving or exceeding some measured

Incentive compensation Reward system that provides monetary (extrinsic) rewards based on measured results. Also called *pay-for-performance systems.*

[2] See A. Kohn, "Why Incentive Plans Cannot Work," *Harvard Business Review,* September–October 1993, pp. 54–63.

performance. Thus, organizations need performance measurement systems that gather relevant and reliable performance information. The reward can be based on absolute performance, performance relative to some plan, or performance relative to that of some comparable group. Measures of absolute performance include:

1. the number of acceptable quality units produced (such as a piece-rate system)
2. the organization's results (such as profit levels or an organization's balanced scorecard measures of customer or employee satisfaction, quality, and rate of successful new product introductions)
3. the organization's share price performance (such as stock option plan)

Examples of rewards based on relative performance are those tied to the following:

1. the ability to exceed a performance target level (such as paying a manager for accomplishing his or her goals under budget, or paying a production group a bonus for beating a benchmark performance level)
2. the amount of a bonus pool (such as sharing in a pool defined as the organization's reported profits less a stipulated return to shareholders)
3. the degree to which performance exceeds the average performance level of a comparable group.

Occasionally, compensation policy can be affected by government regulations. For example, since 1994, most organizations in the United States cannot claim as an expense the portion of any employee's salary that exceeds $1 million for the purpose of computing taxable income. This will certainly (1) reduce the use of salary and perquisites (such as company cars and club memberships) and (2) increase the use of variable pay based on performance.

EFFECTIVE PERFORMANCE MEASUREMENT AND REWARD SYSTEMS

In this section we discuss six attributes of a measurement system that must be in place in order to motivate desired performance.

1. The employees must understand their jobs and the reward system and believe that it measures what they control and contribute to the organization. This attribute ensures that the employee perceives the reward system as fair and predictable. If employees do not understand their jobs or how to improve their measured performance, then a reward system based on performance measures is ineffective. In this case, employees perceive no relationship between effort and performance and, ultimately, outcomes. Similarly, if the reward system is complex, employees are unable to relate perceived performance improvements to changes in outcomes, and the motivational effect of the reward system will be lost.

   Additionally, if the reward system does not measure employees' controllable performance, they conclude that measured performance is independent of their efforts, and again the incentive effect of the reward system is lost. Specifying and developing a clear relationship among effort, performance, and result and ensuring that all employees understand this relationship is a critical management role. Therefore, the centerpiece of incentive compensation systems is the performance measurement system, which becomes the focus of the employees' attention. The decisions that employees make in pursuing the performance measures that ultimately provide valued personal outcomes move the organization toward achieving its goals if the performance measures are aligned with the organization's goals.
2. Related to the first attribute, designers of the performance measurement system must make a careful choice about whether it measures employees' inputs or outputs. In general, the greatest alignment between employees' and the organization's interests is provided when the performance measurement system monitors

and rewards employee outputs that contribute to the organization's success. However, outputs often reflect circumstances and conditions that are beyond the employee's control, and when they do, the perceived link between individuals' efforts and measured results is reduced, thereby decreasing the motivation provided by the reward system. Under circumstances when outcome measurement is problematic, organizations often choose to monitor and reward inputs (such as employee learning, demonstrated skill, and time worked). For example, in some manufacturing organizations, employees can take on-site night classes to increase their skills. Once these classes are completed, and the new skills mastered, the employees are moved to a higher wage level. The choice of the mix of performance measures and the decision about whether those measures are input based, output based, or a combination of measures comprise one of the most difficult tasks in the design of performance measurement and compensation systems.

3 The elements of performance that the performance measurement system monitors and rewards should reflect the organization's critical success factors. This attribute ensures that the performance system is relevant and motivates intended performance that matters to the organization's success. Moreover, the performance measurement system must consider all facets of performance so that employees do not sacrifice performance on an unmeasured element for performance on an element that the reward system measures. This is the role and purpose of measuring and rewarding employees across a set of balanced and comprehensive measures as proposed in the balanced scorecard. For example, if a supervisor tells a telephone operator that productivity (such as the number of help requests handled per shift) is important, the operator may sacrifice the quality and courtesy offered to customers in order to handle as many questions as possible.

4 The reward system must set clear standards for performance that employees accept. Standards help employees assess whether their skills and efforts create results that the performance measurement system captures and reports as outcomes. This attribute determines employees' beliefs about whether the performance system is fair. If performance standards are either unspecified or unclear to employees, the relationship between performance and outcome is ambiguous and therefore reduces the motivational effect of the performance reward system.

5 The measurement system must be calibrated so that it can accurately assess performance. This attribute ensures that the performance measurement system establishes a clear relationship between performance and outcome.

6 When it is critical that employees coordinate decision making and other activities with other employees, the reward system should reward group, rather than individual, performance. Many organizations now believe that, to be effective, employees must work well in teams. These organizations are replacing evaluations and rewards based on individual performance with rewards and evaluation based on group performance.

In most organizations, pay is more than simply what is required to keep an employee from leaving the organization. Pay is part of the complex bundle of factors that motivate people to work in the organization's best interests. Therefore, organizations must consider pay issues within the larger context of motivation.

CONDITIONS FAVORING INCENTIVE COMPENSATION

Not all organizations are suited to incentive compensation systems. Centralized organizations require most of the important operating decisions to be made in the head office. Such organizations are unsuited to incentive compensation systems for their front-line employees, because employees in these organizations are expected to follow rules and have no authority to make decisions. In fact, it is more appropriate to call compensation systems in these organizations "enforcement systems," because employment continues only if people follow the rules and standard operating procedures. Here the task of the management accountant is to design internal control systems and conduct internal audits to verify that people are following rules and procedures.

Incentive compensation systems work best in organizations in which employees have the skill and authority to react to conditions and make decisions. We previously discussed organizations that face continually changing environments—ones in which it is either impractical or impossible to develop standard operating procedures to deal with these changing conditions. Such organizations can develop incentive compensation systems to motivate employees to identify changes in the environment, to apply their skills and knowledge accordingly, and to make decisions that best reflect the organizations' goals.

When the organization has empowered its employees to make decisions, it can use incentive compensation systems to motivate appropriate decision-making behavior. In these organizations, the focus of control changes from telling people what to do, to asking employees to use their skills and delegated authority to do their best to help the organization achieve its stated objectives.

INCENTIVE COMPENSATION AND EMPLOYEE RESPONSIBILITY

The incentive compensation system must focus primarily on outcomes that the employee controls or influences. Consider an incentive compensation plan that rewards the performance of a production worker only when the sales department meets its sales target. Assuming that the worker is only responsible for the amount of resources used in the production of a product and its quality, it would be demotivating to base the employee's compensation on a sales target, because the sales department and not the product department controls the level of sales.

Employees' incentive compensation should reflect the nature of their responsibilities in the organization. Employees whose roles are to plan, coordinate, and control day-to-day activities should receive rewards based on their ability to manage these daily operations effectively and to make the best short-term use of available resources. Their rewards should be tied to short-term controllable performance measures, such as efficiency and the ability to meet customer quality and service

IN PRACTICE

Long-Term Performance Incentives

A Conference Board survey report indicated that most industry sectors use long-term performance plans designed to link the employee's interests with the organization's. The primary method of securing commitment to long-term goals is to link employee rewards to the achievement of financial performance goals over a time period of three to five years.

The survey report also indicated that participation in these plans is usually limited to a small group of senior executives in the organizations surveyed and that less than one half of one percent of employees regularly receive long-term incentive rewards.

The report suggested that the size of the performance rewards are correlated with the individual's position in the organization and range from 48% for CEOs to 21% for the lowest level individuals—the average being 32%.

Source: *BNA Pension & Benefits Reporter,* June 26, 1995, Volume 22, Number 26, p. 1486.

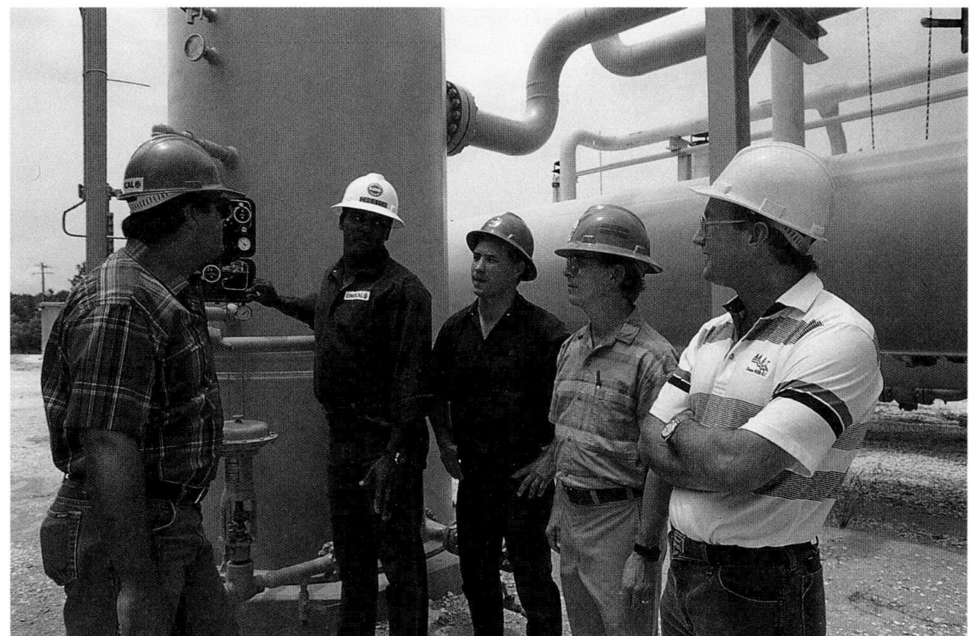

This team of Unocal employees earned a team bonus for designing a system to reduce the time taken to perform the annual maintenance on a natural gas liquids plant from 8 days to 3.5 days. The faster turnaround saved Unocal maintenance costs and reduced the amount of lost production time. Asked to describe his reaction to the reward, the employee shown to the far right seemed to derive more satisfaction from having his views "listened to and acted on" than from the monetary reward. The satisfaction expressed by this employee is a form of intrinsic reward related to satisfaction from a job that provides an opportunity for thinking and contribution. (Alan Whitman/Unocal)

requirements. Employees whose roles are to plan long-term projects, such as building new facilities or acquiring significant capital equipment, should be rewarded based on the long-term growth or improvement in the organization's operations that results from their strategic choices. These rewards should be based on the organization's performance compared with its stated objectives. In some cases, rewards also can be based on how an organization's performance compares with other similar organizations. This mix of rewarding both short- and long-term outcomes is consistent with the goals of the balanced scorecard approach.

REWARDING OUTCOMES

Another consideration in the design of effective incentive compensation systems is the manner in which performance is measured. Incentive compensation schemes tie rewards to the outputs of employee performance rather than to inputs such as their level of effort. Moreover, incentive compensation based on outcomes requires that organization members understand and contribute to the organization's objectives.

However, rewards can be based on inputs in three instances:

- when it is impossible to measure outcomes consistently
- when outcomes are affected by factors beyond the employee's control
- when outcomes are expensive to measure

Input-based compensation measures the time, knowledge, and skill level that the employee brings to the job, with the expectation that the unmeasured outcome is correlated with these inputs. Many organizations use some form of knowledge-based remuneration. This type of remuneration bases the rate of pay on an employee's training and job qualifications, which can be upgraded by on-the-job training. The employee's compensation is the product of the number of hours worked (time input) and the hourly rate (a reflection of the deemed level of skill input). Organizations use knowledge-based pay to motivate employees to continuously upgrade their job skills, thereby allowing them to receive a higher base pay.

MANAGING INCENTIVE COMPENSATION PLANS

Considerable evidence indicates that organizations have mismanaged incentive compensation plans, particularly those for senior executives. Many articles have appeared in influential business periodicals arguing that executives, particularly executives of U.S. corporations, have been paid excessively for mediocre performance.

Experts debate whether compensation systems motivate goal-seeking behavior and whether they are efficient, that is, whether they pay what is needed and no more. Some studies show a positive correlation between executive compensation and shareholder wealth. Other studies report finding no, or even a negative, correlation between organization performance and executive compensation. Until recently, shareholder value was decreasing downward, while executive compensation was climbing even higher. Some believe it is particularly inappropriate for companies to continue operating compensation systems in which executive rewards bear no relation to corporate performance.

Despite economic data showing an association between executive compensation and company performance, many professionals still argue that the amounts are excessive and reflect high status rather than good performance. The issue of fairness has also surfaced. Surveys indicate that, on average, CEOs in the United States earn 300 times the amount of the lowest paid employee. In Japan, however, the relationship is only 30 times the lowest paid worker. That these questions are raised reflects perceptions of unfairness and a degree of cynicism that average people feel about the role of incentive compensation in organizations.

TYPES OF INCENTIVE COMPENSATION PLANS

The most common incentive compensation plans are cash bonuses, profit sharing, gainsharing, stock options, performance shares stock, stock appreciation rights, participation units, and employee stock ownership plans (usually called ESOPs). These different plans pose varying challenges for the management accounting system.

We can group compensation plans into two broad categories: (1) those that rely on internal measures, invariably provided by the organization's management accounting system, and (2) those that rely on performance of the organization's share price in the stock market.

Management accountants get involved in the first group of plans—those that revolve around rewards based on performance that the organization's management accounting system monitors and reports. Most employees who participate in financial incentive plans take the plans very seriously. These people are both interested in, and concerned about, the performance measurement system that monitors and reports the performance measures used to compute and distribute financial rewards. Many practicing management accountants have found that the most contentious debates arise from issues relating to performance measurement used for financial rewards. Therefore, management accountants take the matter of developing performance measures for financial reward systems very seriously.

Cash bonus
A payment method that pays cash based on some measured performance. Also called lump-sum reward, pay for performance, and merit pay.

Cash Bonus. A **cash bonus** plan—called a lump-sum reward, pay for performance, and merit pay—pays cash based on some measured performance. Such a bonus is a one-time award that does not become part of the employee's base pay in subsequent years.

Cash bonuses can be fixed in amount and triggered when measured performance exceeds the target, or they can be proportional to the level of performance relative to the target. They can be based on individual or group performance, and they can be paid to individuals or groups.

For example, in the late 1980s, General Motors eliminated automatic salary increases based on increases in the cost of living and replaced them with a **pay-for-performance system** that rewarded managers based on their results. Managers were required to group their employees into four groups: high performers (the top 10%), good performers (the next 25%), average performers (the next 55%), and low performers (the last 10%). Supervisors used these groupings to award merit pay and enforce salary differences based on assessed performance.

Pay-for-performance system
Reward system that provides monetary (extrinsic) rewards based on measured results. Also called *incentive compensation.*

Profit Sharing. **Profit sharing** is a cash bonus calculated as a percentage of an organization unit's reported profit. Profit sharing is a group incentive compensation plan focused on short-term performance.

Profit sharing
A cash bonus calculated as a percentage of an organization unit's reported profit; a group incentive compensation plan focused on short-term performances.

All profit-sharing plans define what portion of the organization's reported profits is available for sharing, the sharing formula, the employees who are eligible to participate in the plan, and the formula for each employee's share.

Many profit-sharing plans are based on residual income now called economic value added. In these plans, the reported profit will be reduced by some percent (say 15%) of the shareholders' investment in the organization. This allotment provides the shareholders with the required return on their investment. The resulting pool is shared between employees and shareholders on some fractional basis, such as 40% for employees and 60% for shareholders. The plan also may specify a limit on the total amount of profits that can be distributed to employees. Finally, the profit-sharing plan specifies how it will distribute the money in the pool to each employee. Some plans provide equal distribution; others distribute the bonus pool based on the employee's performance relative to individual performance targets.

In the performance compensation approach, employees receive a performance score that reflects how well they achieved specific performance goals for that year. The employee's score divided by the total scores of all employees in the profit-sharing agreement is the individual's share of the pool total. Some profit-sharing plans distribute rewards to each employee in an amount proportional to the base wage or salary, because their designers believe this reflects the employee's contribution to the overall result.

Profit-sharing plans require a number of contributions from the organization's accounting systems in general, and from the management accounting system in particular. First, the organization must prepare a means to calculate profits. This process usually is monitored and attested to by an external auditor. Second, when a deduction is to be made from the pool that is based on the owners' investment, the management accounting system must provide a measure of invested capital. Third, when the profit sharing is based on some measured level of performance (e.g., a composite score that reflects the employee's ability to meet a set of performance targets), the management accounting system must provide the underlying measures of performance and the overall performance score.

Gainsharing. **Gainsharing** is a system for distributing cash bonuses from a pool when the total amount available is a function of performance relative to some target. For example, employees in a designated unit receive bonuses when their performance exceeds a performance target. Gainsharing is a group incentive, unlike the pay-for-performance cash bonus, which is an individual reward. In its usual form, gainsharing provides for the sharing of financial gains in organizational performance.

Gainsharing
A system for distributing cash bonuses from a pool when the total amount available is a function of performance relative to some target.

The gainsharing plan usually applies to a group of employees within an organization unit, such as a department or a store. It uses a formula to specify the amount and distribution of the rewards and a base period of performance as the benchmark for comparing subsequent performance. This benchmark is not changed unless a major change occurs in process or technology. When performance exceeds the base period performance, the gainsharing plan pays a bonus pool.

Gainsharing promotes teamwork and participation in decision making. It requires that employees have the skills to participate and that the organization encourages participation. Consider these companies that have used gainsharing effectively:

- The Herman Miller Company, a furniture manufacturer that is frequently rated as one of the 10 best-managed U.S. corporations, has used a gainsharing plan for many years. The company also uses a strategy of employee involvement that supports and enhances the motivational effect of the gainsharing plan.
- Grumman Corporation developed a performance bonus plan for the crew in its Long Life Vehicle project that it used in conjunction with its Grumman Quality program. Employees focused on processes that involved rework, scrap, and excessive maintenance costs. Half the savings from improved performance were divided equally among the crew members working on the project.

The three most widely used gainsharing programs are improshare, the Scanlon plan, and the Rucker plan.

Improshare
A gainsharing program that determines its bonus pool by computing the difference between the target level of labor cost given the level of production and the actual labor cost.

Scanlon plan
A form of gainsharing program.

1. **Improshare** (improved productivity sharing) determines its bonus pool by computing the difference between the target level of labor cost given the level of production and the actual labor cost (the direct labor efficiency variance). The plan specifies how the difference will be shared between the shareholders and the employees and how to calculate the amount distributed to each employee.
2. The **Scanlon plan** is based on the following formula, computed using the data in some base period.

$$\text{Base ratio} = \frac{\text{Payroll costs}}{\text{Value of goods or services produced}}$$

For example, if in the base period payroll costs are \$25 million and the deemed value of production or service is \$86 million, then the base ratio would be 0.29 (\$25 million $\div$ \$86 million). In any period in which the ratio of labor costs to the value of production or service is less than the base ratio, the deemed labor savings are added to a bonus pool. Therefore, continuing the above example, if actual payroll costs were \$28 million in a period when the deemed value of production was \$105 million, then the amount added to the bonus pool would be:

$$\begin{aligned}\text{Amount added to bonus pool} &= (\text{Value of production this period} \times \text{Base ratio}) \\ &\quad - \text{Actual payroll costs} \\ &= (\$105{,}000{,}000 \times 0.29) - \$28{,}000{,}000 \\ &= \$2{,}450{,}000\end{aligned}$$

When labor costs are more than the base ratio, some organizations deduct the difference from the bonus pool. Periodically, usually once a year, the pool is apportioned between the company and the employees in the pool using the plant ratio, which is often 50%/50%.

Rucker plan
A form of gainsharing program.

3. The **Rucker plan** is based on the following formula, which reflects the data from a representative period:

$$\text{Rucker standard} = \frac{\text{Payroll costs}}{\text{Production value}}$$

where production value is measured as net sales − inventory change − materials and supplies used. As in the Scanlon plan, the idea in the Rucker plan is to define a baseline relationship between payroll costs and the value of production and then reward workers who improve efficiency. Efficiency is measured as lowering the ratio of payroll costs to the value of production. When actual costs are less than the Rucker standard, the employees receive a bonus.

Gainsharing plans must reflect performance levels that are reasonable in order to work. As you might expect, management and the employees who are subject to these plans often have very different ideas about what is fair. Management usually seeks tighter standards or targets, and employees want the opposite. This plan requires that management, the management accountant, and employees participate in seeking the performance level that will serve as the standard or benchmark for the plan. Many management accountants relish their role as the honest brokers between management and the employees who are subject to these plans.

The people who designed gainsharing plans believed, from the beginning, that monthly or even weekly performance awards are best. They provide rapid feedback and therefore additional motivation as rewards reinforce the desired type of behavior. While rapid feedback may improve the motivational effect of rewards (expectancy), short-cycle feedback can put strains on the organization's management accounting system when the need for recording and accruing labor costs increases both the cost and potential for error in the management accounting system.

Recall that since gainsharing plans are team-based rewards, they have the associated problem that some team members may not be doing their fair share and could earn rewards based on the work of others. For example, students often complain about group projects, particularly when they cannot choose their own groups, because there is often someone in the group who refuses to do or is incapable of doing the work. Students, like employees, are often uncomfortable about disciplining, or reporting, their peers. The early proponents of gainsharing recognized this phenomenon and observed that, for gainsharing to work, the organization culture must promote cohesive relationships within the group and between the group and management.

Finally, corporate culture has a significant effect on the potential of gainsharing plans. These programs rely on employee commitment and involvement. Therefore, a corporate culture that respects employees, encourages their involvement, and actively supports employee learning and innovation reinforces the motivational potential of a gainsharing program. Finally, like all incentive programs, gainsharing programs work best when they are simple to understand and monitor. A test of this attribute is whether employees can compute their own bonuses. In addition, such programs should be perceived as fair, as being directly affected by employee performance, and as being conducive to promoting teamwork.

Gainsharing plans usually rely on performance measures reported by an organization's management accounting system, which plays a primary supporting role in the gainsharing process. Most gainsharing plans focus on management accounting measures relating to labor costs and the relationship of actual labor cost to some standard, or budgeted, level of labor cost. Therefore, the key issues in performance measurement relate to measuring labor costs accurately and consistently and to having the ability to establish a cost standard that is perceived as fair.

Stock Options and Other Stock-Related Compensation Plans. Judging by the published remarks of compensation experts, stock options are the most widely known, misused, and maligned approach to incentive compensation. A **stock option** is the right to purchase a unit of the organizations stock at a specified price, called the option price.

Stock option
The right to purchase a unit of the organization's stock at a specified price, called the option price.

This employee is part of a gain sharing plan at Georgia-Pacific, a paper products manufacturer. The plan pays employees cash bonuses based on productivity improvements. A motivationally desirable feature of the Georgia-Pacific gain sharing plan is that it pays these productivity bonuses even when the company's net income is negative. (John Chiasson/Liaison Agency, Inc.).

A common approach to option pricing is to set the option price at about 105% of the stock's market price at the time the organization issues the stock option. This method is intended to motivate the employee who has been granted the stock options to act in the long-term interests of the organization, thereby increasing the value of the firm so that the market price of the stock will exceed the option price. For this reason, compensation system designers usually restrict stock options to senior executives, because they believe these people have the greatest effect on increasing the market value of the organization. Others have argued, however, that operations staff, as they carry out short-term operating plans, can make significant and sustainable process improvements. This would provide the organization with a competitive advantage, thereby increasing the organization's market value.

The critics of stock option plans have argued that organizations have been too generous in rewarding senior executives with stock options. For example, the organization may issue a senior executive many thousands of stock options with an option price that is very near, or even below, the market price at the time the stock option is issued. This is an implementation issue, not a fundamental defect of stock options. Some critics have argued, however, that stock price increases often reflect general market trends that have nothing to do with the performance of the individual organization. For this reason, many incentive compensation experts have argued that the stock option price should be keyed to the performance of the organization's shares relative to the performance of the prices of comparable shares. In this case, the stock option would be valuable only if the organization's share price increases more rapidly than the share prices of comparable organizations. Since management accountants are often involved in studies or systems that rely on external benchmarks, organizations sometimes delegate the role of developing the appropriate performance standards for relative stock option plans to a team that includes a management accountant.

Organizations use many other forms of stock-related incentive compensation plans, including performance shares stock, stock appreciation rights, participation units, and employee stock ownership plans that are beyond the scope of issues in management accounting. These plans provide incentive compensation to the participants when the stock price increases. The idea behind such plans is to motivate employees to act in the long-term interests of the organization by engaging in activities that increase the organization's market value. Therefore, all these plans assume that stock markets will recognize exceptional behavior in the form of increased stock prices.

In general, the use of employee stock ownership plans assumes that employees will work harder when they have an ownership stake. Avis, the automobile rental company, used an employee stock ownership plan to improve employee motivation, which, in turn, resulted in both higher sales and a higher margin on sales. Salomon Brothers, a Wall Street investment house, provided huge bonuses for high-performing employees during the 1980s and early 1990s. For example, one bond trader was paid a $23 million bonus in 1990. Reacting to this, Salomon Brothers' largest shareholder, Warren Buffett, whom Forbes identified as the wealthiest person in the United States in 1993 and who was interim chairman at the time, indicated that he wanted Salomon Brothers' employees to earn rewards through owing shares, not by free riding on the owners' investment. To align the interests of the firm's employees and its shareholders and provide for more reasonable performance rewards, Mr. Buffett, through the Salomon Brothers' Compensation Committee, developed an incentive plan that paid employees up to half their pay in company stock, issued at below market prices, that could not be sold for at least five years after issue. However, Mr. Buffett failed to weigh a consideration that is vital in designing any compensation plan, namely, how other investment banking firms were compensating their employees. While some people applauded the rationality of Mr. Buffett's plan, many employees left the firm to join other investment banking firms that were using compensation practices similar to the ones abandoned at Salomon Brothers. These departures precipitated a crisis which, eventually, led to the scrapping of the new plan.

SUMMARY

In the opening vignette to this chapter, Nathaniel Young thought he had not been careful enough to involve employees in designing his new MACS. He wondered about the kinds of behavioral characteristics that he needed to manage.

In this chapter we outlined four key behavioral characteristics that comprise a well-designed MACS. The choice of the four characteristics is based largely on an acceptance of the human resources model of human motivation. Understanding these characteristics should provide Nathaniel guidance for designing his new MACS.

The first is embedding the organization's ethical code of conduct into MACS design. At the core of a well-designed MACS is the organization's ethical code of conduct. Ethical codes of conduct help organizations deal with ethical dilemmas or conflicts between individuals and organizational values and those that exist between the organization's stated and practiced values. The elements of an effective ethical control system are presented together with a specific decision model that can be applied when attempting to resolve ethical issues.

Organizations spend a lot of time determining how to motivate employees. One way is to align the goals of employees with those of the organization. However, even if goals are aligned, organizations cannot always rely on employee self-control to achieve targeted performance. In many instances, organizations must set up task or results control systems. Task control uses either preventive control devices or relies on monitoring, whereas results control focuses on comparing actual results to desired performance. Development and use of the right kinds of performance measures are tied directly into the second behavioral characteristic, which involves using a mix of short- and long-term qualitative and quantitative performance measures. We labeled this the balanced scorecard approach.

The balanced scorecard is the first systematic

attempt to design a performance measurement system that translates an organization's strategy into clear objectives, measures, and initiatives. The scorecard is built around four perspectives—the financial perspective, the customer perspective, the internal business perspective, and the learning and growth perspective. For each of these, specific performance measures are developed. Having such perspectives allows an organization to manage themselves in a balanced fashion, as no particular perspective gets overemphasized at the expense of the others.

The third characteristic is empowering employees to be involved in decision making and MACS design. This characteristic acknowledges that people are the organization's greatest asset. Providing a voice through participation has a twofold benefit. First, participation in decision making has been shown to increase employee morale, commitment to a decision, and job satisfaction. Second, by allowing employees to participate, the organization is able to gather information about jobs and processes from the individuals who are closest to those jobs and processes. Such information provides managers with insights that they would not normally be able to obtain simply by performing cursory inspections of how people are working. Continuing to educate employees in the information they are using and being evaluated on is another critical aspect of employee involvement. For example, without a clear understanding of how their actions translate into a score on a performance measure, employees are left without direction and may take actions detrimental to the organization.

Both intrinsic and extrinsic rewards are used by organizations to motivate employees. However, intrinsic rewards come from inside an individual and may simply be the result of an employee liking a specific job. Organizations try to hire individuals who will match a particular job and thus be intrinsically motivated. But even if intrinsic motivation exists, many organizations still rely on extrinsic rewards, such as financial incentives, for motivational purposes.

Developing an appropriate incentive system to reward performance is the fourth characteristic. In this chapter we discuss the characteristics of an effective performance measurement system and the most common ways of rewarding results, including cash bonus, gainsharing, and stock options.

KEY TERMS

Balanced scorecard, 408
Cash bonus, 418
Data falsification, 407
Employee self-control, 403
Ethical control system, 400
Extrinsic reward, 413
Gainsharing, 419
Gaming the performance indicator, 406
Goal congruence, 403
Human relations movement, 396
Human resources model of motivation (HRMM), 396
Improshare, 420
Incentive compensation, 413
Intrinsic rewards, 412
Monitoring, 404
Motivation, 396
Pay-for-performance system, 419
Preventive control, 403
Profit sharing, 419
Results control, 405
Rucker plan, 420
Scanlon plan, 420
Scientific management school, 396
Stock option, 421
Task control, 403

ASSIGNMENT MATERIALS

QUESTIONS

10-1 What are the four major behavioral considerations in MACS design? (LO 1)

10-2 What is the scientific management view of motivation? (LO 2)

10-3 What is the human relations movement view of motivation? (LO 2)

10-4 What is the human resources model view of motivation? (LO 2)

10-5 What are the four requirements of ethical conduct by which certified management accountants (CMAs) have to abide? (LO 4)

10-6 What are some choices that individuals can make when ethical conflicts arise? (LO 4)

10-7 What is an ethical control system, and what are its key elements? (LO 4)

10-8 What are the three key dimensions of motivation? (LO 3)

10-9 What is goal congruence? (LO 3)

10-10 How does task control differ from results control? (LO 3)

10-11 List and explain the two categories in task control. (LO 3)

10-12 List three quantitative financial measures of performance in a manufacturing organization of your choice. (LO 3)

10-13 List three quantitative financial measures of performance in a service organization of your choice. (LO 3)

10-14 List three quantitative nonfinancial measures of performance in a manufacturing organization of your choice. (LO 3)

10-15 List three quantitative nonfinancial measures of performance in a service organization of your choice. (LO 3)

10-16 List three qualitative measures of performance. (LO 3)

10-17 What is gaming? (LO 3)

10-18 What is data falsification? (LO 3)

10-19 What is a balanced scorecard? (LO 5)

10-20 What are the four measurement perspectives in the balanced scorecard? (LO 5)

10-21 What are two essential elements in employee empowerment? (LO 6)

10-22 What is an intrinsic reward? (LO 6)

10-23 What is an extrinsic reward? (LO 6)

10-24 What is incentive compensation? (LO 6)

10-25 What are the six attributes of effective performance measurement systems? (LO 6)

10-26 What type of organization is best suited to incentive compensation? Why? (LO 6)

10-27 What is a cash bonus? (LO 6)

10-28 What is profit sharing? (LO 6)

10-29 What is gainsharing? (LO 6)

10-30 What is a stock option plan? (LO 6)

EXERCISES

10-31 ***Managerial approaches to motivation*** How do the scientific management, human relations, and human resource schools differ in their views on human motivation? LO 2

10-32 ***Characteristics of a MACS: ethical issues*** List and describe the hierarchy of ethical considerations. LO 4

10-33 ***Characteristics of a MACS: ethical issues*** What should a person do if faced with a conflict between his or her values and those of the organization? LO 4

10-34 ***Characteristics of a MACS: ethical issues*** What should a person do if the organization's stated values conflict with practiced values? What are the individual's choices? Why do you think such conflicts exist? LO 4

10-35 ***Choosing an approach to control*** Think of any setting in need of control. Explain why you think that task control or results control would be more appropriate in the setting that you have chosen. Do not use an example from the text. LO 3

10-36 ***Characteristics of a MACS: multiple performance measures*** What is the advantage of having multiple measures of performance? LO 3

10-37 ***Understanding performance measurement*** Why is it important that people understand what performance is measured, how performance is measured, and how employee rewards relate to measured performance? LO 3

10-38 ***Controllable performance*** Why should performance measurement systems and rewards focus on performance that employees can control? LO 3

LO 3 **10-39** ***Tailoring performance measurement to the job*** In a company that takes telephone orders from customers for general merchandise, explain how you would evaluate the performance of the company president, a middle manager who designs the system to coordinate order taking and order shipping, and an employee who fills orders. How are the performance systems similar? How are the performance systems different?

LO 3, 6 **10-40** ***Characteristics of a MACS: rewards*** Can goal congruence be increased if rewards are tied to performance? Explain.

LO 3 **10-41** ***Nongoal-congruent behavior*** What distinguishes data falsification and gaming activities?

LO 3 **10-42** ***Nongoal-congruent behavior*** List some methods of gaming performance indicators.

LO 3 **10-43** ***Nongoal-congruent behavior*** Can you think of instances when gaming behavior is appropriate in an organization?

LO 6 **10-44** ***Characteristics of a MACS: participation*** What are the advantages for the individual in being able to participate in decision making in the organization, and what are the advantages for the organization in allowing the individual to participate in decision making?

LO 6 **10-45** ***The nature of intrinsic and extrinsic rewards*** Do you believe that people value intrinsic rewards? Give an example of an intrinsic reward that you would value and explain why. Why are extrinsic rewards important to people? If you value only extrinsic rewards, explain why.

LO 6 **10-46** ***Choosing what to reward*** Explain when one would reward outcomes or outputs, reward inputs, or use knowledge-based pay.

LO 6 **10-47** ***Choosing the reward level*** You work for a consulting firm and have been given the assignment of deciding whether a particular company president is overpaid both in absolute terms and relative to presidents of comparable companies. How would you undertake this task?

LO 6 **10-48** ***Using cash bonuses*** When should an organization use a cash bonus?

LO 6 **10-49** ***Using profit sharing*** When should an organization use profit sharing?

LO 6 **10-50** ***Using gainsharing*** When should an organization use gainsharing?

LO 6 **10-51** ***Using stock options*** When should an organization use stock options?

LO 6 **10-52** ***Rewarding group performance*** How would you reward a group of people that includes product designers, engineers, production personnel, purchasing agents, marketing staff, and accountants, whose job is to identify and develop a new car? How would you reward a person whose job is to discover a better way of designing crash protection devices in cars? How are these two situations similar? How are they different?

PROBLEMS

LO 1 **10-53** ***MACS design motivation*** Explain why an understanding of human motivation is essential to MACS design.

LO 1 **10-54** ***Behavioral considerations in MACS design*** List the four key behavioral considerations in MACS design, and explain the importance or benefits of each.

10-55 ***Ethics quiz*** Refer to *The Wall Street Journal* Workplace-Ethics Quiz in the In-Practice box on page 401. Discuss reasons why individual respondents might feel justified answering as they did. LO 4

10-56 ***Ethics*** Suppose you are the CEO of a manufacturing firm that is bidding on a government contract. In this situation, the firm with the lowest bid will win the contract. Your firm has completed developing its bid and is ready to submit it to the government, when you receive an anonymously sent packet containing a competitor's bid that is lower than yours. If your firm loses the bid, you may need to lay off some employees and your profits will suffer. What are some possible options in this situation, what are the possible consequences, and what would you do? LO 4

10-57 ***Characteristics of MACS design: ethical issues*** During data collection for the transition from an old management accounting system to a new activity-based cost management system, you see a manager's reported time allotments. You know that the data supplied by the manager is completely false. You confront the manager and she states that she is worried that if she reports how she actually spends her time, her job will be altered, and it will also be found out that she is really not performing very well. She implores you not to tell anyone because she has needed to take time off to care for her chronically ill parents and she needs the pay to help cover her parents' medical expenses. What actions should you take? Please explain. LO 4

10-58 ***Approaches to control*** Cite two settings or jobs where each of the following approaches to control would be appropriately applied. Identify what you feel is the definitive characteristic of the setting that indicates the appropriateness of the approach to control that you have identified. LO 3

(a) preventive control

(b) monitoring

(c) results control

10-59 ***Characteristics of MACS: types of information*** Under what circumstances should both quantitative and qualitative performance measures be used to evaluate employee, workgroup, and divisional performance? Provide examples to support your answer. LO 1, 3

10-60 ***Designing a balanced scorecard*** Consider the manager of a store in a fast-food restaurant chain. Construct a balanced scorecard to evaluate that manager's performance. LO 5

10-61 ***Evaluating system performance*** Suppose that you are the manager of a production facility in a business that makes plastic items that organizations use for advertising. The customer chooses the color and quantity of the item and specifies what is to be imprinted on the item. Your job is to ensure that the job is completed according to the customer's specifications. This is a cut-throat business that competes based on low price, high quality, and good service to the customer. Recently you installed a just-in-time manufacturing system. How may you evaluate the performance of this system given the characteristics of your organization? LO 1, 3

10-62 ***Characteristics of MACS design: participation and education*** Explain how participation in decision making and education to understand information contribute toward employee empowerment in MACS design. LO 6

10-63 ***Characteristics of MACS design: rewards*** What are some pros and cons of tying an individual's pay to performance? LO 6

LO 6 **10-64** ***Designing reward structures*** Answer these two questions about the organization units listed below:

- What behavior should be rewarded?
- What is an appropriate incentive system?

(a) A symphony orchestra

(b) A government welfare office

(c) An airline complaint desk

(d) A control room in a nuclear generating facility

(e) A basketball team

LO 6 **10-65** ***Designing a compensation plan*** Suppose that you are the owner/manager of a house-cleaning business. You have 30 employees who work in teams of three. Teams are dispatched to the homes of customers where they are directed by the customer to undertake specific cleaning tasks that vary widely from customer to customer.

Your employees are unskilled workers who are paid an hourly wage of $8. This wage is typical for unskilled work. Turnover in your organization is quite high. Generally, your best employees leave as soon as they find better jobs. The employees that stay are usually ones who cannot find work elsewhere and have a poor attitude.

The hourly rate charged customers per team hour is $40. That is, if a team spends 1.5 hours in a customer's home, the charge is $60.

You want to develop an incentive system to use in your organization. You would like to use this incentive system to motivate good employees to stay and motivate poor workers either to improve or to leave. What type of system would you develop? If the system relies on any measurements, indicate how you would obtain these measurements.

LO 6 **10-66** ***Motivating desired performance*** Darlington Engineering is a research and development company that designs equipment for nuclear generating stations. The company consists of an administrative unit, a research laboratory, and a facility used to develop prototypes of new designs. The major costs in this company are the salaries of the research staff, which are substantial.

In the past, the research scientists working at Darlington Engineering have been rewarded based on their proven scientific expertise. Salaries of these research scientists are based on the level of education achieved and the number of research papers published in scientific journals. At a recent board of directors meeting, an outside director criticized the research and development activities with the following comments:

> There is no question that we have the most highly trained scientists in our industry. Evidence of their training and creativity is provided by the number of research publications that they generate. However, the knowledge and creativity are not translating into patentable inventions and increased sales for this company. Our organization has the lowest rate of new product introduction in our industry, and we have one of the largest research and development teams. These people are too far into basic research, where the rewards lie in getting articles published. We need these people to have more interest in generating ideas that have commercial potential. This is a profit-seeking organization, not a university research laboratory.

REQUIRED

(a) Assuming that the director's facts are correct, do you agree that this is a problem?

(b) The board of directors has ordered the president of Darlington Engineering to increase the rate of new products and the time devoted to new product development. How should the president go about this task?

10-67 ***Profit-sharing plan at Hoechst Celanese*** Hoechst Celanese, a pharmaceutical manufacturer, has used a profit-sharing plan, the Hoechst Celanese Performance Sharing Plan, to motivate employees. To operationalize the plan, the Hoechst Celanese Executive Committee set a target earnings from operations (EFO). This target was based on the company's business plans and the economy's expected performance. The Performance Sharing Plan also used two other critical values: the earnings from operations threshold amount and the earnings from operations stretch target. The targets for 1994 are shown in Exhibit 10-5. LO 6

The plan operates as follows. If earnings from operations fall below the threshold value, there is no profit sharing. If earnings from operations lie between the threshold amount and the target, the profit-sharing percent is prorated between the threshold award of 1% and the target payment of 4%. For example, if earnings from operations were $285 million, the profit-sharing percent would be 2.5%.

$$\text{Profit-Sharing Percent} = 1\% + 3\% \times \left[\frac{285 - 250}{320 - 250}\right] = 2.5\%$$

$$\text{Profit-Sharing Pool} = 2.5\% \times \$285{,}000{,}000 = \$7{,}125{,}000$$

If earnings from operations are between the target and the stretch target, the profit-sharing percent is prorated between the target payment of 4% and the stretch-sharing payment of 7%. For example, if earnings from operations were $350 million, the profit-sharing percent would be 5.29% and the profit-sharing pool would be $18.5 million:

$$\text{Profit-Sharing Percent} = 4\% + 3\% \times \left[\frac{350 - 320}{390 - 320}\right] = 5.29\%$$

$$\text{Profit-Sharing Pool} = 5.29\% \times \$350{,}000{,}000 = \$18{,}500{,}000$$

If earnings from operations equal, or exceed, the stretch target level, the profit-sharing pool would be $27.3 million:

$$\text{Profit Sharing Pool} = 7\% \times \$390{,}000{,}000 = \$27{,}300{,}000$$

REQUIRED

(a) List, with explanations, what you think are desirable features of the Hoechst Celanese Performance Sharing Plan.

EXHIBIT 10-5

Hoechst Celanese Performance Sharing Plan: 1994 Targets

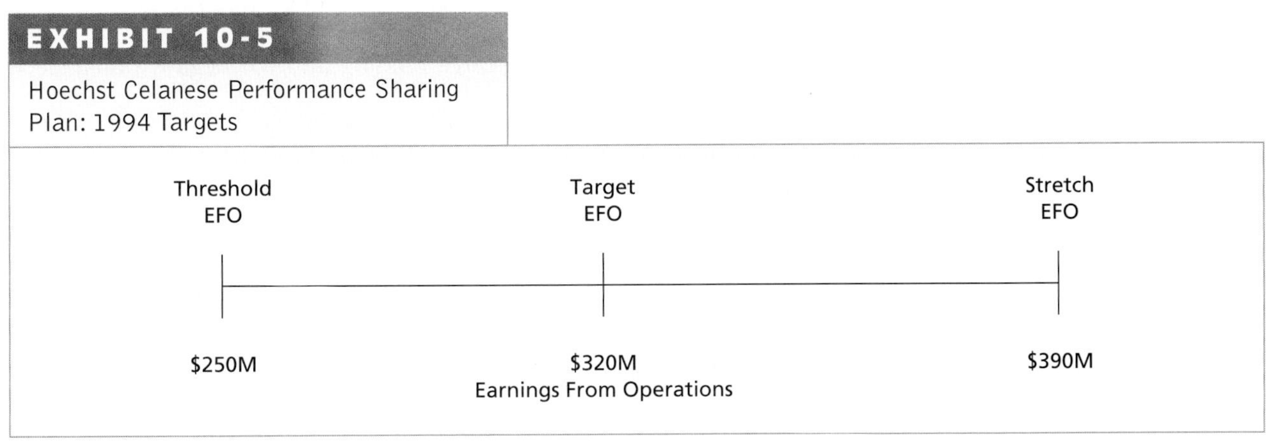

(b) List, with explanations, what you think are the undesirable features of the Hoechst Celanese Performance Sharing Plan.

(c) The EFO for 1994 was $332 million. Compute the size of the profit-sharing pool.

(d) In 1995 the Performance Sharing Plan parameters were threshold EFO—$420 million; target EFO—$490 million; and stretch EFO—$560 million. What do you think of the practice of raising the parameters from one year to the next?

LO 6 **10-68** ***Profit sharing*** Peterborough Medical Devices makes devices and equipment that it sells to hospitals. The organization has a profit-sharing plan that is worded as follows:

The company will make available a profit-sharing pool that will be the lower of the following two items:

1. 40% of net income before taxes in excess of the target profit level, which is 18% of net assets, or
2. $7 million

The individual employee is paid a share of the profit-sharing pool equal to the ratio of that employee's salary to the total salary paid to all employees.

REQUIRED

(a) If the company earned $45 million of profits and had net assets of $100 million, what would be the amount available for distribution from the profit-sharing pool?

(b) Suppose that Marg Watson's salary was $68,000 and that total salaries paid in the company were $25 million. What would Marg's profit share be?

(c) What do you like about this profit-sharing plan?

(d) What do you dislike about this profit-sharing plan?

LO 6 **10-69** ***Gainsharing*** Lindsay Cereal Company manufactures a line of breakfast cereals. The production workers are part of a gainsharing program that works as follows. A target level of labor costs is set based on the achieved level of production. If the actual level of labor costs is less than the target level of labor costs, the difference is added to a cumulative pool that is carried from year to year. If the actual level of labor costs exceeds the target level, the amount of the excess is deducted from the cumulative pool.

If the balance of the pool is positive at the end of any year, the employees receive half the balance of the pool as part of a gainsharing plan and the balance of the pool is reset to zero. If the balance of the pool is negative at the end of any year, the employees receive nothing and the negative balance is carried to the following year.

In any year when the target level of costs exceeds the actual level of costs, the target level for the following year is based on the actual level of cost performance in the previous year.

REQUIRED

(a) Suppose that the target level of performance is set using the following labor use standards: (1) 0.15 labor hours per case of cereal A, (2) 0.10 labor hours per case of cereal B, (3) 0.20 labor hours per case of cereal C, and (4) 0.25 labor hours per case of cereal D.

During the last year, production levels of cereal A, B, C, and D were 200,000 cases, 220,000 cases, 130,000 cases, and 240,000 cases, respectively. The company used 120,000 labor hours during the year, and the average cost of labor was $16 per hour. What is the amount available for distribution to employees under this gainsharing program?

(b) What do you like about this program?

(c) What do you dislike about it?

10-70 ***Scanlon plan*** Bathurst Company manufactures household paper products. During a recent quarter, the value of the products made was $50 million and the labor costs were $3 million. The company has decided to use a Scanlon plan with this quarter being used to establish the base ratio for the plan. LO 6

The formula is to be applied quarterly with differences, positive or negative, added to the bonus pool. The pool is to be distributed on a 35%/65% basis between the employees and the company at the end of the fourth quarter.

The following production and cost levels were recorded during the first year of the plan's operation.

QUARTER	PRODUCTION VALUE	PAYROLL COSTS
1	$45,000,000	$2,475,000
2	60,000,000	3,480,000
3	55,000,000	3,575,000
4	48,000,000	2,832,000

REQUIRED

(a) How much would be distributed to the employees at the end of the year?

(b) What assumptions does the Scanlon plan make about the behavior of payroll costs?

(c) What formula should be used to determine each employee's share?

(d) Management proposes to adjust the base ratio using the lowest ratio experienced in any year. Do you think this is a good idea?

10-71 ***Characteristics of MACS design: ethical issues*** You are a management accountant working in the controller's office. Rick Koch, a very powerful executive, approaches you in the parking lot and asks you to do him a favor. The favor involves falsifying some of his division's records on the main computer. The executive states that if you do not do as he asks, he will have you fired. What do you do? Please explain. LO 4

10-72 ***Designing a balanced scorecard*** The following exhibit appeared in Weirton Steel Corporation's 1990 annual report: LO 5

We are bound together in these common beliefs and values. We must . . .

For the Customer

1. Have a total quality commitment to consistently meet the product, delivery, and service expectations of all customers.
2. Give customers increased value through processes that eliminate waste, minimize costs, and enhance production efficiency.

For the Employee

1. Reward teamwork, trust, honesty, openness, and candor.
2. Ensure a safe workplace.

3. Recognize that people are the corporation and provide them with training and information that allows for continuous improvement.
4. As employee-owners, obligate ourselves to provide a high level of performance and be accountable for our own actions.
5. Respect the dignity, rights, and contributions of others.

For the Company

1. Continuously invest in new technology and equipment to ensure competitiveness and enhance stockholder value.
2. Manage our financial and human resources for long-term profitability.

For the Community

1. Commit to environmental responsibility.
2. Fulfill our responsibility to enhance the quality of community life.

REQUIRED

Develop a balanced scorecard that Weirton Steel Corporation may use to measure performance on each of these imperatives.

LO 5 **10-73** ***Developing a balanced scorecard for a university*** Develop a balanced scorecard that the dean or director of your school may use to evaluate the school's operations. Be specific and indicate the purpose of each balanced scorecard measure.

LO 6 **10-74** ***Choosing what to reward*** During the late 1970s, Harley-Davidson, the motorcycle manufacturer, was losing money and was very close to bankruptcy. Management believed that one of the problems was low productivity and, as a result, asked middle managers to speed up production. The employees who made the motorcycles were told that the priority was to get the motorcycles made and shipped on schedule, which was usually very tight. Middle managers were judged by their ability to meet shipment schedules.

REQUIRED

(a) What is the rationale that would lead to a desire to speed production in the face of increasing costs and declining productivity?

(b) What type of behavior do you think that this performance measurement system would create in the sense of the priorities that middle management would establish for the production process?

(c) What type of problems would this performance measurement system create?

(d) How, if at all, would you modify this system?

LO 6 **10-75** ***Characteristics of MACS design: participation vs. imposition*** Denver Jack's is a large toy manufacturer. The company has 100 highly trained and skilled employees who are involved with six major product lines, including the production of toy soldiers, dolls, etc. Each product line is manufactured in a different city and state. Denver Jack has decided to make all of the production decisions for the toy lines himself, including which products to eliminate. The managers of each toy line believe he is making a mistake.

REQUIRED

What are the pros and cons of Denver Jack's approach?

LO 6 **10-76** ***Evaluating a compensation plan*** Beau Monde, Inc., a manufacturer and distributor of health and beauty products, made the following disclosure about its compensation program:

Our compensation philosophy is based on two simple principles: (1) we pay for performance; and (2) management cannot benefit unless our shareholders benefit first.

Executive compensation at Beau Monde consists of three elements: base salary, bonus, and stock awards. Frankly, we see base salaries and the underlying value of restricted stock as what you have to pay to get people in the door—fixed costs, if you will. Incentives, in the form of annual cash bonuses and gains tied to increases in the price of our stock, are the performance drivers of our pay equation—the variable costs.

The first element is base salary. Our philosophy is to peg salary levels at median competitive levels. In other words, we pay salaries that are sufficient to attract and retain the level of talent we require.

The second element of our executive compensation is our bonus plan. This plan is based on management by objectives. Each year, the compensation committee approves objectives and performance measures for the corporation, our divisions, and our key individual managers. At year end, bonuses are paid on the basis of measurable performance against these objectives.

The third element of our executive compensation program is stock incentives, namely, restricted stock and stock options.

Our restricted stock program is very straightforward. Stock option grants are made each year at market value. Our options vest over time periods of two to six years to encourage long-term equity holding by management.

In 1991, we instituted an innovative stock incentive plan called the Stock Option Exchange Program. Under this program, management can purchase stock options by exchanging other forms of compensation, such as the annual bonus or restricted stock, for the options. The price charged for the options is determined by an independent investment banker using pricing mechanics.

Our compensation committee is made up entirely of independent outside directors. There are no interlocking directorates, in which I serve on the compensation committee of one of my director's companies and he or she serves on mine. The compensation committee uses outside advisers chosen independently to ensure that recommendations are fair to all shareholders.

What do you think of this incentive compensation plan?

10-77 ***The mix of salary and commission*** Belleville Fashions sells high-quality women's, men's, and children's clothing. The store employs a sales staff of 11 full-time people and 12 part-time people. Until recently, all sales staff were paid a flat salary and participated in a profit-sharing plan that provided benefits equal to about 5% of wages. Recently, the manager and owner of Belleville Fashions announced that in the future all compensation would be commission based. The initial commission rate was set equal to the rate that would have caused the actual wage bill based on the old system to be equal to what the wage bill would have been under the commission system. Profit sharing was discontinued. LO 6

REQUIRED

(a) What do you think of this change?

(b) Describe some of the reactions that the owner might hear from the sales staff when announcing this change.

(c) Do you think that the method of determining the commission rate was appropriate?

(d) Describe what you think will happen under the new system.

LO 6 **10-78** ***Salary and job responsibilities*** Marie Johnston, the manager of a government unemployment insurance office, is paid a salary that reflects the number of people she supervises and the number of hours that her subordinates work.

REQUIRED

(a) What do you think of this compensation scheme? What incentives does this compensation scheme provide to Marie?

(b) What would you recommend as an appropriate performance measurement and reward system?

LO 6 **10-79** ***Distributing a bonus pool*** Four broad approaches to distributing the proceeds of a bonus pool in a profit-sharing plan are listed below.

(1) Each person's share is based on salary.

(2) Each person receives an equal share.

(3) Each person's share is based on position in the organization (larger payments to people at higher levels).

(4) Each person's share is based on individual performance relative to some target.

REQUIRED

(a) For each of these alternatives, give two reasons to support the alternative.

(b) For each of these alternatives, give two reasons to oppose the alternative.

(c) Pick the alternative that you think is best and support your choice with an argument of no more than 100 words.

CASES

LO 1, 3 **10-80** ***Characteristics of MACS design: types of information*** Chow Company is an insurance company in Hong Kong. Chow hires 55 people to process insurance claims. The volume of claims is extremely high and all claims examiners are kept extremely busy. The number of claims that have mistakes runs about 10%. If a claim has an error, it must be corrected by the claims examiners. After looking at the data, Judy Choy, senior manager of the division, was not satisfied with the volume of claims processed. She instructed Anne Wu, the manager, to motivate the claims examiners to work faster. Judy believes that the claims examiners are working as fast as they possibly can. She is also concerned that, by working faster, the examiners will make more errors.

REQUIRED

(a) How should Anne Wu handle this situation?

(b) On what performance measures is the organization relying?

(c) What performance measures should the organization use?

LO 5 **10-81** ***Implementing the balanced scorecard*** Find either by visiting a site or from a description in a published article a description of the implementation of a balanced scorecard.

REQUIRED

(a) Document in detail the elements of the balanced scorecard.

(b) Identify the purpose of each balanced scorecard element.

(c) Describe, if the facts are available, or infer, if the facts are not available, how the balanced scorecard elements relate to the organization's strategy.

(d) Evaluate the balanced scorecard by indicating whether you agree that the choice of balanced scorecard measures is complete and consistent with the organization's plan and stakeholder set.

10-82 ***Rewarding long-term performance*** In 1983, Johnson Controls Inc. developed a seven-year performance plan for two of their most senior-level executives. In each of the seven years, the base amount of the plan (consisting of $300,000 and $100,000 for the two executives, respectively) is multiplied by a percentage that varies between 0% and 150%. The determination of each percentage is based upon the ratio of the average annual total shareholder return for Johnson Controls (over the 10-year period ending with the current year) to the average total shareholder return for a peer group of Fortune 500 companies over the same period. Then each of the yearly awards is invested in a hypothetical portfolio consisting of the stock of Johnson Controls. The payment of the total value of this hypothetical portfolio is deferred until the end of the seven-year performance period. LO 6

There are several interesting aspects of this performance plan. First, the term of the contract extends approximately three years beyond the retirement of the two executives. This feature appears to be an attempt to lengthen the decision-making horizons of the two executives, especially in the case of those near retirement age. This contract explicitly motivates the executives to consider the impact of their decisions on the company after they leave the corporation.

Second, the scorecard for the annual changes in the value of the performance plan is formally tied to changes in shareholder wealth over the prior 10 years. This is unusual because performance plans are typically based on earnings per share or return on equity growth rates. One explanation for the choice of changes in shareholder wealth is that the board of directors is attempting to lengthen the executive's decision-making horizon by selecting a scorecard that has a longer performance evaluation horizon than yearly accounting numbers.

Finally, the performance plan is based on relative changes in shareholder wealth. This appears to be an attempt to isolate that portion of changes in shareholder wealth that is under management's control from economy- and industry-wide effects. The choice of a 10-year period for assessing the performance of the company may be an attempt to wash out other random effects that affect performance in a single year.

Comment on this incentive compensation plan. Identify what you like and what you do not like about it.[3]

[3]Richard A. Lambert and David F. Larcker, "Executive Compensation. Corporate Decision-Making and Shareholder Wealth: A Review of the Evidence." Joel M. Stern, G. Bennett Stewart III, and Donald H. Chew (eds.), *In: Corporate Restructuring and Executive Compensation.* Cambridge, MA, Ballinger Publishing Company, 1989.

chapter 11

Using Budgets to Achieve Organizational Objectives

AFTER READING THIS CHAPTER, YOU WILL BE ABLE TO

1. identify the primary role of budgets and budgeting in organizations
2. demonstrate the importance of each element of the budgeting process
3. explain the different types of operating budgets and financial budgets and their interrelationships
4. describe the way that organizations effectively use and interpret budgets
5. use cost-volume-profit analysis to evaluate the operating and financial consequences of alternative decisions
6. undertake what-if and sensitivity analyses—two important budgeting tools used by budget planners
7. identify the role of budgets in service and not-for-profit organizations
8. recognize the behavioral effects of budgeting on an organization's employees

John Elk III/Stock, Boston

THE FINANCING CRISIS IN RIDGETOWN

Ridgetown was a thriving and growing city whose population had recently topped 750,000 people. The residents were proud of their city, which boasted a vibrant downtown, extensive community services in the form of recreational facilities, and a clean and relatively crime-free environment.

The city's industries were primarily light industrial and white collar. Industries included some automobile parts manufacturing plants, a university, a head office for a major insurance company, and a head office for a major software development company.

In 2001, the projected city revenues were about $2.5 billion, of which 50% were collected from property taxes, 20% from business taxes, 20% from user fees and profits of the city-owned public utility, and 10% in grants from the federal government. There was a general feeling that the city council had to hold the line on tax increases, that user fees were not likely to increase over the foreseeable future, and that grants from the federal government were unlikely to increase and, in fact, might fall while Washington wrestled with chronic deficits.

Proposed expenditures for 2001 were slightly higher at approximately $2.7 billion, of which about 60% were for education, 20% for police and fire services, 5% for recreation (parks, arenas, and classes), 4% for debt servicing, 3% for transit, 2% for road maintenance, 2% for garbage collection and processing, 1% for the library, and 3% for other services.

Mayor Sandra Moore and the city council were concerned about the projected deficit for two reasons. First, the city was not allowed to run deficits. Second, the mayor and the majority of council believed that residents expected to continue to enjoy the high level of services and quality of life currently provided in Ridgetown. The city's budget committee was at an impasse concerning how to deal with the difference between projected revenues and expenditures.

Determining the Levels of Capacity-Related and Flexible Resources

Thus far we have discussed costs as they relate to short- and long-term decisions. Those that varied with the activity level in the firm were referred to as variable, or flexible, costs, whereas those that did not change with changes in activity levels were referred to as fixed, or capacity-related, costs.

In many business decisions, especially those made in the short term, capacity-related costs are thought of as given, and thus most relevant costs are flexible costs. In an ideal situation, the supply of capacity resources, such as people and equipment, is based on the demands for the services provided for projected levels of product volumes and mix. The budgeting process also highlights the reality that some resources, once acquired, cannot be disposed of easily if demand is less than expected. In this chapter, we discuss the **budgeting process**—the process that determines the planned level of most flexible costs. Budgeting for capacity-related resources was discussed in Chapter 8.

Budgeting process
The process that determines the planned level of most flexible costs.

The Budgeting Process

Most members of households have at some time developed a financial plan to guide them in allocating their resources over a specific period. Usually the plan reflects spending priorities and demands, including specific categories on which money will be spent such as the mortgage, utilities, property taxes, and essential items such as food and clothing. Family budgets often are the result of negotiations between parents, children, and others reflecting their different needs and objectives. For instance, money left over after required spending on food, clothing, medicine, insurance, and housing

The cost of this equipment is a capacity-related cost which reflects a long-term commitment of resources to acquire capacity. (Louise Gubb/The Image Works)

EXHIBIT 11-1

Planning and Control and the Role of Budgets

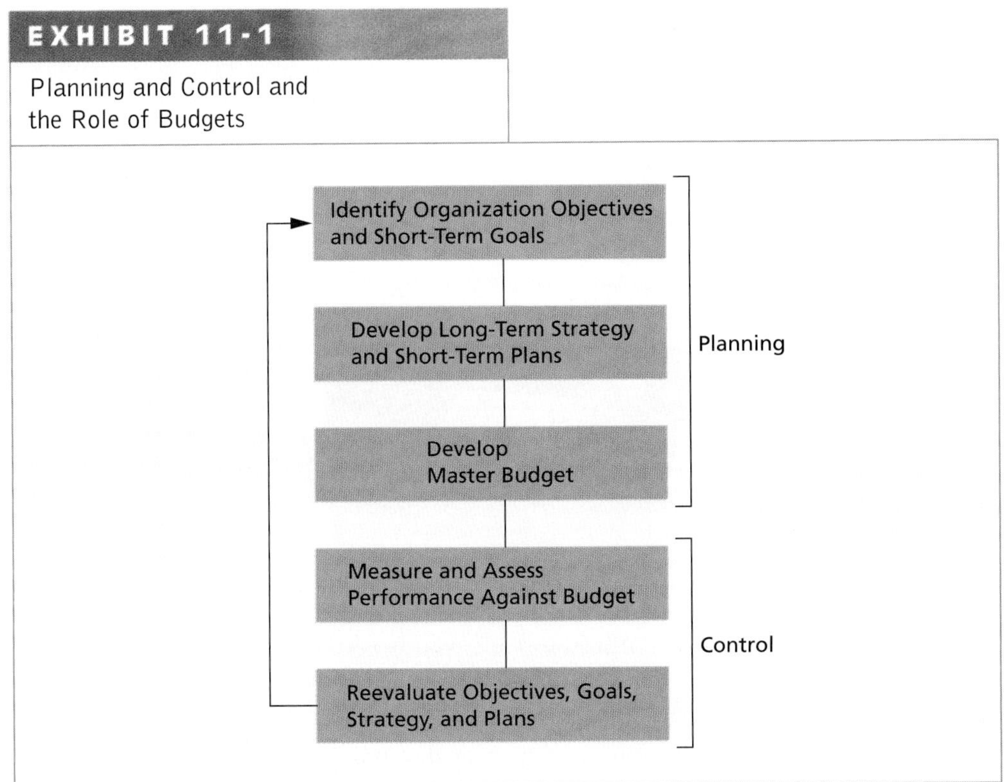

may go into savings or be used for other purposes; one parent may want to use most of the remaining disposable income for a vacation, whereas the other may want to use the money to paint the house. Within the same household, a teenager may ask the parents for help in financing the purchase of a used car. The family budget is a planning tool, but it also serves as a control on the behavior of family members by setting limits on what can be spent within each budget category. Without a budget, the families have no way of knowing how much of their money is being spent. Such a situation can easily lead a family into unexpected debt and severe financial difficulties.

Budgets play a similar planning and control role for managers within business units and are a central part of the design and operation of management accounting systems. Exhibit 11-1 shows the central role played by budgets and the relationship between planning and control. Note the distinct but linked steps for each function—three for planning and two for control.

As in a household, budgets in organizations reflect in quantitative terms how to allocate financial resources to each organizational subunit, based on its planned activities and short-run objectives. For example, a bank manager may want to increase local market share, which may require a larger spending budget than in the previous year in order to increase the amount of local advertising, implement a training program among the staff to improve customer service, and renovate the building to make it more appealing to customers. Thus, a **budget** is a quantitative expression of the money inflows and outflows that reveal whether a financial plan will meet organizational objectives. **Budgeting** is the process of preparing budgets.

Budget
A quantitative expression of the money inflows and outflows that predicts the consequences of current operating decisions and reveals whether a financial plan will meet organizational objectives.

Budgeting
The process of preparing budgets.

Budgets also provide a way to communicate the organization's short-term goals to its members. Budgeting activities of organization units can reflect how well unit managers understand the organization's goals and provide an opportunity for the organization's senior planners to correct misperceptions about the organization's goals. For example, suppose that an organization recognized quality as a critical success

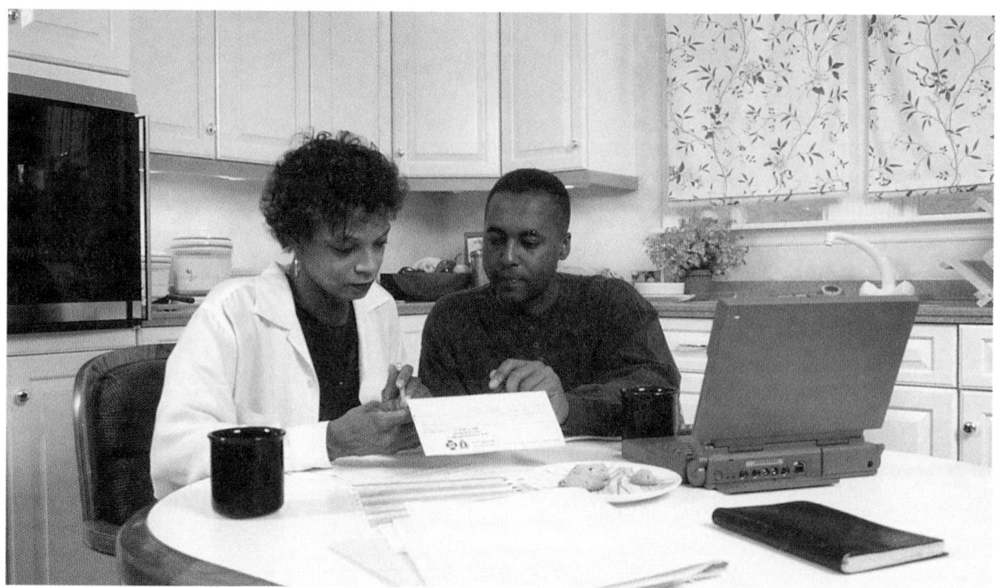

Most households are familiar with the notion of a budget, which is a plan that involves estimating cash inflows and outflows. (Blair Seitz/Photo Researchers, Inc.)

factor and wanted to promote quality awareness. If a department prepared a budget that reflected no expenditures on employee quality training, a senior planner would recognize that the importance of quality training had not been communicated properly.

Budgeting also serves to coordinate the organization's many activities. For example, budgets show the effect of sales levels on purchasing, production, and administrative activities and on the number of employees that need to be hired to serve customers. Therefore, budgeting is a tool that forces coordination of the organization's activities and helps identify coordination problems. Suppose, for example, that the sales force plans to significantly expand sales. By comparing selling plans with manufacturing capacity, planners might discover that the manufacturing operations are unable to support the planned level of sales. Powerful desktop computers are invaluable in this coordination role, because they allow planners to simulate easily the impact of different decisions on the organization's financial, human, and physical resources. Simulation (what-if) analysis helps managers choose a course of action

Part of planning is to coordinate the organization's various activities such as planning and selling. Where sales are seasonal, the organization will have to make plans to produce in advance and store product for the crucial selling season. (The Image Works)

among many alternatives by identifying a decision's consequences in a complex system with many interdependencies.

By considering interrelationships among operating issues, using budgets can help to anticipate potential problems and can serve as a tool to help provide solutions to these problems. For example, organizations such as canneries that engage in seasonal production must invest large amounts of cash in inventory during the canning season. Then, during the year, the organization sells its inventory and recovers cash. Budgeting reflects this cycle and provides information to help the organization plan the borrowing needed to finance the inventory buildup early in the cycle. If budget planning indicates that the organization's sales potential exceeds its manufacturing potential, then the organization can develop a plan to put more capacity in place or to reduce planned sales. The ability to anticipate problems is important, since it usually takes organizations several months to several years to put new capacity in place.

Budgets are prepared for specific time periods to allow managers to compare actual results for the period with planned results. Differences between actual results and the budget plan are called **variances.** Variances provide a signal that operations did not go as planned and are part of a larger control system for monitoring results. Supervisory personnel often use variances as an overall check on how well the people who are managing day-to-day operations are discharging their responsibilities. Variances also show the effectiveness of the control systems that operations people are using and the organization's effectiveness relative to other organizations. Other types of information—such as trends in actual production rates, numbers of defects and yields, and cycle times—provide additional information to help employees detect and correct problems as they arise and learn about and improve operations. We will develop the role of information and variances for feedback, learning, and improvement in more detail in Chapter 12.

Variances
The differences between planned and actual costs.

Budgeting generally involves forecasting the demand for three types of resources over different time periods:

1. Flexible resources that create variable or flexible costs. These can be acquired or disposed of in the short term
2. Intermediate-term capacity resources that create capacity-related costs
3. Long-term capacity resources that create capacity-related costs

In the next section we will discuss the overall framework for budgeting in organizations. The discussion will begin with the budgeting process and lead to formulation of the overall master budget. We will then break down the master budget into the two major types of budgets.

1. **Operating budgets** summarize activities such as sales, purchasing, and production.
2. **Financial budgets,** such as balance sheets, income statements, and cash flow statements, identify the expected financial consequences of the activities summarized in the operating budgets.

Operating budget
The document that forecasts revenues and expenses during the next operating period including monthly forecasts of sales, production, and operating expenses.

Financial budgets
Those budgets that identify the expected financial consequences of the activities summarized in the operating budgets.

We will present a comprehensive example of the budgeting process using this framework; and then turn to the behavioral and organizational aspects of budgeting. Budgets are critical to many people in organizations. Therefore, we need to understand behavioral issues that arise from the participants in the budget-setting process, and the kinds of games (such as distortion and manipulation) that people sometimes play with budgets. Exhibit 11-2 summarizes many different components of the budgeting process. The dotted lines from the projected financial statements (box 12) and statement of expected cash flows (box 11) to organization goals (box 1) show how the estimated financial consequences from the organization's tentative budgets can influence the organization's plans and objectives. The dotted lines illustrate an iterative process in which planners compare

EXHIBIT 11-2

The Master Budget

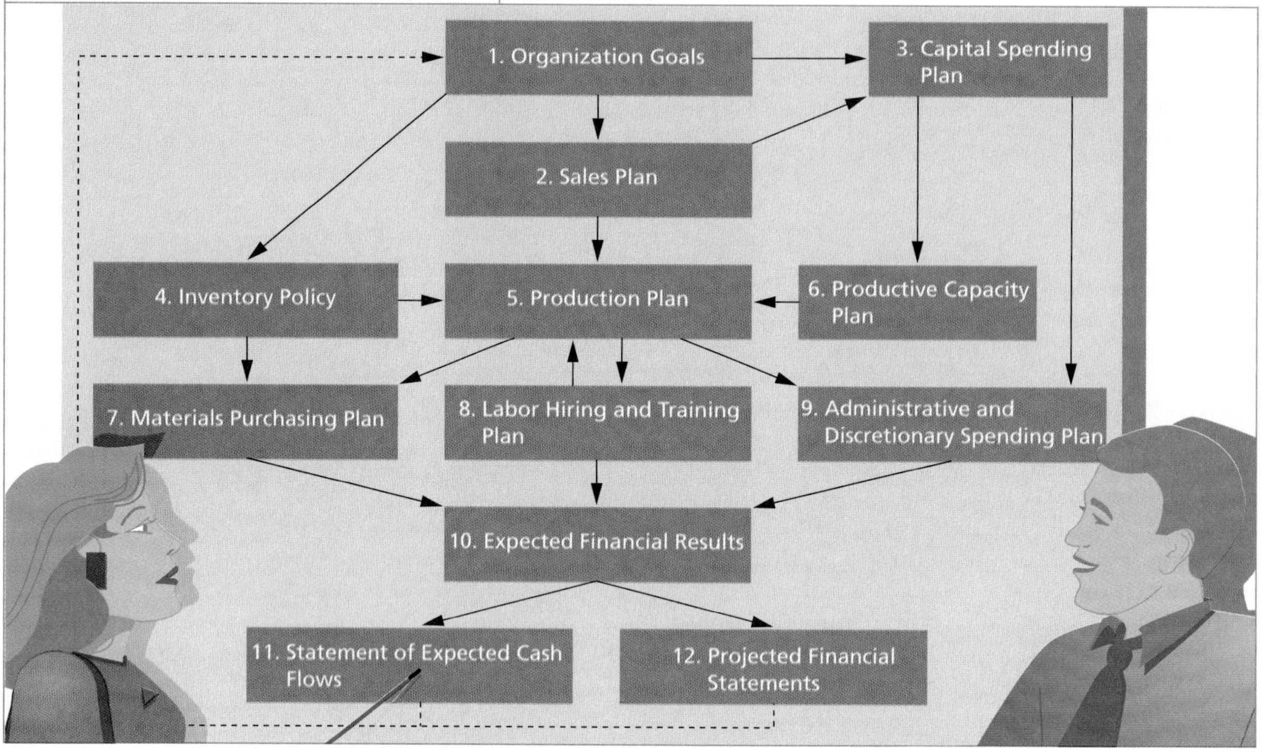

1. Organization Goals
2. Sales Plan
3. Capital Spending Plan
4. Inventory Policy
5. Production Plan
6. Productive Capacity Plan
7. Materials Purchasing Plan
8. Labor Hiring and Training Plan
9. Administrative and Discretionary Spending Plan
10. Expected Financial Results
11. Statement of Expected Cash Flows
12. Projected Financial Statements

projected financial results with the organization's financial goals. If initial budgets prove infeasible or unacceptable, planners repeat the budgeting cycle with a new set of decisions until the results are both feasible and financially acceptable.

The budgeting process describes the broad activities performed during the budget period. Planners can select any budget period but usually choose one year. We will assume a one-year cycle in the following discussion.

Master Budget Outputs

The master budget in Exhibit 11-1 (third box) includes two sets of outputs from Exhibit 11-2: the plans or operating budgets that operating personnel use to guide operations [sales plan (box 2), capital spending plan (box 3), production plan (box 5), production capacity (box 6), materials purchasing plan (box 7), labor hiring and training plan (box 8), and the administrative and discretionary spending plan (box 9) in Exhibit 11-2] and the expected or projected financial results (box 10). Planners usually present the projected financial results, or financial budgets, in three forms:

1. A statement of expected cash flows (box 11)
2. The projected balance sheet (box 12)
3. The projected income statement (box 12)

Pro forma financial statements The projected balance sheet and projected income statement.

The projected balance sheet and projected income statement are generally called **pro forma financial statements.**

OPERATING BUDGETS

Operating budgets typically consist of these six operating plans (shown in Exhibit 11-2):

1. The sales plan (box 2) identifies the planned level of sales for each product.
2. The capital spending plan (box 3) specifies the long-term capital investments, such as buildings and equipment, that must be made to meet activity objectives.
3. The production plan (box 5) schedules all required production.
4. The materials purchasing plan (box 7) schedules all required purchasing activities.
5. The labor hiring and training plan (box 8) specifies the number of people the organization must hire or release to achieve its activity objectives, as well as all hiring and training policies.
6. The administrative and discretionary spending plan (box 9) includes administration, staffing, research and development, and advertising.

Operating budgets specify the expected requirements and results of any selling, capital spending, manufacturing, purchasing, labor management, and administrative activities during the planning period. Operations personnel use these plans to guide and coordinate the level of various activities during the planning period. Exhibit 11-3 illustrates information to be used to determine operating budgets in the future.

FINANCIAL BUDGETS

Planners prepare the projected balance sheet and income statement to evaluate the financial consequences of proposed decisions. Financial analysts use the statement of projected cash flows in two ways:

1. To plan when excess cash will be generated so that they can undertake short-term investments
2. To organize how to meet any cash shortages

Exhibit 11-4 illustrates the manufacturing of high volumes of high-quality, low-cost glass bottles by the Ball Corporation glass plant. Although the product layout

EXHIBIT 11-3

Combining Operating and Financial Data

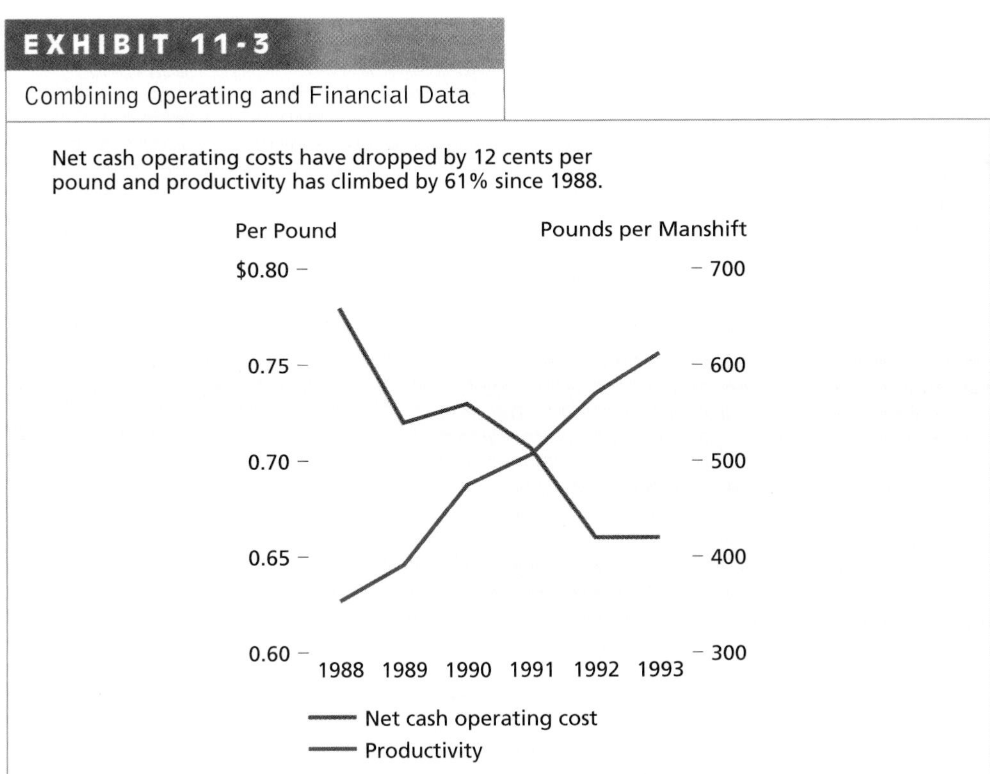

Although operating budgets and financial budgets focus on different types of information, the numbers are interrelated. Exhibit 11-3, prepared by Magma Copper Company, shows how cost per pound of copper fell while pounds of copper produced per person shift increased between 1988 and 1992. This relationship and these trends would be reflected in the labor and cost budgets prepared by Magma Copper planners. Source: *Magma Copper Company promotional brochure.*

EXHIBIT 11-4

Inside a Ball Glass Plant

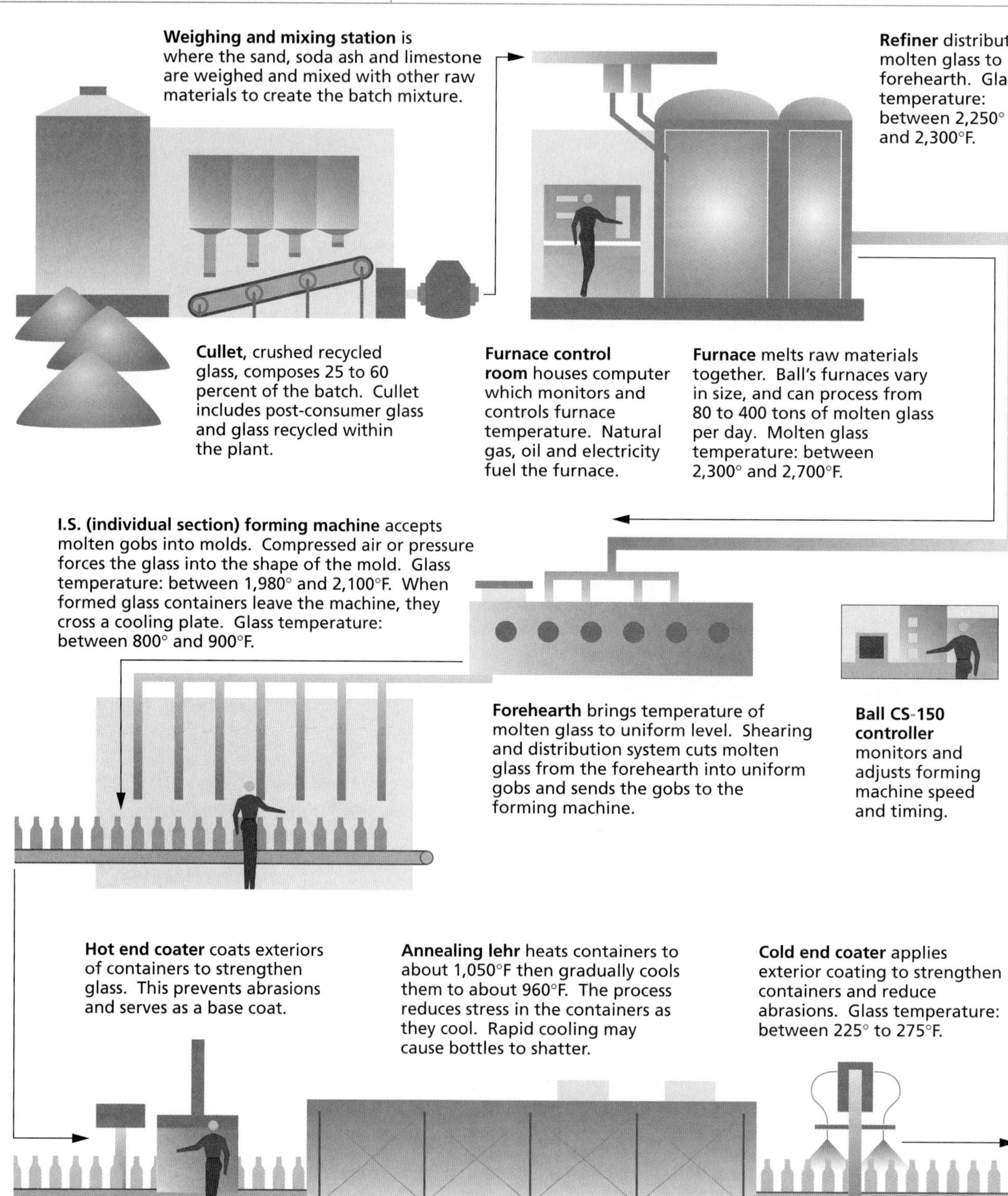

Weighing and mixing station is where the sand, soda ash and limestone are weighed and mixed with other raw materials to create the batch mixture.
Refiner distributes molten glass to forehearth. Glass temperature: between 2,250° and 2,300°F.
Cullet, crushed recycled glass, composes 25 to 60 percent of the batch. Cullet includes post-consumer glass and glass recycled within the plant.
Furnace control room houses computer which monitors and controls furnace temperature. Natural gas, oil and electricity fuel the furnace.
Furnace melts raw materials together. Ball's furnaces vary in size, and can process from 80 to 400 tons of molten glass per day. Molten glass temperature: between 2,300° and 2,700°F.
I.S. (individual section) forming machine accepts molten gobs into molds. Compressed air or pressure forces the glass into the shape of the mold. Glass temperature: between 1,980° and 2,100°F. When formed glass containers leave the machine, they cross a cooling plate. Glass temperature: between 800° and 900°F.
Forehearth brings temperature of molten glass to uniform level. Shearing and distribution system cuts molten glass from the forehearth into uniform gobs and sends the gobs to the forming machine.
Ball CS-150 controller monitors and adjusts forming machine speed and timing.
Hot end coater coats exteriors of containers to strengthen glass. This prevents abrasions and serves as a base coat.
Annealing lehr heats containers to about 1,050°F then gradually cools them to about 960°F. The process reduces stress in the containers as they cool. Rapid cooling may cause bottles to shatter.
Cold end coater applies exterior coating to strengthen containers and reduce abrasions. Glass temperature: between 225° to 275°F.

This diagram of a Ball Corporation Glass plant shows a product layout designed to produce high volumes of high-quality, low-cost glass bottles. Planners need operating and financial budgets to estimate the operating and financial consequences of their operating plans and to evaluate the implications, both operating and financial, of changing plans. (Ball Corporation)

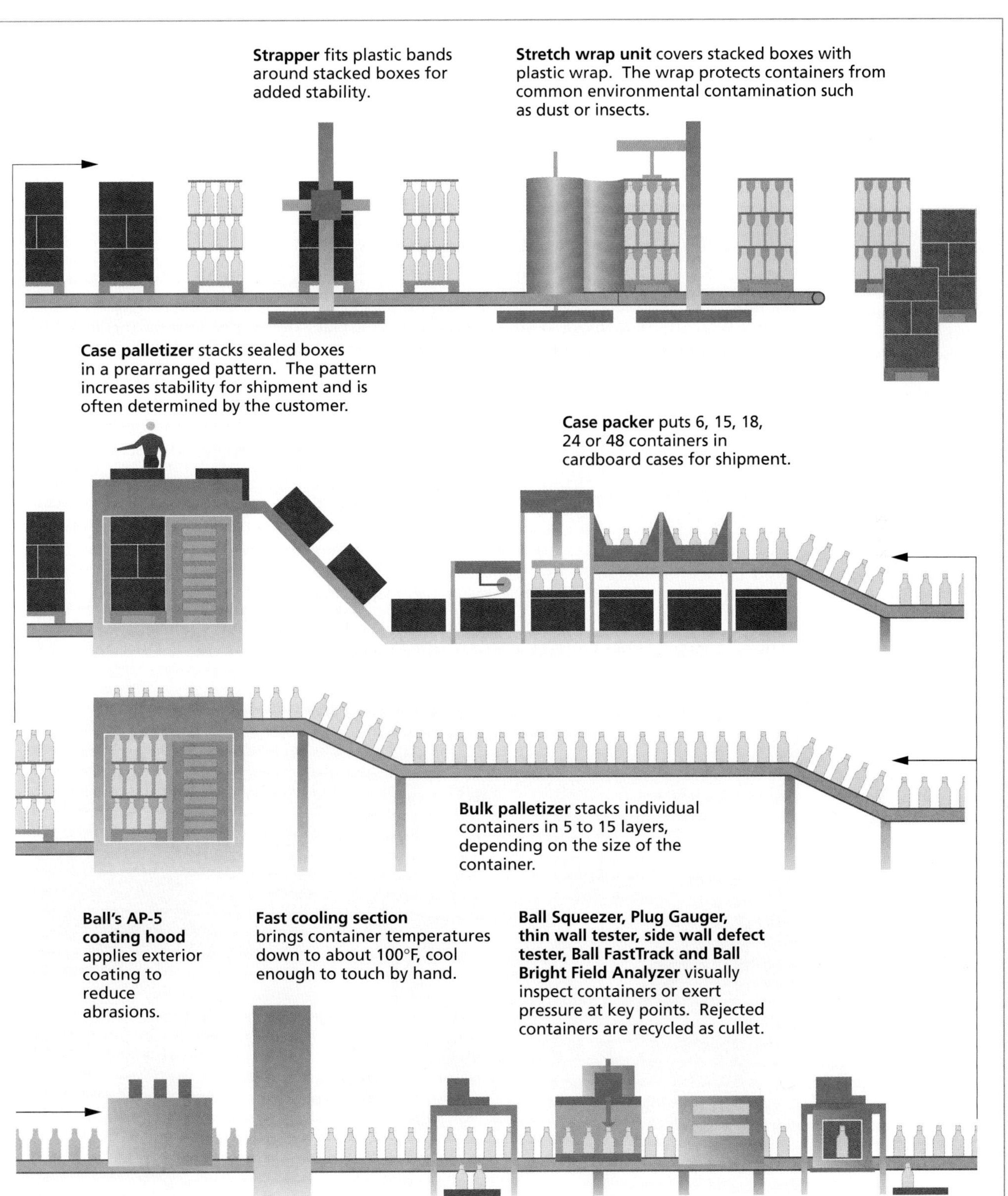

Strapper fits plastic bands around stacked boxes for added stability.
Stretch wrap unit covers stacked boxes with plastic wrap. The wrap protects containers from common environmental contamination such as dust or insects.
Case palletizer stacks sealed boxes in a prearranged pattern. The pattern increases stability for shipment and is often determined by the customer.
Case packer puts 6, 15, 18, 24 or 48 containers in cardboard cases for shipment.
Bulk palletizer stacks individual containers in 5 to 15 layers, depending on the size of the container.
Ball's AP-5 coating hood applies exterior coating to reduce abrasions.
Fast cooling section brings container temperatures down to about 100°F, cool enough to touch by hand.
Ball Squeezer, Plug Gauger, thin wall tester, side wall defect tester, Ball FastTrack and Ball Bright Field Analyzer visually inspect containers or exert pressure at key points. Rejected containers are recycled as cullet.

(Exhibit 11-4, *cont.*)

appears straightforward, planners need operating and financial budgets to estimate the operating and financial consequences of their operating plans. These budgets are also used to evaluate the implications if specific aspects of the operating budget, such as the sales, production, and materials purchasing plans, change.

The Budgeting Process Illustrated

The budgeting process can sometimes be frustrating and time consuming. Some organizations invest thousands of hours over many months to prepare the master budget documents just described. We will illustrate an entire budgeting process with a simplified but still comprehensive exercise that covers many budgeting elements.

ONTARIO TOLE ART, BUOY DIVISION

Ontario Tole Art sells high-quality wooden and metal objects, both new and antique, painted by the owner, Gael Foster. Until recently each object was unique and Gael did all the work by herself. Two years ago, however, Gael developed a new product line that she intended to sell in larger volumes because she wanted to expand her business. The new products are two models of painted fishing buoys—Santa, a buoy painted to look like Father Christmas, and Danny Buoy, a buoy painted to look like an Irish fisherman. Gael set up a new operation for this new product called Ontario Tole Art, Buoy Division (hereafter called Ontario Tole Art). Gael did the planning for this operation and hired a manager, Ross Lopes, to handle the daily operations of the new business.

The production process begins when Gael purchases, for $2.25 each, used fishing buoys from local fishers. An artist sands the used buoys to remove old paint and debris and applies a base coat of primer paint. When the base coat is dry, the artist hand paints the image of the Santa or the fisherman onto the buoy. Once the image dries, the artist applies a finishing coat of varnish. When the varnish dries, the artist wraps the finished buoy in packing material and inserts it into a specifically designed mailing container that Ontario Tole Art ships directly to the customer.

(Anthony Atkinson)

IN PRACTICE

Budgeting in Government

In profit-seeking organizations, revenues and expenditures are interrelated; organizations spend money to earn revenues. In many cases, there is a physical relationship between the amount of money spent (on things such as raw materials) and the amount of revenue. In government organizations, however, revenues and expenditures are independent. Governments develop revenue budgets, which are estimates of the amount of money that they will raise or will be allocated. Legislatures approve expenditure budgets, which provide public servants with the authority to spend government revenues on specific projects. Occasionally governments pass laws (often called *balanced-budget requirements*) limiting government expenditures to the amount of revenues raised, but revenues and expenditures are separate. For most governments, controlling government expenditures means ensuring that authorized government spending has not been exceeded by actual spending rather than assessing whether the programs on which money was spent accomplished their objectives.

Source: Stanley C. Beiner, "Budgeting in Not-for-Profit Organizations," *CMA Magazine*, November-December 1987, pp. 20–27.

Ontario Tole Art has two types of customers, retail and dealer. Retail orders arrive by mail and are prepaid. The retail price per unit, including packing and shipping charges, is $80. If capacity exceeds retail demand, Gael sells to dealers at the lower per unit price of $55. Gael loses dealer orders that she does not fill immediately, because dealers will buy alternative products from other suppliers.

Sales to dealers are on account; stated terms call for the dealers to pay the full amount of the invoice within 30 days of billing. Receipts from dealers, however, are often delinquent. Typically only 30% of dealers pay in the month following the sale; 45% pay in the second month following the sale, 20% in the third month following the sale, and 5% of sales to dealers are never collected.

Ontario Tole Art hires local area artists to paint the buoys. Due to local employment conditions, Ontario Tole Art must hire artists for periods of three months. The artists receive a fixed monthly salary of $2000 and work a maximum of 160 hours per month. The Ontario Tole Art manager makes staffing decisions at the start of each quarter, beginning January 1. The total time to sand, base coat, paint, and pack each buoy is 0.8 labor hour.

Paint costs $3.15 for each buoy. Other manufacturing costs, including sandpaper, brushes, varnish, and other supplies, amounts of $2.75 per buoy. Packing materials cost $1.95 per buoy and shipping by courier costs $7.50 per buoy.

Ontario Tole Art rents space in a local industrial mall where the employees work on the buoys. The one-year lease stipulates that rent is to be paid quarterly in advance. Ontario Tole Art can rent shops of several sizes that would provide the following monthly capacities in buoys: 600, 800, 1000, and 1200. The quarterly rents for each of these units are $3600, $4800, $6000, and $7200, respectively. All production takes place to order, and Ontario Tole Art acquires supplies only as needed.

SHOP SPACE TYPE	SHOP CAPACITY (NUMBER OF BUOYS)	QUARTERLY RENT
A	600	$3600
B	800	4800
C	1000	6000
D	1200	7200

Insurance, heating, lighting, and business taxes are $20,000 per year and advertising expenses amount to $40,000 per year. Ross, the manager of Ontario Tole Art, receives $30,000 per year to supervise the operation, manage the raw materials acquisitions, handle all the order taking and billing, and do the accounting. All operating expenses are incurred and paid in equal monthly installments.

Realized sales for October, November, and December of 2000 and forecasted demand for 2001 appear in Exhibit 11-5. Based on this demand forecast, Gael and Ross have decided to rent an 800-capacity unit for 2001 and hire two painters in the first quarter, two painters in the second quarter, one painter in the third quarter, and three painters in the fourth quarter.

Gael plans to withdraw $20,000 from the company at the start of each six-month period for a total of $40,000 per year as her compensation for functioning as owner and planner. She also wants to maintain all the firm's cash in a separate bank account for her business with a minimum cash balance of $5000 (see Exhibit 11-6). She has arranged a $50,000 line of credit with her bank to provide her with short-term funds for the company. At the start of each month, the bank charges interest at the rate of 1% on the balance of the line of credit as of the end of the previous month. The bank pays interest at the rate of 0.6% on any cash in excess of $5000 held in the account. The bank pays interest on the first day of each month based on the balance in the account at the end of the previous month.

EXHIBIT 11-5

Ontario Tole Art
Forecasted Unit Demand 2000–2001

	DEMAND		
Month	**Retail**	**Dealer**	**Total**
October 2000*	275	510	785
November 2000*	420	425	845
December 2000*	675	175	850
January 2001	100	375	475
February 2001	105	400	505
March 2001	95	425	520
April 2001	115	350	465
May 2001	75	300	375
June 2001	60	250	310
July 2001	50	300	350
August 2001	55	325	380
September 2001	75	300	375
October 2001	150	300	450
November 2001	290	350	640
December 2001	350	400	750

*Actual

EXHIBIT 11-6

Ontario Tole Art
Proposed Balance Sheet, January 2001

Cash	$ 5,000	Owner's Equity	$34,948
Accounts receivable	29,948		
Total assets	$34,948	Total liabilities and owner's equity	$34,948

DEMAND FORECAST

An organization's goals provide the starting point and the framework for evaluating the budgeting process (see box 1, Exhibit 11-2). For example, at Ontario Tole Art, the goals are to produce high-quality products and to expand the business. To assess the plan's acceptability, Gael compares the projected financial results from the tentative operating plan with the organization's financial goals.

As shown in Exhibit 11-5, the budgeting process is influenced strongly by the demand forecast, an estimate of sales demand at a specified selling price. Organizations develop demand forecasts in many ways. Some use sophisticated market surveys conducted either by outside experts or by their own sales staff. Other organizations use statistical models to generate demand forecasts from trends and forecasts of economic activity in the economy and the relation of past sales patterns to this economic activity. Other companies simply assume that demand will either grow or decline by some estimated rate over previous demand levels.

Regardless of the approach used to develop the demand forecast, the organization must prepare a sales plan for each key line of goods or services. The sales plans provide the basis for other plans to acquire the necessary factors of production such as labor, materials, production capacity, and cash. Production plans are sensitive to the sales plan; therefore, most organizations develop budgets on computers so that planners can readily explore the effects of changes in the sales plan on production plans.

Choosing the amount of detail to present in the budget involves making tradeoffs. A greater level of detail in the forecast improves the ability of the budgeting process to identify potential bottlenecks and problems by specifying the exact timing of production flows in the organization. Conversely, forecasting and planning in great detail for each unique item in organizations with thousands of products of production is prohibitively expensive and overwhelming to compute. Therefore, most organizations rely on the judgment of their production planners to strike a balance between the need for detail and the cost and practicality of detailed scheduling. Planners do this by grouping products into pools of products so that each product in a given pool places roughly equivalent demands on the organization's resources.

Because Ontario Tole Art has only one basic product, a painted buoy with only two variations, its budget can be detailed and comprehensive. Organizations with many products and services may choose, however, to budget at a more aggregated level such as by product line.

THE PRODUCTION PLAN

Planners match the completed sales plan with the organization's inventory policy and capacity level to determine a production plan (see box 5, Exhibit 11-2). The plan identifies the intended production during each subperiod of the annual budget. Budget subperiods may be daily, weekly, or monthly.

Planners use the inventory policy (box 4, Exhibit 11-2) and the sales plan (box 2, Exhibit 11-2) to develop the production plan (box 5, Exhibit 11-2). Therefore, the inventory policy is critical and has a unique role in shaping the production plan. Some organizations use a policy of producing goods for inventory and attempt to keep a predetermined, or target, number of units in inventory at all times. This inventory policy often reflects a level production strategy that is characteristic of an organization with highly skilled employees or equipment dedicated to producing a single product. A level production strategy reflects a lack of flexibility. Highly skilled production workers cannot be used to do various jobs in the organization. Therefore, they must be kept busy in the job that they know. Similarly, dedicated equipment that can be used for only one job must be kept busy to justify its expense. In these organizations, monthly sales draw down the inventory levels, and the production plan for each month attempts to restore inventory levels to their predetermined target levels.

Other organizations have an inventory policy of producing for planned sales in the next budget subperiod. Organizations moving toward a just-in-time inventory policy produce goods to meet the next subperiod's demand as an intermediate step on the path to moving to a full just-in-time inventory system. Each subperiod becomes shorter and shorter until the organization achieves just-in-time production. In this setting, the inventory target is the level of next week's or next month's planned sales, and the scheduled production is the amount required to meet the inventory target. Implementing a just-in-time inventory policy requires flexibility among employees, equipment, and suppliers and a well-designed production process. In organizations using this strategy, demand drives the production plan directly; that is, the production in each period equals the next period's planned sales. This is the inventory policy that Ontario Tole Art uses (see box 4, Exhibit 11-2).

AGGREGATE PLANNING

Throughout the production planning process, planners who often use computer-based planning tools compare the production plan implied jointly by the sales and

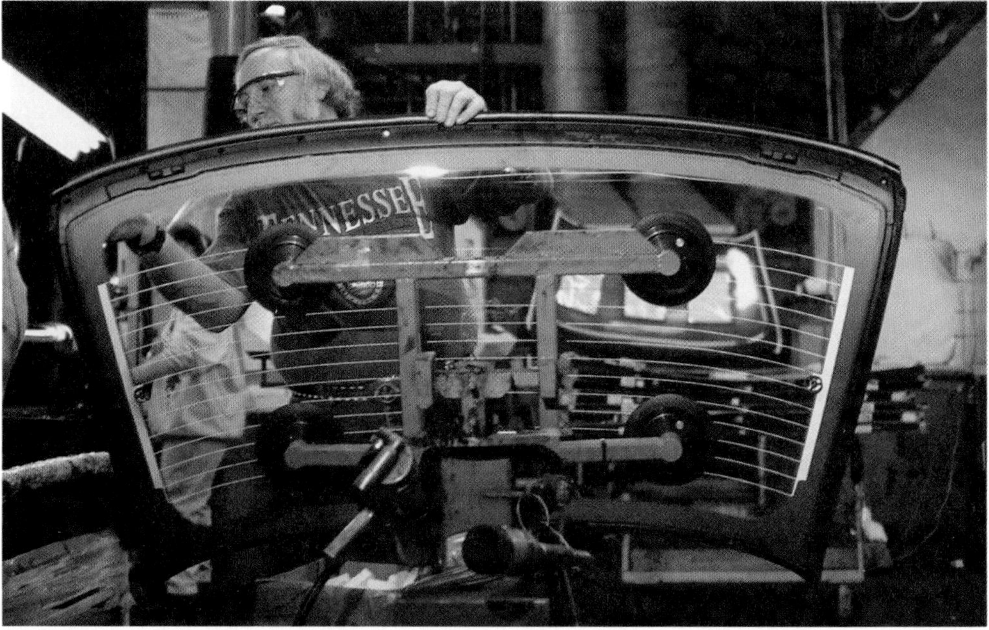

The production plan for this assembly plant must be fixed in advance of actual production so that suppliers can know exactly when they have to deliver their parts and components. (George Haling/Photo Researchers, Inc.)

inventory plans with the amount of available productive capacity. This comparison assesses the feasibility of the proposed production plan. Planners call this **aggregate planning.**

Aggregate planning The process that compares the production plan with the amount of available productive capacity; this comparison assesses the feasibility of the proposed production plan.

Aggregate planning does not attempt to develop a detailed production schedule that people use to guide daily production in the organization. Rather, aggregate planning determines whether the proposed production plan can be achieved by the production capacity the organization either has in place or can put in place during the planning period. Even planning at this aggregate level can be complicated, because planners may need to consider ways to modify existing facilities that would otherwise constrain planned procedures.

DEVELOPING THE SPENDING PLAN

Once planners have identified a feasible production plan, they can make tentative resource commitments. The purchasing group prepares a materials purchasing plan to acquire the raw materials and supplies that the production plan requires (see box 7, Exhibit 11-2). Materials purchasing plans are driven by the cycle of the organization's and the suppliers' production plans. These plans notify suppliers of the quantity of materials they should supply and the timing of those deliveries. Because sales and production plans change during the year, the organization and its suppliers must be able to quickly adjust their plans based on information received during the operating period. At some point, however, the budget planning subinterval production and purchasing plans are committed for that subperiod. For most organizations, this commitment point occurs anywhere from one day to one quarter before the anticipated production date.

The personnel and production groups prepare the labor hiring and training plan (see box 8, Exhibit 11-2). This plan works backward from the date when the personnel are needed in order to develop hiring and training schedules that will ensure the availability of these personnel. This plan can include both expansion and contraction activities. In the case of contraction, the organization uses retraining plans to redeploy employees to other parts of the organization or develops plans to discharge employees from the organization. In the case of employees who lose their employment, discharge plans may include retraining and other activities to help them find new jobs. Because discharging employees reflects moral, ethical, and legal issues and may involve high severance costs, most organizations attempt to avoid this action unless no other alternative can be found.

Staff and other groups prepare an administrative and discretionary spending plan, which summarizes the proposed expenditures on activities such as those for research and development, advertising, and training (see box 9, Exhibit 11-2). Discretionary expenditures provide the infrastructure required by the emerging production and sales plan. The term *discretionary* is used because actual sales and production levels do not drive the amount spent. Rather, the senior managers in the organization determine the amount of discretionary expenditures. Once determined, however, the amount to be spent on discretionary activities becomes fixed for the period because it is unaffected by product volume and mix.

For example, if a fast-food restaurant plans to make 3000 hamburgers during some planning interval, it knows the quantity of materials that it will use because there is a physical, or engineered, relationship between ingredients such as meat, buns, condiments, and packages and the number of hamburgers made. However, no direct physical, or engineered, relationship exists between the number of hamburgers sold and the discretionary amounts spent on advertising and employee training.

Finally, the appropriate authority in the organization approves the capital spending plan for putting new productive capacity in place (see box 3, Exhibit 11-2). Because capital spending projects usually involve time horizons longer than the period of the operating budgets, a long-term planning process rather than the one-year cycle of the operating budget drives the capital spending plan. The spending plans for material, labor, and support resources are based on a forecast of the activities the organization must complete to achieve the production targets identified in its production plan. As the planning period unfolds and time reveals the actual production requirements, production planners make commitments to detailed production schedules and the required related purchasing requirements.

CHOOSING THE CAPACITY LEVELS

At Ontario Tole Art these three types of resources determine the monthly production capacity:

1. *Flexible resources that the organization can acquire in the short term.* Paint and packing supplies are examples. If suppliers either do not deliver these resources or deliver unacceptable products, then production may be disrupted. This problem was not identified as an issue for Ontario Tole Art, but it is a practical concern for many organizations. Organizations spend a great deal of time and money developing supplier relationships so that they will receive zero-defect materials and purchased parts just when needed.
2. *Capacity resources that the organization must acquire for items for the intermediate term.* Between July 1 and September 30, Ontario Tole Art plans to employ one painter. Because each painter works 160 hours per month and because each buoy requires 0.8 hour to complete, the monthly capacity provided by intermediate-term activity decisions between July 1 and September 30 is 200 (160/0.8) units.
3. *Capacity resources that the organization must acquire for the long term.* Gael plans to rent a shop that provides a monthly capacity of 800 units. Gael requires a simple setting with a relatively short commitment period. Other organizations may take several years to acquire long-term capacity that may last for 10 years or more, whose cost is justified only if it is used that long. Consider the amount of time an oil company takes to build an oil refinery or the time that a municipality needs to build a hospital. Capacity resources are expensive and are called "committed" because they are the same regardless if the facility is used, and the level of capacity and capacity-related costs are very difficult to change in the short term. Therefore, capacity resources impose risk on the organization.

As summarized in Exhibit 11-7, the nature of the resources determines whether they are short term, intermediate term, or long term. Many organizations develop sophisticated approaches for choosing a production plan that balances the use of short-term, intermediate-term, and long-term capacity to minimize the waste of resources. For example, the size and the number of service areas in a bank represent the capacity available for use during any period provided by long-term building decisions. The level of long-term capacity chosen reflects the organization's assessment of its long-term growth trend.

For Ontario Tole Art, which is renting capacity, long-term capacity is defined by the lease stipulations, which equals one year. If Ontario Tole Art were building this capacity, long-term capacity would be defined by the time needed to plan and build the facility.

The number of full-time staff employed by a bank determines the long-term capacity available for the intermediate term. For example, if the plan were to acquire capacity that the organization could use increasingly as sales grew, the intermediate-term capacity decisions would put in place other elements that require intermediate-term commitments. These would include defining the number of people and banking equipment necessary to allow the bank to use its long-term capacity. The

EXHIBIT 11-7

Summary of Capacity Types and Commitment Time

TERM	TYPE OF CAPACITY ACQUIRED	EXAMPLES
Flexible resources required in short term (less than several weeks)	Provides the ability to use existing capacity	Raw materials, supplies, casual labor
Committed resources acquired for the intermediate term (several weeks to six months)	General-purpose capacity that is transferrable between organizations given time	People, general purpose equipment, specialty raw materials
Committed resources acquired for the long-term (more than six months)	Special purpose capacity is customized for the organization's use	Buildings, special purpose equipment

intermediate-term capacity decision reflects the longer of the time needed to put intermediate-term capacity in place or the contracting period for intermediate-term capacity. For Ontario Tole Art this is the contracting period for artists, which is three months.

Finally, the number of part-time or temporary staff employed by a bank determines its capacity on a day-to-day basis. Such short-term capacity decisions reflect the cyclical demands that the bank may face daily, weekly, monthly, or annually. The short-term capacity decision reflects the time needed to put short-term capacity in place. For Ontario Tole Art, this is the time period that suppliers require for delivery, which is assumed to be virtually instantaneous. However, if Ontario Tole Art had to order and wait for supplies, it would become very important to plan acquisitions so that in the very short term Ontario Tole Art would not have to stop production while it waited for supplies to arrive. In this sense, supplies provide the short-run capacity to use longer term capacity.

This discussion raises the question of how production planners choose capacity levels. Organizations use many different approaches to plan capacity. The process that Ontario Tole Art used was to choose a level of shop capacity (one of 600, 800, 1000, or 1200) and then to hire the number of painters in each quarter that, given the forecasted demand and chosen shop capacity, provided the highest level of expected profits.

We can classify the resource-consuming activities for Ontario Tole Art into three groups, which are typical of all organizations.

1. *Activities that create the need for resources and, therefore, resource expenditures in the short term.* For Ontario Tole Art, these short-term activities include the purchasing, preparation, painting, packing, and shipping of buoys. Acquiring the resources for these short-term activities requires expenditures that vary directly with the production levels because the inventory policy is to produce only to order.
2. *Activities undertaken to acquire capacity for the intermediate term.* For Ontario Tole Art, this is the quarterly acquisition of painting capacity, that is, hiring the painters to paint the buoys.

3. *Activities undertaken to acquire capacity that must be acquired for the long-term.* For Ontario Tole Art, this includes the annual choice of the level of shop capacity, level of advertising, the manager and manager's salary, and expenditures for items such as insurance and heat.

Planners classify activities by type because they plan, budget, and control short-, intermediate-, and long-term expenditures differently. Analysts evaluate short-term activities using efficiency and effectiveness considerations and ask questions such as the following:

1. Is this expenditure necessary to add value to the product from the customer's perspective?
2. Can the organization improve the execution of this activity?
3. Would changing the way this activity is done provide more customer satisfaction?

Analysts evaluate intermediate- and long-term activities by using efficiency and effectiveness considerations and asking questions such as the following:

1. Are alternative forms of capacity available that are less expensive?
2. Is this the best approach to achieve our goals?
3. How can we improve the capacity selection decision to make capacity less expensive or more flexible?

Choosing the capacity plan—making the commitments to acquire intermediate-term and long-term capacity—commits the firm to its intermediate-term and long-term expenditures. Choosing the production plan, that is, choosing the level of the short-term activities, fixes the short-term expenditures that the master budget summarizes.

HANDLING INFEASIBLE PRODUCTION PLANS

Although the relationships between planning and production at Ontario Tole Art are simple, the company's planning process reflects how planners use forecasted demand to plan activity levels and provide required capacity. If planners find the tentative production plan infeasible because of resource or capacity constraints, then they have to make provisions to acquire more capacity or reduce the planned level of production. For example, if the labor market is tight and Ontario Tole Art can hire only two artists between January and June, then Gael would have to revise her capacity and production plans to reflect this constraint.

INTERPRETING THE PRODUCTION PLAN

Exhibit 11-8 summarizes the production plan that Ontario Tole Art has developed for 2001. The three elements that drive planning are (1) demand, which is what people are willing to buy at the stated price; (2) the capacity levels chosen; and (3) production output. Ontario Tole Art makes no products until it receives an order. Therefore, production is the minimum of demand and capacity. In equation form, we may write this:

$$\text{Production} = \text{Minimum (Total demand, production capacity)}$$

At Ontario Tole Art these equations apply:

$$\text{Production capacity} = \text{Minimum (Shop capacity, Painting capacity, supplies capacity)}$$

$$\text{Total demand} = \text{Retail demand} + \text{Dealer demand}$$

In Ontario Tole Art's case, the production capacity is the minimum of the long-term capacity (the productive capacity of the shop), the intermediate-term capacity

EXHIBIT 11-8

Ontario Tole Art: Demand and Sales Data, Number of Units, 2001

	JAN.	FEB.	MARCH	APRIL	MAY	JUNE	JULY	AUG.	SEPT.	OCT.	NOV.	DEC.
Retail demand	100	105	95	115	75	60	50	**55**	75	150	290	350
Dealer demand	375	400	425	350	300	250	300	**325**	300	300	350	400
Total demand	475	505	520	465	375	310	350	**380**	375	450	640	750
Shop capacity	800	800	800	800	800	800	800	**800**	800	800	800	800
Painting capacity	400	400	400	400	400	400	200	**200**	200	600	600	600
Production capacity	400	400	400	400	375	310	200	**200**	200	450	600	600
Retail units made and sold	100	105	95	115	75	60	50	**55**	75	150	290	350
Dealer units made and sold	300	295	305	285	300	250	150	**145**	125	300	310	250
Total units made and sold	400	400	400	400	375	310	200	**200**	200	450	600	600

(the painting capacity provided by hiring artists), and the short-term capacity (the capacity provided by the short-term acquisition of materials). For example, in August the retail demand is 55 units and the dealer demand is 325 units, totaling 380 units. The shop capacity is 800 units and the painting capacity is 200 units. Therefore, production capacity, which is the minimum of the shop capacity and painting capacity, is 200 units. Planned production and sales of 200 units represents the minimum of total demand (380 units) and production capacity (200 units).

THE FINANCIAL PLANS

Once the planners have developed the production, staffing, and capacity plans, they can prepare a financial summary of the tentative operating plans. The financial results for Ontario Tole Art implied by the production plan developed in Exhibit 11-8 appear in the following exhibits. Exhibit 11-9 presents the cash flows expected from the production and sales plan. Exhibit 11-10 and Exhibit 11-11 summarize the projected balance sheet and income statement, respectively, expected as a result of the production and sales plans. (These are examples of the elements of boxes 11 and 12 in Exhibit 11-2). Planners use the projected balance sheet as an overall evaluation of the net effect of operating and financing decisions during the budget period and the income statement as an overall test of the profitability of the planners' proposed activities. Note that to keep this example relatively simple we are ignoring taxes. Taxes are part of the budgeting and cash flow estimation process of all organizations.

EXHIBIT 11-9

Ontario Tole Art Cash Flow and Financing Data — 2001

CASH INFLOWS	JAN.	FEB.	MARCH	APRIL	MAY	JUNE	JULY	AUG.	SEPT.	OCT.	NOV.	DEC.
Retail sales	$ 8,000	$ 8,400	$ 7,600	$ 9,200	$ 6,000	$ 4,800	$ 4,000	$ 4,400	$ 6,000	$ 12,000	$23,200	$28,000
Dealer collections— 1 Month	2,887	4,950	4,868	5,033	4,703	4,950	4,125	2,475	2,392	2,062	4,950	5,115
Dealer collections— 2 Months	10,519	4,331	7,425	7,301	7,549	7,054	7,425	6,188	3,713	3,589	3,094	7,425
Dealer collections— 3 Months	5,610	4,675	1,925	3,300	3,245	3,355	3,135	3,300	2,750	1,650	1,595	1,375
Total	$27,016	$22,356	$21,818	$24,834	$21,497	$20,159	$18,685	$16,363	$14,855	$ 19,301	$32,839	$41,915
CASH OUTFLOWS												
Flexible Resources:												
Buoys	$ 900	$ 900	$ 900	$ 900	$ 844	$ 698	$ 450	$ 450	$ 450	$ 1,013	$ 1,350	$ 1,350
Paint costs	1,260	1,260	1,260	1,260	1,181	977	630	630	630	1,418	1,890	1,890
Other supplies costs	1,100	1,100	1,100	1,100	1,031	853	550	550	550	1,238	1,650	1,650
Packing costs	780	780	780	780	731	605	390	390	390	878	1,170	1,170
Shipping costs	3,000	3,000	3,000	3,000	2,813	2,325	1,500	1,500	1,500	3,375	4,500	4,500
Committed Resources:												
Painters' salaries	$ 4,000	$ 4,000	$ 4,000	$ 4,000	$ 4,000	$ 4,000	$ 2,000	$ 2,000	$ 2,000	$ 6,000	$ 6,000	$ 6,000
Shop rent	4,800	0	0	4,800	0	0	4,800	0	0	4,800	0	0
Manager's salary	2,500	2,500	2,500	2,500	2,500	2,500	2,500	2,500	2,500	2,500	2,500	2,500
Other shop costs	1,667	1,667	1,667	1,667	1,667	1,667	1,667	1,667	1,667	1,667	1,667	1,667
Interest paid (received)	0	163	127	95	81	48	17	208	177	160	231	145
Advertising costs	3,333	3,333	3,333	3,333	3,333	3,333	3,333	3,333	3,333	3,333	3,333	3,333
Total	$23,340	$18,703	$18,667	$23,435	$18,181	$17,006	$17,837	$13,228	$13,197	$ 26,382	$24,291	$24,205
Net cash flow this month	**$ 3,676**	**$ 3,653**	**$ 3,151**	**$ 1,399**	**$ 3,316**	**$ 3,153**	**$ 848**	**$ 3,135**	**$ 1,658**	**$−7,081**	**$ 8,548**	**$17,710**
FINANCING OPERATIONS												
Opening cash	5,000	5,000	5,000	5,000	5,000	5,000	5,000	5,000	5,000	5,000	5,000	5,000
Cash invested (withdrawn)	−20,000	0	0	0	0	0	−20,000	0	0	0	0	0
Cash available	−11,324	8,653	8,151	6,399	8,315	8,155	−14,152	8,134	6,658	−2,079	13,548	22,710
Opening loan	0	16,324	12,671	9,520	8,121	4,806	1,652	20,803	17,669	16,010	23,089	14,541
Borrowing made	16,324	0	0	0	0	0	19,152	0	0	7,079	0	0
Borrowing repaid	0	3,653	3,151	1,399	3,315	3,155	0	3,134	1,658	0	8,548	14,541
Ending loan	16,324	12,671	9,520	8,121	4,806	1,652	20,803	17,669	16,010	23,089	14,541	0
Ending cash	5,000	5,000	5,000	5,000	5,000	5,000	5,000	5,000	5,000	5,000	5,000	8,168

EXHIBIT 11-10

Ontario Tole Art
Projected Balance Sheet
December 31, 2001

Cash	$ 8,168	Owner's Equity	$35,613
Accounts receivable	27,445		
Total assets	$35,613	Total liabilities and owner's equity	$35,613

UNDERSTANDING THE CASH FLOW STATEMENT

The cash flow statement in Exhibit 11-9 is organized into three sections:

1. Cash inflows from retail cash sales and collections of dealer receivables
2. Cash outflows for flexible resources that are acquired and consumed in the short term (buoys, paint, other supplies, packing, and shipping) and cash outflows for capacity resources that are acquired and consumed in the intermediate term and long term (painters, shop rent, manager's salary, other shop costs, interest paid, and advertising costs)
3. Results of financing operations

In each month, the format of the cash flow statement is as follows:

Cash inflows − Cash outflows = Net cash flow

EXHIBIT 11-11

Ontario Tole Art
Projected Income Statement
For the Year Ended December 31, 2001

Revenue		$279,134
Flexible resource expenses		
Buoys	$10,205	
Paint	14,286	
Other supplies	12,472	
Packing	8,844	
Shipping	34,013	79,820
Contribution margin		$199,314
Committed resource expenses		
Painter's salaries	$48,000	
Shop rent	19,200	
Other shop costs	20,004	
Manager's salary	30,000	117,204
Other expenses		
Advertising	$39,996	
Interest paid	1,452	41,452
Net income		$41,448

In January, for example, ending cash was found as follows:

$$\text{Net cash flows} + \text{Opening cash} + \text{Effects of financing operations} = \text{Ending cash}$$
$$\$3676 + \$5000 = [-\$20{,}000 + \$16{,}324] = \$5000$$

To help you to understand the derivation of the numbers in Ontario Tole Art's cash flow statement, let us study the numbers for July.

Cash Inflows Section. Recall that the pattern of collections at Ontario Tole Art is as follows:

1. Retail orders are paid for with the order at a retail price per unit of $80.
2. Sales to dealers for $55 per unit are on account with a typical collection pattern being 30% in the month following the sale, 45% in the second month following the sale, 20% in the third month following the sale, and 5% never collected.

Therefore, in July, Ontario Tole Art will collect (1) all the retail sales for July, (2) 30% of the dealer sales from June, (3) 45% of the dealer sales from May, and (4) 20% of the dealer sales from April. Exhibit 11-12 summarizes these July collections.

Cash Outflows Section. Exhibit 11-13 summarizes the cash outflow numbers for July. Note that for expenditures on flexible resources that are acquired in the short term, this equation applies:

$$\text{Cash outflows} = \text{Units purchased} \times \text{Price per unit of flexible resource}$$

For expenditures on capacity resources, that is, resources acquired in the intermediate term or long term, this equation applies:

$$\text{Cash outflows} = \text{Monthly expenditure for capacity resource}$$

Financing Section. The financing section of the cash flow statement summarizes the effects on cash of transactions that are not a part of the normal operating activities. This section includes the effects of issuing or retiring stock or debt and buying or selling capital assets. Exhibit 11-14 shows a common format used in the financing section of the cash flow statement with the corresponding numbers for July. Note that the format of the financing section of the cash flow statement is as follows:

$$\text{Cash flows this period} + \text{Opening balance} \pm \text{Changes} = \text{Closing balance}$$

EXHIBIT 11-12

Ontario Tole Art
Summary of Cash Collections
in July, 2001

ITEM	CALCULATION	
Retail sales from July (see Exhibit 11-8)		$ 4,000
30% of June dealer sales*	30% × 250 × $55 =	4,125
45% of May dealer sales	45% × 300 × $55 =	7,425
20% of April dealer sales	20% × 285 × $55 =	3,135
Total		$18,685

*Sales equals units sold multiplied by the selling price of $55 per unit.

EXHIBIT 11-13

Ontario Tole Art
Cash Outflow Calculations for July, 2001

ITEM	AMOUNT	FORMULA	CALCULATION
Flexible Resources:			
Buoy cost	$450	July production × Price per buoy	200 × $2.25
Paint cost	630	July production × Paint cost per buoy	200 × $3.15
Other supplies cost	550	July production × Other supplies cost per buoy	200 × $2.75
Packing costs	390	July sales × Packing cost per buoy	200 × $1.95
Shipping costs	1,500	July sales × Shipping cost per buoy	200 × $7.50
Committed Resources:			
Painters' salaries	2,000	Number of painters in July × Monthly salary	1 × $2,000
Shop rent	4,800	Units of capacity × Capacity cost per unit	800 × $6
Manager's salary	2,500	Annual salary ÷ 12	$30,000 ÷ 12
Other shop costs	1,667	Annual other costs ÷ 12	$20,000 ÷ 12
Interest paid	17	June ending loan balance × 1%	$ 1,652 × 1%
Advertising costs	3,333	Annual advertising ÷ 12	$40,000 ÷ 12

The major sources and uses of cash in most organizations are (1) operations, (2) investments or withdrawals by the owner in an unincorporated organization, (3) long-term financing activities related to issuing or retiring stock or debt, and (4) short-term financing activities.

Short-term financing usually involves obtaining a line of credit with a financial institution. The line of credit may be secured or unsecured. The line of credit allows a company to borrow up to a specified amount at any time and may be secured or unsecured. The line of credit is secured if the organization has pledged an asset that the financial institution can seize if the borrower defaults on the line of credit provisions. The financial institution sets a limit on the line of credit, and the borrower (Ontario Tole Art) pays interest periodically, such as monthly, on the outstanding balance borrowed. See the ending loan row in Exhibit 11-9, and note that Ontario Tole Art's line

EXHIBIT 11-14

Format of Financing Section of
Cash Flow Statement

	Net cash flow from operations	848
+	Opening cash	+5,000
±	Cash invested or withdrawn*	−20,000
±	Cash provided or used in issuing or retiring stock or debt	0
=	Cash available before short-term financing	−14,152
±	Cash used or provided by short-term financing	19,152
=	Ending cash	5,000

*In the case of a private busines such as Ontario Tole Art, this refers to the capital transactions by the owner.

of credit balance varies between $0 and $23,089 during the year, well within the limit of $50,000 that Gael negotiated with the bank.

Note that the format of the financing section of the cash flow statement in Exhibit 11-9 for Ontario Tole Art does not follow the format used in Exhibit 11-14. The financing section of Ontario Tole Art's cash flow statement provides information about the line of credit balance. Many organizations include the line-of-credit information in the cash flow statement, because financial statement readers should be aware of the limits that can potentially constrain operations.

USING THE FINANCIAL PLANS

Ontario Tole Art's cash flow statement, shown in Exhibit 11-9, provides several types of useful information. First, it contains a short-term financing plan that suggests that, if events unfold as expected, Ontario Tole Art's cash balance increases only modestly during the year because of the $40,000 withdrawal that Gael will make from the business. Therefore, the company will use its line of credit agreement heavily. It will be borrowing from the bank for 11 of the 12 months in the year.

Organizations can raise money from outsiders by borrowing from banks, issuing debt, or selling shares of equity. A cash flow forecast helps an organization identify if and when it will require external financing. The cash flow forecast also shows whether any projected cash shortage will be temporary or cyclical, which can be met by a line-of-credit arrangement, or whether it will be permanent, which would require a long-term loan from a bank, further investment by the current owners, or investment by new owners. Based on the information provided by the cash flow forecast, organizations can plan the appropriate mix of external financing to minimize the long-run cost of capital.

The projected income statement and balance sheet provide a general assessment of the operating efficiencies at Ontario Tole Art. If Gael believes that these projected results are unacceptable, she must take steps to change the organizational processes that create the unacceptable results. For example, if the employees consistently use more quantities of any factor of production than competitors use, such as paint, labor, or capacity, Gael should attempt to modify procedures and therefore resource use to be able to compete profitably with its competitors.

Suppose that Ross has studied the projected financial results in the initial budget plans and has decided that the 14.6% profit margin on sales ($40,666 ÷ $279,134 from Exhibit 11-11) is too low. Ross has reached this conclusion because Ontario Tole Art is in the craft industry in which competitors often duplicate attractive products quickly resulting in short periods of product profitability. After determining that this profit margin on sales is too low, the manager may develop a marketing program to improve the cost/revenue performance at Ontario Tole Art.

USING THE PROJECTED RESULTS

The operating budgets, like the production plan, hiring plan, capital spending plan, and purchasing plan for materials and supplies, provide a framework for developing expectations about activity levels in the upcoming period. Planners also use the operating budgets to test the feasibility of production plans. As the period unfolds, production and operations schedulers will make more accurate forecasts and base their production commitments on them. Thus, planners use the budget information to accomplish the following:

1. *Identify broad resource requirements.* This helps develop plans to put needed resources in place. For example, Ross can use the activity forecast to plan when the organization will have to hire and train temporary help.

2. *Identify potential problems.* This helps avoid problems or deal with them systematically. For example, Ross can use the statement of operating cash flows to identify when the business will need short-term financing from its bank. This will help the manager negotiate with a bank-lending officer for a line of credit that is both competitive and responsive to Ontario Tole Art's needs. The forecasted cash flows also will identify when the buoy business will generate cash that Gael can invest in other business opportunities.
3. *Compare projected operating and financial results.* These are compared with those of competitors as a general test of the efficiency of the organization's operating processes. For example, the differences between planned and actual costs at Ontario Tole Art will focus Ross's attention on understanding whether the plans were unrealistic or whether the execution of a sound business plan was flawed. This signals the need for improved planning, better execution, or both.

Cost-Volume-Profit Analysis

In Chapter 2 when we studied cost behavior, we considered the relationship between volume and costs. Many decision makers like to combine cost behavior information with revenue information to project profits for different levels of volume, a process called **cost-volume-profit analysis.**

Cost-volume-profit analysis
The process of combining cost behavior information with revenue information to project revenues, costs, and profits for different levels of volume.

Conventional cost-volume-profit analysis rests on the assumptions that all organization costs are either purely flexible or capacity related, that units made equal units sold, and that revenue per unit does not change as volume changes. With these assumptions, an organization can write its profit equation as follows:

Profit = Revenue − Costs

Profit = Revenue − Flexible costs − Capacity-related costs

Profit = (Units sold × Revenue per unit) − (Units sold × flexible cost per unit)
− Capacity-related costs

Profit = [Units sold × (Revenue per unit − Flexible cost per unit)]
− Capacity-related costs

Profit = (units sold × Contribution margin per unit) − Capacity-related costs

One volume of interest is required to break even. The cost-volume-profit equation can be used to find the break-even volume of sales as follows:

Break-even profit = 0 = (Units sold × Contribution margin per unit)
− Capacity-related costs

Units sold to break even = Capacity-related costs ÷ Contribution margin per unit

We can illustrate cost-volume-profit analysis by returning to Ontario Tole Art. To keep the initial discussion focused and simple, we will simplify the original Ontario Tole Art facts as follows:

1. Ontario Tole Art sells only to retail customers, holds no inventory, and sells on a cash basis only, that is, no credit sales.
2. Four painters are hired for the entire year.
3. The shop capacity, painting capacity, and advertising decisions allow the organization to make and sell up to 800 units per month of 9600 units per year.

To refresh your memory, Exhibit 11-15 summarizes the relevant unit revenue and cost information.

EXHIBIT 11-15

Ontario Tole Art — Summary of Unit Revenue and Cost Information

Revenue per Unit	$80.00
Flexible Costs per Unit	
Cost of used fishing buoys	$ 2.25
Paint costs	3.15
Other manufacturing costs	2.75
Packing materials	1.95
Shipping costs	7.50
Total	17.60
Contribution Margin per Unit	$62.40
Capacity-Related Costs	
Painter's salaries	$ 96,000
Shop rent	19,200
Manager's salary	30,000
Other shop costs	20,000
Advertising costs	40,000
Total	$205,200

EXHIBIT 11-16

Ontario Tole Art — Cost-Volume-Profit Chart

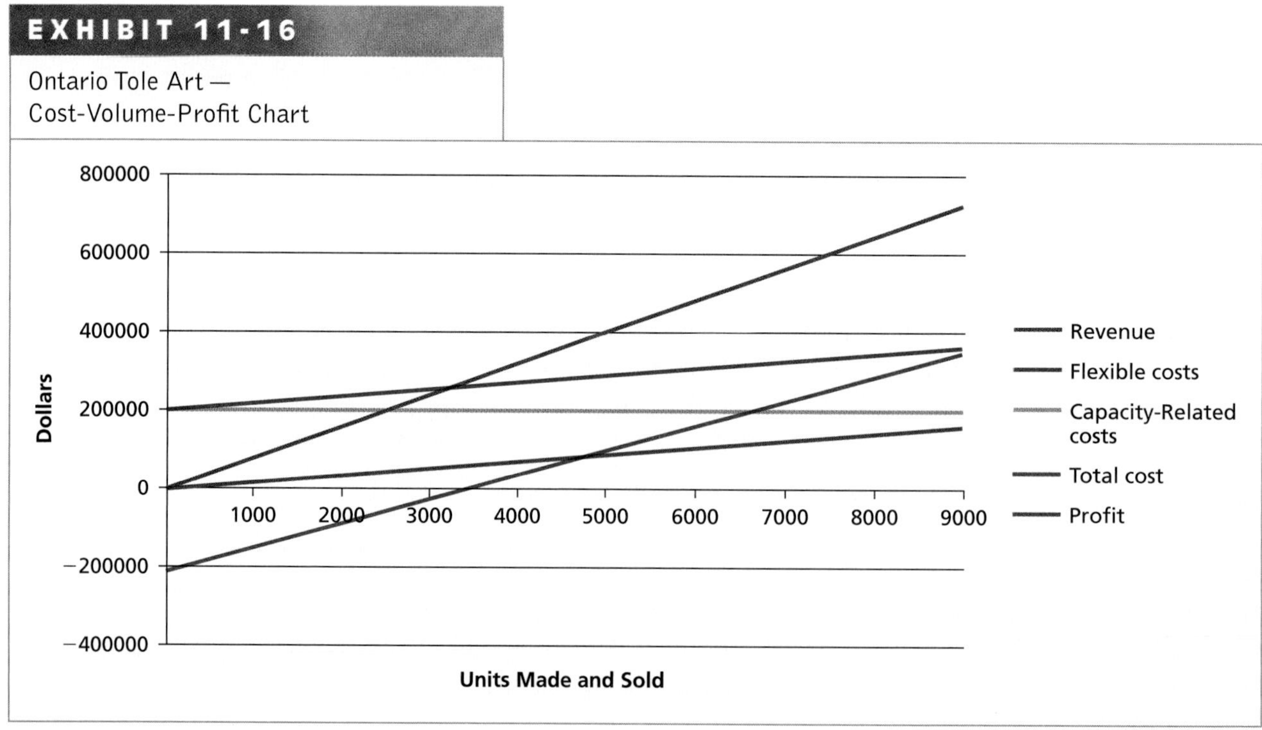

With this information, we can write the profit equation for Ontario Tole Art as follows:

$$\text{Profit} = (\$62.40 \times \text{Units Sold}) - \$205{,}200$$

And we compute the break-even quantity as

$$\text{Break-even quantity} = 205{,}200 \div 62.40 = 3288 \text{ units}$$

Decision makers usually summarize cost-volume-profit information in a cost-volume-profit chart. Exhibit 11-16 summarizes this information for Ontario Tole Art.

The cost-volume-profit chart provides a convenient way of summarizing the relationship between volumes, revenues, costs, and profits and provides a visual way to display the effect of volume changes on profits. The critical line—the primary focus of attention—is of course the profit line. Note that it crosses the horizontal axis, which denotes a zero or break-even level of profits, at about 3300 units of sales, which is what we computed with the profit equation, and reaches a level of about $360,000 at 9000 units, which is the upper bound of production.

Extending Cost-Volume-Profit Analysis for Multiproduct Organizations

As you study the cost-volume-profit chart in Exhibit 11-16, it might occur to you that this type of graphical representation really only works for single-profit organizations, a characteristic that would seriously inhibit its value as a practical organization tool. To overcome this limitation, analysts have proposed an extension to the basic cost-volume-profit analysis that allows it to be applied to multiproduct organizations. To illustrate this extension, consider the activities of Princeton Company. Princeton Company manufactures three products: plastic valves, metal valves, and specialty valves. Exhibit 11-17 summarizes the revenue and cost information for each product and the initial budget for the upcoming year.

The initial budget projects a loss of $1,825,000, and the management at Princeton Company is interested in knowing how much sales would have to increase in order to allow the company to at least break even for the year.

There are infinitely many combinations of sales levels for its three products that would allow Princeton Company to break even. These can be simulated on an electronic spreadsheet by varying the sales levels of the three products and finding combinations that result in total profits being positive, or at least zero. After completing our discussion of cost-volume-profit analysis, we will illustrate this simulation approach.

In the days before powerful desktop computers and spreadsheet packages, cost-volume-profit analysis was done by hand. It was not very practical to manipulate multiple products simultaneously in order to find a mix of production and sales that would be profitable. So decision makers developed an extension of basic cost-volume-profit analysis, which allowed them to continue to use its basic profit equation and graphing techniques.

That extension was to create an average product, which was a weighted combination of the organization's products. The weights were determined by estimating the sales mix. So, for example, if one product made up 30% of the estimated total sales, that product's revenues and costs would be weighted 30% in determining the revenues and flexible costs of the average product. In the case of Princeton Company, the decision maker would construct an average product by weighting each of the three real products—plastic valves, metal valves, and custom valves—according to their respective proportions in the estimated product mix. For example, the revenue per unit of the average product would be computed using the following equation.

EXHIBIT 11-17

Princeton Company

	PLASTIC VALVES		METAL VALVES		SPECIALTY VALVES		TOTAL
	Unit	Total	Unit	Total	Unit	Total	
Unit Sales		500,000		425,000		400,000	1,325,000
Revenue	$60.00	$30,000,000	$80.00	$34,000,000	$100.00	$40,000,000	$104,000,000
Flexible Costs							
Materials	$31.00	$15,500,000	$42.00	$17,850,000	$ 56.00	$22,400,000	$ 55,750,000
Supplies	3.00	1,500,000	6.00	2,550,000	11.00	4,400,000	8,450,000
Selling	6.00	3,000,000	8.00	3,400,000	10.00	4,000,000	10,400,000
Shipping	6.00	3,000,000	9.00	3,825,000	10.00	4,000,000	10,825,000
Contribution Margin	$14.00	$ 7,000,000	$15.00	$ 6,375,000	$ 13.00	$ 5,200,000	$ 18,575,000
Capacity-Related Costs							
Manufacturing	$3,500,000		$2,700,000		$3,200,000		$ 9,400,000
Administrative and other	2,600,000	6,100,000	1,800,000	4,500,000	2,100,000	5,300,000	6,500,000
Product Contribution		$ 900,000		$ 1,875,000		−$ 100,000	$ 2,675,000
Business-Sustaining Costs							4,500,000
Organization Profit							−$ 1,825,000

$$60 \times \frac{500{,}000}{1{,}325{,}000} + 80 \times \frac{425{,}000}{1{,}325{,}000} + 100 \times \frac{400{,}000}{1{,}325{,}000} = \$78.49$$

Similarly, the materials flexible cost for the average product would be computed using the following equation:

$$31 \times \frac{500{,}000}{1{,}325{,}000} + 42 \times \frac{425{,}000}{1{,}325{,}000} + 56 \times \frac{400{,}000}{1{,}325{,}000} = \$42.08$$

Exhibit 11-18 summarizes the calculations for the average product. With this information we can determine the break-even level of the average product, as shown in the following equation:

$$\text{Break-even quantity} = \frac{20{,}400{,}000}{14.0189} = 1{,}455{,}181.696$$

Exhibit 11-19 displays the cost-volume-profit graph for this weighted product.

What does this information mean? How do we interpret the break-even quantity for individual units of production given the computed break-even level for this average product? We simply reverse the process of computing the average. Assuming that the sales mix remains constant, the required sales levels to break even are as follows:

1. Plastic valves = 1,455,181.696 × 500,000/1,325,000 = 549,125.1684
2. Metal valves = 1,455,181.696 × 425,000/1,325,000 = 466,756.3932
3. Custom valves = 1,455,181.696 × 400,000/1,325,000 = 439,300.1347

EXHIBIT 11-18

Princeton Company — Weighted Product Calculation for CVP Analysis

	WEIGHTED AVERAGE	
	Unit	**Total**
Unit Sales		1,325,000
Revenue	$78.49	$104,000,000
Flexible Costs		
Materials	$42.08	$ 55,750,000
Supplies	6.38	8,450,000
Selling	7.85	10,400,000
Shipping	8.17	10,825,000
Contribution Margin	$14.02	$ 18,575,000
Capacity-Related Costs		
Manufacturing	$9,400,000	
Administrative and other	6,500,000	15,900,000
Product Contribution		$ 2,675,000
Business-Sustaining Costs		4,500,000
Organization Profit		−$ 1,825,000

EXHIBIT 11-19

Princeton Company — Weighted Average Product

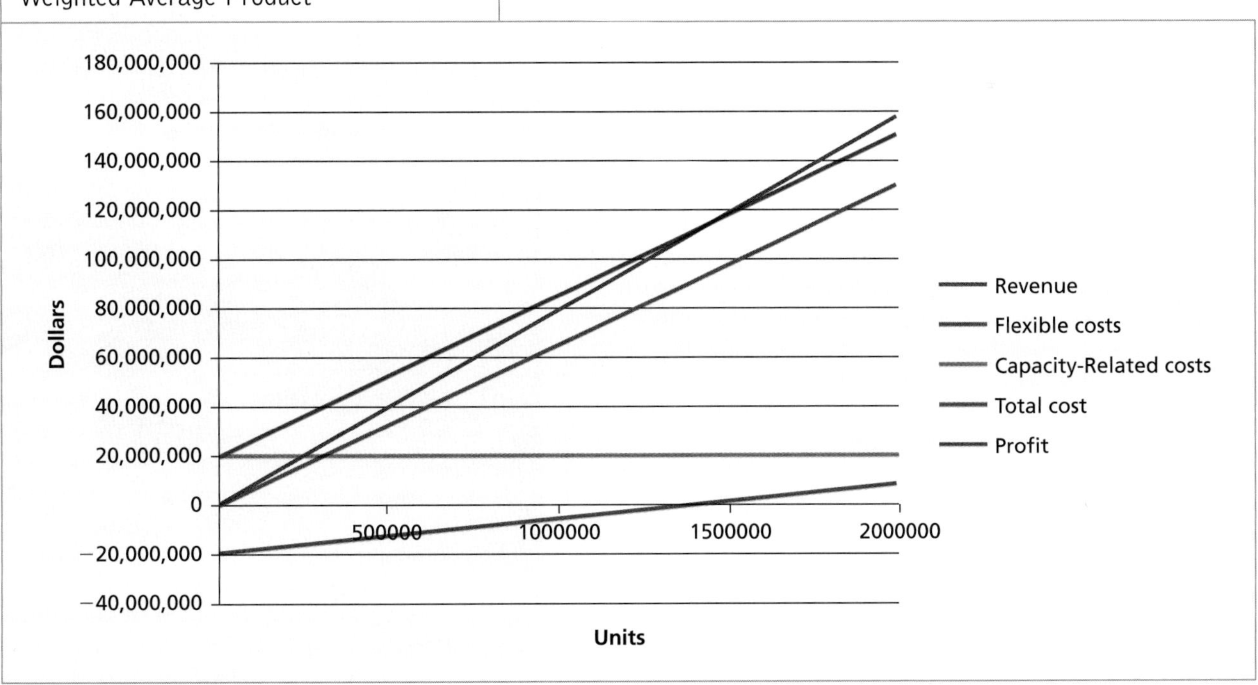

What-If Analysis

Although the conventional CVP analysis provided important insights, as we have seen these insights were limited in that they relied on assuming a constant product mix for the practical implementation of this analysis. The availability of powerful desktop computers and electronic spreadsheets opened up the possibility of modeling the organization directly, without creating hybrid or average products, and allowed management to consider alternative strategies.

What-if analysis
A type of analysis that explores the effect of a change in a parameter on an outcome.

If planners use the computer for the budgeting process, they can use the budgeting framework to explore the effects of alternative marketing, production, and selling strategies. Returning to Ontario Tole Art, Ross may consider raising prices, opening a retail outlet, or using different employment strategies. Alternative proposals take the form of "what-if" questions in a process called **what-if analysis.** What-if analysis includes the insights of conventional CVP analysis as a special case without making the limiting assumptions required by CVP analysis.

Ross may ask: "What if I decrease prices on my retail products by 5% and then sales increase by 10%? Is that desirable?" The answer is that Ontario Tole Art profits will fall from $40,666 to $37,695. (This revised profit number was found by inserting the revised price and demand schedule in the spreadsheet that was used to prepare the original budget figures.) Therefore, this proposed price adjustment is undesirable.

Ross may also wonder: "What if I opened a retail outlet? Suppose that retail sales would increase by 50% if Ontario Tole Art opened a retail outlet that would cost $40,000 per year to operate (including all costs). The retail outlet orders would be shipped by courier to the customer's address. Would this change be desirable?" If Ontario Tole Art follows this strategy, profits will increase to $46,586, which seems to be an improvement over the currently projected profit of $40,666. However, Ross may not want to face the problems associated with operating a retail store for an increment profit increase of only $5920 ($46,586 − $40,666).

The development of powerful electronic spreadsheets which were used for modeling and sensitivity analysis provided a strong impetus for the personal computer market. (Bob Daemmrich/The Image Works)

The structure and information required to prepare the master budget can be used very easily to provide the basis for what-if analysis. (It took only several seconds to answer Ross's questions using the spreadsheet developed to prepare the Ontario Tole Art's cash flow forecast.)

EVALUATING DECISION-MAKING ALTERNATIVES

Suppose that Ross is considering renting a machine to automatically sand the buoys and apply the primer coat. The capacity of the machine is 1300 buoys per month. This machine will reduce the painting time per buoy from 0.8 hour to 0.5 hour, but will increase annual shop costs from $20,000 to $35,000. The reduction in painting time per buoy enables Ontario Tole Art to reduce the number of painters needed for any level of scheduled production.

Exhibit 11-20 shows the revised pro forma income statement reflecting the rental of the sanding and priming machine. Renting this machine will increase projected net income from the original level of $40,666 to $45,484, a 12% increase of $4818.

SENSITIVITY ANALYSIS

What-if analysis is only as good as the model it uses. The model must be complete, it must reflect relationships accurately, and it must use reasonable estimates. If the model is complete and reflects capacity, cost, and revenue relationships accurately, then the remaining issue is the accuracy of the data used. Planners test planning models by varying key estimates. For example, suppose that one machine represents a bottleneck resource for manufacturing operations. Then the productivity (output per hour) of that machine is a key estimate for the production plan. The production planner could test the effect of errors in the estimate of the machine's productivity on the production plan by varying the productivity number by 10% or 20% above and below the estimate used in the planning budget.

If forecasting errors of an estimate used in the production plan have a dramatic effect on the plan, we say that the model is *sensitive* to that estimate. If the consequences from a bad estimate are severe, planners may want to invest time and resources to improve the accuracy of their estimates. **Sensitivity analysis** is the process of selectively varying a plan's or a budget's key estimates. Sensitivity analysis allows planners to identify the estimates that are most critical for the decisions based on that model. For example, the labor that Ontario Tole Art needs to make each

Sensitivity analysis
The analysis of the effect of a change in a parameter on a decision rather than on an outcome.

IN PRACTICE

Budgeting in High-Technology Organizations

Photon Technology International, Inc., is a manufacturer of high-technology equipment used for medical research and diagnostic purposes. Like most growing companies, Photon Technology needed large amounts of cash to finance inventories, investments in capital assets, and accounts receivable. In addition, as a high-technology company, it needed to make large investments in research and development. In response to continuing liquidity problems, Chuck Grant, the chief operating officer, introduced a budgeting cycle. The budgeting cycle allowed the company to identify and anticipate its cash requirements and plan to meet them systematically. Photon undertook three what-if scenarios to develop contingency plans to meet its cash requirements under best-case, worst-case, and most likely situations affecting cash flows.

Source: Janine S. Pouliot, "High-Tech Budgeting," *Management Accounting,* May 1991, pp. 30–31.

EXHIBIT 11-20

Ontario Tole Art
Sanding/Priming Machine Option
Projected Income Statement
For the Year Ended December 31, 2001

Revenue		$282,530
Flexible resource expenses		
Buoys	$10,350	
Paint	14,490	
Other supplies	12,650	
Packing	8,970	
Shipping	34,500	80,960
Contribution margin		$201,570
Committed resource expenses		
Painter's salaries	$30,000	
Shop rent	19,200	
Other shop costs	35,000	
Manager's salary	30,000	114,200
Other expenses		
Advertising	$40,000	
Interest paid	1,886	41,886
Net income		$ 45,484

product is an important parameter in its planning budget. Small changes in this parameter, which is the key productive resource, produce large changes in the profit figure. If Ontario Tole Art can develop a process or redesign the product so that labor time needed to make a buoy would be reduced by 10%, from 0.8 to 0.72 hour per buoy, projected profit would rise from $40,666 to $53,255—a 31% increase. This is a signal to Ross that designing and running the manufacturing process so that the artists can work as efficiently as possible is a key to the success of the business.

Comparing Actual and Planned Results

To understand results, organizations often find it useful to compare expected, or projected, results in the master budget with actual results. In chapter 12 we will discuss the concept of financial control, which shows how organizations can use differences, or variances, between the planned and actual level of costs as a warning signal to trigger a more detailed investigation of the circumstances that led to the variances.

The Role of Budgeting in Service and Not-For-Profit Organizations

To this point, we have discussed the role of budgeting in manufacturing organizations. Budgeting serves a slightly different but equally relevant role in natural resource companies, service organizations, and not-for-profit (NFP) organizations such as charitable organizations and government agencies. As in manufacturing organizations,

EXHIBIT 11-21

Focus of Budgeting in Different Organizations

ORGANIZATION TYPE	MAIN FOCUS OF BUDGETING PROCESS
Manufacturing	Sales and manufacturing activities
Natural resource	Sales, resource availability, and acquisition
Service	Sales activities and staffing requirements
NFP	Raising revenues and controlling expenditures

budgeting helps nonmanufacturing organizations perform their planning function by coordinating and formalizing responsibilities and relationships and communicating the expected plans. Exhibit 11-21 summarizes the main focus of the budgeting process in manufacturing, natural resource, service, and NFP organizations.

In the natural resources sector, the key focus is on balancing demand with the availability of natural resources, such as minerals, fish, or wood. Because the natural resource supply often constrains sales, success requires managing the resource base effectively to match resource supply with potential demand.

In the service sector, the key focus is on balancing demand and the organization's ability to provide services, which is determined by the level and mix of skills in the organization. Although the service sector frequently uses machines to deliver products to customers, most operations remain labor paced; that is, they operate at a pace dictated by their human operators. Therefore, people rather than machines usually represent the capacity constraint in the service sector. A key issue in planning in

▶ *The role for budgeting in planning and control is as important in not-for-profit and government organizations as it is in profit-seeking organizations. (Malcolm Linton/Liaison Agency, Inc.)*

the service sector is to consider the time needed to put skilled new people in place as sales increase. Planning is critical in high-skill organizations, such as in a consulting business, because people capacity is expensive and services cannot be inventoried when demand falls below capacity.

In NFP organizations, the traditional focus of budgeting has been to balance revenues raised by taxes or donations with spending demands. Government agencies call planned cash outflows, or spending plans, **appropriations.** Appropriations set limits on a government agency's spending. Governments worldwide are facing increased pressures to eliminate deficits without raising tax revenues. Therefore, many governments are looking for ways to eliminate unnecessary expenditures and to make necessary expenditures more efficient, rather than just ensuring that government agencies do not spend more than they have been authorized to do. Thus, as part of the planning process, these agencies must establish priorities for their expenditures and improve the productivity with which they deliver services to constituents.

Appropriation
An authorized spending limit in a government department.

Periodic and Continuous Budgeting

The basic budgeting process described in this chapter involves many organizational design decisions, such as the periodicity of the budget process, the basic budget spending assumptions, and the degree of top management control.

The budget process described for Ontario Tole Art is performed on an annual or **periodic budget** cycle. Gael, the owner, prepares budgets periodically for each planning period. Although planners may update or revise the budgets during the period, periodic budgeting is typically performed once per budget period.

Periodic budget
An annual budget prepared for each planning period.

In continuous budgeting, as one budget period (usually a month or a quarter) passes, planners drop that budget period from the master budget and add a future budget period in its place. Therefore, if Ontario Tole Art used continuous budgeting with a one-year cycle, Ross would drop one month from the beginning of the budget period and add a month to the end of the budget period as each month passes. For example, at the end of February 2000, Ross would drop February from the budget and add February 2001.

The length of the budget period used in continuous budgeting reflects the competitive forces, skill requirements, and technology changes that the organization faces. The budget period must be long enough for the organization to anticipate important environmental changes and adapt to them, and yet short enough to ensure that estimates for the end of the period will be reasonable and realistic.

IN PRACTICE

Ethics in Budgeting

Ivan Kilpatrick, a former vice-president of Bombardier, Inc., a large Canadian manufacturer of specialty vehicles, has a complaint. He claims that many management accountants, under pressure from senior executives, knowingly prepare budgets that overstate revenues and understate expenses. As evidence to support his assertion, Mr. Kilpatrick observed that profit variances are almost always unfavorable rather than being unfavorable about 50% of the time, which is what would be expected if the estimates were unbiased. Mr. Kilpatrick observed, "Accountants must remember that we are members of a profession, and we should speak out against the nonsense of fantasy forecasts."

Source: Ivan Kilpatrick, "It's Time to Face the Music on Budgets," *CMA Magazine,* March 1994, p. 6.

Advocates of periodic budgeting argue that continuous budgeting takes too much time and effort and that periodic budgeting provides virtually the same benefits at a smaller cost. Advocates of continuous budgeting argue that it keeps the organization planning, assessing, and thinking strategically year-round rather than just once a year at budget time.

Controlling Discretionary Expenditures

Organizations use three general approaches to budget discretionary expenditures for items such as spending on R&D:

1. incremental budgeting
2. zero-based budgeting (ZBB)
3. project funding

Each has important benefits, which explains why all three are used in practice.

INCREMENTAL BUDGETING

Incremental budgeting bases a period's expenditure level for a discretionary item on the amount spent for that item during the previous period. For example, if the total budget for discretionary items increases by 10%, each discretionary item is allowed to increase 10%. This basic model has variations; for example, if the total spending on all discretionary items is allowed to increase by 10%, then all discretionary spending may experience an across-the-board increase of 5% and the remaining 5% increase in total spending may be allocated to discretionary items based on merit or need.

Incremental budgeting
Bases a period's expenditure level for a discretionary item on the amount spent for that item during the previous period.

Some people have criticized incremental budgeting because it does not require justification of the organization's goals for discretionary expenditures. Incremental budgeting includes no provision to reduce or eliminate expenditures as the organization changes, nor does it have a mechanism to provide disproportionate support to discretionary items that will yield substantial benefits.

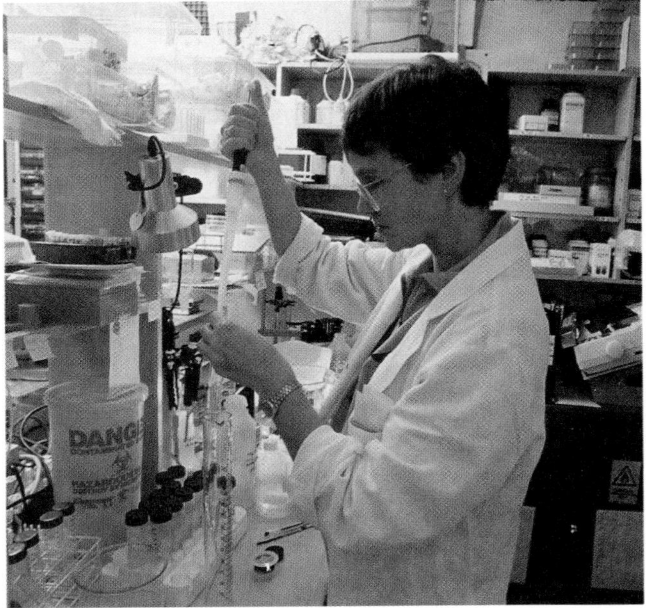

Accountants call research and development expenditures discretionary expenditures, *because they are not determined by the organization's level of production activities. (James Holmes/Glycobiology Unit, Oxford University/Science Pht L/Photo Researchers, Inc.)*

ZERO-BASED BUDGETING

Zero-based budgeting (ZBB)
Requires that proponents of discretionary expenditures continually justify every expenditure.

Zero-based budgeting (ZBB) requires that proponents of *discretionary* expenditures continuously justify every expenditure. (Note that zero-based budgeting is not appropriate for budgeting that relates to engineered costs that vary in proportion to production.) For each planning period, the starting point for each budget line item is zero. Zero-based budgeting arose, in part, to combat indiscriminate incremental budgets since that approach can require very little thought and result in misallocation of resources and in part to combat projects that, once activated, take on a life of their own and resist going out of existence.

Under ZBB, planners allocate the organization's scarce resources to the spending proposals they think will best achieve the organization's goals. While seemingly logical, the zero-based approach to planning discretionary expenditures is controversial. This approach has been used primarily to assess government expenditures. In profit-seeking organizations, ZBB has been applied only to discretionary expenditures such as research and development, advertising, and employee training.

Traditionally, ZBB ideas do not apply to engineered costs (short-term costs that have an identifiable relationship with some activity level). Engineered costs are controlled by measuring and using reports of the amounts of resources consumed by operating activities and by the cost variances described earlier. But even for engineered costs, ZBB could be effective when combined with the reengineering approach. For example, reengineering a product or process involves developing a vision of how a product should perform or how a process should work independently of current conditions. It is possible to use ZBB as a tool to provide baseline costs to new products or processes.

ACTIVITY-BASED BUDGETING

Activity-based budgeting
A budgeting approach based on the insights of activity-based costing.

A recent phenomenon involves the rise of **activity-based budgeting,** which is an approach to budgeting that is based on the insights of activity-based costing, as discussed in Chapter 5. Activity-based budgeting uses knowledge about the relationship

EXHIBIT 11-22

Paris Packing Components—Product Data

	PRODUCT A		PRODUCT B		PRODUCT C	
	Units	$/Unit	Units	$/Unit	Units	$/Unit
Revenue		$1900		$2500		$2600
Flexible Costs						
Materials		$ 125		$ 140		$ 210
Components		230		260		290
Supplies		35		40		60
Shipping		60		70		110
Contribution Margin		$1450		$1990		$1930
Capacity-Related Costs						
Moving @ $35	4	$ 140	6	$ 210	9	$ 315
Fabricating @ $110	8	880	7	770	9	990
Assembly @ $85	3	255	9	765	6	510
Unit Profit Contribution		$ 175		$ 245		$ 115

EXHIBIT 11-23

Paris Packing Components — Master Budget

	PRODUCT A		PRODUCT B		PRODUCT C	
	Units	$	Units	$	Units	$
Revenue	6000	$11,400,000	4000	$10,000,000	5000	$13,000,000
Flexible Costs						
Materials		$ 750,000		$ 560,000		$ 1,050,000
Components		1,380,000		1,040,000		1,450,000
Supplies		210,000		160,000		300,000
Shipping		360,000		280,000		550,000
Contribution Margin		$ 8,700,000		$ 7,960,000		$ 9,650,000
Capacity-Related Costs						
Moving @ $35	24,000	$ 840,000	24,000	$ 840,000	45,000	$ 1,575,000
Fabricating @ $110	48,000	5,280,000	28,000	3,080,000	45,000	4,950,000

between production units and the activities required to produce those units to develop detailed estimates of activity requirements underlying the proposed production plan. There are two major benefits of activity-based budgeting. First, it identifies situations when production plans require new capacity. Second, it provides a more accurate way to project future costs.

The following simple example illustrates the insights provided by activity-based budgeting. Paris Packing Components manufactures three products. Exhibit 11-22 summarizes the revenue, flexible cost, and capacity consumption data for each of the three products.

For example each unit of product A consumes four activity units in moving, eight activity units in fabricating, and three activity units in assembly.

Exhibit 11-23 summarizes expectations regarding total revenues, flexible costs, and capacity consumption given the production plan for the upcoming period, which is to produce 6000 units of product A, 4000 units of product B, and 5000 units of product C. Note how the activity information not only allows a projection of the production cost that will be allocated to production (the actual cost incurred, which will be the budgeted amount, will equal the total units of capacity for each capacity resource multiplied by its rate), but also projects the demand on capacity for the production plan. If any of the proposed uses of capacity of the current production plan exceeds the capacity available, the organization will either have to take steps to expand capacity or find a production plan whose capacity use does not exceed availability.

PROJECT FUNDING

Critics of zero-based budgeting have complained that it is expensive, because it requires so much employee time to prepare. These critics have proposed an intermediate solution between the two extremes of zero-based budgeting and incremental budgeting to mitigate the disadvantages of each. The intermediate solution is called **project funding,** which is a proposal for discretionary expenditures with a specific time horizon or sunset provision. Projects with indefinite lives are sometimes called *programs* and should be continuously reviewed to ensure that they are living up to their intended purposes.

Project funding
A proposal for discretionary expenditures with a specific time horizon or sunset provision.

THE TECHNOLOGICAL EDGE

The Benefits of E-Budgeting

Mention the word *budgeting* to many managers and you will often get looks of frustration and pain. The annual budgeting process in many organizations, especially large ones, often can take 9 months (or more). One major reason for the lengthy process is the number of rounds of submissions and resubmissions of requests and changes. Budgeting also can lead to mountains of paperwork, endless spreadsheets, and the need for a large amount of coordination among the parties involved.

Enterprise-wide budgeting and planning conducted over the internet (e-budgeting) has begun to significantly reduce the amount of work involved in the dreaded budgeting process. Web-based systems can be either designed for specific applications or integrated with the general ledger. Being tied to the general ledger allows the use of a centralized administrative system.

Some benefits of e-budgeting are fewer administrative costs and tasks, increased levels of service to employees, and the ability to shift people's attention away from spreadsheets and on to helping implement strategy. Administrative costs are reduced as the need for numerous spreadsheets—and constant reconciliation—is diminished. Service to employees is increased as organizational participants worldwide can log on to the internet and check the status of their budgets. E-budgeting also increases the number and kind of people involved in the budgeting process. Research has shown that participation in the budgeting process increases commitment to the final budget. Finally, e-budgeting gives the finance department personnel the opportunity to spend their time on strategic activities rather than on coordinating the flow and reconciliation of spreadsheets.

Source: Steve Hornyak, "Budgeting Made Easy," *Management Accounting*, October 1998, pp. 18–23.

Proposers of discretionary expenditures state their request in terms of a project proposal that includes project duration and cost for each period during the project's life. Planners approve no discretionary spending for projects that have indeterminate lengths or spending amounts. If the planners approve the project, then they agree to provide the level of support requested in the plan. Requests to extend or modify the project must be approved separately. The advantage of providing sunset provisions is they strike an intermediate balance between the high cost resulting from the need for close scrutiny and continuous justification provided by zero-based budgeting and the much lower cost of incremental budgeting.

Managing the Budgeting Process

Who should manage and oversee the budgeting process? Many organizations use a budget team, headed by the organization's budget director, sometimes the controller, to coordinate the budgeting process. The budget team usually reports to a budget committee, which generally includes the chief executive officer, the chief operating officer, and the senior executive vice presidents. The composition of the budget committee reflects the role of the budget as a key planning document that reflects and relates to the organization's strategy and objectives. The danger of using a budget committee is that it may signal to other employees that budgeting is something that is relevant only for senior management. Senior management must take steps to ensure that the organization members affected by the budget do not perceive it and the budgeting process as something beyond their control or responsibility.

Behavioral Aspects of Budgeting

Because of the human factor involved in the entire process, budgets often do not develop in a smooth, frictionless manner. How do people try to affect the budget and, in turn, how do budgets affect people's behavior? These questions have led social scientists to engage in extensive study about the human factors involved in budgeting.

Regardless of whether you are developing a family budget, a budget for a small company like Ontario Tole Art, or a budget for a major multinational company, you should be aware that the ways in which people interact with budgets are essentially the same. In this section, we discuss two interrelated behavioral issues in budgeting.

1. *Designing the budget process:* How should budgets be determined, who should be involved in the budgeting process, and at what level of difficulty should the budget be set to have the greatest positive influence on people's motivation and performance?
2. *Influencing the budget process:* How do people try to influence or manipulate the budget to their own ends?

DESIGNING THE BUDGET PROCESS

Where do the data come from that planners use to prepare the master budget and supporting plans? How should budgets be determined and who should be involved in the budgeting process?

The three most common methods of setting budgets are authoritarian, participation, and consultation. **Authoritative budgeting** occurs when a superior simply tells subordinates what their budget will be. The benefit to the organization is that the process is straightforward and efficient—it allows superiors to assign budgets and promotes overall coordination among subunits in the organization because it is done from a single perspective. Managers who want to impose a budget in a top-down manner often want control and have authoritarian aspects to their personalities. One disadvantage of imposing budgets is that superiors may have no clear idea about the appropriate target levels within the budget. Targets are the goals related to each part of the budget. In this instance, the superior indicates the goals to the subordinates. Under authoritative budgeting, a subordinate who has high aspirations for the coming year regarding new goals may now become frustrated and debilitated. A second problem is the lack of motivation and commitment to the budgeted goals because of the lack of employee participation in establishing the budget. Worse yet, if the superior sets high goals and only provides a small budget for resource spending, motivation can decrease significantly and individuals and the organization can fail to attain their goals.

Authoritative budgeting
A budget-setting method in which a superior tells a subordinate what the budget will be.

Research shows that the most motivating types of budgets are those that are tight, that is, those with targets that are perceived as ambitious but attainable. Recently, companies such as Boeing and General Electric have implemented what are known as **stretch targets.** In the past, both companies used an incremental approach in which targets from the previous year were increased slightly. Stretch targets exceed previous targets by a significant amount and usually require an enormous increase in a goal over the next budgeting period. **Stretch budgeting** means that the organization will try to reach much higher goals with the current budget. The rationale for this approach is that stretch targets push an organization to its limits. The theory is that only in this manner will companies completely reevaluate the ways in which

Stretch targets
A target that exceeds previous targets by a significant amount and usually require an enormous increase in performance during the next budgeting periods.

Stretch budgeting
A budgeting method that attempts to reach much higher goals than the current performance.

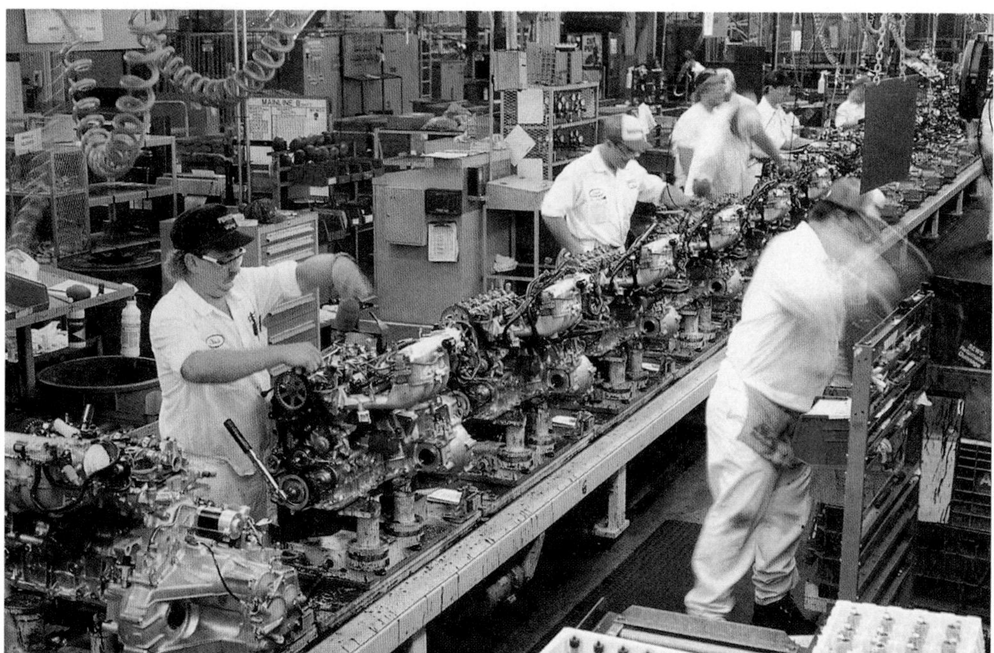

Research evidence suggests that when employees have a part in setting the budgets or targets for their work, they tend to accept these budgets more willingly and strive harder to achieve them. (Andy Sacks/Stone)

they develop and produce products and services. While some employees thrive in this type of environment, the pace of work and difficulty of achieving stretch targets can frustrate many and cause others to quit their jobs. Further, whereas employees may be able to push themselves very hard to meet the stretch target in the short run, they may not be able to sustain an enormously high level of effort in every subsequent period. Organizations need to make sure that they provide resources and a plan so that employees believe that stretch targets are achievable.

Participative budgeting A method of budget setting that uses a joint decision-making process in which all parties agree about setting the budget targets.

Participative budgeting is a method of budget setting that uses a joint decision-making process in which all parties agree about setting the budget targets. Allowing employees to participate in decision making provides an opportunity for them to use their private or specific information to jointly set their goals and negotiate the level of their budget. Participation has many benefits for employees, such as greater feelings of commitment to the budget and, therefore, a higher level of motivation to attain goals and keep within the budget. Research on participative budgeting has shown that employees generally feel greater job satisfaction and higher morale due primarily to their having greater control over their jobs. In some instances, higher levels of performance can result.

Allowing participation offers an additional benefit for management, because it often induces subordinates to reveal what is called their *private information,* or *data* about how well they can perform their jobs, or to introduce new ideas that may help improve existing processes. As a result of discussing the budget jointly, subordinates indirectly reveal this information and their level of aspiration to management. Then it can be incorporated into the planning process.

Consultative budgeting A method of budget setting used when managers ask subordinates to discuss their ideas about the budget, but no joint decision making occurs.

The third method of setting the budget is called **consultative budgeting.** Consultative budgeting occurs when managers ask subordinates to discuss their ideas about the budget, but no joint decision making occurs. Instead, the superior solicits the subordinates' ideas and determines the final budget alone. For many large organizations in which complete participation is impractical, consultation is the norm. A variant of the consultative form of budgeting may occur when subordinates believe

IN PRACTICE

Five Ways to Manage People Facing Stretch Targets

In an interview with *Fortune,* Steve Kerr, described as the "Chief Learning Officer" at General Electric, states that "Most organizations don't have a clue about how to manage stretch goals." He offers the following advice:

1. By definition, stretch goals are very difficult to meet. Don't punish people for not hitting them.
2. Don't set goals that stretch your employees crazily.
3. Understand that stretch targets can unexpectedly affect other parts of the organization.
4. Don't give tough stretch goals to those people already pushing themselves to the limit.
5. Share the wealth generated by reaching stretch goals.

Source: Strat Sherman, "Stretch Goals: The Dark Side of Asking for Miracles," *Fortune,* November 13, 1995, pp. 231–232.

that their input will be used directly in setting the budget, even though their superior really has no intention of considering their inputs. This process is called pseudo-participation and can have a debilitating effect on subordinates if they find out that the superior was insincere.

INFLUENCING THE BUDGET PROCESS

Clearly, the budgeting process is not simple or mechanical. It highlights the need for interactions about resource allocation, organizational goals, and human motivation and performance. In large organizations, as in families, budgets represent the outcomes of negotiations among individuals. Some individuals will do all that they can to increase the size of their budgets because they believe a large budget is a symbol of power and control.

Although the budget is used as a tool for planning, coordinating, and resource allocation, it also serves to measure performance and ultimately to control and influence behavior. In addition, many managers have their incentive compensation tied directly to budget and goal attainment. When incentives and compensation are tied to the budget, some managers engage in behavior that is dysfunctional to their organizations. Managers have been known to play **budgeting games** in which they attempt to manipulate information and targets to achieve as high a bonus as possible. One well-known way that managers engage in budgeting games is through the participation process.

Budgeting games A process in which managers attempt to manipulate information and targets to achieve as high a bonus as possible.

Participation provides employees the opportunity to affect their budgets in ways that may not always be in the best interests of the organization. For instance, subordinates might ask for resources above and beyond what they need to accomplish their budget objectives. This results in a misallocation of resources for the organization as a whole. Another risk is that subordinates will distort information by claiming that they are not as efficient or effective at what they do as they appear, thereby attempting to lower management's expectations of their performance. Subordinates may want some additional cushion in performance requirements in case there is an unforeseen change in the work environment that detrimentally affects resources or impairs their ability to meet the budget. If subordinates succeed in this type of negotiation, they will find it easy to meet or exceed their budgeted objectives. Again the organization suffers, because it is not obtaining the most accurate information available to assess, and thereby improve, its operations. Both these acts—requiring

IN PRACTICE

"Oh the (Budgeting) Games People Play Now, Every Night and Every Day Now, Never Meaning What They Say, Never Saying What They Mean" (with apologies to Joe South; Capital Records, 1969)

In this humorous article, Sigmund Ginsburg describes the nine classic types of approaches that managers use in negotiating their budgets. Do you recognize any of these characters?

- **The Gardner** is known for "watering" his budget so that all the bushes and trees grow many new shoots. Each shoot represents something he doesn't really desire such as a new coffee machine or a training seminar for his staff. At budget time, the gardner makes slick presentations that justify his requests; however, by that time the garden has grown into a jungle. Trying to cut his budget is exhausting and that is how the gardner always fares well with his budget.
- **The Duck Hunter** knows how to use decoys well. She peppers her budget with ducks, some of which are real and some of which are decoys. The decoys are often an expensive new project presented in very complex terms. The duck hunter's strategy is to focus your attention on the details relating to the decoy so that you will not notice her real programs. She will try to get you so intrigued with the decoys that you could spend an entire day discussing them and not the real issues.
- **The Entrepreneur's** song is "I need the right kind of investment and management support for my new idea." The entrepreneur is flamboyant, gutsy, and innovative. He uses graphs and charts to illustrate how with very little money he will make the company a fortune. The problem is that many of the entrepreneur's ideas are untested. If he fails, he will simply tell you that he was implementing a high-risk proposition.
- **The Gambler** has a perfect poker face when it comes to negotiations. His air is that of an old-time riverboat confidence man. He needs his budget to achieve a big score and he is willing to take enormous risks to win. His threat is "Cut my budget and I'll resign." He's hoping that you won't call his bluff.
- **The Surgeon** enters your office looking very grim. She has just performed a major operation on her budget. You can almost see the bloodstains on her gown. She laments that the patient cannot take any more as she has cut everything to the bare bone. Any more surgery will damage the vital organs. When you suggest that she cut some more, she tells you that she won't take responsibility if her department cannot meet its objectives.
- **The Good Soldier** is a true company person and follows all company policies and believes in all company objectives. She claims to have adhered strictly to your orders regarding a bare bones budget. As she is turning over her battle plan to you, she states that she will leave it up to you to make any changes. Since every officer needs a good soldier to depend on, you may feel that you should trust her judgment and give her the money. If you do, you may find that with her experience she has successfully padded the budget.
- **The Drowning Man** makes his budget presentation as if it were his last. "We are going down for the last time." He requests more money so that he and his employees can keep their heads above water. Using guilt, the drowning man wants you to feel that you have always underfunded him. Now is the time to help him he cries. Faced with such a plea, you have to decide whether now is the time to fund him.
- **The Savior** approaches you and says, "I'm not here to talk about saving some funds for my department, I'm here to talk about saving the entire firm." Speaking in an impassioned manner, the savior says that his department needs a great deal of money not only to achieve its objectives but to carry the entire company. It appears that he is willing to take on the weight of the company; however, he is also implying that if you don't fund him, the company's future is at stake. Do you believe him?
- **The Honest Guy** is a very rare animal indeed. This is someone who really means what he

says. His budget seems to be accurate and realistic. He does not dwell on past accomplishments and discusses his department's problems in a straightforward manner. He guarantees that there is no fat in his budget. In dealing with the honest guy, you have to follow your instincts and give him his budget. If you cut him arbitrarily, he may turn into the drowning man—something you certainly do not want to happen.

Source: Sigmund G. Ginsburg, "Negotiating Budgets: Games People Play," *INC.*, September 1981, pp. 89–91.

excess resources and distorting performance information—fall under the heading of creating **budget slack.**

Budget slack
Involve the acts of requiring excess resources and distorting performance information.

Consider a manager who is worried that a supplier will be unwilling to sell raw materials at an historically budgeted price. The manager may decide to increase the allowance requested for purchasing raw materials, which would build slack into this budget line item. The request leads to the assignment of excess resources for this purpose and hence fewer resources for other purposes. Other distortions can arise from arbitrary increases in resource requests, because the resulting established standard costs for products will be incorrect. Further, subordinates are also concerned about standards or budgets that are too difficult to attain; if their bonuses are based on attaining a budget, then they will opt for an easier budget. To counter the problem of low target setting, management may design an incentive system that provides higher levels of bonuses based on attaining higher targets.

Budgeting games can never be eliminated, although some organizations have devised methods to decrease the amount of budget slack. They can use an iterative process to formulate the budget, for example, developing a very lengthy budgeting cycle that may last as long as a year. Then subordinate managers submit a preliminary budget, which is modified by senior management and sent back to subordinate managers for modification. The modifications usually require justification for each line item in painful detail. This process continues for several iterations until senior managers are convinced that they have eliminated as much slack as possible from the subordinate manager's budget. The other benefit to this process is that by the time both parties agree to the budget, everyone has developed a strong commitment to it. This commitment gives them confidence that they can achieve their goals for the coming year.

RESOLVING THE BUDGETING CONCERNS IN THE CITY OF RIDGETOWN

Sandra, the mayor of Ridgetown, instructed Shawn Dawson, the senior analyst in the finance group, to develop a budget that reflected the nature and type of costs facing the municipality. The result is Exhibit 11-24. The projected shortfall was $200 million ($2.7 billion – $2.5 billion), and Shawn's role was to identify ways to eliminate this projected shortfall.

Shawn began by identifying the various revenue and cost elements in the municipal budget. After a detailed investigation, each cost element was divided into three groups.

1. *Committed costs, which were costs that were contractually committed and could neither be reduced nor varied. These costs totaled $2,340,630,000.*

EXHIBIT 11-24

Ridgetown Budget Analysis

REVENUES			
Property taxes	50%		1,250,000,000
Business taxes	20%		500,000,000
User fees	20%		500,000,000
Grants	10%		250,000,000
Total			2,500,000,000
Expenditures			
Education	60%		1,620,000,000
Committed	85%	1,377,000,000	
Discretionary	12%	194,400,000	
Cost reduction potential	3%	48,600,000	
Policing and fire services	20%		540,000,000
Committed	90%	486,000,000	
Discretionary	8%	43,200,000	
Cost reduction potential	2%	10,800,000	
Recreation	5%		135,000,000
Committed	77%	103,950,000	
Discretionary	22%	29,700,000	
Cost reduction potential	1%	1,350,000	
Debt servicing	4%		108,000,000
Committed	100%	108,000,000	
Discretionary	0%	0	
Cost reduction potential	0%	0	
Transit	3%		81,000,000
Committed	94%	76,140,000	
Discretionary	5%	4,050,000	
Cost reduction potential	1%	810,000	
Road maintenance	2%		54,000,000
Committed	72%	38,880,000	
Discretionary	27%	14,580,000	
Cost reduction potential	1%	540,000	
Garbage collection	2%		54,000,000
Committed	96%	51,840,000	
Discretionary	1%	540,000	
Cost reduction potential	3%	1,620,000	
Library	1%		27,000,000
Committed	75%	20,250,000	
Discretionary	24%	6,480,000	
Cost reduction potential	1%	270,000	
Other services	3%		81,000,000
Committed	97%	78,570,000	
Discretionary	2%	1,620,000	
Cost reduction potential	1%	810,000	
Total			2,700,000,000
Total Committed Costs		2,340,630,000	
Total Discretionary Costs		294,570,000	
Total Committed and Discretionary		2,635,200,000	
Cost Reduction Potential		64,800,000	
Total Costs		2,700,000,000	

2. *Discretionary costs, which were costs that could be reduced by eliminating the programs or activities that created them. These costs totaled $294,570,000.*
3. *Reengineering or redesign program costs with a cost-reduction potential. These totaled $64,800,000 and had, on average, a two-year payback period. That is, their costs would be recovered in two years by the savings they generated. Therefore, the net effect in the current year of implementing these cost-reduction programs would be to increase cash outflows by about $65,000,000.*

Armed with this analysis, Shawn had an informal meeting with most of the members of the city council. Since the cost-reduction activities would create additional costs before their savings were realized, it was evident to Shawn that the immediate problem was to choose which discretionary expenditures would have to be cut in the short run, and he communicated this to the council members. The council members were strongly divided not only about which programs to cut, but also over the principle of whether any programs should be cut.

The councilors agreed that tax increases on residential properties were out of the question. Residential property taxes were above the average for comparable communities, and earlier election promises indicated no increases for at least three years. The councilors agreed to a modest increase in business taxes, on the ground that these taxes were below the average for communities with comparable services to businesses. In addition, a study of licenses issued for construction and new retail businesses indicated that there would be a natural increase in business taxes resulting from planned expansions that would come on line in the next year. The result was that the forecast for business tax collections was increased by 5% or $25 million.

The councilors instructed Shawn and his group to look into increasing the profits from user fees and from the municipally owned power company. After a careful analysis, Shawn's senior analyst, Karen Brown, indicated that a moderate price increase was possible and would generate about $30 million in additional revenues. Moreover, the utility could sell off excess equipment, which would generate cash inflows of about $10 million.

These changes would cover the short-run costs of the cost-reduction programs, leaving the benefits to be enjoyed in future years. This left Shawn with the original $200 million deficit to resolve.

Recognizing that the current budget numbers were projections of the costs incurred in the most recent two years—a form of incremental budgeting—Shawn instructed his staff to study those costs. Two important results emerged. First, police and fire expenditures had been significantly higher in the last two years because of major capital expenditures. Like most municipalities, Ridgetown did its accounting on a cash flow basis rather than an accrual basis. This analysis suggested that projected expenditures for police and fire services were likely overstated by $30 million. There was no evidence that this type of effect on costs was evident in any other expenditure class.

Following the rule of thumb to look for opportunities to reduce costs in the area where most expenditures were made, Shawn studied the education budget. This study *confirmed what Shawn already suspected: The cost per student enrolled in the public school system in Ridgetown was significantly higher than in any comparable community. Through modest increases in class size and the creation of split campuses at two schools, Shawn identified savings of about $60 million.*

Finally, Shawn's staff investigated the federal government grant proposal. A careful analysis suggested that there had been significant underpayments of these grants, which were based on legislation. The town's solicitor indicated that these underpayments were between $20 million and $30 million. Shawn took the midpoint of $25 million as his estimate of what was owed.

Shawn was still about $85 million short of his cost-reduction target ($200 million − $30 million − $60 million − $25 million) and concluded that there were no more cost savings to be gleaned from scrutinizing current operations or recasting projections. Shawn advised the city council that the next step would have to be either to reconsider raising residential taxes or to start cutting into discretionary expenditures. The proposal of increasing residential tax expenditures was again flatly rejected, and the council was now preparing to debate which discretionary expenditures would be eliminated.

In this regard, the council approved a motion that Shawn hire a consultant to survey community attitudes concerning which programs to eliminate. A consensus quickly developed to eliminate several programs whose costs totaled $55 million, leaving $30 million of cost cuts on the table.

Council now turned to the political process of deciding which discretionary programs would be eliminated to achieve these target cuts. Shawn was told that the council wanted to use zero-based budgeting to prioritize the discretionary cost spending in order to target the remaining cost cuts.

SUMMARY

A budget is a quantitative expression of the money inflows and outflows used to determine whether a financial plan will meet organizational goals. A budget supports the management roles of planning and control by providing a way to express plans and the foundation for control activities. In many short-term decisions, only flexible costs are relevant, whereas capacity-related costs are thought of as given. In this chapter, we discuss the budgeting that determines the level of capacity-related costs. In an ideal situation, the supply of capacity resources is determined based on the demands for the services the resources provide for projected levels of product volumes and mix.

The budgeting process forces the organization to do the following:

1. Identify its long-term objectives and short-term goals and be specific in setting goals and evaluating performance relative to those goals.
2. Recognize the need to view the organization as a system of interacting components that must be coordinated.
3. Communicate the organization's goals to all organization members and involve them in the budgeting process.
4. Anticipate problems, thereby handling them proactively rather than reactively.

The master budget is the set of operating and financial plans that summarizes the organization's activities for the upcoming budget period, which is usually one year. The financial plans developed in the master budget include a projected or pro forma cash flow statement, balance sheet, and income statement. Planners use the projected balance sheet and income statement to evaluate the financial consequences of a proposed short-term business plan. Financial managers use the statement of projected cash flows to plan when the business will generate excess cash to help plan short-term investments or ways to meet their cash shortages in the least expensive manner.

The chapter presents a detailed master budgeting exercise and develops the financial plans for a set of given operating plans. Organizations make financial commitments when they acquire special-purpose facilities or capacity in the long term and general-purpose facilities or capacity in the intermediate term. In the short term, organizations acquire other resources, such as materials and casual labor, as needed, allowing them to use longer-term capacity to produce products and services.

We discuss conventional cost-volume-profit analysis and how decision makers can use it to understand and portray the relationship between volume and profits. In particular, cost-volume-profit analysis highlights the level of sales at which the organization breaks even.

The insights of what-if analysis, a modeling exercise that explores the operating and financial consequences of varying a proposed plan, allows decision makers to plan effectively. In addition, sensitivity analysis explores the sensitivity of operating decisions and financial results to the estimates used in the planning model.

The source of information used in budgeting models is important in two ways. First, the information source should be credible and reliable. Second, the potential use of planning information for control can create a potential behavioral conflict. Budgeting in nonmanufacturing environments, such as the natural resource sector, the service sector, and the nonprofit sector, were discussed. The chapter also described incremental budgeting and compared it with zero-based budgeting, which bases the appropriations in the current budget on those in the previous budget. Finally, there are important behavioral considerations regarding the budgeting process, such as who should be involved with the process, the concept of budget slack, and stretch budgets and commitment.

KEY TERMS

Activity-based budgeting, 472
Aggregate planning, 451
Appropriations, 470
Authoritative budgeting, 475
Budget, 439
Budgeting, 439
Budgeting games, 477
Budgeting process, 438
Budget slack, 479
Consultative budgeting, 476
Cost-volume-profit analysis, 461
Financial budgets, 441
Incremental budgeting, 471
Operating budgets, 441
Participative budgeting, 476
Periodic budget, 470
Pro forma financial statements, 442
Project funding, 473
Sensitivity analysis, 467
Stretch budgeting, 475
Stretch targets, 475
Variances, 441
What-if analysis, 466
Zero-based budgeting (ZBB), 472

ASSIGNMENT MATERIALS

QUESTIONS

11-1 What is a budget? (LO 1)

11-2 What is the difference between flexible and capacity-related resources? (LO 1)

11-3 A student develops a spending plan for a school semester. Is this budgeting? Why? (LO 1)

11-4 How does a family's budget differ from a budget developed for an organization? (LO 1)

11-5 What is a production plan? Give an example of one in a courier company. (LO 1)

11-6 What is a variance? How is a warning light in a car that indicates the oil pressure is low like a variance? (LO 1)

11-7 What is the difference between operating and financial budgets? (LO 3)

11-8 Would a labor hiring and training plan be more important in a university or a municipal government office that hires casual workers to do unskilled work? Why? (LO 3)

11-9 What is the relationship between a demand forecast and a sales plan? (LO 4)

11-10 What is a demand forecast and why is it relevant in budgeting? (LO 4)

11-11 Is employee training an example of a discretionary expenditure? Why? (LO 4)

11-12 What does a capital spending plan do? (LO 4)

11-13 What is an example of a capacity-related expenditure? (LO 4)

11-14 Are food costs in a university residence cafeteria an engineered cost or a capacity-related cost? Briefly explain. (LO 4)

11-15 Are materials always a flexible resource? Why? (LO 4)

11-16 What is a line of credit? How is it useful to a small organization? (LO 4)

11-17 Using the notion of aggregate planning, what problems would municipal authorities face when planning transportation for people attending a rock concert in the city's center? (LO 4)

11-18 What does the term *contribution margin* per unit mean? How is contribution margin used in cost analysis to support managerial decisions? (LO 5)

11-19 What does the term *break-even point* mean? (LO 5)

11-20 What are the similarities and differences between what-if and sensitivity analysis? (LO 6)

11-21 What is an appropriation? Give an example of one in a university. (LO 6)

11-22 What is a periodic budget? (LO 4)

11-23 You are planning your expenses for the upcoming school semester. You assume that this year's expenditures will equal last year's plus 2%. What approach to budgeting are you using? (LO 4)

11-24 You are willing to donate to worthy organizations. However, you believe strongly that each request for a donation should be evaluated based on its own merits. You would not feel bad in any year if you donated nothing. What approach to budgeting are you using? (LO 4)

11-25 What are the two interrelated behavioral issues in budgeting? (LO 8)

11-26 What are the three most common methods of setting the budget? (LO 8)

11-27 What is the most motivating type of budget with respect to targets? (LO 8)

11-28 What is a stretch target? (LO 8)

11-29 What is budget slack? (LO 8)

EXERCISES

LO 2, 3 **11-30** ***Budgeting information*** Consider a company that sells prescription drugs. It has salespeople who visit doctors and hospitals to encourage physicians to prescribe its drugs. The company sells to drugstores. Salespeople are evaluated based on the sales in their territory. Their income is a salary plus a bonus if actual sales exceed planned sales. To plan operations, this company needs to develop estimates of total sales. Where should it get this information?

LO 1, 4, 8 **11-31** ***Budgeting and planning*** Some people say that budgets are great for planning but not for control. What do you think they mean? Do you agree with this sentiment? Explain.

LO 1, 4, 7 **11-32** ***Budgeting: types of resources in a university*** For a university, identify a cost that you think is controllable in the short term and explain why. Identify a cost that you think is controllable in the intermediate term and explain why. Identify a cost that you think is controllable in the long term and explain why. What does this cost structure imply about the university's flexibility in responding to changing student demands and enrollment?

LO 1, 2, 3 **11-33** ***Financial budgets*** Many managers consider the pro forma financial statements to be the most important product of the master budgeting process. Why do you think they believe this?

LO 1, 2, 4, 7 **11-34** ***Consulting company: types of resources*** Budgeting allows an organization to identify broad resource requirements so that it can develop plans to put needed resources in place. Use an example to illustrate why this might be valuable in a consulting company that provides advice to clients.

LO 2, 3, 4 **11-35** ***Canning company: budgeting process*** Budgeting allows an organization to identify potential problems so that plans can be developed to avoid these problems or to deal with them systematically. Give an example of how budgeting might serve this role in a company that buys vegetables and cans them.

11-36 ***Financial budgets: cash flows*** Monthly cash budgets of inflows and outflows are an important part of the budgeting process in most organizations. In the course of preparing a cash budget, the organization must estimate its cash inflows from credit sales. Suppose that in response to projected cash shortfalls the organization decides to speed its collections of credit sales. What effect can this have on the organization? LO 3, 4

11-37 ***Machine shop: comparing financial and operational results*** Budgeting allows an organization to compare its projected operating and financial results with those of competitors as a general test of the efficiency of the organization's operating processes. Explain how this might be valuable for a machine shop that does custom machining work for its customers. LO 1, 3

11-38 ***Break-even analysis for a hospital*** Mariposa Medical Institute operates a 100-bed hospital and offers a number of specialized medical services. Mariposa's hospital facility and equipment are leased on a long-term basis. The hospital charges $100 per patient day. Based on past cost data, Mariposa has estimated its flexible costs as $45.70 per patient day. Capacity-related costs are $91,000 per month. The hospital's administrator has estimated that the hospital will average 2300 patient days per month. How much will the hospital need to charge per patient day to break even at this level of activity? LO 5

11-39 ***Break-even analysis, what-if analysis*** Polar Parkas Company budgets sales revenues at $30 per unit, flexible costs at $19.50 per unit, and capacity-related costs at $147,000 for the year 2000. LO 5, 6

REQUIRED

(a) What is Polar's contribution margin per unit?

(b) Determine the number of units Polar must sell to break even.

(c) Determine the sales revenue required to earn (pretax) income equal to 20% of revenue.

(d) Polar is considering increasing its advertising expenses by $38,500. How much of an increase in sales units is necessary from expanded advertising to justify this expenditure?

11-40 ***What-if-analysis*** Jeren Company is considering replacing its existing cutting machine with a new machine that will help reduce its defect rate. Relevant information for the two machines includes the following: LO 6

Cost Item	Existing Machine	New Machine
Monthly capacity-related costs	$32,000	$40,000
Flexible cost per unit	44	40
Sales price per unit	55	55

REQUIRED

(a) Determine the sales level, in number of units, at which the costs are the same for both machines.

(b) Determine the sales level in dollars at which the use of the new machine results in a 10% profit on sales (profit/sales) ratio.

11-41 ***Sensitivity analysis*** Sensitivity analysis is an important component of any budgeting exercise. Which estimates do you think will be most crucial in developing a master budget? Why? LO 2, 3, 6

LO 6, 7 **11-42** ***Sensitivity analysis: cost cutting*** A university faced with a deficit reacts by cutting resource allocations to all faculties and departments by 8%. Do you think this is a good approach to budgeting? Why?

LO 8 **11-43** ***Method of designing the budget*** How does participation in the budgeting process differ from consultation?

LO 8 **11-44** ***Budget slack*** What are the pros and cons of building slack into the budget from (a) the point of view of the employee building in slack and (b) from a senior manager's point of view?

LO 8 **11-45** ***Budgeting games*** What are budgeting games, and why do employees engage in them?

PROBLEMS

LO 3 **11-46** ***Operating budgets: production plan*** Borders Manufacturing is developing a sales and production plan as part of its master budgeting process. Projected monthly sales, which occur uniformly during each month, for the upcoming year follow:

BORDERS MANUFACTURING
PROJECTED MONTHLY SALES

MONTH	UNIT SALES
January	8742
February	9415
March	7120
April	8181
May	7942
June	9681
July	2511
August	2768
September	2768
October	2283
November	1542
December	1980
January	8725

Production for each month equals one-half of the current month's sales plus one-half of the next month's projected sales. Develop the production plan for Borders Manufacturing for the upcoming year.

LO 3 **11-47** ***Operating budgets: labor hiring and production plan*** Mira Vista Planters provides reforestation services to large paper products companies. It must hire one planter for every 10,000 trees that it has contracted to plant each month. An employee must receive one week of evaluation and training before being profitably employed. For every five prospective employees who enter training, three are deemed suitable for employment. When cutbacks occur, employees are laid off on the first day of the month. Every employee laid off receives severance pay equal to one week's salary, which is on average $400, regardless of how long the layoff will last. Laid-off employees inevitably drift away and new hires must be trained.

The company has been offered the following contracts for the upcoming year. Each monthly contract is offered on an accept or reject basis, that is, if a monthly contract is accepted, then it must be completed in full. Partial completion is not acceptable. The revenue per tree planted is $0.20.

MIRA VISTA PLANTERS
MONTHLY TREE PLANTING CONTRACTS

MONTH	TREES
January	8,692
February	5,765
March	8,134
April	34,400
May	558,729
June	832,251
July	1,286,700
August	895,449
September	733,094
October	203,525
November	29,410
December	9,827

REQUIRED

Prepare a labor plan for the upcoming year, indicating the following for each month.

(a) Whether you feel the company should accept or reject the proposed planting contract.

(b) How many people will be hired for training. (Recall that an employee is not available for planting during the week of training and that only three of the five employees accepted for training can be hired.)

(c) How many people will be laid off. The organization will have two trained employees on January 1.

11-48 ***Operating budgets: materials purchasing plan*** Pasadena Chemical Company manufactures a wide range of chemical compounds. One of the most difficult compounds is a cleaning solvent made from an expensive and volatile raw material called tetrax that is often in short supply. The company uses one liter of tetrax for every 100 liters of cleaning solvent that it makes. LO 3

Tetrax costs $560 per liter and must be stored in space leased in a special warehouse. The storage cost including all related costs is $2 per liter per day stored. The chemical is unstable and on average the loss is 1% of the volume stored per day. The cleaning compound can also be made from monax, which costs $1000 per liter. Because of the prohibitive cost of monax, however, Pasadena avoids using it unless it is absolutely necessary.

The three existing tetrax suppliers have been unreliable. For this reason, Pasadena has refused to begin production of the cleaning compound. Recently, a new supplier joined the field and guarantees the supply of tetrax under three conditions. Customers must be prepared to take weekly deliveries of tetrax, the weekly order must be for precisely the same quantity each week, and the contract must cover one year. If these conditions are met, the supplier will replace any undelivered tetrax with monax.

Because the cleaning compound itself is also volatile, users demand the product when they are ready for it and no sooner. Suppliers carefully estimate the amount of cleaner they require and will not accept less than the ordered amount.

The contracted cleaning compound sales for next year follow:

PASADENA CHEMICAL COMPANY
CLEANING SOLVENT PRODUCT

MONTH	UNIT SALES	MONTH	UNIT SALES
January	41,203	July	41,889
February	48,077	August	42,107
March	53,646	September	47,488
April	60,038	October	49,638
May	46,332	November	49,942
June	50,508	December	37,593

REQUIRED

(a) Set up a spreadsheet for this problem. The spreadsheet should allow you to compute the total cost of a contract with the new supplier. This total cost includes purchase price, storage cost, and the cost, if necessary, of any monax that would be purchased. The spreadsheet should be set up to allow you to vary the purchase quantity of tetrax easily. To simplify the problem, make the following assumptions:

- The loss each month is 1% times the number of days times the sum of (1) the average of the opening and ending inventory (before the loss) and (2) one-half the batch size.
- The cost of carrying inventory each month is two times the number of days times the sum of (1) the average of opening and closing inventory (after the loss) and (2) one-half the batch size.
- Production takes place seven days per week.
- January, March, July, and November have five weeks; the rest of the months of the year have four weeks.

(b) What is the best weekly quantity to contract for purchase from the new supplier?

LO 3 **11-49** ***Operating budgets: labor hiring plan*** Strathfield Motel is planning its operations for the upcoming tourist season. The motel has 60 units and the following table presents the average number of daily rentals expected for each of the 12 weeks of the tourist season.

The motel hires housekeeping staff on a weekly basis. Each person can clean 15 rooms per day. Employees must be hired for the entire week at a wage of $400 per employee per week. Because of the motel's location in a midsize city, there are always trained people available to work on short notice.

The motel does not own its linen and towels but rents them from a rental agency in a nearby city. The rental contract must be signed for a 4-week period and for a fixed amount of linen and towels. Therefore, the motel must sign three contracts for the 12-week tourist season. The contract provides the linen required for each room for $3 per night.

STRATHFIELD MOTEL AVERAGE NUMBER OF DAILY RENTALS			
WEEK	AVERAGE UNITS RENTED	WEEK	AVERAGE UNITS RENTED
1	46	7	55
2	48	8	55
3	54	9	50
4	60	10	45
5	60	11	37
6	60	12	30

REQUIRED

Prepare a weekly budget for the hotel showing the following:

(a) The number of housekeeping staff to employ

(b) The number of linen and towel units to contract

11-50 ***Financial budgets: expense budget*** During the school year, the Homebush School band arranges concert dates in many communities. Because only part of the school's travel expenses are covered by the concert admission fees, the band raises money in the local community through events such as car washes to help defray its operating expenses. LO 3

To estimate its expenses for the upcoming year, the band's manager has estimated the number of concert dates for each of the school months, September through May. For each concert, the manager estimates hotel costs of $900, food costs of $480, bus rental costs of $600, and other costs of $200.

The following table presents the number of planned concerts during the upcoming year.

HOMEBUSH SCHOOL BAND SCHEDULED CONCERTS			
MONTH	SCHEDULED CONCERTS	MONTH	SCHEDULED CONCERTS
September	3	February	4
October	4	March	2
November	5	April	5
December	8	May	7
January	3		

Prepare a monthly schedule estimating the band's travel expenses.

11-51 ***Break-even point, what-if analysis*** Premier Products, Inc. is considering replacing its existing machine with a new faster machine that will produce a more reliable product and will turn around customer orders in a shorter period. This change is expected to increase the sales price and capacity-related costs but not the flexible costs. LO 5, 6

Cost Item	Old Machine	New Machine
Monthly capacity-related costs	$120,000	$250,000
Flexible cost per unit	14	14
Sales price per unit	18	20

REQUIRED

(a) Determine the break-even point *in units* for the two machines.

(b) Determine the sales level *in units* at which the use of the new machine will achieve a 10% target profit-to-sales ratio.

(c) Determine the sales level *in units* at which profits will be the same for either the old or the new machine.

(d) Which machine represents a lower risk of incurring a loss? Explain why.

(e) Determine the sales level *in units* at which the profit-to-sales ratio will be equal with either machine.

LO 6 **11-52** ***What-if-analysis*** Tenneco, Inc. produces three models of tennis rackets: standard, deluxe, and pro. Sales and cost information for 2000 follows:

Item	Standard	Deluxe	Pro
Sales (in units)	100,000	50,000	50,000
Sales price per unit	$30	$40	$50
Flexible manufacturing cost per unit	$17	$20	$25

Capacity-related manufacturing support costs are $800,000, and capacity-related selling and administrative costs are $400,000. In addition, the company pays its sales representatives a commission equal to 10% of the price of each racket sold.

REQUIRED

(a) If the sales price of deluxe rackets decreases by 10%, its sales are expected to increase 30%, but sales of standard rackets are expected to decrease by 5% as some potential buyers of standard rackets will upgrade to deluxe rackets. What will be the impact of this decision on Tenneco's profits?

(b) Suppose that Tenneco decides to increase its advertising by $50,000 instead of cutting the price of deluxe rackets. This is expected to increase sales of all three models by 2% each. Is this decision advisable?

(c) The incentive created by sales commissions has led Tenneco's sales force to push the higher-priced rackets more than the lower-priced ones. Is this in the best interest of the company?

LO 5, 6 **11-53** ***Break-even point, what-if analysis*** The following information pertains to Torasic Company's budgeted income statement for the month of June 2000:

Sales (1200 units @ $250)	$300,000
Flexible cost	−150,000
Contribution margin	$150,000
Capacity-related cost	−200,000
Net loss	($ 50,000)

REQUIRED

(a) Determine the company's break-even point in both units and dollars.

(b) The sales manager believes that a $22,500 increase in the monthly advertising expenses will result in a considerable increase in sales. How much of an increase in sales must result from increased advertising to justify this expenditure?

(c) The sales manager believes that an advertising expenditure increase of $22,500 coupled with a 10% reduction in the selling price will double the sales quantity. Determine the net income (or loss) if these proposed changes are adopted.

11-54 ***Break-even point, what-if analysis*** Air Peanut Company manufactures and sells roasted peanut packets to commercial airlines. Price and cost data per 100 packets of peanuts follow: LO 5, 6

Estimated annual sales volume = 11,535,700 packets

Selling price	$35.00
Flexible costs:	
Raw materials	$16.00
Direct labor	7.00
Manufacturing support	4.00
Selling expenses	1.60
Total flexible costs per batch	$28.60

Annual capacity-related costs:	
Manufacturing support	$192,000
Selling and administrative	276,000
Total capacity-related costs	$468,000

REQUIRED

(a) Determine Air Peanut's break-even point.

(b) How many packets does Air Peanut have to sell to earn $156,000?

(c) Air Peanut expects its direct labor costs to increase by 5% next year. How many units will it have to sell next year to break even if the selling price remains unchanged?

(d) If Air Peanut's direct labor costs increase by 5%, what selling price must it charge to maintain the same contribution margin to sales ratio?

11-55 ***Methods of setting budgets*** Megan Espanoza, manager of the Wells Division of Mars, Inc., a large credit card company, recently received a memorandum about the proposed budgeting process for 2000. For the coming year, senior management at Mars would follow a new procedure regarding the budget-setting process. The process would work in the following manner. Megan and the other division managers would each submit a budget proposal outlining their operating plans and financial requirements. Management would then study the proposals and determine the budget for each division. LO 8

REQUIRED

(a) What is this form of budgeting called?

(b) What are the pros and cons of this approach? Explain.

11-56 ***Methods of designing budgets*** Budgets are usually set through one of three methods—participation, authority, or consultation. LO 8

REQUIRED

Write an essay stating the circumstances under which each method is most appropriate. If you disagree with a particular method, justify your answer.

11-57 ***Financial budgets: cash inflows*** Worthington Company makes cash (20% of total sales), credit card (50% of total sales), and account (30% of total sales) sales. Credit card sales are collected in the month following the sale, net of a 3% credit card fee. This means that if the sale is $100, then the credit card company's fee is $3, and Worthington receives $97. Account sales are collected as follows: 40% in the first month following the sale, 50% in the second month following the sale, 8% in the third month following the sale, and 2% never collected. LO 3

The following table identifies the projected sales for the next year.

WORTHINGTON COMPANY PROJECT SALES			
MONTH	**SALES**	**MONTH**	**SALES**
January	12,369,348	July	21,747,839
February	15,936,293	August	14,908,534
March	13,294,309	September	11,984,398
April	19,373,689	October	18,894,535
May	20,957,566	November	21,983,545
June	18,874,717	December	20,408,367

If the collections from these sales are the only cash inflows in Worthington Company, prepare a statement showing the cash expected each month.

LO 3 **11-58** ***Operating budgets: materials purchasing plan*** Masefield Dairy is preparing a third-quarter budget (July, August, and September) for its ice cream products. It produces five brands of ice cream, and each uses a different mix of ingredients. Its suppliers deliver ingredients just in time provided that they are given two months' notice. The following table indicates the units of each type of ingredient required per unit of each product.

MASEFIELD DAIRY REQUIRED INGREDIENTS					
	PRODUCT				
Ingredients	**A**	**B**	**C**	**D**	**E**
Ice cream	1	2	1	1	1
Ingredient 1	2	0	3	1	4
Ingredient 2	0	1	2	4	0
Ingredient 3	1	3	0	2	2
Ingredient 4	0	2	1	0	2
Ingredient 5	3	1	3	0	1

The following table summarizes the estimated unit sales for each product in each of the months in the third quarter.

MASEFIELD DAIRY ESTIMATED UNIT SALES			
PRODUCT	**JULY**	**AUGUST**	**SEPTEMBER**
A	194,675	162,033	129,857
B	104,856	98,375	76,495
C	209,855	194,575	170,654
D	97,576	75,766	55,966
E	47,867	39,575	20,958

Prepare a monthly purchases budget for the ice cream ingredients.

11-59 ***Financial budgets: wages and expense budgets*** Nathaniel's Motor Shop does major repair work on automobile engines. The major cost in the shop is the wages of the mechanics. The shop employs nine mechanics who are paid $750 for working a 40-hour week. The work week consists of five days of eight hours. Employees actually work seven hours each day, because they are given one hour of breaks each day. They are highly skilled and valued by their employer so these mechanics are paid whether or not there is work available for them to do. They are also paid $30 for every overtime hour or partial overtime hour that they work. LO 3

The machine shop industry estimates that for every mechanic hour actually worked in a shop like this, the employee consumes about $25 of flexible support items, such as lubricants, tool parts, and electricity.

The motor shop has estimated that the following work will be available each week during the next 10 weeks.

NATHANIEL'S MOTOR SHOP
ESTIMATED WORK

WEEK	HOURS OF WORK	WEEK	HOURS OF WORK
1	255	6	280
2	330	7	260
3	300	8	300
4	285	9	340
5	325	10	355

Develop a weekly budget of mechanic wages and flexible support costs.

11-60 ***Financial budgets: cash outflows*** Country Club Road Nurseries grows and sells garden plants. The nursery is active between January and October each year. During January, the potting tables and equipment are prepared. The potting and seeding are done in February. In March and April, the plants are cultivated, watered, and fertilized. May and June are the peak selling months. July, August, and September are the peak months for visiting customers in their homes to provide them with advice and help solve their problems. During October, the equipment and buildings are secured for the winter months, and in November and December, full-time employees take their paid holidays and the business is closed. LO 3

The nursery employs 15 full-time staff and, depending on the season, up to 20 part-time staff. The full-time staff members are paid an average wage of $2700 per month and work 160 hours per month.

The part-time staff members are paid $10 per hour. Because the nursery relies on local students for part-time work, there is no shortage of trained people willing to work the hours that are available. The ratio of full-time employee hours worked to part-time employee hours worked is as follows: January 5:1; February, 5:1; March, 3:1; April, 3:1, May, 1:1; June, 1:1; July, 1:1; August 1:1; September, 2:1; and October, 4:1. Because part-time students are mainly used for moving and selling activities, their work creates very little incremental support costs.

Capacity-related costs, other than wages, associated with this operation are about $55,000 per month. The cost drivers in this operation are the activities that the full-time employees undertake. These cost drivers are proportional to the hours worked by the full-time employees. The flexible costs depend on the season and reflect the common employee activities during that season. Average flexible costs per employee hour worked are as follows: January, $15; February, $15; March, $15; April, $15; May, $5; June, $5; July, $20; August, $20; September, $20; and October, $10. These flexible costs include both support items, such as power and water, and direct items such as soil and pots. Assume that all expenses are paid in the month that they are incurred.

Based on the information provided, prepare a cash outflow statement for the upcoming year.

LO 3 **11-61** ***Operating budgets: labor hiring plan*** Shadyside Insurance Company manages a medical insurance program for its clients. Employees of client firms submit claims for reimbursement of medical expenses. Shadyside processes these claims, checks them to ensure that they are covered by the claimant's policy, notes whether the claimant has reached any limit on coverage, computes any deductible, and issues a check for the claimant's refund.

Three types of clerks work in the claims processing department: supervisors, senior clerks, and junior clerks. The supervisors are paid $42,000 per year, the senior clerks are paid $37,000 per year, and the junior clerks are paid $32,000 per year. For every 150,000 claims processed per year, Shadyside plans to use one supervisor, six junior clerks, and two senior clerks.

Last year, the company processed 2 million medical claims and employed 14 supervisors, 30 senior clerks, and 83 junior clerks.

REQUIRED

(a) Compute the excess costs or cost savings relating to the claims processing staff.

(b) How would you interpret these results? What additional information would you ask for if you were making a determination of the clerical group's processing efficiencies?

LO 3, 4, 5 **11-62** ***Budgeted profit, what-if analysis*** The Monteiro Manufacturing Corporation manufactures and sells folding umbrellas. The corporation's condensed income statement for 1999 follows:

Sales (200,000 units)		$1,000,000
Cost of goods sold		600,000
Gross margin		400,000
Selling expenses	$150,000	
Administrative expenses	100,000	250,000
Net profit (before income taxes)		$ 150,000

Monteiro's budget committee has estimated the following changes for 2000:

30% increase in number of units sold

20% increase in material cost per unit

15% increase in direct labor cost per unit

10% increase in flexible indirect cost per unit

5% increase in indirect capacity-related costs

8% increase in selling expenses, arising solely from increased volume

6% increase in administrative expenses, reflecting anticipated higher wage and supply price levels; any changes in administrative expenses caused solely by increased sales volume are considered immaterial.

As inventory quantities remain fairly constant, the budget committee considered that for budget purposes any change in inventory valuation can be ignored. The composition of the cost of a unit of finished product during 1999 for materials, direct labor, and manufacturing support, respectively, was in the ratio of 3:2:1. In 1999, $40,000 of manufacturing support was for capacity-related costs. No changes in production methods or credit policies were contemplated for 2000.

REQUIRED

(a) Compute the unit sales price at which the Monteiro Manufacturing Corporation must sell its umbrellas in 2000 in order to earn a budgeted profit of $200,000.

(b) Unhappy about the prospect of an increase in selling price, Monteiro's sales manager wants to know how many units must be sold at the old price to earn the $200,000 budgeted profit. Compute the number of units which must be sold at the old price to earn $200,000.

(c) Believing that the estimated increase in sales is overly optimistic, one of the company's directors wants to know what annual profit is likely if the selling price determined in (a) is adopted but the increase in sales volume is only 10%. Compute the budgeted profit in this case.

11-63 ***Competitive contribution margin analysis*** Johnson Company and Smith Company are the two competing firms offering limousine service from the Charlesburg airport. While Johnson pays most of its employees on a per-ride basis, Smith prefers to pay its employees fixed salaries. Information about the cost structures of the two firms is given below: LO 5, 6

COMPETING LIMOUSINE SERVICE BIDS FROM CHARLESBURG AIRPORT PER RIDE DATA

COST CATEGORY	JOHNSON COMPANY	SMITH COMPANY
Selling price	$30	$30
Flexible cost	24	15
Contribution margin	6	15
Capacity-related costs per year	$300,000	$1,500,000

REQUIRED

(a) Calculate the break-even point in the number of rides for both firms.

(b) Draw two graphs plotting profit as a function of the number of rides for the two firms.

(c) Explain which firm's cost structure is more profitable.

(d) Explain which firm's cost structure is riskier.

11-64 (Adapted from CPA May 1993) ***Budget preparation, break-even point, what-if analysis with multiple products*** The following budget information for the year ending December 31, 1999, pertains to Rust Manufacturing Company's operations: LO 3, 4, 5, 6

Budget Item	PRODUCT Ace	Bell	Total Costs
Budgeted sales in units	200,000	100,000	
Selling price per unit	$40	$20	
Direct materials cost per unit	$8	$3	
Direct labor hours per unit	2	1	
Depreciation			$200,000
Rent			$130,000
Other manufacturing costs			$500,000
Selling costs			$180,000
General and administrative costs			$ 40,000

The following information is also provided.

(a) Rust has no beginning inventory. Production is planned so that it will equal the number of units sold.

(b) The cost of direct labor is $5 per hour.

(c) Depreciation and rent are fixed costs within the relevant range of production. Additional costs would be incurred for extra machinery and factory space if production is increased beyond current available capacity.

(d) Rust allocates depreciation proportional to machinery use and rent proportional to factory space. Budgeted usage is as follows:

Depreciation Item	Ace	Bell
Machinery	70%	30%
Factory space	60%	40%

(e) Other manufacturing support costs include flexible costs equal to 10% of direct labor and also include various capacity-related costs. None of the miscellaneous capacity-related manufacturing support costs depend on the level of activity, although support costs attributable to a specific product are avoidable if that product's production ceases. Other manufacturing support costs are allocated between Ace and Bell based on a percent of budgeted direct labor.

(f) Rust's selling and general administrative costs are fixed in the intermediate term.

(g) Rust allocates selling costs on the basis of a number of units sold at Ace and Bell.

(h) Rust allocates general and administrative costs on the basis of sales revenue.

REQUIRED

(a) Prepare a schedule, using separate columns for Ace and Bell, showing budgeted sales, flexible costs, contribution margin, fixed (capacity-related) costs, and pretax operating profit for the year ending December 31, 1999.

(b) Calculate the contribution margin per unit and the pretax operating profit per unit for Ace and for Bell.

(c) Calculate the effect on pretax operating profit resulting from a 10% decrease in sales and production of each product.

(d) What may be a problem with the above analysis?

11-65 ***Multiple break-even points, what-if analysis*** In September 2000, Capetini Capacitor Company sold capacitors to its distributors for $250 per capacitor. The sales level of 3000 capacitors per month was less than the single-shift capacity of 4400 capacitors at its plant located in San Diego. Flexible production costs were $100 per capacitor, and capacity-related production costs were $200,000 per month. In addition, flexible selling and distribution support costs are $20 per capacitor and fixed (capacity related) selling and distribution support costs are $62,500 per month. LO 5, 6

At the suggestion of the marketing department, Capetini reduced the sales price to $200 in October 2000 and increased the monthly advertising budget by $17,500. Sales are expected to increase to 6800 capacitors per month. If the demand exceeds the single-shift capacity of 4400 capacitors, the plant needs to be operated in two shifts. Two-shift operation will increase monthly capacity-related production costs to $310,000.

REQUIRED

(a) Determine the contribution margin per capacitor in September 2000.

(b) Determine the sales level *in number of capacitors* at which the profit-to-sales ratio would be 10%.

(c) Determine the two break-even points for October 2000.

(d) Determine the sales level *in number of capacitors* at which the profit-to-sales ratio in October is the same as the actual profit-to-sales ratio in September. Is there more than one possible sales level at which this equality would occur?

11-66 ***Break-even analysis, what-if analysis*** The Herschel Candy Company produces a single product—a chocolate almond bar which sells for $0.40 per bar. The flexible costs for each bar (sugar, chocolate, almonds, wrapper, and labor) total $0.25. The total monthly capacity-related costs are $60,000. During March 2000, bar sales reached 1 million. However, the president of Herschel Candy Company was not satisfied with its performance and is considering the following options to increase the company's profitability: LO 5, 6

(a) Increase advertising

(b) Increase the quality of the bar's ingredients and simultaneously increase the selling price

(c) Increase the selling price with no change in ingredients.

REQUIRED

(a) The sales manager is confident that an intensive advertising campaign will double sales volume. If the company president's goal is to increase this month's profits by 50% over last month's, what is the maximum amount that can be spent on advertising that doubles sales volume?

(b) Assume that the company increases the quality of its ingredients, thus increasing flexible costs to $0.30 per bar. By how much must the selling price be increased to maintain the same break-even point?

(c) Assume next that the company has decided to increase its selling price to $0.50 per bar with no change in advertising or ingredients. Compute the sales volume in units that would be needed at the new price for the company to earn the same profit as in March 2000.

11-67 ***Budgeting: motivational issues*** Manoil Electronics manufactures and sells electronic components to electronics stores. The controller is preparing her LO 8 annual budget and has asked the sales group to prepare sales estimates. All members of the sales force have been asked to estimate sales in their territory for each of the organization's 10 major products.

The marketing group is paid a salary and a commission based on sales in excess of some target level. You have discovered that the sales manager uses the sales estimates to develop the target levels at which commissions begin. Specifically, the sales manager takes the sales estimate, adds 10%, and the result becomes the sales hurdle level. If sales are less than the hurdle level, no commissions are paid. If sales are above the hurdle level, commissions are paid at varying rates.

REQUIRED

(a) What is the motivation of the sales force if they know the relationship between their estimate and the target level of sales?

(b) What is the likely consequence of basing the organization's budgets on these estimates?

(c) If you were the controller in this situation and were responsible for both the reward system and the budgeting system, what would you do?

LO 8 **11-68** ***Budget slack*** Mike Shields was having dinner with one of his friends at a restaurant in Memphis. His friend, Woody Brooks, a local manager of an express mail service, told Mike that he consistently overstated the amount of resources needed in his budget requests for his division. He also told Mike that year after year he was able to obtain the budget requested. When Mike asked him why he did this, Woody replied, "It's a dog-eat-dog world out there. If I'm going to succeed and move up the ladder, I've got to perform well. Having those extra resources really helps!"

REQUIRED

Write an essay discussing Woody's point of view related to budgeting. Is he justified in his approach? Please explain.

CASES

LO 3, 4, 5 **11-69** ***Budgeting: comprehensive problem*** Judd's Reproductions makes reproductions of antique tables and chairs and sells them through three sales outlets. The product line consists of two styles of tables, three styles of cabinets, and two styles of chairs. Although customers often ask Judd Molinari, the owner/manager of Judd's Reproductions, to make other products, he does not intend to expand the product line.

The planning group at Judd's Reproductions prepares a master budget for each fiscal year, which corresponds to the calendar year. It is December 2000, and the planners are completing the master budget for 2001.

Unit prices are $200, $900, and $1800, respectively, for the chairs, tables, and cabinets. Customers pay (1) by cash and receive a 5% discount, (2) by credit card (the credit card company takes 3% of the revenue as its fee and remits the balance in the month following the month of sale), or (3) on account (only exporters buy on account). The distribution of cash, credit card, and exporter sales is 25%, 35%, and 40%, respectively. Of the credit sales to exporters, Judd's Reproductions collects 30% in the month following the sale, 50% in the second month following the sale, 17% in the third month following the sale, and 3% go uncollected. Judd's Reproductions recognizes the expense of cash discounts, credit card fees, and bad debts in the month of the sale.

Judd's employs 40 people who work in the following areas: 15 in administration, sales, and shipping; 2 in manufacturing supervision (director and a scheduler); 9 in manufacturing fabrication and assembly (carpenters); and 14 in manufacturing, finishing, and other (helpers, cleaners, and maintenance crew).

The carpenter hours required to make the parts for and assemble a chair, table, or cabinet are 0.4, 2.5, and 6, respectively. Production personnel have organized the work so that each carpenter hour worked requires 1.5 helper hours. Therefore, production planners maintain a ratio on average of 1.5 helpers for every carpenter. The company pays carpenters and helpers $24 and $14 per hour, respectively (including all benefits).

Judd's Reproductions guarantees all employees their pay regardless of the hours of work available. When the employees are not doing their regular jobs, they undertake maintenance, training, community service, and customer relations activities. Judd's pays each employee weekly for that week's work. If an employee works 172 hours or less during the month, Judd's pays the employee the product of his hourly rate and 172. The company pays 150% of the normal hourly rate for every hour over 172 that the employee works during the month. Planners add new carpenters if the projected total monthly overtime is more than 5% of the total regular carpenter hours available. Judd's has a policy of no employee layoffs. Any required hiring is done on the first day of each month.

Judd's Reproductions rents a converted warehouse as a factory; it costs $600,000 per year. The company pays rent quarterly beginning January 1 of each year. Judd's pays other capacity-related manufacturing costs, which include manufacturing supervision salaries and which amount to $480,000, in equal monthly amounts.

The capital investment policy is to purchase, each January and July, $5000 of machinery and equipment per carpenter employed during that month. Judd's recognizes depreciation at the rate of 10% of the year-end balance of the machinery and equipment account. Statistical studies of cost behavior have determined that supplies, flexible support, and maintenance costs vary with the number of carpenter hours worked and are $5, $20, and $15, per hour, respectively.

The units of wood required for chairs, tables, and cabinets are 1, 8, and 15, respectively. Each unit of wood costs $30. The inventory policy is to make products in the month they will be sold. Two suppliers deliver raw materials and supplies as required. The company pays for all materials, supplies, flexible support, and maintenance items on receipt.

Annual administration salaries, capacity-related selling costs, and planned advertising expenditures are $300,000, $360,000, and $600,000, respectively. Judd's Reproductions makes these expenditures in equal monthly amounts. Packaging and shipping costs for chairs, tables, and cabinets are $15, $65, and $135, respectively. Flexible selling costs are 6% of each product's list price. Judd's Reproductions pays packaging, shipping, and flexible selling costs as incurred.

Using its line of credit, Judd's Reproductions maintains a minimum balance of $50,000. All line-of-credit transactions occur on the first day of each month. The bank charges interest on the line-of-credit account balance at the rate of 10% per year. Judd's pays interest on the first day of each month on the line-of-credit balance outstanding at the end of the previous month. On the first of each month, the bank pays interest at the rate of 3% per year on funds exceeding $50,000 in the company's cash account at the end of the previous month.

Realized sales for October, November, and December 2000 appear in the following table:

JUDD'S REPRODUCTIONS UNIT SALES 2000			
ITEM	**OCTOBER**	**NOVEMBER**	**DECEMBER**
Chairs	900	975	950
Tables	175	188	201
Cabinets	90	102	95

Sales staff estimates the unit demand for 2001 as follows: chairs, 1000 plus a random number uniformly distributed between 0 and 50 plus 15% of the previous month's sales of chairs; tables, 200 plus a random number uniformly distributed between 0 and 20 plus 15% of the previous months sales; and cabinets, 100 plus a random number uniformly distributed between 0 and 10 plus 15% of the previous month's sales of cabinets. This estimation process resulted in the demand forecasts and the sales plan found in the following table.

JUDD'S REPRODUCTIONS PROJECTED UNIT SALES 2001			
MONTH	**CHAIRS**	**TABLES**	**CABINETS**
January	1020	200	109
February	1191	237	120
March	1179	243	119
April	1195	250	126
May	1200	252	122
June	1204	255	125
July	1194	242	123
August	1199	253	121
September	1222	243	127
October	1219	248	126
November	1207	244	126
December	1192	255	119

Planners project the Judd's Reproductions balance sheet at January 1, 2001, to be as follows:

JUDD'S REPRODUCTIONS BALANCE SHEET, JANUARY 1, 2001			
Cash	$ 50,000	Bank loan	$ 0
Accounts receivable	575,008		
Machinery (net book value)	360,000	Shareholder's equity	985,008
Total	$985,008	Total	$985,008

REQUIRED

(a) Prepare a sales forecast, staffing plan, production plan, cash flow statement, pro forma income statement, and pro forma balance sheet for 2001.

(b) The level of bad debts concerns the Judd's Reproductions controller. If Judd's insists on cash payments from exporters who would be given the cash discount, the sales staff expects that total sales to exporters in 2001 will fall by 5% (sales in 2000 will not be affected). Based on the effect of this change on profitability, is it desirable? (Round sales forecasts to the nearest unit.)

(c) Ignore the changes described in (b) and return to the data in the original example. The sales staff is considering increasing the advertising budget from $600,000 to $900,000 and cutting prices by 5%. This should increase sales by 30% in 2001 (sales in 2000 will not be affected). Based on the effect of this change on profitability, is it desirable? (Round sales forecasts to the nearest unit.)

(d) Is there a criterion other than profitability that may be used to evaluate the desirability of the changes proposed in (b) and (c)? If yes, what is that criterion and why is it important? If no, why is profitability the sole relevant criterion?

11-70 ***Budgeting: motivational issues*** Nate Young is the dean of a business school. LO 4, 7, 8
The university is under strong financial pressures, and the university president has asked all the deans to cut costs. Nate is wondering how he should respond to this request.

The university receives its operating funds from three sources: (1) tuition (60%), (2) government grants (25%), and (3) gifts and endowment income (15%). The money flows into the university's general operating fund. A management committee consisting of the university president, the three vice presidents, and the nine deans allocates funds to the individual schools. The university's charter requires that it operate with a balanced budget.

The initial allocation of funds reflects (1) capacity-related costs that cannot be avoided, primarily the employment costs of tenured faculty and (2) capacity-related costs relating to support items, such as staff, building maintenance, and other operations costs. The balance of funds is allocated to discretionary activities, such as scholarships, program changes or additions, and sports.

The various deans compare their respective funding levels. The basis of comparison is to divide total university expenditures by the number of full-time students to get an average cost per student. Then the average cost per student is multiplied by the number of full-time students to get the target funding for each school. On average, the actual funding for the business school has been about 70% of the target funding, which is the second lowest in the university. (The lowest is the arts school.)

Because of the rapid growth of capacity-related and administrative costs, the amount of funds allocated to discretionary activities has been declining from a historic level of about 10%. This year, the projected revenues will not even cover the projected capacity-related costs. In response to this development, the president has called on all deans to "do your best to reduce the level of expenditures."

The president's request has been met with skepticism by many deans, who are notorious for digging in their heels, ignoring requests for spending cuts, and then being bailed out by funds released from other activities or raised to meet the budget shortfall. Many deans believe that the departments that sacrificed and reduced their budgets would only create funds that would be used by the university to support other schools that had made little or no effort to reduce their budgets. Then these schools would be asked to make even more cuts to make up for the lack of cuts in schools that made little progress in cost reduction. On the other hand, the deans also believe that if there were no reaction to the president's initial request for cost reductions arbitrary cutbacks would be imposed on the individual schools.

In response to this situation, Nate is wondering what to do. He knows that by increasing class sizes slightly, using some part-time instructors, and eliminating some optional courses that seldom attract many students, he can trim about $800,000 from his operating budget of $11,000,000. However, making these changes would create hardships for both the students and faculty in the business school and, given the historic relationship of the school's average funding to its target funding, Nate is wondering whether the business school should be asked to make additional sacrifices.

Nate knows that he has several alternatives:

- Do nothing, arguing that the business school is already cost effective relative to others and it is time for others to reduce their cost structures.
- Make the cuts that he has identified but stretch them out over a number of years and stop making them if other schools are not doing their share in cutting costs.
- Make the cuts unilaterally and advise the administration that the business school budget can be reduced by about $800,000.

Explain what you would do if you were Nate and why. Your explanations should include your analysis of the motivation of all schools to cut costs in an environment that traditionally has taken advantage of those that cooperate.

LO 3, 6, 7 **11-71** ***Budgeting and cost drivers*** Dinkum Company provides package courier services. Each afternoon its couriers pick up packages; they drive trucks operating out of local terminals. Packages are returned to the terminal and are transported to the central hub that evening. In the hub, packages are sorted during the late evening and are sent to the destination terminal overnight. The next morning couriers from the destination terminal deliver packages to the addresses.

Most of the routes that the couriers follow are fixed. Each day the couriers have both scheduled and unscheduled pickup and drop-off stops. However, studies have shown that adding an unscheduled stop to a route or picking up an additional shipment at a scheduled stop creates negligible additional costs. The key costs in terms of the courier's time, the vehicle, and the fuel costs are determined by the route itself. Therefore, most of the costs at Dinkum result from decisions that reflect the planned level of activity rather than decisions that reflect the actual volume of activity. The major exception is the sorting cost in the hubs and terminals. Because sorting labor is hired on a part-time basis as required, the sorting cost varies with the number of shipments handled.

Linda Price, the manager of the Miami terminal, is preparing an expense budget for the upcoming year. She plans to base this year's budget on the trends from the previous years. The following table shows the level of costs in the previous two years.

DINKUM COURIER COMPANY ACTIVITY COST LEVELS			
ITEM	**1998**	**1999**	**2000**
Shipments handled	8,500,000	10,300,000	11,100,000
Administrative costs	$ 300,000	$ 315,000	$ 320,000
Truck depreciation and maintenance	$ 750,000	$ 830,000	$ 850,000
Courier fuel costs	$ 600,000	$ 660,000	$ 670,000
Courier wages	$1,750,000	$1,810,000	$1,850,000
Terminal support costs	$ 240,000	$ 280,000	$ 260,000
Labor costs in terminal	$ 120,000	$ 150,000	$ 170,000

REQUIRED

(a) Identify what you think are the cost drivers for each of the items in this table.

(b) Given the information provided, prepare an expense budget for the upcoming year, assuming that the volume of shipments handled is expected to be 14,000,000 units.

Responsibility Centers and Financial Control

chapter 12

AFTER READING THIS CHAPTER, YOU WILL BE ABLE TO

1. describe the form and nature of variance analysis and apply its basic insights
2. explain why organizations use responsibility centers
3. identify the issues to consider and basic tools to use in assessing the performance of a responsibility center
4. describe the common forms of responsibility centers
5. assess the issues and problems created by revenue and cost interactions in evaluating the performance of an organization unit
6. identify the transfer-pricing alternatives available to organizations and the criteria for choosing a transfer-pricing alternative
7. use return on investment and economic value added as financial control tools
8. identify the limitations of financial controls

Georgia Institute of Technology

FINANCIAL CONTROL IN ACTION[1]

Like many universities, Georgia Tech University developed and operated athletic programs to generate revenue, to attract top students, and to support alumni fund raising. However, the early 1990s saw the costs of athletic programs at many universities spiraling out of control, and Georgia Tech was not spared.

The situation created a demand for information that would identify the total costs of the various athletic programs and help administrators monitor and evaluate both costs and revenues. This need for cost information was heightened when Title IX of the Equal Rights Amendment was passed, requiring that all institutions receiving federal funding treat men's and women's athletic programs on an equivalent basis. The new requirement had two effects. First, equity demanded some comparison of the costs of the men's and women's programs, and these costs were unavailable. Second, the requirement clearly meant that Georgia Tech would need to expand its offering of women's sports dramatically. This increase would increase costs, but without an understanding of the costs of the current programs, the amount of the increase could not be evaluated.

While administrators were reasonably confident that the football and basketball programs at Georgia Tech were self-supporting, the other 12 varsity sports were nonrevenue generating. Moreover, the problems of identifying program costs was exacerbated, because many costs were buried in the university's general overhead and not allocated or associated with the sports that created them. One university administrator observed that the tightening cost environment created a situation of desperation that called for the development and implementation of a system of financial control for varsity sports.

[1] This description is adapted from Strupeck, Milani, and Murphy, "Financial Management at Georgia Tech," *Management Accounting* (US), February 1993, pp. 58–63.

IN PRACTICE

Focusing on Cash Flow

Mike Maskall, director of international tax services at Price Waterhouse, feels that institutional investors do not trust earnings numbers because despite GAAP they can be easily manipulated.

Instead, Mr. Maskall and his colleagues argue that financial control should focus on cash flow (which they feel cannot be as easily manipulated as GAAP income) and have identified what they feel are the seven key drivers of cash flow: sales growth, operating profit margin, cash tax rate, working capital, fixed assets, cost of capital, and the length of the growth period. The idea is to measure performance on these seven elements and benchmark them against competitors or best-in-class performers.

Source: Simon Caulkin, *The Observer,* March 5, 1995, p. 9.

Financial Control

Chapter 2 discussed the organization's goals and control systems and described how many organizations today provide employees with information to help them achieve both local and organizational goals. This chapter addresses the issue of financial control, which involves using financial information for operational control. Decentralization was the phenomenon that prompted the original use of financial control in organizations in the early 1900s.

During the twentieth century, most organizations developed and used financial control methods to monitor, assess, and improve operations. Financial control uses financial numbers, such as costs or expenses, as broad indices of performance or measures of the resources used by a process or operating unit. Financial control involves comparing actual financial numbers with targets from a standard or budget to derive variances. An unfavorable variance serves as a warning signal and should trigger a

IN PRACTICE

Financial Control at Ford Motor Corporation

In the 1940s, Ford Motor Corporation was in big trouble as profits and sales were both falling. In response to this crisis, Ford hired Charles Tex Thornton and a group of 10 people that came to be known as Thornton's whiz kids. The whiz kids revolutionized management at Ford and replaced the autocratic secretive management style at Ford with a disciplined system of financial controls. At the heart of this philosophy was the belief that organizations could and should be controlled by financial numbers and that a detailed knowledge of markets and operations was unnecessary for control.

For many years, these controls worked well and Ford's fortunes improved. Financial control was hailed as a success and Ford's savior. However during the 1970s and 1980s, Ford's fortunes, as well as those of the other big three North American automobile manufacturers, sagged under relentless pressure from Japanese competitors. Many experts attributed the inability of Ford and the North American manufacturers to respond to the competitive pressures presented by the Japanese to their preoccupation with financial control and a lack of a basic understanding of or monitoring of the manufacturing and distribution processes that create financial results.

In a high-volume business like a courier company, cost control is crucial for success. What is equally important, however, is to provide customers with the service they have been promised. (Etienne DeMalglaive/Liaison Agency, Inc.)

sequence of activities to identify, investigate, and correct the cause of the unfavorable performance. We begin our discussion of financial control with variance analysis, a tool that is perhaps the hallmark of organization control.

Variance Analysis

Variance analysis has many forms and can result in complex measures, but its basic principle is quite simple—an actual (cost or revenue) is compared with a target (cost or revenue), and the difference, or variance, is isolated. The essence of a variance is that it represents a departure from what was expected. Its nature and size will trigger an investigation to determine its cause and what should be done to correct it.

IN PRACTICE

Using Other Performance Indicators for Cost Centers

A manufacturing facility making computer chips was evaluated using conventional manufacturing cost variances. The facility made computer chips on a large disk called a wafer. The wafer was tested and defective chips were marked, cut out of the wafer, and discarded. Processing costs were not affected by the number of good or bad chips.

In this environment, the facility had little interest in controlling quality. The result was poor quality—the average chip yield was about 60%, meaning that only about 60% of the chips on each wafer were usable.

Then the performance measurement system was changed from assessing the manufacturing group's ability to control costs relative to a standard (a one-dimensional focus on an internal cost standard) to cost per good chip compared to that of a competitor.

The facility quickly became concerned with quality because yields were the critical driver for decreasing the cost per good chip produced. Designs, processes, equipment, and employee training were reevaluated and changed to improve yield. Yield increased, leading to dramatic reductions in the cost per good chip produced.

THE TECHNOLOGICAL EDGE

Another Kind of Variance Analysis: Meeting Expectations

The idea of comparing expected with actual performance has many applications. Consider this report by a consulting group called Benchmarking Partners of Cambridge, Massachusetts, which studies gaps (variances) between anticipated and actual results of enterprise resource planning (ERP) systems.

Some results showed that expectations were below what was actually achieved (negative variances):

- Of the 164 decision makers surveyed, about 25% anticipated that ERP would reduce information technology (IT) costs. Only 12% actually realized any savings.
- About 45% anticipated reductions in IT and business staff, but only about 34% achieved them.

Or, some enterprises actually exceeded their expectations (favorable variances):

- About 18% of the respondents predicted an improvement in order management/cycle time; 33% realized such savings.
- Less than 5% believed on-time deliveries would improve, but almost 10% realized improvements in deliveries.

Other findings were as follows:

- The biggest obstacle to achieving benefits was a need for better change management, cited by 65% of those surveyed.
- Lack of adequate training also was an obstacle, cited by 40% of those surveyed. This ranked evenly with issues concerning adequacy of internal staff skills.

Debra Hoffman of Benchmarking Partners stated, ". . . you must manage the benefits . . . and if they're not up to expectations, find out why. Keep everyone focused on the true purpose of an ERP implementation. It's not just about going live on time and on budget. It's about getting business value."

Source: Excerpted from N. Wreden, "ERP Systems—Promise vs. Performance," *Beyond Computing,* September 1999, pp. 17–22.

BASIC VARIANCE ANALYSIS

Variance analysis The set of procedures used by managers to help them understand the source of differences (variances) between actual and budgeted costs.

Variance analysis is a set of procedures managers use to help them understand the source of differences (variances) between actual and targeted costs. It is valuable in several ways. If managers learn that specific actions they took on some jobs helped lower the actual costs of these jobs, then they can obtain further cost savings by repeating those actions on similar jobs in the future. If they can identify the factors causing actual costs to be higher than expected, then managers may be able to take the necessary actions to prevent those factors from recurring in the future. And if they learn that cost changes are likely to be permanent, they can update their cost information when bidding for future jobs.

▶ *The operator of this machine is responsible for controlling the use of raw materials and meeting quality requirements. The operator's control of raw materials cost can be assessed through the use of variances. (Lawrence Migdale/Stock, Boston)*

CANNING CELLULAR SERVICES

Canning Cellular Services (CCS) is a national provider of cellular phone services. Cellular services are highly competitive, and cost control is a major component of remaining profitable. For this reason CCS has undertaken a major study of its costs to understand the nature of cost behavior and to provide a continuing basis for cost reduction. The two major costs in the cellular business are equipment costs and personnel costs.

As part of its effort to control personnel costs, CCS has documented in eurodollars the cost associated with connecting a new customer—which are estimated to be €95.50. Exhibit 12-1 reports the results of the study, which identified three relevant costs: direct materials costs, direct labor costs, and support costs.

The direct materials costs relate to the welcoming package that is provided to each new customer. This package defines the range and nature of the various cellular services offered by CCS.

EXHIBIT 12-1

Canning Cellular Services—Total Cost per Activated Customer

	UNIT	COST/UNIT	TOTAL COST
Direct Material			
Welcome package	1.00	25.00	25.00
Direct Labor			
Sales staff	0.50	25.00	12.50
Technical staff	0.25	40.00	10.00
Support Cost			
Data processing	0.20	15.00	3.00
System activation	0.15	300.00	45.00
Total cost per activated customer			95.50

There are two components of direct labor costs. The first is the cost of the salesperson, who describes the various services available and writes up the sales contract. On average, the salesperson spends 0.5 hour with each new customer and is paid 25 eurodollars (€25) per hour. The second component is the cost of the technical staff person, who activates the new cellular telephone by calling the control center and providing the telephone's electronic serial number and such customer-related information as name, address, and payment details. This requires 0.40 hour of time and technical staff are paid €40 per hour.

The third element of customer-related cost is support cost. There are two components of support cost. The first is the cost of the data processing staff who enter the customer-related information into the CCS customer database. This information is used for billing and advertising purposes. On average, it takes 0.20 hour to enter the information for each customer and the data processing clerks are paid €15 per hour. The second component is the system activation cost. This includes the cost of the computing and data processing systems that support the process of entering each new customer into the system and activating the customer on the system. On average, the activation process takes 0.15 hour on the computer, and the cost of computer time is estimated at €300 per hour.

Based on these cost estimates and the projected addition of 1 million new customers during fiscal 2000, CCS developed the estimate of costs for the upcoming year as shown in Exhibit 12-2.

The document summarizing these costs, which are variously referred to as budgeted, estimated, projected, target, or forecasted costs, is called the master budget. Note that the budgeted costs of €95,500,000 depend on three elements:

1. The projected volume of activity, which in this case is 1 million customers
2. The standards for the use of each of the budgeted items
3. The standards for the cost per unit of each of the budgeted items

We can anticipate, before we go any further, that if any of these items differ from the forecasted amount, the actual total costs will differ from the master budget total.

FIRST-LEVEL VARIANCES

Several weeks after the 2000 year end, the company comptroller forwarded the summary shown in Exhibit 12-3 to the manager of new customer accounts. Exhibit 12-3 displays the **first-level variances** for different cost items. The first-level variance for

First-level variance For cost items, the difference between the actual and master budget costs for that cost item.

EXHIBIT 12-2

Canning Cellular Services—
Master Budget

	UNITS/CUSTOMER USE	COST/UNIT	TOTAL COST
Direct material			
Welcome package	1.00	25.00	25,000,000
Direct labor			
Sales staff	0.50	25.00	12,500,000
Technical staff	0.25	40.00	10,000,000
Support cost			
Data processing	0.20	15.00	3,000,000
System activation	0.15	300.00	45,000,000
Total customer-related costs			95,500,000

EXHIBIT 12-3

Canning Cellular Services—Summary of First-Level Variances

	MASTER BUDGET	ACTUAL COSTS	DIFFERENCE
Direct material			
Welcome package	25,000,000	29,700,000	4,700,000
Direct labor			
Sales staff	12,500,000	14,850,000	2,350,000
Technical staff	10,000,000	10,890,000	890,000
Support cost			
Data processing	3,000,000	3,960,000	960,000
System activation	45,000,000	42,900,000	−2,100,000
Total customer-related costs	95,500,000	102,300,000	6,800,000

a cost item is the difference between the actual and master budget costs for that cost item. By convention, we compute variances by subtracting master budget costs from actual costs. Therefore, variances are "favorable," or "F," if the actual costs are less than estimated costs, that is, if the variance is negative. "Unfavorable," or "U," variances arise when actual costs exceed master budget costs, that is, when the variance is positive. In this example, the first-level cost variance for sales staff, for example, is €2,350,000 unfavorable.

Sharon Mackenzie, the manager of new customer accounts, was surprised by the report, since she had directed her staff to undertake a number of important initiatives related to employee training and equipment improvement to reduce costs. Not only had costs not decreased, but they had increased by €6,800,000, which was significant. There was no explanation in this exhibit to help the manager understand what went wrong. Therefore, Sharon demanded an explanation for why costs had not decreased following the cost-cutting initiatives.

DECOMPOSING THE VARIANCES

Following up on Sharon's request, the financial group prepared Exhibit 12-4 and forwarded it to her. Fred Liang, the CCS comptroller, explained to Sharon that Exhibit 12-4 uses a concept called the **flexible budget,** in which the forecast in the master budget is adjusted for the difference between planned and actual volume. Therefore, the flexible budget reflects a cost target or forecast based on the level of volume that is actually achieved, rather than the planned volume, which underlies the master budget. Fred referred Sharon to Exhibit 12-4, which provides the details of the flexible budget calculations. Therefore, the cost differences between the master budget and the flexible budget, which are called **planning variances** because they reflect the difference between planned and actual output, arise entirely because the planned volume of activity was not realized. Therefore, based on the result that 1.1 million new customers were added instead of the planned 1 million, the projected or target level of costs are now €105,050,000.

Flexible budget
The forecast of the projected level of cost given the volume and mix of activities undertaken.

Planning variances
The cost differences between the master budget and the flexible budget; reflect the difference between planned and actual output.

Sharon immediately noted three things in Exhibit 12-4. First, the volume of customers exceeded the number that had been used to forecast costs. Second, the unit cost of four of the five items in the budget exceeded the standard used to develop the forecast. Third, the per unit use of both labor items and one of the two support costs was lower, reflecting the results of the process improvements that Sharon had

EXHIBIT 12-4

Canning Cellular Services—Summary of Second-Level Variances

	MASTER BUDGET 1,000,000			FLEXIBLE BUDGET 1,100,000			ACTUAL RESULTS 1,100,000		
	U/C	Cost	Total	U/C	Cost	Total	U/C	Cost	Total
Direct material									
Welcome package	1.00	25.00	25,000,000	1.00	25.00	27,500,000	1.00	27.00	29,700,000
Direct labor									
Sales staff	0.50	25.00	12,500,000	0.50	25.00	13,750,000	0.45	30.00	14,850,000
Technical staff	0.25	40.00	10,000,000	0.25	40.00	11,000,000	0.22	45.00	10,890,000
Support cost									
Data processing	0.20	15.00	3,000,000	0.20	15.00	3,300,000	0.24	15.00	3,960,000
System activation	0.15	300.00	45,000,000	0.15	300.00	49,500,000	0.12	325.00	42,900,000
Total customer-related costs			95,500,000			105,050,000			102,300,000

commissioned. The per unit use of the other support item was higher, but only because midway through the year Sharon had developed a more comprehensive form that required more input for new customers. Sharon asked the finance group to isolate the effects of these various price and use effects.

PLANNING AND FLEXIBLE BUDGET VARIANCES

Flexible budget variances
Shows the difference between the flexible budget and the actual results.

The finance group responded to Sharon's request for more information with Exhibit 12-5.

Fred explained that the differences between the flexible budget and the actual results, called the **flexible budget variances,** reflect variances from the target level of costs *adjusted for the achieved level of activity,* and that this should be the focus of

EXHIBIT 12-5

Canning Cellular Services—Second-Level Variance Summary

	MASTER BUDGET	PLANNING VARIANCE	FLEXIBLE BUDGET	FLEXIBLE BUDGET VARIANCE	ACTUAL RESULTS
Direct material					
Welcome package	25,000,000	2,500,000	27,500,000	2,200,000	29,700,000
Direct labor					
Sales staff	12,500,000	1,250,000	13,750,000	1,100,000	14,850,000
Technical staff	10,000,000	1,000,000	11,000,000	−110,000	10,890,000
Support cost					
Data processing	3,000,000	300,000	3,300,000	660,000	3,960,000
System activation	45,000,000	4,500,000	49,500,000	−6,600,000	42,900,000
Total customer-related costs	95,500,000	9,550,000	105,050,000	−2,750,000	102,300,000

attention to determine whether the cost-cutting activities had been successful. Since the total flexible budget variance was €2,750,000—a favorable variance—overall costs were lower than the projected or target costs for the achieved level of activity. Fred pointed out to Sharon that the planning variance and flexible budget variance are called **second-level variances,** because together they comprise the first-level variance.

Second-level variances
The planning variance and flexible budget variance, which combined are the *first-level variance.*

Sharon was pleased with this information but still concerned. She pointed out to Fred that these flexible budget variances reflect both use variances (the difference between the planned and the actual use rates per unit of output) and cost variances (the difference between the price or cost per unit of the various cost items). Sharon asked Fred whether he or his staff could prepare an exhibit that would highlight the incremental effects of use and price variances.

USE AND PRICE VARIANCES FOR MATERIAL AND LABOR

Direct material and direct labor variances can be decomposed further into efficiency (use) and price (rate) variances which, using the logic to name the second-level variances, we might call third-level variances, because together they explain the flexible budget component of the second-level variance. Returning to Exhibit 12-4, note that the amount of direct materials used equals the volume of production achieved (1.1 million) multiplied by that actual use rate, which was 1, giving an actual use of direct materials of 1.1 million. The flexible budget allowance is the volume of production achieved (1.1 million) multiplied by the planned or target use rate, which was 1, giving a planned or target use of direct materials of 1.1 million.

Material Use and Price Variances. The material use variance is determined by using the following formula:

$$\begin{aligned}\text{Use variance} &= (AQ - SQ) \times SP \\ &= (1{,}100{,}000 - 1{,}100{,}000) \times €25 \\ &= 0\end{aligned}$$

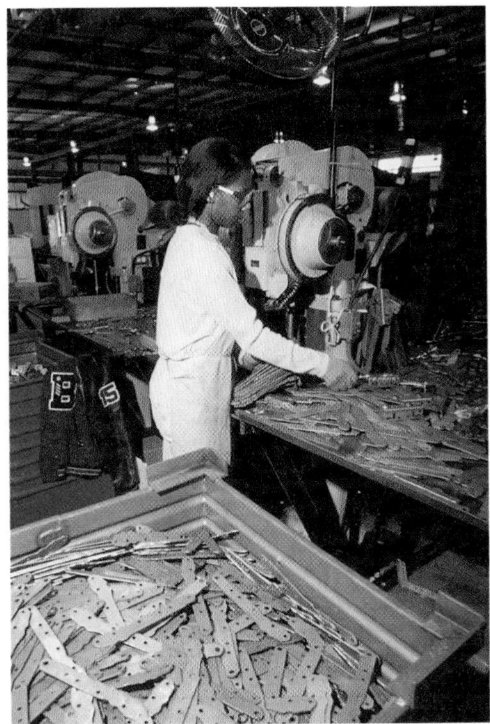

If this worker is paid hourly and based on the work available, her wages are considered to be direct labor costs. When this worker takes less time to do a job than what was allowed or budgeted for the work done, she generates a positive labor use variance. (Kenneth Murray/Photo Researchers, Inc.)

where

AQ = actual quantity of materials used
SQ = estimated or standard quantity of materials required
SP = estimated or standard price of materials

Material price variance for direct materials is calculated using the following formula

$$\begin{aligned}\text{Price variance} &= (AP - SP) \times AQ \\ &= (€27 - €25) \times 1{,}100{,}000 \\ &= €2{,}200{,}000 \text{ U}\end{aligned}$$

where

AP = actual price of materials
SP = estimated or standard price of materials
AQ = actual quantity of materials used

We have now decomposed the total variance for the cost of the welcoming package, which is the direct material in this example, into a material use and a material price variance. When we add these two second-level variances (€0 + €2,200,000 U), we obtain the total variance for direct materials (€2,200,000 U).

The general result of decomposing the variances is easily verified by adding together the algebraic formulas for material use and price variances. The sum of the decomposed variances is

$$\begin{aligned}\text{Sum of decomposed variances} &= \text{use variance} + \text{price variance} \\ &= [(AQ - SQ) \times SP] + [(AP - SP) \times AQ] \\ &= (AQ \times SP) - (SQ \times SP) + (AP \times AQ) - (SP \times AQ) \\ &= (AP \times AQ) - (SQ \times SP) \\ &= \text{Actual cost} - \text{Budgeted cost} \\ &= \text{Total variance}\end{aligned}$$

What does this variance and its decomposition tell Sharon, who is the manager ultimately responsible for these costs? First, Sharon knows that the use was consistent with the number of customers, no more and no less. Second, Sharon knows that the cost of €27 per unit exceeded the planned or target cost of €25. Perhaps this cost increment reflected changes in the planned welcoming package, or perhaps additional costs billed by the supplier. Given the magnitude of the variance, Sharon would follow up to determine its cause. However, it is important to point out that as a good manager, she might already be well aware of the variance, and the value of the variance analysis is to confirm its magnitude.

Efficiency and Wage Rate Variances for Direct Labor Costs. The labor cost variances are determined in a manner similar to that described for material use and price variances. The formulas are as follows:

$$\begin{aligned}\text{Efficiency variance} &= (AH - SH) \times SR \\ \text{Rate variance} &= (AR - SR) \times AH\end{aligned}$$

where

AH = actual number of direct labor hours
AR = actual wage rate
SH = estimated or standard number of direct labor hours
SR = estimated or standard wage rate

As before, total cost variance is computed as follows:

$$\begin{aligned} \text{Efficiency variance} + \text{Rate variance} &= (AH - SH) \times SR + (AR - SR) \times AH \\ &= (AH \times SR) - (SH \times SR) + (AR \times AH) - (SR \times AH) \\ &= (AR \times AH) - (SR \times SH) \\ &= \text{Actual cost} - \text{Estimated cost} \\ &= \text{Total cost variance} \end{aligned}$$

Let us compute the efficiency and rate variance for the technical staff. The total hours of technical staff use is 495,000 (0.45 × 1,100,000), and the total planned target level of use, given the achieved level of production, is 550,000 (0.5 × 1,100,000).

Therefore the efficiency variance for technical staff labor cost is

$$\text{Efficiency variance} = (AH - SH) \times SR = (495{,}000 - 550{,}000) \times €25 = €1{,}375{,}000 \text{ F}$$

The efficiency efforts commissioned by Sharon evidently paid off in terms of less use of technical staff time than planned for the achieved level of income, resulting in cost savings of €1,375,000.

The price or rate variance for technical staff labor is

$$\text{Rate variance} = (AR - SR) \times AH = (€30 - €25) \times 495{,}000 = €2{,}475{,}000 \text{ U}$$

In other words, for the number of hours worked, the technical staff was paid €2,475,000 more than was planned when the master budget was developed. This increase might reflect a corporate-wide wage adjustment that is beyond Sharon's control; or perhaps it reflects the hiring of more skilled and qualified technical staff who were responsible for the favorable efficiency variance. These facts would be established by an investigation, which would be triggered by a variance this size.

Note that, as required, the sum of the rate variance and the efficiency variance equals the total flexible budget variance for technical staff costs.

$$\begin{aligned} \text{Total flexible budget variance for technical staff cost} &= €1{,}375{,}000 \text{ F} - €2{,}475{,}000 \text{ U} \\ &= €1{,}100{,}000 \text{ U} \end{aligned}$$

Detailed Analysis of Support Activity Cost Variances. We have considered the decomposition of direct material and direct labor costs. What about support costs? Support costs can reflect flexible or capacity-related costs. The quantity of capacity-related costs may not change from period to period, but the spending on them may fluctuate. Engineers can travel, take courses, vacation, quit, and be replaced with someone else. So it is possible and desirable to monitor spending variances on capacity-related resources, even when you cannot monitor efficiency variances which will show up as changes in used and unused capacity.

What about flexible support costs? These support costs reflect behind-the-scenes operations that are proportional to the volume of activity but are not directly a part of the product or service provided to the customer. For example, an indirect support cost in a factory would be the wages paid to employees who move work in process around the factory floor as the product is being made.

In CCS these support costs are two-fold. First, they reflect the time and cost of the equipment and personnel who input customer data each time a new customer is added to the CCS customer file. Second, they reflect the time and cost of equipment and personnel each time a new customer is activated on the computers that control access to the cellular system.

Investigation by Sharon revealed that the cost of the data processing staff had two components—a wage rate and a system access charge incurred when the data processor was accessing the system. These cost components are summarized in Exhibit 12-6.

EXHIBIT 12-6

Canning Cellular Services—Clerical Budgeted Cost Per Hour

	UNITS	RATE	TOTAL
Clerical wage	1	10.00	10.00
Computer access time	0.1	50.00	5.00
Total cost per hour			15.00

The actual hourly clerical wage is €10, and for each hour the clerk works, the database is accessed for 0.1 hour. The system access fee is €50. This yields a blended total cost of €15 per data processing clerk hour. Note that when a blended rate per hour is constructed in this way, the rate variance will reflect both the use and the cost of the components used to compute the rate. With this understanding of how the rate was computed for a flexible support item, we can use cost analysis to undertake an investigation of the variance associated with a support cost item.

In view of the size of the variance associated with system activation costs, Sharon directed Fred to undertake an analysis of its source. Exhibit 12-7 summarizes the calculation used to develop the €300 hourly charge for the hourly activation rate, which has two components. The first reflects the wage paid to the technical staff, which is €40 per hour. The second component is the system access fee, which is charged at the rate of €520 per hour of access. On average the technical staff accesses the activation system for half an hour for each hour worked, yielding the blended rate of €300, which was used in developing the budget.

Investigation yielded the information in Exhibit 12-8 to explain the actual access fee. Note that the actual rate differs from the budget rate for three reasons. First, the wage paid to the technical staff was €15 higher than the budgeted rate. Second, the computer access time per hour worked by technical staff was lower than budgeted. Third, the rate for computer access time was higher than budgeted.

These three elements combined with the data in Exhibit 12-4, allow Fred to develop the information in Exhibit 12-9, which explains the total flexible budget variance for system activation support costs.

Now that we have discussed and considered the elements of variance analysis, which was originally designed to support the process of decentralization, we can now turn to consider the nature and scope of decentralization.

EXHIBIT 12-7

Canning Cellular Services—Technical Budgeted Hourly Cost Calculation

	UNITS	RATE	TOTAL
Technical staff	1	40.00	40.00
Computer access time	0.5	520.00	260.00
Total cost per hour			300.00

EXHIBIT 12-8

Canning Cellular Services—Actual Calculation of Cost Per Hour

	UNITS	RATE	TOTAL
Technical staff	1	55.00	55.00
Computer access time	0.45	600.00	270.00
Total cost per hour			325.00

Decentralization

Chapter 1 argued that **centralized** organizations reserve most of the decision-making power for senior executives. In contrast, **decentralized** organizations delegate a good deal of decision-making authority to lower-level managers.

Centralized responsibility Reserving decision-making power for senior management levels.

Decentralized responsibility Refers to the authority that local-division managers have in order to make their own decisions without having to seek higher approval on various business operations.

Most highly centralized organizations are unable to respond effectively or quickly to their environments; therefore, centralization is best suited to organizations that are well adapted to stable environments. People used to cite power, gas, and telephone utilities and companies such as couriers, fast-food operations, financial institutions, and natural resource industries as examples of organizations facing stable environments. This meant that there were no major information differences between the corporate headquarters and the employees who were responsible for dealing with customers or running the operations that make the organization's goods and services. Therefore, there was no need for a rapid response to a changing environment or for delegation of decision making to local managers.

In such organizations, technology and customer requirements were well understood and the product line consisted mostly of commodity products for which the most important attributes were price and quality. When price is critical, so too are cost control and quality. To accomplish this, organizations often develop standard operating procedures to ensure that (1) they are using the most efficient technologies and practices to promote both low cost and consistent quality, and (2) there are no deviations from the preferred way of doing things.

EXHIBIT 12-9

Canning Cellular Services—Decomposition of Flexible Budget Variance for System Activation Support Costs

Use variance for system activation support	(0.12 − 0.15) × 1,100,000 × €300 = €9,900,000 F
Price variance for system activation support	1,100,000 × 0.12 × (€325 − €300) = €3,300,000 U
due to additional labor use	[(1,100,000 × 0.12 × 1) − (1,100,000 × 0.15 × 1)] × €40 = €1,320,000 F
due to additional labor rate	(1,100,000 × 0.12 × 1 × (€55 − €40) = €1,980,000 U
due to additional computer use	[(1,100,000 × 0.12 × 0.45) − (1,100,000 × 0.15 × 0.5)] × €520 = €12,012,000 F
due to additional access rate	1,100,000 × 0.12 × 0.45 × (€600 − €520) = €4,752,000 U

For example, McDonald's Corporation has developed the application of standard operating procedures almost to a science. Its restaurant layout, product design, form of raw materials, and prescribed operating procedures are all intended to keep cost low and quality high. McDonald's is not looking for a chef who wants to be creative either in preparing food or in introducing new items to the menu. Rather, it wants someone who can follow standardized procedures to promote consistent quality and low costs.

Today, in response to increasing competitive pressures and the opening up of former monopolies to competition, many organizations—even utilities, couriers, and financial institutions that were once thought to face stable environments—are changing the way they are organized and the way they do business. This is necessary because they must be able to change quickly in a world where technology, customer tastes, and competitors' strategies are constantly changing.

For example, in the past, financial institutions developed rigid and authoritarian management systems to protect assets and meet regulatory requirements. Although these systems have helped to meet such goals, in many cases they have not served well in dealing with customers. Providing high-quality customer service means remaining open in the evenings, installing automated teller machines to provide 24-hour banking services, offering on-line banking that customers can access via telephone or personal computer, offering new products and services such as credit and debit cards, and responding more quickly to customer requests, such as approving car loans and mortgages in minutes rather than weeks.

Being adaptive generally requires that the organization's senior management delegate or decentralize decision-making responsibility to more people in the organization. Decentralization allows motivated and well-trained organization members to identify changing customer tastes quickly and gives front-line employees the authority and responsibility to develop plans to react to these changes.

There are many degrees of decentralization. Some organizations restrict most decisions to senior and middle management. Others delegate important decisions about how to make products and serve customers to the employees who perform these activities. The amount of decentralization reflects the organization's trust in its employees, the employees' level of training, and the employees' ability to make the right choices. It also reflects the organization's need to have people on the front lines who can make good decisions quickly.

Three conditions are necessary for effective decentralization:

1. Employees must be given, and must accept, the authority and responsibility to make decisions.
2. Employees must have the training and skills they need to accept the decision-making responsibility.
3. The organization must have a system in place that guides and coordinates the activities of decentralized decision makers.

Controlling Operations Using Financial Control

Decentralization requires that someone who has the responsibility to make decisions know what is important to the organization's success, have the information to help evaluate alternatives, and be skilled in evaluating those alternatives and choosing the appropriate course of action. The major purpose of decentralization is to give decision makers the responsibility to make operating decisions, which creates a need for operations control. However, operations control has a different perspective than financial control and effective overall control requires that the two perspectives of financial and operational control be aligned.

IN PRACTICE

Improving Performance at Liz Claiborne

After experiencing extraordinary growth in the 1980s, Liz Claiborne, Inc., a designer of womens' apparel, failed to recognize the change in what women want and are willing to pay for in clothing—a failure that resulted in lost sales and declining profits.

The company hired Paul Charron, an expert in designing and using financial controls, who promised to cut operating costs; eliminate unprofitable lines of clothing; reduce the time to design, make, and deliver clothes to retailers from 40 weeks to 30 weeks; and, in an unusual step in the fashion industry, speak to customers to find out what they want in clothes.

Critics remained skeptical, arguing that Mr. Charron's skills and efforts were misplaced because existing financial controls were already keeping costs reasonably competitive. These critics felt that Mr. Charron should have focused on developing a better system to identify and track changing customer tastes, that is, they felt that the organization should develop a sharper focus on operations control.

Source: James F. Peltz, "Fashioning a New Strategy at Claiborne," *Los Angeles Times,* May 21, 1995, Part D, p. 1.

Operations control considers control from the perspective of process improvement, whereas **financial control** assesses an organization's financial success by measuring and evaluating its financial outcomes. Operations control focuses on finding the best operating decisions; financial control focuses on an overall assessment of how well operations control is working to improve financial performance. Financial control information signals when operations control is not working well and, hence, needs to be evaluated and improved.

Performance measures in financial control vary. Those most widely used include revenue, cost, profit, return on investment, and economic value added. Before discussing particular forms of financial control, we must first understand the nature and role of responsibility centers, which are the different types of decentralized units in organizations to which financial controls are applied.

Operations control
The process of providing feedback to employers and their managers about the efficiency of activities being performed.

Financial control
A process used to assess an organization's financial success by measuring and evaluating its financial outcomes.

IN PRACTICE

Choosing Between Operations and Financial Control

Some people believe that financial control is inappropriate under any conditions and refuse to use financial numbers for control. Instead, these people promote using performance measures like quality, cost, or service, which are defined by the organization's critical success factors, for control purposes. These people believe that, if the organization has chosen critical success factors appropriately, particularly those related to customer satisfaction, financial results will follow.

People who promote the use of financial control believe that it is an overall, shareholder-relevant test of the efficacy of the strategic and operating decisions that the organization has made. Most organizations use a combination of both types of control.

Responsibility Centers

Responsibility center An organization unit for which a manager is made responsible.

A **responsibility center** is an organization unit for which a manager is made responsible. Examples of responsibility centers include a hotel in a chain of hotels, a workstation in a production line that makes computer control units, the data processing group in a government office that handles claims for payment from suppliers, a claims processing unit in an insurance company, or a shipping department in a mail-order business.

A responsibility center is like a small business, and its manager is asked to run that small business to promote the best interests of the larger organization. The manager and supervisor establish goals for their responsibility center. Goals provide employees with focus and should therefore be specific and measurable. They should also promote both the long-term interests of the larger organization and the coordination of each responsibility center's activities with the efforts of all the others. Let us look at how this coordination is accomplished.

COORDINATING RESPONSIBILITY CENTERS

For an organization to be successful, the activities of its responsibility units must be coordinated. Suppose we divided the operations in a fast-food restaurant into three groups: order taking, order preparation, and order delivery. Imagine the chaos and customer ill will that would be created if the communication links between any two of these organization groups were severed. Unfortunately in large organizations, sales, manufacturing, and customer service activities are often very disjointed, resulting in diminished performance.

Consider the operations of a courier such as Federal Express. Nationwide couriers establish local stations or collector points (called terminals) from which they dis-

Kinko's Copy Centers have become successful by designing processes and systems that minimize costs. However, to ensure success, Kinko's Copy Centers have expanded their focus beyond cost control to incorporate quality and service considerations as well. (Gregg Mancuso/Stock, Boston)

patch trucks to pick up and deliver shipments. Shipments that are bound for other terminals are sent to the Federal Express hub in Memphis where they are sorted and redirected. The formula for success in the courier business is simple and has two key elements: (1) meeting the service commitment to the customer politely, on time, and without damage, and (2) controlling costs. The only way to achieve success is to ensure that all the pieces of the system work together effectively and efficiently to achieve these two critical elements of performance.

Suppose that management has determined that each terminal is to be treated as a responsibility center. How should the company measure the performance of each terminal, its managers, and its employees?

First, the company can measure the drivers of efficiency in each terminal. To focus on efficiency, it may measure the number of parcels picked up, sorted, or delivered per route, per employee, per vehicle, per hour, or per shift. To focus on efficiency and customer satisfaction, it may count for productivity purposes only those shipments that meet customer requirements, for example, on-time pickup and on-time delivery to the right address.

Second, the organization's ability to meet its service commitment to customers in a highly integrated operation like a courier business reflects how well the pieces fit together. The company should measure how much each group contributes to the organization's ability to meet its commitments to customers. There are two important elements of terminal-hub interaction for a courier.

1. The proportion of the time that the terminal meets its deadlines, that is, whether the trucks and containers are packed and ready to leave for the hub when they are required to leave (often called a percent correct measure)
2. When terminals are required to sort shipments, the number of shipments sorted to the wrong destination or that travel by the wrong mode (often called a percent defect measure)

Third, the company must assess service to the customer at a more detailed level. For example, it can measure the following:

1. The number of complaints (or percent of shipments with complaints) the terminal operations group receive
2. The average time taken by the operations group to respond to complaints
3. The number of complaints of poor or impolite service received by the company's customer service line

In general, controlling the activities of responsibility centers requires measuring the nonfinancial elements of performance, such as quality and service that create financial results. The key message is that properly chosen nonfinancial measures anticipate and explain financial results. For example, increased employee training that improves quality in this period should improve revenues and profits in subsequent periods. Therefore, we must always be careful to use financial results as aggregate measures of performance and rely on nonfinancial results to identify the causes or drivers of the financial results.

ACCOUNTING FOR RESPONSIBILITY CENTERS

Organizations use financial control to provide a summary measure of how well their systems of operations control are working. When organizations use a single index to provide a broad assessment of operations, they frequently use a financial number such as revenue, cost, profit, or return on investment, because these are the measures that describe the primary objectives of shareowners in profit-seeking organizations.

RESPONSIBILITY CENTER TYPES

The accounting report prepared for a responsibility center reflects the degree to which the responsibility center manager controls revenue, cost, profit, or return on investment. When preparing accounting summaries, accountants classify responsibility centers into four types:

1. Cost centers
2. Revenue centers
3. Profit centers
4. Investment centers

Cost centers
Responsibility centers in which employees control costs but do not control revenues or investment level.

Cost Centers. **Cost centers** are responsibility centers in which employees control costs but do not control revenues or investment level. Virtually every processing group in service operations (such as the cleaning plant in a dry-cleaning business or the check-clearing department in a bank) or in manufacturing operations (such as the lumber-sawing department in a sawmill or the steelmaking department in a steel mill) is a candidate to be treated as a cost center.

Cost center reporting, especially for repetitive operations such as stamping car body parts, reflects the perspectives and uses of the reporting methods described in Chapters 4 and 5 to provide cost information that managers use to monitor and assess operations. Organizations evaluate the performance of cost center employees by comparing the center's actual costs with target or standard cost levels for the amount and type of work done. Therefore, cost standards and variances figure prominently in cost center reports. Moreover, because standards and variances are used to assess performance, the process of setting standards and interpreting variances has profound behavioral effects on employees, particularly relating to misrepresenting performance potential and performance results.

We will now use the cost center, the activity costing concepts developed in Chapter 5, and the variance analysis tools developed earlier in this chapter to show how financial control might be applied in a cost center.

Comparing Budgeted and Actual Costs

The cost budget shown in Exhibit 12-10 was prepared for the manufacturing unit in Moncton Carpet Products, a manufacturer of carpet-cleaning products. This budget represents a cost target for the cost performance of the manufacturing group and shows that total center costs are budgeted at $9,891,820. The actual costs reported by the manufacturing group are $9,978,050. Exhibit 12-11 provides details of these actual costs.

The evaluation of this cost center involves identifying the causes for the differences between the budgeted costs in Exhibit 12-10 and the actual costs in Exhibit 12-11. Exhibit 12-12 provides a summary of these cost differences. Recall from our earlier discussion in this chapter, the variances reported equal the actual cost minus the budgeted cost.

Because the reported variance equals actual cost minus budgeted cost, a positive variance means that the actual cost was more than expected. A variance is unfavorable when the actual cost is higher than the planned cost, and a variance is favorable when the actual cost is less than planned cost. Therefore, positive cost variances are unfavorable and negative cost variances are favorable.

Exhibit 12-12 reports a mix of positive and negative variances. For example, for products 1 and 3, the unit-related costs are higher than planned, and for products 2 and 4 they are lower than planned. In total, the unit-related costs and batch-related costs are lower than planned and the product-sustaining and business-sustaining costs are higher than planned.

EXHIBIT 12-10

Moncton Carpet Products
Master Budget

	Product 1	Product 2	Product 3	Product 4	Totals
Units made	245,000	385,000	636,000	1,250,000	
Units per batch	500	2,500	1,500	5,000	
Number of batches	490	154	424	250	
Cost per unit	$5.40	$3.20	$4.25	$1.45	
Cost per batch	$325.00	$680.00	$400.00	$135.00	
Unit-related costs	$1,323,000	$1,232,000	$2,703,000	$1,812,500	$7,070,500
Batch-related costs	$159,250	$104,720	$169,600	$33,750	$467,320
Product-sustaining costs	$125,000	$168,000	$256,000	$355,000	$904,000
Facility-sustaining costs					$1,450,000
Total costs					$9,891,820

Based on this initial analysis, we might conclude that the manufacturing group at Moncton Carpet Products is able to control unit-related and batch-related costs but does not do well controlling its product-sustaining and business-sustaining costs. A closer examination of Exhibits 12-10 and 12-11, however, casts doubt on the validity of these conclusions. We can see in one of these exhibits that the number of units produced differs from the planned number of units for each product. Similarly, as we can see from line 2 of these exhibits, the actual number of units per batch differs from the planned number of units per batch for each product. Because of these volume differences, it is not meaningful to compare the cost targets in the master budget with the actual cost results. When actual volume differs from budgeted or planned volume, accountants use a flexible budget to evaluate actual costs.

EXHIBIT 12-11

Moncton Carpet Products
Actual Results

	PRODUCT 1	PRODUCT 2	PRODUCT 3	PRODUCT 4	TOTALS
Units made	297,000	345,000	675,000	960,000	
Units per batch	600	2,300	1,800	6,000	
Number of batches	495	150	375	160	
Cost per unit	$5.43	$3.18	$4.33	$1.40	
Cost per batch	$335.00	$670.00	$387.00	$144.00	
Unit-related costs	$1,612,710	$1,097,100	$2,922,750	$1,344,000	$6,976,560
Batch-related costs	$ 165,825	$ 100,500	$ 145,125	$ 23,040	434,490
Product-sustaining costs	$ 133,000	$ 163,000	$ 259,000	$ 362,000	917,000
Facility-sustaining costs					1,650,000
Total costs					$9,978,050

EXHIBIT 12-12

Moncton Carpet Products
Simple Cost Analysis

	MASTER BUDGET (FROM EXHIBIT 12-10)	VARIANCE	ACTUAL RESULTS (FROM EXHIBIT 12-11)
Unit-related costs:			
Product 1	$1,323,000	$289,710	$1,612,710
Product 2	1,232,000	(134,900)	1,097,100
Product 3	2,703,000	219,750	2,922,750
Product 4	1,812,500	(468,500)	1,344,000
Total	$7,070,500	($93,940)	$6,976,560
Batch-related costs:			
Product 1	$159,250	$ 6,575	$165,825
Product 2	104,720	(4,220)	100,500
Product 3	169,600	(24,475)	145,125
Product 4	33,750	(10,710)	23,040
Total	$467,320	($32,830)	$434,490
Product-sustaining costs:			
Product 1	$ 125,000	$ 8,000	$ 133,000
Product 2	168,000	(5,000)	163,000
Product 3	256,000	3,000	259,000
Product 4	355,000	7,000	362,000
Total	$ 904,000	$ 13,000	$ 917,000
Facility-sustaining costs	1,450,000	$200,000	1,650,000
Total costs	$9,891,820	$ 86,230	$9,978,050

Using the Flexible Budget

Producing a product requires production activities that, in turn, create costs. For example, increased production levels require more production activities that, in turn, create higher costs. Recall that the preparation of the master budget occurs before the start of production and is based on the planned level of production and production-related activities. However, organizations seldom realize their production plans exactly. There usually are differences between the actual level of production and planned production, causing actual production activity levels to differ from planned production activity levels. Thus, it follows that the cost targets, or budgets, in the master budgets reflect different activity levels than do the actual costs incurred. It is therefore inappropriate to compare actual cost results with a budget that reflects cost targets based on a different level of production activities.

As shown in Exhibit 12-4, a flexible budget recasts cost targets in the planned or master budget to reflect the actual level of production. The flexible budget develops the cost target levels based on the actual level of activity. Thus, flexible budgets allow comparisons of actual results to targets based on the achieved level of production.

Exhibit 12-13 presents the flexible budget for Moncton Carpet Products. The cost standards in this exhibit reflect the same cost per unit or cost per batch standards as the master budget. It is common to refer to the target for a unit cost as a standard

EXHIBIT 12-13

Moncton Carpet Products
Flexible Budget

	PRODUCT 1	PRODUCT 2	PRODUCT 3	PRODUCT 4	TOTALS
Units made	297,000	345,000	675,000	960,000	
Units per batch	500	2,500	1,500	5,000	
Number of batches	594	138	450	192	
Cost per unit	$5.40	$3.20	$4.25	$1.45	
Cost per batch	$325.00	$680.00	$400.00	$135.00	
Unit-related costs	$1,603,800	$1,104,000	$2,868,750	$1,392,000	$6,968,550
Batch-related costs	$ 193,050	$ 93,840	$ 180,000	$ 25,920	492,810
Product-sustaining costs	$ 125,000	$ 168,000	$ 256,000	$ 355,000	904,000
Facility-sustaining costs					1,450,000
Total costs					$9,815,360

EXHIBIT 12-14

Moncton Carpet Products
Flexible Budget Cost Analysis

	1 MASTER BUDGET	2 PLANNING VARIANCE	3 FLEXIBLE BUDGET	4 FLEXIBLE BUDGET VARIANCE	5 ACTUAL
Unit-related costs:					
Product 1	$1,323,000	$280,800	$1,603,800	$8,910	$1,612,710
Product 2	1,232,000	(128,000)	1,104,000	(6,900)	1,097,100
Product 3	2,703,000	165,750	2,868,750	54,000	2,922,750
Product 4	1,812,500	(420,500)	1,392,000	(48,000)	1,344,000
Total	$7,070,500	$(101,950)	$6,968,550	$8,010	$6,976,560
Batch-related costs:					
Product 1	$159,250	$33,800	$193,050	$(27,225)	$165,825
Product 2	104,720	(10,880)	93,840	6,660	100,500
Product 3	169,600	10,400	180,000	(34,875)	145,125
Product 4	33,750	(7,830)	25,920	(2,880)	23,040
Total	$467,320	$25,490	$492,810	$(58,320)	$434,490
Product-sustaining costs:					
Product 1	$ 125,000	0	$ 125,000	$ 8,000	$ 133,000
Product 2	168,000	0	168,000	(5,000)	163,000
Product 3	256,000	0	256,000	3,000	259,000
Product 4	355,000	0	355,000	7,000	362,000
Total	$ 904,000	0	$ 904,000	$ 13,000	$ 917,000
Facility-sustaining costs:	$1,450,000	0	$1,450,000	200,000	1,650,000
Total costs	$9,891,820	($76,460)	$9,815,360	$162,690	$9,978,050

and the target for total cost, which is computed by multiplying a standard by the projected or actual volume, as the budget.

As we saw earlier in the chapter, the key feature of a flexible budget is the adjustment in the volume levels relative to the master budget which reflects the achieved level of activity. For example, Moncton Carpet Products actually made 345,000 units of product 2. At the standard batch size of 2500, there should have been 138 (345,000 ÷ 2500) batches of product 2 made. At a standard unit cost of $3.20 and a standard batch cost of $680, the unit-related and batch-related costs for product 2 should have been $1,104,000 ($3.20 × 345,000) and $93,840 ($680 × 138), respectively. We can now adjust the master budget targets for the changes in volume to provide a volume-adjusted cost standard to compare with actual costs, as shown in Exhibit 12-14.

Exhibit 12-14 reconciles the actual cost to the master budget target through the flexible budget. The variances between the master budget (column 1) and the flexible budget (column 3), which accountants call planning variances (column 2), reflect the cost adjustments resulting from the differences in production volume between the master budget (planned volume) and the flexible budget (achieved volume). This planning variance is computed by subtracting the flexible budget amount from the master budget amount for each item. A negative variance indicates a cost reduction because of a lower volume, and a positive variance indicates a cost increase because of a higher volume.

Planning variances have little meaning. Their value lies in showing the effect of volume change on revenues, costs, and profits. They facilitate adjustments to the master budget target amounts for differences between planned and actual volumes so that the cost targets become comparable to the actual cost levels.

The flexible budget variances are the focus of cost control in a cost center. We can see that the flexible budget variance for unit-related costs for product 1 was $8910 (column 4), signaling that cost expenditures for unit-related items relating to product 1 were $8910 higher than they should have been, given the level of volume achieved. This flexible budget variance is the sum of the price and quantity variances.

For batch-related costs, the flexible budget variance reflects a mix of the difference between the planned and actual cost per batch and the number of batches given the actual level of activity. Note that the variance for batch-related costs for product 1 was −$27,225 (column 4). This favorable variance indicates that batch-related costs were $27,225 less than the target specified in the flexible budget.

The favorable variance arises from two factors. First, as we can see by comparing the cost targets in Exhibit 12-10 with the actual costs in Exhibit 12-11, the standard cost per batch and actual cost per batch for product 1 were $325 and $335, respectively. Therefore, the batch-related costs for product 1 reflect an increased, or unfavorable, cost, which equals the increased cost per batch of $10 multiplied by the actual number of batches, a total of $4950 ($10 × 495).

Second, we can see that when comparing the actual results in Exhibit 12-11 with the flexible budget amounts in Exhibit 12-13, given the achieved level of activity, the actual number and standard number of batches were 495 and 594, respectively. The manufacturing group increased the average batch size for product 1 from 500 to 600, thereby reducing the number of batches from the planned level, to create part of the reported savings in batch-related costs. By reducing the number of batches by 99 (594 − 495), the manufacturing group saved $32,175 ($325 × 99) in batch-related costs.

The total flexible budget variance for the batch-related costs for product 1 is −$27,225 ($4,950 − $32,175) and reflects the combined effect of (1) fewer than the standard number of batches given the production level achieved and (2) a higher than standard cost per batch. We also can investigate the causes of other flexible budget variances reported for the various costs for each product in a similar manner.

Other Cost Control Approaches

When an organization unit's output mix and output level are constant, it is possible to compare current cost levels with those in previous periods to promote an environment of continuous cost improvement. Interperiod cost comparisons can be misleading when the production mix or the production level is changing. Under these conditions, there exists noncomparability of cost levels between periods; however, when circumstances warrant, organizations are often able to plot cost levels on a graph and look for downward cost trends, which imply improved efficiencies in the processes that are creating costs.

Addressing Other Issues in Cost Center Control

Many organizations make the mistake of evaluating a cost center solely on its ability to control and reduce costs. The Federal Express example illustrates that quality, response time, the ability to meet production schedules, employee motivation, employee safety, and respect for the organization's ethical and environmental commitments are other critical measures of a cost center's performance. If management evaluates cost center performance only on the center's ability to control costs, its members may ignore unmeasured attributes of performance. Therefore, organizations should never evaluate cost centers using only the center's cost performance. Rather, performance measures also should reflect the contributions the cost center makes to the organization's success.

Revenue Centers. **Revenue centers** are responsibility centers whose members control revenues, but do not control either the manufacturing or the acquisition cost of the product or service they sell or the level of investment made in the responsibility

Revenue center
A responsibility center in which members control revenues but do not control either the manufacturing or the acquisition cost of the product or service they sell or the level of investment made in the responsibility center.

This hotel has many facilities that allow it to attract convention business. While, on the surface, the dining rooms or the meeting rooms may not appear profitable, if these services were unavailable, the hotel would be unable to earn the room revenues from the convention business. In many organizations, there is a complex interaction between the different business segments that influence the organization's overall profits. (Richard Pasley/Stock, Boston)

center. Examples are a department in a department store, a regional sales office of a national or multinational corporation, and a unit in a large chain of units.

Some revenue centers control price, the mix of stock carried, and promotional activities. In these centers, revenue will measure most of their value added activities and will indicate in a broad sense how well they carried out their various activities.

Consider the activities of Napanee Service Center, a gasoline and automobile service station owned by a large oil refiner. The service center manager has no control over the cost of items such as fuel, depreciation on the building, power and heating costs, supplies, and salary rates, but the manager has a minor influence, through scheduling and staffing decisions, on total labor costs. Levels of gasoline sales and repair activities determine all other costs. The service manager also has no control over the wages paid to employees—the head office staff controls them; and the central marketing staff controls all promotional activities. The major controllable item in this service station is customer service, which distinguishes its gasoline sales and repair services from those offered in similar outlets and helps to determine the service station's sales levels.

The revenue center approach evaluates the responsibility center based solely on the revenues it generates. Most revenue centers incur sales and marketing costs, however, and have varying degrees of control over those costs. Therefore, it is common in such situations to deduct the responsibility center's traceable costs, such as salaries, advertising costs, and selling costs, from its sales revenue to compute the center's net revenue.

Critics of the revenue center approach argue that basing performance evaluation on revenues can create undesirable consequences. For example, sales staff rewarded solely on sales may (1) promote, or agitate for, a wide product line that in turn may create excessive diversity-related costs (both production and logistic), or (2) offer excessive customized services. In general, focusing only on revenues causes organization members to increase the use of activities that create costs to promote higher revenue levels.

Profit center
A responsibility center in which managers and other employees control both the revenues and the costs of the product or service they deliver.

Profit Centers. **Profit centers** are responsibility centers in which managers and other employees control both the revenues and the costs of the product or service they deliver. A profit center is like an independent business, except that senior management, not the responsibility center manager, controls the level of investment in the responsibility center. For example, if the manager of one outlet in a chain of discount stores has responsibility for pricing, product selection, purchasing, and promotion, then the outlet meets the conditions to be evaluated as a profit center.

Most individual units of chain operations, whether they are stores, motels, or restaurants, are treated as profit centers. It is doubtful, however, that a unit of a corporate-owned fast-food restaurant such as Burger King, or a corporate-owned hotel such as Holiday Inn, meets the conditions to be treated as a profit center, because the head offices make most purchasing, operating, pricing, and promotional decisions. These units are sufficiently large, however, so costs can vary due to differences in controlling labor costs, food waste, and the schedule for the facility's hours. Revenues also can shift significantly based on the unit's service level. Therefore, although these organizations do not seem to be candidates to be treated as profit centers, local discretion often affects revenues and costs enough so that they can be.

Numerous organizations evaluate units as profit centers even though the corporate office controls many facets of their operations. The profit reported by these units is a broad index of performance that reflects both corporate and local decisions. If unit performance is poor, it may reflect unfavorable conditions: (1) that no one in the organization can control, (2) poor corporate decisions, or (3) poor local decisions. For this reason, organizations should not rely only on profit center results for performance evaluations. Instead, detailed performance evaluations should include quality, material use (yield), labor use (yield), and service measures that the local units can control.

Investment Centers. **Investment centers** are responsibility centers in which the manager and other employees control revenues, costs, and the level of investment in the responsibility center. The investment center is like an independent business.

Investment center A responsibility center in which the manager and other employees control revenues, costs, and the level of investment in the responsibility center.

In 1993, Canada Post, Canada's national postal service, purchased Purolator Canada Limited, a courier service, and announced that Purolator would continue as an independent operation with its own management and policies. Purolator is an example of an investment center within the Canadian postal system.

Exhibit 12-15 summarizes the characteristics of the various types of responsibility centers.

EVALUATING RESPONSIBILITY CENTERS

Using the Controllability Principle to Evaluate Responsibility Centers. Underlying the accounting classifications of responsibility centers is the concept of controllability. The **controllability principle** states that the manager of a responsibility center should be assigned responsibility only for the revenues, costs, or investment that responsibility center personnel control. Revenues, costs, or investments that people outside the responsibility center control should be excluded from the accounting assessment of that center's performance. Although the controllability principle seems to be appealing and fair, it can be difficult, often misleading, and undesirable to apply in practice.

Controllability principle States that the manager of a responsibility center should be assigned responsibility only for the revenues, costs, or investment that responsibility center personnel control.

A significant problem in applying the controllability principle is that in most organizations many revenues and costs are jointly earned or incurred. Consider the

EXHIBIT 12-15

Summary of Responsibility Centers

FACTORS	COST CENTER	REVENUE CENTER	PROFIT CENTER	INVESTMENT CENTER
Controlled by center management	Costs	Revenues	Costs, revenues	Cost, revenues, and significant control over investment
Not controlled by center management	Revenues, investment in inventory and fixed assets	Costs, investment in inventory and fixed assets	Investment in inventory and fixed assets	
Measured by the accounting system	Costs relative to some target (usually a budget)	Revenue relative to some target (usually a budget)	Profit relative to some target (usually a budget)	Return on investment relative to some target
Not measured by the accounting system	Performance on critical success factors other than cost	Performance on critical success factors other than revenue	Performance on critical success factors other than profit	Performance on critical success factors other than return on investment

(Table header: TYPE OF RESPONSIBILITY CENTER)

operations of an integrated fishing products company that is divided into three responsibility centers: harvesting, processing, and marketing and distribution. The harvesting group operates ships that go out to sea and catch various species of fish. The ships return to one of the company's processing plants to discharge their catches. The plants process the fish into salable products. Finally, the marketing and distribution group sells products to customers.

As in most organizations, the activities that create the final product in this company are sequential and highly interdependent. The product must be of the right species, quality, and cost to be acceptable to the customer. The performance of the harvesting, processing, and marketing and distribution jointly determine the organization's success.

Evaluating the performance of harvesting, processing, and marketing and distribution requires the firm to consider many facets of performance. For example, it is possible to evaluate harvesting's operations by measuring its ability to

1. Catch the entire quota allowed,
2. Minimize the waste and damage done to the fish caught,
3. Minimize equipment failures, and
4. Control the costs associated with operating the ships.

Similar measures can be developed for processing, and the evaluation of marketing and distribution may be based on their ability to meet delivery schedules and improve market share.

As part of the performance evaluation process, the organization may want to prepare accounting summaries of the performance of harvesting, processing, and marketing and distribution to support some system of financial control. The management accountant undertaking this task immediately confronts the dilemma of how to account for highly interrelated organization centers as if they were individual businesses. For example, costs of harvesting are easy to determine, but what are the harvesting revenues? Harvesting does not control sales or prices—its role is to catch the fish, maintain raw material and product quality, and meet the schedules determined jointly by it (processing, and marketing and distribution).

Evaluating the department that manufactured this wafer of computer chips based solely on the cost per chip would motivate that department's personnel to ignore quality-related issues. Performance measures must be broad enough to motivate desired performance, for example, cost per good chip that is produced on time. (Zigy Kaluzny/Stone)

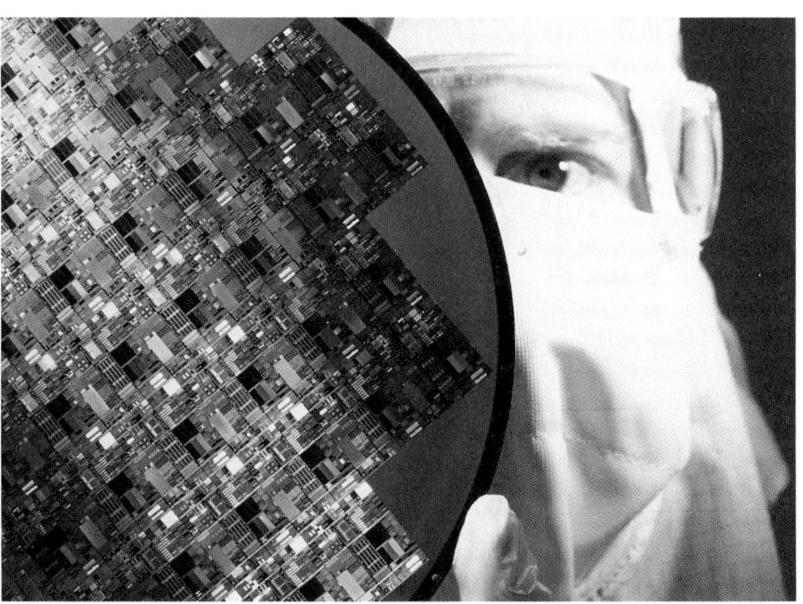

IN PRACTICE

Segment Margins and Financial Control

Business Week reports that one of the first activities of Nobuhiki Kawamoto when he took over as the President of the ailing Honda Motor Co. in 1990 was to divide "the company by product lines so that the robust motorcycle and power-equipment groups wouldn't disguise the trouble in cars."

Source: Karen Lowry Miller, Larry Armstrong, and David Woodruff, *Business Week,* September 13, 1993, p. 64.

If the company evaluates harvesting as a cost center, what about indirect organization costs such as corporate administration that reflects overhead resources used by the cost center? What about other important performance facets, such as maintaining quality, catching the full quota of fish, and delivering the required species of fish, when required, to the processing group? Should harvesting be asked to bear some of the costs of the head office groups, such as personnel, planning, and administration, whose services it uses? If so, how should its share of the costs of those services be determined?

We could probably conclude that processing should be evaluated as a cost center, but then what about the marketing and distribution group that through its general marketing efforts probably has the most direct impact on sales? What costs does this group control? It does not control harvesting and processing costs. The only costs that marketing and distribution controls are marketing and distribution costs that, in most integrated fishing products companies, are less than 10% of total costs. The harvesting group, through its ability to catch fish and maintain their quality, and the processing group, through its ability to produce quality products, are also influential in determining the organization's sales level. However, some people do not agree that the controllability principle is the best way to view performance evaluation, as we will now see.

Using Performance Measures to Influence versus Evaluate Decisions. Some people argue that controllability is not a valid criterion to use in selecting a performance measure. Rather, they suggest that the choice of the performance measure should influence decision-making behavior.

Consider a dairy that faced the problem of developing performance standards in an environment of continuously rising costs. Because the costs of raw materials, which were between 60% and 90% of the final costs of the various products, were market determined and, therefore, thought to be beyond the control of the various product managers, people argued that evaluation of the managers should depend on their ability to control the *quantity* of raw materials used rather than the *cost.*

Senior management of the dairy announced, however, that it planned to evaluate managers on their ability to control total costs. The managers quickly discovered that one way to control raw materials costs was to make judicious use of long-term fixed price contracts for raw materials. These contracts soon led to declining raw materials costs. Moreover, the company could project product costs several quarters into the future, thereby achieving lower costs and stability in planning and product pricing.

This example shows that managers, even when they cannot control costs entirely, can take steps to influence final product costs. When more costs or even revenues are included in performance measures, managers are more motivated to find actions that can influence incurred costs or generated revenues.

Using Segment Margin Reports. Many problems can occur when organizations treat responsibility centers as profit centers. These problems concern identifying responsibility for the control of sales and costs. In particular, this means deciding how to assign the responsibility for jointly earned revenues and jointly incurred costs. Therefore, as we now consider the form of the accounting reports that accountants prepare for responsibility centers, remember the assumptions and limitations that underlie these reports.

Despite the problems of responsibility center accounting, the profit measure is so comprehensive and pervasive that organizations prefer to treat many of their organization units as profit centers. Because most organizations are integrated operations, one of the first problems that designers of profit center accounting systems must confront is handling the interactions between the various profit center units.

To address this issue, consider the activities at Earl's Motors, a full-service automobile dealership organized into five responsibility centers: new car sales, used car sales, the body shop, the service department, and leasing. Each responsibility center has a manager who is responsible for the profit reported for that unit. The responsibility center managers report to Earl, using the quarterly reports as shown in Exhibit 12-16.

Exhibit 12-16 illustrates a common form of the segment margin report for an organization that is divided into responsibility centers. There is one column for each profit center. The revenue attributed to each profit center is the first entry in each column. Variable costs are deducted from its revenue to determine the contribution margin, which is the contribution made by operations to cover its costs that are not proportional to volume (see "Other costs" in Exhibit 12-16).

Next, the costs not proportional to volume are deducted from each center's contribution margin to determine that unit's segment margin, which is the performance

EXHIBIT 12-16

Earl's Motors
Quarterly Segment Margin Report for the Period July 1 to September 30, 1993

Item	New Car Sales	Used Car Sales	Body Shop	Service Department	Lease Sales	Total
Revenue	$976,350	$1,235,570	$445,280	$685,210	$635,240	$3,977,650
Variable costs	764,790	954,850	235,450	427,400	517,360	2,899,850
Contribution margin	$211,560	$ 280,720	$209,830	$257,810	$117,880	$1,077,800
Other costs	75,190	58,970	126,480	185,280	46,830	492,750
Segment margin	**$136,370**	**$ 221,750**	**$ 83,350**	**$ 72,530**	**$ 71,050**	**$ 585,050**
Allocated avoidable costs	69,870	74,650	64,540	65,290	22,490	296,840
Income	$ 66,500	$ 147,100	$ 18,810	$ 7,240	$ 48,560	$ 288,210
Unallocated costs						325,000
Dealership profit						($ 36,790)

measure for each responsibility center. The unit's segment margin measures its controllable contribution to the organization's profit and other indirect costs. Allocated avoidable costs are the organization's administrative costs, such as personnel-related costs and committed costs for facilities. These costs can be avoided if the unit is eliminated and the organization has time to adjust its capacity levels by selling excess facilities or by reducing the number of administrative staff. Allocated avoidable costs are deducted from the unit's segment margin to compute its income. Finally, the organization's unallocated costs (sometimes called shutdown costs), which represent the administrative and overhead costs incurred regardless of the scale of operations, are deducted from the total of the five profit center incomes to arrive at the dealership's profit.

Evaluating the Segment Margin Report. What can we learn from the segment margin report for Earl's Motors? First, we know that conventional accrual accounting reports a loss of $36,790 for this quarter. This loss may signal a long-term problem, or it may have been expected. Perhaps this quarter is a traditionally slow quarter and operations in the year's other three quarters make up the deficiency. Perhaps there is a disproportionate amount of committed costs incurred in this quarter and they will be lower in subsequent quarters.

What Do the Statements Tell the Reader? As we look at the statements for the individual responsibility centers, we can see that each showed a positive income. The contribution margin for each responsibility center is the value added by the manufacturing or service-creating process before the costs that are not proportional to volume.

A unit's segment margin is an estimate of its short-term effect on the organization's profit. It also represents the immediate negative effect on corporate income if the unit is shut down. The unit's income is an estimate of the long-term effect of the responsibility center's shutdown on the organization's profit after fixed capacity is allowed to adjust. For example, if the lease sales operation is discontinued, then the immediate effect is to reduce the profit at Earl's Motors by $71,050. After some period of time, however, perhaps a year or even several years, when capacity has been allowed to adjust for this loss of activity, the estimated net effect of closing the lease operation would be to reduce corporate profits by $48,560. The difference between the unit's segment margin and income reflects the effect of adjusting for business-sustaining costs, which are committed in the short run.

Good or Bad Numbers? Organizations use different approaches to evaluate whether the segment margin numbers are good or bad. Following are the most popular sources of comparative information.

1. *Past performance.* Is performance this period reasonable, given past experience?
2. *Comparable organizations.* How does performance compare with similar organizations?

Evaluations include comparisons of absolute amounts, such as cost levels and revenue levels, and relative amounts, such as each item's percentage of revenue. For example, in evaluating the performance of Earl's Motors, the manager of the service department may note that variable costs (the costs of flexible resources) are about 62% of revenue. This may compare favorably with past relationships of variable cost to revenue. By joining an industry group that provides comparative information for dealerships in similar-size communities, however, Earl's Motors may find that, on average, variable costs in automobile dealerships are only 58% of revenue. This suggests that Earl's Motors should investigate why its variable costs are higher than the industry average. Management should make similar evaluations for all cost items in this report.

EXHIBIT 12-17

The Operation of a Typical Mobil Corp. U.S. Refinery

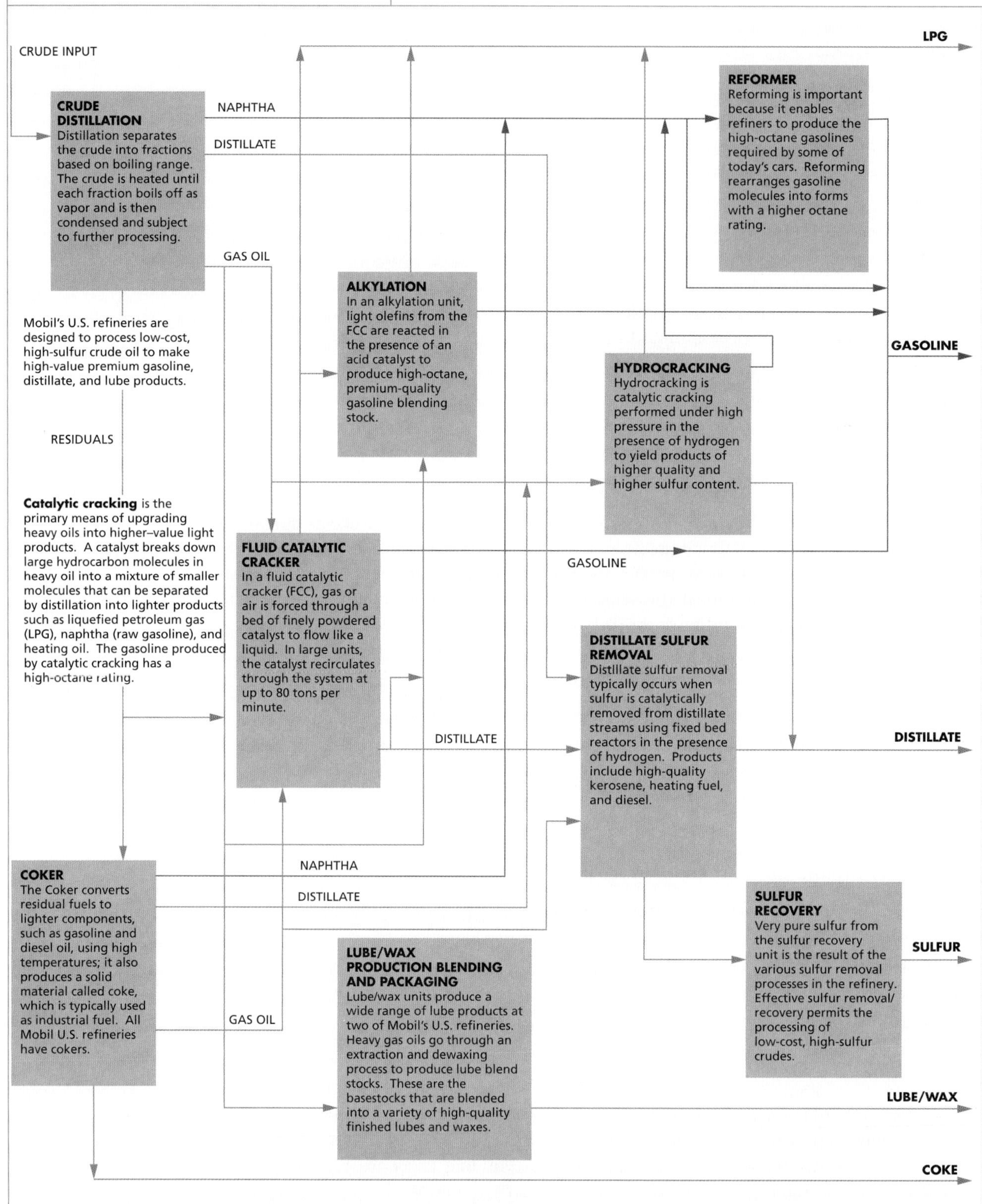

CRUDE INPUT
CRUDE DISTILLATION
Distillation separates the crude into fractions based on boiling range. The crude is heated until each fraction boils off as vapor and is then condensed and subject to further processing.
NAPHTHA
DISTILLATE
GAS OIL
LPG
REFORMER
Reforming is important because it enables refiners to produce the high-octane gasolines required by some of today's cars. Reforming rearranges gasoline molecules into forms with a higher octane rating.
ALKYLATION
In an alkylation unit, light olefins from the FCC are reacted in the presence of an acid catalyst to produce high-octane, premium-quality gasoline blending stock.
Mobil's U.S. refineries are designed to process low-cost, high-sulfur crude oil to make high-value premium gasoline, distillate, and lube products.
GASOLINE
HYDROCRACKING
Hydrocracking is catalytic cracking performed under high pressure in the presence of hydrogen to yield products of higher quality and higher sulfur content.
RESIDUALS
Catalytic cracking is the primary means of upgrading heavy oils into higher–value light products. A catalyst breaks down large hydrocarbon molecules in heavy oil into a mixture of smaller molecules that can be separated by distillation into lighter products such as liquefied petroleum gas (LPG), naphtha (raw gasoline), and heating oil. The gasoline produced by catalytic cracking has a high-octane rating.
FLUID CATALYTIC CRACKER
In a fluid catalytic cracker (FCC), gas or air is forced through a bed of finely powdered catalyst to flow like a liquid. In large units, the catalyst recirculates through the system at up to 80 tons per minute.
GASOLINE
DISTILLATE SULFUR REMOVAL
Distillate sulfur removal typically occurs when sulfur is catalytically removed from distillate streams using fixed bed reactors in the presence of hydrogen. Products include high-quality kerosene, heating fuel, and diesel.
DISTILLATE
DISTILLATE
COKER
The Coker converts residual fuels to lighter components, such as gasoline and diesel oil, using high temperatures; it also produces a solid material called coke, which is typically used as industrial fuel. All Mobil U.S. refineries have cokers.
NAPHTHA
DISTILLATE
SULFUR RECOVERY
Very pure sulfur from the sulfur recovery unit is the result of the various sulfur removal processes in the refinery. Effective sulfur removal/recovery permits the processing of low-cost, high-sulfur crudes.
SULFUR
LUBE/WAX PRODUCTION BLENDING AND PACKAGING
Lube/wax units produce a wide range of lube products at two of Mobil's U.S. refineries. Heavy gas oils go through an extraction and dewaxing process to produce lube blend stocks. These are the basestocks that are blended into a variety of high-quality finished lubes and waxes.
GAS OIL
LUBE/WAX
COKE

This graphic, developed by Mobil Corporation, shows the processing activities used in a typical U.S. refinery to refine a barrel of crude oil into its resulting, or joint, products. The complex and interrelated nature of the products simultaneously produced in a refinery creates profound problems in determining the individual costs of those products. (Mobil Corporation)

Interpreting Segment Margin Reports with Caution. The segment margin statement may seem to be a straightforward and interesting approach to financial control. Segment margin statements should be interpreted carefully, however, because they reflect many assumptions that disguise underlying issues.

First, like all approaches to financial control, segment margins present an aggregated summary of each organization unit's performance. It is important to consider other facets relating to critical success factors, such as quality and service. For example, companies may use customer surveys to establish a customer satisfaction index for each department, or they might compute quality statistics that report error or recall rates for each department.

Second, the segment margin report contains numbers that can be quite arbitrary, because they rest on subjective revenue and cost allocation assumptions over which there can be legitimate disagreement. (Accountants often call these arbitrary numbers *soft numbers*). Each subsequent amount shown down each column becomes less controllable by the responsibility center's manager and is affected more by the assumptions used in allocating costs. Although a unit's segment margin is assumed to be controllable, the manager may have less than complete control over the costs used to compute it; and the manager may have almost no control over the costs allocated to compute the unit's income. In a typical refinery, for example, joint use of facilities creates problems when managers attempt to allocate the costs of expensive processes, such as those of the crude distillation unit, to the outputs that it produces (naphtha, distillate, gas, oil, and residuals) (see Exhibit 12-17).

Third, and perhaps most important, the revenue figures reflect important assumptions and allocations that sometimes can be misleading. These assumptions relate to the transfer pricing issue, which focuses on how the revenues the organization earns can be divided among all the responsibility centers that contribute to earning those revenues.

Transfer Pricing

Transfer pricing is the set of rules an organization uses to allocate jointly earned revenue among responsibility centers. These rules can be arbitrary when a high degree of interaction exists among the individual responsibility centers. Exhibit 12-18 shows the possible interactions among the responsibility centers at Earl's Motors.

Transfer pricing
The set of rules an organization uses to assign the prices to products transferred between internal responsibility centers.

EXHIBIT 12-18

Transfer Pricing Interrelationships

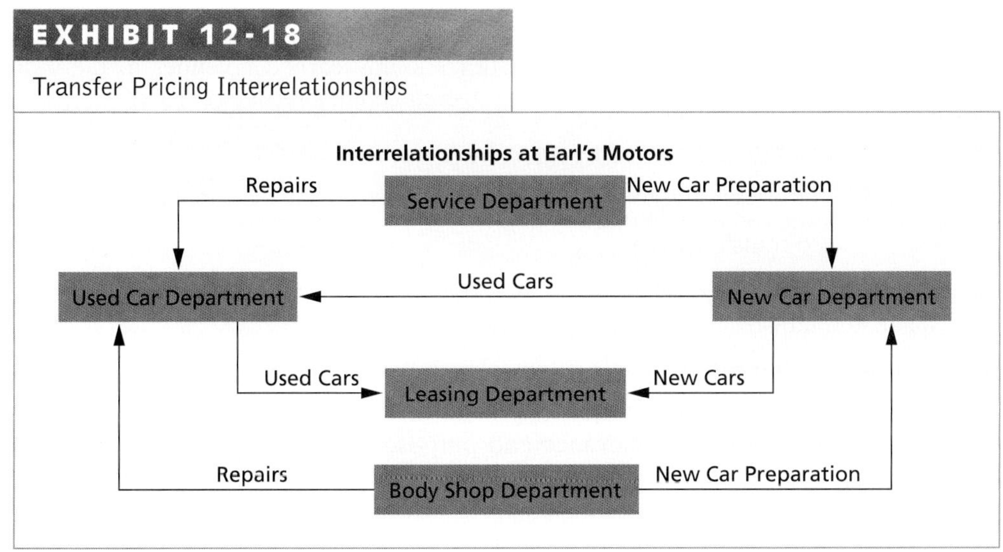

There are many interactions among the responsibility centers in an automobile dealership. When these responsibility centers are evaluated on a profit basis, these transfers must be priced. For example, the new car department sells a used car taken in on trade to the used car department and the service department sells repair services to the used car department. (Bob Daemmrich/The Image Works)

To understand the issues and problems associated with allocating revenues in a simple organization such as Earl's Motors, consider the activities that occur when a customer purchases a new car. The new car department sells the new car and takes in a used car as a trade. Then Earl's must transfer the used car to the used car department, where it may undergo repairs and service to make it ready for sale, or may be sold externally as in the wholesale market.

The value placed on the used car transferred between the new and used car departments is critical in determining the profits of both departments. The new car department would like the value assigned to the used car to be as high as possible because that makes its reported revenues higher; the used car department would like the value to be as low as possible because that makes its reported costs lower.

The same considerations apply for any product or service transfer between any two departments in the same organization. The rule that determines the values of the internal transfers will allocate the organization's jointly earned revenues to the individual profit centers and, therefore, will affect each center's reported profit.

APPROACHES TO TRANSFER PRICING

Organizations choose among four different approaches to transfer pricing:

1. Market-based transfer prices
2. Cost-based transfer prices
3. Negotiated transfer prices
4. Administered transfer prices

Before we review the basic transfer-pricing methods that organizations use, it is worthwhile to recall that the relevance and purpose of transfer prices depend upon whether the transfer price has the intended effect on organization decision makers. Transfer prices serve different purposes; however, the usual goal is to motivate the decision maker to act in the organization's best interests. Accountants must always remember that the primary purpose of producing management accounting numbers is to motivate desirable behavior regarding managers' planning, decision making, and resource allocation activities, not to create accounting reports.

Market-Based Transfer Prices. If external markets exist for the intermediate (transferred) product or service, then market prices are the most appropriate basis for pricing the transferred good or service between responsibility centers. The market price provides an independent valuation of the transferred product or service, and of how much each profit center has contributed to the total profit earned by the organization on the transaction. For example, the selling division, instead of transferring the good internally, could sell it externally. Similarly, the buying division could purchase externally rather than receiving the internal transfer.

Unfortunately, such competitive markets with well-defined prices seldom exist. Consider Earl's Motors. Dealers trade used cars in well-organized markets that publish prices. A given used car could be valued using this information. The wholesale value of a used car depends, however, on its mechanical condition, which is only imperfectly observable and at a cost. In addition, the used car's value depends on its visible condition, which is a matter of subjective evaluation. Therefore, it is not clear that it is possible to easily determine an objective wholesale price for a given used car.

Some dealerships avoid this problem by asking the used car manager to value any used car being taken in on trade. This value becomes the transfer price. Because people often react to risk and uncertainty by requiring a margin of safety, the used car manager may discount the perceived value of the used car to provide a margin of safety that covers the repair of any hidden problems that become evident when the car is prepared for resale. If the value is excessively low, however, the new car manager complains that this is impeding the ability of the new car department to sell new cars. Therefore, the new car manager may be given the option to shop a potential trade-in to other used car dealers to find a better price. This allows the transfer price to better reflect market forces.

Cost-Based Transfer Prices. When the transferred good or service does not have a well-defined market price, one alternative to consider is a transfer price based on cost. Some common transfer prices are variable cost, variable cost plus some percent markup on variable cost, full cost, and full cost plus some percent markup on full cost.

Proponents of each of these types of transfer prices have arguments to support their respective choices. Economists argue, however, that any cost-based transfer price other than marginal cost (assuming that it can be computed) leads organization members to choose a lower than optimal level of transactions, causing an economic loss to the overall organization. For example, if the transfer price is higher than the marginal cost, the supplying unit wants to sell more than the optimal quantity and the purchasing unit wants to buy fewer than the optimal quantity. Because supply and demand must be equal, and because no organization unit can be forced to buy or sell more than it wants, the amount that is ordered and supplied is always equal to the lesser of what is offered and what is wanted. The dilemma here, however, is that if the supplying division charges marginal cost as the transfer price and marginal costs decline with volume, then the marginal cost will be less than average cost and the supplying division will always show a loss.

There are other problems with using cost-based transfer prices. Cost-based approaches to transfer pricing do not support the intention of having the transfer pricing mechanism support the calculation of unit incomes. Moreover, organization units prefer to be treated as profit centers, not cost centers, because profit centers are considered more prestigious.

Transfer prices based on actual costs provide no incentive to the supplying division to control costs, since the supplier can always recover its costs. This is a well-known problem in government contracting and utility regulation where prices or rates are often based on actual costs. One solution is to use a standard cost as the transfer price. Under this approach, the difference between the actual costs that a center incurs and the standard costs that are charged out become a measure of the unit's operating efficiency.

Using a cost-based transfer price assumes that the organization can compute a product's cost in a reasonably accurate way. Chapters 4 and 5 show that developing and operating accurate costing systems is quite a challenge. People are likely to complain and become frustrated if they believe the organization is using an inaccurate costing system for transfer-pricing purposes.

A final problem with cost-based approaches is that they do not provide the proper economic guidance when operations are capacity constrained. When an organization is operating at capacity, production decisions should reflect the most profitable use of the capacity rather than cost considerations only. In this case, the transfer price should be the sum of the marginal cost and the opportunity cost of capacity, where opportunity cost reflects the profit of the best alternative use of the capacity.

One interesting approach to transfer pricing is the so-called dual rate approach, in which the receiving division is charged only for the variable costs of producing the unit supplied and the supplying division is credited with the net realizable value of the unit supplied. This procedure has the desirable effect of letting marginal cost influence the decisions of the buying division while, at the same time, giving the selling division credit for an imputed profit on the transferred good or service.

Another interesting cost-based approach charges the buying division with the target variable cost. That amount includes the number of standard hours allowed for the work done multiplied by the standard cost per hour, in addition to an assignment of the supplying division's committed costs. The assignment should reflect the buying division's share of the supplying division's capacity. For example, if the service department acquired capacity expecting that 10% of its capacity would be supplied to the new car department, then the new car department would receive a lump-sum assignment of 10% of the service department's capacity costs, irrespective of the amount of work actually done for the new car department during the period. In this situation, the service department's income is the difference between the actual and target cost of the work it completes.

Cost-based transfer prices raise complex performance measurement, equity, and behavioral issues. Such issues are addressed more thoroughly in advanced texts.

Cost Allocations to Support Financial Control

Despite the difficulties of measuring responsibility center performance, many organizations want to develop responsibility center income statements. In effect, although revenue and cost allocation rules are arbitrary, people seem satisfied as long as the ones chosen and put in place are fair and consistently applied. Organizations need to design and present responsibility center income statements so that they isolate the discretionary components included in the calculation of each center's reported income. Refer back to Exhibit 12-16, which presents one possible format.

The format shown in Exhibit 12-16 helps to identify what the center controls directly. It shows the revenue and variable costs separately from the other costs in the profit calculation, which are the indirect or joint costs that are allocated. Like the allocation of jointly earned revenues, the allocation of indirect or joint costs can cause considerable distortions and can misdirect decision making.

Consider the operations of Shirley's Grill and Bar, which has three operating units: a restaurant, a billiards room, and a bar (see Exhibit 12-19). The segment margin of $110,256 reported for the restaurant includes all revenues from selling food, all

EXHIBIT 12-19

Shirley's Grill and Bar
Responsibility Center
Income Statements
Indirect Cost Allocation
Based on Benefit

	RESTAURANT	BILLIARDS	BAR	TOTAL
Attributed revenue	$354,243	$32,167	$187,426	$573,836
Less segment costs	243,987	12,965	127,859	384,811
Segment margin	**$110,256**	$19,202	$ 59,567	$189,025
Less allocated costs	**87,791**	15,289	47,430	150,510
Segment income	$ 22,465	$ 3,913	$ 12,137	$ 38,515

food costs, all costs of kitchen and serving staff, and all costs of equipment and supplies relating to the kitchen and the seating area. These revenues and costs are directly attributable to the operation of the restaurant. Indirect costs in the $87,791 allocated to the restaurant operations include depreciation and taxes on the building, advertising, and franchise fees.

In general, the restaurant's accountant can choose among many different activity bases to select a method to allocate indirect costs, for example, a responsibility center's direct costs, floor space, and number of employees. Suppose that Shirley's decides to allocate indirect costs in proportion to the presumed benefit, as measured by segment margin, provided by the capacity these allocated costs reflect. Many people believe that allocating indirect costs in proportion to benefit is fair. It is a widely used criterion to evaluate an indirect cost allocation method.

The segment incomes reported in Exhibit 12-19 may seem straightforward and reasonable, but as in the case of all results involving indirect cost allocations, the numbers need careful interpretation. Suppose that a cost driver analysis revealed the following:

1. A significant portion of total indirect costs reflects depreciation on the building.
2. Allocating building costs based on floor space is considered to be the most reasonable approach to handling building costs.
3. The amount of floor space occupied by the restaurant, billiards, and bar operations is 40%, 25%, and 35%, respectively.

An allocation of costs based on floor space occupied yields the results summarized in Exhibit 12-20.

Do these alternative results have any meaning? On the one hand, we might argue that the indirect cost allocations based on floor space provide more meaningful economic results, because the floor space allocation reflects depreciation—the major component of indirect costs, and its driver, floor space. Even if floor space is the cost driver for indirect costs in the short term, the revised results may suggest nothing significant, because the allocated depreciation cost is likely to be a committed cost that cannot be avoided in the short term.

The allocations based on floor space may seem to suggest that the contribution to profit per square foot of floor space is lowest in the billiard operation, and that Shirley's should reduce the scope of the billiard operations in favor of adding more

EXHIBIT 12-20

Shirley's Grill and Bar
Responsibility Center
Income Statements
Indirect Cost Allocation Based on Floor Space Occupied

	RESTAURANT	BILLIARDS	BAR	TOTAL
Attributed revenue	$354,243	$32,167	$187,426	$573,836
Less segment costs	**243,987**	**12,965**	**127,859**	**384,811**
Segment margin	$110,256	$19,202	$ 59,567	$189,025
Less allocated costs	**60,204**	**37,627**	**52,679**	**150,510**
Segment income	$ 50,052	($18,425)	$ 6,888	$ 38,515

floor space to the bar or restaurant. This conclusion, however, does not necessarily follow. Suppose that without the billiard operation to attract customers the bar sales would be cut in half. How could the responsibility center income statements reflect this? They probably cannot. With this supplementary information, it would be possible to determine the economic effect of closing the billiards operation. Conventional segment margin statements cannot capture the interactive effects of such actions.

The message here is that responsibility center income statements have to be interpreted with considerable caution and healthy skepticism. They may include arbitrary and questionable revenue and cost allocations and often disguise interrelationships among the responsibility centers.

Negotiated Transfer Price. In the absence of market prices, some organizations allow supplying and receiving responsibility centers to negotiate transfer prices between themselves. Negotiated transfer prices reflect the controllability perspective inherent in responsibility centers, since each division is ultimately responsible for the transfer price that it negotiates. Negotiated transfer prices, and therefore production decisions, may, however, reflect the relative negotiating skills of the two parties rather than economic considerations.

In an economic sense, the optimal transfer price results when the purchasing unit offers to pay the net realizable value of the last unit supplied for all the units supplied. The net realizable value of a unit of transferred material is the selling price of the product less all the costs that remain to prepare the final product for sale. If the supplying unit is acting optimally, it chooses to supply units until its marginal cost equals the transfer price offered by the purchasing unit. This leads to the optimal quantity of the transferred units being supplied.

Problems arise when negotiating transfer prices, because this type of bilateral bargaining situation causes the supplying division to want a price higher than the optimal price, and the receiving division to want a price lower than the optimal price. When the actual transfer price is different from the optimal transfer price, the organization as a whole suffers, because it transfers a smaller than optimal number of units between the two divisions.

Administered Transfer Price. An arbitrator or a manager who applies some policy sets *administered transfer prices*, for example, market price less 10% or full cost plus 5%. Organizations often used administered transfer prices when a particular transaction occurs frequently. However, such prices reflect neither pure economic considerations, as market-based or cost-based transfer prices do, nor accountability considerations, as negotiated transfer prices do. Exhibit 12-21 summarizes the four major approaches to transfer pricing.

Returning to the example of Earl's Motors, Earl may order that the transfer price for body shop work done for the new and used car departments will be charged out at 80% of the normal market rate. This may seem reasonable and may reflect a practical approach to dealing with the issues associated with market-based and cost-based transfer prices; but this rule is arbitrary and, therefore, provides an arbitrary distribution of revenues and costs between the body shop and the units with which it deals. Administered transfer prices inevitably create subsidies among responsibility centers. Subsidies obscure the normal economic interpretation of responsibility center income and may provide a negative motivational effect if members of some responsibility center believe that the application of such rules is unfair.

Transfer Prices Based on Equity Considerations

Administered transfer prices are usually based on cost; that is, the transfer price is cost plus some markup on cost or market. Thus, the transfer price is some function (e.g., 80%) of the market price. However, sometimes administered transfer prices are based on equity considerations that invariably are designed around some definition of a reasonable division of a jointly earned revenue or a jointly incurred cost.

As an example, consider the situation in which three responsibility center managers need warehouse space. Each manager has undertaken a study to determine the

EXHIBIT 12-21

Summary of Transfer Pricing Approaches

APPROACH	MARKET-BASED	COST-BASED	NEGOTIATED	ADMINISTERED
Measure Used	**Market Price**	**Product Cost**	**Direct Negotiations**	**Application of a Rule**
Advantage	If a market price exists, it is objective and provides the proper economic incentives.	This is usually easy to put in place because cost measures are often already available in the accounting system.	This reflects the accountability and controllability principles underlying responsibility centers.	This is simple to use and avoids confrontations between the two parties to the transfer-pricing relationship.
Problems	There may be no market or it may be difficult to identify the proper market price because the product is difficult to classify.	There are many cost possibilities and any costs other than the marginal cost will not provide the proper economic signal.	This can lead to decisions that do not provide the greatest economic benefits.	This tends to violate the spirit of the responsibility approach.

cost for an individual warehouse that meets the responsibility center's needs. The costs are as follows: manager A—$3 million; manager B—$6 million; and manager C—$5 million. A developer has proposed that the managers combine their needs into a single large warehouse, which would cost $11 million. This represents a $3 million savings from the total cost of $14 million if each manager were to build a separate warehouse. The issue is how the managers should split the cost of this warehouse.

One alternative, sometimes called the *relative cost method*, is for each manager to bear a share of the warehouse cost that is proportional to that manager's alternative opportunity. This would result in the following cost allocations:

Manager A's share = $11,000,000 × $3,000,000/$14,000,000 = $2,357,143
Manager B's share = $11,000,000 × $6,000,000/$14,000,000 = $4,714,286
Manager C's share = $11,000,000 × $5,000,000/$14,000,000 = $3,928,571

This process is fair in the sense of being symmetrical. All parties are treated equally and each allocation reflects what each individual faces. Another approach, which reflects the equity criterion of ability to pay, is to base the allocation of cost on the profits that each manager derives from using the warehouse. Still another approach, which reflects the equity criterion of equal division, is to assign each manager a one-third share of the warehouse cost. Thus, each of the many different approaches to cost allocation reflects a particular view of equity.

Assigning and Valuing Assets in Investment Centers

When companies use investment centers to evaluate responsibility center performance, there are all the problems associated with profit centers plus some new problems unique to investment centers. The additional problems concern how to identify and value the assets used by each investment center. This task presents troubling questions that have no clear answers.

In determining the level of assets that a responsibility center uses, the management accountant must assign the responsibility for (1) jointly used assets, such as cash, buildings, and equipment; and (2) jointly created assets, such as accounts receivable. Once the decision makers have assigned the organization's assets to investment centers, they must determine the value of those assets. What cost should be used—historical cost, net book value, replacement cost, or net realizable value? These are all costing alternatives for which supporting arguments can be made (see advanced cost accounting texts).

The culmination of the allocation of revenues, costs, and assets to operating divisions is the calculation of the division's return on investment. To consider this, we return to the Dupont Company as discussed in Chapter 1, one of the earliest and most prolific users of the return-on-investment criterion.

Efficiency and Productivity Elements of Return on Investment

Referring back to the discussion in Chapter 1 about the Dupont Company, recall that one of Dupont's major challenges was to develop a way to manage the complex structure caused by its diverse activities and operations. In the early twentieth century, most organizations were single-product activity operations. These organizations approached the evaluation of the investment level of the organization by considering the ratio of profits to sales and the percent of capacity used. Dupont, however, being a multiproduct firm, pioneered the systematic use of return on investment to evaluate the profitability of its different lines of business. Dupont's approach to financial control is summarized in Exhibit 12-22. At Dupont, the actual exhibit used to summarize operations was extremely detailed and contained 350 large charts that were updated monthly and permanently displayed in a large chart room in the headquarters building.

Recall from Chapter 1 that return on investment (ROI) is the ratio of operating income to investment. The Dupont system of financial control focuses on return on investment and breaks that measure into two components: a return measure that assesses efficiency and a turnover measure that assesses productivity. The following equation illustrates this idea:

$$\text{Return on investment} = \frac{\text{Operating income}}{\text{Investment}} = \frac{\text{Operating income}}{\text{Sales}} \times \frac{\text{Sales}}{\text{Investment}}$$

Alternatively, we can compute return on investment in two other ways:

$$\text{Return on investment} = \text{Return on sales} \times \text{Asset turnover}$$

$$\text{Return on investment} = \text{Efficiency} \times \text{Productivity}$$

The ratio of operating income to sales (also called return on sales, or sales margin) is a measure of efficiency—the ability to control costs at a given level of sales activity. The ratio of sales to investment (often called asset turnover) is a measure of productivity—the ability to generate sales for a given level of investment.

The Dupont approach to financial control develops increasingly more detailed subcomponents for the efficiency and productivity measures by focusing on more detailed calculations of costs and different groups of assets. The upper portion of

EXHIBIT 12-22

The Dupont Return on Investment Control System

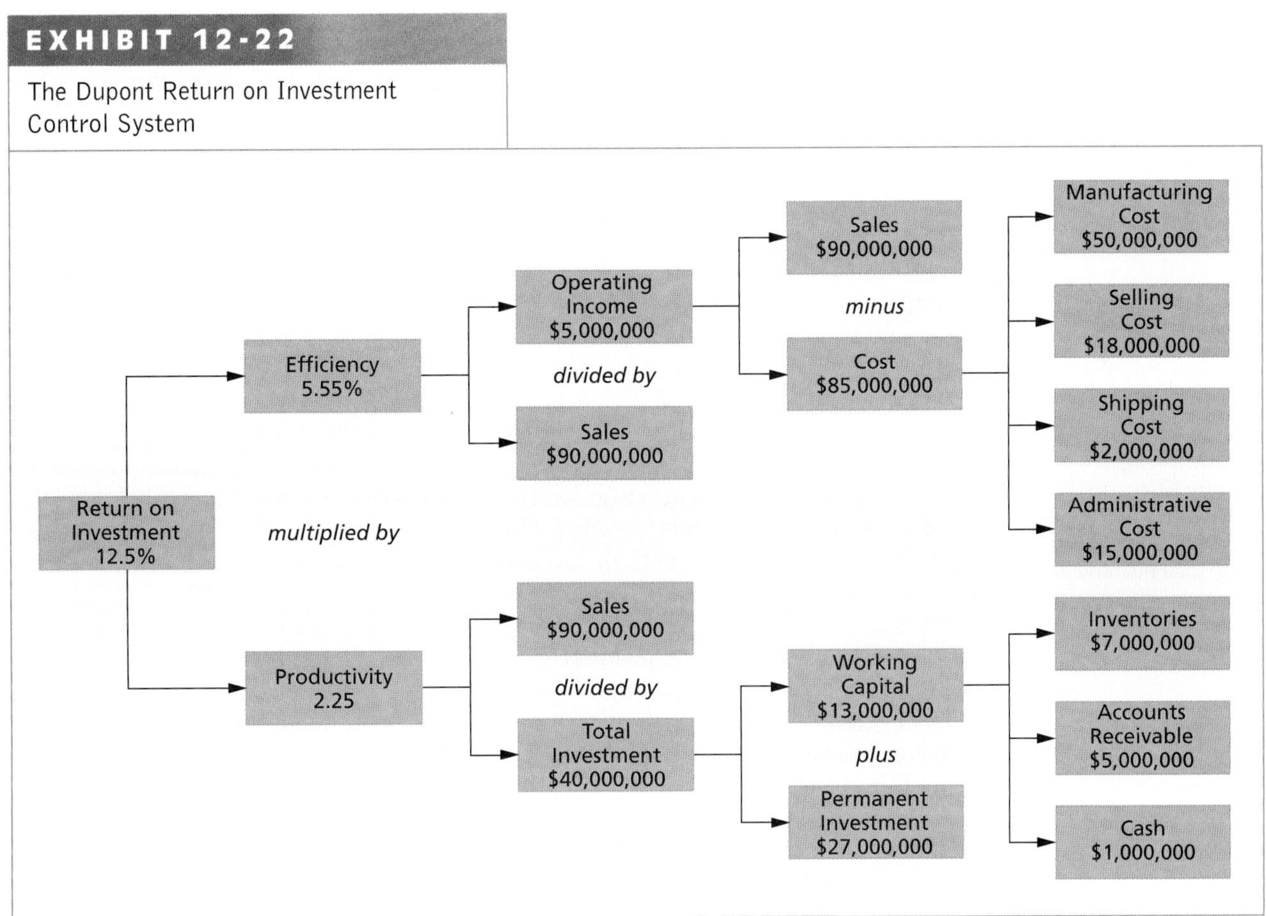

Exhibit 12-22 shows the efficiency measure factored into its components; and the lower portion of the exhibit shows the productivity measure factored into its components. For example, by looking at the efficiency ratio of operating income to sales, we can examine the various components of costs (manufacturing, selling, shipping, and administrative), their relationship to sales, and their individual trends to determine whether each is improving. Then it is possible to compare these individual and group efficiency measures with those of similar organization units or competitors, in order to discover where to make improvements.

The productivity ratio of sales to investment allows development of separate turnover measures for the key items of investment—the elements of working capital (inventories, accounts receivable, cash) and the elements of permanent investment (equipment and buildings). Comparisons of these turnover ratios with those of similar units or those of competitors can suggest where improvements are required.

We now consider the two elements of return on investment. First we discuss efficiency and then productivity, which is one of the most interesting and widely used applications of financial control.

ASSESSING ORGANIZATION EFFICIENCY USING FINANCIAL CONTROL

Most accounting approaches to assessing efficiency stress comparing costs with some standard. For example, if a standard cost is \$10 and the actual cost is \$12, the efficiency measure is standard cost divided by actual cost or, in this case, 83.3%. In this particular approach, the benchmark efficiency measure is 100%. An efficiency measure below 100% implies inefficient operations, whereas a measure above 100% implies efficient operations.

$$\text{Operations efficiency} = \frac{\text{Standard cost}}{\text{Actual cost}}$$

ASSESSING PRODUCTIVITY USING FINANCIAL CONTROL

The most widely accepted definition of productivity is the ratio of output over input. For example, if a worker produces 50 items in a seven-hour shift, the workers' productivity (often called labor productivity) is 7.1 units per hour. Labor-intensive industries monitor their labor productivity closely, because labor costs are a big fraction of total costs.

Organizations develop productivity measures for all factors of production, including people, raw materials, and equipment. For example, in the fishing industry, the ratio of weight of salable final products to the weight of the raw fish is typically 30%. This ratio of raw material in the finished product to the total quantity of raw material acquired is called **raw material productivity** or **yield.** Most organizations in the natural resource industry keep a close watch on raw material productivity, because the cost of acquiring raw materials is a large proportion of total costs. For example, Weirton Steel, a U.S. steel products manufacturer, once estimated that each percentage point increase in its raw material yield is equivalent to a \$4.7 million decrease in operating costs. This gives a practical example of how organizations can use a financial control number, such as raw material yield, to make inferences about how well the underlying manufacturing operations are working.

Raw material productivity
The ratio of raw material in the finished product to the total quantity of raw material acquired.

Finally, many organizations in continuous process industries, such as paper manufacturing, monitor their machine productivity ratios (output per hour or per shift of machine time). Investment in the machine represents a huge fixed cost invested in capacity, and profitability depends on how well that capacity is used. Again, a measure like machine productivity provides organizations with an effective method to relate process results and financial results.

EXHIBIT 12-23

Dorchester Manufacturing
Balance Sheet

Cash	$ 1,000,000	Accounts payable	$ 2,000,000
Accounts receivable	5,000,000	Other liabilities	1,000,000
Inventory	7,000,000	Long-term debt	7,000,000
Plant and equipment (net)	27,000,000	Shareholders' equity	30,000,000
Total	$40,000,000	Total	$40,000,000

Assessing Return on Investment

USING RATIO TRENDS

Trend analysis and cross-sectional analysis provide useful insights for assessing return on investment. Consider the operations of Dorchester Manufacturing, which makes custom windows for the residential construction industry. Dorchester Manufacturing's most recent balance sheet and income statement appear in Exhibits 12-23 and 12-24.

The first decision to make when applying the return on investment approach to financial control is to determine how to define investment. This example measures investment as total assets employed net of accumulated depreciation. With this assumption, and using the previous equation for calculating ROI, we compute the return on investment for Dorchester Manufacturing as follows:

$$\text{Return on investment} = \frac{\text{Operating income}}{\text{Investment}} = \frac{\text{Operating income}}{\text{Sales}} \times \frac{\text{Sales}}{\text{Investment}}$$

$$= \frac{\$5{,}000{,}000}{\$40{,}000{,}000} = \frac{\$5{,}000{,}000}{\$90{,}000{,}000} \times \frac{\$90{,}000{,}000}{\$40{,}000{,}000}$$

$$= 0.0556 \times 2.25 = 12.5\%$$

EXHIBIT 12-24

Dorchester Manufacturing
Income Statement

Sales		$90,000,000
Less cost of goods sold:		
Materials and supplies	$25,000,000	
Labor	10,000,000	
Overhead	15,000,000	50,000,000
Gross margin		$40,000,000
Selling expenses	$20,000,000	
Administrative expenses	10,000,000	
Taxes	5,000,000	35,000,000
Net income		$5,000,000

TIME SERIES COMPARISONS

Dorchester Manufacturing earned a return of 12.5% on the net book value of its assets invested. This equals net income of 5.5% of sales multiplied by the 2.25% of sales to total assets ratio. It is possible to evaluate trends for these numbers and to compare them with data for other organizations, as shown in Exhibit 12-25. This form of financial benchmarking is common, since decomposing an ROI number into its components and evaluating the trend of these components and the performance of competitors provides additional insight about recent performance.

CROSS-SECTIONAL COMPARISONS

The top two lines of Exhibit 12-25 show that Dorchester Manufacturing is earning a lower return on investment than its competitor. The efficiency and productivity portions of the exhibit explain why. The middle portion of Exhibit 12-25 shows that the efficiency of operations (return on sales) at Dorchester Manufacturing is declining while the competitor's efficiency is improving continuously. The bottom portion of the exhibit shows that Dorchester's productivity (asset turnover) is also lower than its competitor's productivity.

It is possible to further examine the efficiency and turnover ratios by decomposing them into their individual components. Exhibit 12-26 summarizes the individual components of costs as a cumulative percent of sales for Dorchester Manufacturing and shows a comparison of these numbers to those of its best competitor.

The bar chart shows that for Dorchester Manufacturing, materials, labor, overhead, selling, and administrative costs are approximately 28%, 11%, 17%, 22%, and 11% of sales, respectively, and approximately 30%, 9%, 14%, 20%, and 8%,

EXHIBIT 12-25

Dorchester Manufacturing ROI Trends

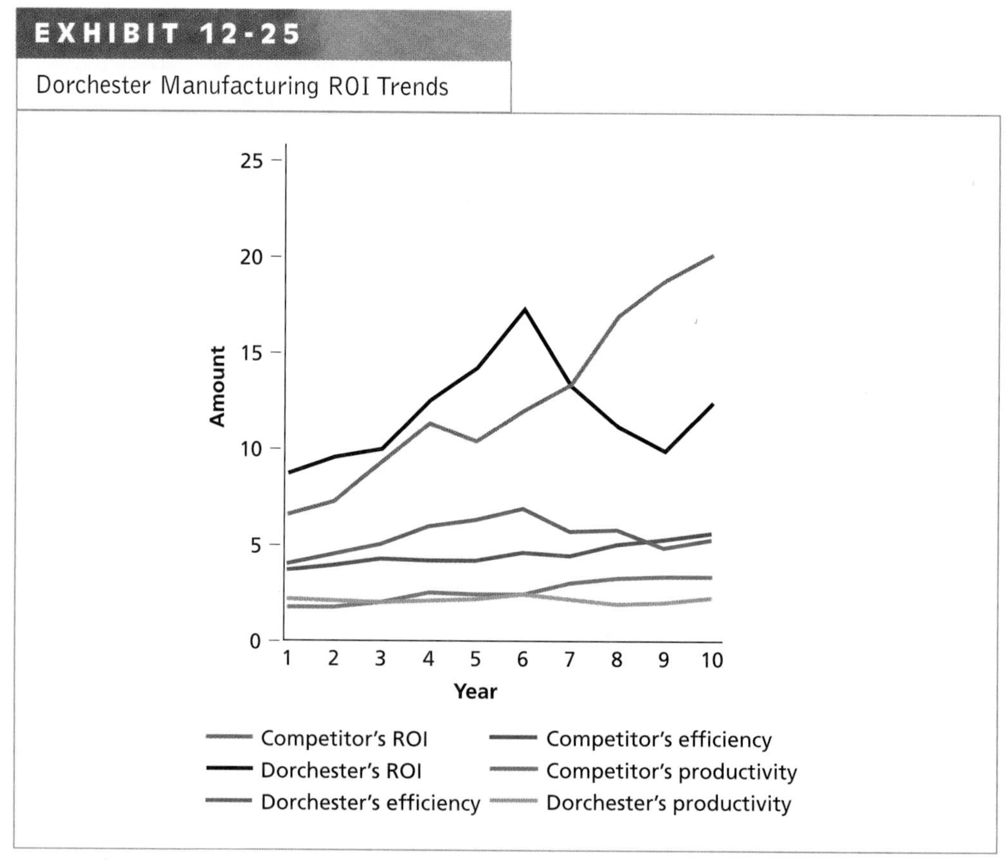

EXHIBIT 12-26

Dorchester Manufacturing Costs as a Cumulative Percent of Sales

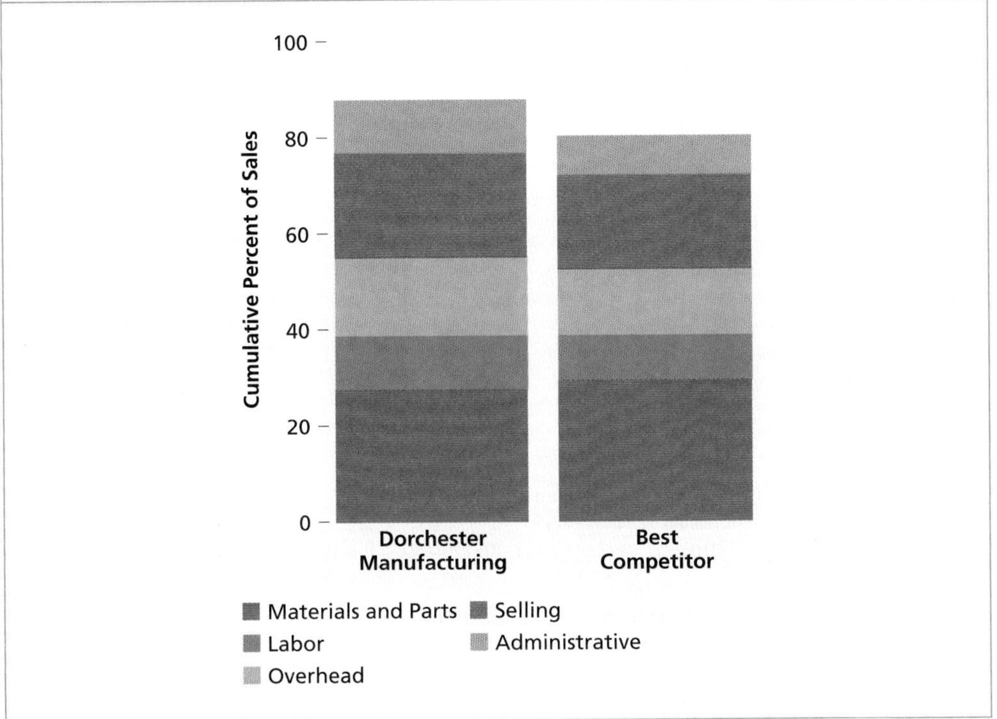

respectively, for the best competitor. These figures suggest that labor, overhead, selling, and administrative costs in total are too high at Dorchester Manufacturing relative to the competitor's costs, and that it may be advisable for Dorchester to conduct an investigation to determine why these differences exist.

Exhibit 12-27 summarizes the ratios of sales to assets, the productivity contribution to the return on investment, for individual asset accounts and compares these ratios with those of Dorchester's best competitor. It shows that the ratios of sales to cash and sales to inventory are, respectively, about 90 and 15 for Dorchester Manufacturing and about 100 and 55 for the best competitor. This comparison suggests that, given its level of sales, Dorchester Manufacturing holds too much cash and inventory compared with its competitor. Perhaps the competitor is using just-in-time production to reduce costs, reduce the investment in inventory, improve quality, and increase return on investment. This is an important manufacturing strategy that Dorchester Manufacturing can consider.

This discussion illustrates two important attributes of the Dupont method of financial control. First, these measures are most useful when evaluating trends and when comparing the numbers with those of the best competitor. Second, these comparisons neither identify the problem nor show how to solve it. Rather, they are signals suggesting where to look for a problem.

For most organizations, a major portion of the investment number used to compute return on investment is the commitment made for long-term capacity. Therefore, it is important to recognize that the return on investment criterion is an evaluation of the desirability of a long-term investment, rather than a measure of the short-term performance of the manager of a facility.

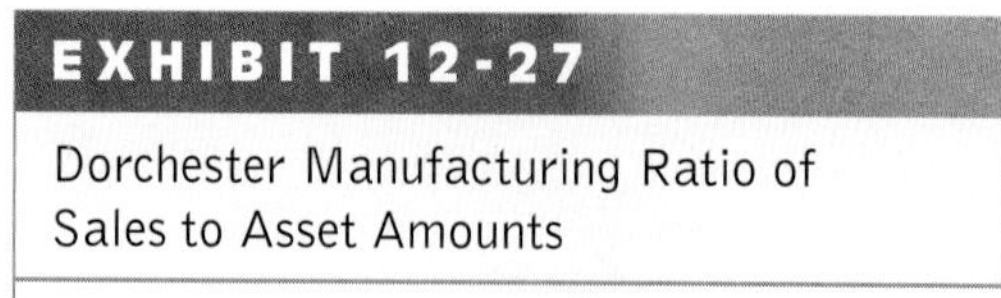

Dorchester Manufacturing Ratio of Sales to Asset Amounts

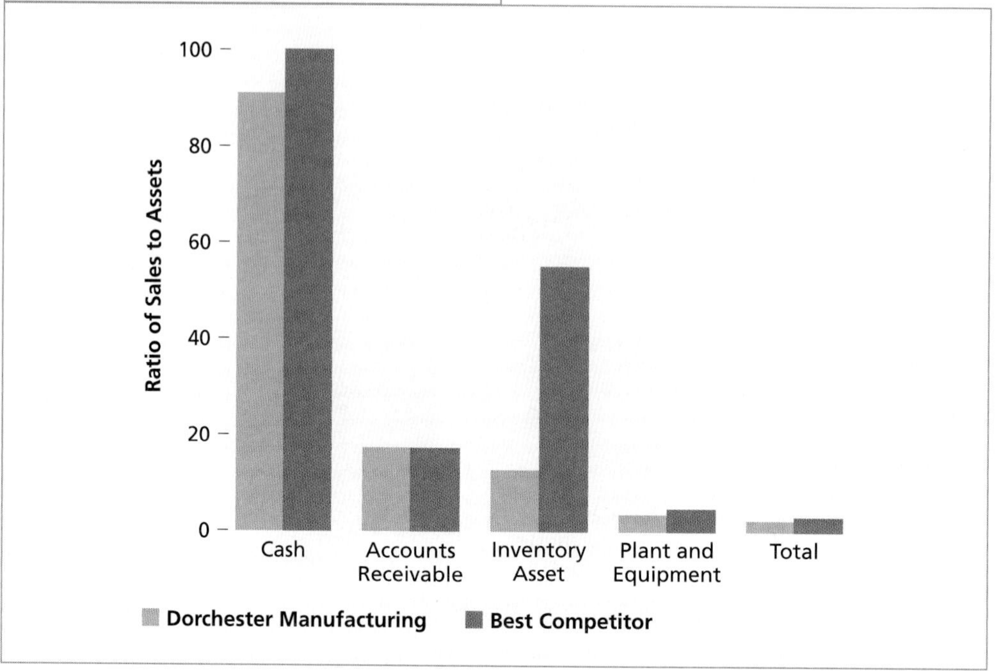

For example, consider the plight of a manager who is employed by an organization that owns a chain of fast-food restaurants. The manager has been asked to manage a restaurant located in an area that is turning from residential to commercial and industrial use. Because of the lack of a residential base to support sales, the restaurant faces declining sales prospects. As a result, the restaurant's return on investment will be low, indicating that it is a marginal investment and a candidate for liquidation if the property has other uses. A good manager may mitigate or slow the decline of ROI by organizing innovative promotions to attract business customers at lunchtime. In such a case, the manager may do an outstanding job given the circumstances, even while the restaurant shows a return on investment below the company's cost of capital.

To evaluate a manager's performance, we must compare actual performance with the performance potential inherent in the circumstances. The desirability of an investment is a different matter, however. An investment may be liquidated because of its declining potential even though a manager has been doing an outstanding job delaying the decline. Therefore, performance evaluation is relative to the potential and circumstances of the setting. The return on investment evaluation is relative to other investment opportunities.

QUESTIONING THE RETURN ON INVESTMENT APPROACH

Despite its popularity, return on investment has been criticized as a means of financial control. Some critics object to the sole use of any financial measures as being too narrow for effective control. They argue that the most effective approach to control is to monitor and assess the organization's critical success factors, such as quality, service, and employee skills and knowledge.

Others who accept the need for financial measures still find weaknesses with the return on investment measure. They observe that profit-seeking organizations should make investments in order of declining profitability until the marginal cost of capital of the last dollar invested equals the marginal return generated by that dollar. Unfortunately, financial control based on return on investment may not yield this result.

For example, consider a manager who is evaluated based on return on investment. Suppose that the current return on investment is 15% and the manager is contemplating an investment that is expected to return 12%. The manager would be motivated to decline this investment opportunity, because accepting it would lower the division's total return on investment and, thus, conflict with what is in the organization's best interests. For example, if the organization's cost of capital were only 10%, then the manager should accept the investment because its expected return exceeds the investment's cost of capital.

USING ECONOMIC VALUE ADDED

People have responded to this criticism of return on investment by creating a different investment criterion. Economic value added, previously called residual income, equals income less the economic cost of the investment used to generate that income. For example, if a division's income is $13.5 million and the division uses $100 million of capital, which has an average cost of 10%, the economic value added can be computed as follows:

$$\begin{aligned}\text{Economic value added} &= \text{Income} - \text{Cost of capital}\\ &= \$13{,}500{,}000 - (\$100{,}000{,}000 \times 10\%)\\ &= \$3{,}500{,}000\end{aligned}$$

Like return on investment, economic value added evaluates income relative to the level of investment required to earn that income. Unlike return on investment, however, economic value added does not motivate managers to turn down investments that are expected to earn more than their cost of capital. Under the economic value added criterion, managers are asked to do whatever they think is necessary to make

One purpose of using economic value added is to motivate managers to divest the organization of excess resources. (Richard Pasley/Stock, Boston)

IN PRACTICE

Economic Value Added at Coca-Cola

In the late 1980s Coca-Cola applied economic value added to its product lines. The analysis suggested that many of Coca-Cola's product lines were unprofitable. As a result, Coca-Cola decided to refocus its attention on its soft-drink business and eliminated investments in many other businesses, including pasta and wine.

economic value added as large as possible. For example, recall the previous situation in which the manager faced an investment opportunity with an expected return of 12% when the cost of capital was 10%. If the project requires an investment of $100 million, then the economic value added if the investment is made and the expected return is realized is $2 million [$100,000,000 × (12% − 10%)]. Therefore, if rewarded based on economic value added, the manager will accept this investment opportunity.

Organizations Adopt Economic Value Added for Different Reasons. SPX Corporation supplies specialty service tools and original equipment components to the automotive industry. In its 1995 annual report, SPX identified the following reasons for adopting shareholder value analysis:

SPX adopted EVA because it

treats the interests of shareholders and management the same, encouraging SPX people to think and act like owners

is easily understood and applied

fits into operational improvement efforts, because success requires continuous improvement of EVA

correlates closer to market value than any other operating performance measure

links directly to investor expectations through EVA improvement targets

focuses on long-term performance by using a bonus bank and predetermined improvement targets

provides a common language for performance measurement, decision support, compensation and communication

The notion of a bonus bank, mentioned in the sixth point above, is particularly interesting. In years when performance exceeds the economic value added target, two-thirds of all bonuses are set aside in a bonus bank that is carried forward and is only payable if the manager achieves economic value added targets in subsequent years. When performance falls below target, the bonus is negative and is deducted from the bonus bank. The bonus bank turns what is nominally a short-run performance measure and reward into a longer run measure.

It is possible to compute the economic value added for every major product or product line to evaluate a product line's contribution to creating shareholder wealth. Recently, economic value added has been extended to adjust GAAP income to correct for the conservative approach that GAAP uses to determine income and value assets.

For example, GAAP requires the immediate expensing of research and development costs; yet, when shareholder value analysis income is computed, research and

IN PRACTICE

Trade Loading at R. J. Reynolds

Although most organizations recognize the cost savings that come with eliminating trade loading, many hesitate to eliminate the practice because sales, and therefore profits, will be depressed while waiting for the glut of inventory to be cleared from the system. For example, R. J. Reynolds saw earnings fall $360 million in the year after it eliminated trade loading because production and sales were curtailed while billions of cigarettes were eliminated from the distribution system. Eliminating the excess inventory is now saving R. J. Reynolds about $50 million a year in inventory-holding costs. Meanwhile, Philip Morris, one of R. J. Reynolds' main competitors, continues to trade load.

development costs are capitalized and expensed over a certain time period, such as five years. The intent of the adjustments prescribed to compute shareholder-value-added income from GAAP income is to develop an income number that better reflects the organization's long-run earnings potential.

Organizations are beginning to use economic value added to identify products or product lines that are not contributing their share to organization return, given the level of investment they require. These organizations have used activity-based costing analysis to assign assets and costs to individual products, services, or customers. This allows them to calculate the economic value added by product, product line, or customer.

Organizations can also use economic value added to evaluate operating strategies. Quaker Oats Company, a food manufacturer, used economic value added to support its decision in June 1992 to cease trade loading, which is the food industry's practice of using promotions to obtain orders for two or three months' supply of food from customers. Trade loading produces quarterly peaks in production and sales that, in turn, require huge investments in assets, including the inventory itself, warehouses, and distribution centers. Through higher prices, customers pay the costs of the higher inventory levels created by this cyclical pattern of inventory. An article in *Fortune* estimated that trade loading is primarily responsible for the $75 to $100 billion in groceries that are always in transit between manufacturers and consumers, and that supporting this inventory "adds some $20 billion to the $400 billion that U.S. consumers annually spend on groceries.[2]

Quaker Oats' economic value added analysis suggests that even though sales levels may be reduced by the elimination of price reductions associated with trade loading, it is more profitable for the company and its trading partners to forego the large inventories and the required warehouse space. Also, to produce food at even levels rather than in peaks reduces the level of production capacity needed. Quaker Oats motivates managers to end trade loading by basing bonuses on efficiency and cycle times rather than on annual sales.

A measure of the increasing importance of economic value added in organizations is the seniority of people who are usually appointed to manage economic value added implementation projects in organizations. For example, in 1995, Olin Corporation's new president and chief executive officer was heading the company's economic value added steering team at the time of his appointment.

[2] Patricia Sellers, "The Dumbest Marketing Ploy," *Fortune*, October 5, 1992, pp. 88–94.

IN PRACTICE

Financial Versus Operations Control

Consider the following statement by Tom Peters, the management consultant, expressing his views on the efficacy of financial control. This is an articulate presentation of the case some people advance against financial control.

"What do you think of EVA as a barometer of business performance?" asked a participant at a recent seminar in the Netherlands. "Not much," I replied. I'm no expert on the pluses and minuses of Economic Value Added. I admitted as much, and then confessed that neither was I that keen on earnings per share or return on investment.

Sure, I understand the importance of profitability, in my business as well as in others', and debate over various measures has merit. It is just that they mostly put the cart before the horse.

The horse is what you make. The financial measure—important as that is—is a derivative of the goodness and acceptance of the product.

Source: Tom Peters, "Legacies With Value Added," *The Independent,* February 5, 1995, p. 10.

The results of economic value added suggest interesting insights into financial control applied at all levels of the organization. However, they should be treated with caution. Like return on investment calculations, economic value added analysis requires complex and potentially problematic allocations of assets, revenues, and costs to divisions, product lines, products, or customers, depending on the focus of the analysis, in order to be an effective motivational and evaluation tool. However, many organizations believe that these problems can be solved and that the insights provided by economic value added analysis are well worth the effort.[3]

The Efficacy of Financial Control

Although financial control is widely practiced, many people have questioned its true insights and effectiveness. Critics have argued that financial information is delayed—and highly aggregated—information about how well the organization is doing in meeting its commitments to its shareowners, and that this information measures neither the drivers of the financial results nor how well the organization is doing in meeting its stakeholders' requirements, a leading indicator of future financial performance.

Financial control may be an ineffective control scorecard for three reasons:

1. First, it focuses on financial measures that do not measure the organization's other important attributes, such as product quality, the speed at which the organization develops and makes products, customer service, the ability to provide a work environment that motivates employees, and the degree to which the organization meets its legal and social obligations to society. Because these elements and others are important to the organization's long-term success, they also deserve to be measured and monitored. The argument is that financial control measures only the aggregated results of how the organization achieved its target financial performance. This limitation of financial control led to the development of the balanced scorecard, which we mentioned briefly in Chapter 1 and in more detail in Chapter 10. Recall that the balanced scorecard uses a range of nonfinancial measures of performance in the area of customer requirements, process characteristics, and learning

[3] The December 11, 1995 issue of *Fortune* magazine included several articles describing the nature of economic value added analysis and named some of the organizations where it has been applied. Included among the avid users of economic value added analysis are AT&T, Eli Lilly, Georgia-Pacific, and Tenneco.

and growth to both explain and predict financial results. Therefore, the balanced scorecard provides a means of managing financial results, which is something not possible when the organization focuses exclusively on financial results since these are an aggregate measure of what happened, not why it happened.

2. Financial control measures the financial effect of the overall level of performance achieved on the critical success factors, and it ignores the performance achieved on the individual critical success factors. For this reason, many people believe that financial control does not suggest how to improve performance on the critical success factors or on financial performance. Critics argue that, at best, financial results only act as a broad signal of how well the organization manages the tasks that create success on the critical success factors that, in turn, create financial returns. The argument is that effective control begins with measuring and managing the elements or processes that create financial returns, rather than measuring the financial returns themselves. The balanced scorecard addresses this problem, as discussed in Chapter 10, by focusing on both financial results (such as return on investment), and measures of process performance (such as employee skills, knowledge, and satisfaction; customer satisfaction; cycle times; the rate of process improvement and innovation; and quality) that create the financial results.

3. Financial control is usually oriented to short-term profit performance. It seldom focuses on long-term improvement or trend analysis but instead considers how well the organization, or one of its responsibility centers, has performed this quarter or this year. This is the result of the misuse of financial control rather than an inherent fault of financial control itself. The preoccupation with short-term financial results is debilitating, however. It motivates an atmosphere of managing short-term financial results that provides disincentives for the types of management and employee initiatives that promote long-term success, particularly in the area of investing in training, equipment, and process changes. One major reason given for taking public organizations private is to provide senior management with the opportunity to manage for long-term results rather than being forced into inappropriate concerns with short-term performance caused by financial analysts who have that preoccupation.

In summary, how should we interpret these facets of financial control? Financial control is an important tool in the process of control. If used properly financial results provide crucial help in assessing the organization's long-term viability and in identifying processes that need improvement. It is a tool to be supported by other tools since it is only a summary of performance.

Financial control does not try to measure other facets of performance that may be critical to the organization's stakeholders and vital to the organization's long-term success. It can, however, provide an overall assessment of whether the organization's strategies and decisions are providing acceptable financial returns. Organizations can also use financial control to compare one unit's results with another. This financial benchmarking signal indicates whether the organization's operations control systems, which seek to monitor, assess, and improve performance on the critical success factors, are operating well enough to deliver the desired financial results.

FINANCIAL CONTROL REMEDIES AT GEORGIA TECH

In response to its financial crisis brought on by the increasing costs of athletic programs, Georgia Tech implemented what it called its responsibility center approach (RCA), which focuses on computing a cost per sport. The preliminary analysis looked at four sports: football, basketball, baseball, and track. All other sports were combined into a fifth category. In effect, five responsibility centers were created.

EXHIBIT 12-28

Georgia Tech Responsibility Center Approach

	FOOTBALL	BASKETBALL	BASEBALL	TRACK	OTHERS	TOTAL
Revenues	$5,278,970	$4,070,519	$526,858	$254,940	$1,303,174	$11,434,461
Direct expenses	4,111,908	1,800,892	426,662	317,854	1,221,638	7,878,954
Contribution margin	$1,167,062	$2,269,627	$100,196	−$ 62,914	$ 81,536	$ 3,555,507
Allocated costs	1,975,390	723,915	241,522	163,224	782,474	3,886,525
Segment margin	−$ 808,328	$1,545,712	−$141,326	−$226,138	−$ 700,938	−$ 331,018

Exhibit 12-28 summarizes the results of the analysis that assigned revenues, direct costs, and indirect costs to these five responsibility centers.

Georgia Tech invested considerable effort in identifying both the direct and indirect costs associated with each responsibility center so that its entire cost could be identified. Indirect costs created a particular challenge, however, because they were currently buried in general university overhead. These costs had to be identified, along with a suitable and acceptable basis for allocating them to the individual responsibility centers.

The analysis revealed that all sports, with the exception of basketball, were a net drain on the university's resources and that, in total, the net cost of the varsity sports to the university was about $750,000.

Most important was the insight provided by the RCA at Georgia Tech and how it improved decision making related to varsity sports. First, the RCA created a basis for both accountability and fiscal responsibility, which was vested in the various coaches. It also provided both an incentive and a basis for program administrators to focus on and manage the costs and revenues associated with the program for which they were responsible. Second, it provided the basis for cost control by requiring that any proposals that would increase costs be accompanied by a proposal to increase revenues to cover those projected cost increases.

SUMMARY

We began this chapter by reviewing the motivation that drives organizations to decentralize decision-making responsibility. Decentralized decision makers create the need for control, and one approach to control is financial control.

The foundation of financial control is the concept of a responsibility center, an organization unit assigned with the responsibility to achieve specified financial results. Organizations classify and evaluate their responsibility based on the presumed control that their members exercise over cost, revenues, profits, and return on investment.

A major tool used in financial control is the segment margin report, which computes responsibility center profit. The segment margin provides insights into the financial contribution or loss attributable to a particular responsibility center. Because of the assumptions that underlie this report, particularly relating to cost and revenue allocations, its calculation must be carefully done and should include an understanding of the potential for distortion caused by any arbitrary allocations used to compute the responsibility center's profits.

Transfer pricing is an important tool used to allocate revenues to responsibility centers. Transfer prices can be based on market prices, costs, or negotiation, or they can be set administratively.

Return on investment is a widely used tool in financial control and, when used properly, can provide insights into the profitability of invested assets. Economic value added is an alternative to financial control that overcomes some problems associated with the return on investment criterion.

In summary, the chapter argues that financial control is an important component of control to use with other control tools that monitor and assess the organization's performance on its critical success factors.

KEY TERMS

Centralized responsibility, 517
Controllability principle, 529
Cost centers, 522
Decentralized responsibility, 517
Financial control, 519
First-level variances, 510
Flexible budget, 511
Flexible budget variances, 512
Investment centers, 529
Operations control, 519
Planning variances, 511
Profit centers, 528
Raw material productivity, 544
Responsibility center, 520
Revenue centers, 527
Second-level variances, 513
Transfer pricing, 535
Variance analysis, 508

ASSIGNMENT MATERIALS

QUESTIONS

12-1 What does financial control mean? (LO 1)

12-2 How does analysis of reasons for variances between actual and estimated costs help managers? (LO 1)

12-3 What is a flexible budget? (LO 1)

12-4 How are first, second, and third levels of variance analysis related? (LO 1)

12-5 Why is it useful to decompose a flexible budget variance into a price variance and an efficiency (use) variance? (LO 1)

12-6 "If more experienced workers work on the job than planned in developing the labor standards, the labor efficiency variance is likely to be favorable but the labor wage variance is likely to be unfavorable." Do you agree with this statement? Explain. (LO 1)

12-7 What effect will the purchase and use of cheaper, lower-quality materials likely have on price and use components of both materials and labor variances? (LO 1)

12-8 What is decentralization? (LO 2)

12-9 What does control mean in a decentralized organization? (LO 2)

12-10 What is a responsibility center? (LO 2)

12-11 What is a cost center? (LO 3, 4)

12-12 What is the assigned responsibility in a revenue center? (LO 3, 4)

12-13 When do organizations use profit centers? (LO 3, 4)

12-14 What is an investment center? (LO 3, 4)

12-15 What does the controllability principle require? (LO 5)

12-16 How do responsibility centers interact? (LO 5)

12-17 What does segment margin mean? (LO 5)

12-18 What is a soft number in accounting? (LO 5)

12-19 What is a transfer price? (LO 6)

12-20 What are the four bases for setting a transfer price? (LO 6)

12-21 Why do organizations allocate revenues to responsibility centers? (LO 3, 6)

12-22 Why do organizations allocate costs to responsibility centers? (LO 3, 6)

12-23 What is return on investment? (LO 7)

12-24 How does efficiency (the ratio of operating income to sales) affect return on investment? (LO 7)

12-25 How does productivity (the ratio of sales to investment) affect return on investment? (LO 7)

12-26 What does economic value added mean? (LO 7)

12-27 What are three reasons financial control alone may provide an ineffective control scorecard? (LO 8)

EXERCISES

LO 1 **12-28** ***Variance analysis, material, and labor*** The following information is available for job K37 for Mandalay Company:

Actual

Materials:	10,500 pounds purchased at $2.50 per pound
Direct labor:	1800 hours at $12 per hour
Units produced:	500

Standard

Materials:	20 pounds per unit at a price of $2.20 per pound
Direct labor:	4 hours per unit at a wage rate of $10 per hour

(a) Determine the material price variance and use variance.

(b) Determine the direct labor rate variance and efficiency variance.

LO 1 **12-29** ***Variance analysis, material, and labor*** Pharout Company uses a standard cost system. Job 822 is for the manufacture of 500 units of the product P521. The company's standards for one unit of product P521 are as follows:

	QUANTITY	PRICE
Direct material	5 oz	$2 per oz
Direct labor	2 hr	$10 per hr

The job requires 2800 ounces of raw material costing $5880. An unfavorable labor rate variance of $250 and a favorable labor efficiency variance of $100 also were determined for this job.

(a) Determine the direct material price variance.

(b) Determine the direct material use variance.

(c) Determine the actual quantity of direct labor hours used on job 822.

(d) Determine the actual labor costs incurred for job 822.

LO 1 **12-30** ***Variance analysis, material, and labor*** Each unit of job Y703 has standard requirements of 5 pounds of raw material at a price of $100 per pound and 0.5 hour of direct labor at $12 per hour. To produce 9000 units of this product, job Y703 actually required 40,000 pounds of the raw material costing $97 per pound. The job used a total of 5000 direct labor hours costing a total of $60,000.

(a) Determine the material price and use variances.

(b) Assume that the materials used on this job were purchased from a new supplier. Would you recommend continuing with this new supplier? Why or why not?

(c) Determine the direct labor rate and efficiency variances.

LO 1 **12-31** ***Standard costs versus actual costs for materials*** Assembly of product P13 requires one unit of component X, two units of component Y, and three units of component Z. Job J372 produced 220 units of P13. The following information pertains to material variances for this job, analyzed by component:

	X	Y	Z
Price variance	160 U	120 F	192 U
Use variance	168 U	100 U	84 F

The actual prices were $0.30 more, $0.20 less, and $0.50 more per unit for components X, Y, and Z, respectively, than their standard prices.

(a) Determine the number of units consumed of each component.

(b) Determine the standard price per unit of each component.

12-32 ***Master and flexible budgets*** An organization plans to make a product in batches of 25,000 units. Planned production is 1,000,000 units, and actual production is 1,125,000 units. What are the planned (master budget) number of batches and the flexible budget number of batches? LO 1, 4

12-33 ***Issues in decentralization*** What control problem does decentralization create in organizations? LO 2

12-34 ***University responsibility centers*** Give an example of a responsibility center in a university. LO 2

12-35 ***Controllability*** Based on your understanding, which of the following—costs, revenues, profits, and investment—does the manager of a cinema control? LO 3, 4

12-36 ***Cost centers*** Give an example of a responsibility center that is properly treated as a cost center. LO 3, 4

12-37 ***Revenue centers*** Give an example of a responsibility center that is properly treated as a revenue center. LO 3, 4

12-38 ***Investment centers*** Based on your understanding of how they are managed, would you agree or disagree that an outlet of a large department store chain should be treated as an investment center? What about the maintenance department within that outlet? What about a single department within the store? LO 3, 4

12-39 ***Multinational companies and investment centers*** Many multinational companies create wholly owned subsidiaries to do business in the countries or regions where they operate. Are these wholly owned subsidiaries examples of investment centers? Explain. LO 3, 4

12-40 ***Computing division income*** A home services company offers renovations, heating, air conditioning, and plumbing services to its customers. Imagine that you are in the process of computing the income for the renovations division. What problems may you encounter in computing this income? LO 3, 4, 5

12-41 ***Controllability and evaluation*** Suppose that you are the manager of a fitness center that is one of many in a chain. Give one example of a cost that you control and one example of cost that you do not control. Why is it important to distinguish between costs that are controllable and costs that are not controllable in this setting? LO 4, 5

12-42 ***Responsibility centers*** Identify three responsibility centers in a fast-food restaurant and explain how they may interact. LO 4, 5

12-43 ***Controllability and motivation*** Give an example of a situation when invoking the controllability principle would have a desirable motivational effect and an example of a situation when suspending the controllability principle would have a desirable motivational effect. LO 5

LO 6 **12-44** ***Domestic and international transfer pricing*** Organizations might desire to use one transfer pricing system designed to support international transfer pricing and another domestic transfer pricing system designed to achieve motivational objectives. Give a reason why you think that organizations would not use two transfer pricing systems—one for international tax purposes and one for motivational purposes.

LO 6 **12-45** ***Choosing transfer prices*** How might a transfer price be chosen for logs in an organization that cuts down trees and processes the logs in a sawmill to make lumber or in a pulp mill to make paper?

LO 6 **12-46** ***Choosing transfer prices*** In a fishing products company, the harvesting division catches and delivers the fish to the processing division that, in turn, delivers the processed fish to the selling division to sell to customers. How can you determine the appropriate transfer price between harvesting and processing and between processing and selling?

LO 6 **12-47** ***Using market-based transfer prices*** What is the main advantage and the main obstacle in using market-based transfer prices?

LO 6 **12-48** ***Soft numbers*** Why did accountants develop the expression "soft number"?

LO 3, 6 **12-49** ***Allocating costs*** A store is divided into four departments: automotive products, home products, paint, and lumber. How would you assign the building costs such as depreciation to each of these departments?

LO 7 **12-50** ***Return on investment*** A business reports an income of $1 million. How would you compute the return on investment for this business?

LO 7 **12-51** ***Characteristic financial ratios*** All organizations face a requirement to earn at least a minimum-level return on investment. Some businesses rely on high ratios of income to sales; other businesses rely on high ratios of sales to investment. Give an example of each of these types of businesses and explain what this characteristic implies about the business.

LO 7 **12-52** ***Productivity ratio*** Give an example of why using units rather than the value of the products produced in the numerator of a productivity ratio may give a misleading picture of the process that produced that output.

LO 7 **12-53** ***Computing economic value added*** A business whose investors require a return on investment of 8% after taxes reports an after-tax income of $1 million on an investment of $20 million. What is the economic value added for this business?

LO 7 **12-54** ***Economic value added in a multiproduct company*** Based on an analysis of operations, a company making sporting goods has determined that the income provided by its golf, ski, tennis, and football product lines are $3.5 million, $7.8 million, $2.6 million, and $1.7 million, respectively. The accountant believes that the investment levels in these product lines are $35 million, $50 million, $45 million, and $23 million, respectively. Use an economic value added analysis to evaluate the performance of each of these product lines, assuming that the organization requires a 10% return on investment.

LO 8 **12-55** ***Single ratio values*** Give an example of why looking at a single value of a financial ratio may give either a misleading or a meaningless result.

PROBLEMS

LO 1 **12-56** ***Variance analysis*** The Sudbury, South Carolina, plant of Saldanha Sports Company has the following standards for its soccer ball production.

Standards

Material (leather) per soccer ball	0.25 yard
Material price per yard	$16
Direct labor hours per soccer ball	0.20 hour
Wage rate per direct labor hour	$10 per hour
Flexible support cost rate	$15 per direct labor hour

Actual Results for October

Used 13,000 yards of raw material, purchased for $205,150
Paid for 8240 direct labor hours at $9.50 per hour
Incurred $131,840 of flexible support costs
Manufactured 40,000 soccer balls

REQUIRED

Determine the following variances for October:

(a) Total direct material cost variance

(b) Total direct labor cost variance

(c) Total flexible support cost variance

(d) Direct material price variance

(e) Direct material use variance

(f) Direct labor rate variance

(g) Direct labor efficiency variance

(h) Flexible support rate variance

(i) Flexible support efficiency (use) variance

12-57 ***Variance analysis*** The Milwaukee, Wisconsin, plant of Englehart Electronics Company has the following standards for component C93: LO 1

Standards

Material	2 units of material B
Material price	$10 per unit of B
Direct labor	1 hour
Wage rate	$10 per direct labor hour
Flexible support cost rate	$25 per direct labor hour

Actual Results for May

Used 4200 units of B, purchased at $9.75 per unit of B
Paid for 2000 direct labor hours at $11 per hour
Incurred $48,000 of flexible support costs
Manufactured 2000 units of component C93

REQUIRED

Determine the following variances for May:

(a) Total direct material cost variance

(b) Total direct labor cost variance

(c) Total flexible support cost variance

(d) Direct material price variance

(e) Direct material use variance

(f) Direct labor rate variance

(g) Direct labor efficiency variance

(h) Flexible support rate variance

(i) Flexible support efficiency (use) variance

LO 1 **12-58** ***Standard versus actual costs*** For each of the following two jobs manufacturing two different products, determine the missing amounts for items (a) through (h).

ITEM	JOB 321	JOB 322
Units produced	200	(e)
Standards per unit		
Material quantity	5 lb	(f)
Material price	$2 per lb	$3 per lb
Labor hours	2 hr	3 hr
Labor rate	$15 per hr	$12 per hr
Actual consumption		
Material quantity	(a)	1000 lb
Material cost	$2000	(g)
Labor hours	(b)	(h)
Labor cost	(c)	$5800
Variance		
Material use	(d)	$100 F
Material price	$ 50 U	$500 F
Labor hour	$100 F	$ 50 U
Labor rate	$ 60 U	$200 F

LO 1, 3 **12-59** ***Computing flexible budget variables*** For Moncton Carpet Products, analyze the flexible budget variances for products 2, 3, and 4 using an analysis similar to that used for product 1 in the text on pages 524–526.

LO 1, 8 **12-60** ***Variances and motivation*** Discuss the possible effect on human behavior of a preoccupation with variances in financial control.

LO 2, 3, 4 **12-61** ***Choosing responsibility center type*** For each of the following units, identify whether the most appropriate responsibility center form is a cost center, a profit center, or an investment center and why you have made that choice.

(a) A laboratory in a hospital

(b) A restaurant in a department store

(c) The computer services group in an insurance company

(d) A maintenance department in a factory

(e) A customer service department in a mail-order company

(f) A warehouse used to store goods for distribution in a large city

(g) A publishing company acquired by a diversified corporation.

LO 3, 6 **12-62** ***Allocating common costs to cost centers*** You have decided to divide a factory into cost centers. How would you allocate depreciation expense on the factory building to its individual cost centers?

LO 5 **12-63** ***Implementing the controllability principle*** One of the most widely accepted and longest held beliefs is the controllability principle, which says that organization units and people should be held accountable only for things that they can control.

REQUIRED

(a) For any job you choose, give one example of something you should be expected to control and one example of something that you should not be expected to control.

(b) Can you think of an example in which making yourself responsible for something that you cannot control would promote a desirable activity?

12-64 ***Segment margins*** Information on Aragon Company's three product lines is provided below. LO 5

	PRODUCT LINE		
	1	2	3
Revenue	$7,160,000	$1,900,000	$4,200,000
Variable cost percentage of sales	60%	50%	40%
Other costs	$ 859,200	$ 237,500	$ 693,000
Allocated avoidable costs	$ 349,000	$ 156,000	$ 698,000

REQUIRED

Construct a segment margin statement for Aragon Company. Use the segment margin statement to explain why the segment margins reported for an organization unit must be interpreted carefully.

12-65 ***Transfer prices and division autonomy*** You are a government controller. A division manager being audited objects to the transfer price he is being charged by the audit group for the audit services. The manager observes, "If I have to pay for these services, I should be allowed to buy them from an outside supplier who is prepared to offer them to me at a lower price." You have been asked to mediate this dispute. What would you do? LO 6

12-66 ***Transfer pricing and outside opportunities*** Deseronto Electronics manufactures motherboards for computers. The company is divided into two divisions—manufacturing and programming. The manufacturing division makes the board and the programming division makes the adjustments required to meet the customer's specifications. LO 6

The average total cost per unit of the boards in the manufacturing division is about $450 and the average total cost per board incurred in the programming division is about $100. The average selling price of the boards is $700. The company is now operating at capacity and increasing the volume of production is not a feasible alternative.

In the past the managers of the two divisions have negotiated a transfer price. The average transfer price has been about $500, resulting in the manufacturing division recognizing a profit of about $50 per board and the programming division recognizing a profit of about $100 per board. Each of the managers receives a bonus that is proportional to the profit reported by his or her division.

Karen Barton, the manager of the manufacturing division, has announced that she is no longer willing to supply boards to the programming division. Sam Draper, the senior purchasing executive for Koala Electronics, a computer manufacturer, has indicated that he is willing to purchase, at $650 per unit, all the boards that Karen's division can supply and is willing to sign a long-term contract to that effect. Karen indicated that she offered the boards to the programming division at $625 per board on the grounds that selling and distribution costs would be reduced by selling inside. Neil Wilson, the manager of the programming division, refused the offer on the grounds that the programming division would show a loss at this transfer price.

Neil has appealed Karen's intention to Shannon McDonald, the general manager, arguing that Karen should be prohibited from selling outside. Neil has indicated that a preliminary investigation suggests that he cannot buy these boards for less than about $640 outside. Therefore, allowing Karen to sell outside would effectively doom Neil's division.

REQUIRED

(a) What transfer price would you recommend? Why?

(b) What recommendations do you have for the programming division?

LO 7 **12-67** ***Return on investment and economic value added*** The Newburg Flyers operate a major sports franchise from a building in downtown Newburg. The building was built in 1940 at a cost of $5,000,000 and is fully depreciated so that it is shown on the company's balance sheet at a nominal value of $1. The land upon which the building was built in 1940 was purchased in 1935 for $10,000 and is valued at this amount for balance sheet purposes. The franchise, which is the company's only other major investment, cost $100,000 in 1940.

The current assessed value of the building is $200,000. The assessed value of the land, which is located in a prime urban area, is $20,000,000 and reflects the net value of the property if the current building is demolished and replaced with an office and shopping complex. The current value of the franchise, assuming that the league owners would approve a franchise sale, is $50,000,000.

REQUIRED

(a) If the team earns approximately $3,000,000 per year, what is the return on investment? (Ignore taxes in this calculation.)

(b) If the team earns approximately $3,000,000 per year, what is the economic value added? Assume that the organization's cost of capital is 15%. (Ignore taxes in this calculation.)

LO 7 **12-68** ***Problems in computing economic value added*** A bank is thinking of using economic value added analysis to identify services that require improvement or elimination. What problems may the bank have in computing the economic value added of any of the services that it offers to its customers?

LO 7 **12-69** ***Evaluating the potential of economic value added*** The owner of a chain of fast-food restaurants has decided to use economic value added to evaluate the performance of the managers of each of the restaurants. What do you think of this idea?

LO 7 **12-70** ***Using economic value added*** As a result of an economic value added analysis, the owner of a company that makes and installs swimming pools has decided to shut down the manufacturing operations which show a negative economic value added for the current year. Is this necessarily the proper response to this information?

LO 7 **12-71** ***Conflicting organization and individual objectives*** Strathcona Paper rewards its managers based on the return on investment of the assets that they manage—the higher the reported return on investment, the higher the reward. The company uses net book value to value the assets employed in the return on investment calculation. The company's cost of capital is assessed as 12% after taxes. The organization's tax rate is 35%.

The manager of the Logistics Division is faced with an opportunity to replace an aging truck fleet. The current net income after taxes of the logistics division is $7 million and the current investment base is valued at $50 million. The current net income after taxes and the current investment base, absent any investment in new trucks, are expected to remain at their existing levels.

The investment opportunity would replace the existing fleet of trucks, which have a net book value of about $100,000, with new trucks costing about $50 million net of the trade in allowance for the old trucks. If kept, the old trucks would last another five years and would have no salvage value. The new trucks would last five years, have zero salvage value, and increase cash flow relative to keeping the old trucks (through increased revenues and decreased operating costs) by about $16 million per year. If purchased, the new trucks would be depreciated for both accounting and tax purposes on a straight-line basis.

REQUIRED

(a) From the point of view of the company, should this investment be made? Support your conclusion with relevant calculations.

(b) From the point of view of the manager, should this investment be made?

(c) If the manager was rewarded based on economic value added, would the manager want to make the investment? Show why or why not.

12-72 ***Strategy and control*** Many people believe that in a successful organization the focus of control reflects the strategic initiatives in the organization. For each of the following organizations, identify what you think are the three most important items assessed by the organization's financial control system and why each is important. For each organization, what critical information is not assessed by the financial control system? LO 1, 3, 4, 8

(a) A company selling cable television services to its subscribers

(b) A symphony orchestra

(c) An organization selling canned soup

(d) A government agency responsible for finding jobs for its clients

(e) An auditing firm

(f) A company selling high-fashion clothing

12-73 ***Variance analysis, material, and labor*** Trieste Toy Company manufactures only one product, called Robot Ranger. The company uses a standard cost system and has established the following standards per unit of Robot Ranger. LO 1

	STANDARD QUANTITY	STANDARD PRICE	STANDARD COST
Direct materials	3.0 pounds	$12 per pound	$36.00
Direct labor	1.2 hours	15 per hour	18.00
			$54.00

During November, the following activity was recorded by the company for the production of Robot Ranger.

(1) The company produced 6000 units during the month.

(2) A total of 21,000 pounds of material were used, purchased at a cost of $241,500.

(3) The company employs 40 persons to work on the production of Robot Ranger. During November, each worked an average of 160 hours at an average rate of $16 per hour.

The company's management wishes to determine the efficiency of the activities related to the production of Robot Ranger.

REQUIRED

(a) For direct materials used in the product of Robot Ranger:
Compute the direct material price variance and the direct material use variance.

(b) The direct materials were purchased from a new supplier who is eager to enter into a long-term purchase contract. Would you recommend that Trieste sign the contract? Explain.

(c) For direct labor employed in the production of Robot Ranger: Compute the direct labor rate variance and the direct labor efficiency variance.

(d) In the past, the 40 persons employed in the production of Robot Ranger consisted of 16 experienced workers and 24 inexperienced assistants. During November, the company experimented with 20 experienced workers and 20 inexperienced assistants. Would you recommend that Trieste continue the new labor mix? Explain.

LO 1 **12-74** ***Variance analysis, hospital*** (Adapted from CMA, June 1989) Mountain View Hospital has adopted a standard cost accounting system for evaluation and control of nursing labor. Diagnosis related groups (DRGs), instituted by the U.S. government for health insurance reimbursement, are used as the output measure in the standard cost system. A DRG is a patient classification scheme that perceives hospitals to be multiproduct firms where inpatient treatment procedures are related to the numbers and types of patient ailments treated. Mountain View Hospital has developed standard nursing times for the treatment of each DRG classification, and nursing labor hours are assumed to vary with the number of DRGs treated within a time period.

The nursing unit on the fourth floor treats patients with four DRG classifications. The unit is staffed with registered nurses (RNs), licensed practical nurses (LPNs), and aides. The standard nursing hours and salary rates are as follows.

	FOURTH FLOOR NURSING UNIT STANDARD HOURS		
DRG CLASSIFICATION	**RN**	**LPN**	**AIDE**
1	6	4	5
2	26	16	10
3	10	5	4
4	12	7	10

STANDARD HOURLY RATES	
RN	$12
LPN	8
Aide	6

The results of operations for the fourth floor nursing unit for the month of May appear below.

ACTUAL NUMBER OF PATIENTS	
DRG 1	250
DRG 2	90
DRG 3	240
DRG 4	140
	720

	RN	**LPN**	**AIDE**
Actual hours	8,150	4,300	4,400
Actual salary	$100,245	$35,260	$25,300
Actual hourly rate	$12.30	$8.20	$5.75

The accountant for Mountain View Hospital calculated the following standard times for the fourth floor nursing unit for May.

DRG CLASSIFICATION	NO. OF PATIENTS	STANDARD HOURS/DRG			TOTAL STANDARD HOURS		
		RN	LPN	AIDE	RN	LPN	AIDE
1	250	6	4	5	1500	1000	1250
2	90	26	16	10	2340	1440	900
3	240	10	5	4	2400	1200	960
4	140	12	7	10	1680	980	1400
					7920	4620	4510

The hospital calculates labor variances for each reporting period by labor classification (RN, LPN, Aide). The variances are used by nursing supervisors and hospital administration to evaluate the performance of nursing labor.

REQUIRED

Calculate the total nursing labor variance for the fourth floor nursing unit of Mountain View Hospital for May, indicating how much of this variance is attributed to the following for each class of nurses:

(a) Labor efficiency

(b) Rate differences

12-75 ***Variance analysis*** Asahi USA, Inc. is a Denver, Colorado, based subsidiary of a Japanese company manufacturing specialty tools. Asahi USA employs a standard cost system. Presented below are standards per unit of one of its products, tool KJ79. This tool requires as direct materials a special chrome steel. LO 1

	STANDARD QUANTITY	STANDARD PRICE	STANDARD COST
Direct materials	8 pounds	$18 per pound	$144
Direct labor	2.5 hours	$8 per hour	20
			$164

During November, Asahi USA started and completed job KJX86 to manufacture 1900 units of tool KJ79. It purchased and used 14,250 pounds of the special chrome steel for tool KJ79 at a total cost of $270,750. The total direct labor charged to Job KJX86 was $37,800. Job KJX86 required 5000 direct labor hours.

(a) For job KJX86, compute the following and indicate whether the variances are favorable or unfavorable:

   (i) direct material price variance.

   (ii) direct material use variance.

   (iii) direct labor rate variance.

   (iv) direct labor efficiency variance.

(b) Provide a plausible explanation for the variances.

12-76 ***Organic and mechanistic organizations*** Researchers have defined two extreme forms of organizations. Organic organizations are highly decentralized with few rules. Most people agree that software development companies are very organic. Mechanistic organizations are highly centralized and use many rules to prescribe behavior. Most people agree that government agencies are very mechanistic. LO 2, 5

Do you agree with these examples? Give your own examples of each of these types of organizations with your reason for giving the organization the chosen classification.

LO 2, 5 **12-77** ***Group and individual conflict*** Think of an example of an organization where it is important that the various functional areas be closely coordinated to promote the organization's overall success. Show how performance measures that focus solely on the performance of an individual unit could create problems in this organization.

LO 2, 3, 4, 5 **12-78** ***Coordinating divisional activities*** For many years, automobile companies have been highly decentralized in terms of functions. The most obvious effect of this heavy decentralization of function is apparent when all the groups must work together to accomplish a goal. The highest order of integration occurs in the design of a new automobile.

Reflecting the functional decentralization of automobile manufacturers, the traditional approach to automobile design is for the marketing group to identify a concept. The design group then creates an automobile that reflects the marketing group's idea, but incorporates engineering requirements and aesthetics identified by the design group. The purchasing group then identifies the parts required by the design and makes further modifications to it to incorporate parts that can be made or purchased. Finally, the manufacturing group modifies the design to reflect the nature and capabilities of the production process. This process takes up to four years and usually results in a vehicle that is far removed from the initial design.

What went wrong here? How might this process be improved?

LO 2, 3, 4, 5 **12-79** ***Choices in financial control*** Bennington Home Products sells home products. It buys products for resale from suppliers all over the world. The products are organized into groups. A few examples of these groups are floor care products, kitchen products, tool products, and paper products. The company sells its products all over the world from regional offices and warehouses in every country where it operates. Because of differences in culture and taste, the product lines and products within those lines vary widely among countries.

The regional offices have administrative staff that manage the operations, do the ordering, and undertake the usual office administrative functions, and a sales staff that does the selling directly to stores within that country. The regional offices are evaluated as investment centers because they have responsibility for revenues, costs, and investment levels. The regional offices make suggestions for new products.

The corporate office manages the regional offices and places the orders received from the regional offices with suppliers. The corporate office does the ordering for three reasons. First, it is believed that one ordering office eliminates duplication in ordering activities. Second, it is believed that one office ordering for all the regional offices gives the organization more power when dealing with suppliers. Third, it is believed that one office can develop the expertise to find and negotiate with suppliers of unique and innovative products.

REQUIRED

(a) Describe an appropriate system of financial control at the regional level.

(b) Describe an appropriate system of financial control at the corporate office level.

(c) Explain why the three systems of financial control should, or need not, mesh.

12-80 ***Assigning responsibility for uncontrollable events*** Some people and organizations believe that the discussion of controllable and uncontrollable events is distracting in the sense that it encourages finger pointing and an excessive preoccupation with assigning blame. These observers argue that it is more important to find solutions than to identify responsibility for unacceptable or acceptable events. LO 5

REQUIRED

(a) What do you think of this argument?

(b) As an organization moves away from assessing and rewarding controllable performance, what changes would you expect to see in its organization structure?

12-81 ***New product opportunities and transfer pricing*** Plevna Manufacturing makes and distributes small prefabricated homes in kits. The kits contain all the pieces needed to assemble the home—all that is required is that the builder erect the home on a foundation. LO 6

Plevna Manufacturing is organized into two divisions—the manufacturing division and the sales division. Each division is evaluated based on its reported profits. The transfer price between the manufacturing division, where the kits are made, and the selling division, which sells the kits, is variable cost plus 10%, a total of about $33,000. The selling price per kit is about $40,000 and selling and distribution costs are about $5,000 per home kit.

The total costs that do not vary in proportion with volume at Plevna Manufacturing amount to about $2,000,000 per year—$1,500,000 in manufacturing and $500,000 in the selling division. Currently the company is operating at capacity, which is dictated by the machinery in the manufacturing division. Each kit requires about 10 hours of machine time and the total available machine time is 5000 per year. Plevna Manufacturing is making and selling about 500 kits per year. Increasing the plant capacity in the foreseeable future is not a viable option.

Willie Scott is the firm's salesperson. Willie has been approached a number of times recently by people wanting to buy cottages to erect on recreational properties. The cottages would be made by modifying the existing home product. The modification process would begin with a completed home kit. The manufacturing division would then incur additional materials and labor costs of $3000 and three hours of machine time to convert a home kit into a cottage kit.

Willie is proposing that the company split the sales division into two divisions—home sales and cottage sales. The new divisional structure would have no effect on existing administrative, personnel, or selling costs.

REQUIRED

Suppose that the new division is created. Discuss the issues in choosing a transfer price in this situation. What transfer price for each of the two products, home and cottage kits, would you recommend and why? (If you feel that the appropriate transfer price for each product can be within a range, specify the range.)

12-82 ***General Motors and economic value added*** Since the firm of Stern Stewart & Co. began ranking firms based on market value added, General Motors has generally been at, or near, the bottom of the list. Undertake an investigation to determine the circumstances that led to this ranking and whether there is any evidence that the situation is improving or getting worse. LO 7

LO 7, 8 **12-83** ***Decision making with return on investment*** You are the controller of a chain of dry-cleaning establishments. You are computing the return on investment for each outlet.

Outlet A, located in a city core, reported a net profit of $130,000. The land on which Outlet A is located was essentially rural when it was purchased for $100,000. Since then, the city has expanded and the land is located in the population center. Comparable undeveloped land in the immediate area of the outlet is worth $2,000,000. The net book value of the outlet building and equipment is $400,000. The replacement cost of the building and equipment is $1,200,000. If the outlet building, equipment, and land were sold as a going concern, the sale price would be $1,500,000. It would cost $250,000 to demolish the building and clear the property for commercial development.

REQUIRED

(a) What is the return on this investment?

(b) How would you decide whether this outlet should continue to be operated, sold as a going concern, or demolished and the land sold?

LO 7, 8 **12-84** ***Market value added, economic value added, and net income*** If you look through *Fortune,* you will find articles that rank organizations by market value added and economic value added. Find one such article and identify three firms: the one with the highest economic value added, the one with the highest market value added, and the one with the highest reported net income. Compare the three firms. Explain the difference in rankings. (In the event that the top-ranked firms by any two of these criteria are the same, do the above for the second-ranked firms.)

CASES

LO 1, 3 **12-85** ***Variance and cost analysis*** Peterborough Food produces a wide range of breakfast cereal foods. Its granola products are two of its most important product lines.

Because of the complexity of the granola production process, the manufacturing area in the plant that makes these two product lines is separated from the rest of the plant and is treated as a separate cost center. Exhibit 12-29 presents the activity and cost data for this cost center for the most recent quarter. The plan data in Exhibit 12-29 reflect the master budget targets for the quarter.

The factory accountant estimates that, with the increased production in line 1, the labor-related product-sustaining costs and the other product-sustaining costs for line 1 should increase by $20,000 and $100,000, respectively. The factory accountant also indicated that the decreased production in line 2 would require several quarters to be reflected in lower product-sustaining costs.

The factory accountant indicated that the labor-related business-sustaining costs and the other business-sustaining costs should increase by $0 and $140,000, respectively, given the net increase in production.

REQUIRED

Prepare a second-level and third-level variance analysis of costs for the granola line cost center. In your analysis, group costs into unit-related, batch-related, product-sustaining, and business-sustaining costs.

LO 2, 3, 4, 5 **12-86** ***Choosing an organization structure*** You are a senior manager responsible for overall company operations in a large courier company. Your company has 106 regional offices (terminals) scattered around the country and a main

EXHIBIT 12-29

Peterborough Food:
Granola Line Products

	LINE 1 PLAN	LINE 1 ACTUAL	LINE 2 PLAN	LINE 2 ACTUAL	TOTAL LINE 1 PLAN	TOTAL LINE 1 ACTUAL	TOTAL LINE 2 PLAN	TOTAL LINE 2 ACTUAL	TOTAL PLAN	TOTAL ACTUAL
Number of boxes	945,000	1,200,000	1,175,000	945,000						
Number of batches	189	200	235	210						
Units per batch	5,000	6,000	5,000	4,500						
Unit-related costs										
Materials										
Grams per box	500	515	350	375						
Cost per gram	$0.0030	$0.0027	$0.0050	$0.0055	$1,417,500	$1,668,600	$2,056,250	$1,949,062	$3,473,750	$3,617,662
Packaging										
Units per box	1.0000	1.0600	1.0000	1.0405						
Cost per unit	$0.0450	$0.0420	$0.0380	$0.0410	$42,525	$53,424	$44,650	$40,489	$87,175	$93,913
Labor										
Hours per box	0.013	0.011	0.009	0.010						
Cost per hour	$18.00	$18.25	$18.00	$18.25	$221,130	$240,900	$190,350	$172,463	$411,480	$413,363
Batch-related costs										
Materials										
Per batch	$1,200	$1,325	$1,525	$1,495	$226,800	$265,000	$358,375	$313,950	$585,175	$578,950
Labor										
Hours per batch	12	11	16	18						
Per hour	$18.00	$18.25	$18.00	$18.25	$40,824	$40,150	$67,680	$68,985	$108,504	$109,135
Product-sustaining costs										
Labor					$256,000	$287,000	$305,000	$323,000	$561,000	$610,000
Other					$2,054,000	$2,123,000	$1,927,000	$2,005,000	$3,981,000	$4,128,000
Business-sustaining costs										
Labor									$145,000	$152,000
Other									$4,560,000	$4,740,000
Total all costs					$4,258,779	$4,678,074	$4,949,305	$4,872,949	$13,913,084	$14,443,023

office (hub) located in the geographical center of the country. Your operations are strictly domestic. You do not accept international shipments.

The day at each terminal begins with the arrival of packages from the hub. The packages are loaded onto trucks for delivery to customers during the morning hours. In the afternoon, the same trucks pick up packages that are returned to the terminal in late afternoon and then shipped to the hub where shipments arrive from the terminals into the late evening and are sorted for delivery early the next day for the terminals.

Each terminal in your company is treated as an investment center and prepares individual income statements each month. Each terminal receives 30% of the revenue from packages that it picks up and 30% of the revenue from the packages it delivers. The remaining 40% of the revenue from each transaction goes to the hub. Each terminal accumulates its own costs. All costs relating to travel to and from the hub are charged to the hub. The revenue per package is based on size and service type and not the distance that the package travels. (There are two services: overnight and ground delivery, which takes between one and seven days, depending on the distance traveled.)

All customer service is done through a central service group located in the hub. Customers access this service center through a toll-free telephone number. The most common calls to customer service include requests for package pickup, requests to trace an overdue package, and requests for billing information. The company has invested in complex and expensive package tracking equipment that monitors the package's trip through the system by scanning the bar code placed on every package. The bar code is scanned when the package is picked up, enters the originating terminal, leaves the originating terminal, arrives at the hub, leaves the hub, arrives at the destination terminal, leaves the destination terminal, and is delivered to the customer. All scanning is done by handheld wands that transmit the information to the regional and then central computer.

The major staff functions in each terminal are administrative (accounting, clerical, and executive), marketing (the sales staff), courier (the people who pick up and deliver the shipments and the equipment they use), and operations (the people and equipment who sort packages inside the terminal).

This organization takes customer service very seriously. The revenue for any package that fails to meet the organization's service commitment to the customer is not assigned to the originating and destination terminals.

All company employees receive a wage and a bonus based on the terminal's economic value added. This system has promoted many debates about the sharing rules for revenues, the inherent inequity of the existing system, and the appropriateness of the revenue share for the hub. Service problems have arisen primarily relating to overdue packages. The terminals believe that most of the service problems relate to missorting in the hub, resulting in packages being sent to the wrong terminals.

REQUIRED

(a) Explain why you believe that an investment center is or is not an appropriate organization design in this company.

(b) Assuming that this organization is committed to the current design, how would you improve it?

(c) Assuming that this organization has decided that the investment center approach is unacceptable, what approach to performance evaluation would you recommend?

12-87 ***Computing objectives and organization responsibility*** Baden is a city with a population of 450,000. It has a distinct organization group, called the Public Utilities Commission of the City of Baden (called the Baden PUC), whose responsibility is to provide the water and electrical services to the businesses and homes in the city. Baden PUC's manager is evaluated and rewarded based on the profit that Baden PUC reports. LO 2, 3, 4, 5, 8

Baden PUC buys electricity from a privately owned hydroelectric facility several hundred miles away for resale to its citizens. Baden PUC is responsible for acquiring, selling, billing, and servicing customers. The maintenance and moving of electric wires within the city are, however, the responsibility of the City of Baden maintenance department (called Baden Maintenance). Baden PUC pays Baden Maintenance for work done on its electrical wires.

Over the years, there have been many squabbles between Baden Maintenance and Baden PUC. These squabbles have usually involved two items: complaints by customers about delays in restoring disrupted service and complaints by Baden PUC that the rates charged by Baden Maintenance are too high. The most recent concerns a much more serious issue, however.

On July 12, at about 10:30 A.M., a Baden city employee working in the parks and recreation department noticed an electrical wire that seemed to be damaged. The employee reported the problem at about 12:15 P.M. to Baden Maintenance during his lunch break. The report was placed on the maintenance supervisor's desk at 1:15 P.M. where it was found at 2:05 P.M. when the supervisor returned from lunch. The maintenance supervisor then called the Baden PUC dispatch office to report the problem and request permission to investigate the report and make any required repairs. The request for repair was placed on the Baden PUC service manager's desk for approval at 2:25 P.M. The service manager received the message when he returned from a meeting at 4:00 P.M., approved the work, and left a memo for a subordinate to call in the request. The request was then mistakenly called in as a request for routine service by a clerk at 4:50 P.M. and logged by the dispatcher in Baden Maintenance. A truck was dispatched the following day at 3:50 P.M. When the repair crew arrived at the scene, it discovered that the wire was indeed damaged and, if any of the children playing in the park had touched it, it would have caused instant death.

The incident went unreported for several days until a reporter for the *Baden Chronicle* received an anonymous tip about the episode, verified that it had happened, and reported the incident on the front page of the paper as an example of bureaucratic bungling. The public was outraged and demanded an explanation from the mayor, who asked the city manager to respond. The initial response from the Baden City manager that "everyone had followed procedure" only fanned the furor.

REQUIRED

(a) Was what happened inevitable given the City of Baden's organization structure? Explain.

(b) Given the existing organization structure, how might this incident have been avoided?

(c) How would you deal with this situation now that it has happened?

(d) Would a change in the organization structure help prevent a similar situation from occurring in the future? Explain.

Glossary

A

Activities the work performed within an organization. An activity brings together people, equipment, materials, energy, and other resources to produce a product or service. Activities should be described using verbs: assemble products, set up machines, respond to customer requests, or design a new service.

Activity a unit of work, or task, with a specific goal; a principle that describes and measures how organizational resources and employees accomplish work.

Activity analysis an approach to operations control that involves the five-step process of identifying the process objectives, charting activities, classifying activities, continuously improving processes, and eliminating activities whose costs exceed their value. Also called *value analysis* or *activity-based management.*

Activity-based budgeting a budgeting approach based on the insights of activity-based costing.

Activity-based costing (ABC) system based on activities that links organizational spending on resources to the products and services produced and delivered to customers.

Activity-based management (ABM) See *activity analysis.*

Activity cost driver rate the amount determined by dividing the activity expense by the total quantity of the activity cost driver.

Activity cost drivers measures that identify the linkage between activities and cost objects; they serve as quantitative measures of the output of activities.

After-sales costs the expenses involved in dealing with customers after the sale.

Aggregate planning the process that compares the production plan with the amount of available productive capacity; this comparison assesses the feasibility of the proposed production plan.

Annuity (*a*) the equal amount, received or paid at the end of each period for *n* periods.

Appraisal costs those costs related to inspecting products to ensure that they meet both internal and external customer requirements.

Appropriation an authorized limit in a government department.

Authoritative budgeting a budget-setting method in which a superior tells a subordinate what the budget will be.

Avoidable costs those costs eliminated when a part, product, product line, or business segment is discontinued.

B

Balanced scorecard a systematic performance measurement system that translates an organization's strategy into clear objectives, measures, targets, and initiatives organized by four perspectives.

Batch-related activities those activities triggered by the number of batches produced rather than by the number of units manufactured.

Beliefs system an explicit set of statements, communicated to employees, of the basic values, purpose, and direction of the organization.

Benchmarking the process of studying and adapting the best practices of other organizations to improve the firm's own performance and establish a point of reference by which other internal performance can be measured.

Benchmarking (performance) gap the specific performance measure on which a firm would like to improve.

Bid price equals the total job costs plus the margin.

Bill of activities the set of activities and costs associated with individual products or customers.

Boundary systems statements that communicate to employees what actions must never be taken; intended to constrain the range of behavior.

Budget a quantitative expression of the money inflows and outflows that predicts the consequences of current operating decisions and reveals whether a financial plan will meet organizational objectives.

Budgeting the process of preparing budgets.

Budgeting games a process in which managers attempt to manipulate information and targets to achieve as high a bonus as possible.

Budgeting process the process that determines the planned level of most flexible costs.

Budget slack involve the acts of requiring excess resources and distorting performance information.

Business-level strategy making the process of choosing the organization's target customers and the broad operating decisions necessary to meet its needs.

Business-sustaining activities those activities required for the basic functioning of the business, independent of production or sales volumes and mix.

C

Capacity-related costs the costs associated with capacity-related resources.

Capacity-related resources those resources acquired and paid for in advance of when the work is completed and whose costs depend upon the amounts required rather than the amount used.

Capital budget the management document that authorizes spending for resources, such as plant and equipment, that will have multiyear useful lifetimes.

Capital budgeting a systematic approach to evaluating an investment in a long-term, or capital, asset.

Cash bonus a payment method that pays cash based on some measured performance. Also called lump-sum reward, pay for performance, and merit pay.

Cellular manufacturing refers to the organization of a plant into a number of cells so that within each cell all machines required to manufacture a group of similar products are arranged in close proximity to each other.

Centralized responsibility reserving decision-making power for senior management levels.

Certified suppliers a set of suppliers who are certified by a company because they are dependable and consistent in supplying high-quality items as needed.

Committed costs those costs that a company incurs before knowing actual production or sales volumes.

Compound interest when interest earned each year on both an initial investment and the interest earned in previous periods is not withdrawn until the fifth year. Also called the compounding effect of interest.

Consultative budgeting a method of budget setting used when managers ask subordinates to discuss their ideas about the budget, but no joint decision making occurs.

Continuous improvement the act of making incremental changes to the process to improve process performance.

Contribution per machine hour a factor obtained by dividing the contribution per unit by the number of machine hours per unit.

Contribution per unit the price per unit less variable costs per unit.

Control refers to the set of procedures, tools, performance measures, and systems that organizations use to guide and motivate all employees to achieve organizational objectives.

Controllability principle states that the manager of a responsibility center should be assigned responsibility only for the revenues, costs, or investment that responsibility center personnel control.

Conversion costs the costs of production labor and support activities to convert the materials or product at each process stage.

Cooperative benchmarking the voluntary sharing of information through mutual agreements.

Cost the monetary value of goods and services expended to obtain current or future benefits.

Cost centers responsibility centers in which employees control costs but do not control revenues or investment level.

Cost driver rates see *activity cost driver rate.*

Cost leadership a business strategy that focuses on delivering products to its customers at the lowest possible cost.

Cost object something for which a cost must be computed.

Cost of capital the return that the organization must earn on its investment to meet its investors' return requirements. Also call *risk-adjusted discount rate.*

Cost of goods sold (COGS) the manufacturing cost of goods sold.

Cost of nonconformance (CONC) to quality standards the cost incurred when the quality of products and services does not conform to quality standards.

Cost of quality (COQ) report a report that details the cost of maintaining quality production processes and products.

Cost of unused capacity an expense determined by the amount of resources unused during production.

Cost-plus pricing a method for setting the price of a product by a markup percentage above cost.

Cost pool a subset of total support costs that can be associated with a distinct cost driver.

Cost-volume-profit analysis the process of combining cost behavior information with revenue information to project revenues, costs, and profits for different levels of volume.

Customer costing the process of assigning marketing, selling, distribution, and administrative costs to individual customers so that the cost of serving each customer can be calculated.

Customer management activities a class of activities directed to understanding customer requirements.

Customer relationship strategy see *niche strategy.*

Customer retention the percent of customers who return for another purchase; a critical long-term success factor for a company.

Customer-sustaining activities those activities that enable the company to sell to an individual customer but are independent of the volume and mix of the products sold and delivered to the customer.

Customer-validated performance measures tools used to reflect customer requirements and help employees manage the value chain's processes and activities in order to please customers.

Cycle time the time required to produce a product from start to finish.

D

Database benchmarking a policy in which companies usually pay a fee and in return gain access to information from a database operator.

Data falsification the process of knowingly altering company data in one's favor.

Decentralized responsibility refers to the authority that local-division managers have in order to make their own decisions without having to seek higher approval on various business operations.

Direct cost a cost of a resource or activity that is acquired for or used by a single cost object.

Direct manufacturing costs costs that can be traced easily to the product manufactured or service rendered.

Discounting the process of computing present value.

Distribution costs the expenses involved in delivering finished products to customers.

Duration drivers represent the amount of time required to perform an activity.

E

Efficient activity an activity that consumes no excess resources.

Employee self-control a managerial method in which employees monitor and regulate their own behavior and perform to their highest levels.

Environmental costing a costing system that computes the cost of the effects an organization has on the environment.

Ethical control system a management control system based on ethics used to promote ethical decision making.

Expenses the costs of goods or services that have expired, that is, have been used up in the process of creating goods and services.

External failure costs those costs incurred when customers discover a defect.

Extrinsic rewards motivating desired behavior by providing an explicit, usually financial, reward.

F

Financial accounting the process of producing financial statements for external constituencies—people outside the organization, such as shareholders, creditors, and governmental authorities. This process is heavily constrained by standard-setting, regulatory, and tax authorities and the auditing requirements of independent accountants (contrast with management accounting).

Financial budgets those budgets that identify the expected financial consequences of the activities summarized in the operating budgets.

Financial control a process used to assess an organization's financial success by measuring and evaluating its financial outcomes.

Finished goods inventory that has been completed but not yet sold.

First-level variances for cost items, the difference between the actual and master budget costs for that cost item.

Flexible budget the forecast of the projected level of cost given the volume and mix of activities undertaken.

Flexible budget variances shows the difference between the flexible budget and the actual results.

Flexible costs those costs that vary with production or sales volumes.

Flexible resources those resources whose supply can be adjusted, in the short run, to actual demands (contrast with *committed costs*).

Full absorption costing a costing method in which all production costs become product costs.

Full costs sum of all costs (direct materials, direct labor, and support) assigned to a product.

Functional benchmarking the study of another organization's practices and costs in relation to functions or processes, such as assembly or distribution.

Future value (*FV*) the amount that today's investment will be after a stated number of periods at a stated periodic rate of return.

G

Gainsharing a system for distributing cash bonuses from a pool when the total amount available is a function of performance relative to some target.

Gaming the performance indicator an activity in which an employee may engage in dysfunctional behavior to achieve a single goal.

General and administrative costs expenses such as legal fees and the CEO's salary that do not fall into any other cost category.

Generally accepted accounting principles (GAAP) the allowable methods for classifying costs for external reporting.

Goal congruence the outcome when managers' and employees' goals are aligned with organizational goals.

Group benchmarking a business alternative in which participants meet openly to discuss their methods.

H

Human relations movement a managerial movement that recognizes that people have needs well beyond performing a simple repetitive task at work and that financial compensation is only one aspect of what workers desire.

Human resources model of motivation (HRMM) a more contemporary managerial view that introduces a high level of employee responsibility for and participation in decisions in the work environment.

I

Improshare a gainsharing program that determines its bonus pool by computing the difference between the target level of labor cost given the level of production and the actual labor cost.

Incentive compensation reward system that provides monetary (extrinsic) rewards based on measured results. Also called *pay-for-performance systems.*

In control refers to a system that is on the path to achieving its strategic objectives.

Incremental budgeting bases a period's expenditure level for a discretionary item on the amount spent for that item during the previous period.

Incremental cost per unit the amount by which the total costs of production and sales increase when one additional unit of that product is produced and sold.

Incremental cost/revenues the amount by which the total costs of production and sales change by a current or proposed action or decision; contrast with *sunk costs.*

Indirect cost the cost of a resource that was acquired to be used by more than one cost object.

Indirect manufacturing costs all manufacturing costs other than direct manufacturing costs.

Indirect/third-party benchmarking a technique that uses an outside consultant to act as a liaison among firms engaged in benchmarking.

Inefficient activity an activity that requires more resources than necessary to produce the desired outcome.

Innovation activities a class of activities that develop new products and services.

Input the variables that the organization puts into a process, such as employee time and production costs.

Intensity drivers used to directly charge for the resources used each time an activity is performed.

Internal failure costs the costs incurred when the manufacturing process detects a defective component or product before it is shipped to an external customer.

Internal rate of return (*IRR*) the actual rate of return expected from an investment.

Intrinsic rewards those rewards that come

from within an individual and reflect satisfaction from doing the job and the opportunities for growth that the job provides.

Investment the monetary value of the assets that the organization gives up to acquire an asset.

Investment center a responsibility center in which the manager and other employees control revenues, costs, and the level of investment in the responsibility center.

J

Just-in-time (JIT) manufacturing a production process method in which products are manufactured only as needed.

Job bid sheet a format for estimating job costs.

Job costs expenses involved with the direct material, direct labor, and support costs for a job.

Job cost sheet format for recording actual job costs.

Job order costing system a process that estimates the costs of manufacturing products for different jobs required for specific customer orders.

K

Kaizen costing a costing system that focuses on reducing costs during the manufacturing stage of the total life cycle of a product.

L

Life-cycle costing a systematic consideration of product costs during the product's lifetime.

Long-run costs the sum of flexible and capacity-related costs associated with a cost object.

M

Make-or-buy decision a decision in which managers must decide whether their companies should manufacture some parts and components for their products in-house or subcontract with another company to supply these parts and components.

Management accounting a value adding improvement process of planning, designing, measuring, and operating nonfinancial and financial information systems that guides management action, motivates behavior, and supports and creates the cultural values necessary to achieve an organization's strategic, tactical, and operating objectives.

Management accounting information financial and operating data about an organization's activities, processes, operating units, products, services, and customers; e.g., the calculated cost of a product, an activity, or a department in a recent time period.

Management accounting and control system (MACS) the larger entity of central performance measurement systems.

Management control the process of providing information about the performance of managers and operating units.

Managing by the numbers the practice of holding managers responsible for meeting financial targets.

Manufacturing costs those costs incurred inside the factory associated with transforming raw materials into a finished product.

Manufacturing cycle the stage of production in which product is produced and that involves the highest level of cost.

Manufacturing cycle efficiency (MCE) a measure used to assess the efficiency of a manufacturing process; evaluates how much of the total cycle time was spent in inventory.

Margin an additional amount added to job costs in order to make a profit.

Marginal cost the increase in cost for a unit increase in the quantity produced and sold.

Marginal revenue the increase in revenue corresponding to a unit increase in the quantity produced and sold.

Marketing costs expenses incurred for advertising and promotion.

Market share the percent of total sales and service in an area that a particular organization or company captures.

Markup percentage See *markup rate.*

Markup rate the percent by which job costs are marked up. Also called *markup percentage.*

Materials requisition note a list of materials required to begin production.

Monitoring inspecting the work or behavior of employees while they are performing a task.

Motivation an individual's interest or drive to act in a certain manner.

Multistage process costing system a system for determining job costs in which conversion costs are applied to products as they pass through successive process stages.

N

Net present value (NPV) the sum of the present values of all cash inflows and outflows associated with a project.

Niche strategy a business strategy that tries to meet the unique requirements of a special market segment. Also called *customer relationship strategy.*

Nonmanufacturing costs the costs of an organization other than those incurred to produce a product; includes *distribution costs, selling costs, marketing costs, after-sales costs, research and development costs,* and *general and administrative costs.*

Number of periods (*n*) in capital-budgeting analysis, the number of periods, usually measured in months, quarters, or years, whose cash flows a proposed long-term investment will affect.

O

Operating budget the document that forecasts revenues and expenses during the next operating period including monthly forecasts of sales, production, and operating expenses.

Operating costs costs, other than direct materials costs, that are needed to produce a product or service.

Operational control see *operations control.*

Operational activity-based management a system that uses information collected by the ABC system at the activity level to identify promising opportunities for reducing costs in indirect and support activities.

Operational excellence a business strategy that emphasizes cost leadership, consistent quality, and ease of purchase.

Operational-level (tactical level) strategy the process of choosing what business the organization is in; reflects the way the organization will pursue its business-level strategy.

Operations activities a class of activities that include designing systems to handle inbound logistics; managing suppliers, operations, and manufacturing; and managing the flow of products to customers.

Operations control the process of providing feedback to employers and their managers about the efficiency of activities being performed. See also *process control.*

Opportunity costs the sacrifices incurred when using resources for one purpose instead of another.

Organization control the activity of ensuring that the organization is on track toward achieving its objectives.

Organizational-level strategy making the process of choosing what business the organization is in.

Outcome the value that a customer places on a product or service.

Out of control a state when a system is not on a path to achieving organizational objectives.

Output a physical measure of what an activity has produced.

Outsourcing the process of buying resources from an outside supplier instead of manufacturing them in-house.

P

Participative budgeting a method of budget setting that uses a joint decision-making process in which all parties agree about setting the budget targets.

Payback period the number of periods required to recover a project's initial investment.

Pay-for-performance systems See *incentive compensation.*

Penetration pricing strategy the act of choosing a low markup for a new product to penetrate the market and win over market share from an established product of a competing firm.

Performance measurement a major management accounting and control process used to evaluate the performance of a manager, activity, or organizational unit.

Period costs those costs related to nonmanufacturing costs, including administrative and marketing costs.

Periodic budget an annual budget prepared for each planning period.

Planning variances the cost differences between the master budget and the flexible budget; reflect the difference between planned and actual output.

Post-implementation audit the process of revisiting the decision to purchase a long-lived asset.

Post-sale service and disposal cycle the portion of the life cycle that begins once the first unit of a product is in the hands of the consumer.

Practical capacity the amount of work that can be performed by resources supplied for production or service.

Present value (*PV*) a future cash flow's value at time zero.

Prevention costs those costs incurred to

ensure that companies produce products according to quality standards.

Preventive control an approach to control that focuses on preventing an undesired event.

Price setter a firm that can determine the prices its customers will pay for its products.

Price taker a firm that accepts the prices set in the marketplace for its products.

Process control the activity of assessing the ability of each unit in the value chain to meet the requirements of the organization's target customers. Also called *operations control.*

Process costing system a costing method that computes and allocates an equal amount of cost to each product.

Processes steps that represent collections of activities for accomplishing organizational objectives.

Processing time time expended to complete a processing activity.

Process layout a production design in which all similar equipment or functions are grouped together.

Process reengineering describes the redesigning or elimination of inefficient processes. Also called *reengineering.*

Product benchmarking the study of another organization's product design and cost.

Product costing the process of measuring and assigning to products and services the costs of the activities performed to design and produce them.

Product costs those costs incurred to produce the volume and mix of products made during the period.

Production departments the departments that have direct responsibility for converting raw materials into finished products.

Product layout a production design in which equipment is organized to accommodate the production of a specific product.

Product leadership strategy a business strategy in which companies develop products that deliver performance superior to that of competitors, and emphasize activities for innovation and for anticipating consumer preferences.

Product-sustaining activities those activities that support the production and sale of individual products but are independent of actual production volumes and batches.

Profitability index a variation on the net present value method, computed by dividing the present value of the cash inflows by the present value of the cash outflows.

Profit center a responsibility center in which managers and other employees control both the revenues and the costs of the product or service they deliver.

Profit sharing a cash bonus calculated as a percentage of an organization unit's reported profit; a group incentive compensation plan focused on short-term performances.

Pro forma financial statements the projected balance sheet and projected income statement.

Project funding a proposal for discretionary expenditures with a specific time horizon or sunset provision.

Q

Q Series of Quality Standards the American version of the ISO9000 quality standards.

Quality refers to how well the product's operating characteristics conform to what the organization promises to customers.

Quality costs those costs incurred on quality-related processes; include *prevention, appraisal, internal failure,* and *external failure costs.*

R

Rate of return (*r*) ratio of net income to investment.

Raw material productivity the ratio of raw material in the finished product to the total quantity of raw material acquired.

Raw materials inventory the purchase cost of resources.

Reengineering See *process reengineering.*

Relevance of information refers to how useful information is for the organization's decision and control processes.

Relevant costs/revenues those factors that are affected by a decision.

Research and development costs expenses for designing and bringing new products to the market.

Research development and engineering (RD&E) a life-cycle concept that involves market research, product design, and product development.

Responsibility center an organization unit for which a manager is made responsible.

Results control the process of hiring qualified people who understand the organization's objectives, telling them to do whatever they think best to help the organization achieve its objectives, and using the control system to evaluate the resulting performance, thereby assessing how well they have done.

Return the increased cash inflows in the future that are attributable to the long-term asset.

Return of investment (ROI) the ratio of net income to invested capital.

Revenue center a responsibility center in which members control revenues but do not control either the manufacturing or the acquisition cost of the product or service they sell or the level of investment made in the responsibility center.

Risk-adjusted discount rate See *cost of capital.*

Rucker plan a form of gainsharing program.

S

Scanlon plan a form of gainsharing program.

Scientific management school a management movement with the underlying philosophy that most people find work objectionable, that people care little for making decisions or showing creativity on the job, and that money is the driving force behind performance.

Scope of a MACS includes the entire value chain of the organization.

Second-level variances the planning variance and flexible budget variance, which combined are the *first-level variance.*

Selling costs those costs incurred for sales personnel salaries and commissions and other sales office expenses.

Sensitivity analysis the analysis of the effect of a change in a parameter on a decision rather than on an outcome.

Sequential allocation method allocates service department costs to production departments and other service departments in a sequential order.

Service the value in use of a good or service.

Service activities a class of activities that provides customers with after-sales service.

Service departments the departments that perform activities that support production but are not responsible for any of the conversion processes.

Short-run costs the flexible costs involved in a process that vary in proportion to production.

Skimming pricing strategy an act of initially charging customers a higher price, who are willing to pay more for the privilege of possessing a product.

Stage 1 allocations assignment of costs accumulated in the service department directly to the production departments or activities.

Stage 2 allocations assignment of costs accumulated in production departments and activities to individual products.

Stock option the right to purchase a unit of the organization's stock at a specified price, called the option price.

Strategic control the process of providing information about the competitive performance of the overall business unit, both financially and in meeting customers' expectations.

Strategic information information that guides the long-term decision making of the organization. Strategic information can include the profitability of products, services, and customers; competitor behavior and performance; customer preferences and trends; market opportunities and threats; and technological innovations.

Strategy the process of choosing target customers and deciding how to serve those customers in a unique, sustainable way.

Strategy benchmarking the study of another organization's strategy and strategic decisions.

Stretch budgeting a budgeting method that attempts to reach much higher goals than the current performance.

Stretch targets a target that exceeds previous targets by a significant amount and usually require an enormous increase in performance during the next budgeting periods.

Sunk costs the costs of resources that already have been committed and cannot be changed by any current action or decision; contrast with *incremental costs.*

Supply chain management a management system that develops cooperative, mutually beneficial, long-term relationships between buyers and sellers.

T

Target cost (C_{tc}) the difference between the target selling price and the target profit margin.

Target costing a method of cost planning used during the planning research development and engineering cycle to reduce manufacturing costs to targeted levels.

Task control the process of developing standard procedures that employees are told to follow.

Theory of constraints (TOC) a management approach that maximizes the volume of production through a bottleneck process.

Throughput contribution the difference between revenues and direct materials for the quantity of product sold.

Time value of money the opportunity cost of using money; that is, money like all commodities has a cost and can earn a return, so its value depends on when it is expended or received.

Total-life-cycle costing (TLCC) describes the process of managing all costs during a product's lifetime.

Transaction drivers used to count the frequency of an activity, the number of times an activity is performed.

Transfer pricing the set of rules an organization uses to assign the prices to products transferred between internal responsibility centers.

U

Unilateral (covert) benchmarking a process in which companies independently gather information about one or several other companies that excel in the area of interest.

Unit-related activities those activities whose volume or level is proportional to the number of units produced or sold.

V

Value analysis See *activity analysis.*

Value chain the sequence of activities that make or deliver a good or service to customers. Each step in the chain should contribute more to the ultimate value of the product than its cost.

Value engineering the process of examining each component of a product to determine whether its cost can be reduced while maintaining functionality and performance.

Value proposition clear and short statement of competitive value that the organization will deliver to its target customers—how it will compete for, or satisfy, customers.

Variable costing a costing method in which only flexible costs are included in product costs.

Variance analysis the set of procedures used by managers to help them understand the source of differences (variances) between actual and budgeted costs.

Variances the differences between planned and actual costs.

W

What-if analysis a type of analysis that explores the effect of a change in a parameter on an outcome.

Work-in-process (WIP) inventory the costs of the resources for each job not yet completed.

Z

Zero-based budgeting (ZBB) requires that proponents of discretionary expenditures continually justify every expenditure.

Subject Index

Page numbers in italics denote illustrations.

C

D

E

F

G

H

I

N

O

P

S

T

U

V

W

Y

Z

Company Name Index

Page numbers in italics denote illustrations.